PENNSYLVANIA COLLEGE OF TECHNOLOGY LIBRARY

5 0608 01129508 5

D1221483

companion encyclopedia
of geography

This completely revised second edition of Routledge's very successful 1996 *Companion Encyclopedia of Geography* provides a comprehensive and integrated survey of the discipline. The revised edition takes the theme of place as the unifying principle for a full account of the discipline at the beginning of the twenty-first century.

The work comprises 64 substantial essays addressing human and physical geography, and exploring their inter-relations. The encyclopedia does full justice to the enormous growth of social and cultural geography in recent years. Leading international academics from ten countries and four continents have contributed, ensuring that differing traditions in geography around the world are represented. In addition to references, the essays also list recommendations for further reading. There is a comprehensive index guiding the reader to specific themes and concepts within the content.

As with the original work, the new *Companion Encyclopedia of Geography* provides a state-of-the-art survey of the discipline and is an indispensable addition to the reference shelves of libraries supporting research and teaching in geography.

Ian Douglas, **Richard Huggett** and **Chris Perkins** are based in the Department of Geography, School of Environment and Development, University of Manchester, UK.

companion encyclopedia of geography

from local to global

second edition

edited by
ian douglas
richard huggett
chris perkins

volume 2

Routledge
Taylor & Francis Group

LONDON AND NEW YORK

LIBRARY
Pennsylvania College
of Technology

One College Avenue
Williamsport, PA 17701-5790

MAY 2 2 2007

First published 2007
by Routledge
2 Park Square, Milton Park, Abingdon, Oxon OX14 4RN
www.routledge.co.uk

Simultaneously published in the USA and Canada
by Routledge
270 Madison Avenue, New York, NY 10016
www.routledge-ny.com

Routledge is an Imprint of the Taylor and Francis Group, an informa business

© 2007 Routledge

Typeset in Bembo and Helvetica by Taylor & Francis Books
Printed and bound in Great Britain by MPG Books Ltd, Bodmin

All rights reserved. No part of this book may be reprinted or reproduced or utilized
in any form or by any electronic, mechanical, or other means, now known or
hereafter invented, including photocopying and recording, or in any information
storage or retrieval system, without permission in writing from the publishers.

British Library Cataloguing in Publication Data
A catalogue record for this book has been requested

Library of Congress Cataloging-in-Publication Data
A catalog record for this book has been requested

ISBN13: 978-0-415-43169-9 (set)
ISBN13: 978-0-415-33977-3 (volume 1)
ISBN13: 978-0-415-43171-2 (volume 2)

Contents

Volume 1

Part I: The nature of place

Part III: Actors in the process

Part IV: Nature, rate, and direction of change

Volume 2

Part V: The geographical imagination

Part VI: Responses to the geographical drivers of change

List of plates

List of figures

List of tables

Part V

The geographical imagination

Chris Perkins

This section discusses the ways in which people have imagined the world through different media, charting the distinctive forms and modalities in which discourses are represented in different contexts. The geographical imagination (Gregory 1994) allows us to create places and envisage futures, but media themselves also constitute difference. The world in words differs from its representation in images, whether they are artistic, photographic, cartographic or filmic. Oral culture creates another altogether different kind of place from multimedia or interactive representations on the World Wide Web.

The novel, the poem, the academic article, the newspaper story, the company annual report, the signpost, the Act of Parliament: each presents a differing reading of geography. The use of language is a continuing and powerful means of understanding geographic relationships. Richard Phillips in Chapter 34 explores the geographical significance of the written word through a consideration of different theoretical approaches to the practices of writing and an evaluation of the politics of the process. This chapter teases out the significance of different contexts in which words represent places, contrasts genres in which words do their work, and unpacks the significance of different media in a consideration of reading. It concludes with a consideration of the textuality of geography itself.

Maps used to be the touchstone of geography, a central method for apprehending places, representing and reducing the diversity of the world in a technology of control, but the map is now only one of a whole suite of practices of scientific visualization that have increasingly come to play significant roles in the representation and management of places. Chapter 35 explores the changing ways that mapping sciences have imagined the world, charting the differences that flow from the application of spatial technologies to the representation of ideas and places. Here Chris Perkins explores the impact of these changing tools upon cultural practices and the sharing of ideas about the world through a consideration of artistic and political contexts, but also focuses upon the ways in which mapping is practised and enacted.

Visual arts also play an important role in the way that people understand our world, and these artistic imaginings are the focus of Chapter 36 by Caitlin DeSilvey and Kathryn Yusoff. The artistic impulse has a rich history that is implicitly placed, but which is contested and debated by many different disciplines. The significance of vision, the symbolic nature of the medium, its subjectivities and its social roles are constantly changing. This chapter explores the interface between geography and art, discussing the ways in which images embody geographical meanings, and the geographical processes involved in their creation and reading, juxtaposing theory with four illustrative vignettes.

Photography as a cultural practice has played a central role in the development of geographical imaginations in the twentieth century. The products, processes and practices of photography fix and freeze the world, naturalizing culture and presenting places and people to an increasingly global audience. Chapter 37 by Chris Perkins discusses different theoretical approaches to the medium, interrogating the apparent neutrality of the photographic image, placing photography in historical and contemporary contexts, and explaining how technology, practice and image deliver social goals. It shows how photographic practices constitute social identities and charts changing roles of the image in digital culture.

However, we also live in a visual culture that increasingly understands the world through film and moving images. In Chapter 38, Stuart Aitken considers the difference that motion makes. He explores the links between film theory and the geographical imagination, assessing the contribution of the medium to our changing notions of the significance of local and global issues. This chapter places film, exploring the nexus of production, the cultural politics of the medium, the depiction of filmic place and the practices of watching film and video, and concludes with a consideration of the emotional geographies called into being by the medium and context.

The immediacy of speaking, listening and responding to the spoken word and music constitutes very different imaginary geographies to those that flow from the permanency of written discourse. Chapter 39 by Andy Bennett explores music as a shared cultural experience, at once embodying universal human values, but also representing local influences: it is implicitly 'placed', yet increasingly global. This chapter explores the changing practices of musical performance and examines how the production of sound relates to differing geographies. It contrasts different theoretical approaches to the links between music and place and unpacks the role of genre and cultural context in the creation of meaning through a consideration of folk, rock, rap and world music.

In the last decade a juxtaposition of profound technological advances has allowed the creation of new geographical imaginaries, constituted through notions of the interactive possibilities offered by multi and hypermedia. Bill Cartwright describes the nature of this shift, characterized by merging, linking and changing interactions, in Chapter 40. Using the example of multimedia mapping systems, he illustrates its geographical significance and also explores the potential of the web as a means of imagining and sharing the world. This chapter assesses the significance of intertextual ambiguities of multimedia presentations and discusses the politics of the virtual.

Reference

Gregory, D. (1994) *Geographical Imaginations*. Oxford: Blackwell.

34

Words

Writing on and about the landscape

Richard Phillips

When we start to notice them, words are everywhere. Looking around the city, we see road signs, notices, names on buildings, letters and words in logos and billboards. The same is true of rural areas, and of the interiors of houses and other buildings. And, of course, the mobile phones and computer screens we spend so much time staring into. We live in a culture that is rich with visual imagery, but it is often the words that allow us to understand places. Words are everywhere, too, in academic geography. And in popular geographies: descriptions and interpretations of places and landscapes in non-academic media such as travel writing, fiction, poetry, newspapers and diaries. Derived from the Greek *geo*, meaning earth, and *graphien*, meaning 'to write', geography is literally 'earth writing' (Barnes and Duncan 1992: 1). Geographers, both academic and popular, spend most of their time working with words. This is why, for instance, geographical study guides are largely devoted to reading, writing and using words in other ways: in spoken presentations, for instance, and in the legends and substance of maps.

Questions about words and their place in the world have increasingly been raised and discussed in human geography. In the early 1990s, Trevor Barnes and James Duncan (1992: 1) could accurately complain that 'Very little attention is paid to writing in human geo-graphy.' This is no longer the case: in recent years geographers have become increasingly self-conscious about the way they write, and have also paid a great deal of attention not only to textual sources but also to the textuality of geography. This chapter begins by exploring written words in material geographies, and asking how people read the landscapes in which they live. It then turns to geographical texts, examining geographical descriptions and asking what such descriptions achieve, theoretically and politically, and how they achieve it.

Writing geographies

To investigate the geography of writing in its most tangible form, I suggest an experiment: set out with a camera and notebook, looking *for* and *at* the words you normally look *through*. I tried this in the east London borough of Tower Hamlets, between Tower Bridge and the Bethnal Green Road. Some of the things I found are shown in Plates 34.1 and 34.2:

537

Plate 34.1. Street signs. Photograph by Richard Phillips.

Plate 34.2. Street graffiti and posters. Photograph by Richard Phillips.

road signs; notices; words on and within buildings; letters in logos and phrases on billboards. In addition to the 'legitimate' words, posted or authorized by government and property owners, I also found unofficial words: illegal posters, graffiti, political slogans, words of art, poetry and humour. I also saw – and heard – words in languages and dialects I know, others that I recognize but cannot fully understand, and many others that I do not know at all. Some of these words orient and inform people, but they do and are more than this; words are part of the place.

It is not only in London that words appear to be everywhere. Elsewhere in England, in smaller towns and villages, in the countryside and national parks, for example, landscapes and interiors are inscribed in some way or another. This is not to say that words are ubiquitous. Writing and reading are obviously more important in times and places with higher levels of literacy. Literacy varies markedly between countries and social groups. Though literacy is near universal in contemporary London, for instance, UNESCO estimates that over 700 million adults (over 15 years of age) are illiterate, many of them in developing countries and women (2005 statistics). The importance attached to writing and reading also varies with culture and religion. In Islamic countries, where the use of visual images is sometimes repudiated on moral grounds, words form the basis of art and the mainstay of architectural ornamentation, both exterior and interior. The importance of words also varies between different social contexts. In London, a heterogeneous city with 7 million residents and a great number of visitors at any one time, a relatively small proportion of communication is by word of mouth, more by overt signs, of which written words are among the most

Plate 34.3. The only street signs in Buenos Aires, Honduras. Photograph by Richard Phillips.

explicit. In contrast, there is less need for written words in many smaller and more intimate communities. The 350 residents of Buenos Aires, a village in northern Honduras, find their way to each other's houses, to the two churches, the school, football field and handful of shops and cooperatives without the need for signs, which many older members of the community would not in any case be able to read. The only such inscriptions in the village are for the benefit of outsiders, announcing the village, providing directions to the nearby national park, and advertising the works of development and aid agencies (see Plate 34.3). Or, as in the words that hang over San Pedro Sula, the industrial capital of Honduras, words advertise companies and products, and symbolize the city and the country's ties with the United States (see Plate 34.4).

As different people attach different values to words in general, the interpretation of particular words within the landscape is more complex than might first be imagined. Moreover, words do not have singular or straightforward meanings. Interpreters of written texts, from literary critics to theologians and lawyers, have shown that texts can invariably be read and used in more than one way (Phillips 2001). Words do not speak for themselves; readers actively generate some of their meaning. Different groups – called 'interpretive communities' (Fish 1980: 320) – read environmental and conventional texts in different ways, which reflect and may reinforce their group identity and enable them to pursue group interests. For example, gang members may be attuned to reading the graffiti and symbols of their own and other gangs, signs that others might not understand or be able to see as anything more specifically legible than vandalism or perhaps art.

Plate 34.4. Coca-Cola sign over San Pedro Sula. Photograph by Richard Phillips.

It is not only their ability to read *words* within the landscape that enables interpretive communities to cohere and function. People read the landscape in much the same way as they read words or a text (see Chapter 2). Landscape critics from John Brinckerhoff Jackson to James Duncan speak metaphorically of environmental literacy and legibility, comparing but not equating the ways in which people read landscapes and – the primary focus of this chapter – words. Having introduced geographies of words in their most concrete forms – letters in the landscape – the next sections turn from tangible to textual geographies, from writing on to writing about the landscape.

Geographical description

Some of the richest geographical data – information about landscape, place and nature, the country and the city – are found in imaginative literature. American geographer Carl Sauer once observed that 'The literature of geography begins with parts of the earliest sagas and myths, vivid as they are with the sense of place and of man's contest with nature' (Sauer, quoted by Phillips 1997: 1). This literature extends to the narratives of explorers, surveyors and academic geographers, and continues in literary and popular culture, including travel writing, fiction and poetry. Travel and adventure writers conventionally describe faraway places; and the great volume of such books, produced and consumed in modern Europe, presented their readers with images of Africa, Asia and the New World (Duncan and Gregory 1999). Cities have been represented in other imaginative literatures, including fiction such as James Joyce's *Ulysses* and poetry such as T.S. Eliot's *The Wasteland* – two complex texts that somehow map modern (early twentieth-century) Dublin and London respectively (Thacker 2003).

A classic example of the literary portrayal of landscape and a region is found in the work of Thomas Hardy, who set most of his novels and short stories in a fictionalized version of nineteenth-century southwest England. His settings are complete with detailed descriptions of hills, rivers, trees, animals and birds, in different weather conditions and times of day. Hardy's rural landscapes are also populated with people and human settlements including farm buildings, lanes, walls and fences. Hardy's reader also learns about towns such as Dorchester, a market town in Dorset, from Hardy's fictional equivalent, Caster-bridge. Other settings correspond less specifically to particular places. Egdon Heath, for example, is a composite of the heaths between Bournemouth and Dorchester. The opening pages of *Return of the Native* provide one of Hardy's best-known geographical descriptions:

A Saturday afternoon in November was approaching the time of twilight, and the vast tract of unenclosed wild known as Egdon Heath embrowned itself moment by moment. Overhead the hollow stretch of whitish cloud shutting out the sky was as a tent which had the whole heath for its floor.

The heaven being spread with this pallid screen and the earth with the darkest vegetation, their meeting-line at the horizon was clearly marked. In such contrast the heath wore the appearance of an instalment of night which had taken up its place before its astronomical hour was come: darkness had to a great extent arrived hereon, while day stood distinct in the sky.

(Hardy 1978/1878: 53)

541

It would be a mistake to read Hardy as a writer who merely recorded the places in front of him; he did not always do this very well (Pite 2002). For instance, he failed to depict many of the harsh realities of nineteenth-century rural life, opting instead for a 'romanticising and pastoral gloss which, from the viewpoint of the social historian, is simplistically misrepresentative' (Snell 1985: 392).

But landscape writers, Hardy included, do not simply depict exterior landscapes. There is both less to their geographies than this, and more. Less, since they leave out some details and get others wrong. And more, because they invent places that did not exist before – Egdon Heath, for instance – and because they animate those places, turning them into settings for stories and people's lives. Geographical images in literature and popular culture not only describe places; they also describe people's *experiences and perceptions* of those places. Humanistic geographers, interested in these things and opposed to the wholesale quantification of geography that was taking place in the 1960s, kept alive the geographical interest in imaginative literature when regional geography declined (Ley and Samuels 1978). As Yi-Fu Tuan (1978: 194) explained, 'Literature provides a perspective for how people experience their world' (see also Simpson-Housley and Preston 1994). Tuan was influenced by the philosopher Gaston Bachelard, whose *Poetics of Space* explained and illustrated how literary sources can be used to understand geographical experience and meaning. Bachelard used novels and poems to trace the meanings people attach to intimate and domestic spaces such as cellars and attics, stairs and windows, drawers, chests, wardrobes and corners of the garden. His understanding of people's attachments to place, which informed humanistic ideas of place and what Tuan called 'topophilia' (the love of place and land), draws upon William Goyen's 1951 novel, *House of Breath*:

> That people could come into the world in a place they could not at first even name and had never known before; and that out a nameless and unknown place they could grow and move around in it until its name they knew and called with love, and call it HOME, and put roots there and love others there; so that whenever they left this place they would sing homesick songs about it and write poems of yearning for it, like a lover.
>
> (Goyen 1951, quoted by Bachelard 1964: 58)

These humanistic geographies, and the geographical literary criticism on which they were founded, have been criticized as socially and politically abstract. More recently, Gillian Rose (1993) has argued that humanistic ideas of home and place appear to be universal but speak specifically of heterosexual men, their desire for home and their power in the home. Implicitly, the humanistic idea of home, informed by writers such as Goyen, is a place in which to be nurtured – by mothers or wives. For many women, of course, nurturing is a job, the home a place of work as well as one of meaning and feeling. Similarly, Paul Carter (1987) shows that ideas of home on a different scale, through which people become attached to the land in which they live, are often embedded in material power relations; making home is connected to the displacement of others.

These criticisms raise important questions about who these imaginative geographies serve – and, more generally, what geographical description is *for*. Edward Said argued that geographical descriptions or representations are more than depictions. They should be judged, not according to 'correctness' or 'fidelity to some great original', but in terms of their 'style, figures of speech, setting, narrative devices, historical and social circumstances' (Said 1978: 21). For Said, the representation is generative and political, always *for* something, and *against* or *instead of* something else. As he puts it, in relation to Orientalism:

My whole point about this system is not that it is a misrepresentation of some Oriental essence – in which I do not for a moment believe – but that it operates as representations usually do, for a purpose, according to a tendency, in a specific historical, intellectual, and even economic setting. In other words, representations have purposes, they are effective much of the time, they accomplish one or many tasks. Representations are formations, or as Roland Barthes has said of all the operations of language, they are deformations. The Orient as a representation in Europe is formed – or deformed – out of a more and more specific sensitivity towards a geographical region called 'the East'.

(Said 1978: 273)

Henri Lefebvre (1991) puts this in another way, which is particularly helpful to geographers who are interested in understanding representations as something other than and more than depictions. He argues that both spaces and texts are cultural productions which function in similar ways, and neither is the *a priori* basis for the other. Responding to the 'seeming separation of a concern with representations, metaphors and discursive constructs from the determinations, violence and messiness of the material world', and drawing upon Lefebvre, Ogborn (2006: 145) stresses the materiality of both text and space, word and geography. As he puts it: 'Some words become material: on the page, the mobile phone, the computer screen. Texts are necessarily geographical in that they exist in particular geographical forms.' Ogborn (2006: 145) argues that we should think, not of texts depicting *a priori* spaces, but of the mutual 'imbrication' of text and space.

So geographers should understand representations, not as depictions of the world but as part of it, both generative and political. As one Hardy scholar put it, 'artists don't copy landscapes, they make them' (Widdowson 1989: 56). The next sections examine in more detail the ways in which geographical words do not simply reflect but actively make, and form part of, geographical worlds and our understandings of them. Andrew Thacker, a literary critic who has studied geographical representations in poetry and fiction, stresses that geographical description should not be seen as an end in itself. He advocates a '*critical* literary geography' which would not simply extract descriptive passages from literary texts, but would ask about their theoretical and political significance. This would 'stress the distance from an effortless mapping of represented landscapes in literary texts, and raise more complex questions about space and power, and how space and geography affect literary forms and styles' (Thacker 2006: 60). This section has explained that literary geographies should be understood as both less and more than *depictions* of exterior and/or mental spaces, and concluded that these geographies should be approached critically, reconnected with theoretical and political questions. In this spirit, the next sections ask what geographical descriptions achieve, conceptually and politically.

The theoretical significance of geographical description

Geographical description can be the vehicle for experimenting with new ways of seeing. Anthropologists George Marcus and Michael Fischer (1986: 15) argue that 'empirical research monographs, through self-conscious attention to their writing strategies, equally become works of heightened theoretical significance'. By putting words to the world, by articulating people's experiences of it, geographical writers can produce what Marxist cultural critic Frederic Jameson (1988: 349) calls 'cognitive maps' – geographical representations that can help people to position themselves within a changing and often disorienting world.

A classic example of geographical writing that does not simply depict, but begins to explain a changing world, is Friedrich Engels' descriptions of Manchester in 1844.

> At the bottom the Irk flows, or rather stagnates. It is a narrow, coal-black stinking river full of filth and garbage which it deposits on the lower-lying right bank. In dry weather, an extended series of the most revolting blackish green pools of slime remain standing on this bank, out of whose depths bubbles of miasmatic gases constantly rise and give forth a stench that is unbearable even on this bridge forty or fifty feet above the level of the water..
>
> (Engels 1958/1845: 60)

There was nothing routine about this description of Manchester. Struggling to describe new levels of social and environmental degradation, Engels conveyed the sense that a new form of industrial society was emerging, a new set of relations between property owners and workers, which could not be put into familiar terms. Struggling to describe this city, he groped towards an understanding of capitalism, which he would develop in more abstract terms with Karl Marx in their joint-authored studies of capitalism.

By writing about places that seem to reveal something more general, such as the future of economic and social relations, successive generations of authors have tried to write geographical descriptions that do not just depict places; they also open new avenues for understanding. Doing so, they have claimed special significance for a range of places, mostly cities in rich countries. Through their novelistic and poetic accounts of Dublin and London, for example, James Joyce and T.S. Eliot examined the flux of modern life (Kearns 2006). Though his Arcades project, consisting of notes and reflections on the geography of Paris, Walter Benjamin developed a broader thesis about modernity (Berman 1982). Through geographical writing, he aimed at something broader. As Benjamin (1986: 5) put it: 'I have long, indeed for years, played with the idea of setting out the sphere of life − bios − graphically on a map.' More recent writers have, to paraphrase Benjamin, tried to set out the sphere of *postmodern* life by writing about Los Angeles. Their geographical descriptions are intended as something more than portraits of a place. In 1986, Ed Soja and Allen Scott (1986: 249) called Los Angeles 'the very capital of the late 20th century', the 'paradigmatic industrial metropolis of the modern world'. By describing Los Angeles, they claimed to offer a glimpse of something more general: emerging regimes of accumulation. Typically, the French philosopher and postmodern theorist Jean Baudrillard claimed to find the essence of postmodernism on the LA freeway:

> The only tissue the city has is that of the freeways, a vehicular, or rather an incessant transurbanistic, tissue, the extraordinary spectacle of these thousands of cars moving at the same speed, in both directions, the headlights full on in broad daylight, on the Ventura Freeway, coming from nowhere, going nowhere . . . the hyperreal scenario of deserts, freeways, oceans and sun.
>
> (Baudrillard 1988: 125–6)

Jameson, meanwhile, found the essence of postmodernism in the architecture of a Los Angeles hotel. He argued that the disorienting effect of reflective surfaces and multiple levels within the Bonaventure Hotel spoke of the mutations of 'postmodern hyperspace' (Jameson 1984: 83). There was much debate in the 1980s and early 1990s about whether the postmodern condition represented a real departure or whether it was merely a distraction from the fundamental continuity of capitalism. Mike Davis, arguing the latter, found the shiny surfaces of ocean freeways and expensive hotels a distraction from the realities of capitalist exploitation, and constructed his description of the city from a different viewpoint:

> The shortest route between Heaven and Hell in contemporary America is probably Fifth Street in Downtown L.A. west of the refurbished Biltmore Hotel, and spilling across the moat of the Harbor Freeway, a post-1970 glass and steel skyscraper advertises the landrush of the Pacific Rim capital to the central city. Here, Japanese mega-developers, transnational bankers and billionaire corporate raiders plot the restructuring of the California economy. A few blocks east, across the no-man's-land of Pershing Square, Fifth Street metamorphoses into the 'Nickel': the notorious half-mile strip of blood-and-vomit-spewn concrete where several thousand homeless people, themselves trapped in the inner circle of Dante's inferno, have become pawns in a vast local power struggle.
>
> (Davis 1987: 65)

Los Angeles continues to figure prominently in debates about postmodernism (e.g. Dear 2000), though writers have turned to many other cities to try to 'cognitively map' postmodernity, particularly in its increasingly global and arguably imperial manifestations.

The attacks of 11 September 2001 brought these issues into focus as never before, demanding a form of cognitive mapping capable of representing New York as a global and contested imperial city (Brooker 2006). The difficulty of representing and reconnecting the local and the global is at the heart of Jameson's concept of cognitive mapping. He argued that the 'truth' of 'limited daily experience' in Western cities such as New York and London lies in 'India or Jamaica or Hong Kong'. And yet, he continued, the 'structural coordinates' of imperialism or globalization 'are no longer accessible to immediate lived experience and are often not even conceptualizable for most people' (1988: 349). Cognitive mapping would 'inscribe a new sense of the absent global colonial system on the very syntax of poetic language itself, a new play of absence and presence' (Jameson 1988: 349). Contemporary geographers struggle to describe this interplay of local and global, just as Engels struggled to describe industrial capitalism (in Manchester). Irit Rogoff (2000: back cover) argues that: 'Geography is a language in crisis, unable to represent the immense changes that have taken place in a post-colonial, post-communist, post-migratory world.' This crisis is not new, but rather renewed, induced by changes that run ahead of people's experiences or vocabularies.

The political significance of description

Engels' description of Manchester bears out Marcus and Fischer's (1986: 15) claim that 'empirical research monographs, through self-conscious attention to their writing strategies, equally become works of heightened theoretical significance', but it also makes it clear that theoretical significance, never 'purely academic', is always already political. Describing Manchester, Engels formulated ideas about capitalism and class, which could be deployed politically, both locally (in Manchester) and generally (nationally and internationally). This illustrates the broader point that geographical description, never neutral, is always *for* something or someone, and often against something or someone else.

The previous discussion of Engels' description of Manchester concluded that the politics of geographical description are fundamentally embedded in its language. Another way of putting this would be to say that geographical writers invoke politically loaded categories and distinctions, even when they appear to be using neutral geographical terms. Developing this argument, the philosopher and cultural critic Roland Barthes (1972) read a range of apparently innocent texts – photographs, travel guides and so on – as 'myths' that cannot be taken at face value. When a photograph or travel guide appears to be describing a mountain, for example, it is really speaking about something else. For instance, Barthes argues that the *Blue Guide* (a travel guidebook) to Switzerland says more about bourgeois taste and Protestant morality than it does about the Alps (Barthes 1972: 74). The politics of geographical writing are not always so implicit, between the lines. The remainder of this section explores some more explicitly politicized geographical words, fleshing these out with examples from geographies of colonialism.

The most fundamental aspect of geographical description – the naming of places – has long been a vehicle for territorial disputes and contests. When European colonists sought to take possession of territory, they enacted rituals of conquest, naming the land as their own. These rituals varied, different European countries adopting different but overlapping practices. All asserted their claims through written documents and maps, but their more tangible practices for making territorial claims varied: the French held theatrical rituals, whereas the Spanish made speeches and the English erected monuments and signs (Seed 1995). The process of claiming land by naming it continued after the moment of conquest and symbolic possession. European conquerors were followed by waves of explorers, surveyors and mapmakers, and by merchants, travellers and settlers, letter-writers and storytellers, writers and artists, who successively assimilated the non-European world, making it their own. Their geographical names and narratives were territorial claims. In *The Road to Botany Bay*, Paul Carter (1987) traces the European naming and mapping of Australian geographical features by white explorers, administrators, settlers and convicts. Carter counters positivist histories of Australia, which regard the land as an *a priori* stage upon which events unfolded, with 'spatial history' that 'begins: not in a particular year, nor in a particular place, but *in the act of naming*' (Carter 1987: xxiv). He continues:

> For by the act of place-naming, space is transformed symbolically into a place, that is, a space with a history. And, by the same token, the namer inscribes his passage permanently on the world, making a metaphorical world-place which others may one day inhabit and by which, in the meantime, he asserts his own place in history.
>
> (Carter 1987: xxiv)

For Carter, Cook's first tentative words opened up a continent, providing him with 'conceptual space in which to move' (Carter 1987: 7).

Carter's spatial history of Australia echoes and politicizes Bachelard. Whereas the latter concentrated upon the experiences of people as they formed attachments to land, Carter asks more questions about how they took possession of it, and from whom. He stresses that, like the names themselves, colonial acts of naming either blatantly ignored or appropriated and incorporated pre-existing Aboriginal names and histories of the land. Aboriginal voices were silenced, Aboriginal histories and geographies erased.

Colonial territorial claims have been contested by critical and counter-narratives. It has been argued that, since naming was a vehicle for colonization, then 'un-naming' can be a means of deconstructing the colonial legacy, and recreating space for those erased and marginalized by colonialism. Un-naming has been effected in a literal sense, through the reversion to pre-colonial place names such as Uluru (formerly Ayers Rock), or the introduction of inclusive place names such as Aoteroa/New Zealand, which acknowledge both the (now permanent) colonizers and also the indigenous peoples (Phillips 2005). Similarly, postcolonial critic Graham Huggan (1994) points to stories and poems that un-name or un-map colonial geographies. Margaret Atwood's *Surfacing* (1973), an important novel of this type, enacts a return to the land in which the identity of an Anglo-Canadian protagonist progressively unravels as she moves from the city to – and into – the bush. Reversing the standard form of exploration narratives, in which heroic explorers map and take possession of the land, the anti-heroine of this story gradually lets go, unburdening herself and reaching a point at which she can start over. By unwriting colonial history and geographies, Atwood clears space in which new stories and places can be written.

The conquest of particular places through geographical writing was accompanied by more general colonial discourse, which asserted territorial claims on a grand scale. As Edward Said put it, the colonial 'struggle over geography' (Said 1993: 6) was fought not only through armed conflict and other tangible forms of domination and resistance, but also through words and stories, contested colonial discourse. Said applied Michel Foucault's concept of discourse to the analysis of colonial power. From this perspective discourse, in which spoken and written words take centre-stage, does not reflect reality in any transparent or straight-forward way; it constructs and organizes social reality and, with it, power relations (Tonkiss 1988). Said (1978) argued that colonial discourse – from scholarly studies of the language or geography of non-European peoples to popular travel books or cultural representations of them (in novels or operas for example) – was important in shaping worldviews. Said stressed that representation did not just depict, it produced geographies, and did so for a reason. As he put it, 'the Orient was almost a European invention' (Said 1978: 1). Europeans invented imaginative geographies in which they could see themselves as legitimate conquerors, non-European peoples as natural colonial subjects. Orientalist discourse produced 'the commonly held view of the Orient as a geographical space to be cultivated, harvested, and guarded' (Said 1978: 219). It was also important, on a more practical level, in facilitating the colonial bureaucracy and day-to-day administration of colonial rule. But, however neatly Orientalist discourse lent itself to the definition of Eurocentric worldviews and colonial projects, discourse could not determine its own effects, as the next section explains.

Geographies of reading

The previous sections have concentrated on written words, whether in the landscape or in textual form. But written words only matter if people read, understand and use them. It is therefore important to look beyond words and authors to ask about reading and readers, the people who animate geographical texts, realizing their potential to make and change worlds.

To see what people do with the written word, with geographical writing, we can begin with a simple example. Returning to Thomas Hardy, we can see that his geographical fiction and poetry has provided a lens through which people have come to see southwest England. Regional identities and tourist promotions revolve around the concept of Hardy's Wessex. Tourist authorities advertise 'pub walks in Hardy's Wessex' (Powers 1997), while the National Trust (the leading UK heritage charity) includes Hardy in a series entitled *Literary Trails: Writers in Their Landscapes* (Hardyment 2000). Both for those who have actually read Hardy and for everyone else, the southwest is 'Hardy country', in much the same way that the Lake District is associated with and seen through the lens of Beatrix Potter and William Wordsworth. But these are simple and rather trivial examples of something more profound: readers animating and using written words.

The recognition that readers produce rather than simply decode meanings raises questions about how *and where* they do so. The spaces in which texts are read have important bearings on *how* they are read. Livingstone (2005) argues for a 'located hermeneutics' in which meaning is interpreted through the local cultural politics of the contexts in which a source is employed. He shows how Darwin's biogeographical theory of evolution by natural selection was interpreted in different ways in different settings. Contexts and geographies of reading are also explained and illustrated in James Secord's *Victorian Sensation* (2000), which traces different readings of a major work of pre-Darwinian evolutionary theory. Robert Chambers' *Vestiges of the Natural History of Creation* (1844) caused a sensation nationally and internationally, but it was understood differently in different places, and its impacts were equally differentiated. Aristocrats in London regarded it as dangerous and endorsed refutations from scientific writers. Unitarians welcomed the book's challenge to the ecclesiastical establishment. To metropolitan progressives it was a bold and visionary work, free of bigotry or prejudice. In Oxford and Cambridge, meanwhile, the *Vestiges* was variously read as supportive of new scientific insights, and vilified as degrading materialism. And in Liverpool, where it was particularly controversial, readings mirrored the social divisions and geographies of the city. It was well received by advocates of urban reform, for example, because it could be taken as scientific justification for social improvement.

These different readings of the same text show that reading is shaped not only by a reader's personality and imagination, but also by their social and political location. Geographies of reading are shaped, not only by readers, but also by interests that shape reading and control the production and circulation of texts. For example, the reading of African 'classics' in Africa has been influenced by publishers such as Heinemann, which launched an African Writers Series in 1962. From a study of this series, Clive Barnett (2006: 7) concludes that publishing is a 'set of distinctively geographical practices that involve the *dissemination* of ideas and materials, and the articulation of texts with multiple contexts'. Publishers interact with other forces and agents in shaping what people read and how they read it. For example, children's reading is influenced by a number of gatekeepers including reviewers and review editors, review publications and literary awards, librarians and teachers, parents and other book buyers (Phillips 2001). In 1960s and 1970s Britain, these gatekeepers intervened to try to change children's reading. One of their main goals was to eradicate the legacies of imperialism, removing colonial representations of people and place, while working to create and promote postcolonial representations. Both these examples – the African Writers Series and children's books in Britain – highlight a second dimension to geographies of reading, concerned not only (like Secord) with the contexts in which reading takes place, but also with the subjects of what is read, including the colonial or postcolonial settings of fiction. And both of these explicitly political examples illustrate how the relationship between geography and reading is reciprocal and politically charged: people read differently in different places, and their readings help to *make* those places.

Developing the thesis that readers use texts to make places, Derek Gregory interprets Orientalist texts and readings as '*performances of space*', producing the effects that they name (Gregory 2004: 18–19, original emphasis). Expanding on the performativity of contemporary Orientalism, he explains that:

> Its categories, codes, and conventions shape the practices of those who draw upon it, actively constituting its object (most obviously, 'the Orient') in such a way that this structure is as much a *repertoire* as it is an archive.
>
> (Gregory 2004: 18–19)

Gregory traces echoes and iterations of Orientalist texts – their colonial tropes and imaginative geographies – in the foreign policies of the United States and its allies in Afghanistan, Palestine and Iraq. The mechanisms of this are often very tangible. For example, English and French travellers in Egypt have often taken books by their predecessors, reading them along the way. They see their own journeys through the lens of other books, which they variously re-enact and use as points of reference. This establishes continuity between travel books and travel experiences, blurring boundaries between imaginative and real travel, textual and material geographies. Writers often try to distance themselves from their colonial predecessors, but those predecessors remain important points of reference. A great deal has been written about colonial travel writing, and how it shaped and legitimated historical forms of colonialism. What Gregory does is to bring this forward, showing how politicians and other people see the contemporary Islamic world through the lens of Orientalist and other colonial fictions and discourses. For example, he examines the words used by George Bush Senior, addressing a joint session of Congress on 11 September 1990, on the crisis in the Gulf following the Iraqi invasion of Kuwait. 'Out of these troubled times, a new world order can emerge,' the President stated, one in which 'the rule of law supplants the law of the jungle.' Gregory (2004: 159) argues that Bush's speech revived a colonial discourse of 'wild untamed spaces' in which 'civilization' was menaced by a reversion to 'barbarism'. Though this kind of imaginative geography, and more specifically through the inertia of its language, the past weighs heavily upon the present.

Conclusion: working with words

This chapter has explained and illustrated the importance of words, which often go unnoticed in both tangible and textual geographies. It has shown that geographical writing, never the mere depiction of places or landscapes, is both conceptually and politically committed. Geographies of writing, shaped not only by authors but also by readers, can sometimes close down political agendas but sometimes open them up. So words do more than depict *a priori* geographies, which would have existed without them. Since they also shape these geographies, they are never superfluous, distractions from material reality. On the contrary, words are both a part of geography and productive of it. This has implications both for the way that geographers write, and for the ways in which we read and understand words and texts.

This chapter has illustrated and explained why geographers use textual sources such as stories and poems for research purposes. Students are encouraged to do the same, though it should be noted that textual analysis is not as straightforward as some other methodologies available to human geographers. As Stuart Aitken explains:

> The adoption of textual analysis and the reading metaphor has given rise to a methodology which is often thought of as being largely implicit and derived from years of apprenticeship and practice. This makes things a little difficult for the beginning researcher who has little training and experience in interpreting texts.
>
> (Aitken 1997: 204–5)

Since textual analysis does not lend itself to easily packaged methodologies, which can be mechanistically learned or applied, textbooks on geographical research methods often struggle to explain this subject. The editors of one such book recently admitted that textual and discourse analysis is 'a craft skill, something like bike riding or chicken sexing, which is not easy to render or describe in an explicit manner' (Hoggart, Lees and Davies 2002: 164). On the other hand, geographical research skills that can be and are applied mechanistically – rote statistics and unimaginative questionnaire surveys – are rarely the most enlightening. Like other research in human geography (including critical statistical analysis and questionnaire research!), textual research is hard to do well, and this chapter has shown that there are good reasons for wanting to do it.

This chapter has also highlighted the textuality of geography itself. This has wide implications, not only for geographers specifically interested in textual data, but also for all those who use words in the course of their work. By looking *for* and *at* words that we normally look *through*, not only in tangible and textual geographies that already exist but also in those we write, this chapter has underlined the need for a self-reflexive approach to writing. As the anthropologist Clifford Geertz put it,

> The ability of anthropologists to get us to take what they say seriously has less to do with either a factual look or an air of conceptual elegance than it has with their capacity to convince us that what they say is a result of their having penetrated (or, if you prefer, been penetrated by) another form of life, truly 'been there'. And that, persuading us that this offstage miracle has occurred, is where the writing comes in.
>
> (Geertz 1988: 4–5)

Geographers need not necessarily worry about writing more beautifully, but we should worry about writing, and write more self-consciously, reflecting always on what we do when we write. As this chapter has shown, geographical writing always involves both less and more than depiction; it is always theoretically and politically committed, and the challenge for geographers is to understand and harness this power.

Further reading

Bachelard, G. (1964) *The Poetics of Space*, trans. Maria Jolas. Boston: Beacon Press.
Carter, P. (1987) *Road to Botany Bay*. London: Faber and Faber.
Gregory, D. (2004) *The Colonial Present: Afghanistan, Palestine, Iraq*. Oxford: Blackwell.
Phillips, R, and McCracken, S. (eds) (2006) The spatial imaginary. *New Formations* 57, 7–149.
Secord, J. (2000) *Victorian Sensation: The Extraordinary Publication, Reception and Secret Authorship of Vestiges of the Natural History of Creation*. Chicago: University of Chicago Press.

References

Aitken, S.C. (1997) Analysis of texts: armchair theory and couch-potato geography. In R. Flowerdew and D. Martin (eds) *Methods in Human Geography*, pp. 197–212. Harlow: Longman.
Barnes, T. and Duncan, J.S. (eds) (1992) *Writing Worlds: Discourse, Text and Metaphor in the Representation of Landscape*. London: Routledge.
Barnett, C. (2006) Disseminating Africa: burdens of representation and the African Writers Series. *New Formations* 57, 74–94.
Barthes, R. (1972) *Mythologies*, trans. Annette Lavers. London: Jonathan Cape.
Baudrillard, J. (1988) *America*, trans. Chris Turner. London: Verso.
Benjamin, W. (1986) *Reflections: Essays, Aphorisms, Autobiographical Writings*, edited by Peter Demetz. New York: Shocken Books.
Berman, M. (1982) *All That is Solid Melts into Air: The Experience of Modernity*. New York: Simon and Schuster.

Brooker, P. (2006) Terrorism and counter narratives: Don DeLillo and the New York imaginary. *New Formations* 57, 10–25.

Davis, M. (1987) Chinatown, Part Two? *New Left Review* 164, 65–86.

Dear, M. (2000) *The Postmodern Urban Condition*. Oxford: Blackwell.

Duncan, J. (1990) *The City as Text: The Politics of Landscape Interpretation in the Kandyan Kingdom*. Cambridge: Cambridge University Press.

Duncan, J. and Gregory, D. (1999) *Writes of Passage*. London: Routledge.

Engels, F. (1958/1845) *The Condition of the Working Class in England in 1844*. Oxford: Blackwell.

Fish, S., (1980) *Is There a Text in this Class?* Cambridge: Harvard University Press.

Geertz, C. (1988) *Works and Lives*. Stanford: Stanford University Press.

Hardy, T. (1978/1878) *The Return of the Native*. Harmondsworth: Penguin.

Hardyment, C. (2000) *Literary Trails: Writers in Their Landscapes*. London: National Trust.

Hoggart, K., Lees, L. and Davies, A. (2002) *Researching Human Geography*. London: Arnold.

Huggan, G. (1994) *Territorial Disputes: Maps and Mapping Strategies in Contemporary Canadian and Australian Fiction*. Toronto: University of Toronto Press.

Jameson, F. (1984) Postmodernism, or the cultural logic of late capitalism. *New Left Review* 146, 53–92.

——(1988) Cognitive mapping. In C. Nelson and L. Grossberg (eds) *Marxism and the Interpretation of Culture*. Chicago: University of Illinois Press.

Kearns, G. (2006) The spatial poetics of James Joyce. *New Formations* 57, 107–25.

Lefebvre, H. (1991) *The Production of Space*, trans. Donald Nicholson-Smith. Oxford: Blackwell.

Ley, D. and Samuels, M.S. (1978) *Humanistic Geography: Prospects and Problems*. Chicago: Maaroufa.

Livingstone, David N. (2005) Science, text and space: thoughts on the geography of reading. *Transactions of the Institute of British Geographers* 30 (4), 391–401.

Marcus, G.E. and Fischer, M.M.J. (eds) (1986) *Anthropology as Cultural Critique: An Experimental Moment in the Human Sciences*. Chicago: University of Chicago Press.

Ogborn, M. (2006) Mapping words. *New Formations* 57, 145–9.

Phillips, R. (1997) *Mapping Men and Empire: A Geography of Adventure*. London: Routledge.

——(2001) Politics of reading; decolonising children's geographies. *Ecumene: A Journal of Cultural Geographies* 8 (2), 125–50.

——(2005) Colonial and postcolonial geographies. In P. Cloke, P. Crang and M. Goodwin (eds) *Introducing Human Geographies*. London: Arnold.

Pite, R. (2002) *Hardy's Geography: Wessex and the Regional Novel*. Basingstoke: Palgrave.

Powers, M. (1997) *Pub Walks in Hardy's Wessex*. Dorchester: Power Publications.

Rogoff, I. (2000) *Terra Infirma*: Geography's Visual Culture. London: Routledge.

Rose, G. (1993) *Feminism and Geography*. Cambridge: Polity.

Said, E. (1978) *Orientalism*. Harmondsworth: Penguin.

——(1993) *Culture and Imperialism*. London: Chatto and Windus.

Seed, P. (1995) *Ceremonies of Possession in Europe's Conquest of the New World, 1492–1640*. Cambridge: Cambridge University Press.

Simpson-Housley, P. and Preston, P. (1994) *Writing the City, Eden, Babylon and the New Jerusalem*. London: Routledge.

Snell, K.D.M. (1985) *Annals of the Labouring Poor: Social Change and Agrarian England, 1660–1900*. Cambridge: Cambridge University Press.

Soja, E. and Scott, A. (1986) Editorial. *Environment and Planning D, Society and Space* 4, 249–55.

Thacker, A. (2003) *Moving Through Modernity: Space and Geography in Modernism*. Manchester: Manchester University Press.

——(2006) The idea of a literary critical geography. *New Formations* 57, 56–73.

Tonkiss, F. (1988) Analysing discourse, in C. Searle (ed.) *Researching Society and Culture*, pp. 245–60. London: Sage.

Tuan, Yi-Fu (1978) Literature and geography: implications for geographical research. In D. Ley and M.S. Samuels (eds) *Humanistic Geography: Prospects and Problems*, pp. 194–206. Chicago: Maaroufa.

Widdowson, P. (1989) *Hardy in History: A Study in Literary Sociology*. London: Routledge.

35

Mapping

Chris Perkins

This chapter explores the role of the mapping in the geographical imagination, charting the powerful differences that flow from the application of spatial technologies to code ideas and places. It investigates maps as technological artefacts of science, charts the role of maps as political and social constructions and artistic imaginings, and explains how mapping can be seen as a suite of cultural actions. But first a story about maps . . .

One day. Many maps. The weather forecast of the BBC. Be careful out there, today it's going to be wild: you can *see* the front sweeping in; *look* how the land disappears under the swathe of animated rain, *watch* as the god-like overview sweeps around the nation, zooming in precisely on script. The forecast conveys certainty and control, orchestrated by the words of the presenter. It all seems so real but also reassuring and entertaining. The next storyline is also illustrated by a map: a more static graphic placing American progress rooting out insurgents in Iraq, sparse and simplified, perhaps covering for a lack of pictures in a breaking story.

Brief interludes to distract from the burning toast. Then up to the station. Early. On the notice-board the schematic map of the line to Manchester carefully directs attention to all that matters – the journey. There is nothing beyond the railway. On the train. Get the book out. A review copy of Katherine Harmon's (2003) *You Are Here*. Striking and artistic images of place, personal and subjective maps of people's worlds.

Out in the crowd at Piccadilly Station – the usual game of 'playing' with the route to the university. Which way today, I wonder? No need for the map, my tracks across the city make the device redundant. And wouldn't it mark you as a stranger, to be seen carrying a map? Past the campus orientation maps with hardly a glance. To work. Ignore the room plan by the lift. Up the stairs. Past the history of cartography such as the Victorian Housing conditions map, framed for visitors to see. Manchester in the past made real for the present. Into the office. Map postcards on the wall, bringing student journeys home to me. Update the PowerPoint slides relating to the first year lecture. How best to tell the story of the difference between aerial photographs and maps – which diagram *works* best? What about the section on cartographic design? Does it really help students with their practical classes? Will the images projected in my PowerPoint presentation be visible from the back of Stopford 3 lecture theatre?

In the afternoon, research on how people play with maps; a chat room discussion with a few 'golf' mappers, designing their own virtual courses. Playing with landscape. Creating maps and places. A focus group after work – talking with groups of walkers about what they want included in some new maps of the city to encourage healthy lifestyles. Show them some prototypes that Nick has drawn up – reactions are mixed – some want the maps to show everything, others like a more selective image; some like the way we integrate photos into one design, others prefer a more pared-down authoritative image of the city. Discuss what the maps are *for*.

One day, *so* many maps. Unnoticed but ubiquitous, icons of fact, indexing the world and making the unknown knowable. Placing everything in a persuasive, powerful and sometimes poetic polemic that enables mobility. Read and unread. So many contexts, so many voices, meanings and actions. Sometimes social, sometimes personal. Was it always like this? And is it like this for everyone, everywhere? A map-immersed society (Wood 1992) or an unrepresentative, partial, personal anecdote from a specialist researcher in an era and culture of fleeting images?

The appliance of science

The vast majority of people who make and use maps still associate them with geography. They mostly assume mapping is 'neutral' and apolitical. Parallels have been noted between the map and science (Turnbull 1993). Maps and scientific theories both appear to show everything, to offer a distanced view from above that suggests objectivity and an uninvolved observer. Both involve the technologies of vision described in Chapter 36. Both work. Both explain. Both naturalize. Both exclude. Both are taken for granted. But what exactly is a map?

Vasiliev *et al.* (1990) carried out an experiment to try to classify what people defined as a map. People thought maps had five components. They *correspond* in some way with locations in geographic space. This correspondence depends on the perspective of image: the more vertical the viewpoint, the more map-like the object becomes. If the subject-matter of the image is the Earth, and in particular the surface of the Earth, that conclusion becomes even more likely. Maps are *graphic*: they tend to be flat and to scale. They are *designed and crafted*: objects in the world appear on the map as pictorial or abstract symbols. The more real the image is the less map-like it becomes.

However, their sample also held pre-conceptions of what a map might be. These were reinforced by the presence of what people saw as typical map-like components, e.g. a key, place names or a grid. The researchers termed this the *prototype effect*. People also recognized objects as maps if they could be used and *function like a map*.

Within these five dimensions lies a huge variation, and the evidence suggests that whilst some maps conform to prototype, many are more 'radial objects', marginal to the core kinds of map and possessing very few of these properties. For example, maps don't have to be tangible: digital maps may be ephemeral images, not artefacts, and many argue that individual cognitive maps allow us to negotiate the world. Nor does a map have to be visible and flat: tactile maps are designed to be read by touch and employ raised relief. The scale of the world represented does not have to correspond to the prototype, either: it is possible to 'map' the atom, the body or the universe as well as the world. Nor does the represented world have to be real: mapping often depicts the imaginary. Perhaps maps don't even have to be communicated or shared: a map stored in a library, or in a computer database, and never used might be no less a map. They need not be crafted or symbolic: remotely sensed imagery appears to be natural and without apparent human input and yet may be employed as if it were a map. So there are serious problems with scientific definitions if you choose to focus only on the artefact.

Perhaps an alternative might lie with technology. Maps are a very specialized way of seeing aspects of the world, and rely upon Western ways of seeing. They depend upon technologies of vision. In the past use these fixed a particular representational view of the world. But technological change is altering the apparently fixed nature of this process.

Data collection has changed from ground-based to aerial-based technologies. Satellites now allow position and elevation to be captured and easily stored in a digital form. Precision and accuracy have increased apace. Sophisticated digital terrain modelling is now routine. Sensors on satellites or airborne platforms capture huge volumes of data in visible, infrared, radar, microwave and sonic ranges. Land covers may be sensed, oceanic survey has been revolutionized and subsurface geological and tectonic features may be analysed. The poles have now been surveyed in detail. Imagery can be generated to provide real-time updates of changing contexts. Mapping technologies help us to manage.

The displays of these data are no longer just static maps. Animated cartography incorporates time into the mapped world and is now commonplace. Digital mapping technologies have separated display from printing and removed the constraint of fixed specifications. We can choose which patterns to display in these images. We can include what we want, and show it as we want. The web allows these images to be widely shared and disseminated at low cost. It also begins to blur the barriers between viewer and viewed: immersive virtual reality systems described in Chapters 33 and 40 allow the user to become a participant in the mapped landscape, instead of an onlooker. These technologies are also increasingly mobile: maps on phones or PDAs and incorporating information derived from GPS now plot your changing real location as you move through the world. And the contexts in which these new mappings are presented themselves depend upon technology – the PowerPoint projected map on the screen in the Stopford lecture theatre can easily be animated and associated with other related data; the same map on an overhead projector is static and inflexible.

People make technologies work. And the new maps achieve their work by *signifying*. Just like the old static maps, they represent something, and in so doing achieve social goals There has been an increasing appreciation that science has to take this context into account, instead of offering universal explanations. Meaning matters, and meaning depends on culture as well as form, content and technology: the schematic map of the railway network is understood because we know what a railway is and understand the conventions for representing a route as an abstracted line without surrounding geographical context. The contexts underpinning this block of chapters concern the *geographical* imagination, so the relationship between map and discipline needs to be considered.

For much of the discipline's history, maps have a been touchstone for geography, employed as an objective tool, to describe regional distributions and as a source for geographical ideas. Practitioners of the geographic art needed to learn how maps were produced and designed, in order to be able to employ them in their research. They studied technologies of production and design. During the Quantitative Revolution in the 1960s and early 1970s there was a retreat from mapping. Model building, theory testing and the wholesale adoption of critical-rationalist approaches to science left little room for unique, factual icons like maps. Remote sensing largely supplanted mapping as a practical tool for physical geographers. The rise of GIS from the mid 1980s and subsequent development of scientific visualization tools reintegrated the mapping sciences back into the mainstream of the discipline. It is now widely accepted that 'maps and cartography comprise a primary part of the geographer's technology, methodology and language' (Bradshaw and Williams 1999: 250). By the mid 1990s a rich variety of visualization could be produced by users. The world of GI science appears to offer great new potential and the map is now only one of a whole suite of practices of scientific visualization that have increasingly come to play significant roles in the representation and management of places (Sui 2004).

Since the Second World War this history has been underpinned by two different scientific approaches. The first emphasized 'cartographic communication' and was based in cognitive scientific research. In this approach the map became an entity in a communication channel, an artefact between a producer and a reader. It mirrored the world. The cartographer's role was to make as good a reflection as possible. Arthur Robinson's influential textbook *Elements of Cartography* came in its later editions to represent this approach to mapping (Robinson *et al.* 1995). Data were acquired and had certain characteristics. They were then mapped following a series of principles established by empirical investigation. These principles covered issues such as how to represent location, direction and distance; how to select information; how best to symbolize these data; how to combine these symbols together; what kind of map to publish, etc. In this view the history of cartography was a story of progress. Over time maps became more and more accurate, knowledge improved, *everything* could be known. The cartographer was separate from the user. And a single optimal map could be produced to meet every need. Mapping was cast as a neutral process independent of any social context. Good maps were made by cartographers who followed the rules. Anything else was outside the remit of map making.

We understand maps today in a very different fashion to what was possible 25 years ago. There has been a profound shift away from the view that maps depict the world in some kind of mimetic process. There are philosophical and pragmatic reasons for this intellectual shift.

Technological changes had rendered problematic a single authoritative view of the world. A whole range of possible ways of seeing the world may now be created by the users of the image, instead of a single carefully crafted view from an authoritative producer (Crampton 2001). Users *explore* their own visualizations now, rather than having to accept a fixed image created by someone else. They can analyse data instead of simply accepting someone else's synthesis. A second hegemonic approach to the mapping sciences responded to these issues and by the mid 1990s had replaced Robinsonian communication as the scientific orthodoxy. The linear inevitability of communication has been supplanted by a multifaceted merging of cognitive and semiotic approaches, centred around representation and strongly influenced by the work of Alan MacEachren (1995). Figure 35.1 offers a visual comparison of these two strands.

The philosophical grounds for rejecting *mimesis* are even more compelling, but they also render scientific representation problematic. There has been an increasing recognition that the image of the world can never fully represent the world, because the process of representing is itself part of the world being represented (King 1996; Pickles 2004). The map-maker and the map would themselves have to be part of the map of the world, and can never, despite the illusion conveyed by the God-like perspective of the image, ever be truly separated from the image (Cosgrove 2001). So science becomes cultural. It has a subjective viewpoint, a politics and a practice despite appearing to have none of these. Social and cultural geographers have rediscovered the power of mapping as a metaphor; along with historians, literary critics, artists and anthropologists in the last 20 years they have begun to research these social contexts, to rethink cartography (Perkins 2003b). The political and cultural contexts in which mapping has been carried out have become crucial.

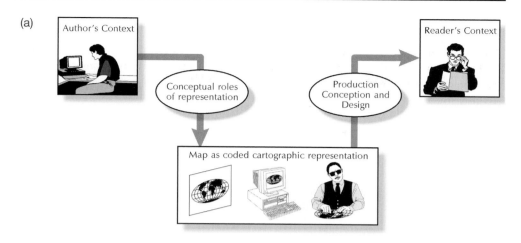

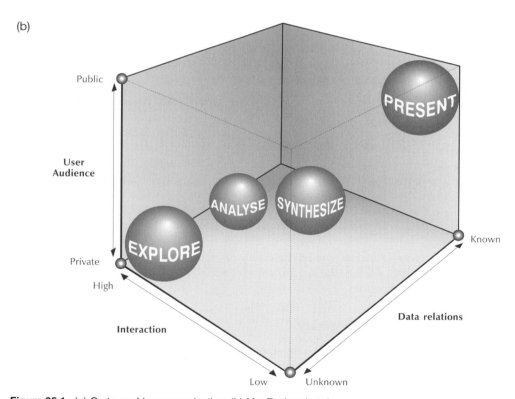

Figure 35.1. (a) Cartographic communication; (b) MacEachren's cube.

557

The power of map representations

In a series of articles published between 1980 and his death in 1991, Brian Harley began to challenge scientific orthodoxy and focus attention on the social role of mapping technologies. He proposed a new research agenda concerned with the roles maps have played in different societies (see Harley 2001 for a posthumous grouping of the most significant papers and Edney 2005 for a systematic and critical overview of his significance).

Harley (1988) argued that maps often reinforced the *status quo* or the interests of the powerful and that we should investigate the historical and social context in which the map has been employed. He later moved on to suggest that mapping could be deconstructed as a form of power-knowledge and to explore the ways in which power has been discursively constructed in the mapping process (Harley 1989). The power of maps, it was argued, lay in the interests that they represented, and often led to people being 'off the map' (Wood 1992). These interests all too often led to subjugation, oppression, control and commerce. Through economic relations, legal evidence, governance or social practice, the power of maps continues to be used to control. It has been argued that many of the social roles played by mapping stem from the modernist project and that mapping partly constitutes modernist enterprise itself (Pickles 2004). Case studies of colonialism, nationalism, military control, gender, landownership and civic governance illustrate the significance of this claim.

Mapping the land: colonial control

Maps have guided the explorer, fostering a sense of inevitable progress and encouraging belief in the march of civilization (Phillips 1997). Local knowledge has been translated into printed working tools, serving the needs of colonizing forces (Lewis 1998). Maps have allowed new territories to be scripted as blank spaces, shown as empty and available for the civilizing Western explorer to claim and name, and subsequently subjugate and colonize. They have employed projection and design elements to naturalize the political process of imperial control and sell imperial values to citizens at home (Cook 1984). The progress of continuing colonial adventures is mapped out nowadays in our news broadcasts, for example in the map of Iraq in the opening vignette. They have been used to govern territory, allocate land, and as an active agent in the creation of newly imperial landscapes (Edney 1997). The settlement of North America, for example, directly followed the surveyors' marks on the ground (Short 2001). Clearly the colonial project relied on the map, and in turn the map relied on colonial aspirations.

Mapping the national imaginary

This imperial context also reveals how maps are part of the geographical imagination of every nation (Dijkink 1996), contributing along with censuses, museums and the printed word to what Benedict Anderson has termed a sense of imagined community that was enormously powerful in fostering the modern development of the nation-state (Anderson 1991). National mapping agencies publish different styles of mapping, designed to different specifications, so that a cultural cartography emerges that parallels national landscapes (Chrisman 1991). National atlases serve as cultural ambassadors for their nations (Monmonier 1994) and ethnic stereotypes are perpetuated through the fixing of place names on officially published mapping (Monmonier 2006). Even the apparently neutral weather forecast map over breakfast maps out the terrain of the British Isles. The representation of the

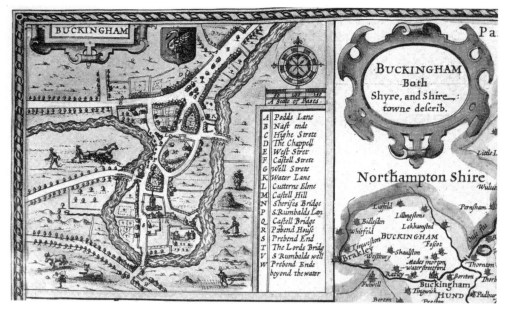

Plate 35.1. County map, England. (John Speed: Buckinghamshire).

nation-state in mapped form may be ambivalent and is often contested. For example, sixteenth-
and seventeenth-century county maps of the Britain reflect a tension between the emerging
early modern state and more local constructions of power (Harley 1983) (see Plate 35.1).

The properties of maps

The property relationship is also closely supported by mapping. Throughout history the
claims, rights and desires of landowners are reflected in maps and in technological changes in
mapping: those without property have all too often been off the map (Kain and Baigent
1992). The estate map served as a practical tool for the administration of a landed estate, as a
means of social control and as an aesthetic statement for its owner (Harley 1983). In a contemporary context the digital land information system in South Africa allows land to be
reapportioned in the wake of apartheid, but also reflects the power of the regime and its
cultural aspirations towards particular projects. The university doesn't only show people how
to find buildings on its orientation map that we walked past, it also proclaims its control over
the campus. Of course, maps are themselves property with a value, often accumulated over
many years and assiduously defended by their owners (Barr 2001). Publication or dissemination is not always in the interests of the powerful: secrecy may have a commercial
rationale; mapping is not always available and leaving out information from a map may also
serve economic interests and reify social relations.

Military interests

Military interests have always had profound impacts on the mapping sciences. National
mapping agencies almost all trace their histories back to military antecedents and military

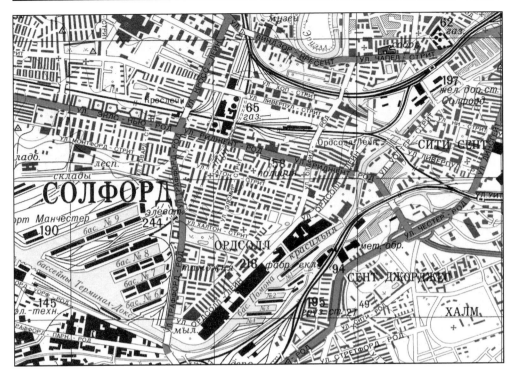

Plate 35.2. Soviet military map.

interests have exerted substantial influences on mapping throughout the history of carto-graphy (see Plate 35.2). Most of the significant technological innovations now accepted as routine in the mapping sciences, such as remote sensing, GIS, terrain analysis and GPS-based technologies, have trickled down from the military (Monmonier 1985). The web has also been influenced by military research. Location-based services stem from military investment and innovation. Multimedia mapping research described in Chapter 40 is fired by military needs for battleground simulation. In high-tech warfare it is in the interests of those prose-cuting the war that military personnel are more distanced from the act of killing. The experience of warfare becomes similar to that of playing a computer game such as *Doom*, where the real landscape morphs increasingly into virtual landscapes familiar to game players. It has been also argued that the interests of the military-industrial complex overlap increas-ingly with those of the entertainment industry (Der Derian 2001), and media mapping representations of recent conflict employ similar technologies to those used by the military to map the battlefield (Clarke 1992).

Governing through watching: maps and surveillance

It has also been argued that visual technologies are employed to facilitate social governance, and that mapping plays an important role in this process by offering a technology that helps to 'discipline' model citizens by marking acceptable and unacceptable forms of behaviour and spaces (Hannah 2000). In this vein Joyce (2003) charts the role of maps in the Victorian city, exploring how the map as a mobile yet immutable form of knowledge was employed to

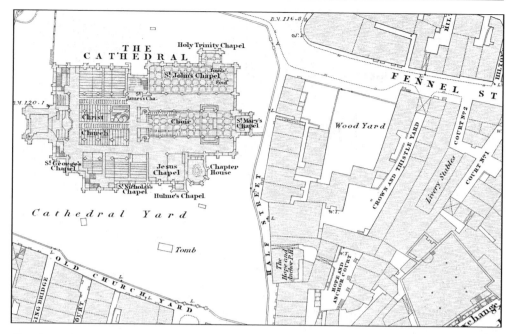

Plate 35.3. OS five-foot plan.

classify and reveal different spaces in the city and in so doing assist in the 'rule of freedom' (see Plate 35.3). In a more contemporary context, national states are much more interested in tracking their citizens after the 9/11 attacks. Crampton (2003) argues that there was a renewed emphasis upon mapping and GIS as surveillant technologies, as part of a strategic and rational governmental response to risks that parallels the invention of thematic mapping as a technology to reinforce a moral order in early nineteenth-century Europe. The nineteenth-century housing condition map of Manchester on the stairs in the opening story plays a similar role, classifying people as a *problem*, subjects demanding attention.

Mapping technologies have the potential to appear to reveal everything. But at the same time there may be moral, political or social reasons for *not* revealing spatial information. Maps remain politically charged documents: there are still huge variations between different nations over what is released into the public domain, and many nations still wish to keep secret the existence of strategic facilities (Parry and Perkins 2000) (see Figure 35.2). The interests of citizens may conflict with the interests of the state: rights to privacy conflict with the all-seeing power of spy satellite, or the real-time web-based tracking of children or criminals (Monmonier 2002).

The man-made map

The authoritative scientific 'all-knowing' gaze of the map has been cast as masculine. In this view the map becomes analogous to a landscape or nature, created as an entity to be seen, controlled and subject to male power, de-corporalized and de-personalized, an objective technology created to do male work (Rose 1995). Mapping practices appear to reinforce this interpretation. In the history of cartography most maps have been made by men. Where

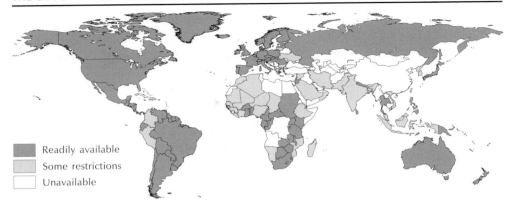

Figure 35.2. Global map availability.

women were involved in the past they were often in positions where they could exercise very little power over the medium. When women were depicted on maps they were often exoticized or eroticized (McClintock 1995: 1–4). The world represented on maps has also tended to be a world of stereotypically male interests: the built environment, emotionless and factual, revealed to be managed. And evidence suggests gender differences in the way maps are read (Harrell *et al.* 2000). However recent interpretation suggests these generalizations may oversimplify – a feminist GIS might empower very different gazes, new themes can be mapped, in new ways (Kwan 2002). A more hybrid vision becomes possible in which power may be subverted.

Subverting power

Subsequent critics of Harley's work have drawn attention to his overly simplistic reading of French post-structuralist thought (e.g. Sparke 1995; Crampton 2001). This has led to a re-interpretation of how power might be articulated in mapping and the increasing realization that power may be employed in many different ways. Emphasis has shifted away from 'power talk', towards a more nuanced and hermeneutic consideration, in which the map is there to be interpreted, its coding of the world conveying impressions of different contexts, cultures and times (Pickles 2004).

New mapping may be published to disseminate alternative views as part of a 'counter-mapping' process. For the last 15 years there has been a profusion of these 'alternative' maps: reaffirming the rights of indigenous peoples; arguing local cases in resource struggles documented in Chapter 57; encouraging community involvement in sustainable lifestyles (like the maps being discussed in our walking-map focus group); reasserting the role of the past in contemporary contexts; or celebrating the aesthetic and the local in an age apparently dominated by uniform and mechanized production and global style.

Pickles (2004) argues that there is never a single interest in the map; instead, mapping may be subverted and interpreted in many different ways. For example, Crouch and Matless (1996) show how the mapping created in the Parish Map Project in Britain articulates many different voices. The same map may at once speak as a political protest, an articulation of local community identity, as aesthetic celebration or as exclusive conservative evocation of a narrowly evoked rural cultural process. It may be classed, gendered and raced. The seeds of alternative readings lie dormant waiting to grow and they flourish in the aesthetic culture of the map.

The aesthetic culture of the map

To appreciate the significance of art in mapping involves four separate relationships: art *in* maps, maps *as* art, maps *in* art and art *as* maps.

(paraphrasing Woodward 1987)

It has long been recognized that aesthetic factors are important for the communication of information in mapped form (Wright 1942). Collectable antiquarian maps are valued as objects of beauty, acquired for their rarity and aesthetic qualities. The visual display of a map is important: maps do more than just inform, they decorate as well. It is widely recognized that mass production and the corporatization of cartographic practice led to a decline in design quality and that the rise of GIS and web mapping has exacerbated this retreat from the aesthetic (Kent 2005). Online maps are functional but ugly. But map users are still able to recognize artistic quality in mapping: individual, subjective, holistic and personal qualities of designs are often contrasted favourably with more utilitarian, depersonalized, analytical and functional qualities associated with map making as a scientific technology. Map users recognize good designs (Wood 1993). 'Good practice' in map design is extolled in texts that systematize artistic qualities: layout, visual hierarchy, name placement, balance, and appropriate levels of generalization are held up as qualities for designers to aspire to (Krygier and Wood, 2005), illustrated in PowerPoint slides in geography lectures (see Figure 35.3). Prizes are given at national and international conferences for the 'best' maps.

Denis Wood has argued that presentational codes allow elements in the map to be combined with associated material such as the title, legends, scale bars, graphs, diagrams, tables,

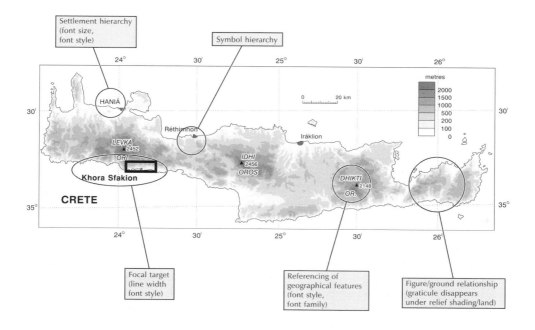

Figure 35.3. Good practice in map design.

cartouches, photographs, borders, vignettes, compass roses, dedications or other associated text in such a way as to set the *tone* for the map (Wood 1992). Subjective combinations of different visual variables result in a design that articulates particular points of view. And tone still matters in the digital era. The animated weather map conveys an *authoritative* impression, its animation and detail conveying almost spurious accuracy to the story of the weather.

The audience reading the map then interprets this aesthetic according to the context in which the map is discursively positioned. A vibrant agit prop image on an alternative weblog will be read differently from a pared-down black-and-white information graphic in *The Times*. So aesthetics depend upon the historical and cultural context of the image. Aboriginal art speaks with a different aesthetic to a Western map of the same area: it is not only *what* is mapped that dictates how the image is employed, it is also *how* features are mapped. Elements in designs themselves allow a map to be dated or even placed. The look of a map immediately encourages preconceptions about the image. Indeed, it has been argued that 'Abstractions of structure order and articulation cannot be cut away from issues of aesthetics or even belief' (Wood 1992: 155).

In the seventeenth-century heyday of decorative European cartography, the worlds of the artist described in Chapter 36 overlapped closely with those of the cartographer. Following the twentieth-century invention of cartography as a science, a much more separate existence became the accepted orthodoxy. Since around the 1980s, however, 'the number and variety of works by contemporary artists based on maps has been remarkable' (Schulz 2001: 1) and books like *You Are Here*, that I was reading on the train, bring this work to a wider audience (Harmon 2003). Artists are increasingly using mapping as a device to draw attention to the way in which we relate to the world. Surrealists, pop artists, situationists (Pinder 1996), land artists (Casey 2005), conceptual artists, community artists (Crouch and Matless 1996), digital media artists and live artists have all employed maps in their work (see Plate 35.4).

Plate 35.4. Map as art: The Thirsk Parish Map.

This turn towards mapping takes place in a time of rapid technological and cultural change. It reflects themes explored elsewhere in this volume: territorial uncertainty in the aftermath of the collapse of the Soviet Union, the global war on terror, American cultural hegemony and neo-liberal orthodoxies are all challenged in this cartographic outpouring. Flux in the information economy, the profusion and dynamism of products and media, increasingly privatized multi-channel and multi-mediated cultures and the rise of virtual places and spaces have all encouraged a focus on the apparently fixed certainties of the map. The blurring of contemporary identities and of divides between genders, ages and social roles, and between nature and culture are all appropriate topics for consideration in mapping. Artists are reflecting changed times but also changing epistemologies. In a Foucauldian sense, maps are entirely appropriate metaphors to explain the heterotopic associations of contemporary spaces. Mapping allows artists to explore the ambivalence of contemporary sign systems, in which reality and the map are increasingly blurred and where the real and the hyper-real coexist. Maps are also mobile and networked, an outcome of a technology that allows cultural messages to be transformed and shared. Artistic mappings also, however, remind us about the pervasive and problematic relations between subjects and objects: mapping can be embodied and its performance reveals the (e)motive and constituitive nature of action.

Acting out the map

Aesthetic approaches alone are insufficient for understanding the significance of mapping for the geographical imagination. Instead, and in parallel with recent research around photography described in Chapter 37, it has recently been argued that mapping needs to be appreciated as a suite of cultural practices (Rundstrom 1991). These involve actions and affects and this kind of mapping reflects a philosophical shift away from representation and towards performance and mobilities (see Thrift 1999 and Chapter 5).

This rethinking of cartography is supported by historical and contemporary work. Researchers concerned with historical contexts increasingly stress the interplay between place, times, actions and theory. David Woodward (1998), for example, argues that mapping in different cultures reflects three traditions: an internal or cognitive set of behaviours involving thinking about space; a material culture in which mapping is recorded as an artefact or object; and a performative tradition where space may be enacted through gesture, ritual, song, speech dance or poetry. In any cultural context there will be a different blend of these elements. So interpreting mapping means considering the context in which mapping takes place and the ways mapping is performed. Instead of focusing on artefacts, performative approaches place mapping as imaginative, material or cultural (Cosgrove 1998).

Central to this theme are the questions of who employs mapping, to what purposes and the kinds of actions this process calls into being, or how the cultures of mapping power are practised (Perkins 2004). In early modernity the culture of printing allowed mass production and dissemination of mapping, and encouraged the map to play its often oppressive role. Detailed examination is needed to chart the actions that this culture brought about. Mapping encounters reveal different meanings. For example Sparke's work (1995) draws attention to the inter-textual field of mapping of native peoples in Canada and employs post-colonial theory to illustrate roles played by native mapping of New-found-land in struggles over identity. Performance is seldom simple; actions are complex and negotiated and mapping interrelates with other cultural performances. For example Schulten's (2001) study of the changing geographical imagination in America situates mapping against a whole suite of geographical and cultural texts.

Contemporary research is also starting to employ ethnographic approaches to carry out empirical investigations to investigate *how* everyday mapping is practised and its relations to identity. Researchers have started to critique representational approaches to mapping and way finding. For example, Tim Ingold (2001: 155) argues mapping is 'the narrative re-enactment of journeys made and of maps as the inscriptions to which such re-enactments may possibly give rise'. Memory leads to action through narrative. Mental maps need not exist as representative structures posited by cognitive psychologists. Brown and Laurier (2005) document the social use of maps by day-trippers planning a car outing and use video evidence to justify mapping as part of the complex social negotiation of day-to-day identity, which changes with the journey and social context. A whole range of tourist mapping experiences and practices are charted in Hanna and del Casino (2003); the postcards on the wall of my office freeze a complex set of placed experiences.

Other recent studies in the context of leisure also illustrate this social emphasis. Perkins and Gardiner (2003) explore how visually impaired people read tactile maps in the real world, but stress that reading depends upon the social interaction between researcher and user and that use does not always constitute reading (see Plate 35.5). Perkins (2006) examines the context of golf mapping and stresses the social function of many different maps employed around the game. Golf course 'planners', for example, serve as functional and often mobile map guides to hole layout, but are also redeployed to help remember the course and game, whilst serving as artefacts in the advertising strategy of the golf course.

In this performative cartography technologies need to be observed in action. This kind of ethnography fits in well with evidence of mapping practice in web-based environments where production and consumption of visualization is increasingly collaborative (Dykes *et al.* 2004). The web brings together mappers as users in collaborative projects grounded in space, for example in mapping hacks and 'mash ups' which subvert existing power structures

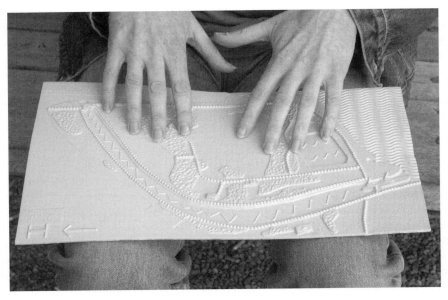

Plate 35.5. Reading the tactile map. Photograph by Chris Perkins.

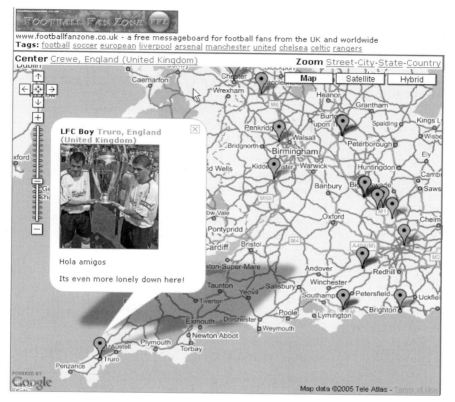

Plate 35.6. Google Maps Frappr site.

(Schuyler *et al.* 2005), or in collaborative urban exploration (Pinder 2005). We can all put ourselves on the map and through the map build new relationships (see Plate 35.6).

New technologies create new stories and performances and evoke many different emotions. Instead of the rational behaviour assumed by the scientific model, or the oppressive behaviour implied in Harleyian takes on the medium, or the aesthetic experience evoked by artists, a performative cartography imagines many different possibilities. Mapping may be sad, playful, proud, painful, revealing, angry, celebratory, boring, reassuring or restless.

Conclusions

The profusion of mapping illustrated in the opening anecdote would not be possible had technologies not shifted profoundly in the last 30 years. But it only touches on the diverse contexts in which mapping has been employed. These contemporary images also reflect a changing political context. They embody power relations in more complex ways than in the era when mapping always seemed to fix, frame and exclude. The apparent neutrality of the mapped image continues to exert a strange power conveyed through the aesthetics of design. We may not notice all these maps around us, but the anecdote certainly reveals the way in which we actively create place through our own mapping performances. Despite their apparently hegemonic assertions about space, maps are there to be imagined, made and remade in the shifting and ambiguous ways that can evoke powerful emotions. The possibilities are endless and other stories are waiting to be played out.

Further reading

Cosgrove, D. (1998) *Mappings*. London: Reaktion Books.
Fawcett-Tang, R. (2002) *Mapping: An Illustrated Guide to Graphic Navigational Systems*. Hove; Mies, Switzerland: RotoVision.
MacEachren, A.M. (1995) *How Maps Work*. New York: Guildford Press.
Perkins, C. (2003) Cartography and graphicacy. In N. Clifford and G. Valentine (eds) *Key Methods in Human and Physical Geography*, pp. 343–68. Sage: London.
Schuyler, E., Gibson, R. and Walsh, J. (2005) *Mapping Hacks*. Sebastopol, CA: O'Reilly.
Turnbull, D. (1993) *Maps are Territories*. Chicago: University of Chicago Press.
Wood, D. (1992) *The Power of Maps*. London: Routledge.

References

Anderson, B. (1991) *Imagined Communities*, revised edition. London: Verso Press.
Barr, R. (2001) Spatial data and intellectual property rights. In R.B. Parry and C.R. Perkins (eds) *The Map Library in the New Millennium*, pp. 176–87. Library Association: London.
Bradshaw, M. and Williams, S. (1999) Scales, lines and minor geographies: whither King Island? *Australian Geographical Studies* 37, 248–67.
Brown, B. and Laurier, E. (2005) Maps and journeying: an ethnographic approach. *Cartographica* 40 (3), 17–33.
Casey, E.S. (2005) *Earth Mapping: Artists Re-shaping Landscape*. Minneapolis: University of Minnesota Press.
Chrisman, N. (1991) Building a geography of cartography: cartographic institutions in cultural context. In M. Blakemore and K. Rybaczuk (eds) *Mapping the Nations: Proceedings of the 15th International Cartographic Association Conference, Bournemouth*. London: International Cartographic Association.
Clarke, K.C. (1992) Maps and mapping technologies of the Persian Gulf War. *Cartography and Geographic Information Systems* 19, 80–7.
Cook, T. (1984) A reconstruction of the world: George R. Parkin's British Empire map of 1893. *Cartographica* 21, 53–65.
Cosgrove, D. (1998) *Mappings*. London: Reaktion Books.
——(2001) *Apollo's Eye: A Cartographic Genealogy of the Earth in the Western Imagination*. Baltimore: Johns Hopkins University Press.
Crampton, J. (2001) Maps as social constructions: power, communication and visualization. *Progress in Human Geography* 25, 235–52.
——(2003) Cartographic rationality and the politics of geosurveillance and security. *Cartography and Geographic Information Science* 30, 135–48.
Crouch, D. and Matless, D. (1996) Refiguring geography the Parish Map Project of Common Ground. *Transactions Institute of British Geographers* 21, 236–55.
Der Derian, J. (2001) *Virtuous War: Mapping the Military–Industrial–Media–Entertainment Network*. New York: Westview Press.
Dijkink, G. (1996) *National Identity and Geopolitical Visions: Maps of Pride and Pain*. London: Routledge.
Dykes J., MacEachren, A.M. and Kraak, M.-J. (eds) (2004) *Exploring Geovisualization*. New York: Elsevier.
Edney, M.H. (1997) *Mapping an Empire: The Geographical Construction of British India*. Chicago: University of Chicago Press.

——(2005) The origins and development of J.B. Harley's cartographic theories. *Cartographica* 40, 1–144.

Fawcett-Tang, R. (2002) *Mapping: An Illustrated Guide to Graphic Navigational Systems.* Hove; Mies, Switzerland: RotoVision.

Hanna, S.P. and del Casino, V.J.J. (2003) *Mapping Tourism.* Minneapolis: University of Minnesota Press.

Hannah, M.G. (2000) *Governmentality and the Mastery of Territory in 19th Century America.* Cambridge: Cambridge University Press.

Harley, J.B. (1983) Meaning and ambiguity in Tudor cartography. In S. Tyacke (ed.) *English Mapmaking 1500–1650*, pp. 22–45. London: British Library.

——(1988) Maps, knowledge and power. In D. Cosgrove and S. Daniels (eds) *The Iconography of Landscape*, pp. 277–312. Cambridge: Cambridge University Press.

——(1989) Deconstructing the map. *Cartographica* 26, 1–20.

——(2001) *The New Nature of Maps.* Baltimore: Johns Hopkins University Press.

Harmon, K. (2003) *You Are Here: Personal Geographies and Other Maps of the Imagination.* Princeton: Princeton University Press.

Harrell, W.A., Bowlby, J.W. and Hall-Hoffarth, D. (2000) Directing wayfinders with maps: the effects of gender, age, route complexity, and familiarity with the environment. *Journal of Social Psychology* 140, 169–78.

Ingold, T. (2001) *The Perception of the Environment.* London: Routledge.

Joyce, P. (2003) *The Rule of Freedom: The City and the Modern Liberal Subject.* London: Verso.

Kain, R.J.P. and Baigent, E. (1992) *The History of Cadastral Mapping.* Chicago: University of Chicago Press.

Kent, A.J. (2005) Aesthetics: a lost cause in cartographic theory? *The Cartographic Journal* 42, 182–7.

King, G. (1996) *Mapping Reality: An Exploration of Cultural Cartographies.* Basingstoke: Macmillan.

Krygier, J. and Wood, D. (2005) Making maps: a visual guide to map design for GIS. New York: Guilford Press.

Kwan, M.P. (2002) Feminist visualization: re-envisioning GIS as a method in feminist geographic research. *Annals of the Association of American Geographers* 92 (4), 645–61.

Lewis, G.M. (1998) *Cartographic Encounters: Perspectives on Native American Mapmaking and Map Use.* Chicago: University of Chicago Press.

McClintock, A. (1995) *Imperial Leather: Race Gender and Sexuality in the Imperial Context.* London: Routledge.

MacEachren, A.M. (1995) *How Maps Work.* New York: Guildford Press.

Monmonier, M.S. (1985) *Technological Transition in Cartography.* Madison: University of Wisconsin Press.

——(1994) The rise of the national atlas. *Cartographica* 31, 1–15.

——(2002) *Spying with Maps: Surveillance Technologies and the Future of Privacy.* Chicago: University of Chicago Press.

——(2006) *Fighting Words: How Names on Maps Claim, Defame, and Inflame.* Chicago: University of Chicago Press.

Parry, R.B. and Perkins, C. (2000) *World Mapping Today.* London: Bowker Saur.

Perkins, C. (2003a) Cartography and graphicacy. In N. Clifford and G. Valentine (eds) *Key Methods in Human and Physical Geography*, pp. 343–68. London: Sage.

——(2003b) Cartography: mapping theory. *Progress in Human Geography* 27, 325–35.

——(2004) Cultures of mapping: power in practice. *Progress in Human Geography* 28, 381–91.

——(2006) Placing the shots: mapping the golf course. *The Cartographic Journal*, forthcoming.

Perkins, C. and Gardiner, A. (2003) Real world map reading strategies. *The Cartographic Journal* 40 (3), 125–30.

Phillips, R. (1997) *Mapping Men and Empire: A Geography of Adventure.* London: Routledge.

Pickles, J. (2004) *A History of Spaces: Mapping Cartographic Reason and the Over-Coded World.* London: Routledge.

Pinder, D. (1996) Subverting cartography: the situationists and maps of the city. *Environment and Planning A* 28, 405–27.

——(2005) Arts of urban exploration. *Cultural Geographies* 12, 4.

Robinson, A., Morrison, J.L., Muehrcke, P.C.A., Kimerling, J. and Guptill, S.C. (1995) *Elements of Cartography*, sixth edition. London: Wiley.

Rose, G. (1995) Geography and gender, cartographies and corporealities. *Progress in Human Geography* 19 (4), 544–8.

Rundstrom, R.A. (1991) Mapping, postmodernism, indigenous people and the changing direction of North American cartography. *Cartographica* 28, 1–12.

Schulten, S. (2001) *The Geographical Imagination in America, 1880–1950*. Chicago: University of Chicago Press.

Schulz, D. (2001) *The Conquest of Space: On the Prevalence of Maps in Contemporary Art*. Leeds: Henry Moore Institute.

Short, J. (2001) *Representing the Republic: Mapping the United States 1600–1900*. London: Reaktion.

Sparke, M. (1995) Between demythologizing and deconstructing the map: Shawnadithit's New-foundland and the alienation of Canada. *Cartographica* 32, 1–21.

Sui, D.Z. (2004) GIS, cartography and the 'Third Culture': geographic imaginations in the computer age. *Professional Geographer* 56, 62–72.

Thrift, N. (1999) Steps to an ecology of space. In D. Massey (ed.) *Human Geography Today*, pp. 295–322. Cambridge: Polity Press.

Turnbull, D. (1993) *Maps are Territories*. Chicago: University of Chicago Press.

Vasiliev, I., Freundschuh, S., Mark, D., Theisen, G. and McAvoy, J. (1990) What is a map? *The Cartographic Journal* 27, 119–23.

Wood, D. (1992) *The Power of Maps*. London: Routledge.

Wood, M. (1993) The map-users' response to map design. *The Cartographic Journal* 30, 149–53.

Woodward, D. (ed.) (1987) *Art and Cartography: Six Historical Essays*. Chicago: University of Chicago Press.

——(1998) Introduction. In D. Woodward and M. Lewis (eds) *The History of Cartography, Volume 2, Book 3: Cartography in the Traditional African, American, Arctic, Australian, and Pacific Societies*. Chicago: University of Chicago Press.

Wright, J. (1942) Map makers are human: comments on the subjective in maps. *Geographical Review* 32, 427–44.

Art and geography

Image and imagination

Caitlin DeSilvey and Kathryn Yusoff

Introduction

Art and geography share a common route in the search for knowledge through the medium of vision. Geography's visual tradition may be traced from the impulse within Enlightenment geographies to give visibility to new worlds, (and metaphors) of looking that are central to contemporary geography's descriptive practice (Livingstone 1992). Many of geography's core tropes and concerns – landscape, sightings, geographical imaginations, the politics of representation, and the society of the spectacle among them – rely on a conception of knowledge as *envisioned*. 'Seeing', conceived of both symbolically and practically, brings new sets of information into the world, whether in the sighting of uncharted coastlands through the telescope, or in the production of a culture of exotic otherness through the circulation of painted images. To consider the relationship between art and geography is to work at this interface, where visual knowledge becomes materialized in image. In this pursuit, we find that visual art's objects – be they paintings or sculptures, decorated artefacts or ephemeral installations – have a curious relation to the geographies they inhabit. People represent the world they know through art, but art also shapes the possibilities of that world, and acts back on it. The practice of art can do social and cultural work, although the effect of that work can vary tremendously depending on the context of its production and reception. Art can be a tool for preserving the status quo, or a tool for understanding and effecting change. It may work to maintain privilege and power, or allow for the expression of resistance. Visual art is a device for imagining the world, but also one of the ways in which the world imagines itself.

This chapter works through three themes to explore the entangled, but often distinct, practices of art and geography; although both base their practices on vision and the visual, their relationship is by no means natural or unmediated. We begin with a discussion of *aesthetics,* broadly understood as the realm where embodied sensation and cultural context combine to generate particular imaginings of the world. Questions of *optics* are taken up in the next section, as we consider the way in which visual instruments have acted to produce certain ways of seeing and acting on the geographies they observe. The complicated relation between art, geography and *power* is considered in the third key theme. Each section uses a few examples to tease out moments of resonant encounter between art and geography. Short sections about specific works of art form a parallel conversation to the main text. Along the way, the chapter's discussion touches on exploration and technologies of vision, ideology and imperialism, desire and visual delight.

As we work through the different themes, a shuttling pattern begins to emerge. If geography's expeditionary and acquisitive visual practices carry new material to artists, then, in a reversal of this influence, art's innovative visual practices can be seen to work back on geography by questioning its assumption of authority and stability. Whether used as a critical tool or considered as part of the 'art of description', art plays an important role in questioning geography's visual methods (Castree and Rogers 2005). A second pattern also emerges from this historical context: there seems to be a transition from a *representational* way of knowing to a more *relational* and situated way of knowing the world. The chapter closes with a discussion of some of the differences that characterize methodological and epistemological approaches underpinning practice in art and geographical discourse.

Illustration 1: *The Geographer*

A shaft of light illuminates the geographer and the instruments of his profession. In Vermeer's 1669 painting *The Geographer* (Plate 36.1) we encounter a telling depiction of the practices of vision (looking, imagining, measuring) which lie at the core of the geographical imagination. The cultural artefacts of seventeenth-century visual exploration order the geographer's room: Hondius's celestial globe, a terrestrial globe, Metius's astrolabe and his 1621 manual on astronomy and geography, a compass, a marine map of Europe, a nautical map, a device for measuring the elevation of the sun and the stars, an optical square (Rohdie 2001: 65–8). The painting documents an historical moment: in the same year that Vermeer painted his geographer, Isaac Newton used curved mirrors to create the first reflecting telescope. Jonathan Crary describes Vermeer's painting as a visualization of the Enlightenment enacted through the episteme of the camera. The light drawn in from outside promises a faithful representation of the world 'out there' (Crary 1990; Gregory 1994: 35); the *camera obscura* effect, working in accord with the 'tools' of geography's visual culture, brings the 'far' near for observation and contemplation.

The sense of interiority and realism that the image aspires to – setting up the dualism of a field 'out there' and the production of objective knowledge 'in here' – still forms a recognizable strand in geographical thinking, despite the influence of critical work that questions such a notion of knowledge production (Crang 2003: 240). The world the geographer looks upon, Mike Crang comments, is divided between the observer and the subjects of (his) observation. Yet, it is precisely the geographer's relation to the instability of vision that makes Vermeer's painting so compelling. The geographer lifts his head away from the map and towards the light, and in doing so he enacts the curiosity that fuelled geographical exploration and the project of the Enlightenment itself (Outram 1999). The geographer seems to be arrested by a fleeting vision. The moment of illumination that holds the geographer captive both confirms and denies a rational separation between observer and observed.

A light from outside the study beckons to the geographer as he makes his measurements and inscriptions. This interference suggests an excessive presence that eludes capture by the lines plotted inside. Vermeer's moment of illumination admits to the profound clarity of vision, while simultaneously affirming the epistemological value of visual endeavour as a means to reach (and, one suspects, have dominion over) the outside world. The delicate

Plate 36.1. *The Geographer, c.* 1668–9, Johannes Vermeer (Stödelsches Kunstinstitut, Frankfurt am Main, reprinted with kind permission).

light, a characteristic of Vermeer's style, expresses the ambiguous and seductive nature of geographical practice. Geography's visual culture summons the imagination, but also holds it at a distance, creating an appetite for that which is in abeyance, or in the terms of the Enlightenment, that which has yet to be discovered. This deferred knowledge of the other animates the drive of discovery and appears as a concentrated energy within Enlightenment science. Vermeer's geographer is not simply a rational observer. While instruments of his discipline attempt to contain the world in a total representation, the geographer glances up from his maps and his measurements to admit the possibility of a more sensual relation with the new worlds opening up beyond the interiority of his study. Vermeer's lucid vision of the

573

geographer bids us today because it suggests as peculative experience of the world, an imaginary relation with the geographies of 'elsewhere', just outside our line of sight.

Aesthetic imaginations

Aesthetics can be understood narrowly as the appreciation of beauty in art, or more broadly as the entire field of sensuous perception, or as a peculiar composite that blends art, affect and culture to arrive at a particular imagining of the world. Visual art is an aesthetic medium, a means for the invention of cultural lenses, which offers glimpses of worlds both familiar and strange. The European exploration of the globe was an aesthetic project as much as a scientific one. Explorers, and the illustrators who accompanied them, were actively involved in 'enframing' (Gregory 1994) the territories they encountered for consumption by those who remained at home (Stafford 1984). Exploration relied on an aesthetic re-description of unfamiliar lands within familiar modes of visual expression – romantic or sublime, picturesque or pastoral (Nash 2000). While the art of exploration varied from place to place (and was often subject to mutation as explorers encountered indigenous modes of expression) aesthetic discipline functioned more often than not as a refuge which sheltered explorers from the overwhelming impact of the new, and as a screen to the economic motives which underlay the exploratory impulse (Outram 1999: 285). Paintings created to provide topographic information followed rigorous 'rules' of practice (Stafford 1984). Yet, as Johannes Fabian has suggested, the reliance on disciplined habits of work may well have been a bulwark of protection against the field's more anarchic and disorienting encounters (Fabian 2000).

The settlement of newly colonized lands required the production of a new aesthetic. In North America, artists recorded on canvas the 'most dearly held beliefs about the meaning of national progress', and fed a mythic imagination about the pastoral transformation of a wild, untamed land (Cronon 1992: 85; John 2004). Images of industrious settlers offered an aesthetic legitimation of the practices of territorial domination. A century later, in Australia, the circulation of picture postcards perpetuated a similar set of frontier mythologies (Waitt and Head 2002). Aesthetics of settlement and belonging form in an uneasy (but symbiotic) relation to aesthetics of exoticism and otherness, evidenced in nineteenth-century British and French romantic paintings of the Orient, which preceded the intellectual colonization of the region by European influences (Said 1979). And, in some instances, a dominant aesthetic takes on a hybrid form, as the colonized take up the visual materials of the colonizers and put them to their own uses (Eaton 2003).

Until the twentieth century, the political and strategic function of aesthetic labour was largely implicit, rather than explicit. An assumption of (or an aspiration to) realist veracity underpinned much of the artistic production. When a discussion of aesthetics and politics came to the fore, responses varied. In the academy, aesthetics was ring-fenced off into the realm of high art, isolated from any association with intellectual or scientific knowledge. A formalist aesthetic project, focused narrowly on the contemplation of artistic beauty, took over from the more eclectic, and implicated, aesthetics of the nineteenth century. Meanwhile, an undercurrent of critical theory and *avant garde* art practice insisted on the impossibility of separating aesthetic considerations from political and cultural ones (Burger 1984; Eagleton 1990; Foster 1996). This resistant trend provided the critical foundation for the 'anti-aesthetic' of the 1970s, a turn which saw artists deliberately refusing to concede to formalist constructions of aesthetic value. These artists and critics were eager to show that aesthetic perception is not universal, but is contingent on changing spatial, temporal and social circumstances (Deutsche 1996; Meyer 2004). An appreciation for the cultural specificity of aesthetic perception developed out of this movement, and out of anthropologists' work on the aesthetic systems of non-Western societies (Geertz 1974).

Within this general epistemic shift, there remains room for a more specifically geographical engagement with the role that aesthetics plays in contemporary life – both inside and outside the art gallery. David Matless's call for a (re) recognition of the mutual constitution of aesthetic and spatial elements of experience cuts to the core of the issue (Matless 1997). The medium of aesthetic communication, no longer the landscape painting or the illustrated travel account, is now more likely to be the authoritative overlays of a GIS program or the Technicolor displays of the satellite image (Gregory 1994: 68). Work that calls attention to this ascendant technological aesthetic comes from both the art world and the academy. Other work tries to make room for another form of aesthetic communication altogether, a 'relational aesthetics' (Bourriand 2002) which centres on processes of dialogue and exchange (Kester 2004).

Illustration 2: *Westward the Star of Empire Takes its Way*

A train moves through a dark forest corridor, its headlamp catching a herd of deer on the tracks as they move towards a stump-scattered clearing where a family stands in front of their raw cabin. The painting *Westward the Star of Empire Takes its Way–Near Council Bluffs, Iowa*, by Andrew Melrose (Plate 36.2), illustrates a moment of aesthetic ambivalence in the history of America's westward colonization. The image suggests at least two possible inflections of meaning: it can be read as a triumphant documentation of the metamorphosis of the wild frontier into a pastoral homeland. In a more muted sense, perhaps, it offers an ironic (or

Plate 36.2. *Westward the Star of the Empire Takes its Way–Near Council Bluffs, Iowa*, 1967, Andrew Melrose (Museum of the American West Collection, Autry National Center, Los Angeles).

575

elegiac) commentary on the gradual destruction of the American wilderness sublime in the name of progress. An understanding of the context of the painting's production hints to the intention that led to the work's commissioning, although this historical context falls short of providing a full account of the image's effects – then or now.

In 1867 the Chicago and Northwestern Railroad commissioned Melrose to produce a painting to celebrate the arrival of the railroad at the Missouri River. Melrose offered this slightly garish tribute, and entitled it *Westward the Star of Empire Takes its Way* in a deliberate (but perhaps not altogether sincere) allusion to the mural of migrating pioneers which Emanuel Gottlieb Leutze had painted on the walls of the US Capitol six years earlier. Leutze's 1862 mural, *Westward the Course of Empire Takes its Way*, borrows its title from a Bishop Berkeley poem (Cronon 1992: 37). In Leutze's representation of America's westward migration, rifle-toting frontiersmen direct a party of hopeful pioneers in their covered wagons over a rugged mountain pass, toward the golden landscape of California (ibid.).

When Melrose painted his image of America's settlement landscape, in the wake of a bloody civil war, the iconography of imperialism had become more ambiguous and troubled. The roughly cleared pasture lies below a stormy sky; the people appear tiny and insignificant in front of their crude shelter. The train cuts through the dark woodland with an uncompromising, and illuminating, force. William Cronon reads this painting as a prophecy of the transformation of the landscape:

> By shuttling between West and East, between frontier and metropolis, between this family and the great markets of Chicago, New York, and London, the railroad knits together the American landscape. It makes far things near, and accelerates the rate at which the pioneer countryside will be transformed.
>
> (Cronon 1992: 73)

The symbolic and topographic suture that occurs through the medium of the painting is not as smooth as Cronon might have it, however. The train's passage through the altered countryside is freighted with an aesthetic and political ambivalence about change within technology and landscape that still haunts the American psyche.

Optical effects

Historically, art and geography display a shared fascination with science and technology, especially in the realm of optics. Although traditionally a term used to describe the workings of the eye, or 'the science of sight and light', optics also refers in a more comprehensive sense to the combined physical, psychological and cultural aspects of vision. This expanded understanding of optics developed out of the recognition that the eye is not cut off from memory and experience. Rather, the act of seeing is located in place, in time and in particular subjectivities. Thus, one might talk of a 'historical optic' or an 'optic of technology', or even the optic of a philosopher such as Walter Benjamin (Coles 1999b). Optical technology has been instrumental in shaping technical and formal approaches to art and geography. As instruments such as lens, telescopes, microscopes, eyeglasses, spyglasses and magic lanterns altered perspectives and revealed newfound wonderment in the world, the desire to see through and beyond that which was optically available to the human eye drove the conditions of engagement and underpinned the Enlightenment pursuit of knowledge (which still has a distinct legacy today).

In a sense, technology forms a prism through which we learn to look. It would be wrong, however, to overemphasize the contribution of technology and in so doing deny the importance of subjectivity and imagination in the production of a historical optic. In the West, the 'science of sight and light' was intricately associated with Judeo-Christian concepts of divinity and truth. The legacy of the Enlightenment invokes this interplay of darkness and luminosity, which the Italians call *chiaroscuro* (bright-darkness). Forms of illumination, whether technically generated or represented as expressions of a godly light, remain a captivating concern of many celebrated art works. Metaphors of light and darkness also play out in the historical geographies of the Western world, whether in invocations of 'Darkest Africa' or in colonial scientific discourses that conflated ideas of darkness and depravity. Illumination itself forms a distinct optic that joins cultural and physical ways of seeing. To read history solely through the lens of technology's optic is compelling, yet it misses the precarious engagement between the observing subject and the seen world. As we change the way we see the world and adopt new optical devices, we also change the way we see ourselves (Crary 1990: 4). 'Images in the field of vision therefore constitute us rather than being subjected to historical readings by us' (Rogoff 2000: 9).

The optical devices of art and geography – such as the mirror, the *camera obscura* and the linear perspective grid – were designed to confer a hitherto unknown objectivity and authority on the observer. 'Impartial' scientific tools and instruments disciplined and legitimized wonder and curiosity in the observational practices of the not-so impartial viewer. In seventeenth-century Holland, visual art aimed, above all, to create an accurate representation of the world through cartographic and optical principles (Alpers 1983). Rationalized systems for observing and representing the world built a new confidence in traversing it. Exploration's optical tools – the telescope, the compass and, later, the camera – codified the way that new lands and peoples were encountered (and consumed by audiences 'back home'). As Sam Rohdie comments, the optic of cartography changed relations of space and altered perceptions of the near and the far, home and away, miniaturizing (in the form of the globe) and multiplying (in the form of maps) distant territories (Rohdie 2001: 65).

As explorers exported their optics to other places, they also found themselves on the receiving end of the observer's gaze. Visual art produced outside the centres of political and economic power reflected those cultures back at themselves, and forced a confrontation with unfamiliar ways of seeing and representing the world (Taussig 1993). Awareness of these 'discovered' cultural frames both troubled and creatively invigorated art's optics (Clifford 1988). Artistic movements such as Primitivism and Surrealism are deeply entangled with exploration's encounters. As such, these movements cannot and should not be considered 'outside' of the colonial geographies that contextualize their cognitive and visual form. One of the more recent ways in which geography's optic meets art's optic is through critical work about place and its representation. A renewed engagement with the products of geography, including technologies of mapping, delineations of the field and site, and graphic forms of geographic information and material culture such as the field notebook, signs, passports, globes and charts (Curnow 1999; Rogoff 2000) has generated many art-based questions about the role of geography in our lives. An increasingly globalized culture raises questions about place, movement and citizenship that make geography's visual culture a potent place within which to think and make work, especially work about the visibilities and invisibilities of certain subjects. Irit Rogoff's work on the 'deterritorialization of the (visual) subject' (Rogoff 2000) suggests a form of optical citizenship which is grounded in multiple positionalities, rather than in traditional conceptions of the singular, bounded viewer who encounters the world as observer.

Illustration 3: *Annual Rings*

The artist Dennis Oppenheim's 1960s experiments in Land Art creatively examine the gap between physical and conceptual systems of landscape information, and so provide a context for understanding how different kinds of information mark and provide way-markers in the landscape. Oppenheim's practice predominately investigated the physical landscape and its traversal by 'lines of information' that refer to 'larger fields of association' (Dickinson 1999: 45). In the work *Annual Rings* (1968) Oppenheim inscribed the geopolitical marker of a border into the landscape boundary between Canada and the US by carving lines through a frozen lake (Plate 36.3). Oppenheim's practice brings into relief the lines of abstract information that transform landscape. Mapping practices use lines, symbols and codes in order to allow landscapes to circulate as dislocated objects (Cosgrove 2005; see also Chapter 35). Oppenheim's piece exacts a critique of the topographic realism for which such practices strive. Essentially, he sutures the map on to the territory, transforming a terrestrial location into a living map that folds abstract information back into the matter of the site. *Annual Rings* refers to geopolitical systems of meaning and demarcation that operate beyond the site, but are not usually visible within it. Oppenheim's emphasis on the 'larger fields of association' that bisect a site changes the object-based artwork to a system-based artwork, which looks at the interplay of relations.

The linking of information systems to landscapes they describe exposes those systems to the temporality of landscape's ecological, geological and anthropological condition. As the snow melts, entropic landscape forces erode the information, and thus call into question the assumptions of logic and fact that placed it there. Matter disrupts the imaginary totality of a

Plate 36.3. *Annual Rings*, 1968, Dennis Oppenheim (Metropolitan Museum of Art, New York).

neutral temporality that the map explicitly assumes. As ice decays over time, so will the geopolitical marks that are inscribed there. By foregrounding the information that acts over the landscape, Oppenheim reveals the indexical function of the map to the site, and the site to the map. Oppenheim's engagement with natural forces of decay sets up a dialogue with real time – art that is made in and subject to time. He uses 'real time systems' to exclude art-historical studio references. The transient nature of the work undermines the modernist narrative about the autonomy of the artwork from natural forces and 'contradicts the idea that an ahistorical or universal set of values might inform art or be embodied in it' (Dickinson 1999: 47). Oppenheim's landscapes are not simply site-specific, in the sense that they take the site as their focus – they focus instead on a relational exploration of the information systems that dictate and inscribe the landscape that forms the site. When engaging in that interrelated space of inscription, the landscape asserts its own forces, which in turn assert the perpetual mobility of site relations and signal the limits of object-hood.

Art and power

As the previous sections have suggested, it is impossible to extricate vision and visuality from questions of power and ideology. The matter of who has the right to decide what is seen, and what remains invisible, is embedded in the history of art and the register of art's effects (Foster 1988; Fyfe and Law 1988; Nochlin 1988). The development of art as a distinct field of cultural production was inextricably linked to the exercise of religious and political influence. Art objects served symbolic and economic roles in the consolidation of wealth and the production of particular forms of privileged subjectivity. As Jonathan Crary comments: 'Vision and its effects are always inseparable from the possibilities of an observing subject who is both historical product *and* the site of certain practices, techniques, institutions and procedures of subjectification' (Crary 1990: 5).

Visual images worked to consolidate other forms of authority, cultural rather than individual. The visual ideology of 'landscape', which emerged as a concept in Renaissance Italy, ordered society and space into hierarchies around class and ownership (Cosgrove 1985). As Lucia Nuti illustrates in her discussion of sixteenth-century attempts to represent urban space, 'modes of observation are not simply sets of formal qualities, but expressions of diverse visual cultures' (Nuti 1999: 98). The visual culture expressed and exercised through the convention of landscape painting was a powerful agent in the European colonization and appropriation of other environments (Nash 2000). The process through which particular imagery works to construct and maintain appropriate social orders, as well as regional and national orders (Brace 1999; Matless 1998) continues, inflected through different visual materials. The complicit relation between vision and power has become a frequent target of analysis in the past several decades. Feminist and political critiques have worked to expose and defuse the authority of the privileged (male) gaze (Foster 1988; Mulvey 1989; Rose 1993). Critical histories of the museum and the high-art establishment have examined art's circulation in (and perpetuation of) systems of authority and exclusive cultural influence (Bennett 1995; MacDonald and Fyfe, 1996).

The flow of other objects into Western art worlds has led to a de-centring of cultural authority, and a recognition that materials, methods and media are subject to complex processes of borrowing, exchange and entanglement (Cerny and Seriff 1996; Lippard 1997; Thomas 1991). In his photographs of the semi-nomadic Arctic people of the Sami, Jorma Puranen reprinted anthropological images on large sheets of glass and placed them back in the landscape through which the people once moved (Osborne 2000: 148). The reflections of the photographic image on to the snow formed fleeting and transient images of peoples within the landscape, in opposition to the dislocated ethnographic framing that had been used to categorize and homogenize the Sami into the nation-state. Puranen's work can be understood as part of an emerging post-colonial art practice that insists on a dynamic and disrupted politics of location, rather than the privileges of position and perspective (Bhabba 1994). Feminist artists have successfully worked to 'render the invisible visible' (Owens 1985), opening up space for the exploration of issues around identity and belonging. And, in countless instances – whether in a forest in Scotland (Mackenzie 2002) or in a Mexican border town where cast-off garage doors from Southern California are decorated with a mural critique of global capitalism (Harding 1997) – art can function as an agent of local resistance. In a recursive, almost redemptive, move, geographers have begun to return to landscape as a useful concept that might be re-imagined to do critical work (Nash 1996).

Illustration 4: *Present Tense*

The small white blocks lie on the stone floor of an art gallery in East Jerusalem. As you walk closer, you catch the scent of olive oil, and then notice the tiny red glass beads pressed into the surface of the blocks in apparently arbitrary patterns. The patterns trace irregular enclosed areas, connecting from block to block. *Present Tense*, an installation piece produced in 1996 by Mona Hatoum at Jerusalem's Anadiel Gallery (Plate 36.4 (a,b)), puzzles at first. The addition of another layer of information forces an expansion of the viewer's perspective into the space outside the gallery: the patterned red beads trace out the territorial divisions of Palestinian and Israeli lands established under the Oslo Agreement (Archer and Hatoum 1996). Hatoum, a Palestinian woman who has spent most of her life in exile, went to Jerusalem to build a map of a controlled and divided territory out of soap – a traditional product whose manufacture carries on in occupied Palestine – and beads.

One visitor to the installation asked: 'Did you draw the map on soap because when it dissolves we won't have any of these stupid borders?' (ibid.). Others, Israeli citizens from Tel Aviv, read in the soap a reference to the concentration camps. 'These two different readings of the work give you an idea of the very different backgrounds and histories of the two cultures trying to co-exist,' Hatoum comments (ibid.: 27). The piece produces a con-catenation of historical, cultural, geographical and emotional effects, capturing a specific moment in a prolonged and unresolved negotiation over the right to occupy a physical location. Hatoum, her own identity gently folded into the work, opens up a space for reflection and recognition otherwise denied to the people who live and work in this contested territory (Araeen 2004).

Methodologies

Geography and art have a shared investment in the production of work through the visual, yet this relationship does not presuppose that they share a common language or set of prac-tices. We might conceive of geography and art as existing in discrete, but overlapping, 'discursive spaces' (Krauss 1999); though their visual cultures exhibit similarities, art and geography arise out of distinct historical and cultural contexts. Rosalind Krauss uses Timothy O'Sullivan's scientific (or expeditionary) photographs of the West to make the point that his

Plate 36.4a. *Present Tense*, 1996, Mona Hatoum (Installation, Anadiel Gallery, Jerusalem; reprinted with the kind permission of Mona Hatoum).

cultural production cannot be considered in the same context as that of contemporaneous painters who painted within the museum context. She argues that although images may be visually comparable they 'mean' differently in different methodological spaces; analysis must take into account the situation of the image's creation. That is to say, modes of production, disciplinary structures and animating networks vary enormously across disciplines and bear upon art objects in complex ways.

Although, as Krauss argues, it is important to acknowledge the context in which an image arises, the fact that modes of production and reception are rarely cleanly delineated (Synder 1994) can make such a differentiation difficult at best, particularly in the context of new modes of digital media communication. In the last few decades of the twentieth century, art

581

Plate 36.4b. *Present Tense*, 1996, Mona Hatoum (Installation, Anadiel Gallery, Jerusalem; reprinted with the kind permission of Mona Hatoum).

historians and art critics responded to this problem of definition with a theoretical move from *formal* (Greenberg 1986) explications of art's effects to *discourse* or *process-based* analyses. The new field of analysis which emerged out of this theoretical shift is often referred to as 'visual culture' (Burgin 1996; Evans and Hall 1999; Rogoff 2000). Taking its direction from feminist, post-colonial and post-structuralist criticism, a visual cultural approach recognizes that vision and visual objects operate in multiple fields of embedded and embodied meanings, and are generative of many different positionalities and forms of spectatorship. The clean white space of the museum wall (which once corresponded to a conceptual space of 'disinterested' context) is now considered to be equally productive of the meanings generated around an image as the material which constitutes the image itself. If, at one time, the prevailing trope for art production was that of a mirror which reflected the world back at itself in an unmediated reproduction, an apt description of the way contemporary art works would be to call on the metaphor of conversation. Irit Rogoff describes contemporary art as 'interlocutor' rather than object of study, an entity that allows for thinking of the world differently (Rogoff 2000: 10), and unravelling and articulating issues around politics, race, geography, gender and nature. In the art movements of the late twentieth and early twenty-first century – site-specific and landscape art, conceptual and critical art practice – the artist takes on the role of catalyst rather than creator (Bishop 2004; Kwon 2002).

In a parallel move, critical geography has moved from an 'art of description' to 'an interventionist art', productive of new and emerging modes of inscription. The debate in geography around the role of vision in the discipline is far from settled (Crang 2003; Rose 2003; Ryan 2003). Historical geographies of place – which once focused on the 'reading' of art images to offer insights about landscape use and iconography – have been aerated with a more reflexive consideration of the networks of communication, materiality and practice in which images of place and culture are situated. These broad intellectual movements in critical geography and visual culture have created some fertile cross-disciplinary areas of exchange. Geographers and other social scientists have engaged in depth with the work of particular artists (Gandy 1997; Matless and Revill 1995), and explored the performance of material meaning in art's museum and display spaces (Yaneva 2003; Hetherington 1997, 2000; Gell 1996). Those working within the conceptual framework of non-representational theory have been keen to communicate a sense of the embodied and practised aspects of art's production and reception. The sub-discipline of museum studies has opened up a critical discussion of the cultural politics of visual art and forms of public engagement (Cooke and Wollen 1995; Karp and Lavine 1991).

Where art and geography may be said to diverge in their conceptual and intellectual terrain is over ideas of methodology and utility. Though social scientists may claim to actively intervene in the social fabric through their research (often with the intention to address issues of inequality or injustice), artists are often less inclined to accept such a utilitarian model of work. Theodor Adorno, who argued against the application of standards of utility or social function to artworks (Adorno 2004), appreciated art for its capacity to transform perceptions, rather than for any rational or political function as an agent of social change. Adorno celebrated art as that which not only avoids but also exposes the fantasy of utility and its propensity to obscure the violence underpinning structures of reason. For Maurice Blanchot, art requires a degree of risk and experimentation that embraces the possibility of failure as a condition of that engagement. He argues that art cannot know itself entirely in advance: it always exists in a condition of *becoming*, and there, Blanchot suggests, lies the possibility for the 'originality of experience' (Blanchot 2000). Art risks itself (through failure) to become art, working at the limit of the legible; the object cannot be grasped through reason alone. Art cannot serve any purpose other than its own becoming, Blanchot argues, and in this becoming it has to become more than itself, *to animate* beyond the rational limits of the object.

In raising questions of subjectivity, place, desire and vision, art challenges the rational methodologies of geography. Traditional geographical discourse mediated against risk through elaborate strategies of technological and political control. Recent trends in critical geography, however, point to a sightline that appears more sensitive to the ground it travels over, and more open to the possibilities of getting lost. Visual knowledge production as a shared process common to artists and geographers can become a form of collaborative co-production that shapes knowledge in unfamiliar ways through joint work (Dunn and Leeson 1997; Driver *et al.* 2002; Lorimer and Foster 2005) and borrowed methodologies. On the whole, artists have perhaps been more willing to take on the mantle of social scientist – as ethnographer (Coles 2000; Foster 1996), archaeologist (Coles 1999a) or sociologist (Heim 2003) – than geographers have been to shed their professional identities and experiment with artful forms of academic production (though see Lorimer and Spedding 2005). If such instances of collaboration and performance are to bring forth challenging new questions about the geographies of vision and geography's visual culture, they need to acknowledge the specific histories and concerns that define both disciplines – histories intimately entangled with issues of aesthetics, optics, and power.

Further reading

Driver, F., Nash, C. and Prendergast, K. (2002) *Landing: Eight Collaborative Projects between Artists and Geographers*. Available at http://www.gg.rhul.ac.uk/vg/landing/ (accessed 5 August 2003).

Foster, H. (1988) *Vision and Visuality*. Seattle: Bay Press.

Gregory, D. (1994) *Geographical Imaginations*. Cambridge, MA, and Oxford: Blackwell.

Kennedy, R. (2005) The artists in hazmat suits. *The New York Times*, 3 July, 1 and 21.

Kwon, M. (2002) *One Place after Another: Site Specific Art and Locational Identity*. Cambridge, MA: MIT Press.

Livingstone, D.N. (1992) *The Geographical Tradition*. London: Blackwell.

Osborne, P. (2000) *Travelling Light: Photography, Travel and Visual Culture*. Manchester: University of Manchester Press.

Perry, G. (2003) Visibility, difference, and excess. *Art History* 26, 319–39.

Rogoff, I. (2000) *Terra Infirma: Geography's Visual Culture*. London: Routledge.

References

Adorno, T. (2004) *Aesthetic Theory*. London: Continuum.

Alpers, S. (1983) *The Art of Describing: Dutch Art in the Seventeenth Century*. Chicago: University of Chicago Press.

Araeen, R. (2004) The success and failure of black art. *Third Text* 18, 135–52.

Archer, M and Hatoum, M. (1996) Interview: Michael Archer in conversation with Mona Hatoum. In M. Archer, G. Brett and C. de Zegher (eds) *Mona Hatoum*, pp. 7–31. Phaidon: London.

Bennett, T. (1995) *The Birth of the Museum*. London: Routledge.

Bhabba, H. (1994) *The Location of Culture*. London: Routledge.

Bishop, C. (2004) Antagonism and relational aesthetics. *October* 110, 51–79.

Blanchot, M. (2000) The original experience. In C. Cazeaux (ed.) *The Continental Aesthetics Reader*, pp. 344–55. London: Routledge.

Bourriand, N. (2002) *Relational Aesthetics*. Dijon: Les Presses du Reel.

Brace, C. (1999) Gardenesque imagery in the representation of regional and national identity: the Cotswold garden of stone. *Journal of Rural Studies* 15, 365–76.

Burger, P. (1984) *Theory of the Avant-garde*. Minneapolis: University of Minnesota Press.

Burgin, V. (1996) *In/Different Spaces*. Berkeley: University of California Press.

Castree, N. and Rogers, A. (2005) *Questioning Geography*. London: Blackwell.

Cerny, C. and Seriff, S. (eds) (1996) *Recycled, Re-seen: Folk Art from the Global Scrap Heap*. New York: Harry N. Abrams.

Clifford, J. (1988) *The Predicament of Culture*. Cambridge, MA, and London: Harvard University Press.

Coles, A. (1999a) The epic archaeological digs of Mark Dion. In A. Coles and M. Dion (eds) *Archaeology*, pp. 25–33. London: Black Dog.

——(ed.) (1999b) *The Optic of Walter Benjamin*. London: Black Dog.

——(2000) *Site-specificity: The Ethnographic Turn*. London: Black Dog.

Cooke, L. and Wollen, P. (eds) (1995) *Visual Display: Culture beyond Appearances*. Seattle: Bay Press.

Cosgrove, D. (1985) Prospect, perspective and the evolution of the landscape idea. *Transactions of the Institute of British Geographers* 10, 45–62.

——(2005) Maps, mapping, modernity: art and cartography in the twentieth century. *International Journal for the History of Cartography* 57, 35–54.

Crang, M. (2003) The hair in the gate: visuality and geographical knowledge. *Antipode* 35, 238–43.

Crary, J. (1990) *Techniques of the Observer*. Cambridge, MA: MIT Press.

Cronon, W. (1992) Telling tales on canvas: landscapes of frontier change. In J.D. Prown, N.K. Anderson, W. Cronon, B.W. Dippie, M.A. Sandweiss, S. Prendergast Schoelwer and H.R. Lamar (eds)

Discovered Lands, Invented Pasts: Transforming Visions of the American West, pp. 37–87. New Haven: Yale University Press.

Curnow, W. (1999) Mapping and the expanded field of contemporary art. In Denis Cosgrove (ed.) *Mappings*, pp. 253–68. London: Reaktion.

Deutsche, R. (1996) *Evictions: Art and Spatial Politics*. Cambridge, MA: MIT Press.

Dickinson, J. (1999) Journey into space: interpretation of landscape in contemporary art. In D. Nye (ed.) *Technologies of Landscape*. Amherst: University of Massachusetts Press.

Dunn, P. and Leeson, L. (1997) The aesthetics of collaboration. *Art Journal* 56, 26–37.

Eagleton, T. (1990) *The Ideology of the Aesthetic*. Oxford: Blackwell.

Eaton, N. (2003) Excess in the city? The consumption of imported prints in colonial Calcutta, c. 1780–c. 1795. *Journal of Material Culture* 8, 45–74.

Evans, J. and Hall, S. (1999) *Visual Culture: The Reader*. London: Sage.

Fabian, J. (2000) *Out of Our Minds, Reason and Madness in the Exploration of Central Africa*. Berkeley: University of California Press.

Foster, H. (1988) *Vision and Visuality*. Seattle: Bay Press.

——(1996) *The Return of the Real: The Avant-garde at the End of the Century*. Cambridge, MA: MIT Press.

Fyfe, G. and Law, J. (1988) *Picturing Power: Visual Description and Social Relations*. London: Routledge.

Gandy, M. (1997) Contradictory modernities: conceptions of nature in the art of Joseph Beuys and Gerhard Richter. *Annals of the Association of American Geographers* 87, 636–59.

Geertz, C. (1974) Art as a cultural system. *Modern Language Notes* 91, 1473–99.

Gell, A. (1996) Vogel's net: traps as artworks and artworks as traps. *Journal of Material Culture* 1, 15–38.

Greenberg, C. (1986) *The Collected Essays and Criticism*, edited by J. O'Brien. Chicago: University of Chicago Press.

Gregory, D. (1994) *Geographical Imaginations*. Cambridge, MA, and Oxford: Blackwell.

Harding, D. (1997) Maclovio Rojas: an exercise in social sculpture. *Variant* 2, 4–5.

Heim, W. (2003) Slow activism: homelands, love and the lightbulb. In B. Szerszynski, W. Heim and C. Waterton (eds) *Nature Performed: Environment, Culture and Performance*, pp. 183–202. Oxford: Blackwell.

Hetherington, K. (1997) Museum topology and the will to connect. *Journal of Material Culture* 2, 199–218.

——(2000) Museums and the visually impaired: the spatial politics of access. *The Sociological Review* 48, 444–63.

John, G.E. (2004) Benevolent imperialism: George Catlin and the practice of Jeffersonian geography. *Journal of Historical Geography* 30, 597–617.

Karp, I. and Lavine, S.D. (eds) (1991) *Exhibiting Cultures: The Poetics and Politics of Museum Display*. Washington: Smithsonian.

Kester, G. (2004) *Conversation Pieces: Community and Communication in Modern Art*. Berkeley: University of California Press.

Krauss, R. (1999) Photography's discursive spaces. In J. Evans and S. Hall (eds) *Visual Culture: The Reader*, pp. 193–211. London: Sage.

Kwon, M. (2002) *One Place after Another: Site Specific Art and Locational Identity*. Cambridge, MA: MIT Press.

Lippard, L. (1997) *The Lure of the Local: Senses of Place in a Multicentered Society*. New York: The New Press.

Lorimer, H. and Foster, K. (2005) *Liquid Geography: Cross-bills*. London: Proboscis/Diffusion.

Lorimer, H. and Spedding, N. (2005) Locating field science: a geographical family expedition to Glen Roy, Scotland. *British Journal for the History of Science* 38, 13–33.

MacDonald, S. and Fyfe, G. (1996) *Theorizing Museums: Representing Identity and Diversity in a Changing World*. Cambridge, MA: Blackwell.

Mackenzie, F. (2002) Re-claiming place: the Millennium Forest, Borgie, North Sutherland, Scotland. *Society and Space* 20, 535–60.

Matless, D. (1997) The geographical self, the nature of the social, and geoaesthetics: work in social and cultural geography 1996. *Progress in Human Geography* 21, 393–403.

——(1998) *Landscape and Englishness.* London: Reaktion.

Matless, D. and Revill, G. (1995) A solo ecology: the erratic art of Andy Goldsworthy. *Ecumene* 2, 423–48.

Meyer, J. (2004) Aesthetic/anti-aesthetic: an introduction. *Art Journal* 63, 14–23.

Mulvey, L. (1989) *Visual and Other Pleasures.* London: Macmillan.

Nash, C. (1996) Reclaiming vision: looking at landscape and the body. *Gender, Place and Culture* 3, 149–69.

——(2000) Breaking new ground: landscape. *Tate Magazine* 60–5.

Nochlin, L. (1988) *Women, Art, and Power and Other Essays.* London: Thames and Hudson.

Nuti, L. (1999) Mapping places: chorography and vision in the renaissance. In D. Cosgrove (ed.) *Mappings*, pp. 90–108. London: Reaktion.

Osborne, P. (2000) *Travelling Light: Photography, Travel and Visual Culture.* Manchester: University of Manchester Press.

Outram, D. (1999) On being Perseus. In D. Livingstone and C. Withers (eds) *Geography and Enlightenment*, pp. 281–95. Chicago: University of Chicago Press.

Owens, C. (1985) The discourse of others: feminists and postmodernism. In Hal Foster (ed.) *Postmodern Culture*, pp. 57–77. London: Pluto Press.

Rogoff, I. (2000) *Terra Infirma: Geography's Visual Culture.* London: Routledge.

Rohdie, S. (2001) *Promised Lands: Cinema, Geography, Modernism.* London: British Film Institute.

Rose, G. (1993) *Feminism and Geography: The Limits of Geographical Knowledge.* Cambridge: Polity Press.

——(2003) On the need to ask how, exactly, is geography visual? *Antipode* 35, 212–21.

Ryan, J.R. (2003) Who's afraid of visual culture? *Antipode* 35, 232–7.

Said, E. (1979) *Orientalism.* New York: Random House.

Stafford, B.M. (1984) *Voyage into Substance: Art, Science, and the Illustrated Travel Account, 1760–1840.* Cambridge, MA: MIT Press.

Synder, J. (1994) Territorial photography. In W.J.T Mitchell (ed.) *Landscape and Power*, pp. 175–203. Chicago: University of Chicago Press.

Taussig, M. (1993) *Mimesis and Alterity.* London: Routledge.

Thomas, N. (1991) *Entangled Objects: Exchange, Material Culture, and Colonialism in the Pacific.* Cambridge, MA: Harvard University Press.

Waitt, G. and Head, L. (2002) Postcards and frontier mythologies: sustaining views of the Kimberley as timeless. *Society and Space* 20, 319–44.

Yaneva, A. (2003) Chalk steps on the museum floor: the 'pulses' of objects in art installations. *Journal of Material Culture* 8, 169–88.

37

Photography

Chris Perkins

Introduction

There is a cultural consensus that modernity relies strongly upon vision; its truths depend upon seeing (Sui 2000). Contemporary life is richly permeated with visual imagery. More than ever before, we live in societies that employ images across almost all realms of human experience, from popular culture, through communication, education and commerce to our judicial systems. Our culture is increasingly visual (Sturken and Cartwright 2001). In the last half of the twentieth century, technologies that generate these images have proliferated, but digital and multimedia systems, film, television and video all employ photographic images. Indeed, photography as a cultural practice has played a central and changing role in the development of geographical imaginations in the twentieth century.

This chapter explores the nature of the products, processes and practices of photography. It understands the photograph as a static image relating to a place, person, event or object, captured using the mechanical apparatus of the photographic or digital camera (moving images are considered in Chapter 38). The key difference from artistic images described in Chapter 36 lies in the ability of the camera to generate a mass-produced, quasi-mechanical image. This reveals a key tension in photography between the technological and the aesthetic.

The ways in which photography has been understood have changed, with theoretical approaches to the photograph shifting over time. The certain vision of modern progress has come increasingly to be replaced by a more postmodern appreciation of contingent complexity (Rose 2001). This chapter seeks to illustrate something of this shift by encouraging readers to link examples of photographic practice to more theoretical material. Its focus is upon the meanings that may be derived from photographic imagery. The argument follows that of Gillian Rose (1996), who justifies how meanings are made at three different sites: those relating to the image itself, to its production and to the contexts in which the photograph is seen by an audience. It can also be argued that we need to understand these meanings through the context of three different modalities: the *compositional* qualities of the photograph itself; the *technological* tools and equipment used to make structure and display the image; and 'the *social*, economic, political and institutional practices that produce, saturate and interpret' (Rose 2001: 188).

THE GEOGRAPHICAL IMAGINATION

There are certain shared features associated with photography. The medium fixes and freezes the mobile world, naturalizing culture, reifying a single viewpoint. The technology of the camera purports to capture reality. This chapter starts by considering how this apparent neutrality of the photographic image has been achieved. It then moves on to consider the ways in which photography operates as an aesthetic form, relating composition to artistic expression. The next section evaluates Foucauldian and psychoanalytical approaches and explores how photography reflects and also creates social difference. Our culture invests diverse meanings in photographs, which evoke memories, allow us to record events, call on us to act, tantalize, give us pleasure, shock us, persuade us and attract our attention. People respond differently to photographs: there are different audiences, and a single photograph can mean different things to different people; serve many different purposes and, will be seen in very different contexts. I consider these complex and contested roles by using semiotic approaches using examples from contemporary commodity culture and the role of the photograph in advertising. The medium is, however, also increasingly being analysed as a set of practices, where meaning resides beyond the representation alone.

These arguments reflect three central concerns: that photographs travel, representing places and people and bringing shared ideas to an increasingly global audience; that their meanings vary through time and across space; and that the shift to digital photography is changing the very nature of visual culture. Above all else, though, this chapter explores and explains why *geographers* should attend to the photographic product, process and practice.

Photographic truth

Photographic images appear to show the world as it is, in some kind of mimetic process offering a mirror-like reflection of objective reality. It has been argued that the development of photographic technologies in the early nineteenth century offered a more accurate way of representing the world than previous artistic technologies and that a positivist scientific ethos came to claim the photograph for its own (Sturken and Cartwright 2001). Nineteenth-century obsessions with classification helped photographs to possess the world but the 'initial emphasis on the realism and truthfulness of photography effectively masked the subjectivity inherent in the decision of what to record' (Schwarz and Ryan 2003: 3). Photographs thus came to be associated with 'truthful' representation of a reality, with some kind of evidential quality. Photographic machinery still appears to 'skim' qualities of an event or place on to the paper on which the image is printed, and we believe in the veracity of the visual representation. This common-sense belief in the neutrality of photographic imagery may well be reinforced by the often-unthinking way in which people accumulate 'snapshots' with their own cameras and subsequently employ these images to evoke personal memories (Wheeler 2002).

Photographic evidence continues to be employed as 'source material' in historical geographies – local histories employ old photographs as evidence of changing places or ways of life (see Chapter 35 for examples of the use of aerial photographic images to record change, and Robbins 2001 for the problematic and political nature of this work). This legacy of objectivity is preserved and continues to exercise considerable power in contemporary contexts. Crang (2003), for example, argues that geographers almost always still employ photographs and other visual material in lectures as evidential support for arguments conveyed in words. Photographs are also still usually employed in an acritical fashion in published academic articles, and in books such as this: they serve as factual support for the more slippery words that carry arguments forward. Their apparent neutrality masks an often dangerous bias (e.g. Myers 2001 on textbook stereotypical representations of Africa). In this chapter images serve as a counterpoint to the text: I have chosen not explain their specific roles: the reader is invited to look at them in conjunction with the words, to reflect on their bias rather than using them as evidence.

In a wider context beyond the academy society places considerable value on this evidential quality. Certain types of photography are more likely to trade upon this 'myth of veracity', to act as a testament. Photojournalism and documentary photography both rely upon an implied correspondence between image and reality. Their status as 'truth bearing' genres generates considerable power for those employing the images. War photographers also trade strongly on the moral imperative of 'documenting' scenes of raw emotional power, despite the often clearly constructed nature of their images. The paparazzi rely upon the apparent veracity of their images of the stars. Judicial practice recognizes photographs as key documentary evidence of events, able to help 'prove' a case. Photographic evidence of a crime scene stands for the scene itself. A still image of a sporting controversy proves the ball went over the line, or that it would have hit the stumps (see Plate 37.1).

Scientific practice also relies heavily on the evidential quality of photography. Sturken and Cartwright (2001) describe several examples from different contexts to illustrate this point. In the nineteenth century physiognomic discourse depended on the classification of visual outward bodily signs of inner, moral, social and intellectual characteristics, and photography allowed anthropometric study to catalogue these traits. Nowadays medical imaging technologies allow doctors to 'know' the body in different ways: the Visible Human Project from the US National Library of Medicine has 'captured' very high resolution 'normal' male and

Plate 37.1. The photograph as evidence: howzat!

female three-dimensional photographic imagery. Kember (1998) likens this monumental visual archive to a virtual Frankenstein, in which the formerly real subjects have been objectified, normalized and put to use through the processes of vision.

In all of these cases photographic technologies have made objects of people or events: a truth has been 'seen' by science, and rendered useful for art, governance or commerce. We need to understand how this process operates and view the photograph in these different contexts.

Compositional qualities: art and the aesthetic

The composition of a photograph may be the most important influence on what the image comes to mean. The image itself may be described, interpreted, evaluated and theorized (Barrett 2000). Photographs have a content. They may depict a landscape, offer a portrait of someone, or depict an object. The subject of the image may be seen in a wide-angle view or in detail more zoomed closely detail; very small objects may be enlarged, or the scale of large objects may be reduced in order to place them into context. They may show a static scene or depict motion. Photographs are also composed. The image has a spatial organization. It has a perspective and eye level, detail is laid out and the position of the viewer can be important when considering what the photograph means. The composition of the image influences what the eye is drawn to – focalizing qualities of photographs may be enhanced by framing a subject, or by carefully arranged lighting. The focus of an image conveys meaning, as does depth of field: it has been argued that the authority of photographic realism depends on the Euclidean cone of vision and that focused images are seen as being geometrically and therefore optically true (Kember 1998: 25). The colour of the image also affects how it is read: we see a sepia print as signifying something old or old-fashioned.

These technical qualities contribute to an overall aesthetic that guides the eye. We under-stand the image without necessarily appreciating why it makes us feel what we do, just as we use the increasingly sophisticated camera equipment without necessarily understanding the technical processes that allow it to capture a scene.

This content is often understood in relation to the photograph as part of a genre char-acterized by different spaces of representation (Rose 1997: 278). These may appear to be less expressive than the artistic genres described in Chapter 36, but photographic genre also profoundly affects what the photograph comes to mean (see Table 37.1). Personal photo-graphs, as mementos of rites of passage, snapshots or holiday souvenirs, for example, may have very different agendas to those that are published and disseminated (see later and Rose 2003 and Haldrup and Larsen 2003 for a consideration of these issues).

The genre that trades most upon the aesthetic is the creation of photography as art. Here the image is contextualized by being shown in galleries or museums, or published as a portfolio of a particular photographer's work, or acquired as a collectable artefact to decorate

Table 37.1. Published photographic genres

Architectural	Holography	Scientific
Artistic	Landscape	Sports
Commercial	Nature and wildlife	Stock
Erotic	Photo-journalism	Travel
Fashion	Portraiture	

Plate 37.2. Photograph as art. Photograph by Nick Scarle.

or inspire (Wells 2004). (See Plate 37.2.) The spaces of representation that the image occupies help us understand what the photograph means, but its significance as a genre extends beyond the white gallery walls. Artistic photographs emphasize compositional and expressive qualities.

Of course, these contexts are never isolated. Photographs taken in one context may be translated to another: fashion photography may subsequently be displayed as an artistic image in a gallery. However, it is clear that the initial rationale for the spread of the technology, its apparent ability to capture the truth, becomes problematic when one considers the inherent subjectivities involved in the composition of a photograph. Instead, these subjectivities invite questions about the power of the image, the time when the photograph was captured and the place it depicts, as well as the ways in which it has been subsequently employed.

The cultural power of photography: race, class and gender

It has long been recognized that along with other pictorial images photographs carry multiple meanings and are therefore subject to matters of politics as well as aesthetics (Berger 1972). This section explores the complex and changing politics of photography, by focusing on class, imperial power, race and gender and stressing how these are reflected in but also constituted by photography. Geographical difference emerges through this discursive process.

It has been argued that the documentary tradition of photography has been particularly complicit in the articulation of surveillance and social control (Price 2004: 105). Until after the Second World War, cameras were mostly in the hands of middle-class people and middle-class values framed photography. Photographers began to record the cultural life of poor people in British cities towards the end of the nineteenth century, from curiosity, for philanthropic reasons or as part of a more sinister desire to pathologize and control. By the interwar period a genre had developed that cast its subjects as social problems, which the camera revealed as part of a reformist liberal campaign. The problem was diagnosed and visually classified, but the context precluded any radical or revolutionary solutions. So an archive of images of subjects developed, in middle-class hands, that partly served as a means of social control. Tagg (1988: 11) argues that 'to be pictured here was not an honor, but a mark of subjugation'. The photograph stigmatized, and 'othered' its subjects, as part of a Foucauldian apparatus of social control and policing.

The regular use of visual technologies to police society, discipline citizens, and support the rule of law has expanded apace in the last 15 years. Now CCTV images allow society to watch its citizens and control their activities by giving photographic proof that an event has taken place, whether a speeding offence or an infringement of an ASBO curfew. In so doing the photographic image and its surveillant qualities in turn contribute to the creation of new kinds of urban spaces (Koskela 2000).

Visual imagery was also frequently employed as part of the apparatus of imperial governance (Ryan 1997; Schwartz 1996) and it has been argued that 'photographs were spaces where facts, in visual form, were stored and communicated, ordered and conceptualized, reconstituted and transformed by an imperial gaze into the myths and metaphors of place and identity' (Schwartz 2003: 155). The invention and popular dissemination of photography coincided with the expansion of the British Empire in the late nineteenth century. It allowed a new imaginative geography of empire to be circulated to citizens at home, which traded upon the scientific rationality embodied in the new medium. The traveller's photograph became a pretext for travel, but also a surrogate for the experience for those unable to visit the terrain or people presented in pictures (Schwartz 1996). These photographic practices carried important messages across the globe. They brought a 'real' empire home, but also allowed the geographical imaginary of the home nation to be presented to the imperial subject. Lantern-slide lectures and illustrated textbooks promulgated views of imperial civilization to children at home and abroad (Ryan 1997). At the same time, the more distant fringes of empire articulated their identities through photographic practices.

Very particular kinds of places were represented in these images. Travellers were able to domesticate, organize and understand alien landscapes through the careful and systematic design of imagery, so that civilized, rational imperial practices were reified (Ryan 1997). Exploration relied increasingly upon the photography as a device for bringing the discovery home. The photograph was also part of the military armoury, employed alongside mapping in imperial campaigns; it also celebrated of male power over nature in big game hunting (Ryan 1997). Photography became a means of converting unknown spaces into knowable places and a justification for imperial practice, but as a tool of governance its use was always negotiated and depended on institutional power. For example, Foster (2003) shows how tensions between commercial interests and civil servants are revealed in South African railway pictures: the images reflect aspirant South African nationalism, British colonial rule and also the emerging narratives of white travel. The ideologies underpinning changing representations of landscape also reflect cultural norms: for example, Nye (2003) shows how the Grand Canyon has been transformed in representations from serving as a national icon, as a geological wonder, a tourist destination and as a place representing fragile nature. The photographs of the canyon reveal how the medium has been employed in the westward advance of American civilization.

The photograph also allowed new imaginary geographies of nation-states to be constituted: through a shared depiction of architectural heritage, e.g. Boyer (2003) on France; by focusing upon landscape, e.g. Jäger (2003) on German and British landscape photography; and by capturing the process of immigration and settlement (Osborne 2003). These images reveal the complex, negotiated and imagined nature of nationality. A contemporary analogy is available in Kinsman's (1995) discussion of black artist Ingrid Pollard's work, which involves a critique of national identity but also reinscribes contemporary black British identities.

The depiction of people in imperial photographs also reveals values of the colonial project and the nature of the colonial encounter. Native 'others' were presented as dark subjects on whom the photographic light of progress would fall (Ryan 1997; Bale 1999). Representations of race in photographs reveal the politics of photographic encounters. For example, Edward Curtis devoted his life to the photographic study of North American Indians and took around 40,000 photographs in the first three decades of the twentieth century, many of which were published as part of a monumental 20-volume work (Jackson 1992). These sepia-tinted images depict a carefully staged 'authentic' romanticized view of the pre-contact Indian as 'noble savage'. The photographer reconstructed what had already vanished, and imposed his own notions into the apparently realistic images. Scenes were staged, props were used, photographs were touched up and cropped to support the rhetoric of Curtis's documentary project. Jackson argues that Curtis's way of seeing Indian cultures and landscapes reflects a scientific racist ideology and a process that 'others' the native subjects as somehow separate from the mainstream of American history. Its nostalgic presentation needs to be understood in the light of the context in which it was created, but also in the light of subsequent political and cultural change (see Plate 37.3).

It is possible to employ the apparatus of more quantitative social science to analyse the cultural construction of these photographic images. Lutz and Collins (1993), for example, explore the changing ways in which *National Geographic Magazine* has used photographs to instruct us about distant cultures. They argue this also reveals the core values of the magazine and the Society as a key arbiter of taste, wealth and power in middle-class America. Photographers, editors and designers select images and text to represent Third World cultures and in so doing negotiate standards of objectivity, visual beauty and informational content. A content analysis of around 600 photographs shows how they depict privilege, progress, race, gender and modernity through the use of pose, colour, framing and vantage point, but also reveals how the magazine celebrates diversity whilst at the same time relegating non-Western people to an earlier stage of progress. This quantitative analysis is supplemented by a consideration of the ways in which photographic images of exoticized and sometimes eroticized

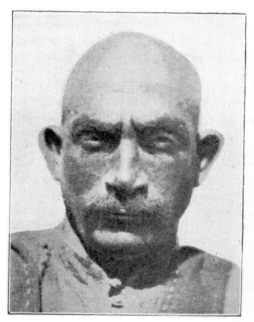

KURD

Plate 37.3. Native as other.
Source: Childe (1926).

subjects may be understood as points of intersection of multiple gazes: the photographer, magazine reader, non-Western subject, Western travelling subject and non-Western subject's view of themselves are all shown in the magazine's photographs, and are in turn subject to an academic gaze. Lutz and Collins argue that the relations of these multiple view-points allow us to make connections to the social world in which the photograph is deployed.

Gendered power relations are embodied in many photographic images, and the nature of 'looking' has preoccupied feminist cultural theorists in the last quarter of the twentieth century. It has been argued that men look, whilst women are cast as the photographic, artistic or filmed subject of male desire (Berger 1972: 47). Feminist critiques of this process problematize the viewer or reader of the photograph as a voyeur and position the conventions of the medium within the confines of patriarchy (Rose 2001). Employing psycho-analytical techniques derived from Freud or Lacan, they have sought to empower the female subject and substitute more complex readings of photographic representation. With regard to photography, it has been the more domestic genres that have been most analysed from a feminist and psychoanalytical stance. The personal snapshot, for example, is often read as reminding the viewer of death and absence, and carries notions of uncertainty, desire or loss (Rose 1997: 278). But Rose also argues that sexual difference in representation and practice transcends genre: a radically uncertain femininity may be revealed once complex spaces of representation are analysed. Female photographers such as Cindy Sherman have increasingly sought to challenge the assumptions of a single patriarchal gaze and substituted their own complex, challenging, embodied visions in an era when postmodern consumption practices and persuasion increasingly matter in the construction of meaning.

Consuming passions: persuasion

It has been argued that Western consumerist values are nowadays the most powerful force in global culture and that advertising is the cultural form that most characterizes our way of life: 'barely a space in our culture is not already carrying a commercial message' (Twitchell 1996: 2). The advert as a form relies to a significant degree on its visual qualities (Williamson 1978; Messaris 1997). So the majority of photographs that people see are explicitly designed to create a particular impact and play a central role in complex carefully designed, ephemeral but often global campaigns.

This proliferation of photographic imagery emerged gradually in the interwar years. Earlier adverts in the imperial era sometimes carried photographic imagery (see, for example, Domosh 2003 on the way the Singer Sewing Machine Company adverts were related to American identity and economic imperialism), but it was not until the 1960s and the growth of commodity culture that numbers of photographic images in advertisements really increased.

The photograph is a tool to express commodity culture, but has also itself been commo-dified (Ramamurthy 2004). Image banks have grown to house huge numbers of 'stock' photographic images to service the needs of the advertising industry (Machin 2004). These generic and bland photographic images offer largely de-contextualized, stereotypical but technically highly competent photographs: the imagery sends symbolic signals, but fails to denote anything directly. These photographs are able to absorb whatever meaning the client wishes them to sell: the photographic world is reduced to a culture of banal corporate spectacle, where politics or exploitation is absent (Ramamurthy 2004). Indeed, photographs in adverts mostly conceal social or labour relations, and perpetuate gendered or racialized stereotypes

The advertisement as a medium is clearly subject to textual analysis as a sign system and semiotic approaches remain a very popular means of analysing the significance of photography and exploring the ways in which photographs relate to other elements of an advert and to other cultural texts. A semiotic approach allows the image to be taken apart, and the relation of different elements of the text to be explored. The figure of Roland Barthes is hugely influential here. Barthean semiotics evokes a structural analysis of how signs in visual material can operate in a cultural context. Signification is the process by which a *signifier* (the material object in the image) comes to stand for the *signified* (a meaning) (Williamson 1978). The form of the signifier comes to represents a concept in a cultural coding process. Barthes argued that this process may progress into a second more ideological stage, which results in a cultural myth.

Messaris (1997) recognizes three key attributes of all photographic images that enable adverts to do their cultural work. First they are *iconic* and able recognizably to stand for something that is real. Photographs in adverts are often there to attract the viewer's attention, by visual parody, metaphor, an obvious violation of reality, a direct gaze from the subject, rear or blocked views, an odd viewing distance or a highly subjective camera angle. This iconic role may also elicit emotion, through sexual attraction, status envy or environmental preferencing. It also operates through the form and style of the advert. Shape and colour, simplicity and order can all be employed to signify particular gender or sexual roles, youth or social status.

His second attribute is to argue for the *indexical* qualities of the photography: photos can stand as proof that something happened, or for the existence of factual referent. Despite this indexical quality images may be staged, edited, carefully selected, manipulated or mislabelled in the process of digital photography.

Messaris's (1997) third attribute is the *syntactical indeterminacy* of the photograph. Whereas words have a precise link between their appearance and language is largely unambiguous, visual materials must be interpreted: they can establish an implicit link, between different images and to attributes of the commodity being sold, that would be all too literal in words. Messaris suggests that visual propositions in adverts may imply causality, signify contrast through juxtaposition, employ analogy or suggest generalization (see Plate 37.4).

We read these adverts in a sophisticated cultural process, where context encourages the reader to interpret the photograph in the light of many other cultural cues. The banner advert on the web works in a different way to the printed advert in a colour supplement. The catalogue is understood differently from the billboard. The logo on a letterhead is read in a different way from the direct mail shot.

The content of some adverts may create a context that is particularly geographical. Place advertising has been a rich field for geographical analysis. The role of the photograph in the marketing of tourist destinations has been analysed in many different contexts (for example, Wyckoff and Dilsaver 1997; Nelson 2005). Postcards as a medium of place marketing have received particular attention (Markwick 2001; Waitt and Head 2002). (See Plate 37.5.) At a completely different scale the global photographic image offers an ambivalent symbol to which many different meanings may be attached (Cosgrove 1994).

Advertisements themselves are also increasingly mobile and meaning is contingent on the context in which the image is received. The global flow of persuasive imagery parallels globalizing forces described throughout the first section of this book. On the one hand, it reflects an increasingly mobile population, able to accumulate experience and artefacts that

Plate 37.4. Advert for product: sexual attraction and class.

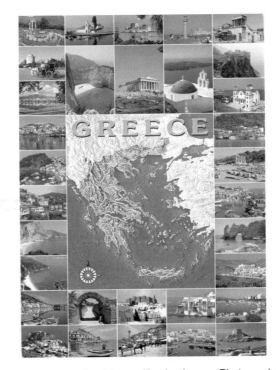

Plate 37.5. Postcard as place advertising: selling landscape. Photograph by Chris Perkins.

memorialize their tourist gazes (Osborne 2000; Urry 1990). On the other hand, the global flow of images reflects the internationalization of commodity culture. Whilst language may be culturally specific, corporations are sometimes marketing a global product, and campaigns by Benetton and Coca-Cola rely upon a belief that photographic imagery has a wider currency. Semiotic analysis of images in the annual reports of Fortune 500 companies (transnational companies) reveals how these TNCs use imagery to support their belief in globalization, but also that they have multiple and often ambiguous global aspirations (Robbins 2004).

However, the viewer is an active agent constructing possible alternative meanings from the same advertisement: these may be the dominant image encoded by the advertiser, but they may also be negotiated or even oppositional (Ramamurthy 2004). There is increasing evidence that context is much more important in the way in which the photographic image is interpreted. For example, in a recent study of global advertising in China Zhou and Belk (2005) show how consumer values continue to be inflected by local cultural practice. Instead of focusing upon semiotic readings of photographs as representations, there may be very good arguments for examining how people employ the technology that creates the image.

Practices

Since the 1990s the practices of photography, rather than the meaning of photographic images, have increasingly been studied. Geographers have shifted away from focusing on the photograph as a representation, towards looking at the social worlds and actions of different kinds of photographic activity. In the past geographers employed photography as part of fieldwork to generate data (e.g. Butler 1994). Now it becomes increasingly possible to use the (digital) camera as a device and technology with which to explore particular encounters with place, representation and the performance of identity (e.g. Sidaway 2002). The technological change that allowed images to be created more cheaply has also enabled a more active and critical engagement with the process by which photographs might be captured, in which field-based discussion of practice can be married to preview, presentation or printing of photographic images.

This shift has also involved a more critical consideration of everyday life, and an increasing concern for the more common uses of photography by everyday people, instead of just exploring professional published products. The emphasis has shifted towards reflexivity, the social nature of photography and embodied performance (Haldrup and Larsen 2003). It increasingly stresses the different kinds of technology and the different kinds of gaze that may be fixed by different photographic practices. It has also shifted away from the image and towards a longer time-span of studies emphasizing practices around the image, from its capture, through to its role as an object in domestic space (Rose 2003), or as an artefact in an archive or museum (Rose 2000).

Personal photography is very much about taking 'snapshots' and focuses largely upon leisure. The family is a central unit in the production and staging of these activities (Spence and Holland 1991), and family photographs enact narratives around social relations. They establish, for example, a particular set of gendered relations and even after the capture of the image the photograph as family artefact is displayed or stored in domestic spaces in ways that contribute to an often nostalgic emotional domestic politics (Rose 2004). These relations also reveal 'a certain tension between the visible record pictures provide, the concrete moment where experience is refracted, and how they may be interpreted' (Crang 1997: 368).

It is during the tourist experience that most images are captured. Indeed, it has even been argued that 'travel is a strategy for the accumulation of photographs' (Sontag 1977: 9). Mobility is frozen as a peg from which to hang memory. In the past these tourist activities were seen as almost scripted: tourists shot in a pre-programmed way, capturing the sights they expect to consume. But there are very many different tourist gazes (Urry 1990). Recent studies suggest that instead of focusing upon the consumption of place we should interrogate the embodied empirical practices that generate these different images (Crang 1997). These practices involve people taking photographs, people being photographed, other disinterested onlookers and subsequent viewers of the images. The interactions are much more complex than the scenarios suggested by Cohen *et al.* (1992). An ethnography of practice is required. (See Plate 37.6.)

For example, it has been argued that many Western holiday experiences are represented through a family gaze in which photographic practices are concerned with producing 'extraordinary ordinariness of intimate social world', rather than being directed at recording tourist sights and sites as 'extraordinary material worlds' (Haldrup and Larsen 2003: 23).

These family snapshots are, of course, also strongly influenced by technological change. The digital camera allows more images to be taken, encourages a rather different concern with composition, and enables the immediate past to be previewed. It also allows images to be amended, and whereas the material printed photographs are seen as being permanent, the digital photograph is worryingly transient. Family events and images of children are, however, often still employed in photographic narratives. The album may have changed into a photo-blog (Cohen 2005) but viewing photographs is still a social event, and images are still organized into a sequence to tell a story. Digital photographs are also shared; they may be distributed via email or direct from camera phones. The sharing may be much closer in time to the capture of the image. Despite having readily available software, however, digital annotation only rarely takes place and most images are un-amended. (See Plate 37.7.)

Plate 37.6. Constructing the tourist gaze: photographing photographers. Photograph by Chris Perkins.

Plate 37.7. The family snapshot. Photographs by Chris Perkins and family.

The social practice after capturing the image appears to have only changed slightly in the world of personal photography. Van House *et al.* (2004) carried out ethnographic work on the social roles played by the digital camera and personal photography. They found photographs continue to be used for three main social reasons: to evoke personal and collective memories; to create and maintain social relationships; and for self-expression and presentation.

Conclusions

It can be argued that the shift to digital technology has eroded the mimetic quality of the photographic image, encouraged new aesthetics, changed the power relations embodied in images, altered the cultural reading of photographs and also changed the practices of photography. Tabloids trade upon carefully manipulated images, the web serves instant images to a global audience, and we can all now enhance the quality of the scenes we capture. Yet in spite of the technological change following the shift to digital camera technology and the consequent ease with which photographic images may be manipulated in packages such as PhotoShop, the eye continues to be drawn in a natural way to a photograph. Wheeler (2002: 4) recognizes that even in a digital era 'the inherent believability of photograph has continued to exceed that of the printed or spoken word'. Digital developments have certainly facilitated an incredible proliferation of images, available in many new contexts. The consensus, however, amongst visual theorists is that the technological changes through which photography is passing signal a cultural continuity, not a new post-photographic age (Lister 2004).

Further reading

Berger, J. (1972) *Ways of Seeing*. Harmondsworth: Penguin.

Lutz, C.A. and Collins, J.L. (1993) *Reading National Geographic*. Chicago: University of Chicago Press.

Rose, G. (2001) *Visual Methodologies: An Introduction to Interpreting Visual Objects*. London: Sage.

Schwarz, J.M. and Ryan, J.R. (eds) (2003) *Picturing Place: Photography and the Geographical Imagination*. London: I.B. Tauris.

Sturken, M. and Cartwright, L. (2001) *Practices of Looking: An Introduction to Visual Culture*. Oxford: Oxford University Press.

Wells, L. (ed.) (2002) *The Photography Reader*. London: Routledge.

——(2004) *Photography: A Critical Introduction*, fourth edition. London: Routledge.

References

Bale, J. (1999) Foreign bodies: representing the African and the European in an early twentieth century 'contact zone'. *Geography* 84, 25–33.

Barrett, T. (2000) *Criticizing Photographs: An Introduction to Understanding Images*, third edition. New York: McGraw-Hill.

Berger, J. (1972) *Ways of Seeing*. Harmondsworth: Penguin.

Boyer, M.C. (2003) La Mission Héliographique: architectural photography, collective memory and the patrimony of France. In J.M. Schwarz and J.R. Ryan (eds) *Picturing Place: Photography and the Geographical Imagination*, pp. 21–54. London: I.B. Tauris.

Butler, D.R. (1994) Repeat photography as a tool for emphasizing movement in physical geography. *Journal of Geography* 93, 141–51.

Childe, V.G. (1926) *The Aryans: a Study of Indo-European Origins*. London: K. Paul, Trench, Trubmer and Co.

Cohen, E., Nir, Y. and Almagor, U. (1992) Stranger–local interaction in photography. *Annals of Tourism Research* 19, 213–33.

Cohen, K.R. (2005) What does the photoblog want? *Media Culture Society* 27, 883–901.

Cosgrove, D. (1994) Contested global visions – one-world, whole-Earth and the Apollo space photographs. *Annals of the Association of American Geographers* 84 (2), 270–94.

Crang, M. (1997) Picturing practices: research through the tourist gaze. *Progress in Human Geography* 21, 359–73.

——(2003) The hair in the gate: visuality and geographical knowledge. *Antipode* 35, 238–43.

Domosh, M. (2003) Selling America: advertising, national identity and economic empire in the late nineteenth century. In A. Blunt, P. Gruffudd, J. May, M. Ogborn and D. Pinder (eds) *Cultural Geography in Practice*, pp. 154–71. London: Arnold.

Foster, J. (2003) Capturing and losing the lie of the land: railway photography and colonial nationalism in early twentieth century South Africa. In J.M. Schwarz and J.R. Ryan (eds) *Picturing Place: Photography and the Geographical Imagination*, pp. 141–61. London: I.B. Tauris.

Haldrup, M. and Larsen, J. (2003) The family gaze. *Tourist Studies* 3, 23–45.

Jackson, P. (1992) Constructions of culture, representations of race: Edward Curtis' 'way of seeing'. In K. Anderson and F. Gale (eds) *Cultural Geographies*, pp. 89–106. Melbourne: Longman.

Jäger, J. (2003) Picturing nations: landscape photography and national identity in Britain and Germany in the mid-nineteenth century. In J.M. Schwarz and J.R. Ryan (eds) *Picturing Place: Photography and the Geographical Imagination*, pp. 117–40. London: I.B. Tauris.

Kember, S. (1998) *Virtual Anxiety: Photography, New Technologies and Subjectivities*. Manchester: Manchester University Press.

Kinsman, P. (1995) Landscape, race and national identity: the photography of Ingrid Pollard. *Area* 27, 300–10.

Koskela, H. (2000) 'The gaze without eyes': video-surveillance and the changing nature of urban space. *Progress in Human Geography* 24 (2), 243–65.

Lister, M. (2004) Photography in the age of electronic imaging. In L. Wells (ed.) *Photography: A Critical Introduction*, pp. 295–336. London: Routledge.

Lutz, C.A. and Collins, J.L. (1993) *Reading National Geographic.* Chicago: University of Chicago Press.

Machin, D. (2004) Building the world's visual language: the increasing global importance of image banks in corporate media. *Visual Communication* 3, 316–36.

Markwick, M. (2001) Postcards from Malta – image, consumption, context. *Annals of Tourism Research* 28, 417–38.

Messaris, P. (1997) *The Role of Images in Advertising.* London: Sage.

Myers, G.A. (2001) Introductory human geography textbook representations of Africa. *The Professional Geographer* 53, 522–32.

Nelson, V. (2005) Representation and images of people, place and nature in Grenada's tourism. *Geografiska Annaler Series B: Human Geography* 87b (2), 131–43.

Nye, D.E. (2003) Visualizing eternity: photographic constructions of the Grand Canyon. In J.M. Schwarz and J.R. Ryan (eds) *Picturing Place: Photography and the Geographical Imagination*, pp. 74–95. London: I.B. Tauris.

Osborne, B.S. (2003) Constructing the state, managing the corporation, transforming the individual: photography, immigration and the Canadian National Railways, 1925–30. In J.M. Schwarz and J.R. Ryan (eds) *Picturing Place: Photography and the Geographical Imagination*, pp. 74–95. London: I.B. Tauris.

Osborne, P.D. (2000) *Travelling Light: Photography, Travel and Visual Culture.* Manchester: Manchester University Press.

Price, D. (2004) Surveyors and surveyed: photography out and about. In L. Wells (ed.) *Photography: A Critical Introduction*, pp. 65–112. London: Routledge.

Ramamurthy, A. (2004) Spectacles and illusions: photography and commodity culture. In L. Wells (ed.) *Photography: A Critical Introduction*, pp. 193–244. London: Routledge.

Robbins, P. (2001) Fixed categories in a portable landscape: the causes and consequences of land-cover categorization. *Environment and Planning A* 33, 161–79.

——(2004) Global visions and globalizing corporations: an analysis of images and texts from fortune global 500 companies. *Sociological Research Online* 9 (2). Available at http://www.socresonline.org.uk/9/2/robbins.html

Rose, G. (1996) Teaching visualised geographies: towards a methodology for the interpretation of visual materials. *Journal of Geography in Higher Education* 20, 281–94.

——(1997) Engendering the slum: photography in East London in the 1930s. *Gender, Place and Culture* 4, 277–300.

——(2000) Practising photography: an archive, a study, some photographs and a researcher. *Journal of Historical Geography* 26, 555–71.

——(2001) *Visual Methodologies: An Introduction to Interpreting Visual Objects.* London: Sage.

——(2003) Family photographs and domestic spacings: a case study. *Transactions of the Institute of British Geographers* 28, 5–18.

——(2004) 'Everyone's cuddled up and it just looks really nice': an emotional geography of some mums and their family photos. *Social and Cultural Geography* 5, 549–64.

Ryan, J.R. (1997) *Picturing Place: Photography and the Visualization of the British Empire.* Chicago: University of Chicago Press.

Schwartz, J.M. (1996) The geography lesson: photographs and the construction of imaginative geographies. *Journal of Historical Geography* 22, 16–45.

——(2003) Photographs from the edge of empire. In A. Blunt, P. Gruffudd, J. May, M. Ogborn and D. Pinder (eds) *Cultural Geography in Practice*, pp 154–71. London: Arnold.

Schwarz, J.M. and Ryan, J.R. (2003) *Picturing Place: Photography and the Geographical Imagination.* London: I.B. Tauris.

Sidaway, J.D. (2002) Photography as geographical fieldwork. *Journal of Geography in Higher Education* 26, 95–103.

Sontag, S. (1977) *On Photography*. London: Penguin Books.

Spence, J. and Holland, P. (eds) (1991) *Family Snaps: The Meanings of Domestic Photography*. London: Virago.

Sturken, M. and Cartwright, L. (2001) *Practices of Looking: An Introduction to Visual Culture*. Oxford: Oxford University Press.

Sui, D.Z. (2000) Visuality, aurality, and shifting metaphors of geographical century. *Annals of the Association of American Geographers* 90 (2), 322–43.

Tagg, J. (1988) *The Burden of Representation*. London: Macmillan.

Twitchell, J.B. (1996) *Adcult USA*. New York: Columbia University Press.

Urry, J. (1990) *The Tourist Gaze*. London: Sage.

van House, N.A., Davis, M., Takhteyev, Y., Ames, M. and Finn, M. (2004) *The Social Uses of Personal Photography: Methods for Projecting Future Imaging Applications*. Available at http://info.berkeley.edu/~vanhouse/van%20house_et_al_2004a.pdf

Waitt, G. and Head, L. (2002) Postcards and frontier mythologies: sustaining views of the Kimberley as timeless. *Environment and Planning D: Society and Space* 20, 319–44.

Wells, L. (2004) On and beyond the white walls: photography as art. In L. Wells (ed.) *Photography: A Critical Introduction*, pp. 245–94. London: Routledge.

Wheeler, T. (2002) *Phototruth or Photofiction?: Ethics and Media Imagery in the Digital Age*. Mahwah, NJ: Lawrence Erlbaum Associates.

Williamson, J. (1978) *Decoding Advertisements: Ideology and Meaning in Advertising*. London: Marion Boyers.

Wyckoff, W. and Dilsaver, L.M. (1997) Promotional imagery of Glacier National Park. *Geographical Review* 87, 1–26.

Zhou, N. and Belk, R.W. (2005) Chinese consumer readings of global and local advertising appeals. *Journal of Advertising* 33 (3), 63–76.

38

Moving images

Contriving the stories of our lives

Stuart C. Aitken

I want to begin this chapter with a story that I related a number of years ago in *The Journal of Geography* (Aitken 1999). It involves my son and his passion for video-games. At the time of the story's first telling, my son is seven years old and piloting his first X-wing fighter in one of LucasArts *Star Wars* video-games. I speak of the way he deftly avoids missiles and light-beams from enemy fighters and courageously engages the enemy as a Death Star brings its planet-destroying canon on the unsuspecting world below. My interest in his passion for this game was spurred in part by a humiliating inability to get my X-wing fighter out of its launch bay without significant dents. I was also a little bit concerned with his passion, which, in my judgment, bordered on addiction. As I looked over his shoulder, I nonetheless recognized something important about the ways young people engage with these games. I watched my son weave in and out of the canyons that comprise the surface of the Death Star. And like Luke Skywalker feeling the force, he successfully sends his missiles down the postage-stamp opening into the main reactor. Boom. We are treated to a spectacular con-flagration. Next level and a new story-line. He is now ramping down a hierarchy of scaled images towards the planet below. The images coalesce in a way that suspends his disbelief about a myriad of pixels changing hue. Indeed, he has no knowledge of the mechanics of digital animation. He is simply hurtling towards the surface to chase some of the renegade enemy fighters that escaped the conflagration aboard the Death Star. Now he is down in some desert canyons, chasing more enemy fighters. I am impressed at this time with the way he negotiates scale. The pixels change hue to form digital images of dynamic landscapes – aerial photographs if you will – from the planetary scale down to just above the desert floor. I am reminded of the agony emanating from some students taking my introductory geo-graphy course as I try to explain the concept and mathematics of scale. Tortured looks greet my explanation of large scales describing small areas in more detail than small scales repre-senting large areas. It seems to me that George Lucas tells the story much better than I do; so well that it is quite comprehensible to a seven-year-old.

This essay is about the ways film and animation contrives the stories of our lives. It is about the power of moving images to construct spaces and affect societal change. And it is about the subtle pervasiveness of these images in contemporary culture.

At fifteen years of age, my son's passion for video-games is undiminished today. His latest gambit involves 'massive multi-player on-line' games such as *Battlefield 2*, engaging as many as 40 Internet opponents who wear a number of different national guises in a world of strategy, mayhem, battles and death. The view from above, the god-trick, is pervasive as heroes and heroines seek knowledge of their foes' whereabouts. Rapid scale-change is still important as he pilots a Blackhawk helicopter on to an aircraft carrier's deck and swiftly procures a new weapon before jumping into a hovercraft. And, most importantly, his foes are sentient-beings ergonomically fitted into games consoles elsewhere in the world. This is a game of global capacity. And so, once more, I am given pause for thought. It is of great concern to me that these games are part of some morbid training ground. I am reminded of Ben Bachmair's (1991: 531) admonition that moving images seduce us with 'an undreamed of extension of impressions, experiences and fantasies' and, at the same time, bring about 'the loss of the corporeal' and the 'de-contextualization' of experience. And yet, there are important connections, important re-contextualizations. My son has the capacity, for example, to attain instant rapport with a young boy in Tijuana (a short drive away from us in San Diego, and yet a world apart) through their mutual passion for the Japanese-created and affected anime game, *Dragon Ball Z*. And so, too, his passion and competence at *Battlefield 2* gives Ross instant connection, and status, amongst many boys his own age. Holloway and Valentine (2003) suggest the importance of video-games, as opposed to communication technologies such as instant messaging, for enabling boys to engage with each other. So, with this essay, I am also interested in the ways moving images bring people together, and in the particular power of film to tap into but also create shared cultural practices, feelings and actions.

I begin the chapter with a brief consideration of what changed when images began to move. I then speculate briefly on how this became a global phenomenon. In what follows, I try to think about the geographies of moving images from the perspective of mobility. I consider some of the implications of the ways these images contextualize and decontextualize our experiences, and think about what kinds of mobile subjectivities are produced through these experiences. Finally, I consider the ways moving images affect us from the standpoint of emotional engagement and connection.

Images begin to move

It may be argued that our search for a sense of place and a sense of self in the world – perhaps the very heart of geography – is constituted in large part by the practice of looking and is, in effect, the stuff of images. Over the last two decades, there has been increasing recognition of the power of articulate, moving images to intervene in the ongoing transformations of everyday life.

Anglo-European productions

Before images began to move, people did. Nineteenth-century visual experiences in Europe and North America such as the panopticon and the diorama anticipated the contemporary escape offered by cinema, the web and video-gaming. Anne Friedberg (1993) argues that a predominantly male gaze was mobilized at this time through walking, tourism and travel. This gaze became feminized by social changes that allowed leisure shopping. She extends this argument to suggest that the so-called virtual gaze and our contemporary immersion in moving images has a history that develops with, but is not necessarily limited to, cinema.

In and of itself, cinema is movement. In its analogue form, it is a particular kind of movement propagated by immobile picture frames rapidly passing in front of a projection light. In the early part of the twentieth century, cinema emerged as a powerful force in Western society although its impact was virtually ignored by contemporary social theorists. Most of the original adherents to the influential Frankfurt School of the 1930s, for example, viewed movies with distaste and disdain (Denzin 1995: 13). A curious omission at a time when a 'certain madness of vision and sound was created' (Jay 1988: 19) in the form of a complex new scopic, ocular and haptic culture based on what Norman Denzin (1995: 16) calls 'an overarching gaze that turned each individual into a surveillance agent for the state, the self and the other'.

The active promotion of images in motion began in the United States on 13 June 1891 when *Harper's Weekly* announced that Thomas Edison had invented a kinetograph, a combination of a moving picture machine and a phonograph (Davis 1976: 12–13). This technology created a new art form and quickly separated it from its more static predecessors. At first, this technology was not touted as an art form, but rather as a science that could record life and nature with precision. The 1902 *Sears* catalogue described the kinetoscope's ability to render a:

> pictorial representation, not lifelike merely, but apparently life itself, with every movement, every action and every detail brought so vividly before the audience that it becomes difficult for them to believe that what they see before them can be other than nature's very self.

> (quoted in Denzin 1995: 16)

In its early years as silent film, the kinetoscope was technically suited to the representation of the mobile. What was revolutionary about the technology was its power over the image; film could lay claim to the authentic portrayal of real world actions and behaviours. In the 1930s and 1940s, the French poetic realism of Louis Lumière, for example, suggested that the space of film *is* the space of reality, and that film's ambition is to reproduce life (Sadoul 1972). A little later, post–World War II realist filmmakers in Germany and Italy sought natural light, outdoor contexts and non-professional actors in everyday situations, and narratives that detailed the specific events of their lives. At the same time, Soviet filmmakers such as Sergei Eisenstein (1949) were breaking new ground with *Kino-Pravda* (Film Truth). Importantly, Eisenstein's concern was with creating cinematic effects rather than elaborating a seemingly true relationship with the events that were being portrayed. His notion of 'the-image-in-motion-over-time-through-space-with-sequence' was about filmic rhythm and the ways that images could be manipulated for fullest affect (Aitken 1991). For Christian Metz (1974) – the film theorist who famously introduced psychoanalytic theory to film studies – understanding image events and sequence was sufficient for most film analysis.

Eisenstein was influenced by the work of American filmmaker Edward S. Porter, who worked out of Edison's studios. Porter produced two influential films – *Life of an American Fireman* (1903) and *The Great Train Robbery* (1903) – which included the first efforts to follow action with camera movement and to produce more than one shot for a scene. He also developed the cross-cut, which involves the interweaving of two scenes. With the pioneering of these techniques comes the first attempts to manipulate time and space, requiring that the audience learns how to fill in the gaps (see Aitken and Dixon 2006). Eisenstein (1943) took this work into the realm of narrative by creating spectacular montages through what he called a 'collision of ideas' that joined dialectically to create new ideas.

American documentary filmmakers such as Paul Strand and Leo Hutwitz were influenced by Eisenstein and *Kino-Pravda*, but they were more concerned with documenting 'true' relationships with events than creating spectacles through manipulating moving images. Over the years, the truth claims of documentary authenticity have been questioned to the extent that these films are seen now as constructions that cannot accurately mirror reality. Rather, the 'reality effect' of documentary film is, as with fiction film, the outcome of successfully performed narrative conventions that are socially and culturally mediated (see Natter and Jones 1993; Aitken 1994).

What is now seen as revolutionary with the kinetoscope is not its ability to render reality but, rather, its potential to manipulate and re-manipulate moving images, and to rearrange time and space in the process. In short, the vitality of moving images lies in their ability to transcend and transform reality.

Global productions

After its inception cinema rapidly became a global phenomena. Cinema was introduced to the world by the Lumière Brothers, very soon after its invention, through a 1896 travelling exhibition (Sadoul 1972). Moving images today are produced and consumed in a highly interconnected global industry of capital, personnel and ideas, and film discourse is an integral part of this production–consumption matrix. A number of geographers focus their geographic analysis specifically on the economic and cultural processes that underlie this matrix (Jenkins, 1990; MacDonald 1994; Lukinbeal 2004).

MacDonald (1994: 28) suggests that the well-developed division over the last century of the global film industry into First, Second, and Third Cinema was 'in waves of reaction to and against the metropole-centered film industries of the colonial powers, or what is now called First Cinema, the cinema of corporate profits'. Second Cinema, the so-called 'art cinema', is the cinema of the post-World War II European city exemplified by the neo-realist genre described above (see also Natter 1994). Third Cinema, MacDonald (1994) argues, is the radical/subversive cinema that developed in the global majority south with the intent to radicalize directly and call audiences to action. After World War II, he points out, radical political movements throughout the world were not only beginning to be expressed in film, but also were beginning to have an impact on cinematic practice. Films like Mexican director Bruñel's *Los Olvidados* (1950) consciously rejected narrative plot structure and aesthetic visual languages, and sought direct political engagement with the audience. Indeed, this rejection of Western film made Third Cinema filmmakers and critics among the first to understand and articulate the limiting context of film discourses which derived chiefly from the global minority north and reflected imperialist contexts (MacDonald 1994: 35). In addition, during this period, national capital, usually with state support and protection, began to expand cinematic facilities, create university programmes in film production and study and otherwise laid the foundation for expanded national industries that are perhaps more representative of cinema today in the global majority south, particularly in Latin America and India.

Moving images fixing identities

The startling and enduring impact of Hollywood cinema over other global cinematic aesthetics was first raised to academic consciousness by Laura Mulvey's (1975) feminist critique.

Her arguments were particularly important because they spoke to the larger patriarchal forms that informed mainstream cinema. Mulvey's (1975) famous notion of 'the gaze' points to the representation of women as bearers, not makers, of meaning in mainstream Hollywood movies. As such, women's identities are fixed as passive objects of desire while men are fixed as active voyeurs. Put another way, in these films women are never represented as self, but rather as other, the dark continent, the love inspired in the hero, or the values from which the protagonist tries to flee (Aitken and Zonn 1994: 19). Fixing involves the process whereby the male gaze seeks to exercise power over its subject, marking 'her' as the 'bearer of guilt' (Mulvey 1975: 11). Mulvey's militant stance against the conventional voyeurism of male spectators' relation to women in film used psychoanalytic theory to interrogate the relations between patriarchal ideology, filmmakers and spectators (Penley 1988: 6). By pointing out that what happens in Hollywood reflects larger societal processes, Mulvey offered an important mechanism for understanding desire and the objectification of women: 'the spectator looks, the camera looks, the male character looks, and the female character is *looked at*' (Saco 1992: 28).

Steve Neale (1993) points to an important and obvious direction by speculating on men as objects of desire and mystery, but there is another important strand to his discussion. He argues that if power is attained through representing men as voyeurs and active perpetrators, what kind of power lies in the portrayal of men as victims and masochists? This avenue of post-Mulveyian thinking focuses on the paradox that although masculinity derives considerable social and sexual power from representational castration, wounding and lacking, cine-psychoanalytic theory has equated masculinity with activity, voyeurism, sadism and story/narrative, and femininity with passivity, exhibitionism, masochism and spectacle.

Carol Clover (1989) points to this paradox by noting that many men as viewers accept female victim heroes – who she characterizes as 'final girl' – in slasher horror movies. Therein lies the contradiction behind fixed representations. For the most part cine-pychoanalytic theory constructs a monolithic male subject as universal and uncontestable (Cohan and Hark 1993: 2). At one level, these representational conventions provide a means through which the private structuring of desire can be represented in public form. But fears and desires embodied in images of disembowelments, for example, are not just about castration fears, they also reflect and refract what Kaja Silverman (1992) notes as a series of male masochistic fantasies, and these fantasies are a pleasurable point of identification for viewers irrespective of gender (*cf.* Studlar 1988; Lehman 1993). So, the male gaze is not just about voyeurism. Suggesting that the male masochist adopts a feminine position, Silverman (1992: 206) ultimately describes a destabilizing position for masculinity that 'magnifies the losses and divisions upon which culture is based, refusing to be sutured or recompensed'. If masochism, an inherently feminized position according to cine-psychoanalytic theory, is often assumed by men and sadism is adopted by 'final girl', then there is a representational flaw in the dichotomous logic of cine-psychoanalytic theory. If I am to believe Clover's (1989) arguments, I need to accept multiple spectator positions to reconcile the appeal of a female victim-hero to a largely male audience. If Mulvey's preoccupation is with the power of images to gender-fix its spectators in a society that is already constructed under a patriarchal bargain, then Clover is suggesting that perhaps the reverse is also possible: moving images offer spectators shifting and multiple positions and resistance to larger hegemonic norms. This is about a collective acknowledgement of difference because, for Clover, the spectator's identification is shifting, unshackled from ethnicity, biological sex, cultural gender or sexual preference. Clover's and Silverman's suggestions in combination further frustrate the persistence of a comfortable monolithic dichotomy aligning masculinity with domination and femininity with submission and point to understanding mobility more fully as it relates to moving images.

Moving images and mobile identities

Tim Cresswell and Deborah Dixon (2002: 4) argue that mobility, like space and identity, 'has no essential meaning or essence outside of the discursive field into which it is inserted'. Importantly, mobilities are constructed in particular ways to produce, reproduce and/or challenge social relations. For Cresswell and Dixon, mobilities characterize a dissemination of meanings via the circulation of moving images through a variety of media and venues, from the cinema to the TV to the personal computer. According to Paul Virilio (1997), this mobility of the image is in stark contrast to the immobility of the viewer, in that technologies of vision (such as filmmaking) transform the landscape into a reservoir of signs, awaiting interpretation from a distanciated and fixed point of view. From Virilio, it follows that the production of film space is intimately connected to the production of other kinds of space and, particularly, those associated with the practice of viewing.

Alternatively, Friedberg (1993) argues that the movement of images opened an arena of speculation over the relations between visual spectacles and fluid rather than static subjectivities. She argues the need to expand our understanding of mobility to include an account of the cumulative psychic effects of encountering moving images. In her account of cinema's role in contemporary Western culture, Friedberg positions the mobilized virtual gaze as a mode of looking based upon mobility rather than confinement. She describes mobility as a form of temporality that highlights nostalgia. A focus on nostalgia means a focus on the popular and the social, emphasizing ordinary, differentiated people and their relations to periodicity in culture. With reality TV, for example, Friedberg (1993: 126) would question how we can internalize this kind of temporality if the time of an image's production, the time of its fiction and the time of its projection are all conflated into the same moment of viewing. The capacity of image projection systems for pausing, rewinding and instant replaying is perhaps recognition in contemporary culture of a surfeit of nostalgia; it is clearly also the establishment of a commodity form and facilitates rather different emotions in relation to the moving image. The inherent *flânerie* of image spectatorship is intensified with web-cams, DVDs and multiplex cinemas. In terms of nostalgia, perhaps our collective capacity to retain the past resonates with the commodified gains of electronic media.

Mobility in this sense, then, refers to dynamic interrelations between the viewer and the viewed. And there is an important fixedness to these interrelations. As I have suggested elsewhere, a Lacanian analysis may be used to draw out aspects of fixed identity, in that the screen portrays images from which the viewer apprehends the on-screen world as a reflective plane that offers a sense of 'wholeness' – that is, a feeling of being complete and secure in a particular identity (Aitken 2001). And Crang (1997) notes that the attenuation of other senses and emotions within the darkened interiors of theatres contrives a peculiar configuration and practice of viewing which sets up the possibility of the illusory eye/I following the camera.

For Cresswell and Dixon (2002) mobility can be thought of in an even broader sense as a certain attitude, at times openly radical and at times quietly critical, towards fixed notions of people and places. That is, an emphasis on mobility suggests a certain scepticism in regard to stability, rootedness, surety and order. In a recent post-structural appraisal of the ways male

identities are elaborated and reconstituted emotionally through the screen presence of leading men in the violent movies of Quentin Tarantino and Clint Eastwood, I suggest that there
are ways of understanding differentiated male experiences in relation to places and people
(Aitken 2006).

Placing stories

Why is the juggling of space and time possible in film without causing distress to the viewer?
First, the composition and rhythm of a film and the adherence to some known narrative
convention give the effect that some event is actually happening with concomitant suspension of disbelief by viewers. Second, the juggling of space and time creates what Gilles
Deleuze (1986) calls a 'movement-image' and this event is contextualized within some kind
of narrative that suggests scenes diverse in time and space are not arbitrary. Narrative conventions are part of the art of cinematic story-telling. The film space contrives the myth of
meaning production. Film meaning is constituted through a variety of representational
techniques (and, importantly for what I want to say in a moment, some of these have non-
representational impacts) that encourage us, as viewers, to suspend our disbelief. Narrative
conventions co-conspire with various technological developments and camera techniques,
which obscure the filmic apparatus and create the filmic space (Aitken and Dixon 2006).

According to Steven Heath (1981: 24) movement in film is tightly dependent on the
construction and 'holding of place'. His famous work on the narrative space of cinema
lies squarely within the cine-psychoanalytic tradition of Mulvey, and from that he argues that
the role of stories helps elaborate coherent, if shifting, positionalities. For Heath, it is one of
the wonders of moving pictures that they continuously threaten to disrupt the fixity and
coherence of perspectival representations. And narrative is the dominant practice that defends
against or contains this disruptive mobility (Clarke 1997: 8). Thus, as I mentioned earlier, the
Lacanian subject is made aware of its own lack of coherency. And this knowing is facilitated technologically through increased mobility. Early film space is predisposed simply to static background
images; a set of scenes linked to a story. It is only when the background scenes become foreground/
actor – a *mis-en-scène*, a positioned and positioning movement – that cinematic narrative convention becomes important (Aitken and Zonn 1994: 17). And so, for example, David Lean makes
his landscapes work in *Lawrence of Arabia* (1962) when they resonate with the emotions of the
central protagonist. At the beginning of the film Lawrence is in love with the desert and he has a
grand plan for the Arab revolt. Lean portrays sensual sand dunes and symmetrical open vistas.
By the end of the movie, with the Arab revolt in tatters and Lawrence falling into psychosis,
the desert is portrayed as rocky, unbalanced and uninviting (Kennedy 1994: 166).

Another example of an important narrative convention is what I call 'scaling the light
fantastic' (Aitken 1999). As I noted in the story that begins this chapter, with the proliferation of computer graphic techniques, scale change is used most effectively to contextualize
the action in video-games. And this god-trick is planetary in its implications of how we, as
subjects, are placed. As Denis Cosgrove (1994) noted, the representation of the Earth from
space is a particularly affective image. In the recent world calamity film, *The Day After
Tomorrow* (2004), the action of the characters on America's eastern seaboard is contextualized
from space in scenes that dramatize an advancing ice-sheet. This narrative convention is
particularly effective in nature and scientific documentaries: the small scientific camp is
found amongst the openness of the glacier or it is perched precariously on a narrow mountain
ledge. As the audience enters the scalar conventions of this form, a character enters the space

of the film: the scientist steps out of his tent and surveys the panorama. In the award-winning 2001 French 'true-story' documentary *Winged Migration*, computer graphics are used to depict birds seemingly flying in space as their migration routes are delineated below. This is not always a control-oriented god-trick, because the convention works for films with themes involving the juxtaposition of enclosure and openness, or human (bird?) limitations and their potential against the backdrop of a global nature (perhaps a Gaia-trick rather than a god-trick).

Importantly, this kind of positioning of places – which began in the early nineteenth-century cinema – highlights transitions that articulate a construction of space, and which achieve a coherency of place that positions the spectator affectively. This vision of the image is its narrative clarity and that clarity is dependent on the negation of space for place, the constant centring of the flow of images and our affective engagement with that centre. It is about narrative movement and completeness (Heath 1981: 18–19). Put another way, narrative movement instils in us something lacking, and installs a desire to explore, to find out what is missing, or to move into a new scene and the possibility of achieving what is desired (Higson 1984: 3). While moving image-events are predominantly organized in the interests of assuring narrative re-significance, they also develop as something fascinating in and of themselves, a source of visual pleasure, a spectacle (Aitken and Zonn 1994).

Clarke (1997: 8) argues that Heath's narrative account is problematically visual in its exclusive orientation, and can be critiqued in terms of the experiences of moviegoers by considering the question of the haptical nature of cinematic space, which is about reaching out and apprehending. It is this haptical quality of cinema that led Gilles Deleuze (1986) to consider non-representational ways of understanding the power of moving images. There is a touching, an affect, to moving images that is not related directly to their visual acuity. And so an understanding of images requires a movement beyond representation and beyond narrative convention.

Images that move me

Analysing representations became a big part of geography the 1990s, when we looked to textual and visual metaphors as an aid for understanding landscapes and culture (Barnes and Duncan 1992). Some of the first studies of geography and film criticized the discipline's unwillingness to look beyond the material world to the ways culture is co-created with representational and visual imagery (Aitken and Zonn 1994; Benton 1995). Others criticized this move away from the material conditions of lived experience, charging that it was also a move away from saying anything about resilience, resistance and material change (Mitchell 2000). A contemporary move is abroad in the discipline to look more closely at the ways non-representational theory and emotional geographies helps us to understand the complex connections between our material existence and contemporary culture (see Chapters 5 and 24). Part of this move began with a focus on music and soundscapes (Smith 2000; Aitken and Craine 2001), which have obvious and important connections to the ways moving images are experienced. In combination with moving images, soundscapes create what Guiliana Bruno (2002: 245) calls an 'emotional mapping' that is, in and of itself, a quintessential geography that connects to fundamental parts of our being:

> 'What is mobilized in film's own emotional mapping is the plan of an unconscious topography in which emotions can 'move' us, for they themselves are organized as a course … Indeed, emotional cartography is about an itinerary, the carnal knowledge by which one comes to know beings. It is the kind of cosmography whose compositional

lines touch the most tender filaments of our inner cells – a cosmography that draws the universe in the manner of an intimate landscape. This is a drawing whose texture is the very system of our interior, the texture of our inner fabric: a place where pictures become a space, an architecture.

At the very least, there are important connections between the construction of moving images and the overflow of emotions. Issues of difference arise with Deleuze's (1986) theorizing about affect and space. To get to that difference some fairly obvious questions are raised by the preceding discussion on the ways images move us. What precisely is the affective mechanism that engages me? What is its lasting effect? How does it create me as a person? How does it help me relate to you? These are heady questions that I intend to spend most of this conclusion to the chapter tip-toeing around. To delve into their depths assumes, I think, an unhealthy penchant for universality when what I really want to talk about is difference and connectivity.

Deleuze (1986: ix) suggests that movies often present 'pre-verbal intelligible content' that is not about story-lines, linguistically based semiotics, a universal language of images, or some existential or Lacanian lack in the viewer (cf. Aitken 2006). An aspect of this content is what he calls the movement-image, comprising: (1) the *perception-image* that focuses on moving me from total objective and indistinguishable knowledge at the periphery of my universe to a central subjective perception that is distinguished from it by elimination and subtraction; (2) the *action-image* that is part of me perceiving things here at the centre of my universe and then grasping the 'virtual action' that they have on me, and simultaneously the 'possible action' that I have on them; and (3) something in between perception and action, the *affection-image*. Affection 'surges in the centre of indetermination' between the perceptive and the active, occupying it 'without filling it in or filling it up' (Deleuze 1986: 65). Affection re-establishes the relation between 'received movement', as perception moves me from the total objective to the subjective, and 'executed movement' when I grasp the possibility of action. Affect, then, alludes to the motion part of emotion that sloshes back and forth between perception and action. It is a movement of expression that carries stories between different levels of articulation; for example, between the embodied and visceral and the moral and valued (Aitken 2006).

Summarizing a number of writers who are influenced by Deleuze's work, Christopher Harker (2005) points out that affect is about an intensity that exceeds representation and, by extension, the affection-image is the part of moving images that is felt and understood bodily rather than represented in a mechanistic or calculated way. Although it is understood bodily, affect cannot be represented fully because it is about the heart not the head. No definitions adequately express this embodiment. And yet affect is representable in part or it would not exist on the cinema screen. But it is almost impossible for my friends to explain why they cry at certain scenes in movies. Are these tears of joy? Of sadness? Of anger? To answer these questions it is worthwhile looking at the ways emotions and affects differ. Whereas it is not difficult to write about emotions, it is difficult to describe affects. Emotion is a subjective consensual understanding about affect; it is the part of affect that is owned and recognized. I know faces that are angry, sad, fearful or joyous and I empathize with the emotions that they represent. But the totality of affect is something more, something that goes beyond representation. Brian Massumi (2002: 22) argues that affect is about emotional intensity that is not directly accessible to experience and yet is not exactly outside of experience either. This elusive intensity is felt in my body rather than understood in my mind. Gut-wrenching experiences tighten my jaw and stomach, or weaken my legs and bladder. The power of

611

movie scenes to well up tears in my eyes or convulse my throat and chest in sobs goes beyond representation and rationality. These are visceral, embodied reactions that cannot be reduced to simple expressions of fear or anger. Successful directors know how to set up a scene not just for drama and story, but also for affect.

Conclusions

The last 100 years has heralded important changes in the way we see ourselves in the world in relation to the power of moving images. There has been increasing recognition of the power of articulate, moving images to intervene in the ongoing transformations of everyday life.

Current geographic study is about invigorating and reinforcing insights that are not just about mapping spatial metaphors on to moving images. Today, geographers elaborate insights through critical spatial theories so that our studies are not only about filmic representations of space but are also about the material conditions of lived experience and everyday social practices. Recently, these studies have moved beyond issues of production and consumption, and inferences from psychoanalytic theory, to involve the non-representable.

Ultimately, moving images are about myth creation and, as such, they give form and meaning to lived experiences. Those forms and meanings begin with the unrepresentable, in the virtual dimension of affect, before they are registered by conscious thought. It is consequently important to examine how myths of moving images not only create borders, exclusions and dichotomies, but how those processes are about embodied affects that create connections. My son engages with passion, and gets to know, the other players in his massive multi-player on-line gaming. He and I go to movies and often engage passionately in what Iris Young (1990) calls the promiscuous mingling of different people. There is not always a happy ending, and yet this is the scopic, ocular and haptic connection that creates a large part of the stories of our lives.

Further reading

Aitken, S.C. and Dixon, D. (2006) Geographies of film. *Erkunde*. Forthcoming.

Aitken, S.C. and Zonn, L.E. (eds) (1994) *Place, Power, Situation and Spectacle: A Geography of Film*. Lanham, Maryland: Rowman and Littlefield.

Bruno, G. (2002) *Atlas of Emotion: Journeys in Art, Architecture, and Film*. New York: Verso.

Clarke, D. (1997): *The Cinematic City*. London and New York: Routledge.

Cresswell, T. and Dixon, D. (2002) *Engaging Film: Geographies of Mobility and Identity*. Lanham, Maryland: Rowman and Littlefield.

Mulvey, L. (1975) Visual pleasure and narrative cinema. *Screen* 16 (3), 6–18.

Natter, W. and Jones, J.P. (1993) Pets or meats: class, ideology, and space in *Roger & Me*. *Antipode* 25 (2), 140–58.

References

Aitken, S.C. (1991) A transactional geography of the image-event: the films of Scottish director, Bill Forsyth. *Transactions, Institute of British Geographers*. New Series 16 (1), 105–18.

——(1994) I'd rather watch the movie than read the book. *Journal of Geography in Higher Education* 18 (3), 291–307.

——(1999) Scaling the light fantastic: geographies of scale and the web. *Journal of Geography* 98, 118–27.

——(2001) Tuning the self: city space and SF horror movies. In Rob Kitchin and James Kneale (eds) *Lost in Space: Geographies of Science Fiction,* pp. 103–22. London and New York: Continuum.

——(2006) Leading men to violence and creating spaces for their emotions. *Gender, Place and Culture.* Forthcoming.

Aitken, S.C. and Craine, J. (2001) The pornography of despair: lust, desire and the music of Matt Johnson. *ACME: An International E-Journal for Critical Geographers* 1 (1), 91–116.

Aitken, S.C. and Dixon, D. (2006) Geographies of film. *Erkunde.* Forthcoming.

Aitken, S.C. and Zonn, L.E. (1994) Representing the place pastiche. In S.C. Aitken and L.E. Zonn (eds) *Place, Power, Situation and Spectacle: A Geography of Film,* pp. 3–25. Lanham, Maryland: Rowman and Littlefield.

Bachmair, B (1991) From the motor-car to television: cultural-historical arguments on the meaning of mobility for communication. *Media, Culture and Society* 13 (4), 530–9.

Barnes, T.J. and Duncan, J.S. (1992) *Writing Worlds: Discourse, Text and Metaphor in the Representation of Landscape.* London and New York: Routledge.

Benton, L. (1995) Will the reel/real Los Angeles please stand up? *Urban Geography* 16 (2), 144–64.

Bruno, G. (2002) *Atlas of Emotion: Journeys in Art, Architecture, and Film.* New York: Verso.

Clarke, D. (1997) *The Cinematic City.* London and New York: Routledge.

Clover, C. J. (1989) Her body, himself: gender in the slasher film. In J. Donald (ed.) *Fantasy and the Cinema,* pp. 91–133. London: British Film Industry.

Cohan, S. and Hark, I.R. (1993) Introduction. In Steven Cohan and Ina Rae Hark (eds) *Screening the Male: Exploring Masculinities in Hollywood Cinema,* pp. 1–8. London: Routledge.

Cosgrove, Denis (1994) Contested global visions: one-world, whole-earth, and the Apollo space photographs. *Annals of the Association of American Geographers* 84 (2), 270–94.

Crang, M. (1997) Watching the city: video, surveillance and resistance. *Environment and Planning A* 28 (12), 2099–104.

Cresswell, T. and Dixon, D. (2002): *Engaging Film: Geographies of Mobility and Identity.* Lanham, Maryland: Rowman and Littlefield.

Davis, R. (1976) *Response to Innovation: A Study of Popular Argument about New Mass Media.* New York: Arno Press.

Deleuze, Gilles (1986) *Cinema 1: The Movement-Image,* trans. Hugh Tomlinson and Barbara Habberjam. London: The Athlone Press.

Denzin, N. (1995) *The Cinematic Society: The Voyeur's Gaze.* London: Sage.

Eisenstein, S. (1943) *The Film Sense.* London: Faber.

——(1949) *Film Form.* New York: Harcourt.

Friedberg, A. (1993) *Window Shopping: Cinema and the Postmodern.* Berkeley: University of California Press.

Harker, Christopher (2005) Playing and affective time-spaces. *Children's Geographies* 3 (1), 47–62

Heath, S. (1981) *Questions of Cinema.* Bloomington and Indianapolis: Indiana University Press.

Higson, A. (1984) Space, place, spectacle: landscape and townscape in the 'Kitchen Sink' film. *Screen: Incorporating Screen Education* 25 (July/October), 2–21.

Holloway, S.L. and Valentine, G. (2003) *Cyberkids: Children in the Information Age.* New York and London: Routledge.

Jay, M. (1988) Scopic regimes of modernity. In H. Foster (ed.) *Vision and Visuality,* pp 3–23. Seattle: Bay Press.

Jenkins, A. (1990) A view of contemporary China: a production study of a documentary film. In L. Zonn (ed.) *Place Images in the Media: Portrayal, Experience and Meaning,* pp. 207–29. Savage, Maryland: Rowman and Littlefield.

Kennedy, T. (1994) The myth of heroism: man and desert in *Lawrence of Arabia.* In S.C. Aitken and L.E. Zonn (eds) *Place, Power, Situation and Spectacle: A Geography of Film,* pp. 161–82. Lanham, Maryland: Rowman and Littlefield.

Lehman, Peter (1993) *Running Scared: Masculinity and the Representation of the Male Body*. Philadelphia: Temple University Press.

Lukinbeal, C (2004) The rise of regional film production centers in North America, 1984–97. *GeoJournal* 59 (4), 307–21.

MacDonald, G. (1994) Third cinema and the Third World. In S.C. Aitken and L.E. Zonn (eds) *Place, Power, Situation and Spectacle: A Geography of Film*, pp. 27–46. Lanham, Maryland: Rowman and Littlefield.

Massumi, Brian (2002) *Parables for the Virtual: Movement, Affect, Sensation*. London: Duke University Press.

Metz, C. (1974) *Language and Cinema*. The Hague: Mouton.

Mitchell, D. (2000) *Cultural Geography: A Critical Introduction*. Oxford: Blackwell.

Mulvey, L. (1975) Visual pleasure and narrative cinema. *Screen* 16 (3), 6–18.

Natter, W. (1994) The city as cinematic space: modernism and place in *Berlin, Symphony of a City*. In S.C. Aitken and L.E. Zonn (eds) *Place, Power, Situation and Spectacle: A Geography of Film*, pp. 203–28. Lanham, Maryland: Rowman and Littlefield.

Neale S. (1993) Masculinity as spectacle: reflections on men and mainstream cinema. In Steven Cohan and Ina Rae Hark (eds) *Screening the Male: Exploring Masculinities in Hollywood Cinema*, pp. 9–20. New York and London: Routledge.

Penley, C. (ed.) (1988) *Feminism and Film Theory*. New York: Routledge.

Saco, D. (1992) Masculinity as signs: poststructuralist feminist approaches to the study of gender. In S. Craig (ed.) *Men, Masculinity, and the Media*, pp. 23–39. Newbury Park: Sage.

Sadoul, G. (1972) *French Film*. New York: Falcon Press.

Silverman, K. (1992) *Male Subjectivity at the Margins*. New York: Routledge.

Smith, S. (2000) Performing (Sound)world. *Society and Space* 18, 615–37.

Studlar, Gaylyn (1988) *In the Realm of Pleasure: Von Sternberg, Dietrich and the Masochistic Aesthetic*. Urbana: University of Illinois Press.

Virilio, P (1997) *Open Skies*. London: Verso.

Young, Iris Marion (1990) *Justice and the Politics of Difference*. Princeton, NJ: Princeton University Press.

39

Sound

Music and the spoken word

Andy Bennett

Music has long functioned as a resource through which individuals situate themselves, and others, in relation to space and place. Most fundamentally, music that originates in a particular place often becomes part of the symbolic imagery of that place's local culture and tradition, along with things such as local cuisine, dialect, styles of dress, etc. Indeed, this is perhaps the most widely understood perception of music's local significance at the level of the everyday. With the advent of recording and the global dissemination of mechanically reproduced music, however, the relationship between music and place has become increasingly more complex as new factors have come into play. Thus, in the context of media culture, musical genres acquire trans-local audiences whose readings and interpretations of music often carry their own localized meanings (Slobin 1993). Similarly, in a world increasingly characterized by global mobility and diasporic communities, music serves as an important bridging device, spiritually connecting displaced peoples with their cultural roots (Gilroy 1993). Music may also serve as an important medium for the imagining of space and place from without. Through the medium of lyrics, melodic patterns and certain characteristic timbres, specific genres of music create particular of images of space and place which are consumed by global audiences and help frame their perceptions of the specific localities from which these musics have emerged (Frith 1987).

This chapter explores the significance of music as a resource in the articulation of discourses relating to space and place. The chapter begins by contrasting different theoretical approaches to music and place before going on to consider, by way of several specific examples, the role of genre and cultural context in the creation of spatial meanings.

Theories of music and place

Music's most obvious connection to a particular space is as a 'folk' form played *by* the people *for* the people. As Connell and Gibson observe, this perspective on music's connection with place provided a basis for much early work carried out in the field of ethnomusicology:

> Central to the ethnomusicological tradition is a sense of endogeny – of musical expressions emanating from within relatively unique social landscapes, rather than

interacting with outside flows, consuming and reproducing the products of others, or mimicking international sounds.

(Connell and Gibson 2003: 20)

Ethnomusicology's approach to the study of music and place rested primarily on the diffuseness of local cultures outwith the Western sphere of cultural influence. Existing in relative isolation, local music traditions, like language, clothes, religion and other aspects of custom, were considered to be imbued with a sense of distinctiveness, resulting from being tied to their place of origin. The relationship between space and place was thus regarded as inherently organic. This argument was supported by the fact that musical styles which originated in a given region would generally be played by local musicians on locally produced instruments (made from raw materials available in the region) and, as a result of relatively limited geographical mobility, would be listened to by primarily local audiences. Similarly, traditions of song, styles of playing, forms of accompanying dance and so forth, would often be handed down from generation to generation within a particular place.

In more recent years, the increasingly trans-local nature of music production, performance and consumption has prompted a shift in thinking about music's relationship to place. The increasing globalization of music, and culture generally, has also forced new questions concerning the relationship between the global and the local. Thus, it is now widely acknowledged that it is no longer possible to speak of a 'bounded' local, the local culture of a place being always a product of its exposure to, appropriation and/or negotiation of global products and information (see Chapter 14). At the same time, however, it is similarly acknowledged that while globalization has had a profound effect on the cultural territory of the local it has not served to completely eradicate local influences. Thus, as Featherstone observes 'a paradoxical consequence of the process of globalization, the awareness of the finitude of the boundedness of the planet and humanity, is not to produce homogeneity but to familiarize us with greater diversity, the extensive range of local cultures' (1993: 169).

The challenge for academic researchers, then, has been to interpret the ways in which the local and the global interact. Pertinent in this respect is the work of Robertson (1995) which argues that the rise of global culture has resulted in a process of 'glocalization', whereby different aspects of global culture are appropriated by particular local cultures and seamlessly woven into the tapestry of everyday life, to the extent that outside global influences become indistinguishable from aspects of indigenous local culture. Robertson's ideas are developed by Lull (1995) through his concept of cultural re-territorialization. Thus, according to Lull, while global images and products are appropriated by local cultures in unpredictable and often quite arbitrary ways, such appropriation is inevitably constrained by local factors, to the extent that global resources acquire distinctly hybrid meanings – at once part of globalizing trends, but also highly particularized in terms of the specific value and significance they assume in a given locality.

Not surprisingly, such debates concerning the relationship between the local and the global have had a significant impact on the study of music's relationship to place, opening the door for contributions to this work from a broad array of disciplines, including sociology, social anthropology, media studies, cultural studies and geography. Dominant in the fields of sociology, media and cultural studies has been an emphasis on the significance of music in the production and articulation of micro-social relations, typically theorized as subcultures (Hebdige 1979), or scenes (Straw 1991; Bennett and Peterson 2004). Music subcultures are defined as subsets of society, often, though not always, comprising of young people, with an alternative, non-conformist value system articulated through the appropriation of a particular

combination of music and visual style. Subcultures are regarded as inherently local formations and typically extensions of extant communities with whom they may to some extent
share common values (Cohen 1972). Music scenes are also commonly interpreted as locally
generated phenomena, although scenes can also embody trans-local and even virtual characteristics (see Bennett and Peterson 2004). Unlike the concept of subculture, however,
which focuses primarily on interactions within and between artist and audience clusters, the
concept of 'scene' has been applied to the interactions of individuals involved in a far broader
range of music-related activities which, in addition to performance and consumption, also
includes production, promotion, distribution and journalism (Stahl 2004).

A crucially defining aspect of any local music scene is, of course, the wider social context
in which it exists. Context in this case describes everything from local traditions of music in
a particular city or region, relationships between local artists and with their audiences, and
the infrastructure of facilities such as rehearsal space, recording studios and venues that promote local live music. Such factors play an important part in shaping a local music scene and
may ultimately determine its distinctive features (Peterson and Bennett 2004). Social
anthropological studies by Finnegan (1989) and Cohen (1991) have provided a highly
insightful mapping of how the relationship between musical life and its broader local context
have shaped the cultural terrains of local music scenes in two specific UK urban settings –
Milton Keynes and Liverpool. Cohen's work in particular illustrates the impact of local
knowledges and sensibilities upon the nature of local music-making, everything from the
gender composition of the local Liverpool music scene to the widely held perception of
music-making being a worthwhile and 'serious' activity being rooted in the local circumstances
of the city and its inhabitants. As Cohen observes, even the sound of locally produced music
was considered by many to be inherently connected with the context from which it emerged:

> Some suggested that the lack of 'angry' music or music of a more overtly political
> nature reflected the escapist tendency of the bands that produced instead music of a
> 'dreamy' and 'wistful' style. Others pointed out that Merseysiders had understandably
> grown cynical about politics and therefore avoided writing about it.
>
> (Cohen 1991: 15)

Key to the work of Cohen (1991) and Finnegan (1989) is the notion of the local as a relatively fixed space, or at least one in which a common musicalized discourse informs the way
in which this space is constructed. As subsequent work has revealed, however, the musicali-
zation of place may lead to not one but a number of competing discourses. Significant in this
respect has been the work of Bennett (2000) which, drawing on the ideas of social geographers such as Massey (1993), has examined the way in which particular localities give rise
to a variety of distinct music scenes, each of which create its own discourse of space and
place resulting in what Bennett (2000) refers to as 'multiple narratives' of the local. For
example, in the case of the German city of Frankfurt am Main, Bennett demonstrates how
differing local appropriations of rap music have led to differing spatializations of the city.
Thus, hip hop purists, for whom African-American styles of rap constitute its only authentic
form, revel in those physical and cultural aspects of Frankfurt that approximate the urban
cultural terrain of the US and the opportunities that this affords for re-enacting the African-
American hip hop aesthetic. However, for those who have chosen to re-work the rap style
into a more locally associated form, for example, through rapping in German or Turkish
(many young local rappers being the children of Turkish immigrant families) and/or using
rap as a means of discussing the everyday problems of ethnic minorities in the city, Frankfurt

is cast as space in which racism and racial exclusion flourishes at both the institutional and local neighbourhood level. Similarly, competing narratives of place are demonstrated by Shank (1994) in his study of the local music scene in Austin, Texas. Here traditional cowboy song and home-grown punk rock produce glaringly contrasting commentaries on Texan male identity, cowboy song championing the tough, maverick qualities it identifies with the typical Texan male, while punk ridicules these same qualities, dismissing them as backwardly conservative values. Austin then becomes a space crossed by competing musicalized discourses of locality and local identity, each produced through a familiarity with the same local knowledges and sensibilities but using the latter to radically different ends.

As this account begins to illustrate, a major aspect of music's ability to evoke notions of space and place in the context of late modernity is its seductive hold on the geographical imagination. Thus, as Stokes (1994) observes, even as the distinctions between local and global become increasingly blurred, music remains a key means through which individuals are able to articulate a sense of place and, with it, a sense of cultural distinctiveness. Additionally, however, music may also serve as an important medium for the imagining of space and place for a global audience of 'outsiders'. Thus, genres of music such as Chicago blues (Grazian 2003) and Algerian raï (Schade-Poulsen 1995) suggest through their lyrics and musical timbres a series of images of space and place which are consumed by listeners and may make them feel they know a great deal about Algeria or Chicago without ever having been there. Alternatively, an interest in a particular genre or style of music may serve as an impetus for actually travelling to its place of location. This is illustrated by the number of tourists who visit Chicago each year to sample what they consider to be the 'authentic' blues experience (Grazian 2003) or the various Beatles tours and other Beatles-theme attractions that are now incorporated into the Liverpool tourist trail (Cohen 1997). The expectations associated with such locally specific examples of music tourism can be aligned with those identified by Urry (1990) in what he terms the 'tourist gaze'. Thus, argues Urry, in late modern, mediatized societies, individual desires to visit particular places are often driven by mediated images of these places – the latter effectively becoming a primary form of experience upon which tourist expectations are largely based (see also Chapter 37).

New technologies have also had a significant impact on the relationship between music and place, influencing both the phenomenological experience of space and place and facilitating new ways in which space and place are imagined. In his work on personal stereo and iPods users, Bull (2000 and 2005) has illustrated how the personal soundscapes facilitated by these technologies radically influence the way in which individuals experience particular settings, for example the city street, the beach or the countryside. As Bull observes: 'The use of personal stereos replaces the sounds of the outside world with an alternative soundscape which is more immediate and subject to greater control' (2000: 78). Bull goes on to examine what he refers to as the 'cinematic experience', a sensation reported by personal stereo users who often feel as if they are either watching a film or are themselves a film character. Bull's work points to a very different way in which notions of space and place are influenced by the experience of consuming music, not in the ways thus far considered in which music evokes feelings of community and collective identity. Rather, in Bull's work it becomes evident that, through the medium of the personal stereo or the iPod, music facilitates highly individual constructions of space and place. Moreover, on the basis of Bull's findings, it appears that such intensely personal musicalized spatializations often overlay existing discourses of space altogether, becoming in effect supra-spatializations – thus, the local high street may, in the personal stereo listener's imagination, become 'Manhattan', the local river the 'Hudson River', and so on.

Similar forms of musically informed supra-spatialization have also been facilitated by the Internet. As Peterson and Bennett (2004) observe, one significant aspect of Internet technology is that it has allowed for the communication between fans of particular musics diffusely spread around the globe. Unable to engage in the face-to-face interaction that characterizes local music scenes, fans who communicate across the Internet build their own on-line 'virtual' scenes, the latter being facilitated by Internet fansites, chat-rooms and mailing lists (see also Chapter 33). Among the themes and issues discussed by fans in such on-line contexts are the local origins and spatial properties of music. Indeed, physically removed from the cities and regions they discuss, and from each other, their collective geographical imagination assumes an enhanced creative licence, with fans creating rich images of space as a crucial underpinning in the birth of particular moments in music history. A pertinent example of this is offered in Bennett's (2002, 2004) work on the 'Canterbury Sound', a term coined by the British music press and briefly used during the late 1960s to describe the music of several rock groups with Canterbury connections, such as Soft Machine and Caravan. The term was abandoned during the early 1970s, by which time the groups concerned had either disbanded or become associated with more mainstream musical directions. However, during the mid-1990s the term 'Canterbury Sound' was revived through a series of dedicated websites, the latter creating a new generation of fans. As Bennett observes: 'Within this [on-line] context, the Canterbury Sound acquired a new resonance as fans set about exchanging views and opinions on-line as to the defining qualities of the Canterbury Sound and the role of the city in its conception' (2004: 206). A similar phenomenon is noted by Hodgkinson (2004) in his study of post-rock, a loosely defined genre of music created through the use of synthesizers, sampling technology and various electronic effects. As Hodgkinson observes, although an essentially placeless music, much of the on-line discussion relating to post-rock groups attempts to relate the music to its place of origin, claiming that different geographical locations have given rise to locally distinctive styles of post-rock. Significantly, in both the case of the Canterbury Sound and post-rock, the opinions of the fans are not generally shared by the musicians themselves. Bennett (2002) has suggested that on-line communities' preoccupation with grounding music in physical circumstances in this way has much to do with the need, evident in any music scene, to anchor music by giving it a lived, everyday context which, as previously discussed, is a key way in which individuals respond to and ultimately understand music.

In a variety of ways and for widely different reasons then, music articulates notions of space and place. That music is able to function in this way has much to do with the nature of music as a cultural form. Thus, as Frith (1987) observes, individuals often feel that they 'own' music and that it is part of them – feelings which are not so readily associated with other aspects of popular culture. At the same time, however, it is important to note that music's forming of particular notions of space and place, in line with the other types of cultural work it performs, is not an arbitrary process. As Frith notes, 'we are not free to read anything we want into a song . . . music is obviously rule bound' (1987: 139). Over time, particular genres of music acquire particular conventions of performance and consumption, which in turn influences the discourses of space and place which form around them. The concluding part of this chapter considers this issue in relation to a number of different musical genres.

Folk

As noted previously, music's most obvious connection to place is as a 'folk' form. Underpinning the performance and reception of folk music is the notion that it is a 'pure' form of music, that is to say, a 'traditional' as opposed to 'commercial' music. This interpretation of folk music is further enhanced because of the widespread use of acoustic instruments in its composition and performance, acoustic instruments becoming in themselves a symbol of purity and authenticity, while the electric instruments are considered part of the bland and faceless terrain of rock and pop. As Narváez (2001) observes, such beliefs remain true even as folk musicians increasingly rely on state-of-art pick-up technology and PA (public address) systems as a means of amplifying, and thus improving, the sound of their instruments. In the context of the British Isles, the 'local' spirit of folk is further enhanced through the emphasis upon informal performances in small, accessible venues, notably local pubs. Although the British folk music scene itself is a relatively recent development, dating back only as far as the folk revival movement of the 1960s (see MacKinnon 1994), the tradition of pub singing on which it draws is much older (Pickering 1984). It is also a source for many of the regional and 'traditional' songs featured in contemporary folk clubs, a tradition which, as MacKinnon (1994) notes, many folk clubs strive to preserve even as new generations of folk singers and musicians come along with a potentially wider repertoire of songs on which to draw. MacKinnon further notes how the informality associated with folk performances is often proactively enforced by club committees, either through the banning of electric instruments and amplification altogether, or the insistence that these be kept to a minimum. At a collective level, such imposed conventions of performance strive to retain what is considered to be folk music's original and 'authentic' character – its connection with region, nation and 'the people'.

Rock

In comparison to folk music which, as we have seen, depends to some extent on the individuals' willingness to buy into its status as an authentic aspect of 'local' culture, on the surface rock music would appear to have a far more tenuous link to place. Certainly hard rock has often been termed a 'working-class' music, while the origins of much of what became the first wave of British heavy metal in the industrial heartland of central England led to associations between the metal style and the grey, industrial veneer of the British working-class city (see Walser 1993). Clearly, such representations are romanticized. Moreover, they are as much statements about class as about place. Certainly, rock bands often begin as 'local bands', in that they grow out of particular cities or regions and, in their initial years at least, draw heavily on the local as a place in which to perform and generate an audience for their music. As a band becomes more successful, however, such local links gradually fade as the band embarks on national and international tours in pursuit of world markets (Frith 1983). In terms of its sound and musical structure, too, rock music ostensibly appears to be an essentially 'placeless' genre, the melody and general song structure of most rock songs conforming with trans-locally established conventions of harmony and rhythm. Significantly, however, even as rock artists become physically removed from their place of origin, this is often replaced with a romantic or spiritual association. For example, at the height of their commercial success in 1967, the Beatles released a double A-sided single containing the songs 'Penny Lane' and 'Strawberry Fields Forever', which draw upon Paul McCartney and John Lennon's respective memories of growing up in Liverpool.[1] Similarly, US 'Southern Boogie' Lynyrd Skynyrd's song 'Sweet Home Alabama', despite its status as a global rock anthem, is also clearly intended as a celebration of the band's southern roots.[2] Other rock songs containing local references include Canadian band Rush's 'Lakeside Park', a lyrical tribute by drummer Neil Peart to a place where he spent much time during his childhood and teenage years, and German-rock band the Scorpions' 'Winds of Change', a ballad charting the mood and sentiment in Berlin during the time immediately after the fall of the Berlin Wall. The fact of globally established rock musicians drawing on local references, no matter how idealized or imagined these may often be, is a further example of music's function as a form of situating practice in late modernity. In the case of artists themselves, this may be indicative of their quest to retain a sense of place, and with it a sense of belonging which, as noted above, is continually undermined by the rock musician's itinerant, trans-local and inherently 'placeless' lifestyle. From the point of view of the rock audience, the use of such local imagery assumes a different, yet equally romantic, resonance. For example, from an audience's point of view, hearing a rock band singing about its 'home town', or an aspect of its local or national culture, may signal to an audience that the band is remaining 'true to its roots'. In other cases, rock's local connections are made not by the artists themselves, nor by their audiences, but through the creative licence of local media and cultural industries. For example, during the mid-1990s Newcastle-born musician/songwriter Mark Knopfler's 'Theme from Local Hero', written for the film *Local Hero*, was re-inscribed as a local anthem through its use as a jingle on regional television in the north-east of England. Each of these examples demonstrate how rock music, despite its ostensibly placeless nature, can generate notions of locality and local identity – for performers and audiences alike – though its creative manipulation of 'the discursive and the real that continually links the global and the local' (Kahn Harris 2006: 133).

Rap

Of all contemporary popular music forms, rap is arguably the one that demonstrates most strikingly the complex interplay between the global and the local. While it is commonly acknowledged that many popular music styles originate in a particular place before being incorporated by the global music industry, rap has successfully circumvented this one-way flow. Thus, while rap is on the one hand a highly successful commercial style of music – being one of the main genres associated with the global popular music – key to rap's longevity is the way in which it is continually being reappropriated and re-made in local circumstances. Much of this has to do with rap's origins as part of hip hop, a street cultural form that originated in the Bronx district of New York during the early 1970s (see Lipsitz 1994). In comparison to other musical styles that demanded competence on a musical instrument and an ability to compose music, rap made use of existing vinyl recordings, these being creatively mixed or 'mashed' together to create new music (Back 1996). Similarly, rap's vocal style was easily emulated, thus making it an instantly accessible form of expression for urban, inner-city youth (Beadle 1993). Although predominantly associated with African-American youth, the origins of rap included contributions from young people from a variety of different ethnic backgrounds (Flores 1994). The street origins of rap, together with the DIY conventions of composition and performance it embraced, were integral to its ensuing global appeal. From the mid-1970s onwards, rap became the soundtrack for socio-economically disadvantaged youth around the world. Similarly important were the key themes and issues considered key to the rap text – racism, racial exclusion, inter-and intra-racial violence, poverty – these being taken up and explored in relation to different local contexts. In Germany, France and Italy, rap became, among other things, a vehicle for protest against the racism directed at migrant workers and their families (Mitchell 1996; Bennett 2000), while in New Zealand rap was adapted by Maori youth as a means of articulating issues relating to Maori land rights, and the occupation of Maori land by white settlers (Mitchell 1996). In the UK, rap has been successfully merged with bhangra and post-bhangra styles by groups such as Asian Dub Foundation whose music examines issues of place and cultural belonging in relation to Asian youth in contemporary Britain (Sharma 1996). Until quite recently, and despite the feeling among many local rappers that rap's cultural association with non-white ethnic cultures was overlooking its street cultural origins (see Bennett 1999), there was a limited acceptance of white rap performers. This has altered with the success of white rap artists such as Eminem and the Streets, who have each played their part in re-working the rap text as a means of exploring issues of socio-economic disadvantage as this affects youth of all ethnic backgrounds. In the case of the Streets, the focus of his work is the urban terrain of post-industrial Britain. Using a pronounced English working-class accent, the Streets address the everyday hardships of British youth stuck in a cycle of MacJobs interspersed with periods and unemployment, and the strategies – drugs, drink, sex, gambling, etc. – that they use to make life bearable under these circumstances.

World music

The term 'world' music has been regularly criticized, not least because of its attempt to commodify highly diverse and sonically distinctive non-Western musics into a single marketing category. At the same time, some observers complain that the term clumsily exoticizes such music, seducing a global audience whose response to the music remains at the level of affect, rather than an interest in the music's cultural context and its association with culture, politics, or religion. Such criticisms are given added weight as a result of the ways in which 'world' music is often manipulated in the studio, where Western technologies are often used to enhance, and in many cases exaggerate, sounds in ways designed to appeal to the senses of audiences akin to listening to Western popular music. Likewise, Western pop and rock musicians who have drawn inspiration from non-Western music, such as Paul Simon and Peter Gabriel, have often been criticized for what is seen as their commercial exploitation of these music (although in fairness both of these artists have also been proactive in promoting the careers of some of those artists whose music they have drawn upon).

In many ways, however, this is a rather one-sided account of world music's impact. No matter how contrived the concept of 'world' music may be, its everyday appeal cannot be reduced to one of aural fetishism. Through providing a range of music otherwise not readily available to Western listeners, the world music market has, at the very least, prompted new sensibilities of musical taste among Western audiences. Moreover, despite arguments to the contrary, there is evidence that consuming 'world' music can also produce a willingness on the part of audiences to learn more about a particular music's place in relation to its culture of origin. The on-going success of the annual WOMAD (World of Music and Dance) festival, established by Peter Gabriel in 1992, and its various off-shoots such as the Australian WOMAdelaide event (see Bloustien 2004), is one example of this. Similarly, the success of world music has led to various local projects, in schools and community resource centres, aimed around educating people about different cultures of the world through the medium of music. Arguably, then, this is another way in which music engages with the geographical imagination through prompting an interest in the listener to learn more about the cultural context of music – its place and meaning in the everyday lives of particular cultures and communities within these cultures.

Notes

1 These songs were originally intended for what became the Beatles' first studio album *Sergeant Pepper's Lonely Hearts Club Band* (Parlophone 1967), which Lennon and McCartney had initially envisaged as a concept album of songs about Liverpool (see Martin and Hornsby 1979).
2 The song was apparently written in response to Neil Young's satirical 'Southern Man' (see Logan and Woffinden 1976).

Further reading

Bennett, A. (2000) *Popular Music and Youth Culture: Music, Identity and Place*. Basingstoke: Macmillan.
Connell, J. and Gibson, C. (2003) *Sound Tracks: Popular Music, Identity and Place*. London: Routledge.
Logan, N. and Woffinden, B. (eds) (1976) *The NME Book of Rock 2*. London: Wyndham.
Martin, G. and Hornsby, J. (1979) *All You Need is Ears*. London: Macmillan.
Slobin, M. (1993) *Subcultural Sounds: Micromusics of the West*. Wesleyan University Press: London.
Stokes, M. (ed.) (1994) *Ethnicity, Identity and Music: The Musical Construction of Place*. Oxford: Berg.
Whiteley, S., Bennett, A. and Hawkins, S. (eds) (2004) *Music, Space and Place*. Aldershot: Ashgate.

References

Back, L. (1996) *New Ethnicities and Urban Culture: Racisms and Multiculture in Young Lives*. London: UCL Press.
Beadle, J.J. (1993) *Will Pop Eat Itself? Pop Music in the Sound Bite Era*. London: Faber and Faber.
Bennett, A. (1999) 'Rappin' on the Tyne: white hip hop culture in Northeast England – an ethnographic study. *The Sociological Review* 47, 1–24.
——(2000) *Popular Music and Youth Culture: Music, Identity and Place*. Basingstoke: Macmillan.
——(2002) Music, media and urban mythscapes: a study of the Canterbury Sound. *Media, Culture and Society* 24, 107–20.
——(2004) New tales from Canterbury: the making of a virtual music scene. In A. Bennett and R.A. Peterson (eds) *Music Scenes: Local, Trans-Local and Virtual*, pp. 205–20. Nashville, TN: Vanderbilt University Press.
Bennett, A. and Peterson, R.A. (eds) (2004) *Music Scenes: Local, Trans-local and Virtual*. Nashville, TN. Vanderbilt University Press.
Bloustien, G. (2004) Still picking children from the trees? Re-imagining Woodstock in 21st century Australia. In A. Bennett (ed.) *Remembering Woodstock*, pp. 127–45. Aldershot: Ashgate.
Bull, M. (2000) *Sounding Out the City: Personal Stereos and the Management of Everyday Life*. Oxford: Berg.
——(2005) No dead air! The iPod and the culture of mobile listening. In A. Bennett (ed.) Popular Music and Leisure. *Leisure Studies* (special edition) 24, 343–55.
Cohen, P. (1972) *Subcultural Conflict and Working Class Community* (Working Papers in Cultural Studies 2). Birmingham: University of Birmingham.
Cohen, S. (1991) *Rock Culture in Liverpool: Popular Music in the Making*. Oxford: Clarendon Press.
——(1997) More than the Beatles: popular music, tourism and urban regeneration. In S. Abram, J. Waldren and D.V.L. Macleod (eds) *Tourism and Tourists: Identifying with People and Places*, pp. 71–90. Oxford: Berg.
Connell, J. and Gibson, C. (2003) *Sound Tracks: Popular Music, Identity and Place*. London: Routledge.
Featherstone, M. (1993) Global and local cultures. In J. Bird, B. Curtis, T. Putnam, G. Robertson and L. Tickner (eds) *Mapping the Futures: Local Cultures, Global Change*, pp. 169–87. Routledge: London.
Finnegan, R. (1989) *The Hidden Musicians: Music-Making in an English Town*. Cambridge: Cambridge University Press.

Flores, J. (1994) Puerto Rican and proud, boyee! Rap roots and amnesia. In A. Ross and T. Rose (eds) *Microphone Fiends: Youth Music and Youth Culture*, pp. 89–98. London: Routledge.

Frith, S. (1983) *Sound Effects: Youth, Leisure and the Politics of Rock*. London, Constable.

——(1987) Towards an aesthetic of popular music. In R. Leppert and S. McClary (eds) *Music and Society: The Politics of Composition, Performance and Reception*, pp. 133–49. Cambridge: Cambridge University Press.

Gilroy, P. (1993) *The Black Atlantic: Modernity and Double Consciousness*. London: Verso.

Grazian, D. (2003) *Blue Chicago: The Search for Authenticity in Urban Blues Clubs*. Chicago: University of Chicago Press.

Hebdige, D. (1979) *Subculture: The Meaning of Style*. London: Routledge.

Hodgkinson, J. (2004) The fanzine discourse over post-rock. In A. Bennett and R.A. Peterson (eds) *Music Scenes: Local, Trans-Local and Virtual*, pp. 221–37. Nashville, TN: Vanderbilt University Press.

Kahn Harris, K. (2006) 'Roots?' The relationship between the global and the local within the extreme metal scene. In A. Bennett, B. Shank and J. Toynbee (eds) *The Popular Music Studies Reader*, pp. 128–34. London: Routledge.

Lipsitz, G. (1994) *Dangerous Crossroads: Popular Music, Postmodernism and the Poetics of Place*. London: Verso.

Lull, J. (1995) *Media, Communication, Culture: A Global Approach*. Cambridge: Polity Press.

MacKinnon, N. (1994) *The British Folk Scene: Musical Performance and Social Identity*. Buckingham: Open University Press.

Massey, D. (1993) Power-geometry and a progressive sense of place. In J. Bird, B. Curtis, T. Putnam, G. Robertson and L. Tickner (eds) *Mapping the Futures: Local Cultures, Global Change*, pp. 59–83. London: Routledge.

Mitchell, T. (1996) *Popular Music and Local Identity: Rock, Pop and Rap in Europe and Oceania*. London: Leicester University Press.

Narváez, P. (2001) Unplugged: blues guitarists and the myth of acousticity. In A. Bennett and K. Dawe (eds) *Guitar Cultures*, pp. 27–44. Oxford: Berg.

Peterson, R.A. and Bennett, A. (eds) (2004) Introducing music scenes. In A. Bennett, and R.A. Peterson (eds) *Music Scenes: Local, Trans-local and Virtual*, pp. 1–15. Nashville, TN. Vanderbilt University Press.

Pickering, M. (1984) Popular song at Juniper Hill. *Folk Music Journal* 4, 481–503.

Robertson, R. (1995) Glocalization: time–space and homogeneity–heterogeneity. In M. Featherstone, S. Lash and R. Robertson (eds) *Global Modernities*, pp. 25–44. London: Sage.

Schade-Poulsen, M. (1995) The power of love: raï music and youth in Algeria. In V. Amit-Talai and H. Wulff (eds) *Youth Cultures: A Cross-Cultural Perspective*, pp. 81–113. London: Routledge.

Shank, B. (1994) *Dissonant Identities: The Rock n Roll Scene in Austin, Texas*. London: Wesleyan University Press.

Sharma, S. (1996) Noisy Asians or Asian noise? In S. Sharma, J. Hutnyk and A. Sharma (eds) *Dis-Orienting Rhythms: The Politics of the New Asian Dance Music*, pp. 32–57. London: Zed Books.

Slobin, M. (1993) *Subcultural Sounds: Micromusics of the West*. London: Wesleyan University Press.

Stahl, G. (2004) 'It's like Canada reduced': setting the scene in Montreal. In A. Bennett and K. Kahn Harris (eds) *After Subculture: Critical Studies in Contemporary Youth Culture*, pp. 51–64. London: Palgrave.

Stokes, M. (ed.) (1994) *Ethnicity, Identity and Music: The Musical Construction of Place*. Oxford: Berg.

Straw, W. (1991) Systems of articulation, logics of change: communities and scenes in popular music. *Cultural Studies* 5, 368–88.

Urry, J. (1990) *The Tourist Gaze: Leisure and Travel in Contemporary Societies*. London: Sage.

Walser, R. (1993) *Running with the Devil: Power, Gender and Madness in Heavy Metal Music*. London: Wesleyan University Press.

40

Multimedia

William Cartwright

In the last two decades a juxtaposition of profound technological advances has allowed the creation of new geographical imaginaries, constituted through interactive possibilities offered by multi- and hypermedia. Multimedia is an altogether different method for information provision that offers a more holistic approach to the representation and understanding of geographical information. It makes information products 'work' by linking the essential ingredients together and extends media by linking multiple channels of information transparently. This merging and linking of media and in particular its application on the World Wide Web has profoundly changed the communication and meaning of geographical information.

This chapter initially outlines the development of the umbrella technology of which multimedia forms a part. It then provides a description of multimedia and how it has been embraced as a new and innovative form of communication and alternative to printing, tracing the shift from discrete to distributed publication systems. Using a case study of mapping as a geographical exemplar of multimedia (see also Chapter 35), I then illustrate the diversity of information available in these new media. The argument moves on to evaluate the potential of the Web as a means of imagining and sharing the world, assesses the significance of intertextual ambiguities revealed in multimedia, and discusses the politics of hyper and multimedia.

The nature of multimedia

Multimedia has become synonymous with the delivery of information using discrete media like CD-ROM and DV-D, or distributed products using the Internet or intranets. It employs many media – text, graphics, audio, imagery and video – to provide a range of ways through which to explore and experience representations of the real or imagined world. Haptic and olfactive feedback and informing devices have also been incorporated as a means for imparting information. Multimedia is interactive, enabling users to choose from rich information resources, and then to follow a 'path' through information, generally through a process of bifurcation, where users navigate through the branches of the system.

In some ways true multimedia built upon analogue multi-mediated foundations. Some 'conventional' paper-based media, like paper maps, incorporated many different kinds of visual display and it has been claimed that maps were in fact the first multi-media products, as they contain text, diagrams, graphics (as ordered symbols) and geographical facts. And paper atlases could be considered to be analogue virtual reality (VR) tools that provide a means by which armchair travellers could 'go' to places from the comfort of their lounge or study.

Artefacts like maps, air photographs, gazetteers, lists, photographs and videotapes may all cover an area of interest. True multimedia products bring together these formally separated elements into a hyperlinked package through which users can now visualize geographical information, and add very different kinds of interactive possibilities. These depictions come in many formats, including:

- commercial and public CD-ROM atlases and encyclopedias;
- animations in which a temporal dimension is added;
- hypermaps;
- drive/walkthroughs and fly-overs;
- distributed multimedia products on the Internet and Web;
- collaborative working through the provision of maps and GIS on the Web.

To understand this rich diversity it is useful to appreciate the history of developments that underpin contemporary use.

The development of multimedia and hypermedia

Linked information

The beginnings of interactive multimedia can be traced to the foresight and unique ideas of Vannevar Bush (1945) who proposed MEMEX, a multi-dimensional diary with links to all connected things (Raper 1991). He envisaged a machine that would store and retrieve information, plus the information owner's memories (hence MEMEX). Bush saw that this would work on an analogue computer, delivering information via microfilm along with 'archived annotations'. Bush saw three main advantages with his theoretical machine: it would greatly reduce information overload; record intimate thoughts, or 'associated trails'; and engender research leading to human-machine consciousness (Zachary 1997: 158). It can indeed be argued that Bush's writings foreshadowed both the personal computer (PC) and the World Wide Web (Web).

Hypertext

Bush's notion of a multi-dimensional diary was further developed by Californian computer guru Ted Nelson, head of the Xanadu project (Reynolds and Derose 1992). He transformed Bush's idea of associated trails and coined the term 'hypertext' in 1965 (Cotton and Oliver 1994) when the word was first used in a paper presented at the Annual Conference of the Association of Computing Machinery (Nelson 1965). He also examined the implications in terms of the associative linking of facts and ideas and created prototypes (Raper 1991).

The hypertext model can be described as 'a set of nodes connected together by undifferentiated links', where the nodes can be abstractions made up from any kind of text or graphic information (Raper 1991). For example, 'electronic books' produced using hypertext preserve the best features of paper documents, while adding rich, non-linear information structures (hypermedia) and interactive user-controlled illustrations (Reynolds and Derose 1992).

Hypermedia is the very essence of multimedia and makes multimedia products 'work' by linking the essential ingredients together. It extends multimedia by linking the multiple channels of information transparently and in a structured, dynamic and navigable form. Initially the most used form was hypertext, which allowed authors to produce seemingly unstructured texts that enabled readers to move through a publication at their own pace and to follow their own reading pattern.

The first significant interactive hypertext editing system was developed by van Dam and his research associates and implemented in collaboration with Nelson in 1968, as the Hypertext Editing System (HES). This pioneered multiwindowing (sic), seamless text and a 'What You See Is What You Get' (WYSIWYG) interface that debuted on the Xerox Star, the first computer offering a graphic user interface (GUI), from Xerox PARC in 1981 (Reynolds and Derose 1992). Also in 1968, Engelbart first demonstrated his on-line hypertext system NLS (Rheingold 2000). With his concept of hypertext, Nelson published *Dream Machines* in 1974 (Nelson 1987) and began to develop Xanadu, in many ways the conceptual forerunner to the Web (Reynolds and Derose 1992). In 1975, ZOG (later designated the Knowledge Management System, KMS), was developed at Carnegie-Mellon as one of the first distributed hypermedia systems (History of Hypertext Systems 2005). Other hypertext developments continued to occur. TELOS introduced Filevision in 1984, a hypermedia database for the Macintosh, which was released in the same year. In 1985 Norman Meyrowitz and associates at Brown University conceived Intermedia, a hypermedia system that was described as a functional hypermedia system (Landow 2005) and, in 1986 OWL introduced Guide, the first widely available hypertext browser.

The technology and theoretical structures developed in the 1970s and 1980s and were further advanced with inexpensive computer memory, making it possible for Bush's and Nelson's ideas to be implemented in working hyper-mediated systems.

Technical developments

In 1968 the Architecture Machine Group was formed at MIT as a laboratory/think tank that researched radical new approaches to human-computer interfaces. It later became the Media Lab. What has been called the first multimedia-mapping project was devised and undertaken by the Group in 1978 and designated the Aspen Movie Map Project (Negroponte 1995). This groundbreaking package used videodiscs, controlled by computers, to allow the user to 'drive' down corridors or streets of Aspen, Colorado. Every street and turn was filmed in both directions, with photographs taken every three metres. By putting the straight street segments on one videodisc and the curves on the other, an artificial seamless driving experience was provided. It used two screens – one vertical showing video, and the other horizontal on which was displayed a street map of Aspen. Users could point to a spot on the map and jump to that spot, enter buildings, see archival photographs, undertake guided tours and leave a trail like Ariadne's thread. The system was accessed via use of a touch screen. The screen image provided interactive tools that allowed the user to 'walk' through the streets, turn, stop and investigate.

In 1976 the Group devised the notion of a Spatial Data Management System (SDMS), for the Defense Advanced Research Projects Agency. This was to prove a seminal step in the development of multimedia and was designated 'Dataland' (Lewis and Purcell 1984). Negroponte and Donelson, supported by Bolt, developed a demonstration room equipped with an instrumented Eames chair, a wall-size colour display and octophonic sound (Liebhold 2003). Users sitting in the chair could 'fly' over Dataland as if it were a landscape, touching down on calculators, electronic books or maps (Leutwyler 1995). Bolt undertook more development work and produced SDMS II in 1980.

In 1985 Negroponte and Wiesner opened the MIT Media Lab (Negroponte 1995). The Media Laboratory was a multidisciplinary initiative that grew out of the Architecture Machine Group and research conducted by Marvin Minsky in cognition, Seymour Papert in learning, Barry Vercoe in music, Muriel Cooper in graphic design, Andrew Lippman in video, and Stephen Benton in holography. Negroponte, who became the Director of the Lab, promoted the *raison d'être* for its work as being to take human interface and artificial intelligence research in new directions. This idea was marketed to the broadcasting, publishing and computer industries as the convergence of the sensory richness of video, the information depth of publishing, and the intrinsic interactivity of computers. In the 1980s military contractors built working prototypes of similar systems for the field, for use in assisting the protection of airports and embassies against terrorism.

Multimedia started to develop from its videodisc origins on to computer hard disk, but only really began to achieve popular acceptance with CD-ROM (Compact Disc-Read Only Memory). Large corporations which in the past had dealt exclusively with film, computing or communications began to form consortia or envelop other media concerns to produce industry conglomerates that had the ability to publish electronically, produce and distribute video and films, author computer packages and games and provide digital communication facilities worldwide. This led to a convergence of what had been discrete components of the entertainment industry.

Views increasingly differed as to what constituted multimedia and how it would mature. The different players in the early 'pioneering' days had different aspirations. It was seen as a new industry by the Australasian Interactive Multimedia Industry Association (AMIA), and not an extension of the film industry, the toy and games industries, the computer industry, the video industry, or any other pre-existing industry (*Multimedia Digest* 1994). In 1992, when multimedia was beginning to look interesting to domestic consumers, the *Australian Multimedia* magazine asked Apple, Commodore, Microsoft, IBM and Lotus to define the field. Their descriptions are outlined in Table 40.1. Each company's description of multimedia was biased towards what they saw as their future, but they shared a clear commitment to multimedia in their future products.

Multimedia offered the opportunity for geographers to develop tools using a variety of delivery platforms and the ability to integrate picture, sound and movement so as to assemble almost any combination into a package for a particular needs.

Multimedia and geographical information artefacts

Historically, multimedia delivers tools that facilitate geographical exploration in the form of tactile, discrete or distributed systems.

Tactile multimedia are media elements that can be touched, held, folded, annotated by hand and generally used for personal information researching. They include paper maps and

Table 40.1. Industry definitions of multimedia, 1992

Apple	The integration of video, sound, text, graphics, and animation under the control of a computer. It is anything with two or more media forms and is a natural extension of the personal computer. Every Macintosh is a Multimedia computer.
Commodore	The integration of graphics, publishing, presentation, video, audio and interactive design to produce a solution for applications that range from business presentation through to leisure and public entertainment.
IBM	Representing the great information revolutions of our century – computers and television … With Multimedia the ability to access and express information goes beyond the text and graphics of the computer to include images, animation, full-motion video, stereo sound and touch-screen interaction … IBM defines Multimedia as the combination of the audio-visual power of television and the interactive power of the personal computer.
Lotus	A set of capabilities that includes some mixture of digital standard computer text, sound, pictures and movies. Multimedia applications capture, store, edit, retrieve, transmit and play back each of these data types [at that time Lotus intended to integrate multimedia capabilities into future products].
Microsoft	The integration of sound, graphics, film, video and text on computers.

atlases, books, photograph albums, sketches, audio-tapes, video cassettes, plan presses of maps and reams of data collection forms and print-outs.

Discrete multimedia comprise products made available through the use of isolated computers regardless of whether they are desktop, notebook or personal digital assistants (PDA). The packages are stored in digital form on floppy disk, hard disk drive, optical disk, videodisc or computer tape. The 1990s were the heyday of discrete multimedia and it was made available to the general public with the arrival of the Apple Macintosh, and software like Apple's *HyperCard* and Macromedia's *Authorware* and *Director*. During this period 'full functional multimedia' was seen to be composed of three elements (*Pixel Vision* 1991):

- natural presentation of information through text, graphics, audio, images, animation and full-motion video;
- non-linear intuitive navigation through applications for access to information on demand; and
- touch-screen animation.

However, the continual development of optical disk storage, effective product authoring tools, communications systems and innovative approaches to publishing within the new medium promoted the development of a 'multimedia' that extended beyond these three elements.

Finally, *distributed multimedia* uses communication resources to link computers locally or internationally. Multimedia packages are delivered using intranets (computers linked internally, in agencies or corporations), or through the Internet and particularly the World Wide Web, with appropriate 'browsers' and 'plug-ins', providing hyperlinked multimedia resources.

Multimedia components can also be classified according to four continua: interactivity, vividness, accessibility and malleability (Mayer 1997). Interactivity, according to Steuer (1992) is determined by the speed at which input is assimilated, the range of user response variables available in a given moment, and the manner in which controls are integrated into a system. Vividness is what Steuer (1992: 81) describes as an index of 'the way in which an environment presents information to the senses', determined by breadth and depth. Accessibility

Table 40.2. Classifying multimedia in terms of access and malleability

	High malleability	Medium malleability	Low malleability	
High access	Immersive VR Mapping packages Electronic atlas CD-ROM mapping package Personal map annotations Terrain interpretation sketches	Analogue video 'flythroughs' Electronic map production packages	Maps via HDD Mapping games Paper atlas Paper map Travel journal	Discrete multimedia and tactile multimedia
Medium access	On-line GIS data Web-delivered GIS	On-line mapping expeditions Web cameras Maps via fax	Web-delivered maps Email map data attachments	Distributed multimedia
Low access	Field data collection records Second or third party map annotations	Air photograph Orthophotomap Terrain slide show	Paper map in map collection Paper map from publisher Paper map in collection Air photograph at government agency	Tactile multimedia

is the ease with which a user can obtain the multimedia element locally or from remote sources, and malleability is the extent to which a user can modify or change the multimedia element to better suit their needs or purpose of use. Table 40.2 explores the relation between malleability and access. It can be argued that interactivity, accessibility, malleability and vividness are all increasing.

Development of multimedia artefacts for the provision of geographical information

Videodisc

Perhaps the most celebrated interactive geographical information product that replaced a printed book or atlas and used personal experiences to tell a geographical story through maps was the BBC Domesday Project (Goddard and Armstrong 1986; Openshaw and Mounsey 1987; Atkins 1986; Openshaw *et al.* 1986; Rhind and Mounsey 1986; Rhind *et al.* 1988). This project was jointly produced by the British Broadcasting Commission, Acorn Computers and Philips to commemorate the 900th anniversary of William the Conqueror's tally book. Even nowadays this system has still not been matched in terms of national coverage and innovation. Limited as they were, and constrained by underdeveloped user interfaces and interrogation routines, interactive videodisc products heralded the future of the application of hypermedia. Figure 40.1 illustrates the types of information provided at each level. Maps and information were stored on two videodiscs – one containing 'national' information and the second 'community' information and delivered on six levels. Level 0 provided introductory

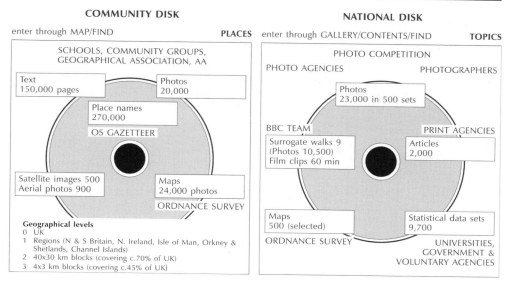

COMMUNITY DISK

enter through MAP/FIND   PLACES

SCHOOLS, COMMUNITY GROUPS,
GEOGRAPHICAL ASSOCIATION, AA

Text
150,000 pages

Photos
20,000

Place names
270,000

OS GAZETTEER

Satellite images 500
Aerial photos 900

Maps
24,000 photos

ORDNANCE SURVEY

Geographical levels
0 UK
1 Regions (N & S Britain, N. Ireland, Isle of Man, Orkney &
   Shetlands, Channel Islands)
2 40x30 km blocks (covering c.70% of UK)
3 4x3 km blocks (covering c.45% of UK)

NATIONAL DISK

enter through GALLERY/CONTENTS/FIND   TOPICS

PHOTO COMPETITION
PHOTO AGENCIES   PHOTOGRAPHERS

Photos
23,000 in 500 sets

BBC TEAM   PRINT AGENCIES

Surrogate walks 9
(Photos 10,500)
Film clips 60 min

Articles
2,000

Maps
500 (selected)

Statistical data sets
9,700

ORDNANCE SURVEY   UNIVERSITIES,
                                   GOVERNMENT &
                                   VOLUNTARY AGENCIES

Figure 40.1. BBC Domesday Disks: types of information, levels, and sources of data.
Source: Adapted from Rhind and Mounsey (1986) and Rhind *et al.* (1988).

map coverage of the whole country. Users could 'zoom' into the next level of maps, Level 1, by clicking the part of the country they wished to move to. Users are able to zoom in further to Levels 2–4. Level 0 and 1 maps were purpose-designed for the project, whilst the more detailed maps on Levels 2, 3 and 4 were scanned from the existing Ordnance Survey coverage. The information on Level 5 provided imagery of mapped areas. At each level users could access text related to the area mapped. Searches were made by place name, region or national grid reference. The hardware/software package, which sold for approximately UK £4,000 in 1985, consisted of two double-sided videodiscs, an Acorn-produced BBC Professional computer, a Philips analogue/digital integrated monitor (multi-format – NTSC/PAL/SECAM) and a Philips videodisc player. Users interacted with the system through the keyboard or through a trackerball. Recently, researchers have 'extracted' this comprehensive multimedia resource of the geography of Britain in the mid-1980s and made it available from http://www.atsf.co.uk/dottext/domesday.html

Compact disc

The CD was jointly developed by Sony of Japan and Philips of the Netherlands in 1982. CD-ROM proved to be a most popular medium, unit costs fell yearly and market penetration increased. Like the laserdisc, compact discs could record information in such a way that it could be read by a beam of light. Formats developed were CD-ROM, WORM (Write Once Read Many), rewritable CDs, CD+ or enhanced CD (combining a music CD with CD-ROM data), Digital Video – Interactive (DV-I), Sony's Minidisc, DVD-ROM, DVD-R and DVD-RAM (rewritable DVD format).

The large storage capacity of CD-ROMs fostered interest in publishing digital maps using the new medium (Rystedt 1987). Products like the Digital Chart of the World (DCW) and the World Vector Shoreline (Lauer 1991) were among the first to exploit this storage

631

Plate 40.1. Topo!

medium. Discrete atlases were also quite quickly produced including the Dorling Kindersley *World Reference Atlas*, Microsoft's *Encarta*, Mindscape's *World Atlas 5* (*NewMedia* 1995) and *The Territorial Evolution of Canada* interactive multimedia map-pack (developed from a proto-type atlas as part of the National Atlas of Canada) (Siekierska and Armenakis 1999). Plate 40.1 illustrates a typical product developed during the early days of using CD-ROM for mapping. *Topo!* from Wildflower Productions was a fusion of digital map information and applications software (Frankel 1996). It contained a seamless set of 50 digitized 1:24,000 United States Geological Survey (USGS) topographic maps covering Yosemite and the San Francisco bay area. Users could pan across the map set, zoom in to any one of five levels and print out any part of the data in colour. The CD-ROM package also included software to access and use the maps.

A number of innovative tools were produced during this period. For example, *T-Vision* (Plate 40.2) described at the time as 'the ultimate world globe' was created by ART+COM, Berlin (Bestor 1996). It consisted of a large projection screen displaying an image of the Earth, compiled from satellite data. The interface was a 1m-diameter sphere, used as a large trackball which the user could spin, and a large screen that kept pace with appropriate displays. A 3D mouse gave access to finer resolutions. Images like weather patterns could be viewed in real-time and the user could 'fly' to any spot on Earth for a more detailed view. This was a discrete media forerunner to *Google Earth*, released almost a decade later.

CD-ROM to DVD

By late 1996 the use of CD-ROM was waning, and new media publishing was shifting to other discrete media and towards distributed formats via the Internet and World Wide Web.

Plate 40.2. T–Vision users navigate the mapping package using the giant trackerball.
Source: After Bestor (1996: 44).

Marketing studies of the time predicted integration of methods and standards for movies, television, publishing and computer technology – all from different traditions, but forced to cooperate under a digital 'umbrella'. Marketing programmes sent messages to consumers regarding opportunities – something that Web-based information providers also began to do during this period. However, the hype of marketing and the Internet in the mid-1990s was viewed with some scepticism: parallels were drawn between predictions about the information superhighway and naive 1950s views of an atomic future (Elliott 1995).

DVD-ROMs provide much more generous storage capacity than the CD-ROM format and CD-ROM was overtaken by DVD-ROM by mid-1996 (Green 1996; Lynch 1996; Ely 1996; Fritz 1996). Some titles previously published on CD-ROM were reissued on the new medium (Hamit 1996). As Ely (1996) saw, this format was the first 'truly (discrete) multimedia' format.

The introduction of DVD storage came about around the same time as the World Wide Web began its inexorable rise. In the mid-1990s there began a shift from discrete to distributed media as a method of making available interactive multimedia, including geographical products. Writers like Negroponte (1995) saw all kinds of package media slowly dying out, as a consequence of the possibilities of 'costless' bandwidth, allowing almost limitless distribution on the Internet; and solid-state memory catching-up to the capacity of CDs of that time, giving the prospect of massive data storage at minimal cost. Many of these predictions have been proved correct by 2006.

Distributed multimedia

Before the Web the Internet was used to deliver mapping products and datasets. Using the File Transfer Protocol (FTP), files, usually compressed, were distributed in this manner. File transfers were quick but the process was burdened with the overheads of file compression and subsequent decompression and the need to have appropriate display software on the 'receiving' computer (Peterson 2001a). Collections of scanned paper maps were constructed and delivered to consumers usually as GIF files. Users still needed to undertake some file manipulations prior to the image being displayed. The Web enabled this problem to be eradicated.

The World Wide Web was proposed by a CERN scientist, Tim Berners-Lee, in the late 1980s (Berners-Lee 2000). With the arrival of the Web and the use of Berners-Lee's browser-driven information displays (Quittner 1999), a different and graphical way of accessing information was made available. The first browser was not all that dissimilar to today's Internet Explorer, and a current-day user of the Web could easily adapt to this original manifestation. Some of the early Web mapping packages used text-heavy interfaces to list the available mapping inventories.

Early mapping sites on the Web such as the *CIA World Fact Book* and the PCL (Perry Castaneda Library) Map Collection (University of Texas at Austin) provided excellent collections of scanned maps, along with other pertinent information. Problems with scanned maps, however, included image quality degradation, warping from improper scanning, coarse scanning resolutions and over-reduction that render many maps unreadable. But users accepted these products because of reduced costs and an almost immediate delivery (Peterson 2001b).

Also quite early in the development of Web mapping, a new genre of 'published' map was made available: those published 'on demand' from databases. *MapQuest*, for example provided a most impressive product for finding streets and business locations, initially in the USA, and later throughout the world. Using *MapQuest* users can pick a country; zoom in to part of it and down to street level. If two addresses are known, maps and routing instructions can be generated and viewed.

The Web changed map publishing for ever. More maps were made available for free or at modest cost, and collections of valuable maps, once only accessible by a visit to a library or map collection, were now made available to researchers and general map users. Web publishing has become prolific and by the new millennium it was recognized that *MapQuest* had become the biggest publisher in the whole history of cartography within five years of being formed.

Mapping services available on the Web include:

- map and image collections;
- downloadable data storages;
- information services with maps;
- on-line map-generation services;
- Web atlases;
- hybrid products.

(Cartwright 2003)

Table 40.3 illustrates the nature of these different resources.

Table 40.3. Mapping services available on the Web

Map and image collections	The extent of map libraries on the Web can be illustrated by the sheer number listed in the University of Minnesota's Web page (University of Minnesota 2000). A large site to access geospatial information is the Alexandria Digital Library (Hill *et al.* 2000). This focuses on the provision of spatially indexed information and comprises a collection of geographically referenced materials and services for accessing those collections. The project is being further developed via the Alexandria Digital Earth Prototype (ADEPT). Increasingly the rarer antiquarian library materials are being scanned and made available via the Web (see, for example, the National Library of Scotland, Project Pont (Fleet 2000)).
Downloadable data storage	Digital geo-spatial information files can be accessed and downloaded on-line. Web repositories have been established by governmental and private mapping organizations to streamline marketing, sale and delivery. These sites reduce distribution costs and maximize revenue.
Information services with maps	Publishers that traditionally published information as paper maps and books now use the Web to provide extra information in support of their paper publications. The sites are numerous, and are provided by organizations like travel information publishers. In Australia, Pacific Access, a wholly owned subsidiary of Telstra Corporation, has actively provided on-line services through its *Whereis* website. This product supplies location information linked to Web versions of both the White Pages and Yellow Pages telephone directories (see http://www.whereis.com.au).
On-line map generation services	A good example to note is ESRI who provide global access to data on-line through its *ArcData Online* site (http://www.esri.com/data/online/quickmap.html). Users are able to select their area of interest and then construct a map by filling in their chosen map 'construction' parameters. This site joins the power of a Geographical Information System with Web-delivered information.
Web atlases	Atlas producers, who face expensive publishing and distribution costs with paper-based products, have embraced the Web as a means of providing atlases of countries and regions. Many different configurations have been assembled, from the very simple to the more complex. One of the earliest to be placed on-line was the *Atlas du Québec et ses Régions*, produced at the University of Québec at Montreal. Another Canadian product that illustrates the effectiveness of providing atlas products via the Web is the National Atlas of Canada *Quick Maps*, which also serves ready-made maps and a service for user-designed output. The atlas was produced by Natural Resources Canada, and it is an excellent example of how atlases can be delivered on-line.
Hybrid products	Combined discrete/distributed products that publish on the Web on CD-ROM and on paper are also being developed. Perhaps one of the most impressive publications of this type is the *Atlas of Switzerland* (2001), published on CD-ROM, on-line via the Web and elegantly published in a bound paper atlas. The atlas has been developed at the Department of Cartography at the ETH in Zurich, on behalf of the Swiss government.

Convergence

By the mid-1990s a digital convergence of communications equipment, office machines, domestic equipment and personal entertainment items meant that almost any digital device could be linked to any other device. This has been brought about by elements talking the same electronic language and by the digitizing of pictures, sounds and video. Zahler, co-director of the Center for Arts and Technology at Connecticut College, New London, Connecticut, has argued that 'with convergence is simplicity . . . it lets every individual find what they want, when they want it, and use it however they like' (*Computer Age* 1995: 26).

Early convergence of computer systems saw the development of hybrid products that linked discrete media to distributed services, enabling information on CD-ROMs to be up-dated using links to sites via the Internet (Glaser 1996). Discrete/distributed hybrid multimedia platforms were developed to complement and enhance interactive multimedia packages, by providing 'value-added' data to formerly isolated mapping packages. 'Hybrid' developers looked forward to the combination of the CD's quick access to local multimedia files with on-line links that provided immediacy and ties to a wide range of related information.

Convergence has now led to multimedia images migrating from the desktop to mobiles, cellular telephones and Personal Digital Assistants (PDAs), which now provide instant, wired and 'at-location' geographical information. Improved connectivity and display technologies are merging with satellite communications technology to serve multimedia images for mobile use, in different real-world contexts. This is facilitated using wires, telecommunications systems, wireless systems like telephony and infrared and proprietary systems such as Bluetooth. You can see where you are on the map on your GPS-enabled palmtop, and watch the dot move across the map as you move through the environment. The implications of this shift are profound.

The implications of the shift to multimedia

By far the most significant use of multimedia in the first decade of the twenty-first century has come from its deployment on the Web. The nature of the multimedia, hypermedia, the particular characteristics of the Web as a global shared environment and the convergence of the Web with other new media (see Sturken and Cartwright 2001 and Lister 2003) have significant implications for producers and users of geographical information and for the wider society. The tensions in the social shift towards multimedia are played out in cultural and political contexts and involve a consideration of intertextuality and meaning (Landow 1992), hyper-reality and the ways in which imagery are related to postmodern times (Baudrillard 1983), and also of how media are able to gain cultural currency and power (Bolter and Grusin 1999).

Multimedia merges linear texts like writing, with more ambiguous and polysemic audio-visual texts. So the multimedia on the Web is part of a complex intertextual field (Sturken and Cartwright 2001). The non-linear nature of hypertext means that the Web is 'self-consciously intertextual': images are borrowed from different media and read in a lateral rather than sequential fashion (Mitra and Cohen 1999). Any one site on the Web is overtly associated with a whole number of other sites and is therefore understood with these sites in mind, in addition to wider and more complex cultural associations. The reader of a map will read it in the light of sites that are associated with the image, other items that appear on the Web page and as part of a wider cultural understanding of what a map means. Most of the earlier theoretical work on hypermedia (for example, Landow 1992) stressed this kind of de-materialized focus upon meaning.

Many of the mapping sites described above turn the reader into the producer and allow people to make their own 'texts' or, in the case of our example, to design their own maps. The nature of the encounter with the information source is shifting with a steady rise in the number of mapping sites that offer interactive possibilities: communication and single answers are being replaced by multiple representations (MacEachren 1995). But the nature of the interaction depends upon ownership structures and power.

The shared nature of the Web and its global spread also affects access to information. More information becomes available to anyone with access to the Web, including an infinite number of possible maps. This profusion of images is also accompanied by a blurring of the real and the hyperreal – fantasy is no longer separate from reality, the virtual worlds described in Chapter 33 resemble real-world experiences and virtual communities interact in simulated spaces. In the postmodern era, *simulation* has replaced representation (Baudrillard 1983) and the play of multimedia imagery plays a central role in the style of our age.

The Web and its hyper-realities are, however, transient. Maps have to be called into existence; they do not reside in any particular tangible medium (Mitra and Cohen 1999). Dead links abide in decentralized hyperspace. File owners may change the data they serve. They may remove data altogether, or may alter the ways you can access data, for example by charging for use.

Early commentators suggested that hypermedia is the successor to print technology (Bolter 1991), but increasingly the complex nature of the shift has been recognized. Moulthrop (1991) considers the medium enhances and intensifies an awareness of how the text has been created; argues that it encourages subjectivity and emotion over reason; and suggests it may empower but is unlikely to replace the printed medium, and that it is much more likely to supplant the television.

The political context in which multimedia is employed is crucial. There are dystopian and utopian narratives at work here. On the one hand, the Web encourages us all to find a voice or weblog, with a rich and active involvement in creating new social and cultural forms. The virtual is becoming more and more important in many people's lives. On the other hand, the Web is enthusiastically dominated by large corporate sites – e-commerce offers a new source for profit and the state sees the medium as offering newly surveillant possibilities and as a medium to be censored and controlled.

Probably the best way to reconcile these diverse strands is to interpret multimedia and the Web as a form of remediation, in which new forms of visual expression gain their cultural significance by paying homage to, rivalling and refashioning, rather than replacing, earlier media (Bolter and Grusin 2000). They argue that hyper-mediation displays a fascination with the medium itself, and that it is through this process of self-referencing that the cultural shift to the Web is occurring.

Conclusion

Historically, the multi-mediated nature of maps has empowered users to exploit these information-rich products. Even hand-drawn paper maps provided multiple communication techniques such as graphics (lines, sketches, renderings and points), text (place names, descriptions and marginalia) and numerics (co-ordinates, values and administrative descriptors and nomenclature). Their electronic counterparts are no longer separate from other media. Instead they form component parts of multimedia packages that may consist of resources linked electronically (as in the case of distributed mapping on the Web), or associated by the human user (combining paper maps, printed reports and other 'tactile' multimedia elements), or linked by the human user interacting with electronics (when using elements stored and retrieved from computer disks, optical disks or videodiscs). Multimedia provides users with a plethora of devices (and their combinations) with which to explore phenomena in real-time, or to access and view stored and related information and data.

The ways in which we understand these new hyper- and multimediated images are in their infancy. Scientific approaches have so far been unable to say with any firm measure of confidence just how effective these new methods are at communicating. There is also considerable debate around the social significance of the Web in contemporary visual culture. All that is certain appears to be the continuing significance of multi- and hypermedia in this process, the continuing rate of change and the continuing obligation on us to research these changes.

Further reading

Bolter, J.D. and Grusin, R. (2000) *Remediation: Understanding New Media.* Cambridge, Mass.: MIT Press.

Cartwright, W.E., Peterson, M.P. and Gartner, G. (eds) (2001) *Multimedia Cartography.* Heidelberg: Springer Verlag.

Cotton, B. and Oliver, R. (1994) *The Cyberspace Lexicon – An Illustrated Dictionary of Terms from Multimedia to Virtual Reality.* London: Phaidon Press.

Landow, G.P. (1992) *Hypertext: The Convergence of Contemporary Critical Theory and Technology.* Baltimore: Johns Hopkins University Press.

Lievrouw, L.L. and Livingstone, L. (2002) *Handbook of New Media: Social Shaping and Consequences of ICTs.* London: Sage.

Openshaw, S., Wymer, C. and Charlton, M. (1986) A geographical information and mapping system for the BBC Domesday optical discs. *Transactions of the Institute of British Geographers* 11 (3), 296–304.

Peterson, M.P. (2001a) *Cartography and the Internet: Implications for Modern Cartography.* Available at http://maps.omaha.edu.NACIS/paper.htm (accessed 5 August 2005).

Peterson, M.P. (ed.) (2003) *Maps and the Internet.* London: Amsterdam: Elsevier.

References

Atkins, S. (1986) The Domesday Project. *Media in Education and Development* 18 (3), 110–11.

Baudrillard, J. (1983) *Simulations.* New York: Semiotexte.

Berners-Lee, T. (2000) *Weaving the Web: The Original Design and Ultimate Destiny of the World Wide Web.* New York: HarperCollins.

Bestor, T. (1996) Real-time globe. *Wired* March, 44.

Bolter, J.D. (1991) *Writing Space: The Computer, Hypertext and the History of Writing.* Fairlawn, NJ: Lawrence Erlbaum Associates.

Bolter, J.D. and Grusin, R. (1999) *Remediation: Understanding New Media.* Cambridge, Mass.: MIT Press.

Bush, V. (1945) As we may think. *Atlantic Monthly* 176, 101–8.

Cartwright, W.E. (2003) Web maps. In M.E. Peterson (ed.) *Maps and the Internet.* Amsterdam: Elsevier.

Computer Age (1995) This is the toaster telling you I'm on fire. Reproduced in *Washington Post* 25 April, 19 and 26.

Cotton, B. and Oliver, R. (1994) *The Cyberspace Lexicon – An Illustrated Dictionary of Terms from Multimedia to Virtual Reality*. London: Phaidon Press.

Elliott, S. (1995) Interactive marketing faces daunting future. *The Age* 6 June, 31.

Ely, M. (1996) Digital video disc pre-mastering: new tools demanded by the new format. *Advanced Imaging* April, 26–9.

Fleet, C. (2000) Distributing images and information over the web: a case study of the Pont manuscript maps. *LIBER Quarterly, the Journal of European Research Libraries* 10, 4.

Frankel, A. (1996) Atlas shrugged. *Wired* July, 140.

Fritz, M. (1996) Digital video discs: compact discs on steroids. *Wired* July, 72.

Glaser, M. (1996) The look of links: CD-ROM/online hybrids. *NewMedia* May, 31–2.

Goddard, J.B. and Armstrong, P. (1986) The 1986 Domesday Project. *Transactions of the Institute of British Geographers* 11 (3), 290–5.

Green, S. (1996) Compounding the issue: multimedia documents and new optical storage options. *Advanced Imaging* September, 38–40.

Hamit, F. (1996) DVD technology: exploding room for images in on-disk multimedia. *Advanced Imaging* September, 42–4.

Hill, L., Carver, L., Larsgaard, M., Dolin, R., Smith, T., Frew, J. and Rae, M.A. (2000) Alexandria Digital Library: user evaluation studies and system design. *Journal of the American Society for Information Science (JASIS)* 51 (3), 246–59. Available at http://www.bren.ucsb.edu/fac_staff/fac/frew/cv/pubs/2000_user_evaluation.pdf

History of Hypertext Systems (2005) http://www.livinginternet.com/w/wi_hyper.htm (accessed August 2005).

Landow, G.P. (1992) *Hypertext: The Convergence of Contemporary Critical Theory and Technology*. Baltimore: Johns Hopkins University Press.

——(2005) *Intermedia: An Introduction*. Available at http://www.scholars.nus.edu.sg/landow/cpace/ht/HTatBrown/Intermedia.html (accessed 17 June 2005).

Lauer, B. J. (1991) Mapping information on CD-ROM. *Technical Papers of the 1991 ACSM-ASPRS Annual Convention, Baltimore: ACSM-ASPRS* 2, 187–219.

Leutwyler, K. (1995) The guru of cyberspace. *Scientific American* September, 40–1.

Lewis, J. and Purcell, P. (1984) Soft machine: a personable interface. Architecture Machine Group, Massachusetts Institute of Technology. Proceedings, Graphics Interface May, 223–6. Available at http://www.idiom.com/~zilla/Work/softMachine/softMachine.html (accessed 17 June 2005).

Liebhold, M. (2003) *Spatial Dataland – 1977*. Available at http://www.starhill.us/spatialdataland.html (accessed 17 June 2005).

Lister, M. (ed.) (2003) *New Media: A Critical Introduction*. London: Taylor & Francis.

Lynch, M. (1996) Separating the hype from the hope. *NewMedia* August, 18.

MacEachren, A. (1995) *How Maps Work*. New York: Guilford.

Mayer, P. A. (1997) Typologies for the analysis of computer media. *Convergence, The Journal of Research into New Media Technologies* 3 (2), 82–101.

Mitra, A. and Cohen, E. (1999) Analyzing the web: directions and challenges. In S. Jones (ed.) *Doing Internet Research: Critical Issues and Methods for Examining the Net*, pp. 179–202. Thousand Oaks, CA: Sage.

Moulthrop. S. (1991) You say you want a revolution? Hypertext and the laws of media. *Postmodern Culture* 1 (3). Available at http://infomotions.com/serials/pmc/pmc-v1n3-moulthrop-you.txt

Negroponte, N. (1995) Affordable computing. *Wired* July, 192.

Nelson, T.H. (1965) A file structure for the complex, the changing and the indeterminate. *Proceedings of the 20th National ACM Conference*, 84–100.

——(1987) *Computer Lib: Dream Machine*, second edition. Redmond: Tempus/Microsoft Press.

NewMedia (1995) You can get there from here. *NewMedia* March, 57.

Openshaw, S. and Mounsey, H. (1987) Geographic information systems and the BBC's Domesday interactive videodisk. *International Journal of Geographical Information Systems* 1, 173–9.

——(2001b) *Cartography and the Internet: Introduction and Research Agenda*. Available at http://maps.omaha.edu.NACIS/CP26/article1.htm (accessed 6 August 2005).

Pixel Vision (1991) IBM 'Ultimedia', 6 (December).

Quittner, J. (1999) The Time 100 – Tim Berners-Lee. *Time* (online). Available at http://www.time.com/time/time100/scientist/profile/bernerslee.html (accessed 10 August 2005).

Raper, J. (1991) Spatial data exploration using hypertext techniques. In *Proceedings of EGIS '91, Second European Conference on Geographical Information Systems*, pp. 920–8. Brussels, Belgium: EGIS.

Reynolds, L.R. and Derose, S.J. (1992) Electronic books. *Byte* June, 263–8.

Rheingold, H. (2000) *Tools for Thought The History and Future of Mind-Expanding Technology*. Cambridge, Mass.; MIT Press.

Rhind, D.W. and Mounsey, H.M. (1986) The land and people of Britain. *Transactions of the Institute of British Geographers* 11 (3), 315–26.

Rhind, D.W., Armstrong, P. and Openshaw, S. (1988) The Domesday Machine: a nationwide geographical information system. *The Geographical Journal* 154 (1), 56–68.

Rystedt, B. (1987) Compact disks for distribution of maps and other geographic information. *Proceedings 13th ICC*. Morelia, Mexico: ICA, IV, 479–84.

Siekierska, E.M. and Armenakis, C. (1999) Territorial evolution of Canada – an interactive multimedia cartographic presentation. In W.E. Cartwright, M.P. Peterson and G. Gartner (eds) *Multimedia Cartography*. Heidelberg: Springer Verlag.

Steuer, J. (1992) Defining virtual reality: dimensions determining telepresence. *Journal of Communication* 42 (4), 73–93.

Sturken, M. and Cartwright, L. (2001) *Practices of Looking: An Introduction to Visual Culture*. Oxford: Oxford University Press.

University of Minnesota (2000) *Map Libraries on the World Wide Web*. Available at http://map.lib.umn.edu/map_libraries.phtml#organizations (accessed 3 July 2005).

Zachary, G.B. (1997) The Godfather. *Wired* November, 152.

Part VI

Responses to the geographical drivers of change

Chris Perkins, Ian Douglas, Richard Huggett

This section focuses upon action. It requires many more chapters than any other section to illustrate the diversity of human responses to change. Places and people respond to different kinds of change and in so doing create new geographies. Paralleling the second block of chapters that documents challenges, this section thematically explores the incredible diversity of approaches to change and evaluates the geographical significance. The early chapters in this section explore people's interactions with the physical environment.

Natural hazards are ever present and are the focus of Colin Green's analysis in Chapter 41. People have always had to cope with earthquakes, volcanoes, tsunamis, floods, avalanches, hurricanes and wildfires. Humans have responded to the threat of natural hazards at a range of scales, from local flood prevention schemes to national and international bodies seeking and monitoring Earth-crossing asteroids. This chapter discusses the relative significance of different threats and explores the ways people deal with risk. Its emphasis is upon management and upon social roles, discourse, governance and development in different contexts. Together the social construction of hazards produces different patterns of adaptability.

During human history, people's responses to climatic variations have changed. They have endeavoured to escape the problem by migrating to other areas, or adjust to it by nomadism, or seasonal spatial shifts in the location of agricultural or pastoral activities. In the short term, in-situ survival for the poor, in a much more crowded world, is aided by relief systems and movement to refugee centres (see Chapter 31), and gradual adjustment guided by greatly improved weather forecasting and climate prediction. In Chapter 42, Rory Walsh emphasizes these temporal changes and spatial-cultural differences in societal impact, response and adaptation to climatic variability. Such responses are spatially and socially variable, reflecting differences in top-down actions by governments and in societal actions and initiatives both to minimize the human impact on the atmosphere and to prepare for climate change.

Catherine Heppell (Chapter 43) explores the relative significance of agricultural and silvicultural practices on the land management. Agriculture occupies 35 per cent of the world's land surface and is the single largest consumer of freshwater resources, using a global average of 70 per cent of surface water supplies. Agricultural expansion is also one of the driving forces behind deforestation and forest land degradation. There are many technological solutions available for minimizing the pollution arising from agricultural and silvicultural practice, either preventative in nature or designed to minimize the delivery and impact of agro-chemicals on the surrounding environment. On their own, however, these technical solutions will not solve the problem of environmental degradation by farming and silvicultural activity. The socioeconomic factors determining how agricultural and silvicultural practices operate have to be changed to achieve greater sustainability of food growing and forest product management.

A small but often locally significant part of the land surface is transformed by waste. Many places reflect their past use as waste dumps but, as Ian Douglas shows in Chapter 44, former landfills are transformed to a host of new uses. Landfill (or landraise) is the least desirable option for waste management. Many of the world's poorest communities are, of necessity, far better than wealthy communities at recycling materials and reusing 'experienced resources'. Providing what consumers expect but at the same time reducing the volume of waste and using resources more efficiently remains a major societal challenge.

Rivers remain attractive and economically valued places for multiple reasons, yet their management has become increasingly challenging. David Sear (Chapter 45) illustrates how the restoration of rivers has become a key component of current river management. From small channels in both urban and rural areas to the world's major rivers, the issues are to retain as many of the amenities of the river environment as possible, with an emphasis on restoring biodiversity and water quality, as well as retaining water supply, power generation, fishery and navigational uses. The chapter presents case studies of river restoration in the UK that demonstrate the complexity of stakeholder interests involved and the need for good scientific understanding. It also discusses broader issues, including dam removal in the USA.

Civilization was made possible by water management – ancient cultures diverted river flow from its 'natural' pathway to use for irrigation. Today, the dual need to ensure adequate water resources and minimize the environmental impact of human activities underpins attempts to move towards sustainable water management. In Chapter 46, Nigel Arnell considers water availability in a global context. Total average annual freshwater flows are approximately 40–47,000 cu. km/year. Global average resource availability (runoff and renewable ground-water recharge) is around 7–8,000 cu. m/capita/year. However, only around 53 per cent of global freshwater flows are available for human use, reducing global per capita availability to closer to 4,000 cu. m/capita/year. The considerable variability in runoff availability from year to year means that in many parts of the world, annual runoff in dry years can be only 10 per cent of the long-term mean. Further, resource availability varies dramatically from region to region, requiring a wide range of strategies to store adequate water, ensure effective irri-gation (the main user of water) and reduce demand, especially in countries with adequate piped supplies.

The saline waters of the oceans contain significant resources that compared to those on the continental land surfaces are under-explored, but often over-exploited. In Chapter 47, Bernd Haupt and Maurie Kelly describe the role of the past and present ocean as biologically diverse habitat, as a resource for life and recreation, most importantly as a stabilizer for our climate. They outline issues related to human impacts on the ocean. Through understanding the role of past and present usage, and the momentous issue of resource exploitation, we can understand how consumerism, industrial and commercial expansion, and insufficient knowledge have led to dramatic changes in the oceans. Co-operative research efforts designed to increase scientific knowledge have enhanced the world's ability to use marine resources more effectively and efficiently, but still greater efforts are needed to ensure that human activities are sustainable.

Coasts are special places for a host of human activities. Competing land uses may lead to complex problems of beach erosion in one place, juxtaposed with harbour siltation in another. Denise Reed (Chapter 48) considers the diverse nature of coastal zone problems and explores practical ways in which these fragile zones may best be managed. The call for coastal management to be based on scientific knowledge of coastal dynamics frequently comes to the fore when hurricanes or non-tropical storms devastate communities and infrastructure. One group advocates systematic retreat from the oceanfront to avoid damage in the future and allow natural processes to heal and adjust to the storm impact. Another reacts to storm damages by calling for increased investment in protecting communities – either through enhancing natural buffers, i.e. beach nourishment, or by strengthening engineered defences such as sea walls. Resolving such contrasted opinions requires good understanding of the environmental and social dimensions of the use of coastal zones.

Global warming has already led to changes affecting low-lying coral atolls in the world's tropical oceans. The main island of Tuvalu was inundated three times in 2003. In Chapter 49, Patrick Nunn explores the special nature of small island environments and communities and discusses their options in a world of rising sea levels. Island decision-makers have the opportunity now to significantly reduce the undesired impacts of future sea-level rise on such islands. The options include gradually relocating vulnerable coastal communities, infrastructure and income-generating activities to higher ground; reducing the dependence, for both subsistence agriculture and cash crops, on lowland areas by relocating farms to higher ground; encouraging new enterprises to operate from higher locations and to have a reduced dependence on lowland-coastal areas; planting vegetation barriers along island coasts, especially, in the tropics, mangrove forests along the most vulnerable stretches of coast; and declaring key coastal areas as reserves to allow natural ecosystems to be restored and to increase coastal resilience to change.

Richard Ladle and Ana Malhado (Chapter 50) explore the 'extinction crisis' and the several factors that are causing a worrying loss of biodiversity – habitat loss, habitat fragmentation, unsustainable exploitation, pollution, the effects of invasive species, and global climatic change. They also consider the responses to biodiversity loss, including the international legislative responses, the establishment of protected areas, and technical responses.

The way we think about nature and the environment structures the way we manage it and thus has material outcomes. Lesley Head (Chapter 51) argues that conceptions of culture and nature as separate entities, symbolized most profoundly in Western thought by the two cultures of the humanities and the sciences, have had many implications for environmental management. For example, natural heritage and cultural heritage are frequently managed by different agencies, or different parts of a single agency, although they may be part of the same landscape. Parts of landscapes are preserved, others have special values to first peoples, such as the Australia Aborigines and the Inuit. Yet even in the world's modern 'extended urban regions' there is a role for nature in the city. For example, it has been suggested that New York could be conceptualized and managed as a Biosphere. While such thinking seems bizarre if we think of nature as existing 'out there', somewhere remote from human activity, it is consistent with the idea that cities are just as much ecosystems as any other area. Such thinking about nature/culture relationships is required for the century ahead.

Population distribution, composition and growth are closely related to local geographies. Analysing demographic structures and changes allows policymakers to project future trends, by unpacking the significance of changing mortality, fertility and migration data. Chapter 52 by Shii Okuno explores the nature of the challenges faced by continuing growth, but also discusses the implications of an aging and stagnating population in parts of Western Europe. It sets population issues into a wider cultural context by discussing the policy options and geographical, social and moral implications of managing change.

In the post-colonial era global power continues to be exercised by the rich and powerful. In Chapter 53, Gavin Bridge focuses in particular on the exploitative nature of uneven development. He charts the nature of commodity chains, explores the continuing significance of ownership and control and documents how these social and economic relations are mapped out in the context of nations or places without mature or complex economies, and in which the trading of single and often primary commodities continues to play a significant role.

Even after the colonial era the global economy continues to be organized around the interests of capital. Its operation depends upon the rapid transfer of funds around the globe, to maximize returns for investors. At a local level, access to financial services is spatially uneven, and communities may be completely unable to borrow. Meanwhile the national debt burden of many countries represents a crippling impediment hindering economic or social development. Chapter 54 by Michael Pryke analyses the nature of these financial underpinnings. It explores why financial centres like Wall Street remain in place and agglomerated, in a world of constant placeless flux and flows. It charts the emergence in the 1970s of new forms of liberalized global finance explaining the particular architecture through which flows are orchestrated. The chapter ends on an optimistic note, arguing that alternative more socially responsible ways of organizing capital are still possible

Finance capital may be footloose and hugely influential, but across the globe people still work, and receive payment for their labour in particular places. The nature of employment practices varies, geographies of the workplace are contested and the social relations of the labour process are in flux. Jobs are exported, created, lost or fought over. Identities are built around work. In Chapter 55, Jane Holgate discusses how work might be placed. She explores how the tensions between capital and labour are played out at different scales across the economic landscape. Global shifts in employment are contrasted with the spatial divisions of labour around class, gender, ethnicity and skills. But labour itself has the power to organize and protect its interests, and in so doing the workers' struggles also create places.

This tension between global change and local action also forms the focus of the next chapter, Chapter 56, in which Simon Dalby explores the significance of geopolitical processes. Geopolitical change may be read as an outcome of a competitive process in which different actors engage and from which flow social, economic and environmental processes. Simon argues that discourse constructs these processes. He explores differing approaches to the placing of power, contrasting the global scales of analysis implicit in much of the literature of critical geopolitics with more local political action. Using case studies around alternative European futures, Nigerian governance and Scottish devolved authority, this chapter argues for a continuing focus upon the local geographical context in any consideration of political change.

Globalization may appear to dominate economic and social life at the start of the new millennium, but forces opposing the global impulse enact a diversity of alternative geographies. Chapter 57 by Paul Routledge charts the significance of these opposing forces, examining the geographies of protest and the ways in which they strive to empower individuals or alternative ways of living. It examines the nature and historical roots of protest movements, and documents aesthetic and poetic responses as well as the political context in which global hegemonic orthodoxy is contested.

Protest may not always be feasible. Often a more rational response is to seek to move. People move to, or for, work; they change their dwelling places; they travel for pleasure or business. Workers in many countries are enabled by new technologies to change their lifestyles;

tourism is globalized and segmented, leisure practices less tied to notions of place, even our representations of place are in motion. Meanwhile mass migration as a result of war or economic and social disparities has increasingly become possible. Movements in turn create responses: improved or cheaper transport, tighter border controls, outsourcing of labour, a weakened local sense of place, more fluid ways of thinking. Many identities are constituted or contested in mobility: 'nomad lives' are becoming more significant and metaphors of the journey frequently appear in our geographical imaginations. Chapter 58 by Ron Skelton travels through this moving terrain and attempts to fix its changing significance.

In a mobile age, where and how people dwell still matters. Geographers have recently increasingly used a dwelling perspective to understand relations between people and nature, between culture and landscape. In Chapter 59, Pau Obrador-Pons critiques earlier approaches to dwelling for being too narrowly focused on authenticity and for not adapting to the flux of modernity. He concludes that dwelling can, however, encompass the global as well as the local, and incorporate the mobile as well as the fixed.

A plethora of communication in many ways characterizes our age. Following on from technological changes in the second half of the twentieth century, communication underpins the move to an information-based global economy. Information is more available, more flexible and more rapidly disseminated than ever before. In Chapter 60, Barney Warf considers differing theoretical and empirical aspects of these changes. He focuses in particular upon the microelectronics revolution as a major facilitator of global communication and considers urban and economic consequences of these changes, with a particular focus on office location, before describing the huge potentials for communication occasioned by the spread of the Internet and the rise of e-commerce. Barney argues that these changes have clearly not yet led to the 'end of geography': how telecommunications are deployed depends upon local circumstances, public policy, culture and ideology.

Shopping and the provision of retail facilities play a growing role in the lives of people from Bangor to Bangalore. Jon Goss considers the differing contexts and changing geographies of these practices in Chapter 61. Through a partial history of shopping, he explores tensions implicit in the ideologies and theoretical understandings of what it means to shop. The cultural significance of shopping and its contradictory anxieties are developed, and the chapter implicitly argues for complexity rather than a narrow or single intellectual focus.

Shopping, like many of the social practices described throughout these volumes, is strongly gendered. The rise of feminist approaches in the social sciences and humanities has paralleled unprecedented global social, cultural and economic changes in the differing roles played by men and women. Women's visions of the world offer hope for less violence, more collaboration, less wasteful competition, greater caring and a more sustainable future. Greater power for women at home, work or in the political process can lead to profound geographical changes. In Chapter 62 Janice Monk explores the philosophical and practical implications of shifting and contested gender roles, charts the nature of changes in different contexts, and explores patriarchal resistance to change.

Social constructionist views of identity and the ways in which it may be placed have recently come increasingly to focus upon notions of performance. Chapter 63 by Jan Penrose and Susan J. Smith explores how gender, race, class, disability and sexuality might be performed and upon some of the ways in which the subject might be enacted in different contexts. They move from identity to explore some of the ways it might be performed, before arguing that a focus on performance circumvents problems of structure and agency, gives emotion and affect a new voice, and activates questions of hybrid relations between humans and non-humans.

The final chapter of this volume is a cartographic plea for action. Danny Dorling presents a striking series of global maps that highlight global challenges described elsewhere in this book. They present us with moral imperatives. Research and books like this should not exist in a policy vacuum. Authors and the readers can think and act. Change can be powered by the rhetoric of academic and policy research. Be moved by these striking global images.

41

Natural hazards

Colin Green

Introduction: the nature of hazards

As a species we live within ecosystems which lie on the interface between two interrelated dynamic systems: the meteorological and the geological/geomorphological. Volcanoes can eject sufficient fine ash into the atmosphere to significantly affect climate, whilst rain, wind, and cold are the primary causes of land erosion and deposition. Not only are these high energy systems, but two-thirds of that interface, the seas, is itself a dynamic system that responds to the dynamic variations in the meteorological and geological systems. The passage of deep atmospheric depressions over the ocean can raise sea levels by seven metres or more. Conversely, flows within the ocean have major long term effects upon local climate, and cyclical variations in temperature flows, notably El Niño and La Niña, have significant short-term effects. The ecosystems, upon which we depend, are in turn adapted to terrestrial or oceanic contexts, and to climatic conditions, and are themselves dynamic. What we label as a 'hazard' is some undesirable perturbation, or extreme of perturbation, in these systems, as generally we have adapted only to a limited part of the dynamic range of conditions, generally seeking to reduce our exposure to extremes. The hidden assumption here is that we expect the world to be a friendly place.

Hence, our obvious interest (e.g. Blaikie *et al.* 2004) in the dramatic perturbations that we call natural hazards, particularly in those parts of the world, notably Japan, which experience a high intensity and variety of perturbations and where everywhere in the entire country is exposed to one or more natural hazard. This chapter argues for a socially mediated view of hazards and risks. It considers the nature of these hazards, and explores how a management policy might best be developed in the light of differing social relations, discourse and governance, with a particular focus on development and adaptability.

Historically, those perturbations that were most crucial were those affecting crops or live-stock, and human diseases. Even as we shifted from subsistence farming to producing a food surplus that would enable cities to develop, buying food still took up the majority of a household's income, as it still does for the poor in developing countries. At the same time, land suitable for arable production has always been scarce. It is only as the ratio of farmers to the rest of the population has fallen that hazards that affect buildings and the infrastructure have gained increasing importance, and only with a global economy and a high degree of interdependence between countries that it has become necessary to be concerned about the impact on national and international economies. In the past, entire civilizations were wiped out by natural hazards but with so little impact on the rest of the world that the problem now is to determine why they disappeared (Fagan 2004).

Some natural hazards represent a perturbation in one of either the meteorological or geological/geomorphological systems. Others are the result of the interactions between the two systems. Two further sources are biological events in ecosystems, notably outbreaks of diseases or pests that affect humans, crops, other plants and animals, and extra-terrestrial, cosmic perturbations including cosmic rays, sunspot activity, meteors and comets. Figure 41.1 explores these different interactions.

In spatial terms, hazards are not randomly distributed so we have quite good knowledge of where each hazard is likely to occur, at least in broad terms. Thus, earthquakes, volcanoes and tsunami are generated along the meeting points of the tectonic plates (Figure 41.2). Similarly, hurricanes, cyclones and typhoons strike coasts to west and north of those areas of ocean where they initially develop. In turn, it is possible to map areas which are at risk from one or more hazards; flood-plain mapping is widely adopted with some countries, such as France and Japan: local maps are published showing the at-risk zones from multiple hazards.

As Figure 41.3 shows, the extent of the risk to different countries varies very markedly across a range of hazards. Over the last 103 years, Asia and the Americas have been hit by more natural disasters than the rest of the world. Over that same period, an average of 27 flood disasters have been reported across the world in each year, with about the same number of wind storm disasters. Conversely, on average, only one disastrous wave/tidal surge event and two volcanic eruptions have been reported in any year. The proportions of events experienced in the different global regions shows a different picture: in Africa, the most

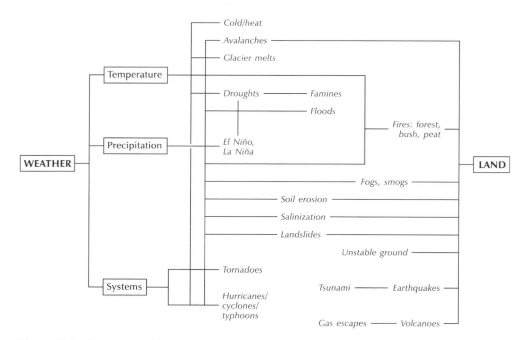

Figure 41.1. The creation of hazards.

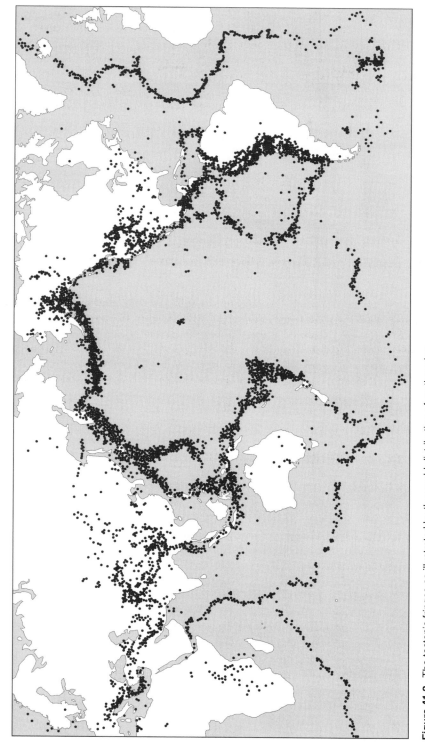

Figure 41.2. The tectonic fringes as illustrated by the world distribution of earthquakes.

Source: Adapted from Ollier (1996).

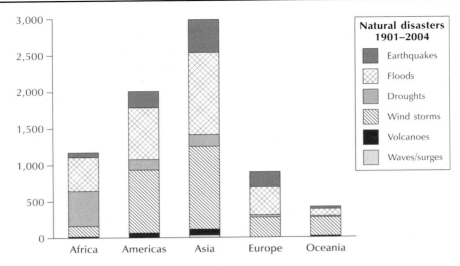

Figure 41.3. Frequency of natural disasters in the period 1900–2006.

frequent disasters are in the form of floods and droughts; in Asia, they are windstorms and floods, and in Europe the most common disaster has been from flooding. This data is taken from the CRED EM-DAT database at the Catholic University of Louvain which is the most complete database of natural disasters (www.em-dat.net).

In compiling any database of disasters, there are a number of problems. The first is that a long time series is needed to generate a sufficient sample size but changes will have occurred over that time. Thus, historically, the greatest number of deaths have occurred from droughts. Droughts are now predictable in advance, food may be moved easily around the world, and relief efforts are much more effective than they were, so deaths on the scale of the past are avoidable. A second problem is what to include: how to define a 'flood' or an 'earthquake', for example. CRED only includes those events which cause harm, and hence those where there are few people or the population is successfully adapted to the hazard are excluded from the record.

Two major changes occurring over time are the increase in populations and the increase in wealth. Consequently, it is very difficult to make good assessments of trends in losses over time because the real value of losses is changing. Probably the best measure would be loss as a proportion of national income but this would emphasize the losses in small, poor countries. For example, a hurricane that would be a national disaster for Jamaica, resulting in a loss that is a significant proportion of national income, would only be a local difficulty for the USA. At the national level, Pielke *et al.* (2002) have shown that there has been no significant change in the real value of per capita flood losses in the USA over the period 1929–2001.

We can identify at least approximately the areas at risk, but are either unable to predict at all when a major perturbation will occur (e.g. earthquakes) or are only able to reliably predict its occurrence a short time in advance (e.g. flash floods). Where we cannot provide adequate warning that a major perturbation will occur, then risks must be lived with and efforts devoted to effective recovery after the event. With longer warnings, emergency preparations are possible; for example, the temporary evacuation of the area at risk.

A major problem with natural hazards is that they provide such exciting still and moving images. This tends to lead us to focus on the exciting, dramatic, most instantly damaging events, seeking bigger threats, and giving such perturbations more attention than more insidious, persistent, less instantaneous disturbances. In turn, this leads us to look at the dramatic rather what than are locally the most frequent threats or those with the biggest effect; to emphasize the acute rather than the endemic or the chronic. It is the latter which often have a greater overall impact than the extremes. For example, in Africa, malaria is estimated to reduce annual economic growth by more than 1 per cent per annum; and to affect 26 per cent of the population (Gallup and Sachs 2001; Malaney *et al.*, 2004). Thirty per cent of pregnant women in South Africa are believed to be infected with HIV and 38 per cent in Botswana. Across Southern Africa, 7.4 per cent of the population as a whole are believed to be infected, with 2.3 million deaths occurring each year. In turn, life expectancy is actually falling in some Southern African countries: in Zimbabwe, life expectancy at birth in 1990 was 52 years; it is estimated to have fallen to 34 years in 2003. Infections with helminths and protozoa are commonplace across much of the world. Globally, amongst schoolchildren, there are estimated to be 320 million cases of roundworm (*Ascaris*); 233 million cases of whipworm (*Trichuris*); and 239 million cases of hookworm (*Necator/Ancyclostoma*). In Africa, some 33 per cent of schoolchildren are believed to be infected with *Schistosoma haematobrium*. Chapter 10 develops these ideas in a greater depth but further epidemiological examples show the potential scale and risks of disease impacts. Across the world, the Spanish Flu pandemic has been estimated to have resulted in 40–50 million deaths at the end of the First World War; the series of plagues between 1328 and 1377 killed between 30 and 50 per cent of the entire population of England, with similar effects across the rest of Europe (Ziegler 1969). It is only after advances in public health over the last 150 years, and consequent dramatically extended life expectancy and reduced infant mortality rates, that other natural hazards have come to prominence.

So, we select some phenomena, the most dramatic, for attention as 'natural hazards' but exclude others which may have more significant effects. The definition of some things as both 'natural' and as 'hazards' reflects a desire to classify things into a formal system of categories: an ontological approach. This may be contrasted with a more epistemological approach to a world concerned with what we can know and how or why we can know it. This clash is also one between an essentially static view of the world and one which is dynamic; the categorizations resulting from an epistemological approach being both provisional and conditional. The remainder of this chapter focuses less upon ontology and more upon the complexity of human responses to hazards arising from just such a provisional and conditional framework.

Grouping a number of different perturbations together implies that they are in some sense similar, or that it is useful to treat them similarly, and that they are in some sense different to other perturbations, notably those that result from human interventions. However, it is generally accepted that the risks of 'natural hazards' can themselves be increased by human activities: deforestation and overgrazing may promote soil erosion and flooding; other land management practices may increase the risk of forest, peat and bush fires as well as the salinization of soils (see Chapter 43). At the grandest scale, human activity is generally accepted to have resulted in climatic change which will result in an increased risk from meteorological perturbations, including the destruction of a number of low-lying small island states (see Chapter 49 for a more detailed treatment of these contexts). Equally, human activity can multiply the effects of a natural disaster: a flood may release chemicals causing widespread pollution and often it is the spread of fire that results in an earthquake becoming catastrophic.

Similarly, one of the messages of the sustainable livelihoods approach (Ashley and Carney 1999) is that to the individual household, all risks are relative. To a particular household the risks from unemployment and illness may be far greater than from local natural hazards; the portfolio of risks faced by a particular household or community should be considered as a whole, rather than a distinction being drawn between natural and unnatural hazards. In order to minimize those other risks, the household may have to choose to accept the risks from those natural hazards. Bangladesh and the Netherlands both support very high population densities and have a very high GDP/sq km. They both occupy flood plains, of Ganges–Brahmaputra and Rhine deltas respectively. The inherent advantages of living on the rich soils of flood plains with a readily available supply of water have historically outweighed the risks of flooding.

In the same way, a nation should not treat natural hazards in isolation but as part of the portfolio of risks to which it is exposed. For most nations, other risks, notably the risks of financial or fiscal crises, are considerably greater than those from acute natural hazards. For example, whilst the 1993 Mississippi flood resulted in US $16 billion of losses, the simultaneous crisis of the Savings and Loans institutions resulted in a loss of US $153 billion (Curry and Shibut 2000). Of course, there are exceptions when an event affects a global financial centre or the whole of a small country. The relative magnitude of the risks and potential losses from financial and natural hazards means that a country should be careful before coupling the two together, lest a financial crisis coincides with a natural disaster, or natural disaster results in a far worse financial crisis.

The focus on the dramatic also tends to lead us to separate out extremes instead of looking at variability. For example, floods and droughts are often examined in isolation rather seeing them as aspects in the variation of water availability over time. This leads, in turn, to efforts to manage each of those extremes rather than to managing hazard variability. But in arid climates floods are the water resource.

Equally, attention to extremes tends to separate 'hazards' from their context, as if natural hazards were somehow distinct, and could be separated, from the problem of delivering sustainable development. In particular, land is scarce and is valued in terms of inherent advantages (e.g. soil, climate, topography), positional advantages (e.g. proximity to water and to fisheries), and in relation to other human activities (e.g. markets, ports). Those advantages may be sufficient to outweigh local natural hazards. The search for the dramatic also dislocates perturbations in time, emphasizing the event itself rather than the longer time-scaled process, or socio-economic development.

From this emerges the notion that, whilst there are not many similarities between what are labelled as 'natural hazards', it is desirable to adopt an 'all hazards management' policy rather than to seek to manage each natural and artificial hazard in isolation. Such a management policy needs to consider social relations and focus on language and governance. It needs to reflect differences in development and be adaptable to a diverse and changing context.

Social roles and relationships

What natural hazards say about us, as individuals and societies, can be more interesting than what we say about them, particularly the way in which our understanding and interpretation of hazards is produced by our relationships between each other, and the social roles which are determined by but also determine those relationships. The most extreme form of this view is 'cultural theory' (Schwartz and Thompson 1990). Governance is the most apparent expression of these relationships. In turn, those relationships are articulated through language, most obviously in those languages which have formal and informal forms for 'you', or where there are distinctions between men's and women's languages, as in Japanese. Language is also used purposefully and specifically often in the attempt to impose the speaker's view of the world.

Central to hazard management are social roles and relationships, particularly the relationships of power and entitlements. These roles and relationships play out before, during and after disasters. Thus, we should not be surprised that women experience a differential burden in terms of households' recovery from disasters (Enarson 2005) because they bear a disproportionate share of household tasks in everyday life. Similarly, the powerful are not only more successful than the poor in gaining access to aid after disasters (Winchester 1991) but are often more able to get protection against disasters in the first place. The poor also are commonly left with the land not occupied by others or not formally approved for residential development, which often means that they occupy the most hazardous hillside and flood-prone areas. Thus, around Rio de Janeiro and Caracas, the poor occupy the unstable hillsides. However, in California similar unstable hillsides are typically occupied by the rich, who value the view. Different power relations create different land values and are a persuasive argument for a management that reflects local needs.

Power can be defined as the degree of influence that can be exerted over the decisions of others; entitlements are the degree to which any one household or group has access to resources of different kinds. The sustainable livelihoods literature defines a number of different forms of resource as being important in this context (Ashley and Carney 1999). Access to resources is a critical coping mechanism in the event of a disaster: Sen (1981) points out that the problem in famines is not the shortage of food but that the poor lack any entitlement to access to the available food. Thus, the !Kung of the Kalahari cope with a highly volatile environment by having geographically widely spread social networks which give them entitlements to support when local resources are scarce. More generally, social relations in the form of 'social capital' (Nakagawa and Shaw 2004) are seen as a key element in the capacity of a society to respond to the challenges which it faces.

The processes by which choices are made, and the outcomes of those choices, also reflect variations in justice or equity (Smith 2000). Collective choice is an exercise in power, and different people and groups have differential access to each form of power. Along with political, physical and financial power, reason itself and information are forms of power. Thus, to adopt a rational approach to decision-making simply gives power to those who are best at deploying reason, or best at establishing a hegemonic definition of reason. It may change the nature of power, and hence perhaps its distribution, although the rich can buy reason in the form of lawyers and experts. The shift to stakeholder engagement as the basis of choice, and away from technocratic methods, will not necessarily result in more just decisions unless the distribution of power is itself more equitable.

Discourse

Language is also tied to individual thought and to communication. Wittgenstein (1961) and semiologists have sought to determine the relationship between words and thought: between what can be said and what can be thought. But we also use language to communicate with one another; we use language in order to change ourselves, or others, or the relationship between us. We may seek to give or get information but we also often want to change opinions or attitudes, to persuade others to adopt our views. Therefore, concepts associated with natural hazards such as 'vulnerability', 'risk' and 'uncertainty' are inherently contested.

Different interest groups wish specific objectives to be pursued, frame the problem in different ways, propose different means of intervention and use language and concepts in ways that support their definition. For example, the reason why we seek to define vulnerability is in order to help us decide what to do to reduce it. Hence a definition of vulnerability implies a course of action, but equally any proposed course of action implies a definition of vulnerability. Both necessarily embody some claim as to the appropriate objectives that should be pursued. 'Vulnerability' is necessarily a contested term because it is relational and links a target, a perturbation and a reason why the target is vulnerable. Hence, it may be argued that the *poor* are vulnerable *to* droughts *because* a high proportion of their income is spent upon food. Those who wish to focus primarily upon poverty alleviation are likely to argue that the poor are inherently vulnerable to multiple perturbations because they are poor. Conversely, those whose concern is primarily on droughts are likely to stress the ways in which droughts affect both different groups within a society and the society as a whole.

Also, definitions of a set of terms often imply relationships between, and roles of, different stakeholders. Those roles form the basis of the claim that a particular definition of vulnerability should be preferred to all others. Thus, claims by scientists to be able to give a universal definition of vulnerability are claims of access to expert knowledge and understanding by reason of being a scientist. Similarly, the label 'risk communication' defines the issue essentially in terms of information transfer; from those who have access to the information, to the public who are considered to lack it. This defines the issue as a one-way communication: as if communication is solely for the purpose of transferring information, and gives power to those who have the information. The discussion in the 1980s of 'acceptable' or 'tolerable' risk (Royal Society 1981) framed the issues in similar terms. Once the experts had determined what level of risk was accepted by the public, it was no longer necessary to consider risk in the choice. Simultaneously, it placed the public in a passive role, the decision being made by the experts. In the same way that Foucault (2003) argued that illness has been turned into the domain of the medical professions, hazard management was made the domain of engineers and other specialists.

Similarly, specialists increasingly both frame risk in terms of probabilities and approach probabilities from the perspective of frequency distributions. The public, on the other hand, is generally much more interested in causality, in order to attribute either responsibility or blame. The danger with framing risk in terms of frequency distributions is that of confusing cause and prediction. Hazards are not a random occurrence; nature does not throw a dice to decide whether there will be an earthquake in a particular area this year: hazards are the outcome of a causal process. But, in our current state of knowledge, we often cannot predict events like earthquakes and floods any better than if they were randomly generated, our best guess as to the likelihood of an earthquake next year being based on historic frequency. Indeed, it may be the case that we will never be able to predict some events any better than we can from assuming that they are randomly generated. However, there is increasing evidence that there are both cycles and trends in the occurrence of some hazards: La Niña has been shown to be associated with the occurrence of flooding in Australia, and the North Atlantic Oscillation with flooding in Scotland (Kiem *et al.* 2003).

A similar contested area is 'uncertainty'. If uncertainty is interpreted as being defined in terms of risk, then the future is knowable within some probabilistic limits and we can assess the likely effectiveness of alternative intervention strategies. Conversely, if uncertainty is understood as inherently different in nature to probability, and the future as being inherently unknowable, then a radically different approach is likely to be necessary to both the assessment of alternative strategies and as a basis for action. A probabilistic definition of uncertainty and the assertion that the future is knowable within specified limits leaves open the option of optimization. The classical definition of uncertainty and the future as inherently unknowable points instead towards intervention strategies that are 'robust' – that is, perform relatively well whatever happens – and also ones which fail gracefully when overloaded.

It is not just engineers who frame such a discourse. The Chicago School of Geographers (White 1945) sought to establish an alternative. By talking of 'flood-plain encroachment', they used language to try to establish a framing in which humans should not occupy or change the flood plains and sought to infer that it is not floods that are the problem but the way in which we use the flood plains. Similarly, there is an ideological argument that market-based relationships, where power is expressed in the form of wealth, should be pre-ferred to the traditional approach of co-operation in the management of natural hazards. Such a market-led approach can seek to promote the use of insurance and market-based approaches to the management of natural hazards. A further example also reveals the importance of discursive framing. Environmental groups seek to use 'natural' to imply not only good but better. So, for example, WWF (2002) has claimed that: 'Traditional forms of flood protection do not work' and asserted that it is necessary to 'restore our wetlands and free us of floods'. WWF seeks to establish a framing in which 'natural is good and works' whereas 'traditional engineering solutions are bad and fail to work'. Again, claims have been made that dams always make floods worse.

So language and the discursive construction of natural hazards have wide-reaching impacts and these arguments are frequently rehearsed in the structures and practice of governance.

Governance

We establish formal and informal structures to manage the risks of natural disasters and to cope with them when they occur. Institutions are defined by sets of informal or formal rules. Consequently, any institution has two forms of boundaries: spatial and functional. Functional boundaries prescribe what that institution may or may not do. One reason for fragmenting the world in this way is to reduce it to manageable pieces. A second is that local democracy is, by definition, local, with narrowly drawn geographical boundaries. There is a conflict between public participation and integrated management; the involvement of communities of place pulls towards small geographical units whilst integration pulls towards institutions that have wider boundaries in spatial and functional terms. Countries vary very widely in terms of the degree and nature of centralization (see Chapter 20). The UK has some 430 units of central, regional and local government for a population of around 60 million people, compared to around 37,000 for a population of 61 million in France (INSEE 2005), and 88,000 for a population of 296 million in the USA (US Census Bureau 2002). A third reason is for accountability; the easiest form of accountability is to test whether an institution is acting beyond its purposes, and defining functional rules which govern what it may do is a comparatively simple way of establishing a test for accountability purposes.

The necessity to set rules partitions the world into parts, whereas managing a dynamic system requires integration. The desire to manage in an integrated way tends towards supra-institutions with wide spatial and functional boundaries. Problems increase as inter-dependency grows between areas; for example, it is quite common and logical to group some combination from agriculture, environment, food, forestry, water and rural development into a single government ministry. However the result is often simply to internalize the problem to the institution. The practical problems are: how to establish and maintain effective communications between institutions, and how to enable co-operation or co-ordination across institutional boundaries. Consequently, it is common to find failures in communication, co-operation and co-ordination in managing the risk from a hazard or in responding to a disaster. It is common to find that different services have radio systems that cannot communicate with each other. The different institutions often have different interests. A hazard management agency will want to keep new development out of high-risk areas, whereas a local community may be concerned with economic and social regeneration on available land that happens to be in high-risk areas. To overcome these issues it can be argued that the primary reason for developing emergency plans and conducting exercises to respond to hypothetical disasters is to build up informal networks of people who know and trust each other.

The purpose of government has concerned philosophers and political theorists for many centuries. But citizens typically judge the competency of their government according to how it performs in a disaster. So, in imperial China, the emperor ruled by the mandate of heaven and a disaster was taken to be a sign that that mandate had been withdrawn, and hence implied that the dynasty had lost its legitimacy. Similarly, in a democracy, a government is the formal expression of the relations between each citizen and political arguments focus upon what those relations should be. A test of government is therefore how far its actions reflect those relations. To argue for less government is to argue that a different network of duties and entitlements should govern the relations between us, one in which greater weight should be given to individual rights over social duties. That network of duties and entitlements is played out in differing philosophies of hazard management. In continental Europe, the emphasis has traditionally been upon 'communal solidarity' as the principle that should govern hazard management. Society in this context provides a form of mutual insurance where natural hazards are amongst the risks covered by the policy.

However, each society is faced with its own internal contradictions and conflicts. The result is that hazard management practices are muddled rather than coherent. The USA is a country where rhetoric is often strongly in favour of less government and strongly in favour of taking individual responsibility for coping with hazards. Thus, some cities have no land-use controls at all, and specifically none concerning development in hazardous zones, because such controls are seen as an infringement of private property rights. But at the same time, the Federal government has had, since 1790, a tradition of compensating victims of disasters (Dauber 2005).

Development

It can be argued that perturbations in different systems have to be seen and managed within the context of sustainable development (Green *et al.* 2000). Losses from natural hazards are, however, not a measure of the success or failure of the sustainable development policy measured against national income, relative to inputs. In narrow economic terms, it is easy to demonstrate that increasing losses from natural hazards are consistent with an increase in economic efficiency, of increasing output per unit input, after netting out both the costs of adjustment to the hazards and losses from those hazards. More generally, the reason why development took place in areas of high natural hazard (e.g. in the flood plains of the Yellow River, Nile, Indus, Euphrates, Rhine) was that the ratio of outputs to inputs, even after considering both flood losses and ameliorative actions, was greater than in alternative areas.

The ratio of losses from natural hazards to national income provides some measure of the relative success or failure of a sustainable development policy, but we should also expect material losses from all forms of hazard to rise with development. The proportion of household income spent upon food (the Engel coefficient) falls with rising income. It is the proportion of household income not spent upon food that is available to be spent upon the housing that may be damaged or destroyed in a disaster. Until the Engel coefficient in a country falls to the region of 0.15 common to the developed world, we should expect losses from natural hazards to rise faster than the rate of economic growth.

The state of development also determines the relative importance given to agriculture. In societies with a heavy reliance upon agriculture and where expenditure upon food takes up a large fraction of household income, communities and government have to be focused upon reducing the risk of crop losses from droughts or floods. It is the relative timings of rainfall and floods to the growing season which dictates flood management policy. If the growing season and rainy season do not coincide then maximum use has to be made of the flood season to grow crops: Egypt is the obvious example here. If there is adequate rain to grow crops but floods coincide with harvest period, then the result tends to be canalized rivers, for example in central Europe and the USA. Here it is necessary to make the best use of the high-quality arable land on the flood plain, but since a flood would destroy the entire harvest, enormous efforts must be placed on protecting agricultural land from flooding. Finally, if there is adequate rainfall to grow crops and floods occur outside of the growing season, then flood risk to agricultural land can often be ignored. Hence, on the big rivers in England, where flooding is a winter phenomenon, agricultural land is largely unprotected and continues to serve to convey and store flood waters.

The big challenge now facing the developing countries is the mass migration of their populations from the rural to urban areas, and particularly to the megacities (see Chapters 9 and 59). The rate of migration links rural and urban development and is a measure of the comparative success of the two. Attempts to manage migration have not been very successful, and in many parts of the world the resulting pressures have overwhelmed attempts to use land-use controls to prevent development in areas of high hazard risks. These pressures have also frequently led to a lack of regulated building standards: urban structures are often too poorly built to resist earthquakes, storms or floods. Given that much of this development is informal and ignores land ownership, this comparative failure is unsurprising. It may be best to understand the effectiveness of land-use controls in terms of a balance of pressures. Where opponents of new development have power, land-use controls can be used to resist the pressure of development. Conversely, land-use controls will be ineffective when the pressure for development exceeds the resistance.

At the same time, planning should always consider multiple objectives and multiple constraints; to base land development solely upon a consideration of the relative risks to different areas of land would be counter-productive. A more constructive policy for managing natural hazard risk might well be one that reflects multiple interests and one anchored in the concept of adaptability.

Adaptability

The conventional approach to hazard management is to focus upon assessing the 'shock' of the disaster itself and the standard approach to measuring the economic consequences of a disaster is to quantify the economic losses in the event. Well-developed methods now exist to deliver such goals (e.g. ECLAC 1999). However, these kinds of approaches are static and often ignore the complexity of adaptation over time. A more dynamic approach focusing upon adjustment can consider loss of quality of life over time (A) rather than the loss (L) in the shock (Figure 41.4). A shift to a dynamic analysis reflects the adoption a systems approach where the change in a perturbation and responses to it over time are the central concern. The 'Household Economy' model (Save the Children 2000) is an example of such an approach and studies how a household redeploys its resources when it experiences a perturbation. Studying how a national or regional economy adjusts, and making recommendations as to how it should re-adjust, in the event of a disaster is, of course, more difficult (Cole 2004).

This shift from a static approach has been mirrored by a change in emphasis of intervention strategies. The traditional approach has been to seek to minimize the impact of the disaster by reducing the magnitude of the impact, or by reducing the susceptibility of the infrastructure, buildings and their contents which support the socio-economic system. There is now an increasing concern with the recovery side of the equation, and particularly with seeking to introduce systems that are resilient (Holling 1973). We would like socio-economic systems that recovered from perturbations quickly and easily, in the same way that a rubber ball bounces back after being squeezed. Whilst the label 'resilience' captures the concept, actually defining what are the necessary characteristics of a resilient system and building those characteristics into socio-economic practices and institutions is considerably more difficult. Too often, 'resilience' seems to be little more than a useful catch-phrase and to amount to no more than a recognition of the need to take a systems approach (Green *et al.* 2000) to hazard management rather than an event-based approach.

Transposing the concept of resilience from ecology to hazard management involves a number of problems. First, can we separate the shock from the recovery phase? In other words, can the recovery cost (A) be independent of the shock (L)? The conventional approach is to seek to reduce L in the expectation that there will be a reduction in A. In drought-prone areas, farmers will often plant a variety of crops that vary in their drought resistance and productivity, those that are drought resistant generally being less productive. Hence, if a drought occurs, they still have a limited harvest from the drought-resistant crop: they reduce their recovery cost by reducing their shock loss.

Second, what is it that we want to be resilient (Folke *et al.* 2005)? In particular, is it desirable that mediating systems filtering the perturbation are themselves resilient, or is it only the socio-economic system that should be resilient? A river system is naturally resilient; it adapts to variations in flows by spreading out over the flood plain, by changing its form, and sometimes its course. When land is scarce, the resilience of the natural system may

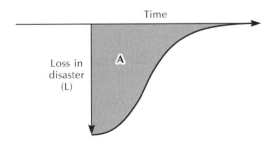

Figure 41.4. Quality of life after disaster.

reduce the resilience of socio-economic processes and institutions. In some circumstances, increasing the resilience of the socio-economic system may require interposing a robust rather than a resilient mediator between the hazard and the society. However, it may be more useful to think in terms of the variation in the response of the mediating system and the socio-economic system to varying degrees of perturbation. In general, we are likely to prefer systems whose output varies relatively smoothly with changes in the perturbation, over those systems that experience a step change at some magnitude of perturbation. Indeed, such a step change might be argued to define a disaster.

Third, ecosystems are self-organizing systems. The effects of human interventions in such self-organizing systems often reduces their resilience. Although, in hazard management, we generally have to design, undertake and operate a system so that it becomes more resilient, and this is a much more difficult task.

Earlier, it was pointed out that definitions of vulnerability are necessarily contested since an intervention strategy follows from the definition that is adopted. Hence, the utility of any definition of vulnerability is essentially the extent to which it gives us new insights into the problem and allows us to find new and better means of intervening. The concept of resilience essentially inverts conventional ideas of vulnerability, since resilience might be defined as the inverse of vulnerability.

There are various other ways of categorizing different possible intervention strategies. Each implies a definition of vulnerability. A classic form of discourse was the distinction between 'structural' means, those conventionally considered by engineers, and 'non-structural' interventions devised by others. But as a means of identifying new forms of intervention, this distinction is not particularly useful. Other possible systems of categorization include those based upon the point of intervention, e.g. reducing the perturbation or the challenge it presents by enhancing the capacity to cope with that challenge before, during or after the event. Another system of categorization is based upon whether the intervention is physical (e.g. flood-proofing, earthquake-resistant construction, reservoirs) or institutional (e.g. land-use planning, insurance, compensation). Other systems of categorization are hazard-specific: for example, for floods, in terms of the processes within the catchment. Similarly, since many hazards are characterized by extreme intensities of energy exchange, intervention strategies can be characterized in terms of how that energy exchange will be managed. For example, for tidal surges such strategies include conversion (the use of mangroves and other coastal wetlands); absorption (such as sand dune systems or beaches); reflection (employed in some forms of sea wall); and resistance such as in rocky breakwaters or groyne systems (Green 2004).

Whatever the form of intervention being considered, it is essential to consider the form and likelihood of possible failures (Green et al. 2000). For example, dike systems, a structural option, and flood-proofing, a non-structural option, share the common characteristic that failure can be catastrophic. In both cases there is the possibility that the building so protected will collapse. Land-use planning is difficult to operate successfully and it has proved difficult to develop warning systems that both are sufficiently reliable and provide an adequate lead time. Warning systems are not possible at all hazards. Common problems with them are the difficulties in converting a forecast into a warning that contains useful information, and difficulties in disseminating that warning to those who need it. People who are warned need to be able to respond, yet they may be unable to evacuate or take other remedial action.

Any intervention can only be as successful as the operation of that system. A virtue of physical interventions is that they often stand a greater degree of neglect than can institutional interventions. If budget cuts and skills shortages occur, it is more likely that a concrete structure will still be there at the end of five years than it is that a warning or building regulation system will still be operating effectively.

The outcome is that layered systems of intervention may be the best option. For example, in the Netherlands, within the areas protected by dikes, in the event of a storm the population were traditionally mobilized to undertake emergency works on the dikes; villages were built on artificial mounds above the level of the flood waters if the dikes failed; and each village kept boats which could be used for evacuation if necessary.

Summary

Natural hazards are characterized by physical features but are also socially constructed. It is the social characterization of natural hazards, including their construction as both 'natural' and a 'hazard', that is of greatest importance, as it is reflected in the intervention strategies adopted. At the same time, the way in which a society approaches these hazards, and sets out to manage them, is a reflection of the social roles and relationships that characterize the society. In turn, the management of hazards is played out in the wider area of the conflicts between different forms of power, different ideologies and different conceptualizations of the world.

In practical terms, it is undesirable to separate out a specific category to be labelled 'natural hazards'; instead, all risks should be considered as part of a portfolio, and risk management should integrate consideration of these risks into the wider concerns of sustainable development as well as integrating management across risks. In considering natural hazards, the focus of our concern should always be: what should we do, should we intervene and how should we intervene? Equally, we should also always be seeking to do 'better', however we define 'better', and hence seek to learn and change. The value of the conflicting perspectives is then the extent to which each can suggest new and better means of intervening.

Further reading

Alexander, D. (1993) *Natural Disasters*. London: UCL.

Blaikie, P. Cannon, T., Davis, I. and Weisner, B. (2004) *At Risk: Natural Hazards, People's Vulnerability, and Disasters*. London: Routledge.

Coch, N.K. (1995) *Geohazards*. Englewood Cliffs: Prentice Hall.

Drabek, T. (1986) *Human System Responses to Disaster*. New York: Springer-Verlag.

Ollier, C.D. (1996) Planet Earth. In I. Douglas, R.J. Huggett and M.E. Robinson (eds) *Companion Encyclopedia of Geography*, first edition, pp. 15–43. London: Routledge.

United Nations Development Programme (2004) *Reducing Disaster Risk: A Challenge for Development*. New York: United Nations.

References

Ashley, C. and Carney, D. (1999) *Sustainable Livelihoods: Lessons from Early Experience*. London: Department for International Development.

Blaikie, P., Cannon, T., Davis, I. and Wisner, B. (2004) *At Risk: Natural Hazards, People's Vulnerability, and Disasters*, second edition. London: Routledge.

Cole, S. (2004) Performance and protection in an adaptive transaction model. *Disaster Prevention and Management* 13 (4), 280–9.

Curry, T. and Shibut, L. (2000) The cost of the Savings and Loan crisis: truth and consequences. *FDIC Banking Review* 13 (2), 26–35.

Dauber, M.L. (2005) The sympathetic state. *Law and History Review* 23 (2), 387–442.

ECLAC (UN Economic Commission for Latin America and the Caribbean) (1999) *Manual for Estimating the Socio-Economic Effects of Natural Disasters*. Santiago: ECLAC.

Enarson, E. (ed.) (2005) *The Gender and Disaster Source Book*. Available at http://www.kroworks.com/gds/

Fagan, B. (2004) *The Long Summer: How Climate Changed Civilisations*. London: Granta.

Folke, C. Hahn, T., Olsson, P. and Norberg, J. (2005) Adaptive governance of socio–ecological systems, *Annual Review Environmental Resources* 30 (8), 8.1–8.33.

Foucault, M. (2003) *The Birth of the Clinic*, trans. A.M. Sheridan. London: Routledge.

Gallup, J.L. and Sachs, J.D. (2001) The economic burden of malaria. Supplement to *The American Journal of Tropical Medicine and Hygiene* 64 (1, 2), 85–96.

Green, C.H. (2004) Evaluating vulnerability and resilience in flood management. *Disaster prevention and management* 13 (4), 323–9.

Green, C.H., Parker, D.J. and Tunstall, S.M. (2000) *Assessment of Flood Control and Management Options*. Cape Town: World Commission on Dams. (Available at http://www/dams.org)

Holling, C.S. (1973) Resilience and stability of ecological systems. *Annual Review of Ecology and Systematics* 4, 1–23.

INSEE (2005) http://www.insee.fr/fr/ffc/chifcle_fiche.asp?ref_id = CMRSOS01207&tab_id = 467

Kiem, A.S., Franks, S.W. and Kuczera, G. (2003) Multi-decadal variability of flood risk. *Geophysical Research Letters* 30 (2), 1035, DOI:10.1029/2002GL015992.

Malaney, P., Spielman, A. and Sachs, J. (2004) The malaria gap. *American Journal of Tropical Medicine and Hygiene* 71, 141–6.

Nakagawa, Y. and Shaw, R. (2004) Social capital: a missing link to disaster recovery. *International Journal of Mass Emergencies and Disasters* 22 (1), 5–34.

Pielke, R.A., Downton, M.W. and Miller, J.Z.B. (2002) *Flood Damage in the United States, 1926–2000 – A Re-analysis of National Weather Service Estimates*. Boulder CO: National Center for Atmospheric Research.

Royal Society (1981) *The Assessment and Perception of Risk*. London: the Royal Society.

Save the Children (2000) *The Household Economy Approach: A Resource Manual for Practitioners*. London: Save the Children UK.

Schwartz, M. and Thompson, M. (1990) *Divided We Stand: Redefining Politics, Technology and Social Choice*. London: Harvester Wheatsheaf.

Sen, A.K. (1981) *Poverty and Famines*. Oxford: Oxford University Press.

Smith, D.M. (2000) *Moral Geographies*. Edinburgh: Edinburgh University Press.

US Census Bureau (2002) *2002 Census of Governments: Volume 1, Number 1, Government Organization*. Washington DC: US Census Bureau.

White, G.F. (1945) *Human Adjustment to Floods* (Research Paper No. 29). Chicago: University of Chicago, Department of Geography.

Winchester, P. (1991) *Power, Choice and Vulnerability*. London: Earthscan.

Wittgenstein, L. (1961) *Tractatus Logico-Philosophicus*, trans. D.F. Pears and B.F. McGuinness. London: Routledge and Kegan Paul.

WWF (2002) *Restore our Wetlands or Face Worse Floods*. Available at http://www.panda.org/epo

Ziegler, P. (1969) *The Black Death*. Harmondsworth: Penguin.

42

Adapting to climate variability and change

R.P.D. Walsh

Introduction

The interrelationship between climate and society has been an enduring theme of geography throughout the history of the discipline. Early studies focused on how climate influenced economy, culture and society and how communities have been able to overcome or adapt to aspects of climate – and particularly its variability and unreliability. Although linkages between historical climatic changes and societal impacts and responses have long formed part of this theme, the global warming issue has resulted in an explosion of concern about its likely environmental and human impacts and how communities might or should respond or adapt. This chapter considers the nature and impacts of climatic change – past, present and future – and in particular explores how responses of societies (and sections of societies) to climatic change have varied through time and space with differing socioeconomic, cultural and technological settings.

This chapter explores the impacts which climatic variability, and particularly longer-term climatic change have posed and will pose for society. Although special emphasis is given to current and predicted future impacts and responses with global warming, the nature of historical impacts are also explored because of the very different contexts in which individuals and communities found themselves.

Climatic variability and climate-related physical responses

Nature and types of climatic variability

The term climatic variability refers to the changeability of climate. Strictly speaking, the term can refer to the year-to-year variability of an essentially stable climate as well as to longer-term climatic fluctuations and change that entail statistically significant differences in climatic means, climatic extremes and year-to-year variability. In Chapter 8 the nature and causes of climatic variability at periodicities ranging from diurnal to 150 m years were examined (Table 8.2 and Figure 8.3). This chapter focuses mainly on shorter-term climatic changes (of two decades to centuries in length) that are produced by a combination and superimposition of a range of cosmic, geological and anthropogenic forcing factors and internal atmospheric dynamics. The question of a 'statistically significant climatic change' on the one hand and an 'environmentally or socially significant change' on the other is important. Climatologists, as objective scientists, have often been concerned with statistical significance in identifying whether or not there has been a change in climate. Society (as well as other aspects of the environment, such as vegetation and geomorphology), however, responds not to statistical significance but to 'real change'. Changes can be statistically significant but too small to be of real significance to communities; equally, sequences of years of anomalous climate can be statistically insignificant, but large enough to produce massive human impacts. Such was the case with the 1965–73 sequence of droughts in the Sahel; despite the famine, loss of life and migrations it caused to the communities affected, it was not until the addition of a renewed sequence of very dry years in the 1980s that the dry epoch actually achieved statistical significance. This was in part because the existing climatic record already contained a period of anomalously dry years in the early twentieth century.

Traditionally, climatic change studies have focused upon changes in climatic averages, particularly of temperature and precipitation, but it is changes in the magnitude and frequency of extreme climatic events (such as droughts, heatwaves, large rainstorms, stormy episodes and tropical cyclones) and also in the year-to-year variability of climate that often have more direct impacts on communities. Predictions of future climatic change, however, are more reliable about changes in mean temperature, less reliable about precipitation changes and their spatial distribution and least certain about changes in the frequency and spatial distribution of climatic extreme events (Parry 2000) (see also Table 8.5). Nevertheless, it is widely predicted that many climates will witness both increased year-to-year variability of climate and increased magnitude-frequencies of some extreme events, such as tropical cyclones, intense Atlantic depressions, large rainstorms and events related to El Niño cycles (Houghton *et al.* 2001).

Climate-related changes in other physical environmental variables

The human impacts of climatic change and variability can be indirect (via changes to hydrological, geomorphological, soil and vegetational systems) as well as direct. Thus precipitation changes may have implications for river flow, evapotranspiration, soil moisture, flood magnitude-frequency, groundwater levels, landslides and erosion, river channel change, vegetation growth rates and character, fire frequency and glacier mass balance. Temperature changes likewise strongly influence evapotranspiration, vegetation, glacier mass balance and sea level. Coastal flooding will be influenced by sea level rise (mainly a function of glacier melt and thermal expansion of seawater – both linked to changes in temperature and precipitation) and changes in hydrology (linked to changes in heavy rainfall frequency). Many of these climate-related changes, however, are simultaneously influenced by the human environment and human responses to climatic change. Identifying, specifying and predicting physical environmental changes that will accompany climatic change is thus a major and often very difficult task – and one that is often made more difficult because many of the variables are (1) related to changes in the frequency of extreme events, about which less is known and there is much greater uncertainty, rather than in climatic means, (2) are simultaneously being influenced by current and past anthropogenic factors, and (3) are incompletely understood.

Human responses to climatic variability and change: overview

Human response systems to climate, climatic variability and climatic change have varied greatly in nature and complexity through time, with particularly profound changes in the last two decades with the growing acceptance of human-induced global warming and the needs both to plan for it and combat it. Through historical time, human communities have adapted to the challenges posed by climate and climatic variability (together with other elements of the physical environment) via a combination of knowledge and experience, technological development, social organization, migration and inter-community interaction (notably trade and forms of aid). In considering interrelationships between climatic variability and society, a range of factors can be considered to influence impacts of climatic change and variability on a community (Table 42.1).

Early societies are generally seen as more directly susceptible to climatic variability (Figure 42.1), but a distinction is generally drawn between hunter-gatherers and rain-fed pastoralist and cultivator communities on the one hand, and more complex societies that generally used some form of irrigation technology and social organization on the other. Because irrigation technology was designed to provide more reliable water supplies for people, livestock and crops and thereby reduce the impacts of spatial and year-to-year variability in rainfall, such societies are generally seen as being less susceptible to climatic variability than the 'simpler' cultures with their direct dependence on rainfall.

This is not entirely the case, however, as most 'simple' traditional cultures had developed mechanisms (such as migration in the case of nomadic pastoralists and food storage and new grain varieties by cultivators) that enabled them to survive climatic adversities (Forde 1934), whereas complex civilizations were subject to catastrophic collapse once sustainability thresholds (where these were not necessarily climatic) were exceeded. All predominantly rural-based societies up to Industrial Revolution times, and many third-world rural areas into the modern era, have been subject to cycles of population growth and drastic reduction, through disease, famine or migration. The timing of adverse climatic events is therefore

Table 42.1. Factors influencing societal impacts of, and responses to, climatic change

1	The nature of the climatic change (or event) in terms of scale, degree of abruptness, climatic and climate-related elements involved (including means and extremes) and perceived or anticipated duration.
2	Past experience of climatic variability or change by the community.
3	The degree of directness of impact on the local society, and its economy and human survival in particular.
4	The choices (and resources) effectively available to that society and sections of it.
5	The nature of the society including its social structure, degree of division.
6	The society's relationship with surrounding communities, regional and global politics and the global economy.

From the 1990s onwards:

7	The *predicted* future climate of the area (provided by science).
8	The *predicted* economic consequences for the area (provided by science and social science, government, various international, governmental and non-governmental agencies and companies/organizations).
9	The degrees to which 7 and 8 are known, transmitted to, believed and acted upon (or capable of being acted upon) by government, agencies/organizations, private companies and individuals, sections of society and the society as a whole.

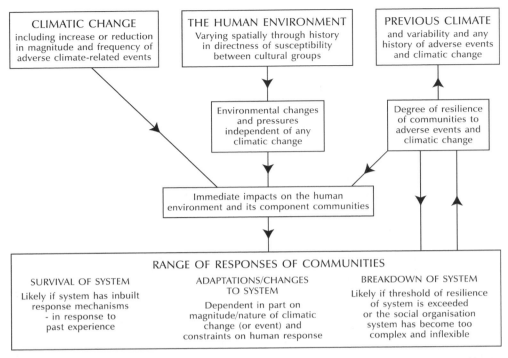

Figure 42.1. A conceptual model of the factors influencing the response of human communities to climatic change and adverse climatic events in the past.

often important, as they will tend to be most damaging when population is high in relation to the technological capabilities of the agricultural system of the time.

Four major developments during the past 150 years have tended to change the nature of human response systems to climate, extreme climatic events and climatic change: (1) the growing dominance of urban over rural populations over the Earth's surface; (2) technological developments in food storage and distribution; (3) the progressive growth in efficiency of trade, aid and news links; and (4) the growth in application of climatic science first to climate-related issues and agricultural and land-use development schemes, and later to climatic change detection and prediction. Urban populations with their access to food links outside the immediate area tend to suffer less than rural subsistence farming communities from famine. Technological developments in food storage (such as refrigeration and tinned foods) and food distribution (first the expansion of shipping trade, then the development of railways, the motor car and air transport) have greatly aided survival of urban and (albeit less so) rural populations during years of failed crops. Trade, relief aid and news information links, developed in the colonial empires and revolutionized in the satellite era, have also enabled more efficient provision of relief aid and helped reduce loss of life following climatic (and non-climatic) disasters. These three factors have together tended to reduce the directness of the old links between climate and societies dominated by largely subsistence agriculture. As a later section will show, the application of climatic scientific knowledge in development schemes particularly since late colonial times can sometimes reduce rather than aid the ability of communities to withstand adverse climatic events and climatic change. Finally, the advent – and growing acceptance by both governments and people – of predictions

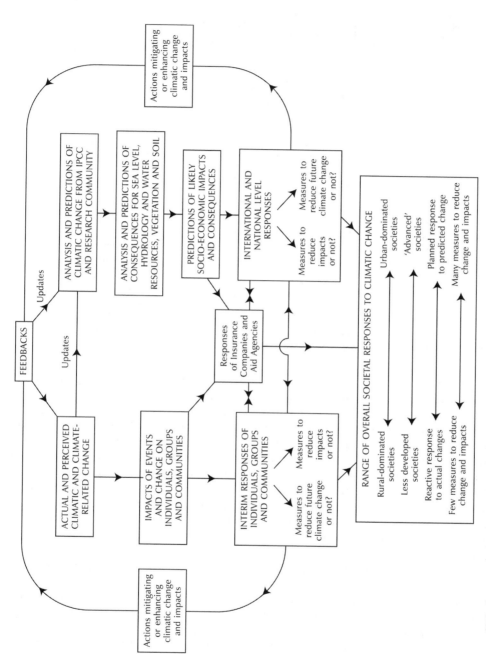

Figure 42.2. A conceptual model of the complex response of human communities to current and predicted future climatic change.

of climatic change with global warming have meant that current and future models of climatic change response now need to incorporate responses, particularly in more developed countries, to *predicted* as well as *actual* climatic change (Figure 42.2). These changes in the nature of societal response to climatic change are now explored in more detail with reference to examples: (1) from different stages in history and (2) in relation to current and future predicted climatic change.

Examples of societal impacts and response in the past

Example 1: Societal impacts and response in Classical times and subsistence societies

Geographers, archaeologists, anthropologists and historians, have long linked some of the past migratory movements of peoples and the rise and fall of past civilizations at least in part to climatic change. Major texts of the first half of the twentieth century (e.g. Taylor 1936/1947; Huntington 1940) incorporated the findings of early climatic change studies (e.g. Brooks 1926) into their arguments about the close relation between climate and society and the history of civilization. Thus Huntington (1940) summarized some of the archaeological and documentary evidence from early studies indicating a significantly wetter climate than now in parts of the Near East and North Africa at the time of the Roman Empire. Claudius Ptolemarus (Ptolemy) recorded climatic information including the days of rain, thunderstorms and wind direction in a remarkable climatic diary in Alexandria in northern Egypt during part of the first century AD. The record indicated a wetter and less seasonal climate than now with westerly winds and thunderstorms in summer more akin to that currently found in northern Greece (though Vita-Finzi (1968) later disagreed with this interpretation and considered that the longer-term climate of the North African coastlands during the Roman era differed little from that at present). Huntington also pointed to the existence of large cities, such as Palmyra in the northern Syrian Desert and Petra in the Dead Sea area, which with the aid of aqueducts supported large populations where there are currently only small villages. Later studies, however, have tended to show that it is often difficult to disentangle the influences of climatic change, social organizational factors and longer-term degradational factors related to the unsustainability of the irrigational or agricultural systems of Classical times. Thus the classic research of Vita-Finzi (1968) demonstrated how anthropogenically enhanced soil erosion and soil conservation measures during Roman times and later climatic deterioration had interacted to produce a complex sequence of valley alluviation and incision. In Greece, both the decline of the Mycenaean civilization and the early Byzantine decline in AD 400–750 have also been argued by Carpenter (1967) to have been due not to invasion but to cyclical climatic change in the Mediterranean basin. In Central America, the decline of the Mayan civilization has been linked by Hodell *et al.* (1995) to drought, though later work has shown that cultural factors that resulted in the lower classes blaming the drought and resultant catastrophic water shortages on the ruling elite and leading to the latter's mass murder played a major role by eliminating the technological capability for the civilization to continue.

The debate between 'environmental determinists' (e.g. Taylor 1936/1947; Huntington 1940), who viewed climate (and other physical factors) as strongly fashioning society (environmental determinism) and the 'possibilists' of the French school, who viewed communities more as free agents able to choose from an array of ways to respond to environmental factors, was an intense one that dominated much of human geography in the first half of the twentieth century. A compromise view of 'probablism' (in which the array of possible responses effectively had different chances of being adopted, with some being more probable than others) was also espoused at the end of this period (Spate 1957). The most productive and enduring work during this period was carried out by open-minded investigators. Thus the classic work of Forde (1934) on habitat, economy and society explored the great variety of interrelationships that characterized responses of traditional hunter-gatherer, cultivator and pastoral nomad communities to environmental factors (including climate and its variability) across the world. He demonstrated clearly that different communities had been influenced by but adapted in different ways to broadly similar habitats (including similar climatic challenges) and he concluded that neither environmental determinism nor what he termed sociological determinism provided a valid approach. Although in general, pastoral nomads and sometimes hunter-gatherers tend to occupy lands where crop cultivation is difficult or impossible because of the unreliability of precipitation and the coldness of the climate, and cultivators occupy lands with more reliable rainfall and crops, Forde highlighted exceptions, where primitive peoples had developed and used drought-resistant and short-season crop varieties, such as the corn and cotton varieties of the Hopi Indians in the American South-West.

Example 2: The Little Ice Age in Europe

Documentary, archaeological and climatic proxy evidence relating to a significantly stormier and cooler climate over much of western Europe from AD 1300 to the late nineteenth century was assembled by Brooks (1926) and greatly expanded upon by Lamb (1977). It is generally considered that summer temperatures were 1.0–2.0°C colder than today and the preceding Mediaeval Warm Period. The period was not uniformly cold, however, and Alpine glaciers attained maximum advance positions on three occasions (AD 1350, 1650 and 1850) during the period. Human impacts were profound. Increased storminess in Britain led to major coastal change and the abandonment and relocation of coastal settlements because of sand dune activity. The formerly active wine industry in Britain disappeared and the era saw the demise of the Norse settlements of Greenland. Poor crop yields following poor summers were in part responsible for famine and population decline in rural areas in Europe.

Example 3: Human impacts of the Sahel drought phase since 1965 in semi-arid Sudan: the deleterious effects of late colonial development based upon inappropriate climatic statistics

Both the impacts of, and societal responses to, the sequence of droughts in the 1960s, 1970s and 1980s in the Sahel can only be explained with reference to factors related to technological and political changes and their influence on the socioeconomic environment. The later colonial era and early independence years saw numerous development schemes, many of which included measures seeking to reduce the constraints stemming from the year-to-year variability and unreliability of rainfall. In the semi-arid and sub-humid zones of the Sudan, for example, programmes were introduced to provide more reliable water supplies to villages in marginal lands either through mechanized deep groundwater boreholes or, if closer to the Nile system, by irrigation canal systems. The programmes thereby enabled the extension of sedentary agriculture into lands that were traditionally devoted to nomadic and semi-nomadic pastoralists (who were often encouraged to become sedentary farmers) or under rain-fed agriculture. Many of these development schemes exacerbated, rather than reduced, the impacts of the 1965–73 droughts and the climatic change to a drier climate that they heralded for several reasons. First, the timing of these schemes was unfortunate, as they followed the rather wet climatic phase of the mid-twentieth century. The climatic statistics available to planners and used in these schemes derived mainly from this period of above-average rainfall and the schemes were themselves implemented towards the end of this wet period. It was later shown using documentary sources (Nicholson and Flohn 1980) that the dry epoch from 1965 onwards was far more typical of the last 1,400 years than the mid-twentieth century wet period. Analysis of the long-term records for the Nile at the Roda Gauge in Cairo stretching back to AD 622 demonstrates this conclusively (Evans 1990). This meant that the expansion of crop cultivation and sedentary agriculture had taken place on land with a longer-term climate that was too dry. Second, many of the schemes designed to ensure increased reliability of water supplies failed due to mechanical breakdown, lack of spare parts,

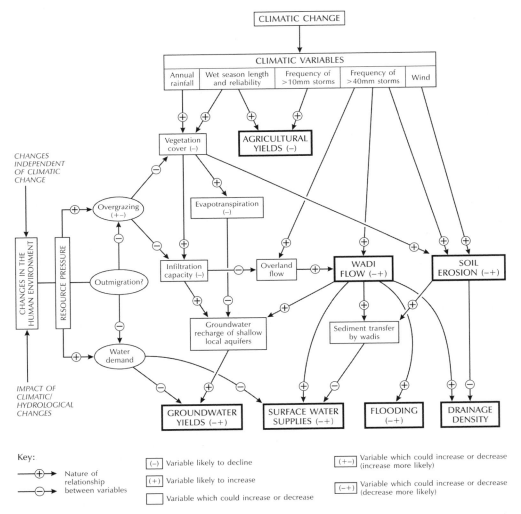

Figure 42.3. A model of the interrelationships between climatic and human variables influencing hydrological, water supply and agricultural yield impacts of rainfall decline in semi-arid parts of the Sudan.

Source: Adapted from Walsh *et al.* (1988).

fuel shortages, poor timing of tractors and (in the case of irrigation schemes) the arrival of water itself. The widespread failure of these supplies, together with the total inadequacy in a drought period of traditional water supplies from small surface reservoirs and shallow–dug wells, meant that much of the greatly expanded sedentary agricultural population had no option but to abandon their lands and villages. This is in contrast to nomadic and semi-nomadic cultures with their inbuilt ability to respond to drought, usually via temporary southward migration to wetter regions, though this adaptive mechanism has been constrained by administrative boundaries and conflicts with sedentary group rights.

These conflicts still persist; thus the violence in 2004–5 in Darfur stems from a conflict between nomadic pastoralists and sedentary farmers, not ethnicity or religion (H.R.J. Davies, personal communication). The fourth new factor affecting impacts and response in the Sahel droughts was that of international famine relief; although this humanitarian aid greatly aids human survival of the event itself, it tends to hinder longer-term recovery. This is in part because: (1) the unequal spatial availability of relief means that people migrate to the foci of more reliable relief (usually major camps near towns); (2) crops are not planted in succeeding years; (3) the comparative reliability of continued relief can become a brake to return of migrants to their home villages; and (4) the famine relief (and later subsidized imports from the developed world) tend to depress local food prices and make agriculture an uneconomic and risky proposition.

Impacts of, and responses to, the 1980s droughts varied considerably locally within White Nile province in semi-arid Sudan in relation to the interaction of human and physical factors and the different cultures of the four main groups inhabiting the area (Trilsbach and Hulme 1984; Hulme 1986; Walsh *et al.* 1988). Figure 42.3 shows how some of the hydrological impacts varied depending on the exact balance of different physical and human factors. It also emphasizes that different parts of the hydrological, water supply and agricultural systems respond to different climatic variables, which do not necessarily change to the same extent as a decline in annual rainfall. Whereas natural vegetation cover including grasses for pastoralists varies with annual rainfall, crop yields depend on the timing, length and structure of the wet season (particularly the continuity of early season rain). Traditional water supplies in rural areas away from the Nile are derived from wells (often dug each year) tapping shallow groundwater aquifers and small surface reservoirs (*hafirs*), in each case located in wide ephemeral river channels (*wadis*); their recharge and water supply capability are dependent on wadi flows in the previous year, where such flows only occur following substantial rainstorms of 20 mm or more. All three climatic variables showed major declines in 1965–84 from early mid-twentieth century (1920–39) levels: (Table 42.2) mean annual rainfall fell by 38–40 per

Table 42.2. Differences in mean annual rainfall, wet season length and the frequencies of large daily falls at locations in White Nile province, Sudan, between the periods 1920–39 and 1965–84

	Annual rainfall			Wet season length			Annual frequency of daily falls		
	mm 1920–39	1965–84	% change	days 1920–39	1965–84	% change	>20 mm 1920–39	1965–84	% change
Khartoum 15°36'N	209	131	−37	47	23	−51	3.40	2.10	−38
El Geteina 14°52'N	245	157	−36	64	39	−39	3.75	2.89	−23
Ed Dueim 13°59'N	356	214	−40	108	63	−42	5.05	2.90	−43

cent, wet season length from 64 to 39 days in the north and from 108 to 63 days in the south, and the frequency of daily falls exceeding 20 mm fell by 23–42 per cent.

Impacts on cultural groups varied significantly. Most badly affected were the Arab el Bahayim, being away from the Nile and dependent on rainfed cultivation of sesame and dukhn (*Pennisetum typhoidum*), rainfed pasture for their cattle, camels, sheep and goats, and on annually recharged shallow aquifers for their water supply. The nomadic groups (Baggara and Kabbabish tribes), in contrast, were able to respond by migrating much farther south than normal, in the 1982 drought as far as Southern Kordofan. Impacts in the irrigation-fed areas (both Nile-fed and from groundwater boreholes) varied depending upon whether the systems remained functional. Throughout the area, however, there was greater pressure on all locations where water supplies did not run out. Ecological and vegetational impacts varied in a complex manner with human impact and response. Ironically, the ecology and vegetation of areas with the least reliable water supply actually recovered as a result of the drought period because people had abandoned the area and migrated to the towns, whereas areas blessed with more reliable water supply suffered enhanced desertification because of in-migration and increased pressure on wood resources and pasture. The model (Figure 42.3) attempts to incorporate variation and uncertainty in local response by including the impacts of variable human response, and indicating hydrological variables that could increase or decrease depending on the magnitude of changes in water demand and grazing pressure that result from varying levels of out-migration.

One of the human impacts of the prolonged drought sequence was paradoxically increased flood risk. Many of the migrants from rural areas resettled in squatter settlements in Khartoum and Omdurman. Many of these settlements' land was in ephemeral watercourses that were liable to flooding in large storm events. The sharp decline in frequency of such events in the drought epoch (Table 42.2) meant that migrants had no experience of the flood risk. This was the main reason why the exceptional 203.5 mm rainstorm over the Khartoum area on 5 August 1988 caused such catastrophic flooding damage mainly in the squatter settlement areas rather than in the older parts of Omdurman and Khartoum (Walsh *et al.* 1994).

Current and projected future responses to global warming

The general context

The context for considering current and future impacts and responses of global warming has arguably become more complex still with the greater involvement of science in terms of the advent of climatic predictions from models, the uncertainties accompanying them, and planning for the predicted changes. Societal response at the current time now encompasses not simply response to *actual* climatic events and change, but planning and implementing responses to *predicted* future climatic change and its likely impacts and hence anticipating changes (Figure 42.2).

Although models are getting better and the overwhelming scientific consensus now accepts that many of the current changes in climate are at least in part the result of human activities, the predictive performance of models remains relatively poor. In general, (1) predictions remain better for temperature than precipitation; (2) models remain poor at predicting spatial patterns at the sub-continental scale even for current and recent past climate; and (3) modelling of changes in extreme events and their spatial distribution is particularly unreliable. There has also been a tendency for the media, governments and poor science to blame everything on global warming rather than human activities and/or government land-use or land management practice policies or inaction. The examples that follow are designed to illustrate both the varying nature (including uncertainties) of current and predicted climatic changes in different parts of the world and the messages and uncertainties involved in predicting the physical and human impacts and appropriate societal adaptive consequences of such changes.

Predicted changes and likely impacts and responses in the UK and Europe

The years since 1990 have seen a mushrooming of studies assessing and predicting the nature and impacts of climatic and climate-related changes associated with global warming and devising strategies to reduce predicted changes and impacts. Many of these are later synthesized by the Intergovernmental Panel on Climate Change (IPCC) in their reports (e.g. IPCC 1996; Houghton *et al.* 2001) or by major texts (e.g. Rayner and Malone 1998a, 1998b). Particularly useful overviews are those produced by the United Kingdom Climate Change Impacts Review Group (1996) and the Europe Acacia Project (Parry 2000) on effects and adaptations in the UK and Europe respectively. The latter project synthesized findings on the current and future predicted climate of Europe and then proceeded to assess the likely effects of the predicted changes on water resources, soil, ecosystems, forestry, agriculture and fisheries, insurance, transport and energy, tourism and recreation, human health, coastal zones and mountain regions. In order to reflect the uncertainties attached to modelling predictions, predicted impacts are often presented for different model scenarios. Examples of such scenario predictions for the 2050s are shown for the frequency of low flows for catchments in different parts of Britain (Table 42.3) and magnitude of peak flows for the Severn and Thames catchments (Table 42.4). In southern Britain summer precipitation and river flows are predicted to decline and drought frequency to increase, whereas in northern Britain increases in precipitation and river flow are predicted for throughout the year. Reliable low flows expressed as 95 per cent exceedance values (which control the reliable water supply, pollution abatement and navigation capabilities of a river) are predicted to fall by 22–39 per cent for the three catchments in eastern, southwest and southeast England (where much of Britain's population reside), but to increase or remain unchanged in northeast England and Scotland (where population is low and water resources are already ample). Because of predicted

Table 42.3. Predicted changes in the frequency of low flows for six catchments in different regions of the United Kingdom by the 2050s relative to 1961–90 under three scenarios

Catchment	Region	% change in flow exceeded 95% of the time			Average annual days below the flow currently exceeded 95% of the time		
		HadCM1 GGa1	HadCM2	HadCM2 GGax	Had CM1 GGa1	HadCM2	HadCM2 GGax
Don	NE Scotland	6	16	2	15	11	17
Greta	NE England	−5	4	−9	20	17	21
Nith	SW Scotland	7	3	−4	16	17	19
Harper's Brook	E England	−22	−5	−24	34	22	36
Medway	SE England	−34	−21	−30	37	28	34
Tamar	SW England	−39	−3	−31	41	20	34

Note: The flow exceeded 95% of the time occurs on average 18 days per year.
Source: After Arnell and Reynard (1999).

673

Table 42.4. Predicted percentage rise in the magnitude of peak floods in the Severn and Thames catchments by the 2050s relative to 1961–90

	Return period				
	2-year	*5-year*	*10-year*	*20-year*	*50-year*
Thames					
GGax-x	10	12	13	14	15
GGax-s	12	13	14	15	16
GGax-x+land use	11	12	13	14	16
Severn					
GGax-x	13	15	16	17	20
GGax-s	15	17	18	19	21
GGax-x+land use	13	15	17	18	20

Notes: GGax-x = GGx scenario with proportional change in rainfall.
GGax-s = scenario with change in storm rainfall only.
GGax-x+land use = GGx scenario with proportional change in rainfall plus 'realistic' land use change.
Source: After Reynard *et al.* (1998).

higher winter precipitation and higher extreme rainstorms, peak flows of all return periods are predicted to increase by 13–21 per cent under all three scenarios, with significant implications for future flood frequency and intensity in the often well-populated floodplain areas.

In Britain, the Environmental Agency and all water companies have already had to draw up assessments of future water supply needs and how they can be met for 50 years ahead, and for this purpose they have used these predictions of future climate. The British government has also changed its policy regarding flood alleviation schemes and planning permissions for floodplain land, in part in response to the predictions of increased areal extent and frequency of flooding. Similar assessments have been made of likely impacts of coastal flooding and erosion (e.g. Bray *et al.* 1997).

A major feature of the British response to predicted climatic change is therefore planning based upon predictions rather than responding to actual changes – though the occurrence of major floods since 2000 (which ironically may be in part linked to changes in land-use and land drainage rather than climatic change) has given the changes additional impetus. Another major driver of response of society (including individuals) to future climatic change is the insurance industry. Their premiums are based upon risk. Avoidance of floodplains by individuals of buying properties or housing developers will probably result more from the inability to obtain insurance, or prohibitive premiums, rather than planning controls alone. The nature of response systems (Figure 42.2), therefore, in developed countries that accept and wish to plan for predicted climatic change impacts, is likely to be very different from that in countries in the less developed world.

Current and future change and response in tropical rain-forest areas

The survival of tropical rain forests is viewed as of key importance to the future of the planet, not least because deforestation is seen as a driver of both regional and global climatic change. This stems from the twin role which rain forests are viewed to play in: (1) maintaining the wetness of the climate of the rain-forest areas themselves through high evapotranspiration (mainly transpiration); and (2) acting as a store of carbon that would otherwise add in part to the atmospheric levels. Rain-forest areas themselves, however, are experiencing significant climatic change already and are considered likely to be subject to greater climatic change in the future. This section considers some of these changes and predicted changes and the implications for rain-forest survival and socioeconomic development of countries within which they lie, using examples from Amazonia and Borneo.

Maslin *et al.* (2005) considered the resilience of the Amazonian rain forest to climatic change by examining how it had responded to past climatic change. Palaeoclimatic and palaeoecological records suggest that rain forest originated in the late Cretaceous and has been a permanent feature in South America for 55 million years, despite large changes in global climate since and atmospheric carbon dioxide levels in the Cretaceous some 4–5 times higher than recent pre-industrial levels (280 ppm). They added that previously held views that the Amazonian forest had retreated into Pleistocene refugia during drier glacial phases had also been revised (Mayle *et al.* 2004). It is now suggested that lower temperatures (and evapotranspiration rates) in glacial periods may have mitigated the effects of reduced rainfall and lower carbon dioxide, thus allowing C3 trees to remain competitive with C4 grasses. (A C3 plant produces, as the first step in photosynthesis, phosphoglyceric acid, which contains three carbon atoms; a C4 plant produces, as the first step in photosynthesis, oxaloacetic acid, which contains four carbon atoms. C3 plants (which include tropical trees) are generally associated with higher nutrient status and lower temperatures and are favoured when atmospheric carbon dioxide levels are high, C4 plants (which include many tropical grasses) are associated with lower nutrient status and higher temperatures and are favoured when atmospheric carbon dioxide levels are low.) Prospects for survival of the rain forest in the twenty-first century with global warming were viewed, however, as less rosy. If deforestation rates continue, rainfall is modelled to fall significantly because of a reduced evapotranspiration supply of atmospheric moisture for rainfall. Although the predicted further increase in carbon dioxide might be expected to enhance photosynthesis by C3 trees, field studies have suggested that this may be concentrated into lianas and fast-growing canopy trees, rather than the traditional forest trees, and may also lead to faster life-cycles of trees. There is extreme concern that these changes and the unprecedented speed of them may exceed the resilience threshold of the forest and lead to replacement of forest by savannah within the next 50 years (Cox *et al.* 2000). This would have consequences not just for forest peoples but for water resources and agriculture of the surrounding agricultural areas.

In Sabah, northeastern Borneo, both the climate and human settings are somewhat different to that of Amazonia. The climate is reliably wet in most years, but subject to dry periods (with a west–east gradient of increasing intensity across Sabah) in major El Niño–Southern Oscillation (ENSO) years. Most of the land surface area was under primary forest until the 1970s, but since then there has been a combination of conversion to plantation agriculture (mostly oil palm) and natural forest management (selective logging of annual coupes on a rotational basis, with the post-logging mosaic left to regenerate). A large area (1 m ha) of southeastern Sabah is managed by the Sabah Foundation (a government charity) and consists of three conservation areas (Danum Valley, Maliau Basin and Imbak Canyon) nested within a large area of regenerating forest logged in blocks at different times (Figure 42.4).

Rainfall records in Sabah are unusually long and reliable for an equatorial location and permit long-term analysis of changes not only in annual and monthly rainfall, but in the magnitude-frequency of dry periods and large daily rainfalls. There is no conclusive evidence of marked changes in annual rainfall at the long-term stations, but there has been a marked upturn since 1999 at the interior station at Danum Valley (Table 42.5). Dry periods in Sabah have increased significantly in both frequency and intensity since the late 1960s compared to the previous 1916–67 fifty-two year period (Figure 42.5), but the period 1877–1915 was

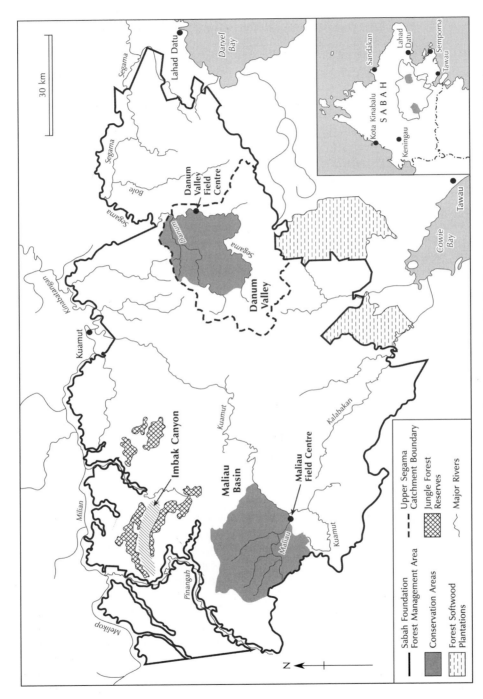

Figure 42.4. The Maliau Basin and Danum Valley conservation areas nested within the Sabah Foundation Forest Management Area in southeastern Sabah.

Table 42.5. Recent changes in the frequency of large daily rainfalls at locations in Sabah

		Mean annual frequency (number of days)			
		1906–40	1953–79	1980–2004	1999–2004
Sandakan	≥50 mm	16.2	14.8	15.3	13.8
	≥100 mm	3.3	2.4	2.9	3.3
Tawau	≥50 mm	5.8	4.6	5.8	6.2
	≥100 mm	0.6	0.3	0.4	0.5
		1986–98	1999–2005	% change	
Danum Valley	≥50 mm	7.92	11.57	+46%	
	≥80 mm	1.77	2.88	+63%	
	≥100 mm	0.85	1.00	+18%	
Annual rainfall mm		2,664	3,062	+15%	

equally drought-prone. There has been an increase in the frequency of large rainstorms in 1980–2005 compared to 1953–79 and the increase since 1999 appears to have intensified (Table 42.5). At Danum Valley (and Tawau) this upswing has been particularly marked and has also been marked by increased year-to-year variability, though frequencies and variability were also high in the 1906–40 period. These trends would appear to conform to a tendency to stronger El Niño (warm) and La Niña (cold) phases of an intensified ENSO cycle in the Pacific, but whether the very recent increase in high rainstorm frequency marks the onset of an impact of a warmer atmosphere and seas, it is too early to say.

When combined with large-scale land-use change and logging activities, however, these drought and heavy rainfall frequency changes have major ecological, conservational and socioeconomic implications for the region. The recent increase in drought magnitude-frequency, which IPCC predictions indicate should become more severe in the future with an intensification of the ENSO cycle (Houghton *et al.* 2001), constitutes a major threat to the species composition and diversity of the remaining forest. This is not because of the droughts themselves, as the forests appear to be resilient to them and in part the outcome of them (Newbery *et al.* 1992; Walsh and Newbery 1999), as drought phases form part of the longer-term climate and were probably more intense in the colder phases of the Pleistocene (Whitmore 1998). The great danger is the increased risk of forest fire accompanying the droughts, because of the increased fuel load in recently logged forest and the proximity of humanity and fire with conversion of adjacent land to plantation farming. The ecological effects of drought-with-fire and drought are very different (Leighton 1984), as fire pre-ferentially destroys the understorey saplings and lianas and leads to a species-poor successor forest dominated by light-demanding and fire-survivor species, whereas following drought alone the understorey saplings provide the replacement canopy trees of the successor forest. The messages for forest management and conservation policy in Sabah were very clear. The policy of maintaining the Yayasan Sabah Forest Management Area as a contiguous forest area with nested conservation areas surrounded by buffer zones and extending west–east across a gradient of varying drought susceptibility: (1) provides maximum protection against fire and; (2) allows the maximum possibility of forest adjustment if drought magnitude-frequency were to increase further in the future. In contrast, a policy of conservation of a larger number of smaller and isolated forest fragments without linking corridors not only is not conducive to maintaining biodiversity (Payne 2001) but also affords little chance of forest adjustment to climatic change and probably will lead to them being damaged by fires.

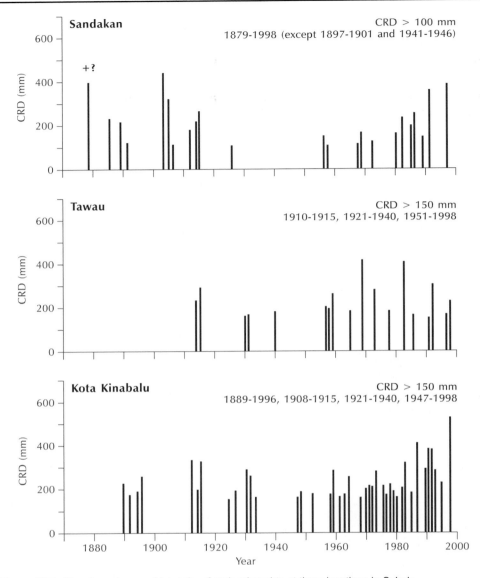

Figure 42.5. The chronology and intensity of major droughts at three locations in Sabah.

The effects of extreme rainstorm events of 162.5 mm on 19 January 1996, 183 mm in 20 hours on 30/31 January 2000 and 182.5 mm on 10 February 2006 at Danum Valley each led to major floods and sediment transport along the Segama River (Figure 42.4). The 2000 floods were widespread in Sabah with the Segama floods exacerbated by logging upstream in 1999 and flooding of plantation land along the Kinabatangan River increased as a result of both logging and forest conversion to plantations in the upper reaches of the catchment. There were again unambiguous messages for forest and land-use management. Impacts of an increase in rainstorm magnitude-frequency can be lessened if the steeper headwater areas of catchments are either left unlogged or only selectively logged using strict 'reduced impact logging' rules. The downstream benefits of protected forest areas and sustainable forest management zones (in terms of safeguarding water supplies, reducing flood risk, protecting against excessive sedimentation and offshore damage to coral reefs) are maximized by a drainage basin oriented conservation and management strategy that protects headwater areas.

Hurricane frequency changes and dilemmas for planning responses in the North Atlantic/Caribbean region

Tropical cyclones have long been forecast to increase in frequency, and perhaps widen their spatial coverage, because of the increase in sea surface temperature accompanying global warming. Because they can cause great damage and, in low-lying parts of the less developed world, sometimes catastrophic loss of life, changes in their frequency, severity and tracks are of great significance to the societies and locations affected. Until very recently, there was no evidence of an overall increase in their frequency in recent decades (Walsh 2000). In the Caribbean/North Atlantic region, frequencies were significantly lower in 1959–95 than in 1929–58 and 1871–1901 (Figure 42.6) and there was evidence of significant shifts in predominant tracks from the late nineteenth century to the present day. Analysis of a longer series back to 1650 for the Lesser Antilles sub-region demonstrated that peak frequencies also occurred in parts of the late eighteenth and early nineteenth centuries (Walsh 2000). Temporal

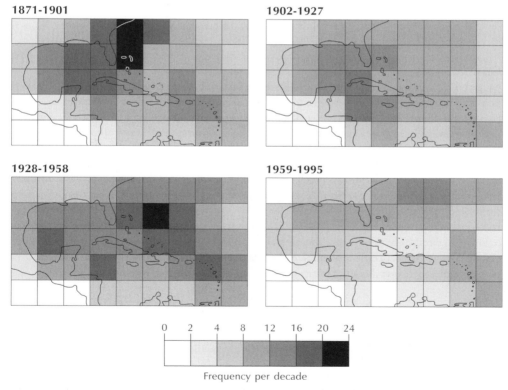

Figure 42.6. Differences in the frequency and spatial distribution of tropical cyclones in the Caribbean for four epochs between 1871 and 1995.

Source: Adapted from Walsh (2000).

patterns of change in different parts of the Caribbean both since 1871 and (for sub-sections of the Lesser Antilles) since 1650 vary greatly. There is currently some evidence of an upsurge in both tropical cyclone frequency and their intensity which, it has been suggested, may be part of the long-awaited rise linked to global warming (Goldenberg *et al.* 2001; Webster *et al.* 2005; Emanuel 2005). Thus the years 1995–2000 saw a doubling of overall activity for the whole North Atlantic basin, a 2.5-fold increase in major hurricanes (greater than or equal to 50 metres per second), and a fivefold increase in hurricanes affecting the Caribbean (Webster *et al.* 2005), though only time will tell whether this trend will be maintained. A number of problems for planners arise from the collective research findings reported before. The first is the mismatch between the regional and sub-regional scales at which most studies provide data and the local spatial scale (individual islands or sections of coast) required for planning by communities. Not only do temporal patterns differ considerably at different scales, but the degree of reliability decreases at more local scales as the number of events upon which they are based falls (Walsh 2000). Second, as spatial patterns and frequencies vary between different periods (Figure 42.6) and the last few years, the question arises as to which is the most appropriate data set or combination to use in calculating hazard probabilities and hazard mapping for future planning purposes. Finally there is the problem of which rate of sea level rise to adopt for the future, as this will greatly affect coastal impacts of future cyclones regardless of changes in cyclone frequency. Further, the lesson of Hurricane Katrina in 2005 is that catastrophic damage is not confined to the less developed countries such as Bangladesh, but also low-lying parts, such as New Orleans, of developed countries like the United States (see Chapter 48).

Conclusions

Societies have always had to respond to climatic changes, but until now they have never had to respond to predicted change. In the past, communities have principally reacted to the extreme events that have heralded a climatic change, but there would not have been the scientific data and analysis to confirm that a change was occurring. Also, in the past, different cultures had their own adaptive mechanisms to help them survive adverse climatic episodes, if not too severe or too often repeated. In the twentieth century, urbanization, westernization, political boundaries, the application of inadequate climatic science and inappropriate technology in agricultural development schemes and, ironically, the side-effects of famine relief have sometimes combined (as in the Sudan example) to reduce the ability of communities to respond effectively to adverse climatic episodes. The challenge of the coming decades is to decide how best to design and implement measures that will aid all types and sections of communities to respond and adapt to the coming climatic changes.

Further reading

Conway, D. (2000) The climate and hydrology of the Upper Blue Nile River. *The Geographical Journal* 166, 49–62.

Houghton, J.T., Ding, Y., Griggs, D.J., Noquet, M., van der Linden, J.P., Dai, X., Maskell, K. and Johnson, C.A. (eds) (2001) *Climate Change 2001: The Scientific Basis: Contribution of Working Group I to the Third Assessment Report of the Intergovernmental Panel on Climate Change: The Scientific Basis.* Cambridge: Cambridge University Press and the Intergovernmental Panel on Climate Change.

Houghton, J.T. (2004) *Global Warming: The Complete Briefing*, third edition. Cambridge: Cambridge University Press.

Intergovernmental Panel on Climate Change (1996) *Review of the Potential Effects of Climate Change in the United Kingdom*. London: Department of the Environment, HMSO.

Maslin, M., Malhi, Y., Phillips, O. and Cowling, S. (2005) New views on an old forest: assessing the longevity, resilience and future of the Amazon rainforest. *Transactions of the Institute British Geographers* NS 30, 477–99.

Parry, M.L. (ed.) (2000) *Assessment of Potential Effects and Adaptations for Climate Change in Europe: The Europe ACACIA Project*. Norwich: Jackson Environment Institute, University of East Anglia.

Reynard, N.S., Prudhomme, C. and Crooks, S. (1998) Impact of climate change on the flood characteristics of the Thames and Severn rivers. In P. Balabanis, R. Bronstert and P. Samuels (eds) *Proceedings of the 2nd International RIBAMOD Conference, Wallingford February 1998*, pp. 49–63. Wallingford: Institute of Hydrology.

Walsh, R.P.D. (2000) Extreme weather events. In: M. Pacione (ed.) *Applied Geography: Principles and Practice*, pp. 51–65. London: Routledge.

References

Arnell, N.W. and Reynard, N.S. (1999) Climate change and UK hydrology. In: M.C. Acreman (ed.) *The Hydrology of the UK*, pp. 3–29. London: Routledge.

Bray, M., Hooke, J. and Carter, D. (1997) Planning for sea-level rise on the south coast of England: advising the decision-makers. *Transactions of the Institute of British Geographers* NS 22, 13–30.

Brooks, C.E.P. (1926) *Climate through the Ages*. London: Ernest Benn.

Carpenter, R. (1967) *Discontinuity in Greek Civilization*. Cambridge: Cambridge University Press.

Cox, P.M., Betts, R.A. and Jones, C.D. (2000) Acceleration of global warming due to carbon-cycle feedbacks in a coupled climate model. *Nature* 408, 184–7.

Emanuel, K.A. (2005) Increasing destructiveness of tropical cyclones over the past 30 years. *Nature* 436, 686–8.

Evans, P. (1990) History of Nile flows. In P.P. Howell and P.A. Allen (eds) *The Nile*, pp. 5–40. London: School of African and Oriental Studies, University of London..

Forde, C.D. (1934) *Habitat, Economy and Society: A Geographical Introduction to Ethnology*. London: Methuen.

Goldenberg, S.B., Landsea, C.W., Mestas-Nunez, A.M. and Gray, W.M. (2001) The recent increase in Atlantic hurricane activity: Causes and implications. *Science* 293, 474–9.

Hodell, D.A., Curtis, J.H. and Brenner, M. (1995) Possible role of climate in the collapse of classic Mayan civilization. *Nature* 375, 391–9.

Houghton, J.T. (2004) *Global Warming: The Complete Briefing,* third edition. Cambridge: Cambridge University Press.

Hulme, M. (1986) The adaptability of a rural water supply system to extreme rainfall anomalies in central Sudan. *Applied Geography* 6, 89–105.

Huntington, E. (1940) *Principles of Human Geography*, fifth edition. New York: John Wiley and Sons.

Intergovernmental Panel on Climate Change (1996) *Review of the Potential Effects of Climate Change in the United Kingdom*. London: Department of the Environment, HMSO.

Lamb, H.H. (1977) *Climate: Present, Past and Future. Volume 2. Climatic History and the Future*. London: Methuen.

Leighton, M. (1984) The El Niño–Southern Oscillation event in Southeast Asia: effects of drought and fire in tropical forest in eastern Borneo. Unpublished report to the World Wildlife Fund.

Maslin, M., Malhi, Y., Phillips, O. and Cowling, S. (2005) New views on an old forest: assessing the longevity, resilience and future of the Amazon rainforest. *Transactions of the Institute British Geographers* NS 30, 477–99.

Mayle, F.E., Beetling, D.J., Gosling, W.D. and Bush, M.B. (2004) Responses of Amazonian ecosystems to climatic and atmospheric carbon dioxide changes since the last glacial maximum. *Philosophical Transactions of the Royal Society of London B* 359, 499–515.

Newbery, D.M., Campbell, E.J.F., Lee, Y.F., Ridsdale, C.E. and Still, M.J. (1992) Primary lowland dipterocarp forest at Danum Valley, Sabah, Malaysia: structure, relative abundance and family composition. *Philosophical Transactions of the Royal Society of London B* 335, 341–56.

Nicholson, S.E. and Flohn, H. (1980) African environmental and climatic changes and the general circulation in late Pleistocene and Holocene. *Climatic Change* 2, 313–48.

Parry, M.L. (ed.) (2000) Assessment of potential effects and adaptations for climate change in Europe: the Europe ACACIA Project. Norwich: Jackson Environment Institute, University of East Anglia.

Payne J. (2001) Protected areas: networks and corridors. In Z. Yaacob, S. Moo-Tan and S. Yorath (eds) *Proceedings of the International Conference on In-situ and Ex-Situ Biodiversity Conservation in the New Millennium 20–22 June 2000, Kota Kinabalu*, pp. 197–210. Kota Kinabalu: Yayasan Sabah/Innoprise Corporation Sdn Bhd and Sabah Museum.

Rayner, S. and Malone, E.L. (eds) (1998a) *Human Choice and Climate Change. Vol. 1 The Societal Framework*. Columbus, Ohio: Battelle Press.

——(1998b) *Human Choice and Climate Change. Vol. 2 Resources and Technology*. Columbus, Ohio: Battelle Press.

Spate, O.H.K. (1957) How determined is possibilism? *Geographical Studies* 4, 3–12.

Taylor, G. (1936/1947) *Environment and Nation*, second edition. Toronto: University of Toronto Press.

Trilsbach, A. and Hulme, M. (1984) Recent rainfall changes in central Sudan and their physical and human implications. *Transactions of the Institute of British Geographers* NS 9, 280–98.

United Kingdom Climate Change Impacts Review Group (1996) *Review of the Potential Effects of Climate Change in the United Kingdom. Second Report.* London: Department of the Environment, HMSO.

Vita-Finzi, C. (1968) *The Mediterranean Valleys*. Cambridge: Cambridge University Press.

Walsh, R.P.D. (2000) Extreme weather events. In M. Pacione (ed.) *Applied Geography: Principles and Practice*, pp. 51–65. London: Routledge.

Walsh and Newbery, D.M. (1999) The ecoclimatology of Danum, Sabah, in the context of the world's rainforest regions, with particular reference to dry periods and their impact. *Philosophical Transactions of the Royal Society of London B* 354, 1869–83.

Walsh, Hulme, M. and Campbell, M.D. (1988) Recent rainfall changes and their impact on hydrology and water supply in the semi-arid zone of the Sudan. *The Geographical Journal* 154, 181–98.

Walsh, Davies, H.R.J. and Musa, S.B. (1994) Flood frequency and impacts at Khartoum since the early nineteenth century. *The Geographical Journal* 160, 266–79.

Webster, Holland, G.J., Curry, J.A. and Chang, H.R. (2005) Changes in tropical cyclone number, duration, and intensity in a warming environment. *Science* 309, 1844–6.

Whitmore, T.C. (1998) Potential impact of climatic change on tropical rain forest seedlings and forest regeneration. *Climatic Change* 39, 429–38.

43

Managing agricultural and silvicultural malpractices

Catherine Heppell

The global importance of agricultural and silvicultural practice

Agriculture occupies 35 per cent of the world's land surface and is the single largest consumer of freshwater resources, using a global average of 70 per cent of surface water supplies (UNEP 1992). Agriculture and forestry are inextricably linked, not least because agricultural expansion is one of the driving forces behind deforestation and forest land degradation (FAO 2003). Forests play an important role in the supply of freshwater, and mountainous forested catchments, in particular, are amongst the most important source of freshwater in the world. So any deterioration in land and water resources arising from agricultural and silvicultural practice is of global importance.

A significant global increase in output from agriculture since the 1960s has been achieved by intensification in both arable agricultural practice and livestock production (increased output per unit of both land and labour) and the expansion of farming into marginal, environmentally sensitive land. Intensification has resulted in the expansion of irrigation practice, and an increasing use of fertilizer and pesticides to achieve higher yields. Grain is particularly important to consider because much of the global population is reliant on food from grain. It is also the most important feed for livestock production (Worldwatch Institute 2003). Cereal agriculture in the industrialized OECD countries relies heavily on high-yielding grain crops and external inputs of modern fertilizers and pesticides. The Green Revolution that began in the early 1960s introduced high-yielding cereals, requiring high inputs of modern fertilizers and pesticides, to the developing world. About half of the rice, wheat and maize areas in developing countries are now planted to these high-yield crops. An increase in the global grain harvest from 805 million tonnes in 1961 to 1833 million tonnes in 2002 has been driven primarily by the intensification of farming practices. The global average harvest was 1.24 tons ha^{-1} in 1967, and had risen to 2.82 tons ha^{-1} in 2002, but has been accompanied by only a 4 per cent expansion in land use (FAOSTAT data 2005). Global meat production has risen by over 350 per cent since 1961 with only a relatively small increase in the area of land under permanent pasture (FAOSTAT data 2005). Since the 1990s much of the expansion of both meat production and consumption has taken place in the developing world. Industrial feedlots or factory farms are the most rapidly growing production systems, but increased stocking densities and livestock grazing on marginal land are also playing a role.

Whilst the fundamental importance of agricultural production is clear, public awareness of the negative impacts of agricultural practice on our environment is growing. These impacts are diverse and operate from the local through regional to global scale and include:

- agrochemical (including fertilizers, pesticides, veterinary medicines) point and non-point source pollution of surface waters and groundwaters;
- sediment erosion and subsequent deposition;
- salinization;
- global transport of persistent organic compounds;
- emissions of greenhouse gases to the atmosphere;
- loss of biodiversity;
- loss of habitat;
- water resources issues such as flooding and over-abstraction;
- pesticides and organic contaminants in the food chain.

The impacts of forest management activities (such as cultivation, drainage, road building and harvesting operations) on the environment also arise from the movement of sediment, nutrients, pesticides and other chemicals (such as fire-retardants and fuels) to surface waters. Other negative effects arise from temperature changes in forest streams, and from the direct exposure of foresters and other operators to the chemicals used in silvicultural practices.

This chapter will chiefly consider off-site environmental impacts arising from agricultural and silvicultural practices, focusing on non-point source pollution of freshwaters by sediments and agrochemicals. Non-point source, diffuse pollution arises from land-use management activities such as forestry and agriculture. It is distinguishable from point source pollution, such as the discharge of sewage or industrial effluents, which can be managed by characterizing and controlling the discrete discharges at source.

Environmental problems arising from the intensification of agricultural and silvicultural practices, and land-use conversion

Traditional farming and silvicultural activities may cause land degradation when a population is forced to farm on marginal lands through economic incentives or displacement. There is a long history of environmental problems caused by transformation of forested and grassland areas to cultivated and grazed land, and of exploitation of forest resources for timber, fuel-wood and food. Land degradation through vegetation loss results in water and wind erosion of topsoils, nutrient decline, waterlogging and salinization (Pimentel 1993). Estimates of the global extent and impact of land degradation vary widely. It has been estimated that between 17 and 70 per cent of all drylands (which include arid, semi-arid and dry sub-humid zones) are desertified (Gisladottir and Stocking 2005). The actual extent of soil loss associated with degradation is difficult to assess because many measures are scale-dependent. The extent and rate of soil erosion is frequently quantified using small plot experiments; however, this approach can lead to over-estimate of soil losses when extrapolated to the field or catchment scale (Brazier 2004). Alternatively, measures of sediment loads in the world's rivers can provide a general measure of land degradation and thus the reduction in the world soil resource (Walling and Fang 2003; Syvitski 2003). This technique, however, can result in an under-estimation of on-site soil erosion due to storage within a catchment (e.g. at the foot of a hillslope, or on a floodplain). Nevertheless, such studies indicate that many areas of the world are vulnerable to soil erosion associated with expansion of agriculture and silviculture on to marginal lands. Regions where there are demonstrable environmental problems caused by land degradation associated with the expansion of traditional cultivation activities include the mountainous terrain of the Himalayas and Andes, on the volcanic soils of Asia, in West Africa (Lal 1993) and the humid tropics of Central America and Africa (El-Swaify 1993). More recently techniques developed by physical geographers have also identified soil erosion as a hazard associated with the modernization of farming. This has not only become an issue in temperate environments such as Europe (see, for example, Boardman 2002), but also in other climatic regions where the Green Revolution has resulted in a marked intensification in farming practices. For example agricultural mechanization and high intensive cultivation practices in Bangladesh and India are cited as potential causes of declining crop yield and land degradation in the 1990s (Ali 2004).

Whether arising from land-use conversion or the adoption of intensive agricultural production methods, soil erosion and the associated off-site transport of soil leads to environmental problems such as contamination of drinking water supply and degradation of aquatic ecosystems through processes such as siltation and eutrophication (nutrient enrichment). The transport of eroded soil results in siltation of river channels and lakes, and inundation of roads and property by soil-laden runoff during flooding (Boardman 2002). In areas of intensive farming, sediment will also carry pollutants such as phosphorus and pesticides that may have further impacts on the aquatic organisms of the receiving environments.

Issues arising from fertilizer use

World fertilizer consumption increased from the 1960s until the late 1980s and currently just exceeds 1.4×10^8 Mt per annum. Fertilizers can be both mineral nitrogen and phosphorus-based compounds, or organic in nature (manures and slurries). The 600 per cent increase in global nitrogen fertilizer consumption since 1961 is largely associated with the rise in grain production for both direct human consumption and animal production. Nitrogen fertilizer use is concentrated in Europe, North America and parts of Asia. In other parts of the world nitrogen fertilizer is very expensive and therefore not so widely used (Mosier et al. 2004). Increased use of nitrogen-based fertilizers, larger numbers of livestock, changes in crop types, increased frequency of ploughing and under-drainage are all modern farming practices that have been implicated in the rise of nitrate concentrations of surface and groundwaters in intensively farmed catchments since the 1960s (Burt 2001). Elevated concentrations of nitrate in drinking water were thought to be a cause of infantile methaemoglobinaemia (blue-baby syndrome) and gastrointenstinal cancers. Recommended safe levels of nitrate concentrations in drinking water were set with these health effects in mind. However, both conditions now appear to be declining in those regions of the world where nitrate concentrations in drinking water have risen, and the results of medical and epidemiological studies are now challenging the former views of human health effects (Mosier et al. 2004).

The effect of rising nitrate concentrations in surface waters on aquatic ecosystems is better established. Eutrophication of lakes, reservoirs and coastal zones arising from the enrichment of surface waters by nutrients has become widespread. The Black Sea, the Baltic Sea and the Gulf of Mexico are all examples of large water bodies affected by transboundary eutrophication, arising from the input of nutrients hundreds to thousands of kilometres upstream (Novotny, 2005). Both nitrogen and phosphorus can contribute to eutrophication, with phosphorus being the limiting nutrient in the majority of examples of freshwaters (Great

Lakes and Norfolk Broads; see, for example, Conway and Pretty 1991), and nitrogen the limiting nutrient in estuaries (Chesapeake Bay, USA). The undesirable effects of eutrophication are wide-ranging and include increases in biomass and production of algae, changes in assemblages of aquatic plants, de-oxygenation of water (frequently resulting in fish kills), changes in fish populations and taste and odour problems in public water supply amongst others. The problems of nutrient enrichment and eutrophication arising from agricultural practices can be attributed to organic manure and slurry applications as well as mineral fertilizer usage. Manures produced by cattle, pigs and poultry are used as organic fertilizers throughout the world. Nutrient leaching from these organic sources can be particularly acute in areas of intensive livestock farming where manure production exceeds the capacity of the land to assimilate the waste, or when direct runoff from intensive livestock farming occurs. Only 30 per cent of the N fertilizer used to produce food eaten by livestock is transformed to protein; the remaining 70 per cent is excreted (Goulding 2004). So, at a global scale, consideration of N losses arising from manures is very important.

Issues arising from pesticide use

Pesticide is a general term to describe any chemical used to control any type of pest which can be further subdivided into herbicides used for weed control, insecticides (insects), fungicides (fungi), nematocides (nematodes) and rodenticides for the control of vertebrates. Every year 2.5 billion kg of pesticide are used for agricultural purposes (Pretty 2005), with over 50 per cent of pesticide products used on a few crops: wheat, maize, cotton, rice and soybean. Herbicide use dominates the North American and European pesticide market, whilst insecticides are more commonly used in the Asia-Pacific region (Conway and Pretty 1991). Pesticide usage in agriculture and silviculture, whilst providing recognized benefits in terms of improvements in food and timber yield, also causes problems for human health and the environment. The diverse documented effects of pesticide use include both on- and off-site impacts on flora and fauna, such as the disruption of predator–prey relationships and loss of biodiversity. There are also impacts on human health caused by skin contact and inhalation, for example through exposure to spray drift, and caused by the ingestion of food and water contaminated with pesticide residues. The environmental impacts of some classes of pesticides (including organochlorine compounds such as DDT and its metabolites) have recently been re-evaluated because of fears that they may act as endocrine disruptors. Endocrine disruptors mimic or interfere with the action of hormones in the body. There is increasing evidence that endocrine-disrupting chemicals are having adverse effects on the reproductive health of wildlife, and potentially on human health as well (Pretty 2005; Williams et al. 2000). Reproductive effects resulting from the use of agricultural pesticides have been reported in predatory birds and alligators exposed to organochlorine compounds such as DDT and DDE (Vos et al. 2000), and frogs exposed to atrazine (Hayes et al. 2002). Many laboratory experiments have demonstrated endocrine-disrupting potential for a range of agricultural pesticides (see Pretty 2005); however, studies identifying causative agents in the field are more difficult and the focus of much current research activity (Williams et al. 2000).

Pesticide residues in the Aral Sea: case study

The Aral Sea Basin is one of the world's most dramatic examples of the negative impacts of agricultural practice, potentially affecting almost 36 million people (Usmanova 2003). This case study focuses on the transfer of pesticides residues to human populations in the region.

The Aral Sea is located in the arid zone of Central Asia, and its catchment area encompasses the countries of Uzbekistan, Tadjikistan, Kirgizstan, Turkmenistan, Kazakhstan and Afghanistan (Figure 43.1). Until the 1960s the Aral Sea was considered to be the fourth largest lake in the world by surface area (66,100 sq km). Since the 1960s the water level in the lake has been steadily falling, the surface area of the lake has been reduced by 33 per cent and the salt content has risen from 11 to 30 g l^{-1}. The discharge of the two rivers that flow to the Aral Sea, the Amu Dar'ya and the Syr Dar'ya, have substantially decreased as a result of a combination of damming for hydroelectrical power, and water abstraction for the irrigation of cotton plantations (Usmanova 2003).

Pesticides such as DDT and lindane have been used in the region since the 1950s to increase the cotton yield. These chemicals are hydrophobic (literally 'water-hating') and bind strongly to soils and sediments. Soil erosion is commonplace in the degraded, salinized soils of the region and will contribute contaminated sediment to irrigation return flow that is diverted back to the surface waters of the catchment, eventually to be deposited on the bed of the Aral Sea. Now that 27,000 sq km of the original sea bed has been exposed, wind spreads these polluted sediments around the region. Sediment-rich water used for irrigation

Figure 43.1. The Aral Sea basin.

687

also contaminates the soil with toxic chemicals, which are then taken up by vegetables and other crops. The human populations of the region are, therefore, exposed to these organochlorine compounds through ingestion of the contaminated food chain, and by inhalation of the wind-blown dusts of the region.

Analysis of DDT and lindane in the blood plasma lipids of children from the Aral Sea region of Kazakhstan in 1997 revealed elevated levels of these compounds up to twenty times those of children from Sweden (Jensen *et al.* 1997). Elevated concentrations of the dioxin, TCDD, have been reported in the mothers' milk from the agricultural districts of the region. This toxic compound may have been unintentionally synthesized when the herbicide 2,4,5-trichlorphenoxyacetic acid was manufactured for use in the region. Public health reports from Uzbekistan indicate that up to 80 per cent of children in the Aral Sea region suffer from anaemia, that fertility rates are low, and that 40 per cent of children are born with abnormalities. Further epidemiological studies are required to study the exact role of organochlorine pollutants in diseases found in the people of the region (Jensen *et al.* 1997).

Physical processes responsible for the off-site transport of diffuse pollutants

Understanding technical approaches to addressing environmental problems arising from agriculture and silviculture requires knowledge of the processes and factors controlling off-site pollutant losses. Sediments and agrochemicals, such as fertilizers and pesticides, can all be transported to receiving surface and groundwaters by a variety of different surface and sub-surface hydrological pathways (see, for example, Burt 2001). Many fertilizers, pesticides and organic manures are directly applied to the soil surface, from which they are easily mobilized during the rainfall events that give rise to storm runoff. Agrochemicals can be transported by these hydrological mechanisms in dissolved form within the water and, in the case of over-land flow and some shallow subsurface routes, also in association with the soil material that has been washed from the land.

Soil erosion is a two-stage process consisting of detachment of particles and aggregates from the soil followed by their transport by the erosive agent. Rainsplash, running water and wind can all loosen and detach the soil for transport. Transporting agents can be subdivided into those processes that act areally over the soil's surface (rainsplash and sheet flow) and concentrated water flow in small channels such as rills and gullies. A final process is transport by mass movement such as soil flows, slides and creeps. The factors that control soil erosion warrant further attention here due to the ability of sediment to also carry chemical pollutants, either as a result of sorption to the soil or as part of the organic component of the soil (for example, organic nitrogen and phosphorus compounds). The factors influencing soil erosion can be grouped under three headings: erosivity, erodibility and protection. Erosivity expresses the energy or potential ability of rainfall, runoff or wind to cause erosion. Erodibility describes the susceptibility of the soil to undergo erosion and is a function of the mechanical and chemical properties of the soil. Agricultural tillage and cultivation practices can alter the erodibility of the soil through changing soil structure. Protection factors refer to the effects of vegetation as plant cover offers protection to the soil from rainfall or wind; different land uses will give rise to varying plant cover with different degrees of protection (Morgan 1986).

Nitrogen losses to the environment following fertilizer application occur in various ways: leaching and runoff in dissolved and sediment-associated form; volatilization as ammonia; and denitrification of NO_3 to N_2O and N_2. Factors controlling nitrogen loss by these different pathways include ecosystem type; soil characteristics; cropping, fertilizer and tillage practice; and prevailing weather conditions. So the management of nitrogen losses has to be tailored to a particular region. Take the example of fertilizer type. In the EU and North America, nitrogen-based fertilizers are predominantly ammonium nitrate and calcium ammonium nitrate from which leaching and denitrification account for up to 99 per cent of total nitrogen losses (Goulding 2004). In other parts of the world urea-based fertilizers are predominant. Ammonia volatilization is a relatively more important pathway for nitrogen loss from these fertilizers (e.g. on the Chinese loess plateau, volatilization accounts for up to 50 per cent of total N losses).

Phosphorus occurs in many different forms within the environment; both bound to sediment (apatite, non-apatite inorganic and organic phosphorus) and in dissolved form (as soluble reactive ortho-phosphorus). These different species of phosphorus can dictate the predominant transport pathways to surface and groundwaters. The majority of phosphorus loss from agricultural land occurs in sediment bound form as erosion products. Once transported to the aquatic environment, previously bound forms of phosphorus can be released in a bioavailable, soluble form under anoxic conditions, giving rise to problems of nutrient enrichment (eutrophication) in the water column of lakes and reservoirs.

Pesticide losses to the environment depend on a combination of the chemical properties of the pesticide itself, in addition to the same factors that influence nutrient losses (soil type, application rate and timing, weather conditions and the hydrological properties of the environment to which the pesticide has been applied). The chemical properties of pesticides that are important when considering both mechanisms of transport and environmental impact are solubility, sorption potential, vapour pressure and persistence. There are several different measures of pesticide sorption. In general terms these describe the extent to which a pesticide binds to either soil or sediment surfaces (K_d, the soil–water partition coefficent), or to fatty tissues (K_{ow}, the octanol–water partition coefficient). The former property can be used to predict whether a pesticide will be transported predominantly in dissolved form or associated with sediment. The octanol–water partition coefficient can be used to predict whether a pesticide has the potential to bioaccumulate in the environment. Persistence is an important characteristic because it determines the length of time the pesticide remains intact in the environment before it is broken down into smaller molecules, known as degradation products or metabolites. The more persistent a pesticide, the increased potential there is for a pesticide to cause harm to something other than the target organism.

Knowledge of the chemical properties of an organic agrochemical is important because these data can be used to predict the compound's transport and fate in the environment. For example, the organochlorine group of insecticides, such as DDT and dieldrin, are strongly sorbing molecules and so they are transported in association with soils and sediments. They have a high vapour pressure and are very persistent in the environment, so they can be easily volatilized into the atmosphere and transported long distances to the Arctic and Antarctic, through a process known as global distillation. These compounds are also 'lipophilic'; their high octanol–water partition coefficient means that they have a tendency to bio-accumulate in the body fat of organisms and in this way they can move through the food chain.

Technological control measures for controlling diffuse pollution

A first set of control measures focuses on limiting the amount of overland flow at a site, and the soil available for transport by water. It should be remembered that any technique that prevents soil erosion will also minimize sediment-bound pollutant transport as well. Thus the following techniques are also particularly useful for controlling of off-site phosphorus and sediment-associated pesticide transport.

Most erosion of soil from hillslopes and the transport of this sediment to rivers occurs during rainfall events of moderate frequency and magnitude (return periods of between one and five years). The return period of the dominant events (those responsible for eroding the most soil) will depend on the type of erosion process in operation at a particular site (Morgan 1986). Seasonal erosion patterns on agricultural land occur in response to farming activities combined with rainfall patterns. In agricultural systems the period between ploughing and the growth of the crop beyond seedling stage is a window of high erosion risk due to the lack of vegetation cover. Soil conservation is based on a combination of practical measures frequently targeted to this period of high erosion risk: of covering the soil to protect it from raindrop impact; increasing the infiltration capacity of soil to reduce runoff; improving aggregate stability; and increasing surface roughness to reduce the velocity of runoff and wind. Much research on experimental research stations and in government forestry and agricultural institutions focuses on matching the various alternative technical approaches to the specific soils, climate and topography of a region.

Mechanical methods control the energy available for soil erosion. There are plentiful examples of the use of terraces, bunds and contour strips in upland areas to manipulate surface topography in order to reduce the flow of water or air. Pretty (1995), however, explains how the positive results of many of these costly mechanical works have actually been extremely short-lived. Poor construction of contour banks, terraces and ridges are repeated themes from soil conservation programmes of the 1930s to the 1970s, resulting in sudden structural failure during severe storms which then resulted in extensive gully erosion. Perhaps the most important lesson to learn has been the problems that arose as a result of enforced technology transfer, without adequate consultation or participation with the people whose land was being rehabilitated. These include terraces that were too small or large to support local agricultural practices, structures that rapidly silted up, and projects that expected local people to bear the high costs of maintenance. That said, physical structures to reduce the surface flow of water are a common component of many indigenous agricultural systems throughout the world and there is widespread evidence for improved crop yield and reduced erosion following their installation as part of community-led soil conservation initiatives in many countries. Contour grass strips and planting, where water velocity is reduced by the effect of vegetation growing perpendicular to the direction of flow, is also a form of erosion control that is now widely adopted for soil conservation purposes (see discussion of buffer zones).

Agronomic measures use vegetation cover to help minimize soil erosion, and can thus be categorized as any means of providing protection for the soil from water or wind. These are the preferred conservation measures to employ because they are less expensive and deal directly with the processes that control soil erosion, such as reducing raindrop impact, increasing infiltration (hence reducing runoff volume), and reducing runoff and wind velocity. Morgan (1986) summarizes those crops that are least effective in protecting the soil as those in rows (such as cereals and maize), tall tree crops (rubber and palm oil) and low-growing crops with large leaves (e.g. sugar beet and broccoli). In these cases cover crops can be grown to reduce soil and nutrient losses. Cover crops are vegetation that is either established after the main crop or intercropped to conserve and regenerate the soil. Cover crops can perform a dual purpose, as a soil protection technique and as organic or green manure which is mulched on the soil surface to fulfil plant nutrition requirements. There are plentiful examples of the successful use of other types of mulches that act as physical protection against the rain under a wide range of climatic conditions. Pretty (1995) describes the use of twigs, branches and leaf litter in Niger and Guatemala, and straw residues in China and Ghana as organic mulches spread on to the soil surface to provide protective physical cover. Legumes or grasses can also be grown consecutively to the row crop, in rotation, as a means of offering protective cover and also improving soil fertility. However, unless the fallow crops can be grown as fodder or grazing they have no value to the farmer, and thus this technique is rarely practised in main cereal-growing areas of the world. However, rotation of stock from one pasture to the next is widely practised on grazed grass and rangelands in order to reduce soil erosion and nutrient losses by overgrazing.

Soil tillage on cultivated land can significantly influence the retention of soil and sediment-bound agrochemicals. Conventional tillage (ploughing followed by discing or tining and then planting) inverts and mixes the topsoil, leaving it bare with no vegetative cover until the next crop establishes, whereas conservation tillage practices minimize soil disturbance leaving protective residues on the soil surface which help to reduce runoff, sediment and nutrient loss. For example, in the Pampas region of Argentina; alfalfa residues are used as stubble-mulch to protect against the effects of both wind and water erosion. Not only does this incorporated and mulched stubble offer physical protection, but its bacterially mediated composition produces colloids which stabilize soil aggregates, so improving soil structure (Molina Buck 1993). Conservation tillage is a soil management system that is also growing in popularity in intensively farmed regions such as North America and Europe. For example, conservation tillage is now used on nearly 40 per cent of the land in maize production in the USA (Goulding 2004). It has been the subject of much research, especially on dry, sandy soils; on very clay rich soils; and on soils that lack structure, such as degraded soils containing a high sodium content. Alvarez (2005) reviewed the global evidence for improvements in soil organic carbon (SOC) content under nitrogen fertilizer application and conservation tillage. He concluded that reduced and no-till cultivation does lead to carbon sequestration in soils, and therefore improvements in soil structure which will help protect against soil erosion. There are as yet mixed messages whether conservation tillage reduces pesticide losses from fields. Whilst lateral herbicide losses may decline because of reduced erosion and overland flow, improved water infiltration through continuous networks of macropores formed by earthworm burrows may in fact enhance pesticide transport to surface waters under reduced tillage conditions (see, for example, Tebrugge and During 1999).

For nitrate and those pesticides that are transported predominantly in dissolved form, other techniques can be used to minimize the potential for diffuse pollution. Figure 43.2 illustrates the global balance of annual nitrogen inputs and outputs associated with farming (adapted from Mosier et al. 2004), highlighting the problem that about 60 per cent of nitrogen used each year in agriculture is lost to the environment in gaseous, dissolved or sediment-associated form. A clear link between nitrogen surplus in soils (the amount of nitrogen not removed from the soil by plant uptake) and losses of nitrogen to the environment has led to research focused on two approaches to increasing nitrogen uptake efficiency by crops: first, by careful selection of crop species, and genetic enhancement of the plant; and second, through altering the management options that determine the availability of soil and fertilizer nitrogen for uptake. Nitrogen management techniques require the crop or soil nitrogen status to be assessed prior to (prescriptive nitrogen management) or during the growing season (corrective nitrogen management) as a basis for making appropriate decisions concerning nitrogen application. Remote sensing, chlorophyll meters and near-infrared leaf nitrogen analysis are all emerging techniques for real-time measurement of leaf greenness to

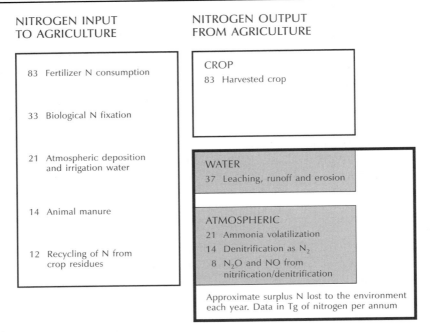

Figure 43.2. Global nitrogen flow arising from agricultural practice.
Source: Data from Mosier *et al.* (2004) based on Smil (1999).

assess crop nitrogen requirements during the growing season. Soil–crop simulation models show potential for making nitrogen prescriptions at the field scale (Giller *et al.* 2004).

As a rule, less than 0.1 per cent of the pesticide applied to the soil surface will be transported by water to surrounding surface or groundwaters. However, the toxicity of trace concentrations of many pesticides in aquatic ecosystems, and the other environmental impacts associated with their use have focused public concern on the effects and costs of pesticide residues in food and drinking water. Using data from Germany, the US and UK, contributors to Pretty (2005) have estimated the considerable annual external costs to OECD countries arising from pesticide use to be of the order of US $3.84 billion. However, the last decade has seen the adoption of both international (FAO Code of Conduct, 2002; Stockholm Convention on Persistent Organic Pollutants) and regional voluntary programmes aimed at reducing pesticide usage, tightening up the registration of new pesticide products, and also the phasing out of persistent, highly toxic pesticides and their replacement with less hazardous alternatives. In industrialized countries consumer concerns about pesticides have resulted in considerable growth in the organic market for food produce, which minimizes application of synthetically derived pesticides and fertilizers. Policy-led programmes designed to reduce pesticide use, combined with consumer pressures on pesticide sales in industrialized countries, have now increased such that the global market for synthetically derived pesticides has declined since early 2000 (Dinham 2005). Despite growing markets for pesticide manufacture and use in developing countries, there is also emerging evidence that community-led integrated pest management programmes that encourage natural pest control mechanisms can reduce pesticide use without decreasing yield (Dent 2005).

Minimizing delivery of pollutants to the stream channel or groundwater

With the intensification of agriculture, many features, such as ditches and hedgerows and wetlands, which to some extent control the transfer of soil and agrochemicals to aquatic ecosystems, have been removed from the landscape. Natural wetlands, in particular, are able to naturally ameliorate high nutrient loadings through processes such as denitrification and plant uptake. However, it is estimated that since the 1950s between 56 and 65 per cent of European and North American wetlands may have been lost, with drainage for agricultural production being cited as the main cause (OECD/IUCN 1996). Techniques for re-introducing such features into the landscape to minimize the delivery of agricultural and silvicultural diffuse pollutants to surface waters include the construction of artificial, vegetated buffer zones and wetlands.

Buffer zones

A buffer zone is a vegetated zone located between a source of pollution and the receiving surface waters. Within the buffer zone agricultural or silvicultural activity is limited or prevented, and the zone should be designed to maximize the capacity of vegetation or soil to attenuate delivery of any potential pollutant to the stream channel.

A simple example of one type of buffer zone is a no-spray area adjacent to a stream channel within which a farmer or forester may not apply pesticide. Such no-spray zones are designed to prevent spray-drift, comprising solutions of high pesticide concentration, from reaching open water bodies. Buffer zones can also comprise vegetated strips designed to minimize the transport of soil and sediment-bound nutrients (particularly phosphorus) and pesticides (Krutz *et al.* 2005) through physical trapping mechanisms. Such zones are usually located adjacent to the stream channel to act as filter and prevent sediment-rich overland flow from reaching surface waters. As agrochemicals are generally surface-applied, their concentrations in overland flow can be markedly elevated, and therefore pose a considerable threat to aquatic ecosystems.

Buffer zones have also been proven to be effective at the hillslope scale for removing nitrate in subsurface flows through denitrification. In fact, buffer strips or non-fertilized grass strips and hedges comprise one component of the 'Code of good agricultural practice' described under the EC Nitrate Directive (91/676/EEC) to control the problems of eutrophication, which are widespread in Europe. Such an application highlights the importance of two practical considerations associated with their use. First, how wide should a buffer strip be to achieve the required reduction in nitrate concentration; and, second, where in the landscape should the buffer zone be located to maximize its potential effect? Both questions require an understanding of the hydrology of the setting in which a buffer zone is to be placed. The hydrological characteristics of the setting will control the travel time of water within the zone, and thus the retention time during which denitrification can occur. The hydrology will also determine whether subsurface flow travels through the soil zone where denitrification is optimized, or bypass much of the soil through preferential pathways. For example, a buffer zone located in a floodplain containing subsurface drainage is unlikely to be particularly effective, as the majority of subsurface flow will bypass the soil profile where denitrification occurs.

Constructed wetlands

A constructed wetland is an artificial wetland environment that simulates the processes found in natural wetlands for the purpose of human use and benefit. Constructed wetlands comprise a synthetic or natural substrate and emergent and/or submerged vegetation through which water flows in either a horizontal or vertical direction. They can be designed to treat a wide range of pollutant types, and increasingly are incorporated into best management practices as a mean of controlling agricultural diffuse pollution. These people-made wetlands provide effective treatment of agricultural effluent and runoff at low costs that are comparable to conventional treatment techniques, but they can require large land areas to be effective in meeting stringent water quality standards. Current research focuses on investigating the processes responsible for removal of pollutants from wetlands, and developing criteria for wetland design and operation. Examples of current agricultural applications of constructed wetlands include treatment of dairy farmyard water (runoff, parlour washings and manure effluents), subsurface agricultural drainage on arable and grazed pasture, and pig effluent prior to land application.

Case study: the Everglades system

The state of Florida in the USA operates over 41,000 acres of constructed wetland, including the largest constructed wetland in the world (16,500 acres) in order to treat water to remove phosphorus before it enters the Florida Everglades. Agriculture is the predominant land use in the contributing watershed with crops comprising sugar cane, vegetables, lawn sod, rice and citrus. The ultimate aim of introducing this technology is to reduce total P concentration in waters of the Everglades to 10 ppb in order to achieve their ecological restoration and protection (http://www.evergladesplan.org/index.cfm).

The constructed wetlands are divided into six Stormwater Treatment Areas (STAs; Figure 43.3). The first STA has been shown to achieve a total phosphorus load reduction of 71 per cent during an initial four-year trial period. Phosphorus is removed from the water flowing through the wetland through uptake by submerged and emergent vegetation, floating plants and algae. The settling out of plant litter and suspended particulate matter also deposits organic and sediment-associated phosphorus on to the floor of the constructed wetland, where it is retained and incorporated into bed sediment.

Guidelines and best management practices

Commonly more than one technical measure has to be implemented to achieve the required environmental improvement. Therefore 'codes of good practice' for forestry and agriculture have been developed to inform land managers of the different management options that are available. In many cases such codes of practice have initially been voluntary in nature, but increasingly are becoming mandatory measures described as 'best management practices' (BMPs).

BMPs have their origin in water quality management in the United States, where they were developed as a means of tackling non-point (or diffuse) sources of pollutants (Ice 2004). Controlling diffuse sources of pollutants is more of a challenge, not least because the sources of the problem are commonly difficult to identify and isolate. Once identified, their management requires an approach that can reduce multiple sources of the pollutant spread over a wide spatial area. BMPs focus on a combination of controlling the activity that gives rise to non-point source pollution in the first instance, and also preventing the pollutant that is generated by the activity from being delivered to the stream channel or groundwater. As explained before, the non-point source pollutants arising from agricultural and silvicultural practices are usually transported to surface and groundwaters during runoff caused by rain or

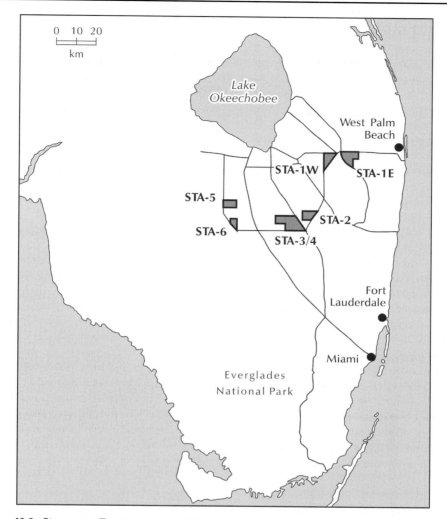

Figure 43.3. Stormwater Treatment Areas (STAs) in the Florida Everglades.

snowmelt. For this reason the effectiveness of a BMP is often linked to the successful iden-tification of where a catchment is most vulnerable, and when the most polluting runoff events might occur.

BMPs differ from other practical guidelines offered by land-use managers for reducing the impacts of agriculture and silviculture in that they are linked to regulatory requirements, and so include enforceable sanctions should the farmer or forester, for example, not comply with the requirements of the best practice. The following case study provides an example of BMPs used for controlling diffuse pollution arising from forestry practices in the USA. Similarly, in the UK the Forestry Commission has drawn up 'Forests and Water Guidelines' in order to provide advice to forest managers on working methods and measures that should be taken to address water quality and quantity issues. Compliance with these guidelines is a necessary requirement to gain approval for any forestry operation on public land, and for obtaining grants to establish or manage forest on private land (Nisbet 2001).

Case study: codes of practice and BMPs in temperate forests

Codes of forest practice generally include the following components:

- requirement for pre-harvest surveys that establish areas where logging should not occur in order to protect species or limit potential for runoff;
- field delineation of coupe boundaries which incorporate environmental factors such as buffer zones to protect streams;
- prescription of harvesting methods, and appropriate road design and drainage;
- prescription of amelioration measures to prevent excessive soil disturbance/compaction;
- sanctions for non-compliance with the code.

(Ferguson 1997)

The US Environment Protection Agency has taken a 'best management practice' approach to forest activities in order to reduce the undesirable effects of mechanized logging, amongst other practices (Ice 2004).

Two-thirds of runoff in the USA originates from its 736 million acres of forested land which are believed to be a significant source of non-point source pollution by sediment, nutrients, forest chemicals and temperature changes. Forested watersheds are often used as source areas for drinking water because of their high quality, and there is public concern about the effects of logging and other forest management activities on the water supply.

Logging and harvesting is split into eight different categories of forest practice. A series of best management practices have been established for each of the categories of: pre-harvest planning; management of streamside zones; protection of forest wetlands; minimizing delivery of pollutants to streams through appropriate road construction and maintenance; guidelines for timber harvesting; re-vegetation post-harvesting; fire management; and forest chemical management practice (Watershed Academy Web 2005). Within each general category there are numerous specific BMPs. For instance, there are 27 BMPS just for the road construction category alone.

The successful implementation of Best Management Practices requires a number of key elements. First, the extent and nature of the diffuse pollution problem has to be identified in order that the most appropriate BMPs can be selected. There is no easy 'one-size-fits-all' solution. Concentrations or loadings of sediment or an agrochemical that are considered acceptable in one catchment may cause unacceptable problems in another sensitive area. D'Arcy and Frost (2001) provides the example of the Loch Leven catchment (Scotland) where yields of soil erosion of 1 t ha^{-1} yr^{-1}, considered acceptable in other catchments, are sufficient to contribute to eutrophication problems. The propensity of a land-use activity to produce diffuse pollution will depend on the resistance and resilience of the landscape to change (Burt 2001). The efficiency with which the pollutant is delivered to the receiving watercourse may depend on the location of the land-use activity within the landscape (e.g. proximity to the river channel). For all these reasons it is desirable for the pollutant loading associated with a particular land-use activity in a particular location to be quantified before a suite of BMPs is prescribed. In practice, quantification of pollutant loads requires either intensive monitoring of storm events (when diffuse pollution events occur), or an accurate means of predicting diffuse pollution at an appropriate scale using mathematical models. The former is extremely costly, and despite much progress in recent years the latter is arguably not yet achievable in practice. The cost-effectiveness of a suite of BMPs should be established, compared with other means of preventing diffuse pollution, prior to the implementation of the management practices, otherwise the BMP may impose financial costs on the land manager without any significant environmental gain. Once it is established, the regulator needs a means of measuring the extent of uptake of any management practice, and must be able to identify any non-compliance. Appropriate sanctions need to be in place to enforce the BMP when the need arises.

Finally, an operational knowledge of the BMPs has to be successfully transferred to the land managers. This requires methods of knowledge transfer that are appropriate to the particular farming or forestry system. Lim and Douglas (2000) ascribe the failure of many soil conservation policies in the tropics to a lack of suitably trained extension services through which farmers are able to receive advice on soil conservation measures. They provide an example of severe land degradation and soil erosion from the steeplands of Malaysia Borneo where a combination of cash cropping with pineapple and partial shifting hill-rice cultivation is practised. At the time of the study government subsidies and technical advice were focused on cash cropping, paying little attention to land management, so that government officers were not trained to give advice concerning improving land management practices.

In summary, the success of BMPs depends not only on how effective they are as a suite of technological measures, but also on a whole host of other socio-economic factors which determine uptake and the extent of their implementation.

Participatory approaches to developing sustainable agricultural and silvicultural practice

It has long been recognized that social and economic factors influence a farmer or a forester's adoption and long-term maintenance of land management practices (Boardman et al. 2003; Craswell 1993). Understanding physical processes and thus designing technical responses to managing diffuse pollution is very important, but in isolation will not prevent unsustainable agricultural or silvicultural practice from taking place because of the interplay of socio-economic factors that also drive polluting activities.

Thus there is increasing recognition that agriculture and silviculture cannot be made sustainable, and diffuse pollution reduced effectively without collective action of those people who are managing the land (see, for example, Douglas 1999). Otherwise consistent, widespread improvements will not occur, as the benefits accrued by any improved farming practice may be undermined by the actions of another farmer in the same catchment. Successful resource management requires the involvement of all stakeholders with a legitimate interest in the outcome of the decision made (Burt 2001). Without the participation and collective action of rural people and land managers, sustainable agricultural practice is unlikely to occur. Studies of agricultural development initiatives show that when people have their own knowledge incorporated into the planning and implementation stage of a project they feel some ownership, so that changes in their practice are more likely to be sustained. Such research suggests that the normal mode of agricultural research, in which the results of experiments from field stations are passed on to the farming community by government officials, are not always the most effective or desirable means of information dissemination regarding best practice. As an alternative to a top-down approach to recommending improved agricultural practices to the rural community, Pretty (1995) advocates the promotion of information exchange between practitioners (e.g. farmer-to-farmer exchange) and support for schemes that encourage training in farmers' own communities and fields.

In the developing world, examples of the socio-economic factors that might influence the success or failure of sustainable agriculture or forestry practice are diverse and include land tenure, poverty, land pressure, labour availability, economic incentives and costs, indigenous technical knowledge, power and social status (Stocking and Murnaghan 2001). For example, Pretty (1995) suggests potential reasons why a farmer may not engage with technologies that aim to conserve soil (and water) as follows:

- a lack of locally appropriate knowledge or skills (perhaps due to recent introduction to agricultural or silvicultural practice, resettlement or migration to new area);
- an unwillingness to invest in economic costs associated with conservation, particularly if in a politically unstable area, threatened by conflict, or where tenure on land is uncertain;
- labour shortages or rising labour costs caused by migration or better opportunities for income earning in other sectors;
- previous conservation programmes they have encountered have been misguided or ineffective;
- response to policies encouraging an increase in food production above conservation.

In the more economically developed countries, legislation is beginning to reflect the importance of stakeholder participation in the development and successful implementation of agricultural practice. One of the earliest examples of the adoption of this approach is the Landcare movement in Australia, which was designed to achieve a more sustainable use of Australia's farming lands, enabling the formation of local groups of stakeholders engaging in community-based action. Landcare has demonstrated that groups of farmers can work together with government and rural communities voluntarily in order to tackle water quality and other land degradation problems (Curtis and De Lacey 1996).

Policy instruments for sustainable agricultural and silvicultural practice

A recognition of the importance of socio-economic factors is encapsulated in the term 'sustainable agricultural and silvicultural development'. Sustainable development in the agricultural and forestry sectors has been described by FAO as 'development [that] ... conserves land, water, plant and animal genetic resources, is environmentally non-degrading, technically appropriate, economically viable and socially acceptable' (Ongley 1996).

The requirements of sustainable agriculture and forestry have resulted in the development of watershed or catchment management programmes that have become the preferred policy instrument by which diffuse pollution from agriculture and forestry is tackled in both the developed and developing world. A catchment management programme can be defined as an holistic employment of management techniques and strategies for an entire river basin. Such programmes are currently considered to be the most appropriate approach to ensure the conservation and sustainability of water and soil resources through addressing environmental, economic and social factors in an integrated manner. As such, their scope extends beyond the environmental concerns arising from agriculture and forestry, to encompass any land use within a catchment which may affect the quality or quantity of the hydrological cycle.

This approach underpins legislation such as the EC Water Framework Directive 2000/60/EC, which requires EU member states to assess and take action to ensure good ecological status of their surface and groundwaters, taking into account social, economic and environmental factors. Key to the implementation of this legislation is the development of river basin management plans. Similarly, in the USA the Total Maximum Daily Load (TMDL) programme requires individual states to develop watershed management plans for polluted water bodies that address both point and diffuse sources. Lim and Douglas (2000) note that watershed management programmes are being developed across Asia with the aim of improving environmental management and planning land use in an integrated manner. Organizations such as the international Food and Agriculture Organization are actively promoting watershed management activities, as an appropriate approach for not only water and soil resource management but also for addressing issues of food security and poverty alleviation. Newson *et al.* (2000) discuss the potential future advantages and major challenges that face catchment management planning in a UK context.

Catchment management plans are just one example of a growing range of communicative, regulatory and economic policy instruments being used to tackle agricultural diffuse pollution across the world. Financial incentives, in particular, are becoming increasingly common. In more economically developed countries farmers are highly influenced by economic incentive and rapidly switch crops and change farming practices in response to changing market prices and quota arrangements (Boardman *et al.* 2003). In countries of the Organization for Economic Co-operation and Development (OECD), agricultural support policies encourage monoculture, intensification (increased production) and/or bringing marginal land into production and hence exacerbating environmental pressures. Examples of support policies identified by the OECD as having the greatest potential impact on production (accounting for three-quarters of the total support to OECD farmers in 2003) are market price support, output payments (per output unit produced), and input subsidies (which may apply to fertilizers, pesticides, water and energy). For instance, in Europe the Common Agricultural Policy (CAP) has been the driving force for advances in technology through high price support (Latacz-Lohmann and Hodge 2003). Throughout north-western Europe farmers have been encouraged, through CAP subsidies, to grow autumn-sown cereals and spring-sown maize on sensitive, erosion-prone land. Similarly, increased fertilizer use, conversion of grassland to arable crops and higher stocking densities, cited as causes of rising nitrate concentrations in surface and groundwaters, can all be attributed to the influence of regional CAP policy. Up until the 1980s economic policies (such as the CAP) did not take into account impacts on the environment but have generally encouraged intensification at any environmental cost. Now we are seeing a gradual shift away from output-related support and towards area-based payments, and payments for the supply of environmental goods. This change in policy direction has come about not just as a result of demand for environmental quality, but also through the budgetary pressures of surplus production and demands for a reduction in global trade-distorting measures.

Conclusion

There are many technological solutions available for minimizing the pollution arising from agricultural and silvicultural practice, either preventative in nature or designed to minimize the delivery and impact of agrochemicals on the surrounding environment. On their own, however, these technical solutions will not solve the problem of environmental degradation by farming and silvicultural activity. The importance of socio-economic factors in determining the nature of agricultural and silvicultural practices, and their consequent impact on the environment, are now fully recognized. The strong influence of economic driving forces, in particular, is being tackled through changes in support policy at a regional and international scale.

At the farm and catchment scale, the participatory involvement of local communities and land managers in integrated land and water management planning for the future is increasingly viewed as an essential component of any initiative to tackle rural diffuse pollution. A further challenge is to develop and refine a range of methodologies and tools to support decision-making at the farm and catchment scale in order to develop environmentally sensitive, sustainable agricultural and silvicultural practice.

Further reading

Burt, T.P. (2001) Integrated management of sensitive catchement systems. *Catena* 42, 275–290.
Mosier, A.R., Syers J.K. and Freney J.R. (2004) Agriculture and the Nitrogen Cycle: Assessing the impacts of fertiliser use on food production and the environment. *Scope* 65, Washington: Island Press.
Pretty, J.N. (2005) *The Pesticide Detox: Towards a more sustainable agriculture*. London: EarthScan Publications Ltd.
Website for the Food and Agriculture Organisation of the United Nations (FAO) http://www.foa.org/

References

Ali, A.M.S. (2004) Technological change in agriculture and land degradation in Bangladesh: a case study. *Land Degradation and Development* 15, 283–98.
Alvarez, R. (2005) A review of nitrogen fertiliser and conservation tillage effects on soil organic carbon storage. *Soil Use and Management* 21 (1), 38–52.
Boardman, J. (2002) The need for soil conservation in Britain – revisited. *Area* 34 (3), 419–27.
Boardman, J., Poesen, J. and Evans, R. (2003) Socio-economic factors in soil erosion and conservation. *Environmental Science and Policy* 6, 1–6.
Brazier, R. (2004) Quantifying soil erosion by water in the UK: a review of monitoring and modelling approaches. *Progress in Physical Geography* 28 (3), 340–65.
Burt, T.P. (2001) Integrated management of sensitive catchment systems. *Catena* 42, 275–90.
Conway, G.R. and Pretty, J.N. (1991) *Unwelcome Harvest: Agriculture and Pollution*. London: Earthscan Publications.
Craswell, E.T. (1993) Soil erosion and conservation in West Africa. In D. Pimentel (ed.) *World Soil Erosion and Conservation*, pp. 257–76. Cambridge: Cambridge University Press.
Curtis, A. and De Lacey, T. (1996) Landcare in Australia: does it make a difference? *Journal of Environmental Management* 46, 119–37.
D'Arcy, B. and Frost, A. (2001) The role of best management practices in alleviating water quality problems associated with diffuse pollution. *The Science of the Total Environment* 265, 359–67.
Dent, D. (2005) Overview of agrobiologicals and alternatives to synthetic pesticides. In J.N. Pretty (ed.) *The Pesticide Detox: Towards a More Sustainable Agriculture*, pp. 70–82. London: EarthScan Publications.
Dinham, B. (2005) Corporations and pesticides. In J.N. Pretty (ed.) *The Pesticide Detox: Towards a More Sustainable Agriculture*, pp. 55–69. London: EarthScan Publications.
Douglas, I. (1999) Hydrological investigations of forest disturbance and land cover impacts in South-East Asia: a review. *Philosophical Transactions of the Royal Society of London B* 354, 1725–38.
El-Swaify, S.A. (1993) Soil erosion and conservation in the humid tropics. In D. Pimentel (ed.) *World Soil Erosion and Conservation*, pp. 233–56. Cambridge: Cambridge University Press.

FAO (2002) International Code of Conduct on the Distribution and Use of Pesticides. Revised version adopted by the Hundred and Twenty-third session of the FAO Council in November 2002. http://www.fao.org/AG/AGP/AGPP/Pesticid/Code/PM_Code.htm (accessed 11th July 2006).

FAO (2003) State of the World's Forests 2003. Rome: Food and Agriculture Organization of the United Nations.

FAOSTAT data (2005) http://faostat.fao.org/ (accessed November 2005).

Ferguson, I.S. (1997) Sustainable Forest Management. Oxford: Oxford University Press.

Giller, K.E., Chalk, P., Dobermann, A., Hammond, L., Heffer, P., Ladha, J.K., Nyamudeza, P., Maene, L., Ssali, H. and Freney, J. (2004) Emerging technologies to increase the efficiency of use of fertiliser nitrogen. In A.R. Mosier, J.K. Syers and J.R. Freney (eds) Agriculture and the Nitrogen Cycle: Assessing the Impacts of Fertilizer Use on Food Production and the Environment (Scope 65), pp. 35–52. Washington: Island Press.

Gisladottir, G. and Stocking, M. (2005) Land degradation control and its global environmental benefits. Land Degradation and Development 16, 99–112.

Goulding, K. (2004) Pathways and losses of fertilizer nitrogen at different scales. In A.R. Mosier, J.K. Syers and J.R. Freney (eds) Agriculture and the Nitrogen Cycle: Assessing the Impacts of Fertilizer Use on Food Production and the Environment (Scope 65), pp. 209–20. Washington: Island Press.

Hayes, T.B., Collins, A., Lee, M., Mendoza, M., Noriega, N., Stuart, A.A. and Vonk, A. (2002) Hermaphroditic, demasculinized frogs after exposure to the herbicide atrazine at low ecologically relevant doses. Proceedings of the National Academy of Sciences 99, 5476–80.

Ice, G. (2004) History of innovative best management practice development and its role in addressing water quality limited waterbodies. Journal of Environmental Engineering 130 (6), 684–9.

Jensen, S., Mazhitova, Z. and Zetterstrom, R. (1997) Environmental pollution and child health in the Aral Sea region in Kazakhstan. The Science of the Total Environment 206, 187–93.

Krutz, L.J., Zablotowicz, R.M. and Matocha, M.A. (2005) Reducing herbicide runoff from agricultural fields with vegetative filter strips: a review. Weed Science 53 (3), 353–67.

Lal, R. (1993) Soil erosion and conservation in West Africa. In D. Pimentel (ed.) World Soil Erosion and Conservation, pp. 7–26. Cambridge: Cambridge University Press.

Latacz-Lohmann, U. and Hodge, I. (2003) European agri-environmental policy for the 21st century. The Australian Journal of Agricultural and Resource Economics 47 (1), 123–39.

Lim, J.N.W. and Douglas, I. (2000) Land management policy and practice in a steepland agricultural area: a Malaysian example. Land Degradation and Development 11, 51–61.

Molina Buck, J.S. (1993) Soil erosion and conservation in Argentina. In D. Pimentel (ed.) World Soil Erosion and Conservation, pp. 171–92. Cambridge: Cambridge University Press.

Morgan, R.P.C. (1986) Soil Erosion and Conservation. Essex: Longman Group UK.

Mosier, A.R., Syers, J.K. and Freney, J.R. (2004) Nitrogen fertilizer: an essential component of increased food, feed and fiber consumption. In A.R. Mosier, J.K. Syers and J.R. Freney (eds) Agriculture and the Nitrogen Cycle: Assessing the Impacts of Fertilizer Use on Food Production and the Environment (Scope 65), pp. 3–18. Washington: Island Press.

Newson, M., Gardiner, J. and Slater, S. (2000) Planning and managing for the future. In M. Acreman (ed.) The Hydrology of the UK, pp. 134–49. London: Routledge.

Nisbet, T.R. (2001) The role of forest management in controlling diffuse pollution in UK forestry. Forest Ecology and Management 143, 215–26.

Novotny, V. (2005) The next step – incorporating diffuse pollution abatement into watershed management. Water, Science and Technology 51 (3–4), 1–9.

OECD/IUCN (1996) Guidelines for Aid Agencies for Improved Conservation and Sustainable Use of Tropical and Sub-tropical Wetlands. Paris: OECD.

Ongley, E.D. (1996) Control of Water Pollution from Agriculture (FAO Irrigation and Drainage Paper 55). Rome: Food and Agriculture Organization of the United Nations. (Available at http://www.fao.org/docrep/W2598E/w2598e00.htm#Contents)

Pimentel, D. (1993) Overview. In: D. Pimentel (ed.) World Soil Erosion and Conservation, pp. 1–6. Cambridge: Cambridge University Press.

Pretty, J.N. (1995) *Regenerating Agriculture: Policies and Practice for Sustainability and Self-reliance.* London: EarthScan Publications.

——(2005) *The Pesticide Detox: Towards a More Sustainable Agriculture.* London: EarthScan Publications.

Smil, V. (1999) Nitrogen in crop production: an account of global flows. *Global Biogeochemical Cycles* 13, 647–62.

Stocking, M.A. and Murnaghan, N. (2001) *Handbook for the Field Assessment of Land Degradation.* London: EarthScan Publications.

Syvitski, J.P.M. (2003) Supply and flux of sediment along hydrological pathways: research for the 21st century. *Global and Planetary Change* 39, 1–11.

Tebrugge, F. and During, R.A. (1999) Reducing tillage intensity – a review of results from long term study in Germany. *Soil and Tillage Research* 53 (1), 15–28.

UNEP (1992) *The World Environment 1972–1992: Two Decades of Challenge.* London: Chapman and Hall.

Usmanova, R.M. (2003) Aral Sea and sustainable development. *Water, Science and Technology* 47 (7–8), 41–7.

Vos, J.G.M., Dybing, E., Greim, H.A., Ladefoged O., Lambre, C., Tarazona, J.V., Brandt, I. and Vethaak, A.D. (2000) Health effects of endocrine-disrupting chemicals on wildlife with special reference to the European situation. *Critical Reviews in Toxicology* 30, 71–133.

Walling, D.E. and Fang, D. (2003) Recent trends in the suspended loads of the world's rivers. *Global and Planetary Change* 39, 111–26.

Watershed Academy Web (2005) http://www.epa.gov/watertrain/ (last accessed December 2005).

Williams, R., Burt, T. and Brighty, G. (2000) River water quality. In M. Acreman (ed.) *The Hydrology of the UK*, pp. 134–49. London: Routledge.

Worldwatch Institute (2003) *Vital Signs 2003.* Washington: Worldwatch Institute.

44

Landscapes of waste

Ian Douglas

Waste is something most people like to forget. People put waste in a bin or throw it away and do not care what happens to it afterwards. It is, as a 1960s UK report on sewage treatment said, 'Out of sight, out of mind', and, as Emmanuelle Le Dorlot says, 'distance' or 'separation' is the key concept in the relation between people and waste (Dorlot 2005): the further away from it as possible, the better. Yet for many people the distance from waste is far less than they might think. Many parts of modern settlements are built over former rubbish dumps and the sites of waste deposition in past centuries. It has changed the character of many places. Waste is part of our lives, our history, our environment and our society. There is a legacy of waste in today's geography and it remains a priority issue for contemporary society and for future generations.

Conventionally, waste is divided into categories according to three main sources: human settlements activities, industrial, and agricultural sources (Table 44.1). It can also be subdivided into liquid and solid wastes, the former conventionally being discharged through sewage systems and the latter being dealt with through collection at source, including the familiar dustbins and waste skips. However, waste can also be classified as coming from either a 'point source' or a 'non-point source'. Point sources are those represented by specific outlets, such as pipes or chimneys, as for example at industrial processing plants. Non-point sources include runoff from urban areas, acid rain and liquid wastes from agricultural fields and grazing lands.

It is preferable to think of waste as resources or materials ready for a new use. The key idea is expressed by the three Rs: Reduce, Re-use, and Recycle (Table 44.2). It has long been recognized that solid wastes are an integral part of the total resources stream and that the entire technology now directed towards disposal, destruction or hiding should be redirected towards a viable resource recovery system (Jacobs and Biswas 1972). In many cases the waste consists of diverse materials mixed together, and many people around the world make a living from sorting waste, from the rag-pickers in the streets and dumps of Indian and African cities to the mechanical engineers developing machinery to separate paper, plastic bags, steel and aluminium from other domestic waste in European and American cities. This sorting is necessary to find the components of waste that have a market value and can be recycled.

More provocatively, waste is now also thought of as an 'experienced resource'. The discipline of industrial ecology that has emerged since 1980 (Erkman 2002) considers that waste

Table 44.1. Major types of waste and associated contaminants

Category	Types of waste	Source	Scale of impact
Human settlements sources			
Domestic rubbish	Metals, plastics, glass, organics, leachates containing nutrients	Point and/or non-point	Local
Sewage	Residual pharmaceuticals, pathogens, fertilizers, organic matter	Point and/or non-point	Local to regional
Hazardous household materials	Cleaners, paints, garden chemicals batteries, solvents	Point and/or non-point	Local
Heating and cooling source emissions	PAHs, particulates	Point and/or non-point	Local to regional
Transport-related emissions	PAHs, nitrogen, particulates (PM_{10}), lubricating oils, coolants, lead	Non-point	Regional
Industrial sources			
Construction and demolition waste	Particulates, paints, lead, PAHs	Point source	Local to regional
Manufacturing and chemical wastes	Highly variable, but particularly solvents, synthetic chemicals and/or metals	Point source	Local to regional
Mining	Metal-contaminated spoil and waters, acid mine drainage waters	Point source	Local to regional
Transportation accidents	Spillages of oils and chemicals	Point source	Local to regional
Energy: power generation (fossil fuels and nuclear)	Metals. PAHs, fixed nitrogen, waste heat. Fly ash, spent radioactive fuel, CO_2, SO_4	Point source	Local, regional and global
Agricultural production			
Livestock rearing (grazing and intensive)	Pathogens, including species-jumping viruses and bacteria, nutrients, slats, organic compounds, pharmaceutical residuals, including antibiotics	Mainly non-point source (except slurry tanks)	Local to regional
Crop production	Residuals from agricultural chemicals, nitrogen and phosphorous, plant debris	Point and non-point sources	Local
Land clearance and rangeland maintenance	PAHs and particulates from fires, nitrogen and greenhouse gases	Point and non-point sources	Local to regional

Table 44.2. Methods of dealing with waste

Process	Advantages	Problems	Examples
Reduction	Ideal solution, now being sought by regulation, such as European Packaging legislation. Per-bag fees for garbage collection reduce waste volumes by about 50 per cent.	Packaging is encouraged by advertising.	'Producer responsibility' for packaging in Europe Per bag fees in Perkasie, Philadelphia, USA.
Re-use	Ability to re-use manufactured items, such as the traditional glass milk bottle. Cuts materials consumption. Reduces materials and energy costs of manufacturing.	May need incentives for re-use, such as deposit on glass bottles as levied in France and some states of the USA.	Re-filling of computer printer ink containers; re-use of office carpet plastic components; re-use of consumer electronica.
Industrial symbiosis	One factory's unused material becomes the raw material for another factory's production.	Relies on consistency in supply from produced to consumer.	The sharing of resources between firms in Kalundborg, Denmark.
Recycling			
(1) Rag picking	Traditional scavenging and separation of re-sellable materials, particularly by slum-dwellers as in Indian cities, or by specific social groups, as in Cairo. Also includes groups living on or around major waste dumps, as in many Asian and Latin American cities.	Only commercially viable materials collected. Major health risks for women and children involved in rag-picking.	Zabaleen in Cairo; minadors on the dumps in Quito.
(2) Composting	Possible at household and at industrial scales. In developed countries requires prior separation, but in developing countries where organic content is over 60 per cent separation is not so important.	Separate collection poses extra costs for municipal collection, but compost can be sold as garden fertilizer. Requires action by individual households at domestic level.	Subsidized provision of household composting bins in UK. Municipal composting in Ahmedabad, India, and Manchester, UK.
(3) Separate household collections	Collection of glass, metal, paper and garden waste separated by the household into different containers. Highly effective where private sector collection is viable, e.g. in affluent areas of low latitude cities.	Municipal services in wealthy countries may have low participation rates and be expensive. Now encouraged by legislation.	Widely practised in Europe and North America.

(Continued on next page)

Table 44.2 (continued)

Process	Advantages	Problems	Examples
(4) Community recycling points	Provision of marked bins at convenient points such as shopping centres for people to deposit glass, aluminium, old clothes, paper, plastic bottles.	Not all sites provide bins for all types of recyclable material. Requires consumer to take initiative. Relatively few opportunities for plastics recycling.	Well-established in Europe.
(5) Industrial links	Recycling of construction and demolition waste, either on-site for new buildings or off-site as aggregate or road foundations. Re-use of office carpet plastic components.	Many agencies may be concerned about possible contamination of construction and demolition waste; consistency of supply and quality of material.	Re-use of power station fly-ash for building-component manufacture.
Open dumping	Easy solution for those getting rid of waste, providing land available; possibilities of on-site scavenging and materials sorting for recycling.	Major human health and environmental risks, especially contamination of nearby water supplies and rivers; release of greenhouse gases.	Major municipal dumps in Asian, African and Latin American cities.
Landfill	Sanitary landfill (and land raise) under controlled containment conditions and contain potentially harmful leachates and permit power generation from methane. Toxic waste requires specific containment measures.	Requires adequate land supply. Many authorities now have to transport material hundreds of kilometres to suitable sites. Aftercare essential to avoid contaminant release.	Former Freshkills landfill, Staten Island, New York; Leslie Spit site, Toronto.
Incineration	Ranges from open burning, to controlled combustion in specially designed plants with controls on emissions to the atmosphere. Controlled incineration greatly reduces the bulk of waste to be deposited in landfill and facilitates energy extraction for electricity generation or for combined heat and power schemes. Metals can be extracted for recycling.	Open burning is dangerous. Emissions from incinerators need to be tightly controlled. Modern high-temperature incinerators can avoid dangerous emissions.	Modern incinerators in European cities, Singapore and elsewhere; open burning of waste in squatter settlements in African cities.
'Fly-tipping'	The easy, but illegal, dumping of waste in any place perceived to be convenient, whether in the street immediately outside the gate of an individual house compound, on a piece of 'waste ground' or in a watercourse.	Major nuisance and pollution problems, including the 'plastics pollution' of windblown plastic bags and problems associated with illegally dumped refrigerators and toxic hospital waste.	Dumping of old furniture and building rubble on derelict land in British cities; dumping of private hospital waste close to stream in Nigeria.

is not inevitable. If industrial systems can be managed to use resources not required in one process in another process, then waste declines. Crushed concrete from the demolition of an old building can be used as aggregate for new construction. In this view waste is an indicator of the inefficiency of our resource-use systems. In nature, the by-products of one organic process supply nutrients to other processes and matter is continually recycled. Industrial ecology argues that by tracking material and energy flows at a variety of scales, from the industrial process to the total city and national flows, and in terms of individual elements like lead and copper to the total urban metabolism, we can optimize resource flows, reduce pollution risks and recycle substances in an environmentally acceptable manner (Lifset and Graedel 2002).

For the present, however, we are far from achieving the industrial ecologists' goal. It is being managed in different ways, and with varying levels of effectiveness, around the world. Much waste, from cigarette packets to building rubble, is simply discarded. Waste is accumulating everywhere, carried by winds and ocean currents into remote seas and wilderness areas, but most particularly on the edge of towns and cities. For centuries the dumping of waste has been changing the character of places.

In thinking of how waste alters the character of places and influences landscapes, the prime concern is solid waste, particularly that from mining, industry and urban living. Many mining landscapes are dominated by heaps of spoil, the waste rock excavated when gaining access to the minerals beneath the ground. Many industrial areas also have waste disposal sites and commercial landfills that receive waste materials, including construction and demolition waste (C&D waste) produced by the construction industry. Most cities have either controlled waste disposal sites or large waste dumps that receive municipal waste from homes and offices. Thus, around all major human settlements, landscapes have been modified by the dumping of waste.

Cities built on waste

In the beginning of the twenty-first century there is a major global contrast between human settlements that have controlled, tightly regulated sanitary landfills and those that have poorly regulated rubbish dumps. Historically, towns and cities had dumps outside their walls which had few controls and little management. Over time, these mounds of waste became the substrate of new extensions of the urban area and waste disposal moved further out, often into the pits created by the extraction of clay for brick-making.

Ancient and mediaeval cities used any convenient place as a waste dump. By 3000 BC, the people of Knossos, Crete, were using landfill sites, where waste was placed in large pits and covered with layers of earth. By 500 BC, the government in Athens had opened the first municipal landfill site 1.5 km outside the city. From about 800 to 1500, at Senlis in Picardy, France, the floor of the first-century Roman amphitheatre was used as a rubbish tip and the surrounding structure as a quarry, so that by the nineteenth century there was just a mound known as 'La Fosse'. Mediaeval London was characterized by dumps of waste from shops, households and markets, with some parts of the city, such as Farringdon Without and Portsoken, being known for their dung-heaps and rubbish dumps (Ackroyd 2000).

In thirteenth-century Britain, waste was burned on open fires in houses, or, with sewage, was thrown out into the streets. Wastes from fishmongers, poulterers and butchers added to the problem. Pigsties were built outside people's doors and rotting food blocked the gutters. Despite the passing in 1297 of a law requiring householders to keep the front of their houses clear, little changed. Further orders and proclamations were ignored. Disease and vermin were constant dangers, with the Black Death in 1348/9 killing two-thirds of the inhabitants of London. From the mid-fourteenth century, men were employed as rakers, to cart the filth away to pits outside the city gates or to the river, to be taken away by boats. In 1408, Henry IV ruled that household rubbish should be kept inside until the rakers took it, and that forfeits should be paid if it were not removed.

As cities expanded they spread over the mounds and hillocks of waste deposited by previous generations, such as the Telld'Hama in Syria, the Kjoekkenmoedingsen in the Netherlands, the Monte Testaccio at Rome, and the labyrinth of the Jardin des Plantes at Paris. Generations of houses are built on the rubbish and the remains of former dwellings. In Chick Lane, London, in 1597, it was found that 12 cottages and 30 tenements had been erected on a former public waste dump (Ackroyd 2000). Several parts of London have the name 'Mount ... '. For example, Mount Pleasant, now the site of the Royal Mail sorting office, was part of a series of rubbish dumps outside the city wall in Clerkenwell that were cleared in 1790 to make way for a new prison. The name is ironical, being described as a reflection of the bad odours emanating from the dump which in 1720 was described as 'a dirty place with a few ill buildings'. Whitechapel Mount, to the east of the city, was an early example of 'uncontrolled landraise' known for its views over Limehouse and Shadwell.

The rebuilding of London on old landfills continues into the twenty-first century, such areas being among the 'brownfield sites', former urban and industrial land, on which new urban development is encouraged by government. For example, Laban, a centre for contemporary dance housed in a translucent building of polycarbonate in the London suburb of Deptford, was built on the site of a former rubbish dump on the banks of a muddy tidal creek. The Deptford creekside had been heavily industrialized for centuries and thus extensive decontamination was required before construction began.

The beginnings of urban recycling

Despite the growth of waste dumps, over the centuries there was also much recycling of waste materials. By 1000 BC, in Europe, bronze was recovered from waste and re-used, and composting was practised in China. People fed vegetable waste to animals and used manure and green waste as fertilizer. During the seventeenth century, Japanese cities organized garbage collection (Hanley 1987), but elsewhere effective municipal waste management began only in the nineteenth century (McNeill 2001). However, by the mid-twentieth century cities in the richer countries that had suffered serious sanitation problems following rapid urban growth had more or less solved issues of waste disposal, sewage collection and waste water treatment (McNeill 2001). They were beginning to look for alternatives to controlled sanitary landfills and to encourage greater recycling. The cities of poorer countries either received organized municipal waste collection systems later than the richer states, or had little chance to develop one, as their populations and the waste-producing potential grew far faster. (See Plates 44.1 and 44.2.)

Waste in the modern world; global disparities and contrasts

Both municipal and industrial solid waste generation continues to expand. Wealth is the key factor in how much solid waste a city produces. As per capita incomes increase in newly industrializing countries, so the per capita waste production grows (Table 44.3). However, the actual trend in waste production in any one city depends on the incentives for waste reduction and recycling, as well as on the degree of increasing affluence. Singapore, for example, has actively encouraged waste minimization (Figure 44.1). Waste in developing country cities has a higher proportion of organic matter than that in wealthy countries,

Plate 44.1. Ragpickers sorting collected waste materials for recycling in a middleman's depot in an Ahmedabad, India squatter settlement. Photograph by Ian Douglas.

Plate 44.2. A modern sanitary landfill in Greater Manchester showing a bulldozer spreading material and a plastic liner. Photograph by Nigel Lawson.

Table 44.3. Per capita municipal waste production in cities around the world

Country	City	Per capita kg per year	Organic %	Data source
USA	Washington, DC	1,246		6
UAE	Dubai	840		2
Australia	Sydney	750	50	1
USA	New York	620	41	2
Oman	Oman	551		7
Kuwait	Kuwait	511		7
Canada	Toronto	510		2
Mexico	Mexico City	485	55	4
France	Paris	475		2
Bahrain	Bahrain	430		7
Indonesia	Padang	360		5
Brazil	So Paulo	352		6
Thailand	Bangkok	321		6
China	Shanghai	320		2
Ecuador	Quito	281		6
Mexico	rural towns	250	65	4
Indonesia	Jakarta	240	up to 75	5
Philippines	Metro Manila	209		7
Turkey	Istanbul	200	48	3
Ivory Coast	Abidjan	200		6
Nigeria	Lagos	90		8

Source: [1] Durney 2002; [2] Fyfe 2002; [3] Kocasoy 2002; [4] Ojeda-Benitez *et al.* 2000; [5] World Bank 2003; [6] WRI 1996; [7] UNEP 2002; [8] Oga 2000.

because traditional rag-picking and waste collection systems remove metals, wood, cardboard, paper, glass and many plastics from the municipal waste stream and because there is a much lower per capita consumption of consumer goods with packaging. Municipal waste in England contains about 38 per cent organic matter, that in India over 60 per cent.

By the twenty-first century, wealthy cities were experiencing rising costs of waste disposal. In the European Community, directives were forcing countries the recycle more, to reduce landfilling and to tightly control toxic waste and packaging materials. Many countries introduced charges encouraging recycling, for example on glass bottles or alternatives, such as the charge on plastic bags in Ireland, or for excess waste, as with the per bag charge for waste collection in parts of Pennsylvania. As land for new waste disposal became both expensive and difficult to acquire, countries such as the United Kingdom found it necessary to introduce landfill taxes, while European legislation forced local authorities to increase the percentage of household waste that was recycled. Incineration was favoured by many waste disposal agencies as a means of reducing the volume of material to go to landfill, increasing the mass of metals available for recycling and gaining the economic benefits of energy from waste to make electricity. Nevertheless, the majority of the world's waste is still being dumped or landfilled. This continues to build up legacies, and perhaps problems, for the future.

The legacy of past waste: changing the character of places

Former waste dumps change their characteristics and land uses over time and eventually only the historical archives and old maps retain the record of their origin. Yet these places are part of one of the most recent geological formations, the deposits created by society and made by human action. They show that in many parts of the world, people are the most powerful geological agent, shifting more material and building up new land surfaces faster than natural processes, even those whose effects are accelerated by human disturbance of ecosystems.

On the edges of many large urban areas, landfills and waste dumps receive hundreds of truck-loads of material per day, so that they grow rapidly. When dumping ceases, they may be left for a decade or more for the material to settle and decompose before they are converted to new uses.

The Diemerzeedijk–Diemerpark, Netherlands

Among the dramatic changes to former landfills are those at the Diemerzeedijk–Diemerpark in the Netherlands, formerly a disposal site for household refuse, construction and demolition waste, mildly polluted dredging mud and chemical waste. High levels of soil contamination occurred, including high concentrations of carcinogenic dioxin. As it was not feasible to remove and remediate this poison, it was decided to isolate the area by installing underground walls all round the site, covering the fill material with foil, and placing a layer of clean soil on top. Water has to be pumped out continuously to prevent it from escaping into the wider environment.

After closure in 1983, the former waste dump was left to nature for 15 years until the start of redevelopment in 1998. Invasions of organisms turned the area into a magnificent wildlife site, rich in wild flowers in summer. A large colony of rabbits, many mice and wood pigeons became staple food for foxes, hawks and ermines (*Mustela erminea*). There were also many song-birds, butterflies and several bumblebee species. Remarkable for its high biodiversity and a high portion of colourful species, the site could be regarded as an emergent ecosystem with novel patterns and levels of interaction between species (Diemerzeedijk–Diemerpark 2005).

Mount Trashmore, Virginia, USA

Near the coastal towns of Hampton and Virginia Beach in the late 1960s, the existing landfill was running out of space to bury waste, so Roland E. Dorer, the director of the State Department of Health, Insect and Vector Control, proposed raising the level of the waste above ground and creating a new land form: making a mountain out of municipal waste. The proposed mountain was to be 100 m wide by 300 m long, built from cells of sanitary landfill covered with six feet of soil. In so doing account had to be taken of the odour from the landfill, groundwater contamination, methane emissions and, most importantly, the stability of the garbage (Smith and Harlow 2002).

Municipal waste and clean soil form the foundation of the mountain; 50 cm square units of garbage and 15 cm of clean soil were compacted. These trash and soil sandwiches were then piled on top of each other and compacted further with bulldozers. Then the mountain was buried under a further 2 metres of clean soil. In 2002, it was capped with rubber to prevent water from running through the mountain.

The residents of Hampton had to endure the odour during construction, but now the new stable landform has been developed into a recreational area open from 7.30 a.m. to sunset attracting approximately 900,000 visitors a year. Facilities include two recreational lakes, four large and many small picnic shelters, playground areas, a basketball court, four volleyball areas, parking, a walking trail, vending machines and restrooms. Soil tests have revealed little or no effects on the area's groundwater. The surface soils are still subject to monthly checks and the accumulated decomposition gases are released through several pipes at prescribed times. Careful construction and post-dumping monitoring help to achieve an attractive landscape that people can enjoy.

The Leslie Street Spit in Toronto, Canada

In 1959, the Toronto Harbour Commissioners (now known as the Toronto Port Authority) began to construct of a spit of land at the base of Leslie Street in anticipation of an expansion of Toronto's port facilities in 1959. It became apparent in the 1970s that these port facilities were not going to be required; however, given ongoing redevelopment pressures in Toronto, the Leslie Street Spit continued receiving construction materials for lakefill. In the 1980s, the Leslie Street Spit was used to contain dredged sediments from the Lower Don River and Keating Channel as part of the Don River flood control activities. It continues to receive dredged sediment from the Lower Don and clean construction material from redevelopment sites. The dredged material was deposited in three cells, each designed as a confined disposal facility. Monitoring of concentrations of polychlorinated biphenyls, metals and pesticides shows that the disposal cells are effective in their containment of the dredged material and that contaminants are not leaking into Lake Ontario (Douglas 2002).

Leslie Street Spit is now 5 kilometres long, provides a land base of 160 hectares and a watered embayment area of 100 hectares. The northern side of the Spit has been renamed Tommy Thompson Park. The citizens' group Friends of the Spit actively works to develop the area as a conservation site for studying natural ecological succession. This Canadian example illustrates that with adequate care and attention, surplus material can be dumped in a creative way to build new landforms and wildlife conservation opportunities.

The Nanjido landfill, South Korea

Since 1980, some 890 sanitary landfills have been built in South Korea (Kim *et al.* 2004). Because these landfills are close to growing urban areas, those that are closed have become potential redevelopment sites. One of the first of these sites to be restored, the Nanjido landfill, took municipal industrial and C&D waste from Seoul from 1978 to 1997, growing to occupy 272 ha with a maximum waste depth of 104 m and a total waste mass of 177 million tonnes. The summit surfaces of the landfill about 96 m above the adjacent Han River have converted into recreation areas, sports grounds and golf courses. However, natural recolonization by grasses, trees and shrubs occurred on the untouched slopes, giving a succession towards natural woodland. The public have come to accept the new vegetation that now blends with the surrounding landscape. The slope vegetation provides a source of seeds for the colonization of other unvegetated areas on the site. However, because the original cover soil for the landfill came from urban construction sites and the sweepings or streets, the new vegetation contains many exotic species (Kim *et al.* 2004) and so may not, over the long term, evolve into a replicate of the natural woodland.

Wider re-use of former landfills

The trend towards redevelopment of landfill sites for recreation found in South Korea, North America and Europe is being replicated elsewhere. With 13 closed landfills in Hong Kong, a restoration programme to reduce the potential safety and health risks of the closed landfills has been launched. The restored landfills are landscaped to provide green areas for urban people to enjoy a healthy living environment. The sites will have such recreational facilities as golf courses, multi-purpose grass pitches, rest gardens and ecological parks. Use of landfill gas provides a non-fossil-fuel energy source, so the gases emitted from the closed landfills are extracted to drive generators, and where that is not possible they are burnt in flares on site.

Many former landfills within 100 km of London, especially those in former brick clay and gravel pits, have been restored to farmland. A landfill site at South Ockendon in Essex, England, was restored in two ways, in one case with 1 m layer of London clay above the rubbish and its capping material, and in the other with a 700 mm layer of London clay together with a top layer of 300 mm depth of screened material. Although both surface layers lacked N and organic matter, they contained adequate available P and K. Experiments showed that additional fertilizer was needed to promote successful crop growth, but although all crops did better on the screenings compared to London clay, establishment was patchy as a result of weed control problems.

Transformations of open waste dumps

Not all transformations of waste dumps are as easy and uncontroversial as the Diemerpark or Mount Trashmore. Perhaps one of the most notorious of the world's waste dumps was the Smokey Mountain in the Philippines, which began to receive waste in 1954, when Manila's then Department of Public Service began to dump garbage close to a peaceful fishing village known as Barrio Magdaragat. Waste effluent from the dump polluted the inshore waters, causing the local fishermen to lose their livelihoods. The fishermen started to scavenge the dump for recyclable materials, soon to be joined by squatters until there were several hundred families living on or immediately around the dump. At its height of activity, the garbage mountain was 40 metres high, occupied 34 ha of Manila Bay, and was receiving 650 tonnes of waste per day from throughout the metropolitan area. When garbage disposal there was stopped and the site stabilized, the Tondo Urban Development Project was started, financed with borrowings from the World Bank through the National Housing Association.

However, a new problem area arose with the alternative dumping site at Payatas, northeast of Quezon City, opened in 1973, and before 2000 receiving up to 2,000 tons of waste every day. The site was not chosen on environmental grounds, but as a matter of political convenience. It was less than 0.5 km from a river contributing to Manila's main water supply. A community of 50,000 to 60,000 people lived on the rubbish, collecting and selling recyclable materials. This precarious way of living exposes people not only to health risks from contaminants and fires, but also to dangers of landslides in the garbage. On 10 July 2000, after a week of heavy rain, a large portion of the Payatas garbage-mountain collapsed, engulfing 400 houses that had been built around the mountain's perimeter. Downed power lines sparked the escaping methane gas, producing large fires despite the rain. Two hundred and twenty people died. Public and government reactions were strong. Communities with similar open dumps blocked access for incoming dump trucks, while in other such areas squatters and salvagers were relocated. The dump was closed in 2000. The only designed landfill in the metropolis, the San Mateo Sanitary Landfill, was closed by a court injunction because the garbage trucks carrying waste to the site were causing severe traffic and air pollution close to expensive, smart houses. A garbage crisis developed. The government tried sending garbage by sea to Semirara Island in the Central Philippines, but local government action on the island stopped the sending of waste from Manila. Metro Manila officials considered eight provinces around Metro Manila as alternative dumpsites. A proposal for a major incineration plant was surrounded by allegations of corruption and failed, while intense lobbying by radical environmental groups succeeded in outlawing incineration in the Congress. Although legally even toxic hospital waste can no longer be incinerated, fires on unofficial open dumps continue to release methane and dioxins and other toxic substances to the atmosphere. Lack of firm action has led to a continuing waste management crisis.

Environmental issues associated with waste dumps

Contamination of soils and rivers by poorly managed waste disposal has been a persistent problem for centuries. Lead from mines worked by the Romans nearly 2,000 years ago still pollutes some rivers in the Pennines in northern England (Berry and Plater 1998). In November 2005, waste from a chemical plant in northeastern China threatened the water supply of the city of Harbin (http://news.bbc.co.uk/2/hi/asia-pacific/4473666.stm). Land-sliding and the collapse of waste dumps frequently threatens homes. One of the worst cases was the mass movement of a coal waste tip on the valley side above the village of Aberfan in Wales in 1966 when 126 people were killed (Nichol 2001).

A good example of the issues concerned with coal mine waste is provided by coal mines in Upper Silesia, Poland, where over 50 million tonnes of waste rock are produced each year (Szczepanska and Twardowska 1999). About 40 per cent of this waste is re-used, either for backfilling underground mines or as construction material and fill in various civil engineering projects. The remainder is added to surface waste mounds. These coal-mine waste dumps are a significant source of groundwater contamination. Total dissolved solid concentrations in groundwater beneath and down-gradient from the dumps have increased by 1–2 orders of magnitude above the natural background levels since 1970, and levels of SO_4, Fe, Zn and Mn have also increased. Acid mine waters drain out towards neighbouring streams affecting aquatic organisms. So severe is the contamination that the water is not fit for any human use. Many communities have had to abandon their groundwater wells and instead have to have piped supplies brought from outside the area (Szczepanska and Twardowska 1999).

Waste dumps that are developed with tight controls from landfilling operations are termed 'landraise'. A case is made for such disposal landforms in terms of the need to allow for settlement and surface drainage, landscape improvements, mitigation of existing sites, creation of viewpoints, provision of recreational after-uses and screening of unsightly developments. Objections to them include the incongruity of the landforms created, closure of views, impacts of bunding, and increased problems with litter, dust and noise (Gray 2000).

Managing waste in the future

Reduction

Major efforts to reduce waste are embedded in legislation concerned with packaging and charges for items such as plastic bags. New technologies have provided challenges, such as for the disposal of redundant, out-dated consumer electronics. Basically the issue is to cut down on materials consumption through greater efficiency in industrial, commercial and daily living processes. However, legislation and incentives to reduce waste seem to be necessary.

Re-use

Many disposable items could be changed for re-usable items, from the commonplace milk bottle to the components of computers or motor cars. Some countries have legislation that encourages return of bottles for re-use, others promote re-use of components. One person's old furniture can be of immense value to someone who does not have enough. Old clothes can be re-used. The ideas even apply to old buildings, from the warehouses converted to smart apartments in cities to the barn conversions to holiday homes in the countryside.

Recycling

Recycling has become a priority for many local authorities faced with rising costs of landfill, opposition to incineration and legislative pressures (Table 44.4). Packaging materials are a major component of the waste put in garbage bins in wealthy cities. In 2000, while Denmark, Austria, Belgium and the Netherlands were achieving a recycling of over 20 per cent of plastics waste, Ireland, Greece and Portugal were recycling less than 10 per cent. Although recycling appropriate plastic waste streams is important, prevention of (unnecessary) packaging has the highest priority. Innovations in packaging will be the most effective way of reducing plastics use and the volume of waste. Together with optimized recycling of selected streams combined with other recovery options, this will ensure the environmental impact is minimized across the whole life-cycle (Mayne 2004).

UK local authorities have to increase the amount of waste that is recycled (Table 44.5). New separate collections of glass, paper, metal and garden waste have been introduced in many areas. In 2005, the UK Department for Environment, Food and Rural Affairs (Defra)

Table 44.4. Current and future targets of the European Packaging and Packaging Waste Directive 1994

Target	Current min–max	Future min–max
Global recovery	50–65%	60–75/85
Global recycling	25–45%	55/65–70/no max
Plastics recycling	15% min	22/22.5% [a]

Note: [a]Possible limitations to mechanical recycling and back to monomer.

Table 44.5. Best and worst local authorities at recycling in England in 2003–4

Council	Recycling and composting rate 2003–4 (% total waste)	Target for 2003–4	Increase since 2002–3
Lichfield	46	26	4
Daventry	42	30	−2
East Hampshire	36	16	11
Isle of Wight	35	26	4
St Edmundsbury	35	33	5
Boston	20	10	13
Newham	6	10	1
Tower Hamlets	5	10	2
Kettering	5	10	1
Liverpool	4	8	2
Isles of Scilly	0	16	n/a

showed that the 2004 recycling rate for household waste was 17.7 per cent – compared to 14.5 per cent in 2002–3. For the first time, the amount of municipal waste being sent to landfill fell, from 29.4 million tonnes in 2002–3 to 29.1 million tonnes in 2003–4, a decrease of about 1 per cent.

Incineration

The first conversion of waste to energy in Britain began in 1874 when the first 'destructor' was designed and constructed in Nottingham. Destructors were prototype incineration plants which burnt mixed fuel, producing steam to generate electricity. During the next 30 years, 250 destructors were built in Britain. They were opposed because of the emissions of ashes, dust and charred paper which fell on to adjacent neighbourhoods. By 1945 incineration was at an all-time low, to re-emerge in the 1960s but with opposition later on the grounds of dioxin emissions. Nonetheless, in many ways incineration is the best option for the waste that remains to be dealt with after all efforts to minimize that which is to be disposed of are put into action.

Materials such as the sludge from sewage treatment plants are appropriate for incineration. Burning of sewage sludge has several benefits. It deals with the problems of release of metals through the spreading of sludge on agricultural land. Although there are fears about the release of dioxins through incineration, the burning of sludge in a modern incinerator actually removes dioxins. Incineration also reduces emissions associated with the traffic involved in the spreading of sludge. It produces electricity through a process that is self-sufficient in energy, and indeed it can be argued that sludge is more valuable as an energy source than it is as a fertilizer. The cement industry and some power stations are already using sludge as a substitute for fossil fuels (Lowe and Hudson 2005). The ash from the incinerators has to go to landfill sites, but the volume involved is small compared to the original volume of the sludge. Total installed incineration capacity for sewage sludge in the UK is approximately 390,000 t per year out of a total sludge production of around 1,200,000 t per year.

The future of landfill

While landfill and landraise continue to change the character of places, their future is under scrutiny. Landfill, even under strictly controlled conditions, is no longer seen as a sensible land use. In 1995 the UK government set a new, aspirational waste management target to reduce the proportion of controlled waste going to landfill to 60 per cent by 2005. UK municipal waste production in 2005 was 25 million tons per year and growing by 3 per cent per year, but landfilling has to be reduced to meet EU Landfill Directive requirements. Twenty-five per cent must go to other forms of waste use and processing by 2010, 50 per cent by 2013 and 65 per cent by 2020 (Alexiou and Moore 2005).

Landfill gas (LFG) is a flammable and potentially harmful mixture of methane, carbon dioxide and a large number of trace constituents produced when waste decays in landfills. The need to prevent harm from LFG emissions is enshrined in site regulations. Control measures such as gas extraction wells and multi-layered liners are now being implemented on a wide scale. Using LFG as an energy source complements the environmental protection requirements and brings in extra income to site operators. First used to generate electricity in the UK in 1985, government support saw 49 power generation projects with a combined capacity of 80 MWe, generating 447 GWh of electricity annually by 1993. In addition, the

12 direct-use schemes using LFG as a fuel for kilns and boilers produced a further 9,200 GJ as heat (Brown and Maunder 1994).

'Fly-tipping'

Although landfill regulation and taxation became a major deterrent to waste disposal, they have had two contrary effects: encouraging responsible people to recycle and to produce less waste, while pushing less responsible people to dump illegally – a process termed 'fly-tipping' in Britain. Collectively, English local authorities are now spending £100–150 million each year on clearing up after fly-tipping (Defra 2004). For example, in the period April 2004 to October 2004, the city of Salford (population 220,000) had 2,986 reports of fly-tipping which cost them £169,622 (Priestley 2004, quoting 'Flycapture' data). While 65 per cent of cases involve bin bags or volumes less than 0.5 cu. m (Webb and Marshall 2004), by mass and volume most of the fly-tipped material is construction and demolition waste (C&D waste) and white goods (refrigerators, washing machines and similar domestic items), both of which are potentially recyclable in some form (Office of the Deputy Prime Minister 2004; Department of Trade and Industry 1999). In north London, more than 70,000 tonnes of construction waste was fly-tipped in 2003, costing more than £1 million to clean up, and avoiding £135,000 in landfill taxes (Vidal 2004). Small businesses, such as the local building repair man, that are liable to pay disposal charges at local authority waste transfer stations, may be tempted to fly-tip to avoid the costs of disposing of rubble and waste. The market forces at the enterprise scale thus become a major factor in waste disposal behaviour.

Sustainable communities and industrial ecology

The link between the economy and the environment provides an important motivation for industrial ecology. Industrial ecology creates symbiotic relationships that promote both environmental quality and economic development, and thus can promote sustainable communities in several ways. First, waste products from one industry can provide input materials for another industry, which can reduce the receiving industry's costs of resource inputs. Economic theory suggests that as non-renewable resources become scarcer, their prices will rise; accordingly, reduced reliance on non-renewable resources can reduce costs of production. This can also promote environmental quality because it reduces the use of raw materials. Second, industrial ecology has the potential to reduce waste disposal costs because waste products now serve as inputs for other industrial or municipal processes. This can reduce pollution because industrial by-products are re-used, rather than discharged directly into the biosphere. Third, industrial ecology can increase industry profits because materials previously regarded as waste now have economic value. Niche industries can evolve to fill in the gaps between other industries to utilize and sell waste materials in an exchange of energy and material flows (Dunn and Steinemann 1998). This view is not without problems. For industrial ecology to mimic the natural model, one should strive towards increasing the flow from producers to recyclers and from consumers to recyclers. This would reduce the energy and raw materials required. In theory, the optimal path towards achieving this would seem to be to physically connect production, consumption and recycling activities in a locally integrated system with short distances between the actors involved. As Life Cycle Analysis (LCA) shows, production and end-consumption are often geographically separated in modern societal systems (Korhonen 2002).

One way of ensuring this ideal re-use of materials is to develop eco-industrial parks in which one industrial process uses substances or energy left over from the operation of another. The Kalundborg EIP in Denmark is the most frequently cited success story of industrial symbiosis, but detailed knowledge of the materials, energy, economic, environmental and social effects of this industry cluster is not widespread (Tibbs 1992; Richards and Frosch 1997; Kibert *et al.* 2000). Kalundborg has attracted world-wide attention for the spontaneous industrial recycling linkages that developed there between four large industrial plants, the municipality and a few smaller businesses (Desrochers 2002; Ehrenfeld and Chertow 2002). The Asnaes power company supplies residual steam from its coal-fired power plant to a Statoil refinery and in exchange receives refinery gas that was formerly flared as waste. The power plant burns the refinery gas to generate electricity and steam and sends its excess steam to a fish farm, to a district heating system serving 3,500 homes and to a Novo Nordisk pharmaceutical and enzyme manufacturing plant. Sludge from the fish farm and pharmaceutical processes becomes fertilizer for nearby farms. Surplus yeast from the biotechnology plant's production of insulin is shipped to farmers for pig food. The fly ash from the power plant is sent to a cement company, while gypsum produced by the power plant's desulphurization process goes to a gypsum wallboard company (Gyproc). Finally, the Statoil refinery removes sulphur from its natural gas and sells it to Kemira, a sulphuric acid manufacturer. The prime motivation is economic.

In Jyväskylä, Finland, an 'industrial symbiosis' evolved around the existing economic and energy supply system structures and emerged because the use of wastes proved profitable. Environmental pressure was not a specific cause for the development of the system, although concerns about air quality and tighter emission standards may prompt the development of more symbiotic practices (Desrochers 2002).

A survey (Gibbs *et al.* 2005) revealed a substantial difference between by-product exchanges in Europe and the USA. Examples of such exchanges included the recycling of shellfish waste into animal feed and soil improvers, together with the recovery of trace elements for healthcare products; the recycling of waste paper into the production of insulation materials; recycling tyres into paving materials; and energy and waste water cascading. Generally this survey indicated that there are few successful sites where interchange of waste and cascading of energy has so far been really successful.

Perhaps the most complete industrial ecology application in the building industry is collaboration between carpet tile manufacturers and raw materials producers for the industry. Much of the polymer material used in the carpet tiles on the floors of commercial premises can be recycled into the manufacture of new carpet backing material. When carpets are being removed for replacement, contractors can peel off the recyclable material and send it back to the manufacturers for re-use. For the first time, manufacturers are competing not only on the function and cost of their products but also on the ability of the materials to be kept in a closed-loop system of manufacture–use–recovery–manufacture (Kibert *et al.* 2000).

Environmental concerns are seldom a prime driver for industrialists to recycle or re-use waste. Examining recycling, remanufacturing and waste treatment (RRWT) firms in Texas, Lyons (2005) found that the majority (and, ultimately all those that survive) do so by identifying and profitably exploiting new market opportunities that have emerge(d) from stricter government regulation, consumer demand, pressure from environmental groups, or technological changes that render unprofitable wastes profitable. However, while there are large numbers of RRWT firms operating today, it is unlikely that they can become central players in the production, consumption and waste cycle loop until fundamental changes in the way we produce and consume products are achieved (Lyons 2005).

Conclusions

Waste continues to transform places. Today the tallest operational chimney in many urban areas is that of the local incinerator or waste transfer plant. Landraise is creating new land-forms and providing new opportunities for innovative redevelopment for recreational, industrial and even residential purposes. There is even talk of landfill mining for aggregates, extracting the sand and gravel material that could have been recycled earlier. Providing what consumers expect but at the same time reducing the volume of waste and using resources more efficiently remains a major societal challenge. Unfortunately, for so much of the time, waste remains 'out of sight, out of mind'. But while the expanding low-latitude cities still have tens of thousands of people who live by rag-picking and waste scavenging, the geo-graphical significance of waste cannot be ignored. As in so many aspects of good environ-mental management, we know what we can do, the technology is there, but the political will is lacking.

Further reading

Ayres, R.U. and Ayres, L.W. (2002) (eds) *A Handbook of Industrial Ecology.* Cheltenham: Edward Elgar.

Clark, M., Smith, D. and Blowers, A. (1992) (eds) *Waste Location: Spatial Aspects of Waste Management, Hazards and Disposal.* London: Routledge.

Fyfe, W. (2002) Waste: the global mass and its management. In Douglas, I. (ed.) *Causes and Consequences of Global Environmental Change* (Volume 3 of *Encyclopaedia of Global Environmental Change,* editor-in-chief Ted Munn), pp. 709–13. Chichester: Wiley.

Hinga, K.R., Batchelor, A., Ahmed, M.T., Osibanjo, O., Lewis, N., Pilson, M., Faruqui, N. and Wagener, A. (2005) Waste processing and detoxification. In R. Hassan, R. Scholes and N. Ash (eds) *Ecosystems and Human Well-being: Current State and Trends, Volume 1. Findings of the Condition and Trends Working Group of the Millennium Ecosystem Assessment,* pp. 417–39. Washington: Island Press.

Jacobs, H. and Biswas, A.K. (1972) *Solid Wastes Management; Problems and Perspectives.* Ottawa: Research Coordination Directorate, Policy Planning and Research Service.

McNeill, J.R. (2001) *Something New Under the Sun: An Environmental History of the Twentieth-century World.* New York: Norton.

Office of the Deputy Prime Minister (2004) *Survey of Arisings and Use of Construction, Demolition and Excavation Waste as Aggregate in England in 2003.* London: Office of the Deputy Prime Minister.

Priestley, W. (Salford City Council Environment Directorate) (2004) Personal communication.

Sellers, G. and Cook, H.F. (2005) *An Investigation into the Growth of Crops on a Closed Landfill Site using London Clay and Screening as Restoration Materials.* Available at http://www.soton.ac.uk/~sunrise/wye.htm (accessed 1 September 2005).

References

Ackroyd, P. (2000) *London – The Biography.* London: Chatto and Windus.

Alexiou, I. E. and Moore, L. (2005) Pilot door-to-door estate recycling services in inner-city London. *WEJ Journal of the Chartered Institution of Water and Environmental Management* 19, 306–11.

Berry, A. and Plater, A.J. (1998) Rates of tidal sedimentation from records of industrial pollution and environmental magnetism: the Tees estuary, north-east England. *Water, Air, and Soil Pollution* 106, 463–79.

Brown, K.A. and Maunder, D.H. (1994) Exploitation of landfill gas. *Water Science and Technology* 30, 145–51.

719

Defra (2004) *Local Environmental Quality: Fly-tipping.* Available at http://www.defra.gov.uk/environment/localenv/flytipping/ (accessed 28 December 2004).

Department of Trade and Industry (1999) *Unwanted White Goods. A Guide to Re-use.* London: Department of Trade and Industry.

Desrochers, P. (2002) Regional development and inter-industry recycling linkages: some historical perspectives. *Entrepreneurship and Regional Development* 14, 49–65.

Diemerzeedijk–Diemerpark (2005) http://www.ecocam.com/nature/Diemerpark.html (accessed 31 August 2005).

Dorlot, E. Le (2005) *Les déchets ménagers: pour une recherche interdisciplinaire,* Strates (online), 11 – Jeune recherche, la vitalité d'un laboratoire. Available at http://strates.revues.org/document410.html (published online 14 January 2005).

Douglas, I. (2002) Geomorphological change for urbanization and industry. In I. Douglas (ed.) *Causes and Consequences of Global Environmental Change* (Volume 3 of *Encyclopaedia of Global Environmental Change,* editor-in-chief Ted Munn), pp. 338–44. Chichester: Wiley.

Dunn, B.C. and Steinemann, A. (1998) Industrial ecology for sustainable communities. *Journal of Environmental Planning and Management* 41, 661–72.

Durney, A. (2002) Industrial ecology: an Australia case study. In R.U. Ayres and L.W. Ayres (eds) *A Handbook of Industrial Ecology,* pp. 311–21. Cheltenham: Edward Elgar.

Ehrenfeld, J.R. and Chertow, M.R. (2002) Industrial symbiosis: the legacy of Kalundborg. In R.U. Ayres and L.W. Ayres (eds) *A Handbook of Industrial Ecology,* pp. 334–48. Cheltenham, Edward Elgar.

Erkman, S. (2002) The recent history of industrial ecology. In R.U. Ayres and L.W. Ayres (eds) *A Handbook of Industrial Ecology,* pp. 27–35. Cheltenham, Edward Elgar.

Fyfe, W. (2002) Waste: the global mass and its management. In I. Douglas (ed.) *Causes and Consequences of Global Environmental Change* (Volume 3 of *Encyclopaedia of Global Environmental Change,* editor-in-chief Ted Munn), pp. 709–13. Chichester: Wiley.

Gibbs, D.C., Deutz, P. and Proctor, A.L. (2005) Industrial ecology and eco-industrial development: a potential paradigm for local and regional development? *Regional Studies* 39, 171–83.

Gray, J.M. (2000) Landraising of waste in England, 1990–2000: a survey of the geomorphological issues raised by planning applications. *Applied Geography* 22, 209–34.

Hanley, S.B. (1987) Urban sanitation in pre-industrial Japan. *Journal of Interdisciplinary History* 18, 1–26.

Jacobs, H. and Biswas, A.K. (1972) *Solid Wastes Management; Problems and Perspectives.* Ottawa: Research Coordination Directorate, Policy Planning and Research Service.

Kibert, C.J., Sendzimir, J. and Guy, B. (2000) Construction ecology and metabolism: natural system analogues for a sustainable built environment. *Construction Management and Economics* 18, 903–16.

Kim, K.D., Lee, E.J. and Cho, K-H. (2004) The plant community of Nanjido, a representative nonsanitary landfill in South Korea: implications for restoration alternatives. *Water, Air, and Soil Pollution* 154, 167–85.

Kocasoy, G. (2002) Waste dumps in megacities: case study of Istanbul. In I. Douglas (ed.) *Causes and Consequences of Global Environmental Change* (Volume 3 of *Encyclopaedia of Global Environmental Change,* editor-in-chief Ted Munn), pp. 707–9. Chichester: Wiley.

Korhonen, J. (2002) Two paths to industrial ecology: applying the product-based and geographical approaches. *Journal of Environmental Planning and Management* 45 (1), 39–57.

Lifset, R. and Graedel, T.F. (2002) Industrial ecology: goals and definitions. In R.U. Ayres and L.W. Ayres (eds) *A Handbook of Industrial Ecology,* pp. 3–15. Cheltenham: Edward Elgar.

Lowe, P. and Hudson, J.A. (2005) Incineration – is there a case? *WEJ Journal of the Chartered Institution of Water and Environmental Management* 19, 286–95.

Lyons, D. (2005) Integrating waste, manufacturing and industrial symbiosis: an analysis of recycling, remanufacturing and waste treatment firms in Texas. *Local Environment* 10, 71–86.

McNeill, J.R. (2001) *Something New Under the Sun: An Environmental History of the Twentieth-century World.* New York: Norton.

Mayne, N. (2004) Status and prospects of plastics waste recovery in Western Europe. Address to Belgian Polymer Group Symposium on Plastics Recycling: Present Status and New Developments, Universiteit Gent, 12 March 2004.

Nichol, D. (2001) Landslides and landslide management in South Wales. *Quarterly Journal of Engineering Geology and Hydrogeology* 34, 415–16.

Office of the Deputy Prime Minister (2004) *Survey of Arisings and Use of Construction, Demolition and Excavation Waste as Aggregate in England in 2003*. London: Office of the Deputy Prime Minister.

Ogu, V.I. (2000) Private sector participation and municipal waste management in Benin City, Nigeria. *Environment and Urbanization* 12 (2) 103–17.

Ojeda-Benitez, S., de Vega, C.A. and Ramírez-Barreto, M.E. (2000) The potential for recycling household waste: a case study from Mexicali, Mexico. *Environment and Urbanization* 12 (2), 163–73.

Richards, D.J. and Frosch, R.A. (1997) The industrial green game: overview and perspectives. In D.J. Richards (ed.) *The Industrial Green Game*. Washington DC: National Academy Press.

Szczepanska, J. and Twardowska, I. (1999) Distribution and environmental impact of coal-mining wastes in Upper Silesia, Poland. *Environmental Geology* 38, 249–58.

Smith, B.S. and Harlow, G.E. (2002) *Conceptual Hydrogeologic Framework of the Shallow Aquifer System at Virginia Beach, Virginia* (Water Resources Investigations Report 01–4262). Seattle: US Geological Survey.

Tibbs, H. (1992) Industrial ecology: an agenda for industry. *Whole Earth Review* 77, 4–19.

UNEP (United Nations Environment Programme) (2002) *Global Environment Outlook 3*. London: Earthscan.

Vidal, J. (2004) Crime gangs fuel explosion in fly-tipping. *Guardian* 22 September.

Webb, B. and Marshall, B. (2004) *A Problem-orientated Approach to Fly-tipping*. London: Jill Dando Institute of Crime Science, University College.

World Bank (2003) *Indonesia Environment Monitor 2003*. Jakarta: The World Bank Indonesia Office.

WRI (World Resources Institute) (1996) *World Resources 1996–97*. Oxford: Oxford University Press.

45

River management

D.A. Sear

Introduction and definitions

River management is a hard term to define! This arises because the practice of managing rivers has evolved over time to incorporate different disciplines and user groups. Further, there is a geographic and cultural dimension to the attitude and practice of river management that influences its objectives. For example, Penning-Rowsell and Tunstall (1996) differentiate between river management objectives of those societies who view the river and floodplain as supporting agriculture (e.g. Nile civilizations), and those whose interest is dominated by protection of aquatic environment. Similarly it is possible to distinguish approaches in terms of hydrological and climatic regime; thus those regions of the world experiencing development in an arid climatic regime have evolved different expressions of river management from those whose climate provides year-long river flows. Cosgrove and Petts (1990), Newson (1997) and more recently Downs and Gregory (2004) all highlight the importance of the historical development of societies in defining what constitutes river management. Technological innovations and the communication of ideas and practice have had a major impact on the evolution of river management. This is perhaps most dramatically expressed in the growth of river impoundments and the reduction in indigenous small-scale, water harvesting (see Newson 1997 for examples). Thus the term 'river management' means different things to different communities at different times in their cultural and political history.

Downs and Gregory (2004) provide a formal definition of river management, drawing on the legal definitions for a river to differentiate between the physical scale of activity (Table 45.1) compared to river channel management and water resource management. It is debateable whether this definition is accurate, since the origin of a river's bed, banks and water is ultimately derived from the upstream catchment through hydrological and geomorphic processes. Thus it is possible to argue that the term 'river management' should include consideration of those actions that are taken by society on the catchment land-surface and within the floodplain and river networks that influence the pattern of natural processes relative to an undisturbed state. However, as Table 45.1 indicates, this scale of emphasis is widely recognized under the term 'catchment management'. Finally, one should recognize that river, catchment and floodplain management are a subset of environmental management.

Table 45.1. Definitions and distinctions between activities that collectively constitute river management

Term	Possible definition	Example
River channel management	The modification or manipulation of the river bed and banks for the benefit of humanity whilst sustaining ecological function in the long term.	Downs and Thorne (1998) – construction of bank protection or restoration of in-stream physical habitats.
Floodplain management	The operation of an overall programme of corrective and preventive measures for reducing flood damage, including but not limited to emergency preparedness plans, flood control works, and floodplain management regulations.	Floodplain Management Group (http://www.floodplain.org/Join%20The%20FMA.htm) – construction of flood dykes (embankments) to contain floodwaters within the channel, or the modification of such structures to restore floodplain ecosystems.
River management	The modification and manipulation of the river bed, banks and flows for the benefits of humanity whilst sustaining ecological function in the long term.	Downs and Gregory (2004) – channel modifications, flow measurement, flow augmentation.
Catchment management	The integration of land and water management practices for the benefit of humanity and the freshwater ecosystem over short–long time periods.	DEFRA (2004) – diffuse pollution control, afforestation for slope stabilization, river channel modification, restoration of floodplain wetlands.
Integrated river basin management (IRBM)	'The process of coordinating conservation, management and development of water, land and related resources across sectors within a given river basin, in order to maximize the economic and social benefits derived from water resources in an equitable manner while preserving and, where necessary, restoring freshwater ecosystems.'	WWF (http://www.gwpforum.org) – definition based on the Global Water Partnership. Similar to catchment management though with a strong emphasis on planning actions in a strategic and coordinated fashion.
Water resources management	The collection, distribution and allocation of surface and subsurface freshwater flows.	Downs et al. (2004) – water grids, flow augmentation and abstraction policies and practice, reservoir construction and operation.
Environmental management	The process whereby the Earth's bioenvironmental systems are used to supply resources to humanity whilst retaining sanative and life–supporting ecosystems.	Goudie (1994) – shoreline management, waste management, management of climate change impacts, river management, soil conservation.

This is helpful since inevitably river systems intersect with other terrestrial, marine and lacustrine environments.

Fundamentally, river management involves the manipulation of channel flows and the physical characteristics of a channel in order to meet human needs and (more recently) those of the other biotic communities. Furthermore, these actions are now required to be undertaken in a manner that does not impose on the ability of future generations to experience these benefits. However, because the definition of river management changes over time, what we undertake today as river management may have as much to do with past actions taken under different social and political conditions, as it does with the goals espoused in current legislation. An extreme example of the influence of past river management activity that is influencing current river management policy and practice is river restoration.

River management is an ongoing activity as rivers tend to 'undo' the modifications made to them by people. For example, dredged channels silt up, sluice mechanisms deteriorate with age, levees and dams may suffer seepage or catastrophic failure. An important component of river management, therefore, is river maintenance – the operation by which the character and function of the managed river is preserved over time.

A brief history of river management

The management of rivers has a long history and as such has played an important part in the development of cultural responses to rivers. Downs and Gregory (2004), building on the work of Cosgrove and Petts (1990) and Newson (1997), identify six chronological phases of river use that influenced way in which rivers were managed (Table 45.2).

In the 1950s–1970s, river management was characterized by flow regulation, channel modification and drainage programmes with little regard for river environments and in-stream biota (Newson 1997; Downs and Gregory 2004). Projects were often large scale (technology permissive) with multi-functional goals (e.g. water supply, flood control, land development). From the 1970s to the early 1990s, river management in developed societies progressively changed in response to recognition of the scale of environmental impact and increasingly strong legislative protection for the environment (e.g. the 1972 Clean Water Act 'to restore and maintain the chemical, physical and biological integrity of the Nation's Water' in the United States and the UK's 1988 Wildlife and Countryside Act). However, in the relatively pristine environments of less developed countries, technology transfer and wealthy-country funding for development resulted in rapid implementation of hydrological regulation and forms of channel management practices that would not have met the new environmental standards (Downs and Gregory 2004; Petts 1995).

A key characteristic of the engineering tradition in river management has been the view of the river channel as a separate, steady state system that is manageable over short timescales and reach-focused spatial scales (Lewin et al. 1988). This was continued through the period of river conservation and into the period of channel restoration. Thus, although transition into the era of environmental preservation and restoration initiated a change in management thinking, as Newson (1988) has commented, this change was only partial. Engineering approaches to river restoration in the period to date, though using information from different disciplines such as geomorphology (Hey and Thorne 1986; Thorne et al. 1996; Downs and Thorne 1998), are characterized by the same static design concepts, often including protection of the river bed and banks in order to maintain the design (River Restoration Centre 1999; Shields 1996). Similarly, both the *Flood Studies Report* from 1975 (NERC

Table 45.2. Six phases of river utilization and associated river management

Phase	Characteristic development	Management methods employed
1 Hydraulic civilizations	River flow regulation Irrigation Land reclamation	Dam construction River diversions Ditch building Land drainage
2 Pre-Industrial Revolution	Flow regulation Drainage schemes Weir construction Navigation Timber transport	Land drainage In-channel structures Can construction Dredging Channelization
3 Industrial Revolution	Industrial mill weirs Cooling water Power generation Irrigation Water supply	Dam construction Canal building River diversions Channelization
4 Late nineteenth–mid-twentieth century	River flow regulation Multiple use and conjunctive river projects Flood defence	Large dam construction Channelization River diversions Hard bank protection River basin planning
5 Second half of twentieth century	River flow regulation Integrated use river projects Flood control Conservation management Re-management of rivers	Large dam construction River basin planning Channelization Hard and soft bank protection River diversions Restoration and enhancement projects Hydrological/hydraulic modelling.
6 Late twentieth–early twenty-first century	Conservation management Re-management of rivers Dam removal Sustainable use river projects Climate change impact management Flood risk management	Integrated river basin planning Re-regulation of flows Restoration and enhancement Hybrid and soft bank protection. Broad scale modelling Formal stakeholder consultation.

Source: After Downs and Gregory (2004); Newson (1997).

1975) and its 1999 revision in the *Flood Estimation Handbook* (Centre for Ecology and Hydrology 1998) explicitly assumed that hydrological regimes were stable (Box 45.1).

The notion of a *dynamic* river system has a deep root in the academic literature (Gregory 1977). The conceptualization of river systems as controllable, steady state systems in which dynamics can be controlled, however, is one of the most pervasive of legacies from the early history of river management. Thus stakeholders within the catchment community have become used to the concept of precise levelling of flood banks, precision cutting of channel dimensions, and a riverscape which has become stabilized. In contrast, Lewin *et al.* (1988) have argued that in an era of environmental change, regime theory is irreconcilable with the emerging picture of dynamic and often geomorphologically sensitive (*sensu* Brunsden 2001) river systems.

Throughout this period approaches to river management have been based around the notion of setting and achieving targets. In flood control, river regulation and water quality management, such targets are often quantified in spuriously 'certain' terms, implicitly

Box 45.1. River and catchment management impacts on a small lowland stream, the Hermitage stream, Hampshire

Prior to 1945, the catchment of the Hermitage stream was predominantly mixed woodland and pasture, with a channel network dominated by sinuous (Sinuosity = 1.4) woodland streams. Urban development was limited and road and rail communications were also modest for a catchment of 19 sq km (Figure 45.1a, catchment map). Urban development policy post-war witnessed a change towards expansion of selected towns to accommodate the rapidly growing population. This resulted in a dramatic change in land use between 1950 and 1990 peaking in the period 1965–1976, during which time the catchment of the Hermitage stream changed from a dominantly woodland and agricultural land use to one dominated by urban development. The channel itself was modified to accommodate this change over a period of 19 years between 1956 and 1975 (National Rivers Authority records).

Table 45.3 compares the land-use cover and length of natural channel before 1945 to those currently found in the catchment, these are illustrated in Figure 45.1. Historical analysis of large-scale

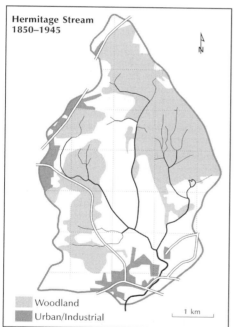
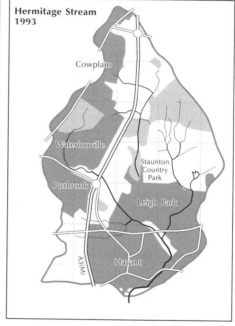

Figure 45.1. Changes in landcover and the river network in a lowland urbanizing catchment (a) 1850–1945 (b) 1993.

Table 45.3. Changes in land cover and channel type within an urbanizing catchment

Attribute	Woodland km²	Urban km²	Farmland km²	Natural channel (km)	Open channel (km)
Pre-1945	8.10 (42.2%)	1.59 (8.3%)	9.51 (49.5%)	26.8	27.8
1995	2.06 (10.7%)	9.34 (48.6%)	7.80 (40.6%)	1.5	22.3

maps back to 1775 reveal that the catchment land use and channel network had remained stable for at least the previous 80 years. It is only in the past 45 years that significant alterations have occurred, and these mainly during the past 30 years.

The hydrology of the Hermitage stream is characterized by a flashy runoff response to rainfall (Base Flow Index = 0.48), caused in part by the impervious clay geology of catchment, and the limited storage opportunity afforded by the confined valley floors. The rainfall runoff response of the catchment has been significantly altered by changes in land use and channelization. Forest clearance would have reduced the opportunity for interception and evapotranspiration from the forest canopy with the probable effects of increasing the surface runoff (Newson 1997; Calder 1976). Urbanization and channelization are known to significantly influence the hydrology of small catchments (Robinson, 1990). Shaw (1994) lists these impacts as:

- increased magnitude of discharge due to greater proportion of precipitation appearing as runoff;
- lag time and time to peak reduced (rate of rise of river increased);
- flood peak magnitudes increased;
- low flows reduced due to reduction in groundwater storage resulting from larger impervious surface post-development;
- reduction in water quality.

Figure 45.2 illustrates that, since the development of the catchment, the time of rise and recession of storm hydrographs has decreased rapidly so that rates of rise and fall in flood stage have significantly increased. Flood magnitudes of the peak flows have not significantly increased, which suggests that for the larger events, the volume of water is being attenuated by the urban storm system. The construction of a dam on the Ryders Lane stream has throttled flood peaks from this significant subcatchment. A visual appraisal of the flood hydrograph records from 1953 to 1994 indicate an increased tendency for multiple peaks, which suggests that flood waters are routed as a series of short rapid flows from the subcatchments and new urban stormwater catchments.

The channel capacity was designed to accommodate floods of 22–24 cumecs based on a large, expensive flooding event in 1966. Urbanization and channelization appear not to have reduced this level of service. The rate of rise and recession coupled with multi-peak flows has probably had the effect of increasing the frequency of moderate flood events, though the duration of floods in general has decreased. Steep rates of rise in flood hydrographs are associated with rapid flow acceleration and high shear stresses.

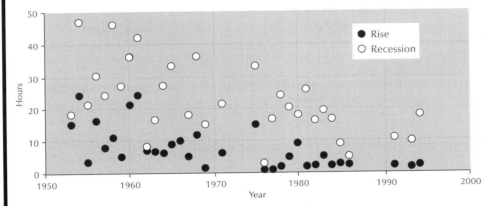

Figure 45.2. Reduction in flood time to peak and recession following urbanization and channelization in a lowland urban catchment.

Channel modification and adjustment

Up to 1950 a few limited straightening schemes had been attempted by individual landowners for the purposes of agricultural land drainage. Since 1945 the length of channel affected by channelization has increased in response to further land drainage (Park Lane stream), and urbanization. Some 10 per cent of the stream length shown on 1:25,000 OS maps has been culverted, whilst the length of channel which appear to be natural has decreased from 96 per cent pre-1945 to 8 per cent in 1995. As these natural channels currently receive modified runoff, it is possible to suggest that 100 per cent of the channel network is now modified in some way.

The modification of the Hermitage stream began in the early 1950s with the initiation of the Hermitage Stream Major Improvement Works Stage 1 in 1952/3. These works were designed to increase the flood capacity of the channel, and to straighten the channel in order to accommodate the planned expansion of development in that area. The design capacity was 8.65 m³s⁻¹, but following flooding in 1955, the design capacity was increased as part of the Hermitage Stream Major Improvement Works Stage 2 to 13.66 m³ s⁻¹ in 1958–9. The channel was concreted and the tidal channel dredged.

During the period 1961–7, the course of the Hermitage stream was straightened, and the old course backfilled with clay (Hampshire River Board records). Channelization was also undertaken on the Park Lane and Riders Lane tributaries. In August 1966, a severe flood event of 22 m³s⁻¹ occurred, which caused local flooding. This flood event significantly exceeded the original design flows, and precipitated the Hermitage Stream Flood Alleviation Scheme of 1971–c.1975. The existing channel was straightened and concreted, and the bed-levels were dropped to accommodate the design flood of 22–24 m³ s⁻¹.

The construction of the channelized reach has significantly affected the hydraulics of the channel. Typical values for Manning's roughness coefficient for concrete channels are 0.015. Measured values of Manning's roughness coefficient for a concrete channel conveying mobile gravel shoals are recorded as 0.030 for a stream in the USA. These contrast with roughness values of 0.060–0.120 for the natural channel sections with coarse woody debris. Removal of woody debris dams from such systems are known to increase flood wave velocities by two to three times (Gregory 1992) and to generate a more efficient sediment transport system. The present channel is an extreme case in point, with limited opportunities for sediment storage and high in-channel velocities (gauged at over 4 m s⁻¹ during a flood in 1995). Maintenance involves removal of gravel and debris from the bed, and the close mowing of the channel banks and berms to reduce hydraulic roughness. The result of urbanization, culverting and channelization of the Hermitage stream typifies the river management of smaller urbanized catchments throughout the world. The focus is on containment of flood waters with the resulting destruction at worst, or modification at best, of the natural watercourses.

---

assuming stability. Clark (2002) and Downs and Gregory (2004) argue that 'targets' are not relevant in a multidisciplinary catchment view of river hydrosystems where dynamism is the norm rather than the steady state. Nevertheless, the notion of 'targets' for river attributes has continued into the twenty-first century, with restoration management demanding targets for specific biota (Sear *et al.* 2004) or physical habitat (Walker *et al.* 2002). The target-focused end state is even enshrined in recent European water legislation (European Commission 2000).

Recent developments in river management

Water quality

In European river management, the most significant recent development has been the publication of the European Commission Directive 'Establishing a framework for Community action in the field of water policy' in December 2000. The Water Framework Directive

(WFD) sets out a European-wide set of objectives that ultimately aim to prevent further deterioration and protect and enhance the status of aquatic ecosystems achieving Good Ecological Status for all surface waters by 2015 (Logan and Furze 2002). Significantly, the Directive recognizes explicitly that rivers are ecosystems and that physical as well as chemical, biological and hydrological 'qualities' are key integrated elements that define Good Ecological Status (Logan 2001). Further, it is the first time that ecological information has been afforded legal value in European water law.

Fundamental to the implementation of the WFD is the notion of the restoration of river ecosystems based on the degree of variation from a 'reference state' condition. This follows in the tradition of target-driven river management, but differs in that the definition of a reference state must vary according to river type and may contain dynamic attributes within the definition.

Flood protection

Recent high-magnitude flooding in Europe, North America and Africa has focused attention on the inability of current river management approaches to provide adequate flood protection (Mance *et al.* 2002). Set against an uncertain future characterized by the probability of increased flooding (OST 2004), such events have led to fundamental changes in river management, captured in the new term 'flood risk management'. In the UK, the Foresight Report on Flooding 2004 concludes that current approaches to flood risk management are unsustainable across all types of future societies from consumerist to participatory. It points towards the need for integrated land and water management to reduce flood risk. The report also highlights the river management paradox that, on the one hand, biodiversity is driven by the dynamics of river channel–floodplain processes and that ecosystem function is dependent on flooding, and yet on the other hand these same processes pose huge economic and social disbenefits. The Foresight Report makes the case for integrated approaches to manage flood risk that work alongside natural processes to increase flood storage and reduce rates of runoff at the catchment scale. The value of ecosystem processes in achieving these is recognized, alongside the reality of dynamic river channels and floodplains in delivering these measures.

River restoration by dam removal

In the United States, stakeholder groups have been increasingly prompting resource managers to consider dam removal as a policy option and as a tool for watershed management. With dam owners facing rising maintenance costs, and the value of rivers as spawning grounds for anadromous fish (fish that ascend rivers to spawn) increasing, dam removal may provide the greatest net benefit to society (Pejchar and Warner 2001). The ecological effects of removal include both environmentally costly changes, such as the invasion of exotic species, and environmentally beneficial outcomes, such as increasing access to spawning habitats for migratory fish (Stanley and Doyle 2003). Restoration of an unregulated flow thus leads to biotic diversity increases through the enhancement of spawning grounds (Bednarek 2001). By returning riverine conditions and sediment transport to formerly impounded areas, riffle/pool sequences, gravel and cobble have reappeared, along with increases in plant, fish and insect diversity. Fish passage has been another benefit of dam removal: for example, the remarkable returns of impressive fish runs following removal of the 162-year-old Edwards Dam on the Kennebec River in Maine (Grossman 2002). However, the disappearance of individual reservoirs may also affect certain publicly desirable fisheries.

Box 45.2. River management for habitat enhancement: case study of the River Nar, Norfolk.

The River Nar has two major channel units: the upland freshwater fluvial catchment draining the plateau and chalk scarp to Narborough, and the lower gradient alluvial and formerly tidal river section draining the lowlands to the eastern margin of the Fen basin at King's Lynn. The two units are marked not only by physical differences but also by the history and type of channel modification. However, the principle controlling difference is channel gradient. The average gradient upstream of Narborough is 0.0020 whilst downstream it is 0.00003. This has a huge impact on sediment transport and channel hydraulics, which in the absence of human modifications would result in very different physical habitats and biotic communities. The River Nar corridor from source to the tidal outfall is a designated Special Site of Scientific Interest (SSSI).

The River Nar is currently not considered to be in a favourable condition with respect to channel morphology, particularly in the lower reaches, where it is essentially a perched drainage channel, uncoupled from the floodplain. The channel is also considered to suffer from excessive fine sedimentation as a result of agricultural intensification in an area of erodible soils (Boar *et al.* 1994). The River Nar has a groundwater-dominated runoff regime with a relative absence of high-energy floods. A relatively subdued relief creates low gradients throughout the river that, coupled with the runoff regime, result in a low-energy river sediment system.

Development of a conceptual model of the River Nar

Despite the detail inherent in the information collected by geomorphological survey procedures it cannot, alone, become the basis for decision support; it requires interpretation, partly by being bridged to larger space and timescales by means of a conceptual model. The conceptual model of channel geomorphology and physical habitat was developed on the basis of published scientific studies undertaken in rivers of similar physiographic and hydrological type. According to this model (Figure 45.3) the geomorphology is strongly controlled by the sequence of past processes evolving through the Quaternary. The river channel metamorphoses from a glacial outwash, sandy/gravel-bedded braided river system to a multiple-channel anastomosing river confined by cohesive floodplain fills and woodland. Subsequent mobilization of fine sediments by forest clearance (typically from *c.*5000 BP) of the valley sides resulted in blocking of multiple channels with fine sediment and the creation of the stable, single-threaded meandering channels occupying the present river course (Brown 2002).

An additional model component applicable to the River Nar was the gravel–sand transition (Ferguson 2003). According to this model, abrupt gradient changes create rapid reductions in shear stress and sediment transport, unless discharge and flow depth are maintained. Size-selective transport processes interact with the abrupt shear stress decline to create reductions in grain size over relatively short distances (Ferguson 2003; Sambrook-Smith and Ferguson 1995). Application of this model component suggests that the River Nar would naturally exhibit a gravel to sand transition in the reaches downstream of Narborough, marking a change in substrate and associated channel geomorphology and biotic communities – essential to consider in decision support.

Applying the conceptual models to the River Nar enabled the development of a channel typology based on hydrology, geomorphology and the operation of dominant process controls like the gravel–sand transition (Table 45.4). Channel management imprints within these channel types yields sub-types of reaches with more or less modification from the semi-natural conditions.

Fluvial audit messages for decision support

The results of the analysis for the Upper Nar support the view that the form and distribution of coarse gravel bed forms of the upper River Nar result from an inherited or relic suite of processes

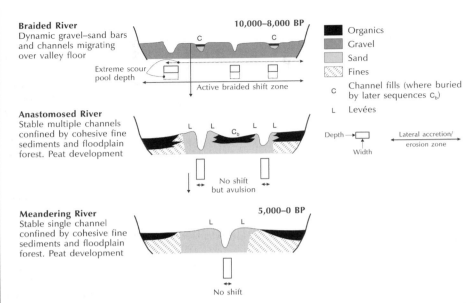

Figure 45.3. Holocene floodplain and channel evolution of the upper River Nar. A conceptual model based on Brown (2002) and Gibbard and Lewin (2003).

Table 45.4. Semi-natural channel typology for the River Nar SSSI river network

Types	Extent	Ref. condition geomorphology and habitat
0	Throughout the main catchment	Dry valley network with spring-sapped headwalls. No historically recorded flow but overland flow and natural pathways for runoff possible. Underlying sediment a mixture of colluvial slope wash and re-worked channel lag deposits.
1	Mileham–East Lexham plus perennial tributary streams in headwaters.	Sinuous single-thread channel system with mixed surface- and groundwater-dominated hydrology. Strong coupling of channel and floodplain leading to wet marsh/woodland/fen community with peat development.
2	East Lexham–Narborough	Sinuous meandering channel formerly multi-threaded with woody debris and limited development of pool-riffle sequence. Groundwater-dominated hydrology with extensive wet fen/Carr floodplain communities underlain by peat. Upwelling groundwater creates mosaic of wetland habitats including pools on floodplain surface.
3	Narborough–tidal influence (Abbey Mill Farm)	Low gradient alluvial channel within broader floodplain with gravel–sand transition in upper reach resulting from marked change in gradient.
4	Abbey Mill Farm–saline limit	Tidally influenced low-gradient mobile sand-bedded channel with adjacent peat-floored marsh and Carr communities on wide floodplain.
5	Saline limit–tidal outfall	Tidal river with saline intrusion supporting increasingly brackish water habitats downstream and adjacent marsh communities.

which created a gravel bed topography and sedimentology characteristic of steeper valley gradients (sea level was far lower) and higher runoff compared with present (and future) conditions. The current distribution of gravel bed forms and channel form is influenced by a long history of channel modification that has altered channel planform, cross-section and bed materials; these impacts persist in the absence of coarse sediment supply and bed mobility.

It is also highly sensitive to increases in fine sediment loads, since the stable bed sediments will tend to accumulate fines without being flushed (this is confirmed to some extent by the reported high levels of fines in chalk stream sediments; Acornley and Sear 1999; Milan *et al.* 2000). Thus the morphology of the River Nar is largely unpredictable, with strong local control on channel form. The morphology is therefore not amenable to 'textbook' restoration designs or importation of existing channel classifications but requires local restoration vision based on understanding processes and modification history. Restoration of natural processes and form must be viewed within this context.

Restoration of the River Nar must therefore proceed within a set of constraints identified by the fluvial audit and MCA (multi-criteria analysis) process. These include the following:

- River processes will not replace dredged gravel substrates.
- River processes will not create extensive coarse gravel features.
- Fine sediment is the only mobile component of the sediment system.
- The Nar is sensitive to increases in fine sediment loads due to a natural inability to mobilize and flush the bed.
- Channel planform, long profile, cross-section form and connectivity with the floodplain are relics of past processes and will not recover to pre-disturbance states.
- Natural processes of recovery will be dominated by fine sediment deposition and growth of aquatic vegetation.
- The hydrological network of the River Nar should be viewed as including roads and associated drainage networks as well as the sequence of field drainage systems. Management of these is as important to the restoration of the River Nar as is physical manipulation of the SSSI river network.

An important element of the restoration vision is based on assessing the extent to which the current channel diverges from the natural condition. Defining 'naturalness' is therefore an important element of the restoration process since it provides the reference conditions. Reference conditions may form the basis of channel designs, and the baseline against which to monitor the effectives of the restoration.

Short-term ecological impacts of dam removal include an increased sediment load that may cause suffocation and abrasion to various biota and habitats. However, several recorded dam removals have suggested that the increased sediment load caused by removal should be a short-term effect. Pre-removal studies for contaminated sediment may be effective at controlling toxic release problems (Bednarek 2001). Although there is a general sense that dam removal will result in positive environmental change, caution is required. Most of the post-removal ecological and geomorphic studies have only lasted for a few years. Both plant and fish communities may respond differently depending on the timing of dam removal, the volume and chemistry of sediment released, and available seed-banks for plant re-colonization. For example, floral communities at former impoundment sites in southern Wisconsin were dominated by monocultures of weedy pioneer species (e.g. stinging nettles) 5–6 years after dam removal (Doyle *et al.* 2000).

The removal of a dam disturbs a fluvial system in a state of partial adjustment to a blockage of the river. This tends to propagate both upstream and downstream through cascades of erosional and depositional processes that are coupled in time and space. What happens upstream drives the downstream response. Little is known about the rate and mechanisms of removal (i.e. knickpoint retreat, fluvial erosion) of sediment from the upstream reservoir in relation to flow regime, grain size, channel and deposit geometry, and method of dam removal. Downstream of the dam site, sediment will be transported through a channel system already altered by the presence of the dam. The temporary storage, over varying residence times, of sediment in the valley-floor corridor (channel bed and floodplain) constrains the making of accurate predictions of how long it will take for sediment to be routed downstream (Grant 2001).

As a result of of the limited monitoring and dam removal studies, continued examination of the possible ecological impacts is important for quantifying the resistance and resilience of aquatic ecosystems. Dam removal, although controversial, is an important alternative for river restoration. Many interests have to be resolved. For example, the controversy over dam removal on the Elwha River on the Olympic Peninsula in Washington State involved a coalition of activists who crafted an ingenious solution that both guaranteed the continuation of cheap power for the Daishowa-owned paper mill and gained the support of a disparate range of interested groups, including wildlife and conservation activists, the dam owners, the Port Angeles Advisory Council (including members of the Port Angeles Chamber of Commerce) and numerous federal and state agencies (Grossman 2002). Across the United States, the main reasons for dam removal are safety concerns and interest in environmental restoration. Rationales for dam removal vary between states, with California leading in removing dams for environmental purposes, while Wisconsin leads in economic and safety rationales. The states with substantial numbers of removals tend to have programmes supporting and funding dam clearing (Pohl 2002).

Future trends in river management

River managers now acknowledge the need to plan for global climate change (OST 2004), aquatic ecologists have recognized that geomorphological and hydrological variability is a key driver of river:floodplain habitat and biodiversity (Tockner *et al.* 2002), flood risk management has moved towards a catchment-based approach (Evans *et al.* 2002) and water quality management has focused on diffuse (catchment) sources (Mance *et al.* 2002). At each transition has come a re-conceptualization of the spatial and temporal scales required to describe, analyse and model the river system to the extent today that government research funding is being specifically focused on integrated multidisciplinary programmes that seek to better understand catchment scale processes.

The rapid change in river management philosophy over the past decade is converging on the overarching ethos of sustainable management of water and associated ecosystem functions within the river catchment (Downs and Gregory, 2004; Sear *et al.* 2004; Graf 2001; Tockner *et al.* 2002). The US National Research Council (1999) presents the concept in terms of 'Watershed Protection' whose features are integrated holistic problem-solving strategies used to maintain and restore the ecological integrity of the watershed whilst protecting human health and providing sustainable economic growth.

Embedded within this ethos are the traditional river management aims of protection against damaging floods and the provision of adequate water supply to the people within the catchment (ICE 2001). However a range of 'new' concerns have also emerged that relate explicitly to the functioning of the aquatic ecosystem – preservation of physical integrity (Graf 2001; Everard 2004), restoration of ecosystem functions (Richards *et al.* 2002; Krysonova and Kaganovich 1994) and management of water, nutrient and sediment fluxes at the catchment scale. As a result, twenty-first-century approaches to river management are more systemic and holistic in their conceptualization (Everard and Powell 2002; Newson 2002), multidisciplinary in their requirement for skills (ICE 2001) and participationary in their implementation (Clark 2002). The latter aspect requires methods of communicating increasingly sophisticated knowledge to a broad range of stakeholders. Furthermore in recognition of the changes occurring within the global environment, river managers have extended the lifetime over which projects are considered for management; have begun to explicitly consider uncertainty within the project planning, design and implementation (OST 2004); and have begun to adopt adaptation as a method of coping with change (Clark 2002) (Box 2).

The restoration of rivers is a key component of current river management, and is widely seen as the process through which its aspirations and targets will be delivered (European Commission 2000; National Research Council 1999). Thus a tremendous diversity of river restoration projects have been undertaken throughout the world in response to a well-documented array of adverse impacts from anthropogenic disturbances (Brookes 1988; Graf 2001; Knox 2003). The restoration science community has responded to the large demands (from the practitioner, policy and stakeholder communities) for ways to restore and mitigate such problems with a rich assortment of approaches, strategies and tools. The combination of these increasingly sophisticated aspirations and targets and more complex multi-disciplinary strategies and tools for delivering river restoration results in more expensive, complex and technically difficult projects, with project lifetimes extending over geomorphologically relevant timescales (Newson 2002; Sear and Arnell, in press). With increasing sophistication come additional risks in terms of our ability to set and meet realistic project targets and to communicate increasingly complex models of river environments to stakeholders from diverse backgrounds of understanding. For example, the results from recent monitoring programmes are beginning to cast doubt on the ability of restoration projects, as practised, to deliver some of these targets (Williams *et al.* 2004; Kondolf 1995). Central to progressing these more sophisticated models of river restoration is our ability to comprehend and communicate the uncertainty in the science to a stakeholder base (that may include other scientific disciplines) that has been brought up with the notion that environments can be managed in a deterministic fashion towards a specific reference point or target. Uncertainty exists throughout the restoration process, yet paradoxically most restoration projects fail to explicitly identify or communicate the uncertainty.

Further reading

Brookes, A. and Shields, F.D. Jr (1996) *River Channel Restoration*. Chichester: John Wiley and Sons.
Calder, I.R. (1976) The measurement of water losses from a forested area using a natural 'lysimeter'. *Journal of Hydrology* 30, 311–25.
Downs, P.D and Gregory, K.J. (2004) *River Channel Management*. London: Arnold.
Hart, D.D. and Poff, N.L. (2002) A special section on dam removal and river restoration. *BioScience* 52, 653–5 (this article introduced a special section of the journal reviewing all aspects of dam removal).

References

Acornley, R.M. and Sear, D.A. (1999) Sediment transport and the siltation of salmonid spawning gravels in a groundwater dominated river. *Hydrological Processes* 11, 447–58.
Bednarek, A.T. (2001) Undamming rivers: a review of the ecological impacts of dam removal. *Environmental Management* 27, 803–14.

Boar, R.R., Lister, D.H., Hiscock, K.M. and Green, F.M.L. (1994) The effects of water resources management on the rivers Bure, Wensum and Nar in North Norfolk. School of Environmental Sciences, University of East Anglia, unpublished final report to NRA.

Brookes, A. and Shields, F.D. Jr. (1996) *River Channel Restoration*. Chichester: John Wiley and Sons.

Brown, A.G. (2002) Learning from the past. *Freshwater Biology* 47, 817–29.

Brunsden, D. (2001) A critical assessment of the sensitivity concept in geomorphology. *Catena* 42, 99–123.

Centre for Ecology and Hydrology (1998) *Flood Estimation Handbook*. Wallingford, UK: NERC.

Clark, M.J. (2002) Dealing with uncertainty: adaptive approaches to sustainable river management. *Aquatic Conservation* 12, 347–63.

Cosgrove, D. and Petts, G.E. (1990) *Water, Engineering and Landscape: Water Control and Landscape Transformation in the Modern Period*. London: Belhaven Press.

DEFRA (2004) *Making Space for Water: Developing a New Government Strategy for Flood and Coastal Erosion Risk Management in England and Wales*. London: DEFRA.

Downs, P.D and Gregory, K.J. (2004) *River Channel Management*. London: Arnold.

Downs, P.W. and Thorne, C.R. (1998) Design principles and suitability testing for rehabilitation in a flood defence channel: the River Idle, Nottinghamshire, UK. *Aquatic Conservation* 8, 17–38.

Downs, P.W., Sklar, L. and Braudrick, C.A. (2004) Addressing uncertainty in prescribing high flows for river restoration. *Eos Trasactions, AGU 83* (47), Abstract H71 F-08.

Doyle, M.W., Stanley, E.H., Luebke, M.A. and Harbor, J.M. (2000) Dam removal: physical, biological and societal considerations. Paper presented to the American Society of Civil Engineers Joint Conference on Water Resources Engineering and Water Resources Planning and Management, Minneapolis, MN, 30 July–2 August.

European Commission (2000) Directive 2000/60/EC of the European Parliament and the Council of 23rd October 2000: Establishing a framework for Community action in the field of water policy. *Official Journal of the European Communities* L327, 1–72.

Evans, E.P., Ramsbottom, D.M., Wicks, J.M., Packman, J.C. and Penning-Rowsell, E.C. (2002) Catchment flood management plans and the modelling and decision support framework. *Civil Engineering* 150 (1), 43–8.

Everard, M. (2004) Investing in sustainable catchments. *Science of the Total Environment* 324, 1–24.

Everard, M. and Powell, A. (2002) Rivers as living systems. *Aquatic Conservation* 12, 329–37.

Ferguson, R.I. (2003) Emergence of abrupt gravel to sand transitions along rivers through sorting processes. *Geology* 31, 159–62.

Floodplain Management Group (2005) http://www.floodplain.org/Join%20The%20FMA.htm (accessed 2006).

Gibbard, P.L. and Lewin, J. (2003) The history of the major rivers of southern Britain during the Tertiary. *Journal of the Geological Society* 160, 829–45.

Global Water Partnership (2006) http://www.gwpforum.org (accessed 2006).

Goudie, A. (ed.) (1994) *Encyclopedic Dictionary of Physical Geography*. London: Blackwell.

Graf, W.L. (2001) Damage control: restoring the physical integrity of America's rivers. *Annals of the Association of American Geographers* 91, 1–27.

Grant, G. (2001) Dam removal: panacea or Pandora for rivers? *Hydrological Processes* 15, 1531–2.

Gregory, K.J. (1977) *River Channel Changes*. Chichester: John Wiley and Sons.

——(1992) Vegetation and river channel process interactions. In P.J. Boon, P. Callow, and G.E. Petts (eds) *River Conservation and Management*, pp. 255–69. Chichester: John Wiley and Sons.

Grossman, E. (2002) *Watershed: The Undamming of America*. New York: Counterpoint.

Hey, R.D. and Thorne, C.R. (1986) Stable channels with mobile gravel beds. *Journal of Hydraulic Engineering* 112, 671–89.

ICE (2001) *Learning to Live with Rivers*. London: Institution of Civil Engineers.

Knox, J.C. (2003) North American palaeofloods and future floods: responses to climate change. In K.J. Gregory and G. Benito (eds) *Palaeohydrology: Understanding Global Change*, pp. 143–64. Chichester: John Wiley and Sons.

Kondolf, G.M. (1995) Geomorphological stream classification in aquatic habitat restoration: uses and limitations. *Aquatic Conservation* 5, 127–41.

Krysonova, V. and Kaganovich, I. (1994) Modelling of ecological and economic systems at the watershed scale for sustainable development. In A.M. Jansson, M. Hammer, C. Folke and R. Costanza (eds) *Investing in Natural Capital: An Ecological Economics Approach to Sustainability*, pp. 215–32. Washington: Island Press.

Lewin, J., Macklin, M.G. and Newson, M.D. (1988) Regime theory and environmental change – irreconcilable concepts? In W.R. White (ed.) *International Conference on River Regime*, pp. 431–45. Chichester: John Wiley and Sons.

Logan, P. (2001) Ecological quality assessment of rivers and integrated catchment management in England and Wales. In O. Ravera (ed.) Scientific and legal aspects of biological monitoring of freshwater, *Journal of Limnology* 60, 25–32.

Logan, P. and Furze, M. (2002) Preparing for the European Water Framework Directive – making the links between habitat and aquatic biota. *Aquatic Conservation* 12, 425–37.

Mance, G., Raven, P.J. and Bramley, M.E. (2002) Integrated river basin management in England and Wales: a policy perspective. *Aquatic Conservation* 12, 339–46.

Milan, D.J., Petts, G.E. and Sambrook, H. (2000). Regional variations in the sediment structure of trout streams in southern England: benchmark data for siltation assessment and restoration. *Aquatic Conservation: Marine and Freshwater Ecosystems* 10, 407–20.

National Research Council (1999) *New Strategies for America's Watersheds*. Washington DC: National Academy Press.

NERC (1975) *Flood Studies Report*. London: HMSO.

Newson, M.D. (1988) Upland land use and land management – policy and research aspects of the effects on water. In J.M. Hooke (ed.) *Geomorphology in Environmental Planning*, pp. 19–32. Chichester: John Wiley and Sons.

——(1997) *Land, Water and Development*, second edition. London: Routledge.

——(2002) Geomorphological concepts and tools for sustainable river ecosystem management. *Aquatic Conservation: Marine and Freshwater Ecosystems* 12, 365–79.

OST (2004) *Foresight: Future Flooding*. London: Office of Science and Technology.

Pejchar, L. and Warner, K. (2001) A river might run through it again: criteria for consideration of dam removal and interim lessons from California. *Environmental Management* 28, 561–75.

Penning-Rowsell, E.C. and Tunstall, S.M. (1996) Risks and resources: defining and managing the floodplain. In M.G. Anderson, D.E. Walling, and P.D. Bates (eds) *Floodplain Processes*, pp. 493–534. Chichester: John.Wiley and Sons.

Petts, G.E. (1995) Changing river channels: the geographic tradition. In A.M. Gurnell and G.E. Petts (eds) *Changing River Channels*, pp. 1–25. Chichester: John Wiley and Sons.

Pohl, M.M. 2002 Bringing down our dams: trends in American dam removal rationales. *Journal of the American Water Resources Association* 38, 1511–19.

Richards, K.S., Brasington, J. and Hughes, F. (2002) Geomorphic dynamics of floodplain: ecological implications and a potential modelling strategy. *Freshwater Biology* 47, 559–79.

River Restoration Centre (1999) *Manual of River Restoration Techniques*. Silsoe, Bedfordshire: River Restoration Centre.

Robinson, M. (1990) *Impact of Improved Land Drainage on River Flows* (IOH Report No. 113). Wallingford: IOH.

Sambrook-Smith, G.H. and Ferguson, R.I. (1995) The gravel to sand transition along river channels. *Journal of Sedimentary Research* 65, 423–30.

Sear, D.A. and Arnell, N.W. (in press) The application of palaeohydrology in river management. *Catena*.

Sear, D.A., Thorne, C.R. and Newson, M.D. (2004) *Guidebook of Applied Fluvial Geomorphology*. Swindon: Environment Agency.

Shaw, E.M. (1994) *Hydrology in Practice*. London: Chapman and Hall.

Shields, F.D. Jr (1996) Hydraulic and hydrologic stability. In A. Brookes and F.D. Shields Jr (eds) *River Channel Restoration*, pp. 24–74. Chichester: John Wiley and Sons.

737

Stanley, E.H. and Doyle, M.W. (2003) Trading off: the ecological effects of dam removal. *Frontiers in Ecology and the Environment* 1, 15–22.

Thorne, C.R., Allen, R.G. and Simon, A. (1996) Geomorphological river channel reconnaissance for river analysis, engineering and management. *Transactions of the Institute of British Geographers.* New Series 21, 469–83.

Tockner, K., Ward, J.V., Edwards, P.J. and Kollmann, J. (2002) Riverine landscapes: an introduction. *Freshwater Biology* 47, 497–500.

Walker, J., Diamond, M. and Naura, M. (2002) The development of physical quality objectives for rivers in England and Wales. *Aquatic Conservation: Marine and Freshwater Ecosystems* 12, 381–90.

Williams, P., Whitfield, M., Biggs, J., Bray, S., Fox, G., Nicolet, P. and Sear, D.A. (2004) Comparative biodiversity of rivers, streams, ditches and ponds in an agricultural landscape in Southern England. *Biological Conservation* 115 (2), 329–41.

46

Global water resources

Nigel W. Arnell

Introduction

It has become a cliché that water resources are essential to life, and that problems with water resources are likely to be the greatest environmental challenge facing human society during the twenty-first century. Approximately a third of the world's population currently live in countries deemed to be water stressed – more than 20 per cent of the available renewable resources are withdrawn for domestic, industrial and agricultural purposes. Around 1.1 billion people lack access to safe water, and 2.6 billion suffer from inadequate sanitation (WHO/UNICEF 2004). Each year, around 140 million people are affected by flooding (IFRC/RCS 2000), and between 2 and 12 million people – mostly children – die from water-related diseases (Gleick 2002).

Pressures on water resources are increasing because of population and economic changes, changes in catchment land use, changes in human use of water, and the effects of global climate change. This chapter summarizes the global water resources issues now and during the twenty-first century, and concludes by reviewing how water management is changing in order to address these concerns.

Global water resources at the beginning of the twenty-first century

The natural resource base

Less than 2.5 per cent of the water in the hydrosphere is freshwater. Around 69 per cent of this freshwater is frozen in ice, and 30 per cent is stored in groundwater, much of which is very deep and inaccessible (Chapter 6): only a very small proportion of the hydrosphere is therefore available for use by humans and ecosystems. Average annual precipitation over the continents is approximately 115 km³/year, or about 860 mm (Arnell 2002). Around 60 per cent of this precipitation is evaporated, and the remaining 40 per cent – 40–47000 km³/year or 290–340 mm – enters the oceans as river flow and, to a much lesser extent, groundwater discharge and the calving of icebergs. There is, however, a very considerable variation across the world both in the volume of runoff and the proportion of precipitation that becomes river flows. Figure 46.1 shows an estimate of long-term average annual runoff across the land surface of the world, and shows considerable variability around the average. In many dry regions much of the runoff generated upstream subsequently infiltrates into the river bed and is evaporated from shallow groundwater: at the extreme, many rivers dry up before they reach the sea. The proportion of precipitation that becomes runoff is shown in Figure 46.2: it varies between under 20 per cent and over 50 per cent in high latitudes and the humid tropics. Annual average renewable groundwater recharge is estimated at around 2500 km^3/ year (Shah *et al.* 2000). Much of this discharges to rivers (or directly to the sea) within the year, but a proportion recharges deep stores which drain only very slowly.

The distribution of river flows through the year is broadly defined by the seasonal cycle of precipitation and evaporation, and is locally modified by the geological characteristics and volume of groundwater and lake storage in the catchment. Figure 46.3 shows some examples of monthly river flow regimes from around the world. The regime for the River Severn in England is typical of that from a humid temperate environment: river flows are highest during the winter and lowest during summer, largely because evaporation is much greater in spring and summer and more of the incoming precipitation is evaporated. The regime for the Niger in Guinea is characteristic of an environment with a very strong seasonal cycle in rainfall: here the highest flows are during the wet season. The regime for the Little Falls River in Minnesota is typical of a climate in which winter precipitation falls as snow. In such a catchment there is little streamflow during winter, and peak flows occur as snow melts in spring.

The figures so far, however, have shown the average hydrological regime. River flows vary considerably from year to year, and it is increasingly clear that there are strong, regionally consistent patterns in flow variability. Figure 46.4 gives an indication of the geographic variation in year to year variability, showing the ten-year return period drought runoff as a percentage of the long-term average runoff. Across much of southern Africa, for example, once every ten years runoff will be less than 20 per cent of the mean; in mid and high latitudes once every ten years runoff will be 60–70 per cent of the mean. This variation is largely determined by the year-to-year variability in precipitation, which generally increases as the average annual precipitation decreases. Consistent patterns in variations in flows from year to year are associated with large-scale atmospheric anomalies associated in particular with ENSO, the North Atlantic Oscillation and, in North America, the Pacific–North America (PNA) pattern. In an ENSO year, for example, river flows tend to be higher than average in western South America and along the Californian coast, but lower in south-east Asia, Australasia and tropical Africa (Arnell 2002). The North Atlantic Oscillation tends to produce consistently high runoff in northern Europe and low runoff across southern Europe and much of the Middle East – and vice versa.

Variations in river flows through the year and variations from year to year are more significant for water availability and management than the long-term average annual volume of flows. Most resource management schemes and plans (down to the farmer scale) are based around providing continuity during low, or high, flow seasons and years.

The maps in this section give a general indication of resource availability across the world – but it is significant that they were produced using a hydrological simulation model driven by inputs of precipitation, temperature and other climatic data. Hydrological data are not collected for large numbers of catchments, particularly in many developing countries, and a key challenge for water management is actually to obtain reliable estimates of the hydrological resource base.

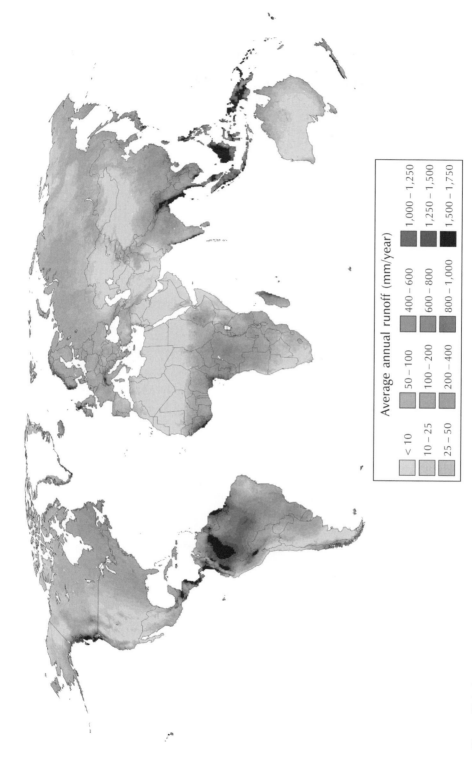

Figure 46.1. Long-term average annual runoff.

Average annual runoff (mm/year)

< 10	400 – 600
10 – 25	600 – 800
25 – 50	800 – 1,000
50 – 100	1,000 – 1,250
100 – 200	1,250 – 1,500
200 – 400	1,500 – 1,750

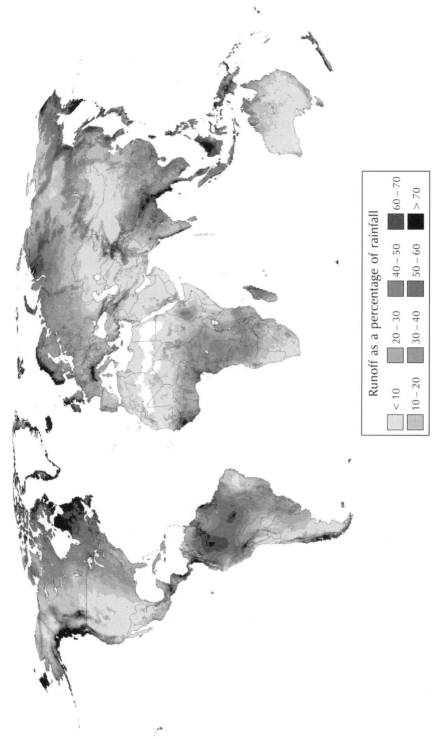

Figure 46.2. Percentage of precipitation that becomes runoff.

Runoff as a percentage of rainfall

< 10   20 – 30   40 – 50   60 – 70
10 – 20   30 – 40   50 – 60   > 70

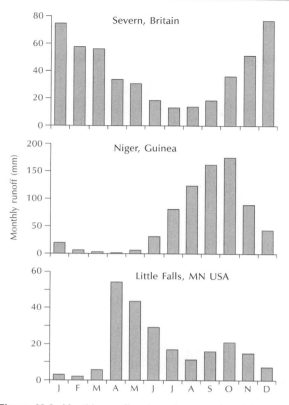

Figure 46.3. Monthly runoff regimes for example catchments.

Human interventions in the global water balance

Human activities have affected hydrological regimes at the local scale for several thousand years, but during the late twentieth century human activities began to have clear and observable effects on the volume, timing and quality of river flows over very large geographic areas. In the most general terms, human activities can affect the *catchment* (through changes in land cover and land use), the *river network* (through impoundments and diversions along rivers), and can intervene directly in the water cycle through *abstractions and returns* of effluent.

The key interventions affecting the surface of the catchment are deforestation and afforestation, the development of agricultural land, and urbanization. Deforestation generally increases streamflows, largely because less precipitation is intercepted by vegetation and hence evaporated (Brown *et al.* 2005), but in some cases partly because the deforestation process alters the surface of the catchment and affects flow generation pathways (e.g. by compacting the land surface – in Borneo, for example: Malmer 1992 – or through the construction of roads – (in the Pacific North West, for example: Jones and Grant 1996). Under such conditions, low flows may decrease even though average flows increase, because less water is stored in the catchment to be released slowly during dry periods. Deforestation also releases nutrients and sediments into the catchment system. The effects of deforestation

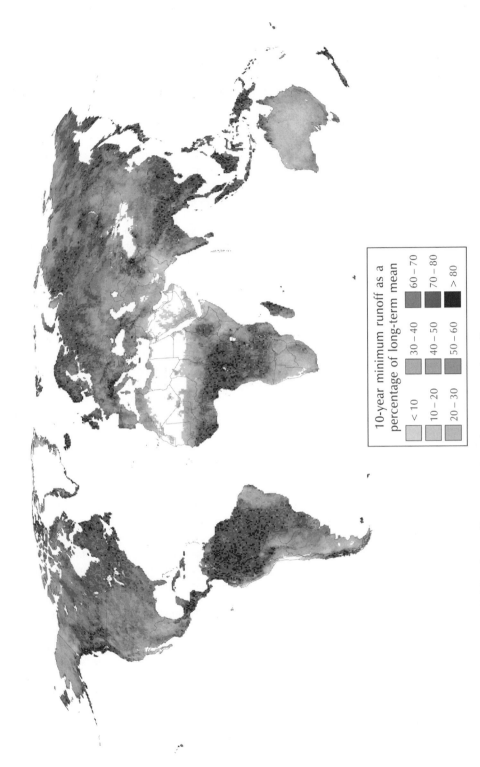

Figure 46.4. Ten-year return period drought runoff as a percentage of average annual runoff.

10-year minimum runoff as a
percentage of long-term mean

< 10
10 – 20
20 – 30
30 – 40
40 – 50
50 – 60
60 – 70
70 – 80
> 80

therefore depend not only on the vegetation type that is removed (and the vegetation type that subsequently develops) and the climate regime, but also on how the deforestation occurs. Afforestation in the medium to long term has the opposite effect to deforestation, leading to reduced runoff, although in the short term the forestry processes associated with forest planting, such as ditching, drainage and the construction of roads, can lead to increased flows, nutrient and sediment fluxes.

Agricultural activities affect the hydrological system partly through changes to the water balance caused by different rates of evaporation between different crop types, but largely through the farming processes associated with agriculture. Field drainage, for example, can accelerate runoff, and areas of bare land and farm tracks can generate disproportionately large volumes of runoff (e.g. in northern Thailand: Ziegler et al. 2004; and southern England: Holman et al. 2003). Ploughing and cultivation practices can release sediments and nutrients to the river system, and over-application of agricultural chemicals can lead to fluxes of nutrients, pesticides and herbicides to rivers and groundwater. Human activities have led to a five-fold increase in total nitrogen flows through the hydrological system across much of Europe, and at least a three-fold increase across most of North America and south and east Asia (Green et al. 2004).

Urbanization affects the hydrological system largely by reducing the impermeability of the catchment and increasing the drainage network; it therefore leads to larger and more rapid runoff from an input of precipitation, and tends to increase flood peaks downstream. Runoff from urban areas also often contains pollutants washed from the land surface (particularly roads) or the drainage network, with particularly large pulses after long dry periods.

Channelization and changes to the geomorphology of river channels affect the timing of river flows during an event, but do not affect the overall volume of flows or their seasonal distribution. Reservoir impoundments, however, can have extremely significant effects on downstream flow regimes. There are currently around 45,000 major dams (over 15 m high or capable of storing more than 3 million m^3 of water), and it is estimated that these dams together store between 6,000 and 7,000 km^3 of water (Shiklomanov and Rodda 2003). In warm regions evaporation from reservoirs reduces the volume of water released downstream, and water is abstracted directly from reservoirs or rivers fed by reservoirs for municipal, industrial and, most significantly, agricultural use. Control of releases from reservoirs changes the hydrological regime downstream, usually reducing substantially flood peaks and enhancing flows during dry periods; more radically, reservoir operation can change completely the seasonal timing of flows (reservoirs in the Ebro catchment in Spain, for example, have the effect of changing the peak flow season from winter to summer, providing water for downstream farmers to abstract for irrigation; Batalla et al. 2004).

Total global water withdrawals are currently approximately 3600 km^3/year (Vorosmarty et al. 2005), mostly in Asia and mostly (70 per cent) for agriculture: between 750 and 800 km^3 of these withdrawals are from groundwater (Shah et al. 2000). Most of the municipal and industrial abstractions are ultimately returned to the hydrological system, although frequently downstream of the point of abstraction and often to another catchment. Such abstractions can therefore locally affect hydrological regimes and water tables (although in a few prominent cases − such as in the Colorado Basin in the US − the interbasin transfers may be over a very large distance). The vast bulk of agricultural abstractions, however, are for irrigation, and much (approximately half: Vorosmarty et al. 2005) is evaporated. This ultimately falls as precipitation somewhere else, but for most practical purposes is lost even to the major river basin. Abstractions for irrigation have therefore had very significant effects on major water resource systems in many parts of the world: two key examples are the Aral Sea (see Chapter

43) and Lake Chad, both of which have reduced considerably in size over the latter part of the twentieth century due largely (Aral Sea) or in large part (Lake Chad) to abstractions from tributary rivers for irrigation. Abstractions from groundwater over renewable recharge rates are very widespread, and have led, for example, to widespread reductions in water table of up to 3.7 m across large parts of China (Shah *et al.* 2000).

These human interventions in the hydrological system are superimposed on to natural climatic variability which, as shown above, may exhibit persistent patterns over both time and space. Attribution of an observed trend to human activities is therefore in many cases problematic: this has important implications for how water resources in a basin are managed.

Patterns of resource availability

Total average annual freshwater flows are approximately 40–47,000 km^3/year. With a world population of around 6 billion in 2000, this means that average resource availability (runoff and renewable groundwater recharge) is around 7–8,000 m^3/capita/year. However, this global figure is highly misleading for a number of reasons. First, only approximately 75 per cent of the available flows are readily accessible to people (Vorosmarty *et al.* 2005: the rest is in sparsely populated areas such as much of the Amazon basin), and approximately 30 per cent of flows are unavailable because they occur during floods (Shiklomanov and Rodda 2003). Only around 53 per cent of global freshwater flows are therefore available for human use, reducing global per capita availability to closer to 4,000m^3/capita/year. Second, as shown in Figure 46.4, there is considerable variability in runoff availability from year to year. In large parts of the world, annual runoff in dry years can be only 10 per cent of the long-term mean. Third, resource availability varies dramatically from region to region, with runoff generation potential (Figure 46.1) and population. Figure 46.5 shows one estimate of resources per capita, by major watershed. Average annual runoff is below 1,000 m^3/capita/year – a widely used criterion denoting water scarcity (Falkenmark and Lindh 1993) – across much of the Middle East, south and east Asia and Europe, and approximately 1.4 billion people live in such water-stressed watersheds (Arnell 2004). Not all of these people actually suffer from water-related problems, because management systems may be in place to ensure reliable supplies, and people living in watersheds with considerably more apparent water per capita can suffer water shortages, but the figure of 1,000 m^3/capita/year generally denotes regions where water management actions are needed to avert water supply problems.

One of the reasons why water scarcity may occur in watersheds with more than 1,000 m^3/capita/year is that excessively large volumes of water may be withdrawn for human use. As mentioned in the previous section, approximately 3,600 km^3 of water was withdrawn annually from rivers and groundwater at the end of the twentieth century, a doubling from 1960 (Shiklomanov and Rodda 2003). This is approximately 16 per cent of the available annual global runoff, but withdrawals are heavily concentrated in areas with large amounts of irrigation (south Asia, east Asia, central Asia, southern Europe and the western United States). Watersheds or regions withdrawing more than 20 per cent of average annual runoff are classified as having medium/high water stress (WMO 1997), and areas with withdrawals greater than 40 per cent are in the high stress class. At the end of the twentieth century, approximately 2.5 billion people lived in countries with medium/high water stress, and 1–2 billion lived in countries where withdrawals were greater than 40 per cent of available resources (WMO 1997). In some regions or entire countries, mostly in the Middle East and parts of North Africa, withdrawals exceed available resources. The 'extra' water comes from

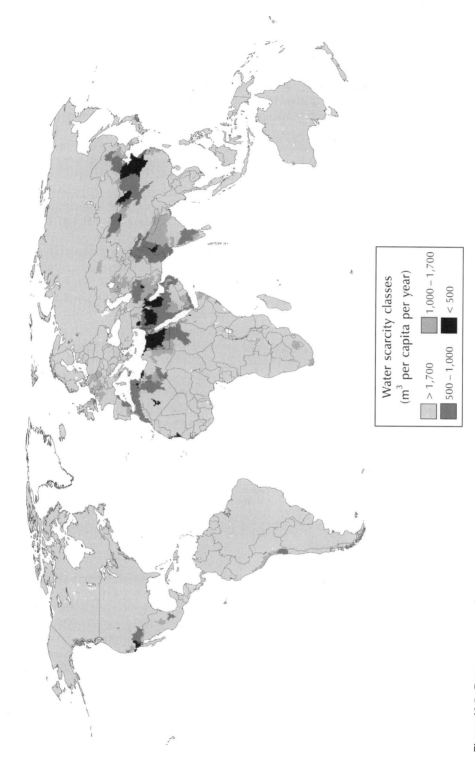

Figure 46.5. Resources per capita by major watershed.

Water scarcity classes
(m³ per capita per year)

> 1,700

1,000 – 1,700

500 – 1,000

< 500

desalination of saline water or, more widely, depletion of groundwater stores at rates in excess of renewable recharge.

Another potential response to geographical variations in the availability of water resources is to move water from one place to another. Whilst this is possible along a river network and for relatively short distances, it is generally very difficult and expensive to transfer bulk water from one place to another (note that there are some significant inter-basin transfers which involve pumping across major watershed boundaries, as in the Colorado basin in the western United States): water shortages in North Africa cannot be solved by importing water from northern Europe, for example. However, regional disparities in water availability can be addressed by the trading of projects which incorporate water. 'Virtual water' is water embedded in commodities (Allan 1998), and by importing these commodities a country or region reduces its need to use water in their production. In practice, the most water-intensive commodity on the international market is grain, so by importing grain a country reduces its demands for water. Each kilogram of grain uses approximately 1 m^3 of water in transpiration, so estimates of flows of virtual water can therefore be made by converting cereal trade volumes into water fluxes. The major cereal exporters (USA, Canada, Australia, Argentina, India and western Europe) export water, and there are net transfers of water in cereal to much of the rest of the world. Most countries receiving virtual water have few available accessible water resources, but some are water rich. Japan, for example, imports a large volume of virtual water through its large imports of rice. In this case, land is a constraint.

The rate of per capita growth in withdrawals reduced towards the end of the twentieth century (Vorosmarty et al. 2005), but population growth meant that total withdrawals continued to increase. In many industrial regions, particularly in both western and eastern Europe, withdrawals of water for industrial use reduced in the latter part of the twentieth century, with the decline in heavy (water-intensive) industry and improvements in water use efficiency. Withdrawals for irrigation in several parts of the former Soviet Union reduced substantially after the collapse of communism as major irrigation schemes fell into disuse. Withdrawals in Moldova, for example fell by close to 50 per cent between 1990 and 1996 (UNEP 1999), reflecting significant economic changes and increases in the efficiency of water use.

Humans are not the only users of the water environment. Freshwater ecosystems within and along the river channel have intrinsic value in their own right (as a component of global biodiversity), but also provide services to humans. These services include fisheries, flood protection (primarily through riparian wetlands storing flood waters), recreation opportunities, and the support of valued landscapes (Revenga et al. 2000). The requirements of freshwater ecosystems for water obviously vary with ecosystem characteristics, but in general terms all require periods of high flows and suffer if low flows become too low. Smakhtin et al. (2004) made a global assessment of environmental water requirements (EWR), assuming that freshwater ecosystems require all flows below the flow exceeded 90 per cent of the time and a variable amount of high flows, depending on the variation in flows through the year. They estimated that the EWR varied between 20 and 50 per cent of average annual runoff, with the highest values where flows are more stable through the year either because precipitation is relatively consistent (e.g. humid tropics) or because lakes sustain river flows. When these requirements are added to direct withdrawals for human use, the apparent pressures on water resources increase considerably. Smakhtin et al. (2004) estimate that basins where current water use means there is not enough water for the EWR cover 15 per cent of the world's land surface, and are home to around 1.4 billion people.

Water resources pressures

The preceding sections have summarized factors affecting water availability: river flows vary through the year, from year to year, and from place to place; human interventions are leading to changes in the volume, timing and quality of flows and groundwater storage. Simple indicators of resource availability highlight strong geographical variations in water resources pressures. These simple indicators, however, do not really characterize the true human and environmental implications and dimensions of water-related stresses and threats. In human terms, the water-related stresses are felt through reliability of safe supplies, access to safe water and sanitation (and attendant ill-health), poor water quality, exposure to floods, and through the potential for water scarcity to trigger conflict between users and regions. In environmental terms, water-related stresses are felt through reductions in the amount of water available to maintain instream and riverine ecosystems, and deteriorations in the quality of water available to support ecosystems.

Reliability of supply is essentially characterized by the difference between the amount of water demanded in a dry period and that which is available. Where demands are low and river flows or lake or groundwater storage plentiful, there is no need for management intervention. Where there is a gap between demand and potential for supply, however, there is a need for some form of intervention, typically through the provision of storage facilities or connections to resources in other catchments, and less frequently through imposed restrictions on demands during deficit periods. The storage facilities may be designed just to ensure continuity of supply during the dry season, with guaranteed replenishment during the wet season. For example, a small-scale farm reservoir may be designed to ensure that the farmer has enough water to irrigate through the spring and summer growing season, and may be small enough that it would be replenished in even the driest winter. More generally, storage or transfer facilities are designed to maintain supplies during infrequent dry years. Most urban supply systems, for example, are designed to maintain supplies in droughts as rare as once in 50 years (although in practice reliability is often higher as emergency measures are generally introduced in extreme droughts).

Access to safe water is not the same as reliability of supply. Where reliability is low, access to safe water is by definition low, but access may also be low even where reliability of supply is high. This occurs in rural areas where people either are a long way from reliable supplies or their access is limited through property rights. In urban areas, access to safe water may be low in the presence of apparent reliability either because the infrastructure to distribute water is lacking (in shanty towns, for example) or because the water is too expensive for the poor to buy. 'Safe' water is defined as water suitable for human use. Essentially, it has to be free of contaminating pollutants. In rural, but more particularly urban, areas most of these pollutants will come from human activities, especially industrial and sewage (raw or treated) effluent. In some areas, natural pollutants may reduce water quality. Groundwater across some parts of Bangladesh, for example, has naturally high arsenic concentrations.

Table 46.1 summarizes the global proportions of urban and rural dwellers with access to safe water and sanitation, and Figure 46.6 maps percentages by country. There is a clear disparity between urban and rural access to safe water and sanitation, and considerably smaller numbers of people actually have access within their home or immediate surroundings, particularly in rural areas. Patterns of access to safe water and sanitation show a clear distinction between developed and developing countries. Almost all African countries, for example, have less than 75 per cent of their population with access to safe water, and in most countries fewer than 50 per cent have access. The access to sanitation map shows even lower

Table 46.1. Population with access to safe water and sanitation (2002)

	Access to safe water			Access to sanitation		
	% with access	% with home connection	Numbers (millions) with no access	% with access	% with home connection	Numbers (millions) with no access
Urban	95	79	161	81	55	568
Rural	72	27	915	37	6	2,051
Total	83	52	1,076	58	30	2,619

Source: WHO/UNICEF Joint Monitoring Programme http://www.wssinfo.org/en/welcome.htm

access rates, and also shows low rates across south and east Asia. There has been an improvement in the numbers of population with access to safe water and sanitation since 1990 (WHO/UNICEF 2004), with most of this improvement in south and east Asia.

Lack of access to safe water for drinking, cooking and washing, and lack of sanitation facilities for removal of waste are together responsible for most of the burden of water-related disease and ill-health. Access to sanitation facilities, like access to safe water, reflects poverty and property rights far more than hydrological characteristics

Humans have long occupied flood-prone locations. Often this is in ignorance of the threat, but often an implicit trade-off is made between exposure to flood risk and the benefits gained from locating on a floodplain. These benefits include access to transport opportunities, control of a trade route (at a river crossing), or access to high-quality agricultural land. Measures to reduce the flood hazard include structural responses to keep floodwaters away from property (e.g. flood control reservoirs, embankments or diversion channels) and nonstructural measures to keep property away from floodwaters (e.g. through flood-resilient design, land-use planning and the use of warnings to allow temporary evacuation). Figure 46.7 shows assessments of the global distribution of flood-related mortality and the economic costs of flood losses (Dilley et al. 2005). Both maps show relative variation across the world, with the lowest category (1st–4th decile) showing the lowest 40 per cent of flooded grid-cells, and the highest category (7th–10th decile) showing the 40 per cent of flooded grid-cells with the highest values. The assessments are based on combining maps of the outlines of major floods over the period 1985–2003 with estimates of the human and economic impacts of those floods, together with estimates of the numbers of people living in flood-affected areas. Areas with the greatest risk to human mortality are concentrated in south and east Asia, central America, south-east Brazil, and parts of northern, eastern and western Africa. Areas with the greatest (relative) economic loss include south and east Asia, but in economic terms floods in Europe and the eastern US become more significant (although when these economic impacts are expressed as a percentage of GDP the relative importance of Europe and the USA declines somewhat).

Freshwater ecosystems, which include lakes, wetlands, riverine wetland and instream ecosystems, are under pressure in many parts of the world (Revenga et al. 2000; Vorosmarty et al. 2005), and their capacity to provide ecosystem services is therefore being degraded. Examples abound of changes in the volume and timing of river flows affecting instream habitats and the frequency of inundation of floodplains, pollution affecting the viability of different species within the river, and realignment and modification of channels and the floodplain leading to habitat degradation.

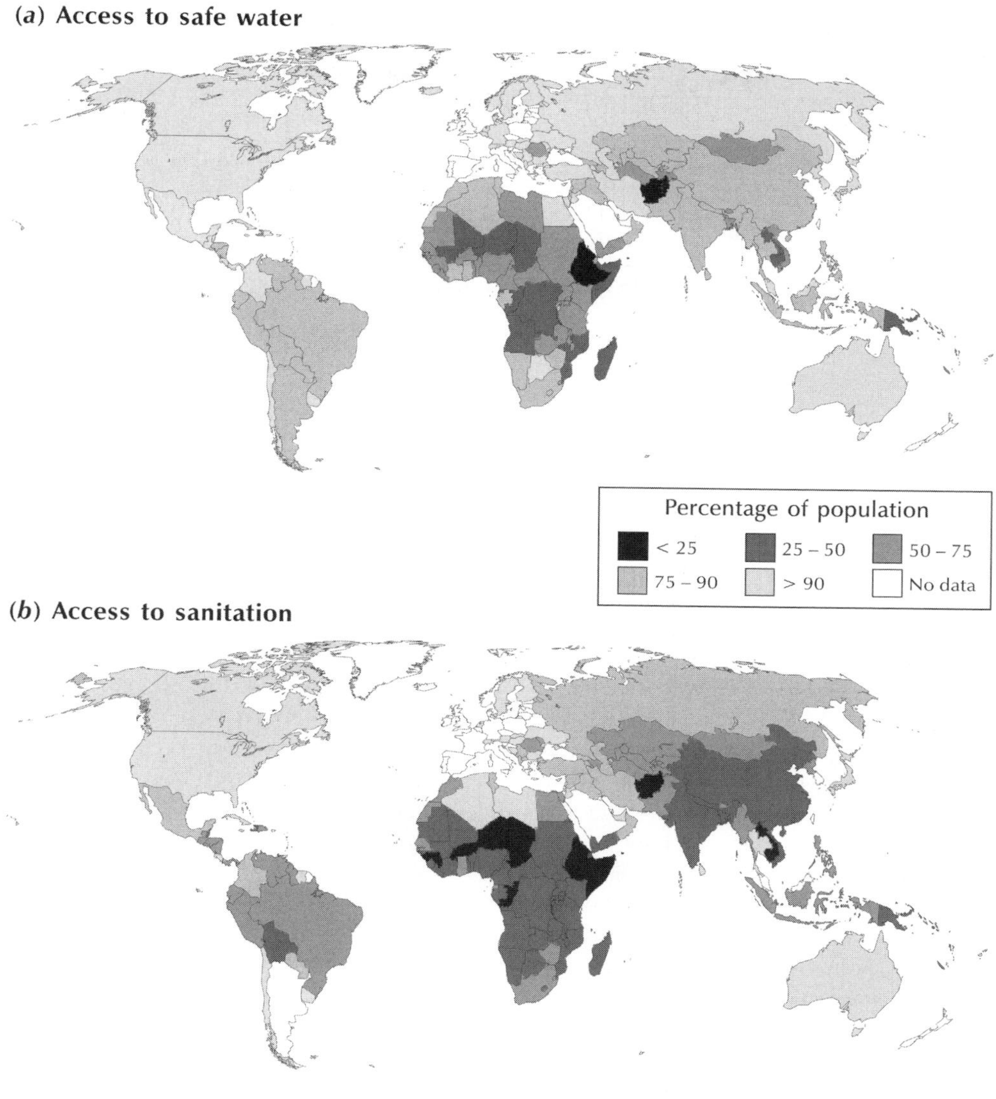

(a) Access to safe water

Percentage of population

- < 25
- 25 – 50
- 50 – 75
- 75 – 90
- > 90
- No data

(b) Access to sanitation

Figure 46.6. Access to safe water and sanitation by country.
Source: WHO.

Conflicts between users of water for access to resources have occurred for generations, and different systems for allocating water rights have evolved to adjudicate between users. Most recently, environmental requirements have added another source of conflict, often challenging rights and practices of existing water users. Similarly, there have long been conflicts between upstream and downstream users, relating not only to the volume of water passed downstream but also its quality. In the vast majority of cases, these conflicts have been settled by negotiation, and a large number of upstream/downstream – and international – treaties have been agreed (in the Nile basin, for example (Metawie 2004) and in the Colorado basin between the United States and Mexico). There are around 263 international river basins (Stahl 2005),

(*a*) **Mortality**

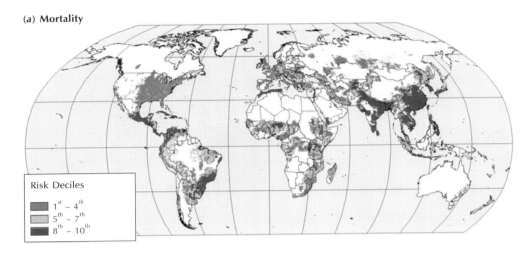

(*b*) **Total Economic Loss**

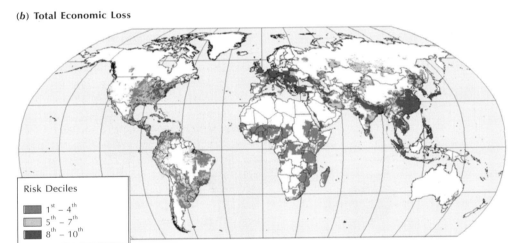

Figure 46.7. Global distribution of flood-related mortality and economic costs of flooding.
Source: Dilley *et al.*, 2005.

covered by over 400 international treaties (http://www.transboundarywaters.orst.edu). The availability of, and access to, water resources, however, has frequently been cited (at least in the popular media) as providing a potential trigger for violent conflict. Widely cited examples include the Jordan, Tigris and Euphrates basins in the Middle East, where many different countries have claims and rights on resources and how they are transmitted downstream. However, although there is a long history of international tensions over resources (between Britain and France in 1898 over control of the Nile, and Syria and Iraq in the early 1970s over control of the Euphrates), water has never – yet – been the sole cause of violent conflict (Gleick 1998). Water resources have, however, been used as a political or military tool and have been targeted during war (Gleick 1998).

Pressures and challenges for the twenty-first century

Projecting the future

The preceding section shows that water resources are seriously challenged at the beginning of the twenty-first century: very large proportions of the world population do not have access to safe water and sanitation, and human activities are in places degrading water resources and the water environment. During the twenty-first century three drivers have the potential to exaggerate further these pressures: population growth and development; further changes in catchment land cover; and the potential effects of climate change on the volume, timing and quality of water resources.

The most conventional approach to estimate the effect of population growth and development on future water resource demands and pressures is simply to extrapolate past trends. A variation on this approach breaks demands and pressures into components (e.g. demand for irrigation), and makes some assumptions about trends in each of these components. This approach has been widely used, for example, to forecast future global water withdrawals. However, experience shows that such projections are usually wrong. Gleick (1998) shows that projections of global water withdrawals in 2000 made between 1967 and the early 1990s gradually reduced from 6,700 to 4,000 km^3/year; as shown previously, it is estimated that withdrawals were actually about 3,600 km^3/year.

A rather different approach does not make forecasts or predictions, but instead estimates what pressures and demands on water resources would be under feasible possible alternative scenarios or 'storylines'. The three most comprehensive sets of scenario storylines have been produced in order to assess potential changes in climate (the IPCC Special Report on Emissions Scenarios (SRES): IPCC 2000), to assess future environmental challenges (the Global Scenario Group scenarios used by UNEP: Kemp-Benedict et al. 2002), and to assess possible changes in ecosystem services and functioning (produced for the Millennium Ecosystem Assessment: Cork et al. 2005). Each is based on a series of assumptions about population change, patterns of economic growth and convergence, energy use, governance, degree of globalization and degree of orientation towards economic (market) or environmental objectives. In each case, possible future water withdrawals and pressures on the water environment vary between storyline and can be described in narrative terms, although none actually make quantitative projections. Rosegrant et al. (2002) developed some specific water storylines, comparing water resources pressures under a 'business as usual' future (no changes in water policy), a 'water crisis' future (increased exploitation of water resources without concern for environmental consequences), and a 'sustainable water solutions' future (increasing concerns for environmental requirements). Table 46.2 summarizes these possible storylines in more detail.

Population and economic development

Future increases in population and economic development will have a number of major direct impacts on the water environment. Figure 46.8 shows one estimate of future resources per capita by 2025 and 2055 under one population scenario. The maps can be compared with those in Figure 46.5, and show increases in water-stressed watersheds with less than 1,700 m^3/capita/year, in particular across much of the Middle East and Central Asia. By 2025, around 2.9 billion people would be living in watersheds with less than 1,000 m^3/capita/year (37 per cent of world population, compared to 24 per cent in 1995), and by 2055

Table 46.2. Water resources pressures under different future storylines

Future world	*Water resources pressures*
'Business as usual'	Slow improvements in efficiency of river basin and irrigation water management
	Declining public investment in irrigation and reservoir construction
	Increased mining of groundwater
	Many households continue to lack access to safe water and sanitation
	Pollution regulations remain weak or poorly enforced
	No increase in share of water allocated to environmental uses
	Increase in water scarcity for irrigation in developing world
'Water crisis'	Reduced investment on irrigation systems and water management infrastructure
	Increasing deforestation and hence land cover change in catchments
	Increased encroachment on to wetlands and exploitation of aquatic ecosystems
	Increased overabstraction of groundwater
	Decline in access to safe water and sanitation
'Sustainable water'	Increased allocation to environmental uses
	Increased access to safe water and sanitation
	Increase in irrigation, municipal and industrial water use efficiency, through financial and technical incentives
	Equitable allocation of resources amongst uses
	Sustainable abstraction from groundwater
	Limited new resource development

Source: Rosegrant *et al.* (2002).

the figure reaches 3.4 billion (39 per cent of world population): higher growth population scenarios produce even greater increases (Arnell 2004).

Future withdrawals of water for municipal, industrial and agricultural use will depend on population growth rates, economic development and changes in water use efficiency. Figure 46.9 summarizes some projections of changes in future global water withdrawals between 'now' (typically 1995) and 2025. Estimates range from an increase of over 50 per cent under a 'business-as-usual' irrigation assumption to a reduction of 20 per cent under a highly optimistic sustainable water use scenario. This last scenario represents an aspiration rather than a serious expectation, and the smallest estimated increase is around 15 per cent. There is, however, considerable variability in changes in withdrawals across the world. Figure 46.10 shows percentage change by region under one business as usual scenario (Alcamo *et al.* 2003). Withdrawals reduce in western Europe, North America and Japan, due to increasing water use efficiency, but increase by between 30 and 40 per cent in south and central America, east Asia and much of Africa: increases in western and central Africa are considerably higher, albeit from a lower absolute base.

The effects of these increases in water stresses and water withdrawals will depend on local and regional contexts. In some cases, increases in withdrawals can be easily accommodated without additional costs or environmental impacts; in others, where pressures are already high, increased withdrawals and demands will have much more serious consequences. Aquatic and riverine ecosystems may be adversely impacted, groundwater resources may be overabstracted, and conflicts between users and regions may be exacerbated. Reductions in the availability of water for irrigation will reduce reliable crop yields, impacting upon food security and risk of hunger. Rosegrant *et al.* (2002) estimate that under a business-as-usual water growth scenario, reduced availability of irrigation water would lead to a global

(*a*) **2025**

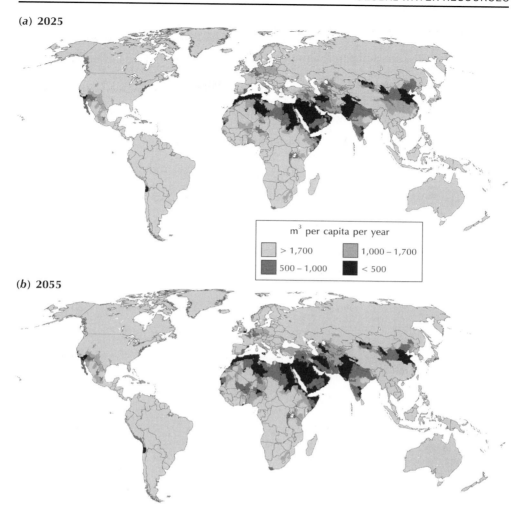

m^3 per capita per year

> 1,700   1,000 – 1,700

500 – 1,000   < 500

(*b*) **2055**

Figure 46.8. Future water resources per capita, 2025 and 2055.

reduction in yield of around 130 million metric tonnes by 2025 (equivalent to the annual rice crop in China in the late 1990s).

Future land use and land cover change

The key future changes to the catchment include deforestation, agricultural intensification, urbanization and continued construction of water resource infrastructure. How these changes manifest themselves depends, however, on future patterns of population and economic development. The effects of such changes on hydrological characteristics must be assessed using credible hydrological models, capable of simulating reliably flows and water quality in a catchment under altered land cover conditions.

A number of global-scale land cover and land use change scenarios have been produced, largely in order to assess changes in global food production, energy use or to estimate changes in carbon and other cycles. The SRES storylines, for example, include changes at the regional scale in cropland, grassland, forest and energy crop production, although the regional projections varied considerably depending on the model used (IPCC 2000). There have, however, so far been no global-scale assessments of the implications of these land use and land cover changes for hydrological behaviour. This partly reflects the inherent uncertainty in making land cover projections, but also reflects the generally coarse scale of most

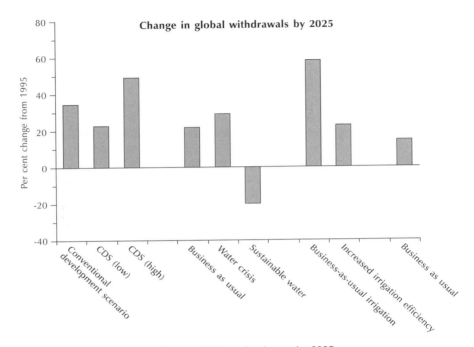

Figure 46.9. Projected future global water withdrawals: change by 2025.

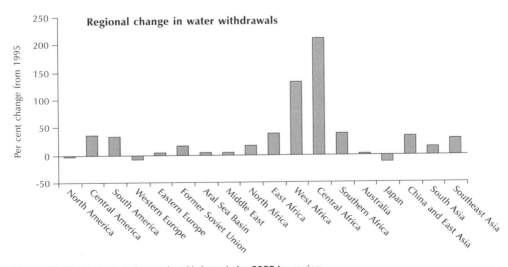

Figure 46.10. Projected change in withdrawals by 2025 by region.

land cover scenarios. Constructing scenarios at finer spatial scales, which can be fed into hydrological models, requires a different, spatially explicit approach which is difficult to apply at greater than the regional scale.

There have, however, been several local and catchment-scale studies that have illustrated the potential effects of land cover change on river flows and water quality. Niehoff *et al.* (2002), for example, showed that possible future changes in urbanization in a small catchment in south-west Germany would result in clear increases in flood peaks, and Van Rompaey *et al.* (2002) showed how relatively small changes in the extent of forest cover in a small Belgian catchment could result in substantial changes in sediment transport to rivers. As scale increases, however, the potential effects of future land cover change on river flows become smaller, as a smaller proportion of the catchment is affected. Future changes in the extent of cropland, forest cover and urbanization in the Rhine catchment, for example, would have little effect on flows in the Rhine itself (Pfister *et al.* 2004).

River flows in major basins, and hence global-scale patterns of resource availability, are therefore unlikely to be significantly affected by changes in catchment land use and land cover; they will be more affected by future water resource developments along the main river networks. The effects of land use and land cover change on resource pressures are therefore most likely to be seen at the local scale. The quality of flows along major rivers, however, is much more sensitive to land use and land cover change than the quantity of flows. In particular, widespread regional changes in agricultural practices – such as the application of fertilizers – would have a cumulative effect across the catchment and be seen in major rivers, and therefore can affect resource reliability through a widespread degradation in quality

Climate change and water resources

In contrast to land cover and land use change, climate change caused by an increasing concentration of greenhouse gases has a clear global-scale impact, although the manifestations of change will vary from catchment to catchment. It is now well established that the use of fossil fuels and deforestation have largely contributed to an increase in global average temperature of around $0.5°C$ over the last century, and could lead to an increase of between 1.5 and $4.5°C$ by 2100 (IPCC 2001). This increase in temperature would be associated with substantial changes in the volume and timing of precipitation, which are probably of greater significance for water resource availability. However, it is not possible to predict precisely the rate and magnitude of future climate change. First, it depends on assumed rates of emissions of greenhouse gases in the future, which is inherently unknowable. Second, the extent to which these additional gases will be absorbed by land and ocean is unknown, and there is also the chance that both positive and negative feedbacks in the earth system could reduce or exaggerate human effects on the atmosphere. Third, the translation of the effects of changes in the composition of the atmosphere into effects on radiative forcing and global climate remains uncertain. Finally, different computer representations of the climate system can give large differences in the regional climatic consequences of increasing greenhouse gas concentrations. There is good qualitative agreement between models in some areas – including high latitudes and the wet tropics – but in others – specifically dry mid latitude regions and south Asia – there is greater variability between models.

Notwithstanding these uncertainties, a large number of studies have used climate scenarios derived from climate models to estimate the potential effect of climate change on river flows and, to a much lesser extent, groundwater recharge and water quality. In general, these studies have tended to show that changes in river flow regimes are largely driven by changes in the volume and timing of precipitation, with increases in evaporation (associated with higher temperature) generally just offsetting to an extent precipitation changes. Figure 46.11 shows estimated change in average annual runoff by the 2050s under four different climate model-based scenarios (Arnell 2003). There is a strong degree of consistency – particularly in high latitudes – but large differences in estimated changes in runoff in southern Asia and parts of North America are apparent.

A much more robust conclusion, however, is that where higher temperatures result in winter precipitation falling as rain rather than snow, the flow regime shifts from spring to winter (Barnett *et al.* 2005). This may have a very significant effect on the effectiveness of

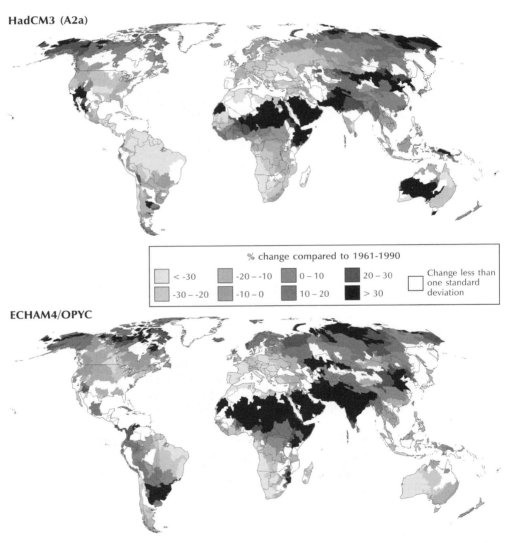

Figure 46.11a. Estimated changes in average annual runoff by the 2050s, under different climate scenarios.

water management systems, particularly those relying on the 'free' reservoir provided by upland areas to sustain flows during summer.

Figure 46.12 shows the potential effects of the climate changes shown in Figure 46.11 on water resources stresses in the 2050s (Arnell 2004). By the 2050s, between 1 and 2 billion people living in watersheds with less than $1,000m^3$/capita/year would experience an increase in water resources stresses because climate change would reduce the amount of water available. Most of these people live in the Middle East and central Asia, around the Mediterranean, in southern Africa and parts of North America. Between 1.8 and 4 billion people in water-stressed watersheds, on the other hand, would experience *increased* runoff. However, this may not alleviate water stresses because there may be little storage available to keep

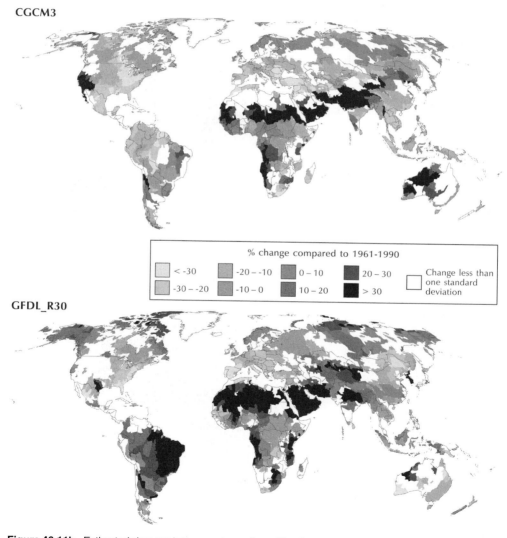

Figure 46.11b. Estimated changes in average annual runoff by the 2050s, under different climate scenarios.

the extra water through the dry season, and in many cases this extra water will come during floods.

From first principles, it would be expected that climate change would generally increase flood risk, because a more active hydrological cycle (more evaporation, more rainfall) will manifest itself in more frequent 'extreme' rainfalls. Across much of the world this is likely to happen with climate change, but there are some major caveats. First, where the higher temperatures mean that runoff occurs right through winter following rainfall rather than in a sudden peak following snowmelt in spring, the absolute maximum flood peaks may be reduced. Second, the effects of changes in extreme rainfall depend on catchment characteristics. Where there is considerable storage in a catchment (in groundwater or a lake, for example), river flows will be relatively unaffected by changes in short-term extreme rainfall, and peak flows will be influenced much more by changes in longer-term, seasonal rainfall. In contrast, where there is little storage, changes in long-term accumulated rainfall will have less effect on flood peaks than changes in short-duration extremes. In other words, an increase in

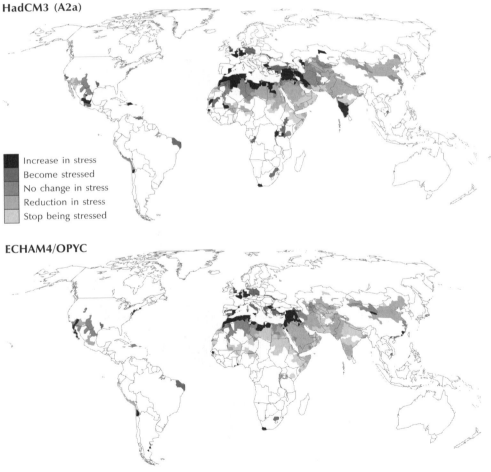

HadCM3 (A2a)

- Increase in stress
- Become stressed
- No change in stress
- Reduction in stress
- Stop being stressed

ECHAM4/OPYC

Figure 46.12a. Change in water resources stress in the 2050s, caused by climate change under different climate scenarions.

seasonal precipitation may not necessarily lead to an increase in flood risk. A corollary, of course, is that flood peaks may increase in frequency even where long-term mean precipitation decreases, if the frequency of flood-producing short-duration rainfall events increases. It is currently difficult to obtain robust estimates of potential changes in extreme precipitation from climate models, primarily because their spatial resolution is too coarse. A variety of techniques have therefore been developed to construct scenarios for changes in rainfall extremes, and much of the variability in estimated impact of climate change on catchment-scale flooding depends on variations in methodology.

In practice, the effects of climate change on resource availability will depend very much on the infrastructure and management systems in place at the catchment scale to deal with water resources and its scarcity, and generalizations are difficult. As with the effects of population and economic change on resource pressures, the effects of climate change will be most strongly felt where resources are already under pressure.

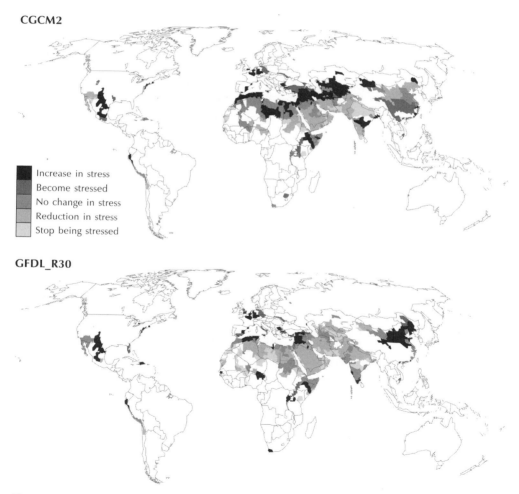

CGCM2

Increase in stress
Become stressed
No change in stress
Reduction in stress
Stop being stressed

GFDL_R30

Figure 46.12b. Change in water resources stress in the 2050s, caused by climate change under different climate scenarios.

Concluding comments: managing water resources in the twenty-first century

This chapter has outlined water resources at the global scale, and summarized both the extent of past human influences on resources and the impacts of possible future trends. The chapter gives a number of examples of degradation of water resources and freshwater ecosystems, and the literature is filled with more case studies. However, it is important to emphasize that this degradation and its adverse effects is being increasingly recognized at all spatial scales.

There are many examples of local-scale initiatives, often at the catchment scale, to restore water environments and operate water management systems in a more equitable, environmentally sustainable, manner. Significantly, moreover, there are an increasing number of global-scale initiatives to improve both access to water and to the management of water resources.

Global-scale interest in water management really crystallized at the 1992 International Conference on Water and the Environment, held in Dublin. This produced the 'Dublin Statement', as a contribution to the 1992 'Earth Summit'. The statement contains four principles – (1) freshwater is a finite, vulnerable and essential resource; (2) water management should be based on a participatory approach; (3) women play a central role in the provision and management of water; and (4) water has an economic value and should be recognized as an economic good – and proposed action under ten headings, most focused around aspects of sustainable water management. Most of these principles are uncontroversial, and indeed increasingly widely accepted and implemented. The fourth principle is, however, more controversial. The price of water is already seen as a burden on urban poor in particular, and the increasingly widespread policy of 'privatizing' the provision of public water supplies has triggered local and international protests.

The Dublin Conference led to two international initiatives. The World Water Council (http://www.worldwatercouncil.org) was proposed at Dublin and established in 1996, with the broad aim of providing a multi-stakeholder platform for the discussion and debate of water management issues. The World Water Council holds a World Water Forum every two years, as a forum for debate: the focus of the 4th World Water Forum in 2006 is on developing local solutions to global problems. The Global Water Partnership (http://www.gwpforum.org) also derives from the Dublin Conference. It is a working partnership of public and private sector organizations involved in water management, with the World Bank, the United Nations Development Programme and donor funding, seeking to undertake specific actions to improve water management. It has programmes in capacity building, strengthening river basin management, mainstreaming gender into water management and, its particular focus, integrated water resources management (IWRM). This differs from 'traditional' water management by considering not only supply-side measures (such as measures to augment supplies or protect against flooding) but also demand-side measures (to reduce demand for water or exposure to floods, for example), and by encouraging explicit consideration of the demands of all users of water resources, including environmental requirements.

These initiatives in water management have been supported by the UN Comprehensive Assessment of the Freshwater Resources of the World (WMO 1997) and, since 2001, the Comprehensive Assessment of Water Management in Agriculture (http://www.iwmi.cgiar.org/assessment/index.htm).

The Millennium Development Goals (MDGs) were agreed at the New York Millennium Summit in 2000, with the broad aim of reducing poverty at the global scale. The seventh MDG, as revised at the 2002 World Summit on Sustainable Development, has the aim of ensuring environmental sustainability, and includes specific targets for water and sanitation: by 2015, the proportion of people without access to safe drinking water and sanitation should be halved, compared to 2000. The costs of this are uncertain, but a cost–benefit analysis (Hutton and Haller 2004) suggests that each dollar invested in meeting the targets results in a return of between $3 and $34, largely the result of reduced ill-health and mortality. Meeting the targets, however, is extremely challenging. Whilst there was considerable improvement between 1990 and 2000, progress was least in sub-Saharan Africa and, more generally, rapid growth in cities is threatening the achievement of both the safe water and sanitation targets (Vorosmarty *et al.* 2005). Problems include not only lack of finance, but also political will to extend services to informal urban settlements, lack of formal land ownership and fragmentation of infrastructure.

Water is indeed one of the key crisis points of the twenty-first century. Pressures on water resources and their management are increasing, due not only to changing human demands but also to changes in resources available to users – and many of the effects of these pressures are uncertain. Water management is changing to reflect these challenges, with an increasing focus on maintaining and sustaining the water environment, accounting explicitly for competing uses, and encouraging efficient water use. Such advances in water management require not only improved monitoring and modelling capabilities (the information base is very poor in many regions), however, but also substantial changes in the politics and governance of water resources. Improving access to safe water and sanitation, ensuring reliable supplies, preventing degradation of the water environment and minimizing the flood hazard requires the development and use of skills from across the disciplines.

Further reading

Arnell, N.W. (2002) *Hydrology and Global Environmental Change*. Harlow: Pearson.
Clarke, R.T. (2004) *The Atlas of Water: Mapping the Global Crisis in Graphic Facts and Figures*. London: Earthscan.
Gleick, P.H. (ed.) (1993) *Water in Crisis: A Guide to the World's Fresh Water Resources*. New York: Oxford University Press.
——(1998) *The World's Water: The Biennial Report on Freshwater Resources 1998–1999*. Washington DC: Island Press.
Raskin, P., Gleick, P., Kirshen, P., Pontius, G. and Strzepek, K. (1997) *Water Futures: Assessment of Long-range Patterns and Problems*. Stockholm: Stockholm Environment Institute.
Seckler, D., Barker, R. and Amarasinghe, U. (1999) Water scarcity in the twenty-first century. *Water Resources Development* 15, 29–42.
Smith, K. and Ward, R.C. (1998) *Floods*. Chichester: John Wiley and Sons.
Young, G., Dooge, J.C.I. and Rodda, J.C. (2004) *Global Water Resource Issues*. Cambridge: Cambridge University Press.

References

Alcamo, J., Döll, P., Henrichs, T., Kaspar, F., Lehner, B., Rösch, T. and Siebert, S. (2003) Global estimates of water withdrawals and availability under current and future 'business-as-usual' conditions. *Hydrological Sciences Journal–Journal Des Sciences Hydrologiques* 48 (3), 339–48.
Allan, J.A. (1998) Moving water to satisfy uneven global needs: 'trading' water as an alternative to engineering it. *ICID Journal* 47, 1–8.
Arnell, N.W. (2002) *Hydrology and Global Environmental Change*. Harlow: Pearson.
——(2003) Effects of IPCC SRES emissions scenarios on river runoff: a global perspective. *Hydrology and Earth System Sciences* 7 (5), 619–41.

763

——(2004) Climate change and global water resources: SRES emissions and socio-economic scenarios. *Global Environmental Change–Human and Policy Dimensions* 14 (1), 31–52.

Barnett, T.P., Adam, J.C. and Lettenmaier, D.P. (2005) Potential impacts of a warming climate on water availability in snow-dominated regions. *Nature* 438 (7066), 303–9.

Batalla, R.J., Gomez, C.M. and Kondolf, G.M. (2004) Reservoir-induced hydrological changes in the Ebro River basin (NE Spain). *Journal of Hydrology* 290 (1–2), 117–36.

Brown, A.E., Zhang, L., McMahon, T.A., Western, A.W. and Vertessy, R.A. (2005) A review of paired catchment studies for determining changes in water yield resulting from alterations in vegetation. *Journal of Hydrology* 310 (1–4), 28–61.

Cork, S., Peterson, G. and Petschel-Held, G. (2005) Four Scenarios. In R. Hassan, R. Scholes and N. Ash (eds) *Millennium Ecosystem Assessment: Ecosystems and Human Well-being: Current State and Trends, Volume 1*, pp. 223–94. Washington DC: Island Press.

Dilley, M., Chen, R.S., Deichman, U., Lerner-Lam, A.L. and Arnold, M. (2005) *Natural Disaster Hotspots: A Global Risk Analysis*. New York: International Bank for Reconstruction and Development/The World Bank/Columbia University.

Falkenmark, M. and Lindh, G. (1993) Water and economic development. In P. Gleick (ed.) *Water in Crisis*, pp. 80–91. New York: Cambridge University Press.

——(1998) *The World's Water: The Biennial Report on Freshwater Resources 1998–99*. Washington DC: Island Press.

——(2002) *Dirty Water: Estimated Deaths from Water-Related Diseases 2000–2020*. Oakland, CA: Pacific Institute for Studies in Development, Environment and Security.

Green, P., Vorosmarty, C.J., Meybeck, M., Galloway, J. and Peterson, B.J. (2004) Pre-industrial and contemporary fluxes of nitrogen through rivers: a global assessment based on typology. *Biogeochemistry* 68, 71–105.

Holman, I.P., Hollis, J.M., Bramley, M.E. and Thompson, T.R.E. (2003) The contribution of soil structural degradation to catchment flooding: a preliminary investigation of the 2000 floods in England and Wales. *Hydrology and Earth System Sciences* 7 (5), 754–65.

Hutton, G. and Haller, L. (2004) Evaluation of the costs and benefits of water and sanitation improvements at the global level. WHO/SDE/WSH/04.04. Geneva: World Health Organization.

IFRC/RCS (2000) *World Disasters Report 2000: Focus on Public Health*. Geneva: IFRC/RCS (International Federation of the Red Cross and Red Crescent Societies).

IPCC (Intergovernmental Panel on Climate Change) (2000) *Special Report on Emissions Scenarios*. Cambridge: Cambridge University Press.

——(2001) *Climate Change 2001: Impacts, Adaptation and Vulnerability*. Cambridge: Cambridge University Press.

Jones, J.A. and Grant, G.E. (1996) Peak flow responses to clear-cutting and roads in small and large basins, western Cascades, Oregon. *Water Resources Research* 32, 959–74.

Kemp-Benedict, E., Heaps, C. and Raskin, P. (2002) *Global Scenario Group Futures: Technical Notes*. Stockholm: Stockholm Environment Institute.

Malmer, A. (1992) Water yield changes after clear-felling tropical rain forest and establishment of forest plantation in Sabah, Malaysia. *Journal of Hydrology* 134, 77–94.

Metawie, A. (2004) History of co-operation in the Nile basin. *International Journal of Water Resources Development* 20 (1), 47–63.

Niehoff, D., Fritsch, U. and Bronstert, A. (2002) Land-use impacts on storm-runoff generation: scenarios of land-use change and simulation of hydrological response in a meso-scale catchment in SW Germany. *Journal of Hydrology* 267 (1–2), 80–93.

Pfister, L., Kwadijk, J., Musy, A., Bronstert, A. and Hoffmann, L. (2004) Climate change, land use change and runoff prediction in the Rhine–Meuse basins. *River Research and Applications* 20 (3), 229–41.

Revenga, C., Brunner, J., Henninger, N., Kassem, K. and Payne, N. (2000) *Pilot Analysis of Global Ecosystems: Freshwater Ecosystems*. Washington DC: World Resources Institute and Worldwatch Institute.

Rosegrant, M.W., Cai, X. and Cline, S.A. (2002) *Global Water Outlook to 2025: Averting an Impending Crisis*. Colombo, Sri Lanka: International Water Management Institute.

Shah, T., Molden, R., Sakthivadivel, R. and Seckler, D. (2000) *The Global Groundwater Situation: Overview of Opportunities and Challenges*. Colombo, Sri Lanka: International Water Management Institute.

Shiklomanov, I.A. and Rodda, J.C. (2003) *World Water Resources at the Beginning of the 21st Century*. Cambridge: Cambridge University Press.

Smakhtin, V., Revenga, C. and Doll, P. (2004) *Taking into Account Environmental Water Requirements in Global-scale Water Resources Assessments*. Colombo, Sri Lanka: Comprehensive Assessment Secretariat.

Stahl, K. (2005) Influence of hydroclimatology and socioeconomic conditions on water-related international relations. *Water International* 30, 270–82.

UNEP (1999) *Global Environment Outlook 2000*. London: Earthscan.

Van Rompaey, A.J.J., Govers, G. and Puttemans, C. (2002) Modelling land use changes and their impact on soil erosion and sediment supply to rivers. *Earth Surface Processes and Landforms* 27 (5), 481–94.

Vorosmarty, C.J., Leveque, C. and Revenga, C. (2005) Fresh water. In R. Hassan, R. Scholes and N. Ash (eds) *Millennium Ecosystem Assessment: Current State and Trends, Volume 1*, pp. 165–207. Washington DC: Island Press.

WHO/UNICEF (2004) *Meeting the MDG Drinking Water and Sanitation Target: A Mid-Term Assessment of Progress*. Geneva: WMO.

WMO (1997) *Comprehensive Assessment of the Freshwater Resources of the World*. Geneva: WMO.

Ziegler, A.D., Giambelluca, T.W., Tran, L.T., Vana, T.T., Nullet, M.A., Fox, J., Tran Duc Vien, Pinthong, J., Maxwell, J.F. and Evett, S. (2004) Hydrological consequences of landscape fragmentation in mountainous northern Vietnam: evidence of accelerated overland flow generation. *Journal of Hydrology* 287 (1–4), 124–46.

47

Ensuring the future of the oceans

Bernd J. Haupt and Maurie C. Kelly

Introduction

The future depends on what we do in the present.

Mahatma Gandhi

Our oceans, which cover more than two-thirds of the Earth's surface and sustain 80 per cent of all known living organisms, were once thought to be an inexhaustible resource that would forever provide sustenance, support economic development, and serve as the primary food source for our growing populations. These expansive and mysterious bodies of water were considered too vast and the biological resources too plentiful to be depleted or to be impacted by the behaviour and needs of the human race. However, over the past several decades an awareness of the precarious condition of our Earth's resources, particularly our oceans, has grown as we have learned more about this unique physical and biological environment which serves as a habitat for fish, birds and mammals, and has a direct impact on climate and thus human existence.

The driving force behind this increased understanding is the ability of scientists and researchers to understand and communicate the intricate and complex phenomena that encompass the geography of the areas known as our oceans. Additionally, media coverage of the development of greenhouse gases, temperature and climatic changes such as alterations in storm tracks and hurricanes, coral bleaching, the melting and formation of Arctic and Antarctic sea ice, airborne pollution and contamination of the oceans though various incidents such as oil spills has led to greater public awareness of the importance and vulnerability of our oceans.

Since the mid-eighties, even greater attention has been focused on the health of our oceans as these factors began to affect economic development and the physical well-being of our population. During this time significant advances in understanding ocean circulation emerged – demonstrating, for the first time, that a global conveyor belt links the Atlantic, Indian, and Pacific Oceans together. Numerical ocean and climate simulations demonstrate that this system of ocean currents is in a delicate balance and, if disturbed, could cause dramatic global climate changes. The swiftness with which these changes could occur is revealed by studies of the geological past that have shown that dramatic changes in our oceans can cause major, rapid climatic changes, sometimes within decades.

This new knowledge and the recognition that the oceans will have to be managed to meet the needs of a population that has increased from less than 1 billion in 1790 to over 6 billion in 2000 (see Chapter 9) as a food resource, as a potential future energy supplier, and even more important as a climate stabilizer, has led to large-scale national and international scientific studies. The goals of these studies were to provide decision makers with more precise predictions and early detection and warning systems to be implemented to help ensure the future of our oceans, and thereby, our own future.

Historical view of detection of environmental changes: air versus water

Undoubtedly, the process of detecting changes in the ocean started much later than the detection of changes in the quality of our air. There are many reasons for this disparate timeline – most notably that the pollution caused by fossil fuel emissions is frequently visible and thus much more obvious to the human eye, while changes in water quality are usually more difficult to trace.

Advances in technology over the past century have been both the cause of increased environmental changes and the basis for analysing those changes. With the onset of the Industrial Revolution, innovations in technology and industry occurred at a rapid pace, enabling immense economic growth, while simultaneously laying the seeds for environmental change (see Chapter 1). The Industrial Revolution changed the population from a largely rural population making a living almost entirely from agriculture to a town-centred society engaged increasingly in manufacturing and industry. These dramatic changes resulted at first in an increase in airborne pollution followed by pollution of streams and rivers, which then carried these toxins via river deltas into marginal or epicontinental seas, then eventually into our oceans.

Western European societies, most notably Great Britain, were particularly affected by the air and water pollution in the earliest years of the Industrial Revolution, since understanding of how industrial waste and pollutants impact humans or the environment was limited and the science of studying our environment was in its infancy. The study of how these massive changes in our societal structure might impact the deep oceans and thus our climate, as well as the technology to perform such studies, was still in the distant future. The earliest scientific tests involved simply taking samples of air and water and examining and weighing the remaining residue. This process was considered adequate for many years for air quality evaluation since most pollution originated primarily from fossil fuel emissions. On the contrary, this early method was less effective for water quality sampling since samples were taken from rivers and streams, or from tidal waters that carried sediment (suspended soil particles), making them appear muddy and turbid. As the turbidity or clarity of water is not a criterion for water quality, other more complex methods like physical and biogeochemical analysis were required to measure factors such as salinity (historically the measurement of the chloride ion concentration in 1 kg of seawater, replaced by measurement of conductivity via the ion concentration), oxygen, pH, pathogens (bacteria and viruses), phosphorus (stimulates the growth of algae), and/or nitrogen (can affect drinking water). For many reasons, extending these types of analyses to the open ocean in the past had been a more difficult process. Pollutants in the open ocean usually originated from local discharge caused by agriculture, factories and towns and cities. The discharge drains from rivers and canals via river deltas into the open ocean, where it becomes diluted. Tides then rapidly disperse the contaminants, making monitoring and detecting changes through traditional water-quality testing an even greater challenge with less reliable results.

Exploration of the ocean, atmosphere and climate

The human impact on the environment and the oceans

The regular recording of weather data began many years prior to the development of metrics for recording regular measurements in the open ocean. It was much easier to install and upgrade land-based weather stations for monitoring purposes. It was simpler to vertically profile the atmosphere than the ocean. A simple look into the sky gives us insight into some of the atmosphere's vertical dynamics, while the ocean allows us only to look only a few metres into its depths – in short, we can see only as far as the light penetrates (even in the twentieth century the deep ocean was seen as a dark and cold place). An example of the ease with which weather data, as opposed to ocean data, are gathered is exemplified by the release of a weather balloon carrying a weather data recording device which profiles the atmosphere. A gas-filled weather balloon rises through the atmosphere and expands with height due to decreasing atmospheric pressure. The recording device drops back to the ground after being either released by a timer or after the balloon bursts at a given height. Unlike the way an atmospheric data gathering device would drop down to Earth, gravity would not return a recording device dropped from a ship into the ocean; it requires more technical finesse to design a pressure withstanding device that rises back to the ocean surface.

As very little was known about the deep ocean, very little attention was paid to any impacts or changes that might be occurring from pollution – industrial or otherwise. In fact, from earliest times, the ocean has been used for the disposal of civilization's wastes and untreated sewage. It provided a so-called economical NIMBY (Not in My Back Yard) outlet for waste disposal.

In Great Britain, the practice of ocean dumping of sewage sludge dates back to the end of the eighteenth century with the dumping of the City of London's wastes into the outer Thames estuary. In the United States, the first dumping of untreated municipal sewage sludge occurred in 1924 in the New York Bight. The expansion of towns and cities around the world, especially in low latitudes since 1950, continues to provoke the release of waste products to the environment, affecting both freshwater and marine environments, even though great progress has been made in waste management and water treatment.

Not surprisingly, the marine pollution severely affecting nearly enclosed seas and deltaic systems for long remained undetected. Large-scale oceanic changes in water quality were first detected in enclosed ocean basins that have a very limited water exchange with the global ocean: the Baltic Sea and Mediterranean Sea are two examples. They are linked to the global ocean via the Oresund (Denmark–Sweden) and Strait of Gibraltar (Morocco–Spain), respectively. Other partially enclosed seas, like the Caribbean Sea and Gulf of Mexico, differ from the Mediterranean and Baltic in two ways: population and ocean currents. Decades to centuries ago, the populations utilizing these seas were much smaller than those of the Baltic and Mediterranean Seas. More importantly, the Caribbean Sea and Gulf of Mexico have a system of ocean currents leaving and entering these two semi-enclosed ocean basins at two different localities ensuring a constant water exchange.

Even though British River Thames became a major transporter of waste to the North Sea, that sea was less affected by waste than other coastal regions such as the New York Bight, the Houston Ship Channel, Japan's Bay of Minamata, the Baltic Sea and the Mediterranean Sea. The

Baltic Sea and Mediterranean Sea are in some ways unique because both have been heavily used for waste disposal by the bordering states, which were unable to agree on 'equal' standards for industrial, agricultural and waste discharges. Over centuries, these enclosed seas bore the burden of the dumping of unregulated discharges, as well as legal and illegal industrial dumping of toxic wastes (including ammunition and chemicals from World War I and World War II) emanating from vessels on the open water.

In the 1970s, the public awareness for environmental problems and coastal pollution began to emerge. Media coverage of organizations such as Greenpeace (since 1971), which campaigned against environmental degradation, showed algae blooms, disfigured and dead fish and seals with high levels of antibiotics and heavy metals, land- and sea-based illegal dumping of toxic waste in costal regions as well on the high seas, decreasing fish and shellfish populations, and other environmental impacts. This enhanced knowledge and access to information propelled the general public into action and helped increase public understanding. The awareness of the impact of the runoff from farms, animal feedlots and streets, and municipal waste water sewage plants, which created huge 'dead zones' in many bays and estuaries, was dawning on the public. Coastal marshes and wetlands, which trap floodwaters, filter out pollution and nurture fish, birds and other wildlife, were disappearing. The more the public learned about habitat deterioration as a result of coastal development and water quality degradation, the more the interest in protecting the oceans emerged. It was at this time, coincidentally, that the bordering states of the Baltic Sea and Mediterranean Sea established 'equal' standards in federal regulations (i.e. inland cities would be economically disadvantaged if coastal cities were allowed to discharge wastes into the ocean because regulations for water usage — and any kind of discharge — in streams and rivers existed much earlier than for the ocean). The ideas of environmental protection and the era of recycling were born. It was as a result of this new awareness and the growth of new technologies that humans intensified efforts in the twentieth century to systematically explore the oceans.

Exploring the ocean: past and present

While understanding of the integrated nature of our environment as a whole and the systematic analysis of our ocean environment may be a more modern phenomenon, it would be a mistake to ignore the early explorers and researchers of past centuries.

Some of the earliest known series of 'expeditions' are those of the Polynesian Seafarers, who sailed the Pacific Ocean about 30,000 years ago, and were known as the 'Masters of Ocean Currents'. These explorers made the earliest forms of navigational or oceanographic maps, called stick charts. Stick charts, which were made of pieces of bamboo or other wood tied together, were used as navigational tools. Shells or knots marked the locations of islands while curved pieces of wood represented the pattern of ocean waves around the island or even the manner in which the waves rocked or shifted their canoes.

During a more active period of exploration covering the past several centuries, many more followed in the footsteps of the Polynesian Seafarers, piecing together the puzzle that is our ocean(s) and our globe. There are too many unique expeditions to mention in this brief text; however a few of the more interesting examples include: more than 1900 years ago sailors from Egypt, Phoenicia, and Crete mapped the regional coastlines to establish some of the earliest trading routes; approximately 650 years ago European explorers like Prince Henry, the Navigator of Portugal, recognized the oceans' importance to trade and commerce; Christopher Columbus sailed westward across the Atlantic Ocean to America and back; about 500 years ago Ferdinand Magellan, the Portuguese navigator, circumnavigated the globe.

Even the famous American statesman and diplomat Benjamin Franklin recognized in the second half of the eighteenth century the complexity and connectedness of our oceans by referring to the Gulf Stream as a 'river in the ocean' (see section 'The global ocean conveyor' for more information).

The beginning of the modern age of ocean exploration and scientific study dates back to the nineteenth century.

The HMS *Challenger* expedition can be considered the first major global oceanographic programme (Committee on Major U.S. Oceanographic Research Programs 1999; Pickard and Emery 1988). The expedition took place from 1872 to 1876 with the goal to investigate 'everything about the sea' – though driven primarily by biological and botanical interests. The expedition led a crew of 243 scientists to all major oceans except the Arctic. It was the first large-scale and interdisciplinary effort to make a systematic series of oceanographic measurements. The gathered data included a wide range of ocean features, including ocean temperatures' seawater chemistry, currents, marine life, and the geology of the sea floor.

A half-century later, another major expedition took place in the North Atlantic, which is also frequently referred to as the first modern oceanographic research cruise: the German navy's *Meteor* expedition (1925–7). The scientific crew focused primarily on collecting physical oceanographic data: 67,400 soundings and detailed current, salinity, temperature and oxygen measurements were collected at 310 stations. The *Meteor* conducted plankton tows, collected a large number of bottom samples, and executed systematic atmospheric tests (using both instrument balloons and kites) while traversing the Atlantic Ocean thirteen times.

These and many more oceanographic programmes that had already taken place or followed had an important impact on ocean and climate science.

Climate study and large-scale oceanographic programmes

The twentieth century introduced the era of modern large-scale oceanographic programmes (Table 47.1) which led to the modern understanding of ocean currents, the role of the ocean in the world's climate, the major chemical fluxes of the modern ocean and the history of both the ocean basins and the world climate through the analysis of sediments on the sea floor and cores from deep drilling into the rocks beneath the oceans.

Many of these projects focused on specific issues or time periods while others, like CLIMAP, GISP, GRIP and GRIP2, focused on the comparison of the past and present (see Alley 2000a, 2000b; and Schäfer *et al.* 2001 for an enhanced list of references).

The global ocean circulation scheme: an overview

The global ocean circulation system transports heat worldwide and affects climate in many areas. In a simple way, ocean currents contribute to the heat transport from the tropics to the poles, partially equalizing Earth surface temperatures. They also affect the routes taken by ships as they carry goods and people across the sea. Early Chinese, Arab and Portuguese navigators used this knowledge in their explorations and trading before Columbus discovered America. In the twentieth century, ocean science advanced our view of the oceans, the currents and their impact on climate.

We learned that ocean currents flow in complex patterns not only affected by wind but also by the water's salinity and heat content, bottom topography and the Earth's rotation. Initially, most studies of the thermohaline circulation concentrated on individual basins.

771

Table 47.1. Large-scale oceanographic programmes

Programme name	Acronym	Area or topic of concern
1969 International Decade of Ocean Exploration	IDOE	Biogeochemical processes in the sea
Climate, Long-range Investigation, Mapping, and Prediction study	CLIMAP	Reconstruction of full glacial climates using fossil evidence from ocean and lake cores
Coastal Ocean Processes		Fluxes of matter in continental margin systems
Coastal Upwelling Ecosystems Analysis	CUEA	Atlantic and Pacific
Coupled Ocean Atmosphere Response Experiment	COARE (part of TOGA)	The region of the western Pacific known as the 'warm pool'
Danish–Swiss–US Greenland Ice Sheet Project	GISP	Greenland palaeoclimate record
Deep Sea Drilling Programme	DSDP	Progenitor of the ODP
French–American Undersea Study		The rift valley of the Mid-Atlantic Ridge
Geochemical Ocean Section Study	GEOSECS	Pacific, Indian and Atlantic
Global Atmospheric Research Programme	GARP	Detailed study of the entire global atmosphere in 1979
Global Ocean Data Assimilation Experiment	GODAE	Regular, complete descriptions of the temperature, salinity and velocity structures of the ocean
Greenland Ice Core Project	GRIP	Greenland palaeoclimate record
Greenland Ice Sheet Project Two	GISP2	Greenland palaeoclimate record
International Geophysical Year 1957–8	IGY	Global investigations: special attention to the Antarctic
International Indian Ocean Expedition 1962–5		Ocean floor and currents in the Indian Ocean
International Southern Ocean Study	ISOS	Antarctic circumpolar current
Joint Global Ocean Flux Study	JGOFS	Processes controlling, regional to global and seasonal to interannual fluxes of carbon between the atmosphere, surface ocean and ocean interior
Mid-Ocean Dynamics Experiment eddies division	POLYMODE	Atlantic current eddies
North Pacific Experiment	NORPAX	North Pacific
Ocean Drilling Programme	ODP	History of the ocean basins
Ridge–Interdisciplinary Global Experiment	RIDGE	Understanding the hydrothermal circulation
The 1974 GARP Atlantic Tropical Experiment	GATE	Role of tropical ocean in global atmospheric circulation
The Russian experiment Polygon70		Discovered synoptic eddies in the open ocean
Tropical Ocean Global Atmosphere	TOGA (related to WRCP)	The tropical oceans and their relationship to the global atmosphere
US Mid Ocean Dynamics Experiment	MODE	Atlantic
World Climate Research Programme	WCRP	Global programme developed from GARP
World Ocean Circulation Experiment	WOCE	Global observations (part of WRCP)

Source: See, for example: Committee on Major U.S. Oceanographic Research Programs 1999; Pickard and Emery 1988; Siedler *et al.* 2001; Wefer *et al.* 1996.

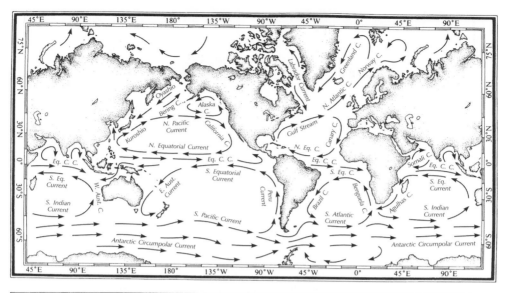

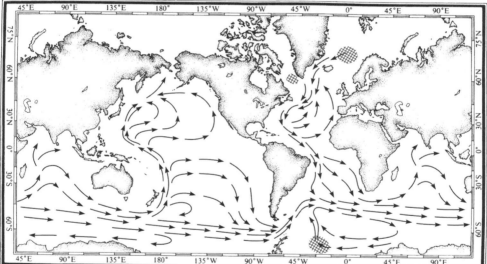

Figure 47.1. The (a) upper and (b) deep ocean circulation. Cross-hatched areas indicate regions of production of bottom water.

Source: Adapted from Stommel (1958).

However, about half a century ago, Stommel (1958) published the first set of global maps showing schemes of surface and deep ocean currents (Figure 47.1). The dominant features are the large anticyclonic subtropical gyres in each ocean basin, the equatorial current systems and the Antarctic Circumpolar Current (ACC). Note that the large anticyclonic subtropical gyres have a common feature: the westward intensification, which means that the western boundary currents are faster and narrower than the eastern boundary currents. Stommel and Arons (1960a, 1960b) have shown that the westward intensification of the

773

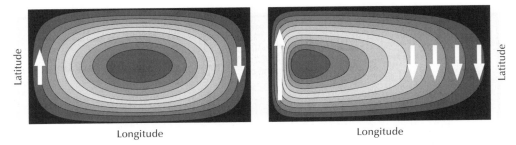

Figure 47.2. Streamlines for a non-rotating ocean (left panel) and a rotating ocean (right panel). The non-rotating ocean shows a symmetrical current system while the rotating ocean shows the westward intensification.

boundary current is due to the Earth's rotation and the fact that the Coriolis parameter is a function of latitude (Figure 47.2).

Further, Stommel (1958) identified the high-latitudinal convection sites in the northern North Atlantic and near Antarctica, where bottom water is formed (Figure 47.1b). At those sites, cool and salty water sinks from the ocean surface water into the deep ocean. The exact nature of impacting this production is still under debate (e.g. Nilsson and Walin 2001). Stommel and Arons's (1960a, 1960b) and Stommel *et al.*'s (1958) ideas of dividing the ocean in a surface and deep ocean with different circulation schemes has been advanced by many scientists.

The global ocean conveyor belt

The present-day thermohaline circulation is seen as a global circulation scheme that is connected primarily through the Antarctic Circumpolar Current (ACC). Bottom water formed in the Weddell Sea and Ross Sea spreads to the bottom of the world oceans, while deepwater formed in the North Atlantic reaches the ACC, where it is partially mixed with the bottom water and spreads to the Pacific and Indian oceans, where it upwells. The deepwater formation in the North Atlantic is compensated by water flux from the Pacific and Indian oceans through certain paths (Figure 47.3). This knowledge has been around for several decades. This fact has been acknowledged and accepted for many years.

However, not until 1991 did Broecker publish his striking idea of describing the global ocean circulation as a 'global ocean conveyor belt' (Broecker 1991). This metaphor, which spread quickly throughout researchers in earth sciences, is also known as 'salinity conveyor belt'. Broecker introduced the concept of a loop of ocean currents connecting the two most distant regions in the world ocean – the northern North Atlantic and northern North Pacific (Figure 47.3; see also Brasseur *et al.* 1999). Broecker's idea was preceded by a number of studies of world ocean circulation as a global entity (e.g. Broecker and Denton 1989; Cox 1989; Gordon 1986; Stommel 1958; Stommel and Arons 1960a).

The sensitivity of the thermohaline circulation and climate shifts

As mentioned earlier, the majority of researchers in earth sciences see the three-dimensional ocean circulation as a continuous conveyor belt. Especially within the last two decades, many research efforts have focused on studying the deep thermohaline circulation (THC) of the

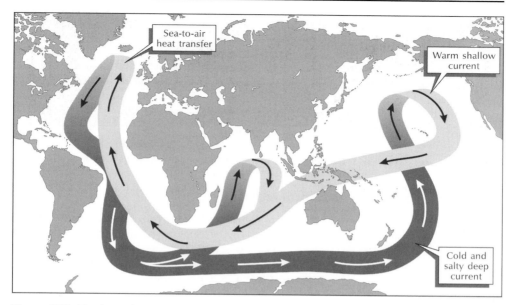

Figure 47.3. The loop of currents connecting the two most distant regions of the world ocean – the northern North Atlantic and northern North Pacific.

world ocean. As computers became more powerful and accessible, numerical models for ocean and climate simulations became more easily available to a wider research community.

Studies using models throughout the hierarchy of complexity (e.g. Blackmon *et al.* 2001; Bryan 1969; Bryan and Cox 1972; Cox 1984; Hughes and Weaver 1994; Manabe and Stouffer 1988; Opsteegh *et al.* 1998; Pacanowski 1996; Petoukhov *et al.* 2000; Rahmstorf 1996; Stommel 1961; Wang and Mysak 2000; Weaver *et al.* 2001) have been used to carry out either ocean-only or coupled ocean–atmosphere experiments. Some of them have indicated that the THC may display regime-like behaviour, and in particular may persist for geologically significant periods of time in circulation states quite different from that observed at the present. Such switches in the configuration of the THC have been implicated in abrupt climate shifts in the geological record and have been predicted to occur in response to increased anthropogenic greenhouse forcing (e.g. Schmittner and Stocker 1999). Scenarios were developed where the THC slowed or collapsed completely, which would have a disastrous effect on our climate and environment considering the ocean's role in transporting huge amounts of heat poleward.

While scientists currently agree that globally rising temperatures, sea level rise, melting icebergs and the retreat of glaciers are partially manmade, there are some climatic events still under debate that have influenced the THC and the climate in Europe.

Great salinity anomalies

Hydrographic time series from the Subarctic Gyre of the North Atlantic throughout the twentieth century show oscillations in temperature and salinity at more or less regular intervals. The Great Salinity Anomalies described during the 1970s (Dickson *et al.* 1988) and during the 1980s (Belkin 2004), however, had particularly large amplitudes and were climatically significant. Both of the Great Salinity Anomalies were described as low salinity anomalies with distinct features: They started out with a high propagation speed in the Greenland–Labrador region and slowed down considerably as they reached the Nordic Seas. There are still discussions about the cause for the low salinity anomalies and the persistence. The most plausible one seems that melting icebergs flowed further south into the Labrador Region than usual (Haekkinen 2002). The release of freshwater on their path/trajectories freshened and de-densified the surface waters, which slowed the production of bottom water, and thus the meridional overturning causing a slowdown of the THC. Seidov and Maslin (1999) showed that there are several sites in the northern North Atlantic that impact the formation of deepwater. The less saline water responsible for the slowed THC hit several of these key areas on its way from the Labrador Region towards the Nordic Seas.

Arctic and Antarctic ice as climate regulator

The THC, now identified as a major climate regulator, depends on a very delicate balance of deepwater formation in high-latitudinal key areas. Computer simulations show that an imbalance between the North Atlantic Deepwater (NADW, i.e. a Northern Hemisphere deepwater source) and the Antarctic Bottom Water (AABW, i.e. a Southern Hemisphere deepwater source) production can cause the global ocean conveyor to either speed up or slow down (e.g. Seidov *et al.*, 2001; Seidov *et al.*, 2001; Seidov *et al.* 2005; Weaver *et al.* 2003). Proxy evidence also gives these indications of strengthening or weakening (Broecker 1991, 1997; Gordon 1986; Gordon *et al.* 1992; Stommel and Arons 1960a). The strengthening or weakening of the THC is accompanied by a heating or cooling of the surface climates in the Earth's two hemispheres (Figure 47.4a). The Northern Hemisphere warms relatively while the Southern Hemisphere cools relatively when the North Atlantic THC strengthens and thus accounts for an increased northward cross-equatorial oceanic heat transport (Figure 47.4b) (Seidov and Maslin 2001). The opposite occurs when the North Atlantic THC is weak: the northward cross-equatorial oceanic heat transport is weak and keeps the Southern Hemisphere warmer relative to the Northern Hemisphere (Figure 47.4c).

The 'speed' of the global ocean conveyor depends on the rate of deepwater formation in both high-latitudinal hemispheres. This rate depends mainly on the density of the seawater and therefore on the water temperature and salinity, the amount of dissolved salt in water. Water becomes denser and heavier the colder and saltier it is, and lighter (less dense) the fresher and warmer it is. A useful rule of thumb is that the same density increase can be achieved by either increase of salinity by approximately 1 psu (practical salinity unit) or by decrease of temperature by about $-5°C$ (Pond and Pickard 1986). Why is this so important, especially in high latitudes in the Arctic Ocean and around Antarctica, where sea ice forms and melts?

As described before, the THC reorganizes itself when temperature and salt are redistributed in the ocean. The deep ocean can become warmer or colder, fresher or saltier. Once a hemisphere warms up because of a relative increase in cross-equatorial meridional heat transport into this hemisphere, the high latitudes become warmer, which can cause sea ice to melt and thus reduce the sea surface salinity. This de-densified (fresher and warmer) water is more buoyant and can reduce or even shut down the deepwater formation (e.g. Knutti *et al.* 2004). In contrast, the opposite hemisphere actually becomes colder due the equatorial heat piracy (Seidov and Maslin 2001). Sea ice formation might increase in this hemisphere, the water becomes saltier due to brine rejection, the water becomes denser, and thus it increases the rate of bottom water formation (There are several studies that confirm

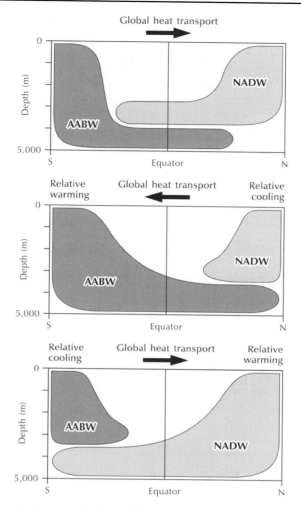

Figure 47.4. Schemes of water mass layering and overturning structure for the Atlantic Ocean: (a) present-day; (b) weakened North Atlantic THC; (c) increased North Atlantic THC. Direction of cross-equatorial oceanic heat transport is shown by arrows above each scheme.

the importance of brine rejection during formation of sea ice on salinity, e.g. England 1992; Stocker *et al.* 1992). This increase in turn reduces the previously observed heat piracy and therefore reverses the whole process. This process, which describes oceanic teleconnections between the hemispheres on millennial time scales and throwing our climate system abruptly from one state into a different one and back, is known as the 'bipolar seesaw' (e.g. Blunier and Brook 2001; Broecker 1998, 2000; Dokken and Nisancioglu 2004; Knutti *et al.* 2004; Robinson *et al.* 2005; Seidov, Haupt, Barron and Maslin 2001; Seidov and Maslin 2001; Stocker 1998, 2002). This bipolarity is not only a feature of our modern world's geometry and climate. Computer simulations show that millions of years ago similar teleconnections existed with land–ocean geometries and climates much different than those observed today (e.g. Haupt and Seidov (2001) who modeled the warm deep ocean during the Mesozoic-cenozoic time).

Exploitation and protection of the ocean

Earth's global commons are those areas that are not under the control of any single nation, the open ocean – essentially a still unexplored habitat – included. Thus, it seems to some as if these resources belong to no one and therefore are easily exploitable. To others, these areas are seen as a global resource, belonging to everyone, and therefore should be protected for the good of all – especially future generations. The ocean commons include only the high seas outside of national jurisdiction. Inside of national jurisdictions exist exclusive economic zones, within which certain economic development rights may be declared – differently handled by different nations, governments and authorities, which may extend 200 miles off a nation's shore. However, as marine wildlife, undersea habitats or pollution do not necessarily respect legal boundaries, protecting the open ocean from harm requires management of coastal and land-based activities on behalf of the global commons. More and more national governments officially cooperate with one another on environmental conservation through several institutions and instruments. This level of cooperation has not always been present and there continue to be many different opinions, regulations and policies about managing the oceans for fishing, mineral extraction and burial of waste, as well as about responsibilities and clean-up efforts after man-made disasters such as oil spills.

On 11 June 2003, the famous ocean explorer Jean-Michel Cousteau said: 'Ocean Exploration enters "Age of Management" to put preservation ahead of exploitation.' He insisted: 'The ocean is national security.'

> With more than half the world's population living in a coastal zone, with global warming delivering its force, and with 75 per cent of all commercial fish populations fished to capacity or already collapsed, we cannot make exceptions to hard fought laws to protect the ocean environment.
>
> (Cousteau 2003)

Despite the development of new technologies and knowledge humankind has gained within the past 25 years about the ocean and what lies beneath its surface, more than throughout all of previous human history, still very few of the ocean's mysteries have been studied and deciphered. In order to protect and ensure the future of the ocean, Cousteau's mission of exploring our global ocean, inspiring and educating people throughout the world to act responsibly for its protection, documenting the critical connection between humanity and nature, and celebrating the ocean's vital importance to the survival of all life on our planet can be seen as a desirable goal.

We should remind ourselves that our oceans hold the key to our future. This is not only a reflection of the wealth of mineral, food and potential medicinal resources existing just under the surface. Just as significant is the magnetism of the oceans, which encourages us to ponder, explore and simply enjoy their abundance. They provide us with life, recreational activities along waterfront communities such as clamming, crabbing, fishing, swimming and boating, and the basis for many cultural traditions handed down from generation to generation.

Advances in technology, medicine, ocean exploration and many more fields give humankind a sense of human progress and heritage. They provide the experience and knowledge necessary to undertake stewardship of the ocean and its resources, and thus set a course for future generations to navigate. What lies ahead is still unknown. Whatever it is, however, will be influenced by what is found through tomorrow's exploration and probably will differ from today's predictions! We should keep in mind that in just a few short decades, research and new technologies have opened doors to ocean exploration and exploitation as well. If humankind is able to avoid further damage of the oceans, this will require a better under-standing of the oceans as ecosystems and part of the climate system. As more information is retrieved and analysed, we may be able to ensure the future of the oceans while extracting resources from them without causing significant damage.

Fisheries

There is no doubt that human impact has altered the biodiversity of the oceans. Pollution has had a significant impact on the health of species such as dolphins and whales. And in recent decades the impact of commercial fishing on ocean ecosystems has increased dramatically. In 2002, 72 per cent of the world's marine fish stocks were being harvested faster than they can produce (GEO Section 2004).

In addition, as transportation and storage mechanisms for food have improved over the past few decades, the demand for fish and seafood has increased, as these once rare food sources, whose availability was previously restricted to coastal areas, become more readily accessible. With increasing demand and over-exploitation of coastal fish stocks, commercial fishing industry has moved to the rich pickings that exist in deep waters. The industry has developed its boats and scaled up its trawl gear to enable it to extend its unsustainable fishing practices into previously unexploited deep waters using a technique called bottom trawling. Many of these deep sea fish stocks are vulnerable to over-fishing.

Many species, such as the orange roughy and Patagonian toothfish in the deeper waters, take a long time to reach sexual maturity, and so stocks can be quickly depleted once most of the older, actively reproducing fish have been harvested. Another aspect of the changing pattern of ocean fishing is that over-exploitation of the species at the top of the food chain means that a growing portion of the total fish catch comes from species on which the tra-ditional commercial fish, such as cod, used to feed. Managing ocean fisheries therefore requires attention to the whole marine ecosystem, not just the species in market demand (GEO Section 2004).

Other large-scale commercial fishing methods are longline and gillnet fishing, as well as whaling. (The motion to resume Japan's commercial whaling after a two-decade ban was defeated in 2005. In the same year, whale burger went on sale in Japan.) These fishing techniques are considered wasteful and are known to decimate populations of fish including tuna, swordfish and sharks, as well as sea birds, turtles and other marine mammals. Millions of these non-targeted species are destroyed every year and are simply considered expendable – as demonstrated by the terms applied to them by the fishing industry – bycatch or discards. In addition, these large commercial fishing operations have a direct economic impact on the small family fishing businesses which operate along the coastlines and help support the economic viability of many smaller communities.

There are some bright spots on the horizon. Frequent media reports of dolphin and whale beachings, mercury in swordfish, and the dire economic situations in some fishing areas, such as those faced by lobster fishing towns along the US coast, have helped to educate the public about the extent of human impacts on ocean ecosystems. In addition, scientists and researchers have mounted national and international efforts to collect information on dis-appearing habitats, as well as the effects of pollution, and have developed exhaustive databases of fish species information. In the United States, the US Geological Survey (http://www.usgs.gov) is working to create a National Biological Information Infrastructure (NBII (http://www.nbii.gov)) which is a series of interconnected thematic and regional Internet nodes focusing on biodiversity information. One component of this effort is specifically focused on Fisheries and Aquatic Resources (FAR (http://far.nbii.gov)). The FAR node works in cooperation with international efforts such as FishBase (http://www.fishbase.org), a global information system containing information on over 25,000 fish species.

As with many issues facing our globe, the health and sustainability of the oceans biodiversity and fisheries stock depends on cooperation, access to information and the continued heightening of awareness through media and scientific activities that help to educate the public and decision makers.

The importance of monitoring our oceans for future protection

Exploring and improving our understanding of the oceans and their influence on global events are among the most important challenges today. The Earth's oceans and the underlying seabed remain one of our planet's last frontiers. Recent trends give some clues as to what lies ahead.

The key element in earth science between the century of the *Challenger* and the last 50 years is adequate and organized sampling. For example, the climatically significant Great Salinity Anomaly (Dickson *et al.* 1988) was detected only by serendipity. Future operational observation systems have to provide spatial coverage that allows anomalies to be recognized, so eliminating any kind of speculation over trends and error bars. One of the most significant contributions to earth observations technology has been the orbital satellites that provide us with consistent time series for trend monitoring and change detection. A systematic monitoring programme is also necessary to ensure that restoration actions, if required or desirable, lead to success. In particular, long-term monitoring allows for the separation of environmental from anthropogenic impacts on changes in temperature, salinity, other chemical and biological parameters, biodiversity and movement of invasive species, ocean fertilization to increase the productivity of fisheries or for CO_2 mitigation, greenhouse gases, THC and sea level changes, and pollutants. Long-term monitoring also allows for early detection of changes.

Ocean observation systems initiatives usually face a common dilemma. High operational costs over an extended period of time require long-term funding commitment from public entities such as government agencies or other large funding mechanisms (e.g. Adams *et al.* 2000). In our more recent past, we have learned that the benefits of an observation/monitoring and forecast system might exceed its costs (e.g. Keller *et al.* 2000, 2004, 2005). For example, in agriculture, many decisions can be improved with a reliable seasonal weather forecast. High resolution satellite imagery can detect and monitor oil threats and sewer overflows that may damage beaches and impact both recreation areas and fishing grounds, affecting local and national economies. For example, in the case of oil spills – by accident or intentionally – detection is the best way of confining the damage and starting the deployment of clean-up equipment; strategies for clean-up depend heavily on oceanographic models that in turn rely on the kind of up-to-date high-resolution ocean circulation data – in time and space – that very often do not exist. Again, given the scale and range of the affected economic activities, an early investment in observational and forecast systems as well in strategic crisis management plans might be beneficial over the long term. Any data collected on major pollution events, if made available, will feed into basic research and into understanding of ecosystem responses, providing valuable indications of the risks that may have to be faced in any future spillage or similar accidents.

It is undeniable that climate change is taking place and will affect future generations. However, there are those who do not believe that global warming is taking place. They often find small faults over a wide array of research, and use these in an attempt to devalue all research that indicates the existence of global warming. Those who deny the existence of any changes are very often those who have an economic interest. Here the public as well as decision and policy makers are asked for help because scientists are not in the business of making policies. They analyse observations and make scientific predictions, assessing the possible outcomes of different strategies. Their role is to provide a sound basis for policies and to consult.

Conclusions

The past and present ocean is a biologically diverse habitat, a resource for life and recreation, and most importantly a stabilizer for our climate. Although this chapter does not provide direct answers to how we should protect the future of our oceans, it has outlined issues related to human impacts on the ocean. Through understanding the role of past and present usage, as well as the more momentous issue of exploitation of resources, we can understand how consumerism, industrial and commercial expansion, and inadequate knowledge have led to dramatic changes in our environment, particularly our oceans. More importantly, this chapter shows that cooperative research efforts designed to increase scientific knowledge have enhanced the world's ability to increase the effective and efficient use of marine resources. It is the job of all of us to change the ways in which our oceans are managed. This means that we must act to ensure that human activities are sustainable: in other words, that they meet human needs of current and future generations without causing harm to the environment.

This requires investing in sciences, global observation systems, the construction of early *in situ* detection and numerical forecast systems for predicting changes in ocean dynamics, and in habitat diversity initiatives. Scientists and researchers need the ability to do independent research to understand and expand existing knowledge about the fragile ecosystem of our oceans – which encompasses Earth and atmosphere, ocean and climate. As scientists and researchers learn more, this information should be disseminated to be used by decision makers, teachers, students and the media as well as the general public. This knowledge can and should be the basis for policy making. It is important that science – including the financial support – and the process of policy and decision making are two separate and independent processes in order to guarantee unbiased observations, scientific predictions and guidance for future ocean management through regulations and education.

A quote found on one of Greenpeace's websites (Greenpeace 2005) should inspire the reader to build their own opinion about 'Ensuring the future of the oceans':

> Every second breath you take comes from the oceans. The oceans give life to our planet and us. In return we are suffocating them; dredging up too many fish, stealing food from needy mouths, carelessly killing countless creatures including whales, turtles, sea birds and thousand year old corals, we fill the oceans with pollution and warm them with climate change.

Further reading

Adams, R., Brown, M., Colgan, C., Flemming, N., Kite-Powell, H., McCarl, B., Mjelde, J., Solow, A., Teisberg, T. and Weiher, R. (2000) *The Economics of Sustained Ocean Observations: Benefits and*

Rationale for Public Funding. National Oceanic and Atmospheric Administration and the Office of Naval Research (NOAA/DOC) Report. Available at http://www.economics.noaa.gov/library/documents/benefits_of_observing_systems/economics-sustained_ocean_observations.pdf

England, M.H. (1992) On the formation of Atlantic intermediate and bottom water in ocean general circulation models. *Journal of Physical Oceanography* 22, 918–26.

Pickard, G.L. and Emery, W.J. (1988) *Descriptive Physical Oceanography – An Introduction*, extended edition. Oxford: Pergamon Press.

Pond, S. and Pickard, G.L. (1986) *Introductory Dynamical Oceanography*, second edition. Oxford: Pergamon Press.

Seidov, D., Haupt, B.J. and Maslin, M.(2001) *The Oceans and Rapid Climate Change: Past, Present, and Future*. Washington DC: AGU.

Siedler, G., Church, J. and Gould, J. (2001) *Ocean Circulation and Climate: Observing and Modelling the Global Ocean*. New York: Academic.

Trenberth, K.E. (ed.) (1992) *Climate System Modeling*. New York: Cambridge University Press.

US Agency for International Development (Bureau for Global Health and Office of Population and Reproductive Health) and US Department of Commerce (Economics and Statistics Administration and US Census Bureau) (2004) *Global Population Profile: 2002* (International Population Reports 226). Available at http://www.census.gov/prod/2004pubs/wp-02.pdf

References

Alley, R.B. (2000a) Ice-core evidence of abrupt climate changes. *Proceedings of the National Academy of Science* 97 (4), 1331–4.

——(2000b) *The Two-mile Time Machine: Ice Cores, Abrupt Climate Change, and Our Future*. Princeton, NJ: Princeton University Press.

Belkin, I. (2004) Propagation of the 'Great Salinity Anomaly' of the 1990s around the northern North Atlantic. *Geophysical Research Letters* 31, 1–4.

Blackmon, M., Boville, B., Bryan, F., Dickinson, R., Gent, P., Kiehl, J., Moritz, R., Randall, D., Shukla, J., Solomon, S., Bonan, G., Doney, S., Fung, I., Hack, J., Hunke, E., Hurrell, J., Kutzbach, J., Meehl, J., Otto-Bliesner, B., Saravanan, R., Schneider, E.K., Sloan, L., Spall, M., Taylor, K., Tribbia, J. and Washington, W.M. (2001) The community climate system model. *Bulletin of the American Meteorological Society* 82 (11), 2357–6.

Blunier, T. and Brook, E.J. (2001) Timing of millennial-scale climate change in Antarctica and Greenland during the last glacial period. *Science*, 291 (5501), 109–12.

Brasseur, G.P., Orlando, J.J. and Tyndall, G.S. (1999) *Atmospheric Chemistry and Global Change*. Oxford: Oxford University Press.

Broecker, W.S. (1991) The great ocean conveyor. *Oceanography* 1, 79–89.

——(1997) Thermohaline circulation, the Achilles heel of our climate system: Will man-made CO_2 upset the current balance? *Science* 278 (5343), 1582–8.

——(1998) Paleocean circulation during the last deglaciation: A bipolar seesaw? *Paleoceanography* 13, 119–21.

——(2000) Was a change in thermohaline circulation responsible for the Little Ice Age? *Proceedings of the National Academy of Science* 97 (4), 1339–42.

Broecker, W.S. and Denton, G.H. (1989) The role of ocean atmosphere reorganizations in glacial cycles. *Geochimica Cosmochimica Acta* 53, 2465–501.

Bryan, K. (1969) A numerical method for the study of the circulation of the world ocean. *Journal of Computational Physics* 4, 347–76.

Bryan, K. and Cox, M.D. (1972) The circulation of the world ocean: A numerical study. Part I, A homogeneous model. *Journal of Physical Oceanography* 2, 319–35.

Committee on Major U.S. Oceanographic Research Programs, National Research Council, NAS (1999) *Global Ocean Science: Toward an Integrated Approach*. Washington DC: The National Academies Press.

Cousteau, J.-M. (2003) http://www.oceanfutures.org/press/2003/pr_06_11_03.asp (accessed April 2006).

Cox, M. (1984) *A Primitive Equation, 3-Dimensional Model of the Ocean. Rep. 1* (Technical Report No. 1). Princeton, NJ: Ocean Group, Geophysics Fluid Dynamics Laboratory, Princeton University.

——(1989) An idealized model of the world ocean, Part I: The global-scale water masses. *Journal of Physical Oceanography* 19, 1730–52.

Dickson, R.R., Meincke, J., Malberg, S.-A. and Lee, A.J. (1988) The 'great salinity anomaly' in the northern North Atlantic: 1968–82. *Progress in Oceanography* 20, 103–51.

Dokken, T.M. and Nisancioglu, K.H. (2004) Fresh angle on the polar seesaw. *Nature* 430 (7002), 842–3.

Geo Section (2004) *Geo Year Book 2003.* Nairobi: United Nations Environment Programme.

Gordon, A.L. (1986) Interocean exchange of thermocline water. *Journal of Geophysical Research* 91, 5037–46.

Gordon, A.L., Zebiak, S.E. and Bryan, K. (1992) Climate variability and the Atlantic Ocean. *Eos, Transactions, American Geophysical Union* 79 (161), 164–5.

Greenpeace (2005) *Defending our Oceans.* Available at http://www.greenpeace.org/raw/content/international/press/reports/defending-our-oceans.pdf

Haekkinen, S. (2002) Freshening of the Labrador Sea surface waters in the 1990s: Another great salinity anomaly? *Geophysical Research Letters* 29 (24), 85-1–85-4.

Haupt, B.J. and Seidov, D. (2001) Warm deep-water ocean conveyor during the cretaceous time. *Geology* 29(4), 295–8.

Hughes, C.W. and Weaver, A. (1994) Multiple equilibria of an asymmetric two-basin ocean model. *Journal of Physical Oceanography* 24 (3), 619–37.

Keller, K., Tan, K., Morel, F.M.M. and Bradford, D.F. (2000) Preserving the ocean circulation: Implications for climate policy. *Climatic Change* 47, 17–43.

Keller, K., Bolker, B.M. and Bradford, D.F.D.F. (2004) Uncertain climate thresholds and optimal economic growth. *Journal of Environmental Economics and Management* 48 (1), 723–41.

Keller, K., Hall, M., Kim, S.-R., Bradford, D. and Oppenheimer, M. (2005) Avoiding dangerous anthropogenic interference with the climate system. *Climatic Change* 73 (3), 227–38.

Knutti, R., Fluckiger, J., Stocker, T.F. and Timmermann, A. (2004) Strong hemispheric coupling of glacial climate through freshwater discharge and ocean circulation. *Nature* 430 (7002), 851–56.

Manabe, S. and Stouffer, R.J. (1988) Two stable equilibria of a coupled ocean-atmosphere model *Journal of Climate* 1, 841–66.

Nilsson, J. and Walin, G. (2001) Freshwater forcing as a booster of thermohaline circulation. *Tellus,* 53A (5), 628–41.

Opsteegh, J.D., Haarsma, R.J., Selten, F.M. and Kattenberg, A. (1998) ECBILT: A dynamic alternative to mixed boundary conditions in ocean models. *Tellus,* 50A (3), 348–67, doi: 10.1034/j.1600-0870.1998.t01-1-00007.x.

Pacanowski, R.C. (1996) *MOM 2. Documentation, User's Guide and Reference Manual* (GFDL Ocean Technical Report 3.2). Princeton, NJ: Geophysical Fluid Dynamics Laboratory/NOAA.

Petoukhov, V., Ganopolski, A., Brovkin, V., Claussen, M., Eliseev, A. and Rahmstorf, S. (2000) CLIMBER-2: a climate system model of intermediate complexity. Part 1: model description and performance for present climate. *Climate Dynamics* 16, 1–17.

Pickard, G.L. and Emery, W.J. (1988) *Descriptive Physical Oceanography – An Introduction.* Oxford: Pergamon Press.

Pond, S. and Pickard, G.L. (1986) *Introductory Dynamical Oceanography,* second edition. Oxford: Pergamon Press.

Rahmstorf, S. (1996) On the freshwater forcing and transport of the Atlantic thermohaline circulation. *Climate Dynamics* 12, 799–811.

Robinson, L.F., Adkins, J.F., Keigwin, L.D., Southon, J., Fernandez, D.P., Wang, S.L. and Scheirer, D.S. (2005) Radiocarbon variability in the western North Atlantic during the last deglaciation. *Science* 310 (5753), 1469–73.

Schäfer, P., Ritzrau, W. Schlüter, M. and Thiede, J. (2001) *The Northern North Atlantic – A Changing Environment.* New York: Springer Verlag.

Schmittner, A. and Stocker, T.F. (1999) The stability of the thermohaline circulation in global warming experiments. *Journal of Climate* 12, 1117–33.

Seidov, D. and Maslin, M. (1999) North Atlantic deep water circulation collapse during the Heinrich events. *Geology* 27, 23–6.

——(2001) Atlantic Ocean heat piracy and the bi-polar climate sea-saw during Heinrich and Dansgaard–Oeschger events. *Journal of Quaternary Science* 16 (4), 321–8.

Seidov, D., Barron, E.J. and Haupt, B.J. (2001) Meltwater and the global ocean conveyor: Northern versus southern connections. *Global and Planetary Change* 30 (3–4), 253–66.

Seidov, D., Haupt, B.J., Barron, E.J. and Maslin, M. (2001) Ocean bi-polar seesaw and climate: Southern versus northern meltwater impacts. In D. Seidov, B.J. Haupt and M. Maslin (eds) *The Oceans and Rapid Climate Change: Past, Present, and Future*, pp. 147–67. Washington DC: AGU.

Seidov, D., Stouffer, R.J. and Haupt, B.J. (2005) Is there a simple bi-polar ocean seesaw? *Global and Planetary Change* 49 (1–2), 19–27.

Stocker, T. F. (1998) The seesaw effect. *Science* 282, 61–2.

——(2002) North–South Connections. *Science* 297, 1814–15.

Stocker, T.F., Wright, D.G. and Broecker, W.S. (1992) The influence of high-latitude surface forcing on the global thermohaline circulation. *Paleoceanography* 7, 529–41.

Stommel, H. (1958) The abyssal circulation. *Deep-Sea Research* 5, 80–2.

——(1961) Thermohaline convection with two stable regimes of flow. *Tellus* 13, 224–30.

Stommel, H. and Arons, A.B. (1960a) On the abyssal circulation of the world ocean, I. Stationary planetary flow patterns on a sphere. *Deep Sea Research* 6, 140–54.

——(1960b) On the abyssal circulation of the world ocean, II. An idealized model of the circulation pattern and amplitude in the oceanic basins. *Deep Sea Research* 6, 217–33.

Stommel, H., Arons, A.B. and Faller, A.J. (1958) Some examples of stationary planetary flow patterns in bounded basins. *Tellus* 10, 179–87.

Wang, Z. and Mysak, L.A. (2000) A simple coupled atmosphere-ocean-sea-ice-land surface model for climate and paleoclimate studies. *Journal of Climate* 13, 1150–72.

Weaver, A.J., Eby, M., Wiebe, E.C., Bitz, C.M., Duffy, P.B., Ewen, T.L., Fanning, A.F., Holland, M.M., MacFadyen, A., Matthews, H.D., Meissner, K.J., Saenko, O., Schmittner, A., Wang, H. and Yoshimori, M. (2001) The UVic Earth System Climate model: Model description, climatology, and applications to past present and future climates. *Atmosphere-Ocean* 39 (4), 1–68.

Weaver, A.J., Saenko, O.A., Clark, P.U. and Mitrovica, J.X. (2003) Meltwater pulse 1A from Antarctica as a trigger of the Bølling-Allerød warm interval. *Science* 299, 1709–13.

Wefer, D., Beger, W.H., Siedler, G. and Webb, D. (1996) *The South Atlantic. Past and Present Circulation.* New York: Springer Verlag.

48

Managing the coastal zone

Denise Reed

Introduction

Nowhere are the pressures of population growth and resource exploitation felt more keenly than at the coast. Already the majority of the US population lives within 130 km of the coast, with 53 per cent of the population living in the approximately 17 per cent of the land area that is considered coastal (Culliton 1998). Increased population density brings pollution and habitat degradation – decreasing the value of many of the resources that initially attract the coastal development. More people mean more infrastructure on or near the coast. Tourist developments, port facilities and fishery processing facilities are normal components of coastal population growth, but as the development increases so does the vulnerability of developed coastal areas to natural hazards. Our ability to predict the paths and intensity of hurricanes and typhoons continually improves (e.g. Kurihara *et al.* 1997) and this should be reflected in reduced risks from storm impacts through better forecasting and preparedness. However, growing population and development at the coast ensures that damages from such hazards will continue to be catastrophic.

The resources on which coastal populations depend are threatened by overexploitation and natural system degradation. Mangrove forests that provide essential nursery habitats for fishery species are harvested for firewood. Aquaculture ponds, producing high-value shrimp, pollute adjacent estuarine waters with their discharges. Rivers that enter the coastal ocean are dammed for power or irrigation, and leveed to prevent flooding of coastal communities, fundamentally changing the nature of estuarine and coastal waters, sediments and natural resources. But in addition to these human pressures which, once recognized could at least theoretically be mitigated, coastal systems face the threats associated with climate change. There is debate over trends in the historical frequency and intensity of tropical cyclones, as the global pattern is complicated by regional variability and decadal scale changes, but recent assessments show that at least in the North Atlantic there has been a significant increase in hurricane frequency since 1995 (Webster *et al.* 2005). This analysis also indicates an increase in the number and proportion of strongest category 4 and 5 hurricanes in the late twentieth century. While many debate the causes of these changes, Timmerman *et al.* (1999) suggest that increasing greenhouse gas concentrations may change the tropical Pacific to a state similar to present day El Niño conditions. Such conditions would suggest that the US would experience fewer Atlantic hurricanes but more extratropical storms on the west coast. More certain perhaps is the trend in sea level, where debate centres on the magnitude and rate of the rise and coastal island states around the globe are clearly vulnerable. Changes will occur in coastal areas in the future, whether from storm impacts, rising sea levels or changes in the magnitude and frequency of freshwater inflows.

Adapting and coping with these changes present a challenge to coastal scientists and managers. In many instances regulatory programmes and management frameworks address the problems of the past. As a society we learn lessons and implement policy frameworks to prevent repeating the mistakes of the past. Perhaps of more importance in the twenty-first century, as the implications of large-scale irreversible changes in the environment come to bear, is applying our knowledge of these systems to proactively plan and manage for what lies ahead.

This chapter illustrates how scientific understanding of coastal processes can provide a foundation for proactive coastal management. Topics addressed include coastal erosion and reclamation, the impacts of tourism and industrial development on coastal systems, and the indirect effects of changes in oceans and watersheds on the sustainability of coastal systems.

The changing coastal landscape

The physical landscape is an underlying control on the location and function of many water-dependent contemporary human activities near the coast, such as ports and resort hotels, as well as the historic communities and cultural resources that have developed in areas both accessible and strategically important to earlier societies. The physiography of the land–ocean margin determines the suitability of specific locations for certain human activities. Many of the great coastal cities of the world, like Hong Kong, Singapore and Rio de Janeiro, are centred on either naturally sheltered deep-water harbours or navigable routes between land-based commercial centres. Even more fundamentally, the geomorphologic character of the coast in terms of both morphology and process controls the nature of coastal ecosystems from coral reefs to sandy barrier islands to rocky intertidal communities, and thus the varied ecosystem services they provide.

The nature of the coast at any time and place reflects a dynamic equilibrium among the energy supplied by waves and tides, the quantity and quality of sediment supply, and the level of the sea. Antecedent conditions that are site specific can also exert control, but whether a coastal system is erosional or depositional in nature is a response to the balance of these factors. The most common sources of sediment are rivers, eroding coastal cliffs and bluffs, and unconsolidated deposits on the continental shelf. Clearly, human activities from dams to coastal protection works can impede sediment supply, resulting indirectly in erosion of shorelines. In the short term, beach profiles adjust to increases in wave energy or temporary rises in sea level – the profile adjusts to accommodate higher energy conditions with flatter profiles dissipating more wave energy. Between storm events, fair-weather wave conditions can produce a readjustment of the beach profile as sand stored in bars is moved onshore and the profile steepens (Wright et al. 1979). Such changes frequently occur seasonally, making the identification of net change in the system difficult without long-term data. However, over decades and centuries the effect of sea-level rise causes shorelines to migrate landward – a coast with a slope of 1:2,000 will be pushed back 1,000 m by a sea-level rise of 0.5 m.

In many cases, the dynamic equilibrium described above is disrupted by direct human interference in sediment transport pathways. Jetties, while keeping inlets open for navigation, interrupt longshore sediment transport. At Ocean City, Maryland, on the Atlantic coast of the US, an inlet created by a hurricane in 1933 was eventually stabilized by jetties. These block longshore transport of sand, estimated at 140,000 m^3 yr^{-1}, leading to dramatic erosion on the southern, or downdrift, side of the inlet. Around natural tidal entrances beaches and nearshore sand bodies act as a 'sand sharing' system with ebb tide shoals providing an important sediment transport pathway around the inlet. When dredging occurs either within the inlet or, more commonly, across the ebb shoals the tendency of the geomorphic system towards equilibrium requires readjustment of form and often results in erosion. The magnitude of these impacts can be huge (Pilkey and Dixon, 1996). It has been estimated that over fifty years, inlet dredging has removed and dumped offshore enough sand to advance the entire 600 km coast of Florida seaward by over 7 m.

Responding to coastal change

Options for protecting eroding shorelines are many but can be simply categorized as stabilization using hard structures, reinforcing the coast by adding sediment, or moving that which is threatened and allowing the erosion to continue. The use of hard structures to mitigate erosion has been the subject of much debate. The most common structures used are seawalls, built on the beach or at the shoreline and that run parallel to the shoreline, and groins, which are walls built perpendicular to the shoreline, that aim to trap sand being transported along the beach in the surf zone. The debate is characterized by the following quotations: 'Properly engineered seawalls and revetments can protect the land behind them without causing adverse effects to the fronting beaches' (National Research Council 1990: 59) and 'Hard stabilization may be the best way to save buildings, but retreating from the problem by removing buildings is the best way to save the beach' (Pilkey and Dixon 1996).

Importantly, the use of seawalls and jetties does not add or remove sand from the coastal system. But such structures can result in redistribution of sand or prevent it entering or moving through the system, preventing the natural seasonal adjustment of the beach to changing energy conditions. The effects of seawalls on beaches can be characterized by three potential types of loss:

- placement loss – when a seawall is built actually on the beach, the part of beach behind the wall is lost to the beach system;
- passive loss – when a beach on a retreating shoreline narrows over time in front of fixed seawall and eventually disappears;
- active loss – during storms, seawalls can concentrate wave energy rather than dissipate it, resulting in a greater loss of sand to offshore than under natural conditions.

The addition of sand to stabilize shorelines is usually termed beach nourishment. This involves the excavation of sand from one site, frequently offshore, on to the beach in order to advance the retreating shoreline seaward. Material is usually placed at a higher than natural beach slope, and a period of equilibrium adjustment then follows placement. Sand should be as coarse as or coarser than the natural beach sand in order to withstand the prevailing energy conditions. The longevity of beach nourishment projects has been the subject of much scrutiny, with many examples on the Atlantic shore of the US where all of the nourished material has been lost from the beach within a few months. Evaluations of beach nourishment projects show that longevity varies directly with the square of the nourished length of the shoreline, indicating that the relationship to bordering erosive areas is important, and inversely with the square of incoming wave height, suggesting that nourishment is more challenging on higher energy shorelines.

Effecting coastal landscape change

Human activities regarding landscape change at the coast are not always defensive. The 'reclamation' of land from the sea using seawalls and other structures to prevent low-lying coastal land from being flooded by the tide has been practised in north-west Europe since at least the Romano-British era. Expertise developed in the Netherlands was exported and reached south-eastern England in the thirteenth century. Over 84,000 ha of marshes have been converted to fastlands (an enclosed parcel of land) in the Wash area of eastern England since Roman times. The driving force for this 'offensive' approach to landscape management was dominantly the provision of lands for agriculture until the nineteenth century, when the need for port facilities grew. In north-eastern England, 3,300 ha or 83 per cent of intertidal land has been claimed since 1720, with most of the work conducted after 1800. Losses of intertidal lands on a similar scale can be noted around the world. In San Francisco Bay, only 8 per cent of the historic marsh land remains, with more than 6,000 ha of tidal marsh converted to ponds for industrial salt production.

In instances where the availability of land limits human activities, the creation of new land by building out into the sea has occurred. Perhaps the most famous example of this is Singapore, where land building began in 1820 but markedly expanded after 1960. The land area of Singapore increased by 6.7 per cent or 39 km^2 between 1960 and 1986, with the new land being used for port facilities, airports, industry and to provide recreational opportunities. Fill for this massive undertaking was obtained from both existing land and sea, with hills levelled with excavators and materials moved by truck to the fill site or transferred to nearshore location using conveyor belts supported by jetty structures. When placing fill into unprotected open waters, additional protection from dispersal by waves and currents is provided by armouring the new land with seawalls, breakwaters or rip-rap revetments.

In the late twentieth century the effects of land claim and land creation on estuaries and coastal waters becomes clearer. Within estuaries, the conversion of intertidal area to fastland leads to increased water depths in the remaining area of tidal influence, and thus longer inundation periods. The reduced intertidal area and the structural defences, usually seawalls, built to protect the reclaimed land from inundation, change the cross-section of the estuary, resulting in alteration of estuarine currents and sediment movements and the establishment of a new equilibrium form for the estuarine system (Townend and Pethick 2002). In addition to these geomorphic changes, the effect of long-term sea-level rise has led to questions regarding the sustainability of estuaries where structures rather than topographic gradients define the limit of tidal inundation. The discussion is similar in many ways to the impacts of seawalls on beaches, described previously. The gradient in habitats from sub-tidal to supratidal driven by tidal inundation means that, in estuaries, some habitats will disappear at the expense of others as sea-level rise causes 'coastal squeeze' and the intertidal zone narrows over time.

These concerns, together with the continued need for protection of communities and infrastructure, even along the sheltered shores of estuaries, has focused attention on the role of intertidal habitats, especially marshes and mangroves, in contributing to protection. Coastal marshes represent a dynamic balance between hydrodynamic forcing of waves and tides and the resistivity of sediments and vegetation. Their ability to dissipate wave energy has been well demonstrated (Möller *et al.* 1999) with studies showing that marshes are four times more efficient at wave dampening than bare sand flats, and that this effect is greatest close to the edge of marshes.

Such studies have led to a new coastal management approach for low-lying historically reclaimed coasts in the UK. The seawalls that back the remaining salt marshes alter the tidal flooding and sedimentation regime relative to a marsh with a gradual landward upland transition. 'Managed realignment' seeks to extend the wave buffer provided by coastal marshes by allowing formerly reclaimed areas to once more be under the influence of the tide and revert to marsh habitats (Townend and Pethick 2002). These 'restoration' sites are essentially marshes almost entirely surrounded by seawalls with one or more breaches that provide the tidal connection. Cahoon *et al.* (2000) have documented early sedimentation patterns within one of these breached sites, and show increased rates in lower elevation areas as might be expected based on flooding frequency–sedimentation relationships for coastal marshes. Studies of sedimentation in UK coastal marshes have frequently pointed to the role of major creeks in supplying sediment (e.g. Stoddart *et al.* 1989). However, marshes which are limited by seawalls at their landward margin, and/or those which have limited tidal connections such as in these levee breach restoration sites, are unlikely to develop extensive creek networks. Reed (1988) showed how sedimentation patterns in a marsh on the Dengie Peninsula in Essex, backed by a seawall, were dominated by sediment delivery across the extensive boundary between the marsh and the intertidal flats. The levee-breach sites do not have such an extensive open boundary – most of the perimeter apart from the breach locations consists of pre-existing seawalls. The sustainability of the recreated marshes must be continually reevaluated as the surrounding estuarine systems adjust to the change in tidal prism and as sea-level rise proceeds.

Tourism

The popularity of coastal areas for their climate, aesthetics and recreational opportunities brings increased pressure over and above that resulting from resident communities and industries. Tourism is the business of trading recreational opportunities for economic gains. The challenge for coastal management and planning is to enhance the users' recreational experience of the coast while protecting and even upgrading the coast as a recreational resource. Making recreation enjoyable and safe must not result in changes that make the area less attractive. The greatest direct impacts of tourism on coastal areas are on wind- and wave-dominated coasts where sand beaches are common due to high energy conditions, although coral reefs areas are also increasing in popularity. On sandy coasts the need for access to the foreshore, down cliffs or across sand dunes can stress habitats by trampling, while the beach itself must be stable with suitable sediment which in many eroding areas produces a need for beach replenishment.

Balancing uses is also a critical area of coastal management, especially in sensitive ecosystems. Some recreational uses are incompatible (e.g. swimming vs boating, windsurfing and jet-skiing) and their promotion requires designation of specific uses. This can be managed by the strategic provisional of facilities (e.g. changing rooms and boat ramps), but managing for indirect impacts of tourism on the local area is more challenging. An influx of people to a coastal area will generate additional waste and pollution requiring additional waste water treatment facilities and water supply, as well as the more obvious accommodations and parking places.

Sustainable tourism

Many have studied the inherent conflicts between tourism and the sustainability of coastal ecosystems. Traditionally, mass tourism and sustainable tourism have been viewed as polar opposites (see Clarke 1997). However, it is also possible to see them converge over time as tourist centres reinvent themselves in a cyclic manner to both avoid conflict and further economic development (Baum 1998). Butler (1980) described a Tourism Area Life Cycle model which recognizes dynamism in the tourist environment, limits growth in tourism and triggers in the environment which can change tourism at a destination.

Butler's model of resort evolution (Figure 48.1) has six key elements:

1 *Exploration*. A few adventurous tourists identify the destination and visits increase by word of mouth.
2 *Involvement*. Local residents begin to provide basic services for visitors, advertise their services, etc. The numbers of tourists begins to grow.
3 *Development*. The provision of facilities and advertising increases. There is increasing control of the tourist trade by outsiders, and an excess of tourists over locals, which may lead to the beginnings of resentment among the local population. This is a period of rapid expansion in tourist numbers.
4 *Consolidation*. The resort has an established recreational business district which may be distinct from that used by the local population. Growth in the number of visitors slows.
5 *Stagnation*. The peak numbers of tourists or the maximum capacity is reached. The resort could be viewed as established but out of fashion. There is little or no growth in the number of visitors.
6 *Rejuvenation or decline* The fate of the resort is now dependent upon new initiatives to revitalize interest. Decline may be offset by renewal projects directed towards the

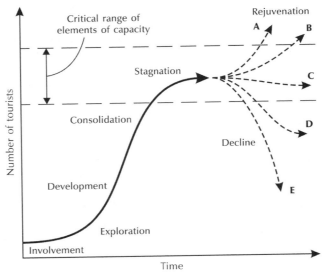

Figure 48.1. The cycle of evolution of a tourism area (Butler model).

original base or refocused towards a new visitor interest group (e.g. ecotourism or gambling).

Some suggest that the environmental pressures associated with tourism can be managed by effective planning using the concept of Limits of Acceptable Change (e.g. Roggenbuck *et al.* 1993). This involves specifying acceptable and achievable environmental and social conditions which can be defined with indicators. Analysis of the relationships between existing and acceptable conditions is then used to identify management actions needed to achieve acceptable conditions. Importantly, continued monitoring of the indicators is required to evaluate the effectiveness of the plan and to allow modifications as necessary (see also Chapter 50).

Tourism in sensitive areas: a case study

The shores of Egypt, Israel and Jordan with their well-developed fringing coral reefs experienced a massive influx of tourists in the late twentieth century. The number of hotel rooms and the number of dive boats in Sharm el Sheik on the Egyptian coast both increased ten-fold between 1988 and 1995. Scuba-diving and snorkelling are the main attractions, as well as a warm climate, which attracts winter tourists from northern Europe. The environmental impacts of this development have included the direct effects of construction such as infilling of coastal habitats and increased sedimentation due to runoff from building sites. Indirect effects in coastal water quality are those associated with sewage discharge, runoff from irrigated lands, and garbage. Increased freshwater demand has led to a major desalinization effort which returns bacteria-laden high salinity waters to the sea. The coral reefs are damaged directly by divers and snorkellers who damage coral through contact and the anchoring and mooring of dive boats close to the reefs (Hawkins and Roberts 1994). Fishery species suffer both from damage to their habitat and from increased fishing pressure due to the increased demand for seafood.

Future solutions to these stresses include the expansion of marine-protected areas and other regulatory approaches on diving and boat access that allow impacted reefs to recover and prevent further damage. Other approaches could include the modification of facilities, e.g. Perspex jetties, to provide access while limiting the damage of structures built into open water, and discharge controls or improved water treatment prior to discharge. The continued viability of the resort facilities on the Red Sea requires such action or, as suggested by Butler's model of the life cycle of tourism areas, the tourism industry could undergo rapid decline.

Industrial effects

The location of industry in coastal areas is dependent upon the basic geography of the system that controls the availability of suitable land for development, the supply of raw materials including water, and access to means of both waste disposal and transportation for finished products. In coastal areas, especially the large areas of reclaimed land discussed earlier, flat land is available for the construction of expansive facilities and ocean access supplies both water and transportation. However, many industrial facilities are vulnerable because of the dynamics of the coastal systems they depend on. For example, many power plants in the UK are located at the coast through land availability and access to cooling waters. One of these is at Dungeness, a shingle cuspate foreland in south-east England. The longshore drift is from west to east, which leads to a deficit of material immediately in front of the nuclear power stations. As a result, beach nourishment is carried out to protect the facilities with material collected at the east of the site and carried by lorry to the west. Longshore drift ensures the material is moved to the shoreline in front of the station and eventually back to where it was originally collected in the east. This recycling must continue to ensure the continued viability of the power station.

Perhaps the most prominent need for management and regulation of industrial activities at the coast is related to their release of contaminants into coastal waters. The record of contaminants in coastal sediments can often provide an insight into the history of human activities and the effectiveness, or not, of different management approaches. One good example of this is the study by Finney and Huh (1989) of sediment cores from basins offshore of Los Angeles. The cores were taken from areas close to outfalls of wastewater treatment plants with anoxic bottom waters, so there was minimal bioturbation. The chronology of contamination was thus well preserved and 210Pb dating was used to date the core profiles. The study detected the onset of Pb, Zn and Cr in sediments in the 1930s and a maximum concentration of these metals between 1960 and 1970. These patterns match trends in the emissions from the waste water treatment plants, but the study also identified peak periods of sewage discharge, associated with organic carbon, and Ba associated with the dumping of drilling muds from oil and gas exploration. A similar coring study in the confined waters of San Francisco Bay (Hornberger *et al.* 1999) shows the effects of regulations on coastal waters. Between 1950 and 1970 cores show severe contamination with DDT, PCBs and PAHs. Post 1970, there is a steep decline in DDT concentrations, reflecting a ban on its use, but a slower decline in PAHs and metals as some inputs continued and the existing inventory was gradually redistributed throughout the bay by tidal circulation.

Industrial impacts on coastal ecosystems: a New Jersey case study

Power plants operated by Public Service Electric and Gas (PSE&G) in Salem, New Jersey, have had dramatic impacts on fisheries in Delaware Bay. The PSE&G facility consists of two pressurized water reactors which use once-through cooling. The pumps for the cooling system have a total capacity of almost 15 billion l/day and the maximum operational withdrawal is just over 13.5 billion l/day. Intake velocity on the pumps is 60 cm/second with each intake cell being protected by mechanically cleaned trash racks to reduce intake of debris into the pumps. Behind the racks fish screens are used to prevent fish from being entrained, and these are cleaned with low pressure washes to encourage fish recovery and return to the estuary. Despite these measures the estimated annual losses due to the cooling intakes are over 7.5 million kg of bay anchovy, over 18,000 kg of white perch and over 5 million kg of weakfish, as well as a substantial take of other locally important fishes such as herring, Atlantic croaker, striped bass and American shad. To mitigate concerns about the potential future impacts of operation on fish populations in the Delaware estuary, the state of New Jersey added special conditions to the discharge permit that allows the plant to operate. These conditions call for the establishment of an estuary enhancement programme, the primary goal of which is the large-scale restoration, enhancement and/or preservation of more than 80 km² of salt marsh and adjacent uplands along the estuary. By 2006 the programme had built thirteen fish ladders and restored thousands of hectares of previously drained land around the margins of the bay. The concept behind the approach is that the restoration will promote increased aquatic resources production and biodiversity in the estuary to offset the losses associated with the power plant cooling.

Indirect effects

While most of the management issues discussed thus far have arisen from the interaction between coastal dynamics and human activities at the coast, the cumulative effects of activities in other areas can result in serious problems for coastal areas. Most pronounced are those resulting from watershed changes in the amount and quality of water and sediment reaching the coast. Land-use changes with implications for downstream areas are many and include alterations in land use and vegetation cover, frequently related to shifts in agricultural practice, and paving and development of formerly wild or agricultural land. The resultant changes in runoff pattern alter the rate of water delivery to the coast, and any increase in the magnitude or change in frequency of flood events can substantially alter the delivery of sediment. Soil losses, and thus potential coastal sediment gains, average only 3 t ha^{-1} yr^{-1} in tropical woodlands but increase to between 54 and 334 t ha^{-1} yr^{-1} when the forest is cleared and cultivated.

Water and river management to support irrigation, municipal and industrial water use, and navigation frequently results in dramatic changes in sediment supply to coastal areas. In Texas, Morton (1979) has documented that the Brazos River discharges only 30 per cent of its pre-dam sediment supply, while the Rio Grande sediment load has likely diminished by 80–95 per cent. The effect of the Aswan High Dam, constructed in 1964, on sediment supply to the Nile delta has also been well documented. Prior to High Dam construction, the Nile delivered 124 million tonnes of sediment per year to the sea. After completion of the dam, this was reduced to 50 million tonnes which resulted in erosion of the delta at rates of up to 30 m/yr. When the erosive forces of the sea are no longer balanced by sediment inputs from the river, erosion will prevail. The Mississippi River shows similar changes. The Missouri River has been principal supplier of sediment to the Mississippi River since the end of the last ice age. After five large dams were completed for hydroelectric power and irrigation above Yankton, South Dakota, between 1953 and 1963, the discharge of sediment from the Upper Missouri River Basin virtually was stopped and the effect could be observed all the way down to the mouth of the Mississippi River. While these losses were somewhat counterbalanced by a five- to ten-fold increase in sediment supply from the Ohio River during the same period due to deforestation and the expansion of row-crop farming, sediment discharges to the Gulf of Mexico in 1992 were less than half of what they were before 1953.

These examples clearly illustrate the magnitude of watershed changes and their influence on the coast. Changes in water quality are equally dramatic. Water quality throughout the Mississippi Basin has been degraded by excess nutrients. Most states in the Basin have significant river miles impaired by high nutrient concentrations, primarily phosphorus, meaning that they are not fully supporting aquatic life uses. When these waters reach the Gulf of Mexico the result is excessive algal growth, driven primarily by excess nitrogen, ultimately causing a decrease in dissolved oxygen in the bottom water. A zone on the Gulf of Mexico's Texas–Louisiana Shelf with seasonally low oxygen levels (-1) develops every year as a result of these watershed inputs. In 2001, it was 20,720 km^2 in extent. The nutrients entering the gulf from the Mississippi River originate from a variety of human activities including: discharges from sewage treatment and industrial waste water treatment plants; stormwater runoff from city streets and farms; and automobile exhaust and fossil fuel power plants via air deposition to the vast land area drained by the Mississippi River and its tributaries. About 90 per cent of the nitrate load to the gulf comes from non-point sources, with 56 per cent contributed by the Upper Mississippi and 34 per cent by the Ohio River Basin.

Problems at the coast frequently occur because of multiple stressors – some direct and some indirect. The cumulative effects may not be immediately apparent until some visible or tangible threshold is crossed. Managing or restoring coastal areas under such conditions requires identification of proximal causes as well as more subtle influence or changes within and without the system.

Indirect effects on coastal systems: a New York case study

Jamaica Bay, located at the south-western end of Long Island, New York, consists of a mosaic of marsh islands separated by intertidal flats and deeper channels. Recent catastrophic losses of tidal marsh vegetation have resulted in a decrease in marsh area from about 930 ha to a little more than 400 ha since 1924, and all marshes will be lost by 2025 if these trends continue. According to the evidence of historical maps and regional geology, the marshes originally developed in the bay when vegetation colonized sandy overwash and inlet deposits that resulted from the east–west movement of Rockaway Inlet, the entrance to Jamaica Bay. Once marsh vegetation was established on these sandy bars, it maintained itself by accumulation of fine sediments and plant matter at a more rapid rate than historical sea-level rise.

A number of man-made alterations have occurred in the Jamaica Bay estuary, many of which alone might not present a major threat to the system, but which cumulatively appear to have stressed the marshes to their limit. The physical dynamics of the bay have changed greatly. The position of Rockaway Inlet was stabilized, potentially reducing the exchange of sediments between the bay and the ocean to below historic levels. Dredging in the vicinity of the inlet has altered the way in which sediment moves into the system from the ocean. The hydrodynamics and circulation of the bay have been severely altered by the construction of a causeway to support a road, the dredging of navigation channels, the dredging of deep borrow pits to provide fill for JFK airport, and the extension of airport runway into the bay. The shorelines around the edge of the Bay have been stabilized and the barrier beach developed, effectively limiting overwash of sands during storms that historically may have contributed sediment to the marshes. The dredging of channels and borrow pits in the bay has resulted in a sediment sink, thus removing a source of sediment that was historically available to maintain marsh elevation against sea-level rise. The lack of sedimentation increases water depth and wave activity across the tidal flats, thus eroding the remaining marsh islands.

As well as these physical alterations, changes in land use and thus runoff within the watershed of the bay have altered the character and amount of freshwater and sediments delivered to the bay. Both landfills and wastewater treatment plants have contributed massive amounts of nutrients and contaminants to the bay. The nutrients appear to have stimulated the growth of dense banks of mussels (*Guekensia demissa*) along the marsh edges which can block small marsh drainage channels. This appears to cause water to pond on the marsh surface for long periods after high tides, waterlogging the marsh soil and stressing marsh vegetation, ultimately leading to interior marsh loss.

While many factors contribute to the marsh loss in Jamaica Bay, the cause–effect relationships are complex, as the multiple human activities described here were not directed at the marshes but at developing economic activities and communities surrounding the bay.

The future of coastal management

Our coast is continually changing – because of human action and natural forces. In many areas, catastrophic storms occur so infrequently that coastal residents have no personal experience of storm impacts. Structures, from houses to roads to industrial facilities, are built in vulnerable areas. Our understanding that future climate change may cause greater impacts than those we have recently experienced (e.g. Webster *et al.* 2005) must be translated into the public context and forthrightly presented to coastal planners. In the ecological sciences, protocols have been developed to link human activities with environmental stressors that produce ecological responses and such approaches are being applied to large-scale ecosystem management (Harwell 1998). However, for the most part these approaches are developed within the scientific community and their direct utilization to develop sustainable approaches to coastal management requires more than just sound science. Cash *et al.* (2003) suggest that for science, technology and knowledge to be effective in developing sustainable solutions, it must be salient, credible and legitimate. These authors also recognize that tradeoffs frequently exist among salience, credibility and legitimacy such that mediation is required. This may entail enhancing legitimacy through increasing transparency and more clearly linking science, technology and knowledge with decision-making. Nowhere is this approach more needed than in the future management of coastal systems.

The call for coastal management to be based on scientific knowledge of coastal dynamics frequently comes to the fore when hurricanes or non-tropical storms devastate communities and infrastructure. Pilkey and Young (2005) set out the opposing approaches to such disasters. On the one hand, are those, such as Pilkey and Young, who advocate systematic retreat from the oceanfront to avoid damage in the future and allow natural processes to heal and adjust to the storm impact. On the other hand, are those that react to storm damages by calling for increased investment in protecting communities – either through enhancing natural buffers, i.e. beach nourishment, or by strengthening engineered defences such as seawalls. Such debate is rarely informed by coastal management regulations. In the United States, the coastal zone management programme was reviewed twenty-five years after initiation by Hershman *et al.* (1999). The programme has five core objectives: protecting estuaries and coastal wetlands; protecting beaches and dunes; providing public access to the coast; revitalizing waterfronts; and accommodating seaport development. The study found that evaluating the effectiveness of the programme was challenging, as monitoring of programme outcomes was rare and mostly inadequate. They point to the need for such programmes both to specifically monitor the perception of success or failure, and to document the outcomes of important trade-off decisions between economy and environment.

Trade-offs between science and engineering, current conditions and future changes, ecology and economy come to the fore at the coast. While decisions must be informed by local knowlwdge, a system-level assessment is essential to ensure the sustainability of coastal geomorphic and ecological systems in the face of increased pressure for homes, ports and recreational facilities. Some have called for strategic planning, which designates not only natural protected areas but also commercial protected areas, as a means to a *priori* establish societal expectations for coastal areas and ensure balance at the regional scale amongst potentially conflicting uses (Weinstein and Reed 2005).

Whether the application of salient, credible and legitimate studies that embrace the range of uses currently in demand at the coast will resolve current coastal management challenges is yet to be seen. Despite high land prices, cyclones and tsunamis, coastal environments continue to be attractive places for people to live, work and recreate. The implications of those activities for the coast have been outlined here. Unfortunately, resolving those conflicts has yet to be achieved at the global scale.

Further reading

Beatley, T., Brower, D.J. and Schwab, A.K. (2002) *Introduction to Coastal Zone Management*. Washington DC: Island Press.

Cicin-Sain, B. and Knecht, R.W. (1998) *Integrated Coastal and Ocean Management: Concepts and Practices*. Washington DC: Island Press.

Viles, H. and Spencer, T. (1995) *Coastal Problems: Geomorphology, Ecology and Society at the Coast*. London: Edward Arnold.

Weinstein, M.P. and Reed, D.J. (2005) Sustainable coastal development: the dual mandate and a recommendation for 'Commerce Managed Areas'. *Restoration Ecology* 13, 174–82.

References

Baum, T. (1998) Taking the exit route: extending the Tourism Area Life Cycle model. *Current Issues in Tourism* 1, 167–74.

Butler, R. (1980) The concept of tourist area cycle of evolution. *Canadian Geographer* 24, 5–12.

Cahoon, D.R., French, J.R., Spencer, T., Reed, D.J. and Möller, I. (2000) Vertical accretion versus elevational adjustment in UK saltmarshes: an evaluation of alternative methodologies. In K. Pye and J.R.L. Allen (eds) *Coastal and Estuarine Environments: Sedimentology, Geomorphology and Geoarchaeology* (Special Publications 175), pp. 223–38. London: Geological Society, London.

Cash, D.W., Clark, W.C., Alcock, F., Dickson, N.M., Eckley, N., Guston, D.H., Jager, J. and Mitchel, R.B. (2003). Knowledge systems for sustainable development. *Proceedings, National Academy of Sciences* 100, 8086–91.

Clarke, J. (1997) A framework for approaches to sustainable tourism. *Journal of Sustainable Tourism* 5, 224–33.

Culliton, T.J. (1998) *Population: Distribution, Density, and Growth* (NOAA's State of the Coast Report). Silver Spring, MD: NOAA.

Finney, B.P. and Huh, C.-A. (1989) History of metal pollution in the southern California Bight: an update. *Environmental Science and Technology* 23, 294–303.

Harwell, M.A. (1998) Science and environmental decision-making in South Florida. *Ecological Applications* 8, 580–90.

Hawkins, J. and Roberts, C.M. (1994) The growth of coastal tourism in the Red Sea: present and future effects on coral reefs. *Ambio* 23, 503–8.

Hershman, M.J., Good, J.W., Bernd-Choen, T., Goodwin, R.F., Lee, V. and Pogue, P. (1999) The effectiveness of coastal zone management in the United States. *Coastal Management* 27, 113–38.

Hornberger, M.I., Luoma, S.N., van Geen, A., Fuller, C. and Anima, R. (1999) Historical trends of metals in the sediments of San Francisco Bay, California. *Marine Chemistry* 64, 39–55.

Kurihara, Y., Tuleya, R.E. and Bender, M.A. (1997) The GFDL hurricane prediction system and its performance in the 1995 hurricane season. *Monthly Weather Review* 126, 1306–22.

Möller, I., Spencer, T., French, J.R., Leggett, D.J., Dixon, M. (1999) Wave transformation over salt marshes: a field and numerical modelling study from North Norfolk, England. *Estuarine, Coastal and Shelf Science* 49, 411–26.

Morton, R.A. (1979) Temporal and spatial variations in shoreline changes and their implications, examples from the Texas Gulf Coast. *Journal of Sedimentary Petrology* 49, 1101–12.

National Research Council. (1990) *Managing Coastal Erosion*. Washington DC: National Academy Press.

Pilkey, O.H. and Dixon, K.L. (1996) *The Corps and the Shore*. Washington DC: Island Press.

Pilkey, O.H. and Young, R.S. (2005) Will Hurricane Katrina impact shoreline management? Here's why it should. *Journal of Coastal Research* 21, iii–ix.

Reed, D.J. (1988) Sediment dynamics and deposition in a retreating coastal salt marsh. *Estuarine, Coastal and Shelf Science* 26, 67–79.

Roggenbuck, J.W., Williams, D.R. and Watson, A.E. (1993) Defining acceptable conditions in wilderness. *Environmental Management* 17, 187–97.

Stoddart, D.R., Reed, D.J. and French, J. (1989) Understanding salt marsh accretion, Scolt Head Island, Norfolk, England. *Estuaries* 12, 228–36.

Timmerman, A., Oberhuber, J., Bacher, A., Esch, M., Latif, M. and Roeckner, E. (1999) Increased El Niño frequency in a climate model forced by future greenhouse warming. *Nature* 398, 694–6.

Townend, I. and Pethick, J.S. (2002) Estuarine flooding and managed retreat. *Philosophical Transactions of the Royal Society of London*, A 360, 1477–95.

Webster, P.J., Holland, G.J., Curry, J.A. and Chang, H-R. (2005) Changes in tropical cyclone number, duration, and intensity in a warming environment. *Science* 309, 1844–6.

Wright, L.D., Chappell, J., Thom, B.G., Bradshaw, M.P. and Cowell, P. (1979) Morphodynamics of reflective and dissipative beach and inshore systems: southeastern Australia. *Marine Geology* 32, 105–40.

49

Managing the present and the future of smaller islands

Patrick Nunn

Preamble

Human existence on islands in the middle of an ocean is, by nature of their remoteness, often comparatively small size with consequently few lifestyle options, and more vulnerable to change than in many other places. The vulnerability of islands to change increases with smaller islands (generally <5000 km² in area[1]), for many of which the entire land area can be classed as 'coastal' and therefore vulnerable to change deriving from the ocean, from the land and from the air.

The combination of small size and remoteness means that humans on such islands may occasionally have their trajectories of social and cultural development disrupted profoundly. A good example comes from remote 506 ha Pukapuka Atoll in the northern Cook Islands whose inhabitants divide their traditional history into two periods separated by *te mate wolo* (The Great Death) about AD 1525 when a huge wave swept across the low island leaving only a handful of survivors (Beaglehole and Beaglehole 1938).

Archaeologists investigating the enigmatic statue-building culture of Easter Island (Rapanui), some 2,250 km from the nearest land (Pitcairn Island) in the southeast Pacific, have long divided the island's history into two (Bahn and Flenley 1992): first, the statue-building period that celebrated a time of plenty; and, second, the statue-toppling and destruction period marking a time when conflict became rampant and culminated in the first written description of the island by Roggeveen in AD 1722 as having a 'wasted appearance'. Some have famously attributed this change to unsustainable human impacts on the land, particularly the cutting of trees (Diamond 2005), while others regard it as the outcome of a natural change (Hunter-Anderson 1998).

Early humans colonized islands for many of the same reasons that tourists flock to them today. Many smaller and archipelagic island environments are capable of sustaining sizable numbers of people because there are diverse sources of sustenance (reefal, lagoonal, deltaic, lowland, upland) that are often neatly compartmentalized through their geography (islands separated from one another by ocean barriers). Small remote land areas generally discourage both overpopulation and the establishment of drawcards for urban population growth (such as industry and manufacturing) that elsewhere have often led to environmental deterioration.

Many tourists visit islands under the illusion that their environments are pristine and largely unchanging, a notion that has underpinned an understanding of traditional human–environment interactions on islands for centuries.

Yet many island environments have been mismanaged, particularly since their (re-) colonization by mostly continental-based colonial powers in the nineteenth century (McNeill 1994; Nunn 2004a).

The introduction of alien fauna and flora into often 'naïve' island environments by people who could hardly foresee the consequences of such action has had calamitous effects for many such islands. Much island environmental management over the past hundred years or so has been based on the assumption that islands are merely miniature continents and thus continental management practices need only to be downsized to be effective (Doumenge 1987). Such practices have compounded in particular the loss of island biotas but could also be considered culpable across a range of environmental problems, ranging from coastal erosion to cash cropping, particularly in steepland areas (Nunn and Mimura, forthcoming; Clarke and Morrison 1987).

The purposeful introduction of the mongoose by 1925 to the larger Fiji Islands, where various plantation crops were being successfully grown, failed to put an end to the rats that plagued these crops but led rather to the extirpation of snakes and ground-dwelling birds (Watling and Chape 1992). The accidental introduction of the snake *Bioga irregularis* to Guam had comparable effects (Savidge 1987). Flax (*Phormium tenax*) on St Helena was originally introduced as an export crop that would invigorate the economy of this remote island. But the initiative failed, and flax has taken over much of upland St Helena, crowding out native species (Cronk 1989). A comparable situation pertains to sisal (*Agave sisalina*) on certain Caribbean islands (Byrne 1980).

Mining has laid barren areas of many smaller islands, most markedly those where thick accumulations of avian phosphate existed. Such islands, including Banaba (Ocean Island) and Nauru in the Pacific, and Christmas Island in the Indian Ocean, were highly attractive to sea birds, both on account of their remoteness and because of the fish-rich waters upwelling around them. Over millennia, the faeces of these birds produced phosphate-rich guano that accumulated in the irregularities of the limestone (karst) surface and even altered the upper parts of the bedrock to create phosphorite. The mining of the phosphate has rendered the flat surface that once existed on these islands into a characteristic pit-and-pinnacle landscape of little use to subsistence agriculturists (Weeramantry 1992). Pollutants emptied into the Jaba River from the Panguna copper mine on Bougainville Island (Papua New Guinea) were a significant cause of the unrest that led to the mine's closure in 1989 (Oliver 1991).

Logging has had comparable effects on island environments, with many of the most regrettable examples coming from the Asia-Pacific region (Dauvergne 2001). Larger islands in Indonesia such as Sulawesi and Sumatra have been almost stripped of the trees that once covered them, with many consequences (Robertson and van Schaik 2001); a similar situation obtains in parts of the Solomon Islands (Hviding and Bayliss-Smith 2000). Logging depletes not only the productive potential of island terrestrial environments for their human inhabitants but also their nearshore (marine) environments.

The singular character of the environmental problems that islands have experienced and the challenges that they face have not gone wholly unremarked. In one of the most effective expressions of concern about the future of smaller-island states, they have banded together as the Alliance of Small Island States (AOSIS) to be heard in international fora where their powerful (multiple-nation) block vote is often actively solicited. AOSIS is supported by the United Nations through the Small Island Developing States network (http://www.sidsnet.org)

established following recognition of the special needs and character of smaller island states (and others) following the first Global Conference on Sustainable Development of SIDS in Barbados in April 1994. Among the various non-government organizations that focus on islands and their environments is the Island Resources Foundation (http://www.irf.org), intended to help the sustainable development of islands (Towle 1971).

Islands – geography and origins

Islands are scattered throughout the world's oceans, most in the largest (the Pacific), most in the tropics. Larger islands, often continental in origin and affinities, lie close to the modern coasts of many continents and include Madagascar, New Caledonia (La Grande Terre) and Svalbard, and many of those in Japan and Indonesia. The smaller islands on which this chapter focuses are commonly farther from continental shores and located within the ocean basins. Most of these are 'oceanic islands', defined as having originated as a result of processes operating in the ocean basins (Nunn 1994).

Oceanic islands have been classified according to their mode of origin (Table 49.1) with the largest and most numerous being found associated with convergent plate boundaries. The reason for this is that these areas are where island-forming processes are most rapid and most persistent. For example, most low-latitude islands in the southwest Pacific between the large island of New Guinea and isolated Niue Island (169°50'W) formed as a result of the oblique convergence of the Pacific Plate and the Indo-Australian Plate within the past 45 million years. Islands tend to retain surface (above-sea) expression longer in the tropics than elsewhere because coral reefs often develop on top of a subsiding (volcanic) island and grow upwards as that subsidence continues, to form an atoll. Most atolls in the equatorial western Pacific, such as those in western Kiribati (Gilbert group), Tuvalu, Tokelau and the Marshall Islands, and those like the Cocos–Keeling group in the eastern Indian Ocean, began forming

Table 49.1. Genetic classification of oceanic islands

Level One	Level Two	Examples
Plate-boundary islands	Islands at divergent plate boundaries	Iceland (Atlantic), Niuafo'ou (Tonga – Pacific)
	Islands at convergent plate boundaries	Lesser Antilles (Caribbean), Vanuatu (Pacific)
	Islands along transverse plate boundaries	Cikobia (Fiji – Pacific), Clipperton (Pacific)
Intraplate islands	Linear groups of islands	Hawaii–Emperor Island–Seamount Chain (Pacific), Kerguelen and Heard Islands (Indian Ocean)
	Isolated islands	Christmas Island (Indian Ocean), Niue Island (Pacific), St Helena (Atlantic)
	Clustered groups of islands	Canary Islands (Atlantic), Galapagos Islands (Pacific)

Source: Adapted from Nunn (1994).

tens of millions of years ago from reefs growing upward from sunken volcanic foundations that are today thousands of metres below the ocean surface.

Smaller islands

While smaller islands exist in most parts of the world's oceans, those that are most commonly discussed as examples of vulnerable locations are those that are also remote. These may be remote from one another – as with Easter Island (see earlier) – or remote from larger (continental) landmasses – as are, by definition, most oceanic islands.

Smaller oceanic islands that are remote are commonly associated with parts of the Earth's surface where island-forming processes are slow or moribund. A good example is the South Atlantic island of St Helena, which probably broke off from the Mid-Atlantic Ridge, now some 960 km distant, some 30–50 million years ago (Baker *et al.* 1967). In the Pacific, Niue Island would probably have stayed beneath the ocean surface had not the plate on which it formed buckled upon approaching the Tonga Trench, thrusting it at least 70 m upwards in the past 600,000 years (Nunn and Britton 2004).

Smallness and remoteness make terrestrial life vulnerable. Plants and animals that are endemic (or native) to smaller islands are well known to lack the ability to resist alien predators; witness this description of uninhabited Howland Island (central Pacific) in 1854: 'the extraordinary tameness of the birds made it necessary to scuffle through them at times as one would if walking through windrows of dead leaves in the autumn' (Howland 1955: 97).

Smallness and remoteness also make human life vulnerable by reducing lifestyle options, particularly in the face of crisis, and rendering mutual (cross-ocean) support networks difficult to sustain. Around AD 1300, many Pacific Island societies were thrown into crisis by a sea-level fall that abruptly reduced food resources by 80 per cent on some islands, leading to conflict (Nunn 2000, 2003).

Today, life on many of the smallest and most remote islands is heavily subsidized to enable the conservation of unique biotas and to allow the island's human occupants to follow their traditional ways of life. Examples include Lord Howe Island in the Pacific, part of which was declared a World Heritage Site in 1982, and Tristan da Cunha Island, a British Dependency in the South Atlantic.

Yet smallness and remoteness also attract some humans. Some islands have been effective prisons. The elusive Napoleon Bonaparte could not escape remote St Helena as he had Elba, dying there in 1821. Two attempts at establishing Norfolk Island (east of Australia) as a penal colony were ultimately abandoned in 1855. Conversely, islands attract many visitors today who are keen to experience what are perceived as the unique qualities of island environments, ranging from pristine ecosystems to unusual cultures. In reality, such qualities are sometimes invented but invariably well marketed to allow tourism to continue and provide often much-needed income to island peoples.

The human inhabitants of smaller oceanic islands have invariably had a closer relationship to the ocean and its resources than many continental dwellers. The first few generations to occupy the islands of Tonga (South Pacific), beginning around 3,000 years ago, appear to have been sustained almost entirely by seafood, largely lagoon-dwelling shellfish (Burley and Dickinson 2001). It is possible that many remoter islands in the world's oceans were colonized initially by 'sea nomads', people who wandered the oceans surviving on ocean foods and only occasionally (or seasonally) making landfall; a modern example comes from the smaller islands off the west coast of mainland Myanmar (Ivanoff 2005).

Plate 49.1. Over-explotation of coral reefs for food around the island of Rarotonga in the southern Cook Islands has led to a revival of traditional taboos, promulgated here in a modern context for the benefit of both local people and tourists. Photograph by P. Nunn.

Modern island peoples, particularly those living outside urban centres, frequently include hunted or gathered sea foods in their diets. As populations have increased, so pressures on particular sea foods has increased, leading to their depletion and, sometimes, the implementation of remedial conservation measures (Plate 49.1). Today tourists target island groups like the Cook Islands (Pacific) and the Maldives (Indian Ocean) largely for their underwater attractions, and a challenge is to diversify the tourism product in such countries to offset the expected degradation of their coral-reef ecosystems over the next few decades (Hoegh-Guldberg 1999).

Island peoples and environments – change and adaptation within the last hundred years

Increasing involvement with the global economy and world trade has affected most smaller-island environments since around 1900. For many such islands, the last hundred years saw them identified for the first time as part of a country, and their inhabitants sought new livelihood opportunities by looking outwards – a contrast to the situation that had prevailed for most of the human history of such islands, whereby their inhabitants identified themselves with a 'tribe' rather than a 'nation' and where livelihoods were largely determined by on-island resources.

A parallel development for many islands has been the unprecedented influx of new migrants, usually with different attitudes from the indigenes towards island resources and commonly seeing money-making possibilities in lands that had previously been used wholly for subsistence. Some migrants introduced diseases to which the indigenous people had little resistance, thereby bringing about widespread mortality and giving the impression to later settlers that many islands were practically devoid of people, an impression that encouraged the introduction of commercial agriculture, for example. Such changes, ably documented for Pacific Islands by McNeill (1994) and globally by Crosby (1986), have led to a situation on many islands whereby human–environment interactions during the twentieth century were quite different from those during earlier times.

Population growth during the twentieth century was fuelled by continued in-migration, urbanization and a tradition of large families on many islands, leading to a situation where many island environments are no longer capable of sustaining existing populations. Unsustainable food-production (and income-generating) strategies exist on many islands and are exacerbated by competing demands on the same environmental resource. This is well illustrated by tourism (also see later) on which many smaller-island economies are increasingly coming to depend. Islanders are being asked to sell or lease productive land, especially nearshore areas, for recreational use; the dilemma is well expressed in the following lament:

> Like an alien
> In we own land
> I feel like a stranger
> And I sensing danger
> We can't sell our whole country
> To please the foreign lobby
> What's the point of progress?
> Is it really success
> If we gain ten billion
> But lose the land we live on?[2]

Deforestation is another major problem for many islands, where traditional landowners, often only partly absorbed within the cash economy, are induced by large cash handouts to sell their valuable hardwoods for a fraction of their true value (Dauvergne 2001). The result is that land which has sustained these people for generations is denuded and the soil eroded, leaving them impoverished long after the money has been spent.

Problems vary between smaller islands depending on whether the nation of which they are part (or with which they are aligned) is largely continental and therefore often rich, or wholly insular and therefore invariably poorer. Thus, for example, the islands of the Hawaii group have environments that are today generally well managed and are likely to remain so in the future because Hawaii is part of the United States. Yet these islands are similar in origin, form and environmental potential to those in independent Samoa where, in contrast, environmental management is under-resourced and producing a situation where 'development' is manifestly unsustainable.

Owing to their locations within the tropics, many smaller islands are particularly vulnerable to climate extremes, notably tropical cyclones (hurricanes) and droughts associated with the El Niño Southern Oscillation (ENSO) phenomenon. In a similar way, many smaller islands are close to lithospheric plate boundaries, and subject to natural disasters arising from the seismicity and volcanism prevalent in many such places, together with the secondary effects of these such as tsunami(s). Particularly since the start of the twentieth century, when the vulnerability of island environments and island populations began increasing markedly, the effects of such phenomena have caused greater disruption than ever before (Pelling and Uitto 2001).

Climate change during the past century has also contributed to problems for island environments and their inhabitants, and is predicted to do so increasingly in the next hundred years (see later). One widespread result of global warming during the past hundred years or so has been a sea-level rise of around 15 cm. This rise has been cited as a cause of shoreline and beach erosion on many islands (Leatherman and Beller-Simms 1997).

Island tourism

Smaller islands generally lack many sources of revenue generation that are available to larger nations and those based on continents, a situation that has noticeably worsened as globalization has gathered pace in the past few decades. One of the few island-specific products for which demand continues to grow is tourism, visitors being attracted, particularly from continents, by a whole range of island attributes.

Yet the development of a tourism product within an island context invariably means replacing existing land cover with other types and changing the uses of particular areas (see calypso mentioned previously and chapter 48). Successful long-term island tourism needs also to be carefully managed, often so that it appears there is no management at all. Often the economic benefits of tourism ensure that developments go ahead on smaller islands irrespective of cautions about their environmental impacts. Thus the out-to-sea extension of the main airport runway on Bali (Indonesia) led to the erosion by 1984 of part of the famed Kuta Beach (Burbridge and Maragos 1985).

The island of Anguilla in the Caribbean saw visitor arrivals more than double in the period 1985–95 and, more significantly, visitor expenditure increase from US $11.3 million to more than US $51 million within the same period. Most visitors to Anguilla are attracted by the island's coasts, yet average beach erosion rates were measured at 0.3 m/year in 1988 (Cambers 1992) and environmental managers have been hindered from implementing any conservation measures that might impact the island's burgeoning tourism. In September 1995, Hurricane Luis hit Anguilla and caused massive erosion of some shorelines; at Maunday's Bay an average recession of the dune front of 9 m was recorded (Plate 49.2a,b). Island managers have now adopted several measures intended to restore Anguilla's coasts and allow for their sustainable development, particularly with tourism in mind. These measures include discouraging beach-front development, planting vegetation along the backs of beaches, and stopping beach-sand mining.[3]

Agriculture

Many inhabitants of smaller islands depend, in part at least, on foods that they can grow, hunt or gather from island environments (including offshore areas). A rise in urban populations in recent decades on many islands has led to a parallel rise in cash cropping, intended to produce surpluses for sale in urban markets, and this has resulted in an overall expansion of areas devoted to agriculture on most islands. Further, some islands have developed niche markets for agricultural products (Plates 49.3 and 49.4) while others continue to produce the same plantation crops that were introduced during colonial times (Plate 49.4); both enterprises are commonly subsidized, either by national governments or through international agreements.

Sugar cane was introduced to the larger Fiji islands during their (British) colonial history (1874–1970) as a plantation crop that produced sugar primarily for the United Kingdom market. The benefits of sugar-cane cultivation in Fiji were that it could be grown at low cost and that, through the government-sponsored infrastructure, a constant supply could be

Plate 49.2a. Changes in the shoreline at Barney Beach on the Caribbean island of Anguilla: September 1994, a classic beach developed for tourism.

Plate 49.2b. The same beach in September 1995, three weeks after Hurricane Luis. Most of the sand has been stripped off the beach to expose a bare rock platform, highly unattractive for tourism. Photographs courtesy of Gillian Cambers.

Plate 49.3. Agricultural niche and plantation crops on smaller islands: oranges from Pitcairn Islands (Pacific Ocean).

practically guaranteed. Following independence, Fiji was regarded as a preferred supplier of cane sugar to the UK (and later the European Union) market, an arrangement subsequently formalized in 1975 under the Lomé Convention. This led to Fiji sugar being bought by the EU at as much as four times what it could have been sold for on the open market (Grynberg 1997). Appeals from other sugar-producing nations to the World Trade Organization in 2004 led to the EU beginning to phase out its subsidy for Fiji sugar, and the creation of a dilemma for this island nation as to how to replace it (Chand 2004).

Water supply and waste disposal

As island populations grow, so too do the challenges associated with supplying those populations with what are commonly viewed as essential services. Among these are the supply of potable water and the disposal of waste, sometimes acute problems on smaller islands where the options for both water supply and waste disposal are limited by size.

Water supply is a problem that is most sustained on arid islands – a recent study of Paros Island in the Aegean Sea concluded that, if population continued to increase, wind-powered desalination plants would have to be built to meet demand (Voivontas *et al.* 2003). But water supply is more of a problem on poorer islands (SIDS) in the tropics where, typically because of ENSO effects, prolonged droughts occur every few years and there are no funds to be proactive (building large reservoirs for long-term storage), only reactive (physically moving water from wet areas to drought-stricken areas). The largest, most populous island in the Cook Islands (Pacific) is Rarotonga where a serious water supply crisis arose in 2002. Of the two reservoirs built in the previous twenty years, one was being used as a landfill, the other

Plate 49.4. Plantation crops: Sugar from Mauritius (Indian Ocean).

was abandoned as being too costly to maintain after just a few years of operation. Funds for water supply were cut from the August 2002 budget and islanders were being asked to boil both drinking and bath water for a minimum of ten minutes before use to avoid disease.[4]

Most water for human consumption/use on such islands comes from surface water (rivers, etc.), groundwater or rainwater. The first two sources are particularly vulnerable to localized pollution, perhaps from nearby pit toilets or pesticides used in agriculture. On islands like those in the Maldives where, for reasons of topography and climate, groundwater is the main source of drinking water, large waves like those associated with the December 2004 Indian Ocean Tsunami can overlay a layer of salt water on the freshwater lens that may persist for years. The presence of this salt water layer may render the water undrinkable for humans and cause those food plants that depend on groundwater to shrivel and die. OXFAM responded in the Maldives by shipping 55 tons of bottled water to the islands in January 2005.[5] Shallow alluvial aquifers in which the level of the water table is controlled by sea level are also affected when this changes. Future sea-level rise on smaller low-lying islands may cause such aquifers to shrink and rise, perhaps even causing freshwater flooding in places.

Waste disposal is an issue for every country in the world but most especially for those, like smaller islands, that have few options. On-land waste dumping has proved a common option but is limited and controversial; incineration and managed (non-polluting) landfills are prohibitively expensive for many countries. For many of the smallest inhabited islands, dumping of solid waste in the ocean or along the beach has become common, with predictably deleterious

Plate 49.5. Niche products: Tuna from the Maldives (Indian Ocean).

effects. Many beaches on Nauru Island (Pacific) now appear blue-green from a distance, a result of all the beer cans discarded there.[6] Waste dumping at sea, from either on-land or offshore sources (like cruise ships), reduces water quality and ecosystem health.

The best solutions to problems of water supply and waste disposal on smaller islands are those that are cheap and sustainable. For water supply, investment in infrastructure, be it rainwater-harvesting systems or desalination plants, may be needed on many islands, with multiple rather than single sources of supply. Roof-top collection, for example, requires little additional investment other than pipes and storage areas; the roofs already exist. By improving water management, both water quality and water storage/supply systems, present problems could be reduced on many islands. An effective short-term solution to waste disposal is to reduce the amount of waste generated, particularly by recycling, but longer-term solutions mostly depend on infrastructural investment.

Sea-level rise – the island problem?

For most of the past 200 years the ocean surface (the sea level) has been rising, causing problems for coastal dwellers the world over (Nunn 2004b). This recent sea-level rise has been accompanied by – probably even driven by – warming, and associated with other manifestations of climate change attributable to the human enhancement of the Earth's greenhouse effect (see Chapter 8). As smaller-island coasts are so long compared to their land areas, many commentators have given the impression that sea-level rise is the main challenge currently facing island communities: in other words, *the* island problem. This is a misleading view that has both:

- hindered appropriate long-term planning for environmental change by those responsible for environmental management of many islands; and
- led to the targeting of issues associated with sea-level rise by international bodies to the effective exclusion of other, equally important, issues of environmental sustainability.

That said, sea-level rise has proved a significant problem for many islands during the recent past, particularly the smaller islands (that have a greater coastline to land area ratio) and the lower islands, such as atolls. The most visible manifestation of sea-level rise has been inundation of low-lying coastal fringes (Plate 49.6). Sea-level rise along sandy shorelines causes their erosion, which is a common condition of many island beaches in recent decades (see Anguilla example above). Sea-level rise has also caused increased salinization of groundwater in low-lying areas with generally undesirable effects for crops grown in such locations.

The most common response to twentieth-century shoreline inundation and erosion has been the construction of artificial structures, usually seawalls built with little acknowledgement of the nature of the shoreline processes causing the erosion (Plate 49.7). Such seawalls typically collapse a year or two after they are built (Plate 49.8) while those that are more appropriately designed may endure (Plate 49.9).

The problems arising from recent sea-level rise have been exacerbated on smaller islands by many other factors. Human-associated factors range from shoreline developments (particularly the construction of inappropriate artificial structures) through shoreline deforestation (particularly the removal of fringing mangrove forests) to nearshore pollution and sedimentation associated with activities in the hinterland (like mining or logging – see previous).

Non-human-linked factors include other manifestations of climate change, notably temperature rise and increased tropical-cyclone frequencies in many areas where smaller islands are found. While the direct effects of recent temperature rise on island environments are difficult to separate from other effects, it is high temperatures (particularly during El Niño events) that appear to have increased stress levels for corals resulting in coral-reef bleaching. Bleaching has become increasingly frequent during the last twenty years, particularly in the warmest areas of the oceans (tropical southwest Pacific, tropical central Indian Ocean), and has led to widespread coral death, a trend that is likely to increase in the foreseeable future (Hoegh-Guldberg 1999). Increased frequencies of tropical cyclones (plus increased geographical range, increased seasonal persistence and increased intensity) have led to increased amounts of damage to smaller islands in the tropics. Such impacts reduce both the resilience of islanders to natural disasters and the ability of island environments to be restored to a condition where they can continue to sustain their inhabitants; a good example is of 5 km^2 Tikopia Island (Solomon Islands), hit by three tropical cyclones within fifteen months in recent years (http://www.afap.org).

Managing island futures

The future of many smaller-island environments and their biotas (including humans) looks bleak. Most such environments are already, it appears, locked into trajectories of unsustainable development (despite many fine words from politicians insisting the opposite) that will

Plate 49.6. The problems and solutions associated with recent sea-level rise around smaller islands: The delta of the Navua River, southern Viti Levu Island, Fiji, has been rapidly inundated in places during the past few decades. Here at Naitonitoni the landowner laments the inundation of some 30 m of beach and coconut plantation within 10 years.

Plate 49.7. The seawall at Nasauvuki Village on Moturiki Island, central Fiji, was built with a view to stopping shoreline erosion caused by the clearance of a 200-m broad mangrove fringe. The wall was built for as long as there was money for cement but has not succeeded in stopping erosion, and at high tide the seawater simply comes around its sides, flooding the lower parts of the village. The people of Nasauvuki are now replanting the mangrove fringe.

only be exacerbated in the next few decades by sharply increased population growth and the various manifestations of climate change (particularly sea-level rise). Recent reviews of this subject have found little to be upbeat about (Zurick 1995; Pelling and Uitto 2001; Nunn 2004a), although there appear to be some initiatives that acknowledge the exigencies of the situation.

International initiatives

In November 1990, at the Second World Climate Conference in Geneva, concern about climate change and sea-level rise prompted the formation of the Alliance of Small Island States (AOSIS), a powerful bloc (in voting terms) that sought to draw attention to the special needs and characteristics of smaller islands and island nations. The first key test of the strength of AOSIS was at the 1992 Earth Summit in Rio de Janeiro, as a result of which through Agenda 21 island nations were acknowledged by the international community as requiring targeted and specific assistance to combat a range of environment threats, including climate change and sea-level rise. Two years later, the Global Conference on the Sustainable Development of Small Island Developing States was held in Barbados, and produced the 1994 Barbados Programme of Action on Small Island Developing States (BPOA). Since 1994 the BPOA has proved a vital guide to development strategies and policies for island countries.

Plate 49.8. A collapsed section of the seawall at Yadua Village, south-coast Viti Levu Island, Fiji, undermined both along its front by wave scour and by the action of ponded water along its landward
side. The village spokesman is being filmed by a Japanese telejournalist for a documentary
intended to raise awareness in Japan of environmental issues in Pacific islands.

In January 2005, an international meeting was convened on the island of Mauritius
(Indian Ocean) to review the BPOA. The meeting concluded that progress in implementing
the BPOA was disappointing. While consensus was achieved at Mauritius on a number of
issues, some of the most pressing matters proved the most contentious. The so-called
Mauritius Strategy for the Further Implementation of the BPOA states that many island
nations are already experiencing 'major adverse effects of climate change' and that policies
needed to be put in place to reverse these. The Mauritius Strategy also urged island nations
to increase their resilience to unwelcome environmental changes, including natural disasters.
To help achieve these goals, island nations were urged to cooperate more with each other
and others, and to continue to draw the attention of the international community to 'the
special circumstances of both their fragile environments and their fragile economies' (Koshy
and Granich 2005: 7).

International resolutions and the pleas of smaller countries for special attention, assistance
and understanding rarely produce lasting results. Many larger nations and funding bodies
need to be convinced by observation rather than simply assertion. It is clear that the message
that island countries sought to get across to the international community at the 2005
Mauritius meeting was significantly amplified by the horrific Indian Ocean Tsunami a few
weeks earlier (Koshy and Granich 2005). It may be that entire nations of low islands will
have to be erased from the map before protocols intended to reverse twenty-first-century
sea-level rise are implemented globally.

Plate 49.9. The seawall that completely surrounds Malé Atoll, the most densely populated in the Maldives Archipelago. The seawall was built with Japanese aid and is designed in a way that is appropriate given the dynamics of the offshore area. This photo was taken before the 2004 Indian Ocean tsunami. Photographs by P. Nunn.

The Kyoto Protocol and smaller islands

One such protocol was drawn up in 1997 at Kyoto in Japan and contained legally binding targets for greenhouse gas emissions. The principal goal for industrialized countries was a 5.2 per cent reduction in emissions of key greenhouse gases by 2012. This was seen as a first step towards reversing the effects of climate change associated with the human enhancement of the greenhouse effect. Despite the refusal of the United States to ratify the Kyoto Protocol, it came into force in 2005. While a victory for AOSIS and island states, the Kyoto Protocol is not enough to significantly reverse current trends of warming and sea-level rise. Yet it does demonstrate that the international community can act together in the common interest, even at a cost to national economies.

One difficulty with agreements like the Kyoto Protocol is that it is issue-specific. It focuses on reducing greenhouse gas emissions to delay the effects of future climate change but it does not, for example, address other issues (such as population growth rates, the spread of HIV/AIDS) that might legitimately compete for the funds being used to fund emissions reductions and will of course add to the problems that smaller-island countries in particular face from climate change.

National strategies

For many island countries, the number of future challenges sometimes appears over-whelming and, combined with a general lack of available funds to address these challenges, often results in inaction unless aid funding (often issue-specific) is available. Many international agreements come with promises of funds to tackle particular environmental issues and this is producing a culture of dependency. In many smaller-island countries, it is non-government organizations (NGOs) that sponsor many particular types of environmental conservation. The salaries of many government employees charged with environmental management come from 'soft money' associated with particular aid-funded projects rather than from governments' recurrent budgets.

Many international bodies support efforts to develop policies for island nations that they believe will ensure their sustainable environmental development. This notion is fallacious because, as in many 'developing' countries, national policies concerned with environmental management in many smaller-island nations, however sensible, are often ignored. Island governments cannot generally provide sufficient personnel to enforce such policies and, even when enforcement is attempted, often the wishes of traditional landowners (particularly in areas remote from capital cities) take precedent over a law that is perceived as anti-development.

For many island countries in the 'developing world', decisions about environmental management are commonly taken at the community level often with no reference to national government and in ignorance of any relevant laws; a good example is provided by Fiji (Turnbull 2004). It seems abundantly clear that effective environmental management on many smaller islands can come only through community empowerment, with community-level 'persons of influence' (not just elected or traditional/hereditary leaders but also religious leaders) targeted rather than government officials.

Islands in the twenty-second century

Much has been said and written, particularly in popular media, about how entire islands could 'disappear beneath the waves' as sea level rises during the twenty-first century. The latest IPCC estimates for sea-level rise this century suggest that it will be at an average rate of three to six times that which occurred during the twentieth century (IPCC WGI 2001). If these estimates of future sea-level rise prove correct, then clearly some low-lying islands will 'disappear' and the geography of island areas will change profoundly. It has even been suggested that entire nations – those that comprise only low-lying atoll *motu*[7] – will cease to exist by the start of the twenty-second century (Roy and Connell 1991).

Even if greenhouse gas emissions were reduced drastically tomorrow, this would have little effect on sea-level rise estimates for the twenty-first century; the emissions reductions promised by the Kyoto Protocol will only postpone warming by a decade or so. Some coral reefs have been known to grow upwards at rates far faster than sea level is likely to rise, but this upgrowth took place when there were no people living near those reefs and at a time when reef ecosystems (particularly species composition) were in upward growth mode as opposed to the lateral growth mode that most reefs have been in for the past few thousand years. It therefore seems unlikely that upgrowth of reefs around tropical islands will occur as sea-level rises.

Some consolation for the disappearance of islands (*motu*) from the surfaces of atoll reefs might be derived from pondering the fact that such islands are young and superficial, forming in the tropical Pacific (where they are most numerous) only a few thousand years ago when sea level fell from its mid-Holocene high (Nunn 1994). But there seems no escaping the likelihood that many such islands will disappear this century, and that their inhabitants will have to move elsewhere.

It will not be only the geography of low-island groups (particularly atoll *motu*) that will change drastically by the start of the twenty-second century. On higher islands, most people live along coasts, most infrastructure and economic activity is located there, so the effect of sea-level rise will be to cause huge disruptions to islander livelihoods. These disruptions will include the following:

- changes to nearshore food supply, particularly reef and lagoonal foods, as a result of increasing wave amplitude (across shallow reef platforms), increased nearshore water and sediment mobility, and increased shoreline erosion;
- changes to lowland agriculture (and other key income-generating activities) through coastal inundation, increased inland reach of storm surges, and groundwater salinization.

Island decision-makers have the opportunity now to significantly reduce the undesired impacts of future sea-level rise on such islands. Some of the ways are as follows:

- gradually relocate vulnerable coastal communities, infrastructure and income-generating activities to higher ground;
- reduce the dependence, for both subsistence agriculture and cash crops, on lowland areas by relocating farms to higher ground, encouraging a more diverse and therefore less vulnerable range of crops together with an appropriate series of strategies for preventing soil loss;
- encourage new enterprises to operate from higher locations and to have a reduced dependence on lowland-coastal areas;
- plant vegetation barriers along island coasts, in particular encourage and, in the tropics, enable coastal communities to plant mangrove forests along the most vulnerable stretches of coast;
- declare key coastal areas as reserves to allow natural ecosystems to be restored and to increase coastal resilience to change.

It is difficult to be overly optimistic that such changes will be enacted and implemented in many island countries. Many islands are part of the 'developing world' and, while their leaders dutifully echo the global rhetoric of 'sustainable development', are consistently following policies that are quite at odds with such a goal. In addition, many island countries are becoming increasingly reluctant to spend their own income (rather than aid money) on projects targeting environmental restoration or long-term sustainability. There is a fear that, as environmental problems worsen for many countries throughout the world in the next few decades, island countries with their comparatively small land areas and populations will be sidelined by potential aid donors in favour of larger, more populous countries. Island governments may be left increasingly to address environmental problems on their own. It is hoped that a new generation of island-environment managers will have emerged by then who are capable of recognizing the singular nature of island environments and persuading their political masters of the imperatives of appropriate actions.

Notes

1 No widely agreed definition of a 'smaller' or a 'small' island exists. The Small Islands Developing States (SIDS) grouping of the United Nations includes larger islands like Cuba and continental countries like Belize and Guyana.
2 The chorus of the 1994 calypso 'Alien' by Rohan Seon of the Caribbean island St Lucia.
3 Reference to undated brochure available at http://unesdoc.unesco.org/images/0013/001325/132554e.pdf viewed on 29 August 2005.
4 Bruce Gray, Rarotonga Environmental Action Programme, October 2002. Accessed from http://www.unesco.org/csi/smis/siv/Pacific/cook3.htm on 30 August 2005.
5 Report on OXFAM website at http://www.oxfamamerica.org/newsandpublications/news_updates/maldiveswater/print.html accessed on 30 August 2005.
6 Environmental News Service 2004, accessed from http://www.ens-newswire.com/ens/mar2004/2004-03-30-05.asp on 30 August 2005.
7 In the Pacific, these nations are Kiribati, Marshall Islands, Tokelau and Tuvalu: in the Indian Ocean, the Maldives.

Further reading

Edmond, R. and Smith, V. (eds) (2003) Islands in History and Representation. London: Routledge.
Insula, a journal about islands
Menard, H.W. (1986) *Islands*. New York: Scientific American Books.
Nunn, P.D. (1994) *Oceanic Islands*. Oxford: Blackwell.
Quammen, D. (1997) *The Song of the Dodo: Island Biogeography in an Age of Extinctions*. New York: Simon and Schuster.
Whittaker, R.J. 1998. *Island Biogeography: Ecology, Evolution, and Conservation*. Oxford: Oxford University Press.

References

Bahn, P.G. and Flenley, J. (1992) *Easter Island, Earth Island*. London: Thames and Hudson.
Baker, P.E., Gale, N.H. and Simons, J. (1967) Geochronology of the St Helena volcanoes. *Nature* 215, 1451–6.
Beaglehole, E. and Beaglehole, P. (1938) *Ethnology of Pukapuka* (Bulletin 150). Honolulu: B.P. Bishop Museum.
Burbridge, P.R. and Maragos, J.E. (1985) Coastal resources management development and environmental assessment needs for aquatic resources development in Indonesia. Report for the International Institute for Environment and Development, and USAID, Bureau of Science and Technology, Washington.
Burley, D.V. and Dickinson, W.R. (2001) Origin and significance of a founding settlement in Polynesia. *National Academy of Sciences, Proceedings* 98, 11829–31.
Byrne, R. (1980) Man and the variable vulnerability of island life: a study of recent vegetation change in the Bahamas. *Atoll Research Bulletin* 240, 1–200.

Cambers, G. (1992) *Coastal Zone Management: Case Studies from the Caribbean* (Latin America and the Caribbean Technical Department, Regional Studies Programme, Report No. 26). Geneva: World Bank.

Chand, S. (2004) Sweet land or sweat land: two proposals for facilitating access to land and adjustment to eroding sugar preferences in Fiji (International and Development Economics Working Paper 04–06). Canberra: Asia Pacific School of Economics and Government.

Clarke, W.C. and Morrison, J. (1987) Land mismanagement and the development imperative in Fiji. In P. Blaikie and H. Brookfield (eds) *Land Degradation and Society*, pp. 76–85. New York: Methuen.

Cronk, Q.C.B. (1989) The past and present vegetation of St Helena. *Journal of Biogeography* 16, 47–64.

Crosby, A.W. (1986). *Ecological Imperialism: The Biological Expansion of Europe, 900–1900*. New York: Cambridge University Press.

Dauvergne, P. (2001) *Loggers and Degradation in the Asia-Pacific: Corporations and Environmental Management*. New York: Cambridge University Press.

Diamond, J. (2005) *Collapse: How Societies Choose to Fail or Succeed*. New York: Viking.

Doumenge, F. (1987) Quelques contraintes du milieu insulaire. In CRET (ed.) *Iles Tropicales: Insularité, 'Insularisme'*, III, pp. 9–16. Bordeaux: CRET, Université de Bordeaux.

Grynberg, R. (1997) *Negotiating a Fait Accompli: The WTO Incompatibility of the Lomé Convention Trade Provisions and the ACP-EU Negotiations*. (ECDPM Working Paper No. 38). Maastricht: European Centre for Development Policy Management.

Hoegh-Guldberg, O. (1999). Coral bleaching, climate change and the future of the world's coral reefs. *Review of Marine and Freshwater Research* 50, 839–66.

Howland, L. (1955). Howland Island, its birds and rats, as observed by a certain Mr Stetson in 1854. *Pacific Science* 9, 95–106.

Hunter-Anderson, R.L. (1998) Human vs climatic impacts at Easter Island: Did the people really cut down all those trees? In C.M. Stevenson, G. Lee, and F.J. Morin (eds) *Easter Island in Pacific Context, South Seas Symposium, Proceedings of the Fourth International Conference on Easter Island and East Polynesia*, pp. 85–99. Los Osos: University of New Mexico and The Easter Island Foundation.

Hviding, E. and Bayliss-Smith, T.P. (2000) *Islands of Rainforest: Agroforestry, Logging and Eco-tourism in Solomon Islands*. Aldershot: Ashgate.

IPCC WGI (2001) *Climate Change 2001: The Scientific Basis*. Cambridge: Cambridge University Press.

Ivanoff, J. (2005) Sea gypsies of Myanmar. *National Geographic*, April, 36–55.

Koshy, K. and Granich, S. (2005) Small island developing states. *Tiempo* 56, 3–7.

Leatherman, S.P. and Beller-Simms, N. (1997) Sea-level rise and small island states: an overview. *Journal of Coastal Research* (special issue) 24, 1–16.

McNeill, J.R. (1994) Of rats and men: a synoptic environmental history of the island Pacific. *Journal of World History* 5, 299–349.

Nunn, P.D. (1994) *Oceanic Islands*. Oxford: Blackwell.

——(2000) Environmental catastrophe in the Pacific Islands about AD 1300. *Geoarchaeology* 15, 715–40.

——(2003) Nature–society interactions in the Pacific Islands. *Geografiska Annaler* 85 B, 219–29.

——(2004a) Through a mist on the ocean: human understanding of island environments. *Tijdschrift voor Economische en Sociale Geografie* 95, 311–25.

——(2004b) Understanding and adapting to sea-level change. In F. Harris (ed.) *Global Environmental Issues*, pp. 45–64. Chichester: John Wiley and Sons.

Nunn, P.D. and Britton, J.M.R. (2004) The long-term evolution of Niue Island. In J. Terry and W. Murray (eds) *Niue Island: Geographical Perspectives on the Rock of Polynesia*, pp. 31–74. Paris: INSULA (International Scientific Council for Island Development).

Nunn, P.D. and Mimura, N. (forthcoming) Promoting sustainability on vulnerable island coasts: a case study of the smaller Pacific Islands. In L. McFadden (ed.) *Managing Coastal Vulnerability: An Integrated Approach*. Amsterdam: Elsevier.

Oliver, D. (1991). *Black Islanders: A Personal Perspective of Bougainville 1937–1991*. Honolulu: University of Hawaii Press.

Pelling, M. and Uitto, J.I. (2001) Small island developing states: natural disaster vulnerability and global change. *Environmental Hazards* 3, 49–62.

Robertson, J.M.Y. and van Schaik, C.P. (2001) Causal factors underlying the dramatic decline of the Sumatran orang-utan. *Oryx* 35, 26–38.

Roy, P. and Connell, J. (1991) Climatic change and the future of atoll states. *Journal of Coastal Research* 7, 1057–75.

Savidge, J.A. (1987) Extinction of an island forest avifauna by an introduced snake. *Ecology* 68, 660–8.

Towle, E.L. (1971) Islands: an endangered species. Presidential Address, 5th Annual Meeting of Caribbean Conservation Association, Puerto Rico.

Turnbull, J. (2004) Explaining complexities of environmental management in developing countries: lessons from the Fiji Islands. *The Geographical Journal* 170, 64–77.

Voivontas, D., Arampatzis, G., Manoli, E., Karavitis, C. and Assimacopoulos, D. (2003) Water supply modelling towards sustainable environmental management in small islands: the case of Paros, Greece. *Desalination* 156, 127–35.

Watling, D. and Chape, S. (1992) *Environment Fiji: The National State of the Environment Report.* Gland, Switzerland: IUCN.

Weeramantry, C.G. (1992) *Nauru: Environmental Damage under International Trusteeship.* Melbourne: Oxford University Press.

Whittaker, R.J. (1998) *Island Biogeography: Ecology, Evolution, and Conservation.* Oxford: Oxford University Press.

Zurick, D.N. (1995) Preserving paradise. *Geographical Review* 85, 157–73.

50

Responding to biodiversity loss

Richard J. Ladle and Ana C.M. Malhado

In a remarkable display of international cooperation 150 nation states signed the Convention on Biological Diversity (usually abbreviated to CBD) on 5 June 1992 at the United Nations Conference on the Environment and Development in Rio de Janeiro. This act put the concept of biodiversity (= biological diversity) at the forefront of the conservation agenda where it has remained as the central theme for both global and local conservation efforts. The adoption of biodiversity as the focus for conservation is surprising when one considers just how recent a neologism it is.

The coinage of 'biodiversity' is attributed to Walter Rosen at the National Forum on BioDiversity [sic] in September 1986. The term was initially intended as nothing more than shorthand for biological diversity but by 1993 the term 'biodiversity' was appearing nearly four times as frequently as 'biological diversity' in *Biological Abstracts* (Takacs 1996). A precise definition, however, has remained frustratingly elusive – Delong (1996) lists 85 different definitions of biodiversity. Perhaps the most widely accepted wording is that provided in Article 2 of the CBD: 'the variability among living organisms from all sources including, *inter alia*, terrestrial, marine and other aquatic ecosystems and the ecological complexes of which they are part; this includes diversity within species, between species and of ecosystems'.

Biodiversity thus refers to the natural variety and variability among living organisms, the space they inhabit, and their interactions with each other and the physical environment (Gaston and Spicer 2004; Redford and Richter 1999). A distinction is thus made between natural patterns of variability and those formed through human influence. Biodiversity is not a value-free term and most definitions imply that biodiversity is a 'good' thing *per se* and that biodiversity loss through human action is therefore 'bad' and should be prevented or minimized.

Wilson (1984) has suggested that valuing biodiversity is universal and may have a biological basis. In his Biophilia hypothesis he conjectures that humans have an innate desire to catalogue, understand and spend time with other life forms. However, with increasing urbanization humans may be losing their emotional connection with nature (Pyle 2003) and, when many children are more familiar with the latest video game than their biological heritage (Balmford et al. 2002), continuing support for conservation action is by no means assured.

Against this background of uncertain public support for the conservation of biodiversity, and those arguing that biodiversity may not even exist as a discrete reality (Escobar 1998), the global environmental movement is engaged in multiple responses to the global loss of species and ecosystems. This chapter will briefly review the evidence that the Earth is in the grip of its sixth mass extinction, highlight the major threats to biodiversity, and discuss the multiplicity of ways in which scientists, governments, communities and individuals are responding to biodiversity loss at different spatial and temporal scales.

The extinction crisis

Although biodiversity is usually defined in terms of the sum total of biotic variation from the level of genes to ecosystems, the international conservation effort has typically focused on species loss. The reason for this may be relative ease with which biological species can be identified and assessed for presence or absence within a site (Purvis and Hector 2000). Species are also the most popular surrogate of biodiversity because the concepts of 'species' and of 'species loss' seem relatively easy to communicate to the general public. Further, certain species, such as the giant panda – the aptly chosen symbol of the World Wildlife Fund (WWF) – are deeply rooted within cultures and have instant global recognition. Thus, the 'biodiversity crisis' has typically been framed as a species extinction crisis and represented in the scientific and popular press in terms of x species going extinct per day or per year.

What is less widely appreciated is how uncertainty exists about how many species currently exist, their geographic distribution and the rate at which they are going extinct. Although scientists have formally described nearly 2 million species this is believed to be a fraction of those that actually exist. Estimates of global species richness vary from around 5 million to 100 million with no real consensus (Pimm et al. 1995; Brown and Lomolino 1998; Groombridge and Jenkins 2000; Whittaker et al. 2005). This knowledge gap is referred to as the Linnean shortfall (Brown and Lomolino 1998) and the problem grows worse as taxonomic groups become smaller and more simple (Whittaker et al. 2005). Even for the species that have been identified and catalogued, scientists often have a poor knowledge of their spatial distribution (termed the Wallacean shortfall by Lomolino 2004) at local, regional or global scales. To make matters worse, Linnean and Wallacean shortfalls are more acute in the tropics, home to the bulk of the Earth's biodiversity, where countries generally have the least technical capacity.

Even with these huge gaps in our basic knowledge of global biodiversity there is still good evidence for an increase in species extinctions relative to historic background rates (Lawton and May 1995). At a recent discussion hosted by the United States National Academy of Sciences on the 'Future of Evolution' the expert panel unanimously agreed that current extinction rates are 50–500 times background and are still increasing (Woodruff 2001). This human-induced crisis began about 30,000 years ago (Wilson 1991) but there is huge uncertainty surrounding its magnitude and significance.

Most estimates of species extinction rates are based upon the well-understood relationship between the area of a habitat and the number of species that inhabit it (MacArthur and Wilson 1967). Empirical studies suggest if the area of a habitat such as a rainforest is reduced by 90 per cent then, on average, it will eventually lose 50 per cent of its species. However, as we don't know the global number of species and we have only a limited knowledge of species-area relationships for many taxa, such estimates can vary immensely. Most estimates based on these methods suggest that between 3,000 and 30,000 species are going extinct each year from a global species pool of about 10 million (Pimm *et al.* 1995; Hughes *et al.* 1997). At least 250,000 species probably went extinct in the last century, and although it is almost absurd to try to extrapolate extinction rates into the future (Pimm *et al.* 1995), most experts agree that ten to twenty times that many will disappear over the next century (Woodruff 2001).

It is important to distinguish between the cautious pronouncements of professional scientists and the sensationalist claims of some environmental activists. One of the earliest and most quoted estimates of 40,000 extinctions per year (Myers 1979) has been very publicly held up as an example of environmental alarmism (Lomborg 2001) with potentially damaging consequences for the credibility of the conservation movement. However, even the most conservative estimates of about 0.7 per cent of species going extinct in the last fifty years, based on observed extinctions in the best-known groups of animals and plants (Groombridge and Jenkins 2000), is still a frighteningly large number, the more so considering that we don't know how the current extinction spasm will affect the future evolution of life or the integrity of the world's environmental (ecosystem) services on which humanity depends (Costanza *et al.* 1998).

Causes of biodiversity loss

Biodiversity decreases when habitat is damaged, fragmented, restructured or completely destroyed; exotic species replace native species; the biophysical conditions change more rapidly than ecological communities can effectively adapt; and/or natural resources are exploited unsustainably. In many ecosystems some or all of these factors are acting to produce local population decline and eventual species extinction. The factors mentioned above, although ultimately responsible for population and species extinction, are not normally the proximate cause. Once a population has been driven to very low numbers, stochastic factors such as demographic shifts, genetic degradation and chance environmental events such as disease outbreaks or unusual weather events usually wipe out the last few individuals.

Habitat loss

Habitat loss is responsible for the greatest reduction of biodiversity loss (Groombridge and Jenkins 2000). Although loss of natural habitats has almost ceased in Europe and North America it is still ongoing in most parts of the tropics, the very place where biodiversity is highest. Tropical forests originally covered between 14 and 18 million square kilometres, but by the late 1980s only about half that area remained (Skole and Tucker 1993). To truly understand the scale of this, imagine the whole of the North American continent as forested and that humans have removed all the trees from the United States.

The wholesale destruction of tropical forests is still ongoing, and although the causes are well known, solutions are more problematic given the economic realities that exist in most of the countries containing these forests. An example of this is the enormous but shrinking Amazon forest of South America stretching across more than 6 million square kilometres and nine countries. The forest still covers 60 per cent of the territory of South America's largest country, Brazil. Of the original forest (whatever this term may mean – see Willis *et al.* 2004), it is thought that 17 per cent has been cleared, mainly for agricultural purposes, and the rate of destruction may be increasing or at least is not being effectively controlled. Provisional estimates from satellite remote sensing indicated that 25,400 square kilometres of forest was cleared in 2002, compared to an average of 17,340 square kilometres over the preceding ten years (Margulis 2004).

In the case of the Brazilian Amazon, the main driver of deforestation is beef ranching that occupies 75 per cent of newly deforested land. A recent World Bank report (Margulis 2004) identified the financial viability of newly created medium to large cattle ranches as the prime motivating factor behind deforestation. New cattle ranches require new roads that, in turn, open up more of the Amazon to settlement and further deforestation. However, it must be noted that Brazil is also restoring considerable areas of forest every year (Margulis 2004), although the positive impact of this on biodiversity will take many years to realize. The Amazon case study illustrates the prime dilemma facing environmentalists around the world – how to allow economic development while sustaining biodiversity at levels that maintain ecological integrity and ecosystem services (Costanza *et al.* 1998).

Given that continuing habitat loss in many ecosystems is inevitable, the key question facing conservationists is not how to prevent further habitat loss but rather 'How much habitat is enough to minimize biodiversity loss?' (Fahrig 2001). Scientists have traditionally approached this question by developing models that predict the area required to sustain a minimum viable population (one with a high probability of continued existence over a substantial period of time) of a species of conservation concern. While this approach is undoubtedly prudent, the current level of international support for conservation means that many other, non-scientific, factors normally determine the size and shape of protected areas (see Figure 50.1) with little reference to whether or not they are large enough to maintain a minimum viable population of a species of conservation concern. The long-term consequences of this strategy remain to be seen.

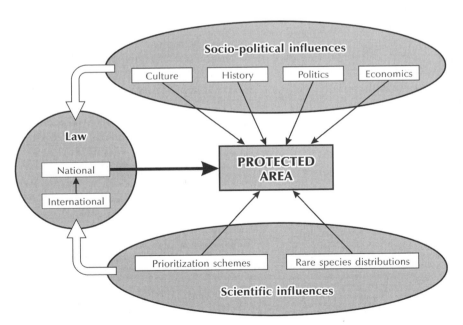

Figure 50.1. Main factors influencing the creation of new protected areas. The creation of a major new protected area is primarily achieved through national legislation but is heavily influenced by socio-political factors and is informed by science.

Habitat fragmentation

Habitat fragmentation has become one of the key foci of biodiversity research. However, it is not easy to define or measure, with authors variously including determinations of patch size, isolation and land cover in their surrogates of landscape fragmentation (reviewed in Fahrig 2003). The process of fragmentation has four main effects on habitat pattern with potential consequences for biodiversity: (1) reduction in habitat amount; (2) increase in number of habitat patches; (3) decrease in size of habitat patches; and (4) increase in isolation of patches. It is important to distinguish the different ways in which these changes in habitat pattern will affect biodiversity. For instance, island biogeography theory suggests that habitat loss has a strong and consistently negative effect on biodiversity, whereas breaking a habitat up (fragmentation without appreciable habitat loss) has much weaker impacts that may be positive or negative (MacArthur and Wilson 1967; Whittaker 1998).

The nature of the habitat between the remaining habitat fragments (known as the habitat or the landscape matrix) will also have a significant influence on impacts of fragmentation. For instance, a recent analysis of woodland bird species in three landscapes from the Canberra area of New South Wales revealed big differences between species and populations in how they responded to different types of matrices in which their woodland habitat was embedded (Watson et al. 2005). This study and others like it call into question the whole conservation paradigm of viewing terrestrial habitat fragments as islands in a sea of uninhabitable land (Whittaker et al. 2005).

Unsustainable exploitation

Over-hunting and over-harvesting may be the second most important cause of extinction after habitat loss (Reid 1992). This is especially problematic in many developing countries where the recent adoption of modern hunting techniques and technologies has led to huge increases in hunting efficiency (Robinson and Redford 1991). A further problem is the over-reliance of many communities living in rainforests on bushmeat (meat from wild caught animals). This is exacerbated by a widespread preference for wild-caught meat and the high status associated with the consumption of species such as chimpanzees and gorillas (Colishaw et al. 2005).

International measures to combat the trade in bushmeat and to reduce hunting in reserves have often had little detectable impact – possibly because of the high levels of corruption in many of the countries that are most affected (Smith et al. 2003). In other instances, such as the hunting of whales by indigenous Inuit communities, restricting the uses of modern technology and the imposition of strict quota systems has proved effective in controlling exploitation while still allowing local communities to follow some of their traditions (Freeman 1998).

Pollution

The impact of pollutants on organisms and ecosystems was one of the main factors responsible for the birth of the modern environmental movement in developed countries. Books such as Rachael Carson's (1963) *Silent Spring* brought the effects of anthropogenic pollutants such as DDT to public awareness and resulted in a concerted move towards lower impact technologies and the imposition of strict emission targets for contaminants. This has led to significant increases in environmental quality in many habitats, especially in riverine ecosystems, over the last thirty years.

Although the threat of pesticides and other toxicants is perhaps less visible than it once was, there has been an increasing recognition of the impact that less toxic, but more widely used, compounds may be having on ecosystems. In particular, nitrogen pollution (mainly from agricultural fertilizers) has recently been dubbed the 'third major threat to our planet after biodiversity loss and climate change' (Lawton, quoted in Giles 2005). Currently Europe and North America are the biggest sources of reactive nitrogen, but by 2020 half of anthropogenic nitrogen pollution will be produced by the developing world with potentially catastrophic consequences for these biodiverse regions.

Invasive species

Humans have always been responsible for the widespread translocation of animals and plants but with the advent of modern transport methods the volume and diversity of organisms being moved intentionally or unintentionally is higher than ever. One consequence of this is the introduction of non-native species that compete with, predate, parasitize and sometimes hybridize with native organisms. These 'exotic' or 'alien' species are often cited as a major cause of species extinction (Groombridge and Jenkins 2000) and habitat transformation, although it is by no means clear whether the incoming species are directly causing biodiversity loss or are merely taking advantage of the 'empty space' created in habitats that have been degraded by other means (Didham *et al.* 2005). The invasive species problem cannot be considered independently from issues of habitat loss and degradation and all these processes may act additively or synergistically to produce the observed patterns of biodiversity loss (Gurevitch and Padilla 2004).

There are, however, many unambiguous examples of invasive species leading to widespread extinctions and habitat transformations. In this respect islands (and enclosed water bodies) appear to have suffered the most serious consequences from the invasion of exotic species. Perhaps the best-known example of bioinvasion leading to extinction is the introduction of the Nile perch (*Lates niloticus* L.) into Lake Victoria, East Africa. The perch is thought to be directly responsible for the extinction of more than 200 species of haplochromine cichlids in Lake Victoria (Goldschmidt *et al.* 1993). Interestingly, more recent work indicates that the number of extinctions may have been over-estimated and that some of the 'extinct' cichlid species may survive at low densities in marginal habitats (Chapman *et al.* 1996).

Global climate change

The current and much debated increase in mean global temperatures could not have come at a worse time for organisms and biomes already struggling to cope with a multitude of other anthropogenic impacts. However, the impacts of climate change on biodiversity are yet to be fully realized and so far there is very little direct evidence of climate change induced extinctions, with the possible exception of the golden toad (*Bufo periglenes* Savage) of Costa Rica (Pounds *et al.* 1999).

Despite this lack of direct evidence there have been many attempts to quantify the future impacts of anthropogenic climate change on biodiversity through the construction of models that seek to capture the relationship between a species distribution and the climate 'space' it occupies. Thomas *et al.* (2004) created one such climate-envelope model to forecast extinction risks for sample regions covering some 20 per cent of the Earth's terrestrial surface. They predicted that 15–37 per cent of species in their sample regions would be 'committed to extinction' (= living outside of their current climate envelope) as a result of climate change between 2004 and 2050. Although this report garnered huge media exposure and led to sensationalist headlines of a 'million species extinct by 2050' (Ladle *et al.* 2004) the huge uncertainties associated with this (Thullier *et al.* 2004), and other similar models, effectively compromise their practical value for conservation planning (Whittaker *et al.* 2005).

Until models forecasting the effects of climate change on biodiversity are further refined, the responses of governments and conservation organizations are likely to be dogged by as much uncertainty as the forecasts that they are using to guide their judgments. Given that climate change is now unlikely to be stopped or reversed, the conservation movement needs to accept that, at all levels of ecological organization, there will be both winners and losers. Managing the effects of climate change on the human and non-human world remains one of the biggest challenges facing humanity, and one without easy solutions or quick answers.

Responses to biodiversity loss

Humans have responded both collectively and individually to biodiversity loss in a wide variety of ways (see Tables 50.1 and 50.2). The most prominent of these responses is probably the creation of protected areas, which cover approximately 11.5 per cent of the Earth's surface (Chape *et al.* 2003). The existence of many of these parks and nature reserves is a direct result of international treaties and conventions that, in turn, have been transposed into national legislation. Both inside and outside of these protected areas environmentalists working for governments or environmental non-governmental organizations (ENGOs) have been developing scientific and pragmatic management strategies to slow, stop and reverse the various causes of biodiversity loss. International agencies, governments and many institutional and individual donors that fund the work of international and local ENGOs are financially supporting this work.

Table 50.1. Actors, responses and funding of the global biodiversity crisis

Main actors	Main response	Funding mechanisms
International community	Multilateral Environmental Agreements (MEAs) ■ CBD[1] ■ CITES[2]	GEF[3] World Bank
National governments	Protected areas Technical responses	Taxes International funds
ENGOs[4]	Global planning frameworks ■ hotspots ■ biogeographic representation ■ important sites Technical responses	Grants Donors
Individuals	Behavioural adaptation ■ ethical consumerism ■ ecotourism Community conservation projects	Free market Economic incentives Grants

Notes: [1] Convention on Biological Diversity; [2] Convention on International Trade in Endangered Species; [3] Global Environment Facility; [4] Environmental non-governmental organizations.

Table 50.2. Technical responses to main threats to biodiversity

Main threats	Responses
Habitat loss	Protected areas. Ecological restoration projects. Systems of quotas and fines.
Habitat fragmentation	Protected areas. Protected area networks.
Habitat degradation	Protected areas. Remediation and restoration measures. Stricter emission controls on contaminants. System of quotas and fines.
Invasive species	Eradication. Biocontrol. Containment. Invasion prevention measures.
Over-exploitation	Anti-poaching measures. Systems of quotas and fines.
Climate change	Protected area networks. Improved forecasting. Translocations and reintroductions.

The international legislative response

The main legislative response of the international community to the biodiversity crisis is the Convention on Biological Diversity (CBD), which has three main aims: the conservation of biodiversity, the sustainable use of its components, and sharing the benefits from the commercial and other utilization of genetic resources in a fair and equitable way. At the heart of the CBD is the acknowledgement that biodiversity is essential for human existence and that the utilitarian (use) value is the key to effective conservation. In essence, biodiversity must pay for itself, but only if the benefits arising from its use are fairly and equitably distributed (Gaston and Spicer 2004).

The CBD, along with Agenda 21 on sustainable development, gives a fairly comprehensive framework for sovereign nations to develop their national legislative response to the biodiversity crisis. This national legislation should outline strategies, plans and programmes that respond to the changing circumstances of biodiversity in particular nations. Many countries have developed national biodiversity strategies (identifying strategic needs) or action plans (identifying practical steps) as ways of fulfilling their obligations to the CBD. However, it should be recognized that the national implementation of the CBD requires parties to engage in an often complex and uncertain legal and political process requiring the use and adjustment of existing domestic institutions. Because domestic implementation of the CBD is complex and extensive many countries, most notably the USA, found the commitments did not mesh sufficiently with their domestic institutions and failed to ratify (Raustiala 1997).

Has the CBD succeeded? The sheer scope and ambition of the CBD makes it very hard to assess its success. There are few measurable targets and deadlines as such (Ten Kate 2002) and because most of the commitments are not fully quantifiable it is impossible to say whether or not it has been successful in its main aims. Even though the Convention acknowledges that biodiversity is a 'common concern' of humankind it also places a firm emphasis on the sovereign rights of states over their own biological resources. This coordination of the different power dynamics makes the effective management of biodiversity within or across national boundaries deeply problematic. Some commentators have suggested that the CBD is too comprehensive to be effective because so many disparate groups see their interests mirrored in the treaty (McGraw 2002). The complexity and comprehensiveness of the CBD also makes it difficult to digest for the mainstream print media and, relatively speaking, it receives far less coverage than its ozone and climate change related counterparts.

Protected areas

The CBD lays great emphasis on *in situ* conservation (Article 8) of viable populations. Among the measures that it calls for are the establishment of protected area networks, the rehabilitation of degraded areas, and the protection of habitats and species conservation in natural surroundings. Governments worldwide have responded to this challenge by building upon (sometimes extensive) existing protected areas, and there are currently more than 100,000 protected areas in 227 countries that occupy 11.5 per cent of the terrestrial environment on Earth (Chape *et al.* 2003). This is a huge figure, but how effective are these protected areas going to be at protecting the Earth's remaining biodiversity?

There have been recent attempts to address this fundamental question by using existing distributional data for terrestrial vertebrates (Rodrigues *et al.* 2004). The analysis revealed more than 1400 'gap species' (species not occurring within any existing protected areas) representing 12 per cent of all of the species analysed. This figure may be even higher because the study conservatively defined 'covered species' as those with a protected area situated in any part of their published geographic range (Rodrigues *et al.* 2004). The abundance of gap species probably reflects the wide variety of historical, cultural, and often political factors (see Figure 50.1) underlying the establishment, placement and dimensions of protected areas (Jepson and Whittaker 2002).

One possible solution to the problem of gap species is to place reserves where they are most needed in terms of biodiversity. Several international ENGOs have attempted to do this by creating protected area planning frameworks of global remit. There are several of these schemes, which use different prioritization criteria but which fall into three broad categories (Whittaker *et al.* 2005): Biogeographical representation approaches set out to identify examples of ecosystem types using established biogeographical or ecological frameworks. An alternative to this largely zonal approach is to target areas ('hotspots') that are rich in species and/or endemism and are under threat – this is sometimes referred to as a 'silver bullet' approach. Alternatively, schemes may use some other criteria of 'importance', such as sites for migration or breeding, to designate areas for protection.

All three of the above frameworks have been adopted, with various degrees of success, by a number of international ENGOs. Perhaps the best known, and certainly the best funded, of these prioritization schemes is the biodiversity hotspots approach of the Washington-based Conservation International (CI). CI scientists have delimited twenty-five hotspots worldwide that have been designated as priority areas for conservation action (Myers *et al.* 2000). The hotspots are defined as areas that possess greater than 1.5 per cent of global plant diversity and which have lost more than 70 per cent of their original habitat. CI claim that these twenty-five areas hold 44 per cent of the world's plant species and 35 per cent of vertebrate species, despite taking up only 12 per cent of the land area of the Earth (Myers *et al.* 2000). Of course, the areas delimited are far too coarse-grained for actual reserve placement, but nevertheless hotspots may have great value as tool for identifying conservation areas and ecosystems most deserving of funding and conservation attention. Conversely, the hotspots programme could be criticized for (possibly unintentionally) drawing funding away from non-hotspot areas with equally pressing conservation needs (Bates and Demos 2001), for representing only a limited set of environmental values (Jepson and Canney 2003), and for the lack of scientific precision and arbitrary nature of many of the geographical boundaries delimiting each hotspot (Whittaker *et al.* 2005). Similar criticisms can be levelled at all of the global conservation planning frameworks mentioned here, which illustrates the pressing need to improve the quality of the data available and increase the spatial resolution of the base maps.

One example of the narrow range of values encapsulated by many of these schemes is the lack of provision in them for indigenous communities living within, and making a living from, protected areas. Although the CBD acknowledges the important role of indigenous peoples in biodiversity conservation, there has often been a conflict between providing livelihoods and conserving biodiversity. One extreme example of this was the expulsion of local peoples from protected areas, leading to social deprivation, poverty and increased environmental degradation on the margins of these areas (Brockington 2002). Such practices are, thankfully, much less prevalent than they used to be, but there are many other social ills that are associated with the creation of protected areas (such as restrictions on hunting, fishing and logging that contribute to local livelihoods).

Ideally, protected areas should be, in the words of the IUCN's director general, 'islands of biodiversity in an ocean of sustainable human development' (quoted in Steiner 2003) with their benefits radiating out beyond their boundaries. Unfortunately, this still remains a largely unfulfilled aspiration. The social impacts of protected areas are a specific example of the more general problem of the tension between conservation and development. Although the proponents of 'pro-poor' conservation support the notion that poverty eradication and bio-diversity protection can occur together (IUCN 2002) there have been very few success stories among projects of this nature. It has been suggested that if conservation projects are to successfully combine biodiversity and social goals, they must find ways to reconcile the diverse interests of different stakeholders in the management of natural resources of biodiverse ecosystems (Adams *et al.* 2004).

Technical responses

Both inside and outside of protected areas there are many on-the-ground approaches to combat the chief threats to biodiversity (see Table 50.2). The main players involved are government departments, ENGOs, communities and, in the developing world, large num-bers of private citizens acting as conservation volunteers. A detailed account of the various technical responses to the main threats to biodiversity is beyond the remit of this chapter, but it is interesting to note that protected areas remain the cornerstone of conservation policy and their strengthening and expansion should be a priority for the global conservation movement for the foreseeable future. However, given that the expansion of the global pro-tected area network will ultimately slow and stop, the focus of biodiversity conservation will have to shift towards conservation within the landscape matrix within which nature reserves are embedded.

Conclusions

The CBD has adopted a target of reducing the rate of biodiversity loss by 2010 (UN 2002). It is doubtful that the international community will even know whether the target has been reached or not. First, the Linnean and Wallacean shortfalls mean that accurate global assessments of biodiversity loss for most taxa are still not credible. Second, there is still no universal scientific consensus on how to measure biodiversity status. In this regard, Scholes and Biggs (2005) have recently proposed a Biodiversity Intactness Index (BII) that meets all the criteria of the CBD for policy relevance. The BII gives the average richness- and area-weighted impact of a set of activities on the populations of a given group of organisms in a specific area. Whether this index will be adopted by the CBD and/or the global conservation community remains to be seen. Even if the 2010 target can be independently and accurately assessed there are many factors that make reaching it problematic. The key impediment to slowing the rate of biodiversity loss is to somehow reduce the rate of habitat loss, particularly in tropical forests. To do this effectively some sort of compromise must be reached between economic development in these areas and the need to protect biodiversity and associated ecosystem services. Sadly, there is no universal panacea and protected areas (existing or planned) may not be sufficient to significantly impact the current global extinction trajectory.

Inadequate funding of protected areas and conservation programmes is also a major impediment to reducing biodiversity loss by 2010. In 1999 the funding of protected areas globally was a paltry $6 billion per year compared to the $27.5 billion per year required for an ecologically representative (e.g. based on a global conservation prioritization scheme such as CI's hotspots) global network of protected areas (James et al. 1999). A further $300 billion would be required annually for a comprehensive global conservation programme that protects biodiversity in the landscape matrix, effectively remediates and restores degraded habitats, and that makes agriculture and fisheries more sustainable (James et al. 1999). These sums, though by no means inconsiderable, are dwarfed by the 'perverse' subsidies that 'support' agricultural production in the developed world. Nevertheless, while conservation issues languish near the bottom of the international agenda the funding shortfall is unlikely to be bridged any time soon.

There are, however, still reasons to be optimistic about the future of biodiversity. The ultimate 'completion' of the global protected area system will lead conservationists to turn their attention away from protected areas and towards more human-dominated habitats. This is already beginning to happen. The term 'reconciliation ecology' has been coined to refer to conservation strategies that work in and with human-dominated habitats (Rosenzweig 2003). Reconciliation ecology is still in its early infancy as an academic discipline but it is the key to the long-term protection of biodiversity because it seeks techniques to give species back their geographical ranges without forcing humans to contract theirs. Examples of such techniques include the 'greening' of agriculture through the adoption of farming practices that are compatible with biodiversity, reforesting state-owned lands to provide new leisure amenities, and creating new management regimes to benefit specific species (Rosenzweig 2003).

Another major conceptual advance is the emergence of 'conservation biogeography' as a strong and vibrant academic sub-discipline. Conservation biogeography is the 'application of biogeographical principles, theories and analysis, being those concerned with the distributional dynamics of taxa individually and collectively, to problems concerning the conservation of biodiversity' (Whittaker et al. 2005: 3). With an increased understanding of the factors that drive global biodiversity patterns at different spatial scales and better models to accurately forecast changes in these patterns, conservation will be able to plan more effectively in a time of unprecedented global change.

A final example encapsulates many of the hopes, uncertainties and difficulties associated with modern conservation practice. In June 2005 it was reported that the 'extinct' ivory-billed woodpecker (*Campephilus principalis* L.) had been rediscovered in the swamps of eastern Arkansas (Fitzpatrick *et al.* 2005). This remarkable and Lazarus-like return of such a large and charismatic bird in the richest country in the world led to a huge outpouring of conservation support culminating in the US Departments of Interior and Agriculture pledging $10 million for efforts to protect the woodpecker and its habitat (Wilcove 2005). Unfortunately, this uplifting story may have an unhappy ending. Recent reports suggest that the sighting of the woodpecker may have been a case of mistaken identity and that the species in Fitzpatrick's video is actually the relatively abundant pileated woodpecker (*Dryocopus pileatus* L.) (Dalton 2005).

Thus, hope springs eternal, but a lack of scientific information, funds and commitment all point to an uncertain future for the world's remaining biodiversity.

Further reading

Adams, W.J. (2004) *Against Extinction: The Past and Future of Conservation*. London: Earthscan.

Borgerhoff Mulder, M. and Coppolillo, P. (2005) *Conservation: Linking Ecology, Economics and Culture*. Princeton: Princeton University Press.

Dinerstein, E., Olson, D.M., Graham, D.J., Webster, A.L., Pimm, S.A., Bookbinder, M.A. and Ledec, G. (1995) *A Conservation Assessment of the Terrestrial Ecoregions of Latin America and the Caribbean*. Washington: World Bank.

Leveque, C. and Mounolou, J.C. (2003) *Biodiversity*. Sydney: John Wiley.

Primack R.B. (2002) *Essentials of Conservation Biology*, third edition. Sunderland, MA: Sinauer.

References

Adams, W.H., Aveling, R., Brockington, D., Dickson, B., Elliott, J., Hutton, J., Roe, D., Vira, B. and Wolmer, W. (2004) Biodiversity conservation and the eradication of poverty. *Science* 306, 1146–50.

Balmford, A., Clegg, L., Coulson, T. and Taylor, J. (2002) Why conservationists should heed pokémon. *Science* 295, 236–37.

Bates, J.M. and Demos, T.C. (2001) Do we need to devalue Amazonia and other large tropical forests? *Diversity and Distributions* 7, 249–55.

Brockington, D. (2002) *Fortress Conservation: The Preservation of the Mkomazi Game Reserve, Tanzania*. Oxford: Currey.

Brown, A.H. and Lomolino, M.V. (1998) *Biogeography*, second edition. Sunderland, MA: Sinauer.

Carson, R. (1963) *Silent Spring*. London: Hamilton.

Chape, S., Blyth, S., Fish, L., Fox, P. and Spalding, M. (2003) 2003 *United Nations List of Protected Areas*. Cambridge: UNEP World Conservation Monitoring Centre.

Chapman, L.J., Chapman, C.A., Ogutu-Ohwayo, R., Chandler, M., Kaufman, L. and Keiter, A.E. (1996) Refugia for endangered fishes from an introduced predator in Lake Nabugabo, Uganda. *Conservation Biology* 10, 554–61.

Colishaw, G., Mendelson, S., and Rowcliffe, J.M. (2005) Structure and operation of a bushmeat commodity chain in southwestern Ghana. *Conservation Biology* 19, 139–49.

Costanza, R., D'Arge, R., de Groot, R., Farber, S., Grasso, M., Hannon, B., Limburg, K., Naeem, S., O'Neill, R.V., Paruelo, J., Raskin, R.G., Sutton, P. and van den Belt, M. (1998) The value of the world's ecosystem services and natural capital. *Ecological Economics* 25, 3–15.

Dalton, R. (2005) Sighting of 'extinct' bird may have been a case of mistaken identity. *Nature* 436, 447.

Delong, D.C. Jr (1996) Defining biodiversity. *Wildlife Society Bulletin* 24, 738–49.

Didham, R.K., Tylianakis, J.M., Hutchinson, M.A., Ewers, R.M. and Gemmell, N.J. (2005) Are invasive species the drivers of ecological change? *Trends in Ecology and Evolution* 20, 470–4.

Escobar, A. (1998) Whose knowledge, whose nature? Biodiversity, conservation, and the political ecology of social movements. *Journal of Political Ecology* 5, 53–82.

Fahrig, L. (2001) How much habitat is enough? *Biological Conservation* 100, 65–74.

——(2003) Effects of habitat fragmentation on biodiversity. *Annual Review of Ecology and Systematics* 34, 487–515.

Fitzpatrick, J.W., Lammertink, M., Luneau, M.D. Jr, Gallagher, T.W., Harrison, B.R., Sparling, G.M., Rosenberg, K.V., Rohrbaugh, R.W., Swarthout, E.C.H., Wrege, P.H., Swarthout, S.B., Dantzker, M.S., Charif, R.A., Barksdale, T.R., Remsen, J.V. Jr, Simon, S.D. and Zollner, D. (2005) Ivory-billed woodpecker (*Campephilus principalis*) persists in continental North America. *Science* 5727, 1460–2.

Freeman, M.M.R. (1998) *Inuit, Whaling, and Sustainability*. Walnut Creek, CA: Altimira Press.

Gaston, K.J. and Spicer, J.I. (2004) *Biodiversity: An Introduction*, second edition. Oxford: Blackwell.

Giles, J. (2005) Nitrogen study fertilizes fears of pollution. *Nature* 433, 791.

Goldschmidt, T., Witte, F. and Wanink, J. (1993) Cascading effects of the introduced Nile Perch on the detritivorous/phytoplanktivorous species in the sub-littoral areas of Lake Victoria. *Conservation Biology* 7, 686–700.

Groombridge, B. and Jenkins, M.D. (2000) *Global Biodiversity: Earth's Living Resources in the 21st Century*. Cambridge: World Conservation Press.

Gurevitch, J. and Padilla, D.K. (2004) Are invasive species a major cause of extinctions? *Trends in Ecology and Evolution* 19, 470–4.

Hughes, J.B., Daily, G.C. and Erlich, P.R. (1997) Population diversity: its extent and extinction. *Science* 278, 689–92.

IUCN (2002) *Beyond Rhetoric: Putting Conservation to Work for the Poor*. Berkeley: University of California Press.

James, A.N., Gaston, K.J. and Balmford, A. (1999) Balancing the Earth's accounts. *Nature* 401, 323–4.

Jepson, P. and Canney, S. (2003) Values-led conservation. *Global Ecology and Biogeography* 12, 271–4.

Jepson, P. and Whittaker, R.J. (2002) Ecoregions in context: a critique with special reference to Indonesia. *Conservation Biology* 16, 42–57.

Ladle, R.J., Jepson, P., Araujo, M.B. and Whittaker, R.J. (2004) Dangers of crying wolf over risk of extinctions. *Nature* 482, 799.

Lawton, J.H. and May, R.M. (eds) (1995) *Extinction Rates*. Oxford: Oxford University Press.

Lomborg, B. (2001) *The Skeptical Environmentalist*. Cambridge: Cambridge University Press.

Lomolino, M.V. (2004) Conservation biogeography. In M.V. Lomolino and L.R. Heaney (eds) *Frontiers of Biogeography: New Directions in the Geography of Nature*, pp. 293–6, Sunderland, MA: Sinauer.

MacArthur, R.H. and Wilson, E.O. (1967) *The Theory of Island Biogeography*. Princeton: Princeton University Press.

McGraw, D.M. (2002) The story of the biodiversity convention: from negotiation to implementation. In P.G. Le Pestre (ed.) *Governing Global Biodiversity: The Evolution and Implementation of the Convention on Biological Diversity*, pp. 7–38. Aldershot: Ashgate.

Margulis, S. (2004) *Causes of Deforestation of the Brazilian Amazon* (World Bank Working Paper No. 22). Washington DC: World Bank.

Myers, N.M. (1979) *The Sinking Ark*. Cambridge: Elsevier.

Myers, N.M., Mittermeier, R.A., Mittermeier, C.G., da Fonseca, G.A.B. and Kent, J. (2000) Biodiversity hotspots for conservation priorities. *Nature* 403, 853–9.

Pimm, S.L., Russel, G.J., Gittleman, J.L. and Brooks, T.M. (1995) The future of biodiversity. *Science* 269, 347–50.

Pounds, J.A., Fogden, M.L.P. and Campbell, J.H. (1999) Biological response to climate change on a tropical mountain. *Nature* 398, 611–15.

Purvis, A. and Hector, A. (2000) Getting the measure of biodiversity. *Nature* 405, 212–19.

Pyle, R.M. (2003) Nature matrix: reconnecting people with nature. *Oryx* 37, 206–14.

Raustiala, K. (1997) Domestic institutions and international regulatory cooperation: comparative responses to the Convention on Biological Diversity. *World Politics* 49, 482–509.

Redford, K.H. and Richter, B.D. (1999) Conservation and biodiversity in a world of use. *Conservation Biology* 13, 1246–56.

Reid, W.V. (1992) How many species will there be? In T.C. Whitmore and J.A. Sayer (eds) *Tropical Deforestation and Species Extinction*, pp. 55–73, London: Chapman and Hall.

Robinson, J.G. and Redford, K.H. (1991) *Neotropical Wildlife Use and Conservation*. Chicago: University of Chicago Press.

Rodrigues, A.S.L., Andelman, S.J., Bakaar, M.I., Biotani, L., Brooks, T.M., Cowling, R.M., Fishpool, L.D.C., da Fonseca, G.A.B., Gaston, K.J., Hoffman, M., Long, J.S., Marquet, P.A., Pilgrim, J.D., Pressey, R.L., Schipper, J., Sechrest, W., Stuart, S.N., Underhill, L.G., Waller, R.W., Watts, M.E.J. and Yan, X. (2004) Effectiveness of the global protected-area network in representing species diversity. *Nature* 428, 640–3.

Rosenzweig, M.L. (2003) *Win–Win Ecology; How Earth's Species Can Survive in the Midst of Human Enterprise*. New York: Oxford University Press.

Scholes, R.J. and Biggs, R. (2005) A biodiversity intactness index. *Nature* 434, 45–9.

Skole, D. and Tucker, C. (1993) Tropical deforestation and habitat destruction in the Amazon: satellite data from 1978 to 1988. *Science* 260, 1905–10.

Smith, R.J., Muir, R.D.J., Walpole, M.J., Balmford, A. and Leader-Williams, N. (2003) Governance and the loss of biodiversity. *Nature* 426, 67–70.

Steiner, A. (2003) An unholy alliance. *New Scientist* 180, 21.

Takacs, D. (1996) *The Idea of Biodiversity: Philosophies of Paradise*. Baltimore: Johns Hopkins Press.

Ten Kate, K. (2002) Science and the convention on biological diversity. *Science* 295, 2371–2.

Thomas, C.D., Cameron, A., Green, R.E., Bakkenes, M., Beaumont, L.J., Collingham, C., Erasmus, B.F.N., Siqiera, M.F., Grainger, A., Hannah, L., Hughes, L., Huntley, B., van Jaarsveld, A.S., Midgley, G.F., Miles, L., Ortega-Huerta, M.A., Townsend Peterson, A., Phillips, O. and Williams, S.E. (2004) Extinction risk from climate change. *Nature* 427, 145–8.

Thullier, W., Araújo, M.B., Pearson, R.G., Whittaker, R.J., Brotons, L. and Lavorel, S. (2004) Uncertainty in predictions of extinction risk. *Nature* 1 July, DOI:10.1038/nature02716.

UN (2002) *World Summit on Sustainable Development: Johannesburg Plan of Implementation*. New York: United Nations.

Watson, J.E.M., Whittaker, R.J. and Freudenberger, D. (2005) Bird community responses to fragmentation: how consistent are they across landscapes? *Journal of Biogeography* 32, 1353–70.

Whittaker, R.J. (1998) *Island Biogeography: Ecology, Evolution, and Conservation*. Oxford: Oxford University Press.

Whittaker, R.J., Araújo, M.B., Jepson, P., Ladle, R.J., Watson, J.E.M. and Willis, K.J. (2005) Conservation biogeography: assessment and prospect. *Diversity and Distributions* 11, 3–23.

Wilcove, D.S. (2005) Rediscovery of the ivory-billed woodpecker. *Science* 308, 1422.

Willis, K.J., Gillson, L. and Brncic, T.M. (2004) How 'virgin' is virgin rainforest? *Science* 304, 402–3.

Wilson, E.O. (1984) *Biophilia*. Cambridge, MA: Harvard University Press.

——(1991) *The Diversity of Life*. Cambridge, MA: Harvard University Press.

Woodruff, D.S. (2001) Declines of biomes and biotas and the future of evolution. *Proceedings of the National Academy of Sciences* 98, 5471–6.

51

Evolving nature–culture relationships

Lesley Head

Introduction

The way we think about nature and the environment, structures the way we manage it and thus has material outcomes. Conceptions of culture and nature as separate entities, symbolized most profoundly in Western thought by the two cultures of the humanities and the sciences, have had many implications for environmental management. For example, natural heritage and cultural heritage are frequently managed by different agencies, or different parts of a single agency, although they may be part of the same landscape. The strongest efforts at the protection of nature have been aimed 'out there', in bounded, pristine spaces such as protected areas, national parks and wilderness areas. A corollary of this is that, in contrast, there has been a denial of nature in cities and other human spaces.

The Western conceptualization of nature and culture as separate realms has been challenged from a number of different directions. These include increasing scientific evidence of humans being embedded in all facets of Earth surface processes, greater attention in the humanities to questions of nature and environment, and the stronger political and intellectual voices of indigenous and non-Western peoples.

Old ideas such as unfettered development clearly do not work. But neither does the notion that we can protect nature as a separate realm by putting a fence around it and imagining we can exclude culture. This chapter, then, explores questions such as how we find a philosophical place for people as part of Earth's ecosystems? How do we manage the environment in a sustainable way? How do we interact ethically with non-humans?

Reconceptualizations of nature and culture

Syntheses of scientific research now show that 'most aspects of the structure and functioning of Earth's ecosystems cannot be understood without accounting for the strong, often dominant influence of humanity' (Vitousek *et al.* 1997: 494). Vitousek *et al.* include as examples the percentages of the following caused by human activity: land surface transformation; atmospheric CO_2 concentration; accessible surface fresh water utilization; terrestrial nitrogen

835

fixation; plant species introduced to Canada; bird extinctions; and marine fishery over-exploitation.

Further, ecological and palaeoecological research now presents such a clear picture of environmental change at a nested set of spatial and temporal scales (e.g. Meadows 1999) that the notion of a pristine baseline to which we can return has lost its empirical power. This rethinking is often referred to as 'the new ecology' or 'non-equilibrium' or 'disequilibrium' ecology. Research is consistently showing that 'change takes place all the time, in all sorts of directions and at all sorts of scales, catastrophically, gradually, and unpredictably' (Stott 1998: 1). Integral to this rethinking is a shift from the cyclical time of systems ecology to historical time.

The rise of non-equilibrium approaches both requires and facilitates a rethinking of the way people are viewed within ecology. Metaphorically, 'people' and 'disturbance' are similarly placed in these debates. In the middle decades of the twentieth century, both were seen as being outside the system. Now they and other examples, such as fire, are more likely to be understood as a normal part of ecosystems rather than an external influence (White and Pickett 1985). The archaeological and palaeoecological records show us that such agents have been operating for many thousands of years (Head 2000a).

Within geography and related social sciences, ideas of hybridity and networks are being utilized to more effectively understand such interactions. The most well-known recent elaboration of ideas of hybridity has been in the work of Haraway (1991), Latour (1993) and Whatmore (2002) and their attempts to break free of the binary categories of society and nature.

A further influence on these debates in the last few decades has been the increasing political voice of indigenous peoples. Indigenous peoples' struggle for representation has become an important influence on thinking about environment, nature and landscape.

The clearest example of these influences converging on a practical environmental issue is in the recent reassessment of the wilderness ideal (Cronon 1996; Head 2000b). Definitions of wilderness have a long history of change, and a shift from negative to positive connotations. The nineteenth-century romantic wilderness ideal – of timeless, unchanging and remote landscapes – underpinned conservation and national parks policy in frontier societies such as the USA and Australia over the past century. The challenge came from diverse lines of evidence, including palaeoecological and archaeological demonstrations of long histories of human occupation, in changing environments, and indigenous voices for whom so-called wilderness areas are home. Influenced by the general critique of social natures, people were forced to ask: what exactly is a natural environment?

Nature in the city

Wilderness is only the most visible of a series of issues swept into this critique. Unsettling the boundaries between human and nature, tame and wild, has also challenged the notion that cities are places of pure culture, outside nature. The increased interest in nature in the city is partly the result of the pragmatic realization that the world is becoming more rather than less urbanized, and that for the first time in human history most of the world's population live in cities (Botkin and Beveridge 1997). Botkin and Beveridge (1997: 3) challenge the 'popular belief that we can ignore cities and perhaps abandon cities in the future of civilization'.

In general, ecologists have been more interested in working in so-called pristine landscapes, although this is changing. For example, there is now a journal called *Urban Ecosystems*, which has taken up the challenge of working in areas dominated by humans. It is also important to recognize that in some cities there is a long history of interest in and study of nature (e.g. Hampstead Scientific Society 1913 and Fitter 1945 on London).

Within the human sciences, interest in urban natures has generated work in diverse areas. These include human–animal relations (e.g. Wolch 2002) as well as human–plant ones (e.g. Jones and Cloke 2002). Detailed focus on nature–culture hybrids such as zoos and agricultural shows (Anderson 2003) has challenged the way the human itself is conceptualized as a unified and separate category. The enmeshments between human and nonhuman worlds extend far beyond the space of the city. Such material connections have been most masterfully demonstrated and elaborated by Cronon (Cronon 1991) for Chicago and more recently by Gandy for New York (Gandy 2002). The networks that connect material and social objects and processes include those which provide food (Winter 2003) and symbols of nature such as cut flowers to city consumers. A quite different approach to similar themes is ecological footprint analysis, which seeks to convert consumption into a single index: a land area that would be needed to sustain a particular population indefinitely (Wackernagel and Rees 1996). Although criticized as being too simplistic, and lacking in regional detail (Lenzen and Murray 2001), such approaches usefully emphasize that the environments that urban consumers transform are much more extensive than the area of the cities themselves.

Traditional ecological knowledge

Increasing recognition of the diverse philosophical bases of human interactions with the nonhuman world has contributed to the growing interest in traditional ecological knowledge (TEK) and its potential contribution to sustainable living. Interest from scientists and environmental managers acknowledges that TEK is built up over long periods of time, and that diversity in knowledge systems is both a cultural and an ecological resource (Folke 2004).

Much has been written in the last few decades about indigenous attachments to land and country, including by indigenous people themselves (Langton 1998). It is important to avoid simplistic representations of these connections in trying to connect them to contemporary environmental concerns; for example suggestions that indigenous people were either 'original conservationists' or inherent 'destroyers' of flora and fauna. The category 'indigenous people' encompasses a great diversity of cultures, each of which has changed in both space and time. Even within a continent such as Australia, where we often talk of Aborigines as a single group, there is great diversity, with some traits in common and some different across groups (see e.g. Keen 2003 for overview and systematic analysis of a sample of these).

Nevertheless, if we closely examine the ways in which different indigenous cultures conceptualize the human place, we are quickly presented with challenges to the Western dualism as the norm. Turner et al. (2000) identify the key elements of TEK within three broad themes. These are practices and strategies for resource use and sustainability (for example, harvesting strategies and monitoring); philosophy or worldview (for example, the spirituality and power of all things); and communication and exchange of knowledge and information (for example, oral histories, traditions and customs). Examples of the practice and strategies that come under the rubric of TEK are summarized in Table 51.1.

An example of TEK and its practical application is provided by Rose's (2005: 299) discussion of the relationships between crocodile egg-laying and other environmental signs. In one part of her Northern Territory study area, at Yarralin, the march flies tell that the crocodiles are laying their eggs. Further upstream at Daguragu, the sign comes when the

Table 51.1. Social-ecological practices and mechanisms in traditional knowledge and practice

Practices / mechanisms	Examples
Management practices based on ecological knowledge Practices found both in conventional resource management and in some local and traditional societies	Monitoring resource abundance and change in ecosystems Total protection of certain species Protection of vulnerable life history stages Protection of specific habitats Temporal restrictions of harvest
Practices largely abandoned by conventional resource management but still found in some local and traditional societies	Multiple species management; maintaining ecosystem structure and function Resource rotation Succession management
Practices related to the dynamics of complex systems, seldom found in conventional resource management but found in some traditional societies	Management of landscape patchiness Watershed-based management Managing ecological process at multiple scales Responding to and managing pulses and surprises Nurturing sources of ecosystem renewal
Social mechanisms behind management practices Generation, accumulation, and transmission of local ecological knowledge	Reinterpreting signals for learning Revival of local knowledge Folklore and knowledge carriers Intergenerational transmission of knowledge Geographical diffusion of knowledge
Structure and dynamics of institutions	Roles of stewards and wise people Cross-scale institutions Community assessments Taboos and regulations Social and religious sanctions
Mechanisms of cultural internalization	Rituals, ceremonies and other traditions Cultural frameworks for resource management
Worldview and cultural values	A worldview that provides appropriate environmental ethics Cultural values of respect, sharing, reciprocity, humility, and other

Source: Adapted from Berkes *et al.* (2000: Table 1).

jangarla tree (*Sesbania formosa*) drops its flowers into the water. Back at Yarralin the flowering of this same tree 'tells that the barramundi are biting'. The system of knowledge is thus both quite localized but also widespread. For Rose, the practical aspects include:

■ each specific concurrence is sufficiently widespread to be useful; you do not have to hang around crocodile nesting places waiting for the right moment to start collecting eggs; you can just wait till the march flies bite;

■ the linkages between ecological information and songs, designs, categories of bodies, and so on, ensure that the information is stored and transmitted along numerous pathways; and

Table 51.2. Areas of complementarity between science and traditional ecological knowledge for population monitoring

Principle	Explanation
Diachronic-synchronic complementarity	Science is good at collecting synchronic data (short time series) over a large area, whereas traditional knowledge tends to focus on diachronic information (long time series), often in small areas, as needed to establish a baseline. Using the two together provides more complete information on both temporal and spatial scales.
Complementarity foci on averages vs extremes	Much of science is based on collecting numerical data, with emphasis on statistical analysis of averages. Holders of traditional knowledge are exceptionally good at observing extreme events, variations and unusual patterns and remembering them through oral history and social memory.
Interplay between quantitative and qualitative information	Science demands quantitative data on parts of the system; traditional knowledge strives for a qualitative understanding of the whole. Given that the understanding of complex systems requires both, the two perspectives are complementary. Qualitative measures can be more rapid and inexpensive, but at the expense of precision.
Traditional knowledge for better hypotheses, science for a better test of mechanisms	Traditional knowledge provides a shortcut to more relevant hypotheses for problem solving but does not usually address mechanisms, i.e. the 'why' question. Science has powerful tools for testing the 'why' but could waste time and effort on trivial hypotheses. The use of the two approaches together takes advantage of their relative strengths.
Complementing objectivity with subjectivity	Science strives to be objective, excluding people and feelings. Traditional knowledge specifically includes people, feelings, relationships and sacredness. Science is good at monitoring populations from a distance, but the incorporation of traditional monitoring incorporates a stronger link between science and community, producing 'science with a heart'.

Source: Moller *et al.* 2004: Table 2.

- the information is calibrated in fine-grained detail at localized levels; it is reliable and can be protected.

(Rose 2005: 299)

Moller *et al.* (2004: 2) have argued that 'traditional ecological knowledge, which is based on learning by doing, is in many ways similar to adaptive management'. As Table 51.2 shows, there are both differences and similarities between TEK and Western science. The differences often lead to situations of complementarity.

Indigenous philosophies on their own terms

However, it would be a mistake to think of TEK primarily in terms of whether or not it matches a scientifically correct view of the world. Some writers have noted that much TEK literature 'tends towards classifying knowledge as data, and towards incorporating data into

Table 51.3. Patterns of connectivity between species and country

- The interests of self and other are enmeshed by being situated within connectivities
- Care of country means caring for others as well as self
- Human care responds to country's communication
- Commensalism co-exists with predation, and there is no singular mode that defines interspecies relationships

existing Western paradigms' (Rose 2005: 294). We need to go beyond this, both to understand indigenous worldviews on their own terms and to bring such philosophies into dialogue with Western attempts to rework the dualisms. Scholars working within anthropological rather than biological traditions have gone further in this regard.

We do not have to go far before we encounter profound challenges to commonsense Western understandings, as for example in the challenging title of Povinelli's paper: 'Do rocks listen?'

> Anthropologists, ecologists, environmentalists, and legal theorists who defend hunter-gatherers' and the fourth world's environmental and human rights ... do so within a theoretical framework imported from the West and built upon Western concepts of what happens when humans act in the natural world. In particular, they partition local cultural beliefs about the limits and meanings of *human* and *environment* from scientifically apprehended 'facts' of ecological and economic systems. For example, they might argue that no matter what indigenous people believe occurs when they act in the environment, this does not alter the fact that they rely on these environmental resources for their livelihood. Or they might argue that by believing the land is sentient or populated by spiritual agents, indigenous people are better able to manage their ecosystems – and this can be shown by measuring their work–leisure ratios, the rate by which they alter their environment, or other aspects of their economic practices. In all cases, however, writers rely on Western notions of human intentionality, subjectivity, and production embedded in the very legal discourses they seek to oppose.
>
> (Povinelli 1995: 507)

Along related lines, Rose (2005: 302) has also discussed the sentience of other species and of country: 'in this Indigenous system, subjectivity in the form of sentience and agency is not solely a human prerogative but is located throughout other species and perhaps throughout country itself'.

These are challenging ideas for those working within a Western mindset, but they also provide the basis for a dialogue about inter-species ethics (Table 51.3).

Implications for environmental management

One of the important contributions of TEK is to show us that the question 'what is sustainability?' is itself culturally loaded, and would be answered in different ways in different cultural contexts. It has been said that there are over 300 definitions of sustainability circulating in the literature (Swart and van der Windt 2005). Swart and van der Windt show how concepts of sustainability are different for a conservation organization, a shellfishing organization and government in relation to the question of shellfish harvesting in the Dutch Wadden Sea. Further, the question of what constitutes the environment to be managed is at issue. For example, the boundary between terrestrial and marine environments is a self-evident (if somewhat fuzzy) one to many environmental managers, and certainly in terms of political frameworks which are centred on land. Indigenous groups, however, may conceptualize seascapes in which territory, rights and responsibilities continue from land out to sea, with no break at the coast.

There are now a number of examples internationally of indigenous joint management of national parks and protected areas, resulting in the incorporation of indigenous skills into management policies. For example, in Kakadu National Park in northern Australia, landscape burning policies aim to incorporate both indigenous and Western scientific aspirations. The aims in relation to fire management are to:

- promote traditional Aboriginal ways of burning within the park;
- involve Bininj/Mungguy in planning and implementing fire management;
- protect life and property within and adjacent to the park;
- restrict fire from spreading so that it doesn't enter or leave the park; and
- maintain biodiversity through effective fire management of species and habitats.

(http://www.deh.gov.au/parks/publications/kakadu-html/index.html)

The example that I focus on here in more depth is the recent evolution in nature–culture relationships within international environmental and heritage management, as expressed particularly in World Heritage, and the UNESCO Man and the Biosphere programme. I examine particularly changes over time and current challenges, occasioned by the influences discussed before.

In her tribute to archaeologist and heritage advocate Isobel McBryde, Sullivan (2005) identifies three characteristics of Western society which, she argues, profoundly influence heritage practice. The first is the emphasis on the material over the spiritual and emotional, leading to a heritage emphasis on 'monumentality, or grandeur, or craftsmanship' (p. 84). There is a gendered aspect here, with the achievements of monument-building men over-emphasized in history. The monumentalist approach almost inevitably contains a systematic neglect of heritage in Oceania, Africa and much of Asia and the Americas (McBryde 2000).

The second is the tradition of perfectability and progress, which stimulates constant change. This in turn leads to increasing discontinuity in society, making heritage conservation increasingly significant, as well as difficult, conscious and artificial. Sullivan contrasts this with a more fluid and continuous connection with the past as seen, for example, in the way Buddhist monks at Mogao in western China continually remade their temples over a number of centuries.

The ideals of perfectability and progress have also led to an emphasis on preserving the 'best' and 'most significant' places, and have made it difficult to find a currency within which to express the significance of ordinary places and attachments.

The third characteristic is the binary or dualistic system of Western reason. This leads us to expect answers to complex questions in yes/no terms: for example, is this site significant or not? The dualism also separates natural from cultural heritage, 'when it is clear that the whole of Australia is a cultural landscape, that our perceptions of it are inescapably cultural, and that every site is an inextricable mixture of natural and cultural values' (p. 85).

Together these characteristics had led, until recent decades, to an emphasis on dead sites over living ones, on dots on the landscape instead of what Sullivan terms 'an ecology of heritage', and a lack of recognition of other ways of thinking about land and landscape, particularly indigenous ones. However, there are a number of recent attempts to engage with the challenges of a more dynamic understanding of land and heritage. Thus, for example, there was discussion and recognition of the importance of journeys and routes of pilgrimage that link a number of places across the landscape. Two important examples are the medieval Christian pilgrim route to Santiago de Compostela in northern Spain (El Camino de Compostela), and the Aboriginal cultural routes leading to the Pukardu Hill ochre deposits in the Flinders Ranges, south Australia (McBryde 2000).

World heritage associative cultural landscapes

The world heritage convention both embodies the old dualisms and attempts to go beyond them. It is written in terms of a distinction between natural and cultural heritage. Natural heritage includes the following:

- natural features consisting of physical and biological formations or groups of such formations, which are of outstanding universal value from the aesthetic or scientific point of view;
- geological and physiographical formations and precisely delineated areas which constitute the habitat of threatened species of animals and plants of outstanding universal value from the point of view of science or conservation;
- natural sites or precisely delineated natural areas of outstanding universal value from the point of view of science, conservation or natural beauty.

These definitions of nature clearly encompass quite a lot of culture. For example the ideas of *value* and *beauty* are ones which are culturally defined. Science is also a cultural activity, privileged in these definitions over other kinds of cultural activity.

Cultural heritage includes three categories: Monuments, Groups of buildings, and Sites. The latter include 'works of man or the combined works of nature and man'. Recognition of the concept of *cultural landscape* as representing these combined works came only in 1992. Cultural landscapes are considered in three main categories. The first and most easily identifiable is the clearly defined and intentionally created landscape, such as gardens and parkland. The second is the organically evolved landscape, such as the irrigated rice terraces of Luzon in the northern Philippines. These are a very obvious human transformation of the physical landscape, with the terraces supported by dry-stone walls on steep mountainsides.

The third category is the associative cultural landscape, whereby powerful religious or cultural associations with nature may have little or no material evidence. This category acknowledges the link between the physical and spiritual aspects of landscape. It was seen to be particularly relevant to the cultural practices of indigenous peoples, and to the Asia-Pacific region with its diversity of living traditions in relation to land and water. In 1993 Tongariro National Park in the North Island of New Zealand, already listed for its natural heritage, became the first property to be inscribed on the World Heritage List under these revised criteria for associative cultural landscapes. As the listing explains:

> The mountains at the heart of the park have cultural and religious significance for the Maori people and symbolize the spiritual links between this community and its environment. The park has active and extinct volcanoes, a diverse range of ecosystems and some spectacular landscapes.

(http://whc.unesco.org/en/list/421)

UNESCO Man and the Biosphere

World heritage is conservative in the sense of trying to preserve things from the past: if not unchanged, at least with integrity comparable to the original. There is an implicit sense of remnants from the past. Man and the Biosphere (MAB) areas, on the other hand are about processes, and explicitly include people.

Biosphere Reserves are described as 'both concept and tool' (UNESCO 2002: 1). They are places where 'the emphasis is on humans as an integral and fundamental part of the biosphere' (p. 1). In other words, they seek to reverse the practices of much protected area management that seek to exclude local peoples. They have three complementary functions: conservation of biodiversity; fostering of sustainable economic and human development; and a logistic function encompassing education, monitoring and research. They are explicitly positioned as a contrast to the 'closed jar' approach of sealing off nature from the human world (p. 2). As at July 2005, there were 482 Biosphere Reserves in 102 countries. Two contrasting examples serve to illustrate some of the problems and potentials.

Smardon and Faust (2006) provide an overview of issues in the four Biosphere Reserves of Mexico's Yucatan peninsula (in 2002 there were thirty-four in the whole of Mexico). They argue that this is a representative example of problems confronting protected area management throughout most of the planet. It is an area with a documented human history covering several thousand years, high biological diversity as a result of its tropical location and complex topography. They point out that many of the areas demarcated for Biosphere Reserves were the ancestral lands of indigenous peoples, perceived as pristine wilderness areas by colonizing invaders. Within this historical context, environmental managers from outside the area, whether the UN, NGOs from North America or educated urban Mexicans, are often perceived as just another set of colonial invaders (Frazier 2006). The generic issues confronting Biosphere Reserve planning and management include the following (Smardon and Faust 2006: 185):

- encroachment from settlement and poaching (NB: It is 'unclear whether the reserve administrators are encroaching on native lands or the natives are encroaching on the reserve'; p. 185);
- lack of personnel to conduct administrative, protection, monitoring, management and development functions;
- funding cycles that do not correspond to long-term needs;
- local participation has frequently been directed by urban professionals with little understanding of rural conditions;
- migration into areas with resources has frequently followed infrastructure development;
- communal land ownership requires re-thinking of methods for working with local communities.

A very different Biosphere Reserve is Kristianstads Vattenrike, in the southern Sweden province of Skåne. Encompassing the lower drainage basin of the River Helge and adjacent coastal waters in the Baltic Sea, the area includes diverse wetland environments of high biological value. For example, it contains 711 species nationally red-listed by Sweden and at least twenty-two species in the IUCN Red List. It is situated in the most densely populated region of Sweden with a highly developed agricultural sector. Further, there is a town of 30,000 people at the heart of the reserve.

For the town of Kristianstad, the watery environment provided by the surrounding lakes, river and high groundwater levels is both threat and opportunity. This ambiguous relationship with water has been central to the town's identity since its establishment in the seventeenth century, in ways comparable to the low-lying areas of the Netherlands to the south. The town was established on a small island by the Danish King Christian IV in 1614. He used the surrounding wetlands as a defence against his enemy, the Swedes (Magnusson 2004). Magnusson outlines shifts in thinking about the wetlands, from waterlogged (*vattensjuk*) to a water kingdom (*vattenrike*).

The successful nomination of Kristianstads Vattenrike as a Biosphere Reserve (declared 2005) was the result of high levels of cooperation between local politicians, the municipality and a range of other stakeholders, working together in a consultative or reference group. It could be argued that the potential for this community to successfully use the Biosphere Reserve concept as a tool for the promotion of sustainability is higher than in the Yucatan, because it has been promulgated by local residents working within a similar cultural frame of reference to the Man and the Biosphere programme. However, it remains an open question whether the concept will capture as much interest and connection among the rest of the town's population as it does among these experts. This is the subject of ongoing research.

If a Biosphere Reserve is 'a laboratory for sustainability' (Alfsen-Norodom 2004: 4), and current examples include towns such as Kristianstad and the urbanized area of Lanzarote in Spain (Dogse 2004), then there is no necessary reason why a major city should not also become a Biosphere Reserve. Indeed, there is now considerable discussion about whether cities such as New York, Rome, Dar es Salaam, Seoul and São Paulo could be conceptualized and managed as Biosphere Reserves (see contributions in Alfsen-Norodom *et al.* 2004, including Alfsen-Norodom *et al.* 2004 on New York). Such thinking seems bizarre if we continue to think of nature as existing 'out there', somewhere remote from human activity. However, it is quite consistent with the idea that cities are just as much ecosystems as any other area, or if we consider the many ways cities are networked into broader ecosystem processes, such as those that supply water (Gandy 2002; Kaika 2005). Incorporating the Biosphere Reserve concept into city planning is one potential tool to manage cities more sustainably. There are, of course, many other means to do this, and a number of countries, including the UK and Australia, now emphasize sustainability in their planning and environmental policies (Australian State of the Environment Committee 2001).

The connections between people and nature in the city go in many directions. One important area of interest is the implications for human health and well-being of contact with nature. Research indicates that access to green space and open space is important to the quality of life of people who live in cities (Burgess *et al.* 1988; Bell *et al.* 2004). There are also socio-economic, ethnic, age and gender differences in patterns of perception and use that managers need to be aware of. For example, Bell *et al.* (2004) found lower levels of use of East Midlands green space among black and minority populations. There are also strong connections to be explored between access to nature in urban areas and physical activity (Carnegie *et al.* 2002). Thus exercise, usually understood as a health issue, connects back to issues of ecological sustainability.

This chapter has offered a brief taste of diverse nature–culture relationships, and many other examples could have been chosen. This diversity will be an important resource in the century ahead as societies face the challenges of environmental change and sustainability.

Further reading

Castree, N. (2005) *Nature.* London: Routledge.

Cronon, W. (1996) The trouble with wilderness; or, getting back to the wrong nature. In W. Cronon (ed.) *Uncommon Ground*, pp. 69–90. New York: W.W. Norton.

Rose, D.B. (1996) *Nourishing Terrains: Australian Aboriginal Views of Landscape and Wilderness.* Canberra: Australian Heritage Commission.

UNESCO (2002) *Biosphere Reserves: Special Places for People and Nature.* Paris: UNESCO.

References

Alfsen-Norodom, C. (2004) Urban biosphere and society: partnership of cities – introduction. *Annals of the New York Academy of Science* 1023, 1–9.

Alfsen-Norodom, C., Lane, B.D. and Corry, M. (eds) (2004) Urban biosphere and society: partnership of cities. *Annals of the New York Academy of Science* 1023 (special issue).

Alfsen-Norodom, C., Boehme, S.E., Clemants, S., Corry, M., Imbruce, V., Lane, B.D., Miller, R.B., Padoch, C., Panero, C.M., Peters, C., Rosenzweig, C., Solecki, W. and Walsh, D. (2004) Managing the megacity for global sustainability: the New York metropolitan region as an urban biosphere reserve. *Annals of the New York Academy of Science* 1023, 125–41.

Anderson, K. (2003) White natures: Sydney's Royal Agricultural Show in post-humanist perspective. *Transactions of the Institute of British Geographers* 28, 422–41.

Australian State of the Environment Committee (2001) *Australia State of the Environment 2001.* Canberra: CSIRO Publishing.

Bell, S., Morris, N., Findlay, C., Travlou, P., Montarzino, A., Gooch, D., Gregory, G. and Ward Thompson, C. (2004) *Nature for People: The Importance of Green Spaces to East Midlands Communities* (English Nature Research Reports 567). Peterborough: English Nature.

Berkes, F., Colding, J. and Folke, C. (2000) Rediscovery of traditional ecological knowledge as adaptive management. *Ecological Applications* 10, 1251–62.

Botkin, D.B. and Beveridge, C.E. (1997) Cities as environments. *Urban Ecosystems* 1, 3–19.

Burgess, J., Harrison, C.M. and Limb, M. (1988) People, parks and the urban green: a study of popular meanings and values for open spaces in the city. *Urban Studies* 25, 455–73.

Carnegie, M.A., Bauman, A., Marshall, A.L., Mohsin, M., Westley-Wise, V. and Booth, M.L. (2002) Perceptions of the physical environment, stage of change for physical activity, and walking among Australian adults. *Research Quarterly for Exercise and Sport* 73, 146–55.

Cronon, W. (1991) *Nature's Metropolis. Chicago and the Great West.* New York and London: W.W. Norton

——(1996) The trouble with wilderness; or, getting back to the wrong nature. In W. Cronon (ed.) *Uncommon Ground*, pp. 69–90. New York: W.W. Norton.

Dogse, P. (2004) Toward urban biosphere reserves. *Annals of the New York Academy of Science* 1023, 10–48.

Fitter, R.S.R. (1945) *London's Natural History.* Collins: London.

Folke, C. (2004) Traditional knowledge in social-ecological systems. *Ecology and Society* 9 (3), 7.

Frazier, J. (2006) Biosphere reserves and the 'Yucatan' syndrome: another look at the role of NGOs. *Landscape and Urban Planning* 74, 313–33.

Gandy, M. (2002) *Concrete and Clay: Reworking Nature in New York City.* Cambridge, Mass.: MIT Press.

Hampstead Scientific Society (1913) *Hampstead Heath: Its Geology and Natural History.* London: Fisher Unwin.

Haraway, D. (1991) *Simians, Cyborgs and Women.* London: Free Association Books.

Head, L. (2000a) *Cultural Landscapes and Environmental Change.* London: Arnold.

——(2000b) *Second Nature: The History and Implications of Australia as Aboriginal Landscape.* Syracuse: Syracuse University Press.

Jones, O. and Cloke, P. (2002) *Tree Cultures. The Place of Trees and Trees in their Place.* Oxford: Berg.

Kaika, M. (2005) *City of Flows. Modernity, Nature, and the City.* London: Routledge.

Keen, I. (2003) *Aboriginal Economy and Society: Australia at the Threshold of Colonisation.* Melbourne: Oxford University Press.

Langton, M. (1998) *Burning Questions: Emerging Environmental Issues for Indigenous Peoples in Northern Australia.* Darwin: Centre for Indigenous Natural and Cultural Resource Management.

Latour, B. (1993) *We Have Never Been Modern.* Cambridge, Mass.: Harvard University Press.

Lenzen, M. and Murray, S.A. (2001) A modified ecological footprint method and its application to Australia. *Ecological Economics* 37, 229–55.

McBryde, I. (2000) Travellers in storied landscapes: a case study in exchanges and heritage. *Aboriginal History* 24, 152–74.

Magnusson, S.-E. (2004) The changing perception of the westlands in and around Kristinastad, Sweden. From waterlogged areas toward a future water kingdom, Kristianstads Vattenrike Biosphere Reserve. *Annals of the New York Academy of Science* 1023, 323–7.

Meadows, M.E. (1999) Biogeography: changing places, changing times. *Progress in Physical Geography* 23, 257–70.

Moller, H., Berkes, F., Lyver, P. and Kislalioglu, M. (2004) Combining science and traditional ecological knowledge: monitoring populations for co-management. *Ecology and Society* 9 (3), 2.

Povinelli, E. (1995) Do rocks listen? The cultural politics of apprehending Australian Aboriginal labor. *American Anthropologist* 97 (3), 505–18.

Rose, D.B. (2005) An indigenous philosophical ecology: situating the human. *The Australian Journal of Anthropology* 16 (3), 294–305.

Smardon, R.D. and Faust, B.B. (2006) Introduction: international policy in the biosphere reserves of Mexico's Yucatan peninsula. *Landscape and Urban Planning* 74, 160–92.

Stott, P. (1998) Biogeography and ecology in crisis: the urgent need for a new metalanguage. *Journal of Biogeography* 25, 1–2.

Sullivan, S. (2005) Out of the box: Isabel McBryde's radical contribution to the shaping of Australian archaeological practice. In I. Macfarlane, M.-J. Mountain and R. Paton (eds) *Many Exchanges: Archaeology, History, Community and the Work of Isabel McBryde* (Aboriginal History Monograph 11). Canberra: Aboriginal History.

Swart, J.A.A. and van der Windt, H.J. (2005) Visions of nature and environmental sustainability: shellfish harvesting in the Dutch Wadden Sea. *Restoration Ecology* 13 (1), 183–92.

Turner, N.J., Ignace, M.B. and Ignace, R. (2000) Traditional ecological knowledge and wisdom of aboriginal peoples in British Columbia. *Ecological Applications* 10 (5), 1275–87.

UNESCO (2002) *Biosphere Reserves: Special Places for People and Nature.* Paris: UNESCO.

Vitousek, P.M., Mooney, H.A., Lubchenco, J. and Melillo, J.M. (1997) Human domination of Earth's ecosystems. *Science* 277, 494–99.

Wackernagel, M. and Rees, W. (1996) *Our Ecological Footprint. Reducing Human Impact on the Earth,* Gabriola Island, BC: New Society Publishers.

Whatmore, S. (2002) *Hybrid Geographies.* London: Sage.

White, P.S. and Pickett, S.T.A. (1985) Natural disturbance and patch dynamics: an introduction. In S.T.A. Pickett and P.S. White (eds) *The Ecology of Natural Disturbance and Patch Dynamics,* pp. 3–13. Orlando, Florida: Academic Press.

Winter, M. (2003) Geographies of food: agro-food geographies – making reconnections. *Progress in Human Geography* 27, 505–13.

Wolch, J. (2002) Anima urbis. *Progress in Human Geography* 26, 721–42.

52

Planning for population growth

Shii Okuno

Population distribution, composition and growth are closely related to local geographies and socio-cultural factors, such as the level of economic development and personal desire for children. Analysing demographic structures and changes allows policy makers to project future trends, by unpacking the significance of changing mortality, fertility and migration data. This chapter explores the nature of the challenges faced by continuing growth, but also discusses the implications of an aging and stagnating population in parts of Western Europe. It sets population issues into a wider cultural context by discussing the policy options and geographical, social and moral implications of managing change.

Projection of population growth

In projecting for future population trends and planning for these changes mortality, fertility, and migration are important elements to be considered. Malthus (1992) in 1803 claimed that population, when unchecked, increases in a geometrical ratio, whilst subsistence could only be increased on an arithmetical scale. The Malthusian view is that insufficiency in food provision will grow larger, and at a certain level may lead to hunger, social unrest or famine, and that rulers may then attempt to reduce the population pressure by every means, even engaging into warfare. But social and medical intervention and the development process have rendered Malthusian predictions doubtful.

World and regional population trends

The world population has increased from approximately 2,500 million in 1950 to approximately 6,000 million in 2000. It is projected to increase further to over 9,000 million persons in 2050, an increase of approximately 6,500 million, or two-and-a-half fold, in a century (see Chapter 9 for more detailed demographic data). Different regions will undergo different rates of demographic change. Africa is expected to rise in its share in total world population from 13 per cent in 2000 to 20 per cent in 2050, whereas Europe will reduce its share from 12 to 7 per cent. Other continents will see little relative change: Asia will decrease from 61 per cent to 59 per cent, and Latin America, North America and Oceania will remain at 9, 5 and 0.5 per cent respectively. Needless to say, nations vary greatly in their natural growth rates (see Table 52.1.).

The Demographic Transition Model

Why is there a difference of population growth between the two groups of nations in 2000: those that are expanding and those where population numbers are stagnant? It can be explained by the Demographic Transition Model, which states that a population's mortality and fertility may decline as a result of social and economic development. It predicts that all nations will go through three demographic transition stages as follows (see Figure 52.1).

Stage I indicates high crude birth rate (CBR) and high crude death rate (CDR) with a resulting stable population growth, as happened in the pre-industrial age in developed nations. The high birth rate is caused by parents' desire for more labour power on their farms, and families need more children to ensure survival of the family and to compensate for the high numbers of children who die young. High death rates are the result of disease and lack of hygiene. The high birth and death rates are both relatively stable and so growth in

Table 52.1. Projection of world regional population (in millions)

	1950	1975	2000	2025	2050
Africa	221	408	796	1,292	1,937
Asia	1,398	2,398	3,680	4,742	5,217
Europe	547	676	728	696	653
Latin America	167	322	520	687	784
North America	172	243	316	394	438
Oceania	13	22	31	40	47
WORLD	2,519	4,068	6,071	7,851	9,076

Source: United Nations (2003, 2005).

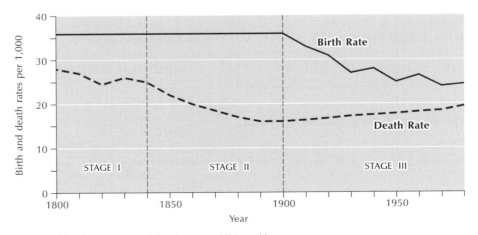

Figure 52.1. The three stages of the demographic transition.

population is held in check. Epidemics may break out occasionally, for example the periodic eruptions of plague throughout Europe in the Middle Ages.

Stage II indicates the pattern of high crude birth rate (CBR) but a lowering crude death rate (CDR), and as a result a large increase in natural growth rate, as in the early stages of industrialization. In the mid-eighteenth century, the death rate in Western European countries fell as a result of improvements in sanitation and the introduction of medicines. The birth rate remained high because of tradition and conventional practice. This resulted in skyrocketing population growth rates. Along with advances in birth control, the crude birth rate in developed countries has been reduced through the twentieth century. Many less-developed countries are currently at this stage of the transition. For example, Ethiopia has a high CBR at 45 per 1,000, but a low CDR at 19 per 1,000 contributed to a continuing high growth rate in the period of 1995–2000.

Stage III indicates that both the CBR and CDR level off and decline to lower rates, following an increasing participation by women in society, and a reduced need for families to have many children. Some nations have a CBR slightly higher than the CDR (as in Denmark, 13 compared to 11 per 1,000 in the year 2000) whereas elsewhere CBR may even have fallen below the CDR (in Sweden, 9.4 against 9.7, over the same period). Countries like China and South Korea are rapidly approaching, or have already entered, Stage III.

This model suggests a general truth but suffers from discrepancies. First, it fails to predict how long it will take for a nation to get from Stages I to III. Second, it assumes that all nations will follow the same path. In practice, however, the CBRs of some nations do not drop because of religious, social or other reasons.

The three components of population projection

Table 52.2 shows the three basic components of population projection – birth rate, death rate and net migration – for a sample of countries. Subtracting the death rate from the birth rate gives the natural rate of increase, and taking the net migration into the calculation, whether it is positive or negative, gives the growth rate for a nation or area. Let us look at some examples in the three different periods of time.

In the 1950s, developing nations like India and Nigeria had a high rate of natural increase. The birth rate rose to over 40 births per 1,000 in many of these countries at a time when death rates were significantly lower. The number of migrants for India and Nigeria was negligible, but Singapore had a net in-migration over 12 persons per 1,000. As a consequence, in 1958 Singapore, part of the newly established nation of Malaya, attained a natural increase rate of 3.4 per cent, whilst India and Nigeria were both also growing between 2 to 3 per cent each year.

By the year 2000, birth and death rates of India and Nigeria were reducing. In India the natural rates of increase had fallen to 1.6 per cent, and Nigerian growth rates had also started to fall. Singapore had attained a much-reduced rate of natural increase of 0.7 per cent. Compared to the slight net migration effect of the other two nations, Singapore experienced a growth rate of 2.2 per cent, almost two-thirds of which was caused by net in-migration.

Canada attained a natural increase rate of 1.8 per cent in 1950, with 27 births per 1,000 and 9 deaths per 1,000. Norway and Sweden had attained rates of natural increase of 1.0 and 0.6 per cent respectively. All three countries had lower birth and lower death rates compared to those of developing nations. Moreover, Norway and Sweden are projected to be stagnant in growth by or before 2050, even allowing for small net in-migration.

Table 52.2. Components of population growth (1950, 2000, 2050)

Country	Year	Births per 1,000	Deaths per 1,000	Net number of migrants per 1,000	Natural increase rate %	Growth rate %
India	1951	45.00	26.00	na	1.9	na
	2000	24.77	8.88	−0.08	1.589	1.500
	2050ᵃ	13.40	9.18	−0.03	0.422	0.400
Nigeria	1953	51.31	26.86	0.00	2.445	2.445
	2000	41.56	17.89	0.31	2.367	2.398
	2050ᵃ	28.82	8.46	0.10	2.036	2.045
Singapore	1958	41.15	6.96	12.42	3.419	4.600
	2000	11.64	3.89	14.58	0.775	2.200
	2050ᵃ	6.43	16.63	0.00	−1.020	−1.000
Canada	1950	27.08	9.04	na	1.804	na
	2000	11.34	7.39	6.20	0.395	1.000
	2050ᵃ	9.81	12.21	4.62	−0.240	0.200
Sweden	1950	16.45	10.02	na	0.643	na
	2000	10.14	10.47	2.58	−0.033	0.200
	2050ᵃ	9.93	12.84	1.65	−0.291	−0.100
Norway	1950	19.11	9.10	7.03	1.001	7.704
	2000	13.19	9.79	2.16	0.340	0.555
	2050ᵃ	9.90	12.54	1.60	−0.264	−0.104

Note: ᵃ Figures of 1950 and 2000 are real whereas those of 2050 are projections.

Source: United States Census Bureau, International Data Base (http://www.census.gov/).

The specific fertility rate

In projecting and planning for growth, the specific fertility rate (SFR) is a useful measure to tell whether the national population can reproduce by itself (see Figures 52.2, 52.3). SFR is the average number of births to women between the ages of 15 and 49.[1]

Between 2000 and 2005, the world average of special fertility rates of different nations stood at 2.69 per cent. The rate required to guarantee 'replacement levels' should not be less than 2.08 per cent. Most of the industrially advanced nations are failing to reach this replacement level. These nations' populations are stagnant in growth or are even in decline. For example, Denmark has an SFR at 1.76, Sweden at 1.71, UK at 1.71, Germany at 1.34, Italy at 1.29, Russia at 1.14. Japan stands at 1.29 and Australia at 1.75 for the SFR. The USA has a higher SFR at 2.04 per cent compared to other advanced nations because a large number of its population originated in Latin America, a region with an average SFR over 2.3. In contrast, the average SFR for Europe is at a level of 1.37 per cent.

In contrast, developing nations show a higher SFR in the period of 2000–5: Africa at 4.57, South Asia at 3.20, Central Asia at 2.94, Latin America and Southeast Asia at 2.36, Oceania at 2.23, while East Asia, with more rapidly industrialized economies, stands at 1.80 per cent. According to the UN's *World Population Prospects: The 2002 Revision*, on the median projection of SFR in the subsequent five-year periods up to 2045–50, developing nations are likely to reduce their SFR whilst advanced nations will probably raise theirs over

Table 52.3. Existing special fertility rate appraisal and policy stance, 2003

	Special fertility rate	Appraisal	Policy stance
France	1.89	Too low	Improving the fertility rate
Germany	1.34	Too low	Non–intervention
Italy	1.29	Too low	Non–intervention
Sweden	1.71	Satisfactory	Non–intervention
United Kingdom	1.71	Satisfactory	Non–intervention
USA	1.04	Satisfactory	Non–intervention
Japan	1.29	Two low	Improving the fertility rate

Source: United Nations Population Division (2003); fertility rates are from European Union (2004); United States Department of Health and Human Services (2003); Japanese Ministry of Welfare and Labour (2004).

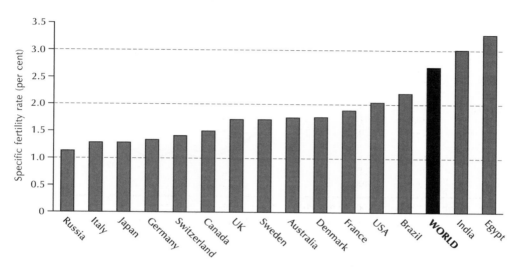

Figure 52.2. Specific fertility rates of selected nations, 2000–5.

the same period (United Nations Population Division 2003). Both of them will converge around 1.85 to 2.40 per cent in half a century from the present period.

For these predicted trends to be realized, however, a number of important policy options will have to be exercised in local contexts. The next two sections of this chapter explore the very different policy challenges for nations which face continuing growing populations, as against those with stagnant or even declining populations.

Nations of continuing growth and their policy options

The population growth trends of India and sub-Saharan Africa raise interesting and significantly different policy options and implications.

The case of India: over-urbanization and the two-children policy

One out of six people on this earth lives in India. It is second to China in population and is projected to overtake China's population by 2040, or even earlier. India had reached 1 billion

851

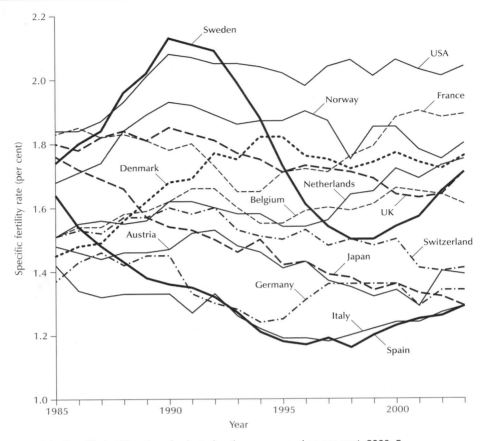

Figure 52.3. Specific fertility rates of selected nations expressed as per cent, 2000–5.

people by the turn of the century. India's population density at 331 persons per square kilometre in 2004 was one of the highest in the world (Register General of India 2000).

With steady population growth, intense pressure on limited land resources forced people to migrate to already crowded urban areas. Increasing urbanization and the growth of cities are generally associated with increasing national gross domestic product and high levels of per capita gross domestic product, but poverty remains a persistent feature of urban life. Low incomes and poor living conditions define life for a vast number of India's urban-dwellers, India's metropolitan regions, such as Delhi, Bombay, and Chandigarh, Hyderabad, Bangalore and other cities.

The rapid increase in urban population, 28 per cent in 2000, has resulted in the growth of slums or squatter settlements with serious social, economic and environmental problems. Roughly 20–25 per cent of India's urban families live in slums, squatter settlements or refugee colonies through the lack of sufficient affordable urban housing stock. Government figures show that the percentage of urban households living in slums is highest in Maharashtra (25 per cent), followed by Orissa (19), Arunachal Pradesh (18), Madhya Oradesh (18) and West Bengal (17) (Register General of India 2000).

A related concern is that of food security. Insufficiency in food is aggravated by the fact that the geographical distribution of poverty is highly uneven in India. Approximately 30 per cent of the people in Bihar, Uttar Pradesh and Andhra Pradesh live below the official poverty line, compared to between 3 and 7 per cent in Himachal Pradesh and Punjab.

Since the 1960s India has launched a series of national family planning programmes (Bhagat 2002). By 2000 her total fertility rate had declined by more than 40 per cent since the 1960s, and today the average number of children per woman is around three.

In the 1970s, the government declared a population 'state of emergency' and began implementing forced sterilization for some people in the nation's poorest regions, despite the unpopularity of the policy initiative amongst sections of India's Hindi population (Bhagat 2002). In 2000, the Indian government announced its national population policy. Its overriding economic and social development objective seeks to improve the quality of lives that people lead, to enhance their well-being, and to provide them with opportunities and choices to become productive assets in society.

The National Population Policy 2000 (NPP 2000) affirms the commitment of government towards voluntary and informed choice and consent of Indian citizens, while providing reproductive health care services and continuing a target-free approach in administering family planning services (Indian National Commission on Population 2000). The NPP 2000 provides a policy framework for advancing goals and prioritizing strategies during the next decade, to meet the reproductive and child health needs of the people of India, and to achieve net replacement levels of 2.1 by 2010. This is based upon the need to simultaneously address issues of child survival, maternal health and contraception while increasing outreach and coverage of a comprehensive package of reproductive and child health services by government, industry and the voluntary non-government sector, working in partnership.

Motivational measures under the policy include: linking of disbursement of the cash awards under the Rural Development Department's maternity benefit scheme in compliance with ante-natal check-ups; an institutional delivery scheme for couples below the poverty line who undergo sterilization with not more than two living children; and a special reward for those who marry after the legal age of marriage, register their marriage, have the first child after the mother reaches the age of 21, accept the small family norm and adopt a terminal method after the birth of the second child.

The policy envisages the setting up of a high-powered commission on population, chaired by the Prime Minister, to monitor and guide planning and implementation of the policy. The Indian Union Health Minister has claimed that the main philosophy behind the policy was that population control could be better achieved by improving the mass poor through greater focus on child survival, empowerment of women and increased participation of men in planning parenthood (Bhagat 2002). The immediate objective was to address the needs for contraception, health-care infrastructure, health personnel and integrated service delivery, while the medium-term objective would be to bring the total fertility rate to replacement levels by 2010.

Population policies for sub-Sahara Africa

In December 1994, World Bank Policy Research outlined the population status of and the population policies for sub-Sahara Africa, comprising the countries of Botswana, Cameroon, Côte d'Ivoire, Ghana, Nigeria, Tanzania, Zambia, Zimbabwe and Senegal (Ainsworth 1994). The population of sub-Sahara Africa is growing at 3 per cent a year. It has already doubled since the 1960s, and its current rate of growth will double again in 22 years. By comparison, the population of South Asia, the developing region with the next highest rate, is growing at 2.2 per cent a year and global population is growing at 1.7 per cent a year. At the same time, economic growth in the sub–Saharan region has been slow. Between 1965 and 1988, per capita gross national product (GNP) for sub-Sahara Africa grew by only 0.2 per cent a year. During the 1980s GNP per capita declined by 2.6 per cent a year. Further, human capital in the form of schooling and other training is low, and in many countries school enrolment rates have fallen.

Today's high birth rate coupled with slow growth in incomes is producing a rapidly growing labour force with low levels of human capital – not a good prospect for improved living conditions. Further, by 2000 the number of people in poverty in sub-Saharan Africa had increased by 100 million since 1985.

Not all of Africa's development problems can be directly attributed to population growth (see also Chapters 10 and 11). Reducing the rate of population growth alone will not be sufficient to improve the quality of life, without other supportive policies. But quality of life, high child mortality and economic uncertainty predispose couples to want large families. This means that slowing population growth must involve policies to reduce high fertility and child mortality while raising quality of life.

Recent demographic surveys show that both fertility and child mortality rate are high in sub-Saharan Africa. The average total fertility rate is between six and seven children per woman, the highest of any developing region. Child mortality has declined steadily since the Second World War. As many as 30–40 per cent of African children died before their fifth birthday in the 1950s, but by the mid-1970s this figure had been reduced to about 20 per cent. Nevertheless, infant and child mortality remains relatively high. In twenty countries infant mortality rates are over 100 per 1,000, and in five countries the rate is greater than 140 per 1,000.

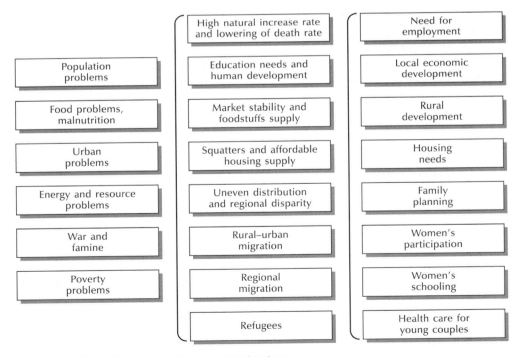

Figure 52.4. Population issues of less developed nations.

There are pockets of women who want fewer children and who lack easy access to family planning. But, by and large, desired family size is still high – between six and nine children per woman. So, lowering fertility and raising contraceptive use will rely on both improving socio-economic conditions associated with reduced demand for children, and increasing the effectiveness of family planning programmes in attracting clients. Designing successful policies depends upon realistic estimates of the impacts of different social programmes on fertility and on contraceptive use.

The World Bank research also points to socio-economic and policy determinants of fertility in sub-Saharan Africa on which effective policies to slow down population growth and to improve population quality are based. Foremost among these factors is women's schooling. With very few exceptions, levels of female schooling are low across the continent. In most cases men's schooling also is relatively low. Schooling policies will also affect the number of children in the short run by prompting couples to improve their lives and have fewer children. Curbing child mortality is another essential policy for lowering fertility. The study also shows that legal frameworks beyond education also affect the status of women and are significant for population planning. These include laws governing marriage and divorce, inheritance, ownership of property, employment opportunities and access to credit.

Figure 52.4 outlines the related issues of population policy taking place in the nations of continual growth, which are mostly developing nations.

Ageing nations and their policy options

The ageing trend

According to the World Health Organization in 1992, the life expectancy of a newborn baby varied from over 80 years to 60 years or below. In descending order, we find Japan at 81.9 years of age, Switzerland at 80.6, Australia and Sweden at 80.4, Canada at 79.8, Germany at 78.7, UK at 78.2, USA at 77.3, Republic of Korea at 75.5, China at 71.1, Russia at 64.6, India at 61.0, and so on. The definition of an aged person is that one's age has become 65 years of age or over. Rising life expectancy has led to an ageing population in many nations (Riley 2001).

Population ageing has a number of important consequences. Comparing the ageing trend of the industrially advanced nations with that of developing nations, one gets results of 8 per cent, 15 per cent, 26 per cent for the former for the years of 1950, 2005, and 2050 respectively, and 4 per cent, 6 per cent and 15 per cent for the latter for the same years.

In 2005 the world population reached approximately 6,465 million, and in 2050 it is projected to reach 9,076 million persons. Amongst the total population, the aged population group at 65 years of age or over will rise from 5.2 per cent in 1950 to 7.4 per cent in 2005, and then 16.1 per cent in 2050. Therefore in the coming half-century the ageing process will increase in pace.

Figure 52.5 shows that Italy, Germany, France and Australia topped the ageing percentage in 1950, but a century later the new aged nations at the top will be Japan, Italy, Germany and France, with the highest share at around 35 per cent of their national population.

If we look at the number of years a nation takes to rise from 7 per cent to 14 percent aged people, we find that France has taken 115 years, Sweden 85 years, Germany 40 years and the United Kingdom 47 years, but that Japan has taken only 24 years.

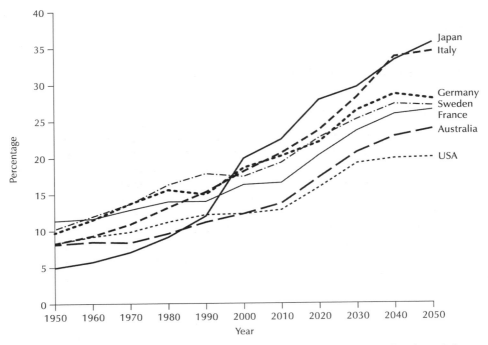

Figure 52.5. Ageing trends of selected nations, 1950–2050, based on percentage of total population over 65 years old.

In Asian societies, where the family link is still strong and aged people are respected, the aged may prefer to live with younger people and maintain a mutual help relationship with each other. Aged people usually care for their young grandchildren, and sometimes prepare meals for the whole family when the younger people are out at work. The Household Register in Japan in 2000 reveals that 20 per cent of older people lived alone in single households, 28 per cent in dual-person households, 16 per cent with unwed offspring, 24 per cent with married offspring, and 12 per cent others (Japanese Ministry of Welfare and Labour 2004). An extended-family lifestyle implies that aged singles or couples receive care or support, but this household pattern is declining, even in Asian cities. Some Asian governments enhance generational links by giving priority, or allocating larger space, in public rental housing or home ownership schemes to households who live with the old parents.

In Denmark and some European nations, group homes for the aged, day-care centres and home-help services are well connected in the local network. Here older people can live in the community and get home-care service free. Moreover, group home facilities are sufficient and nearly 6 per cent of the aged live in group homes now.

Employment for the aged is important if social welfare provision is not yet established in a nation. The aged may need to make new friends in the community, and the community also need them to contribute. In some societies, group activities, learning activities, medical care and regular check-ups, and non-profit-sector participation are provided to help the aged to live a meaningful life.

Social welfare systems are, however, often beset by problems. Pay-as-you-go pension systems are almost completely unsustainable in a period of population ageing. The largest area of expenditure by almost all governments in these contexts is health care, and these costs increase dramatically as the population gets older, requiring higher taxes or a reduction in governmental roles in providing health care.

Stagnating nations and their policy options

The problems of population decline

Most ageing nations or societies face the problem of zero or negative growth in the later stages of their demographic process. This phenomenon is represented by a low SFR, i.e. less than 2.07 per cent for countries with minimal immigration flows. How do industrially advanced nations view their existing SFR and what are their policy stances? France, Germany, Italy and Japan all consider their existing SFR to be too low, but only France and Japan have so far taken policy action to recover fertility: most other nations remain non-interventionist. In contrast, Sweden, the United Kingdom and the USA see their existing SFR as satisfactory and will take no policy action at all (see Figure 52.6, Table 52.3).

Population decline may lead to lowering of gross domestic product when the productivity remains constant, to a stagnant economy because of ineffective demand, and to a competitive and smaller labour market with fewer jobs. In social services, some public schools, clinics or public services often have to be closed if thresholds of demand are not being met, or the costs of service provision per capita has to go up. This may in turn persuade policy makers to raise taxation levies in order to cover costs, or to reduce the level of service provision. Population decline, without technological innovation or higher value-added jobs, leads to smaller GDP, which might cause a contraction in labour markets and therefore fewer jobs for young people or women, and might start off a vicious circle which in turn calls for a smaller population.

A Japanese newspaper surveyed 1,000 adults on the net in August 2005 and reported that over 77 per cent of the respondents regarded the image of a stagnant society as dim (Nippon Keizai Shimbun 2005). Moreover, they feared that: (1) social security systems cannot be

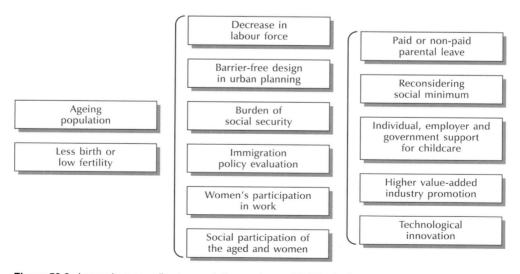

Figure 52.6. Issues in responding to population ageing and fertility decline.

maintained in future; (2) society will lose its vitality; (3) standards of living will fall as the economy contracts; (4) more development problems will be found in peripheral areas; and (5) industries will increasingly lack global competitiveness. The newspaper called on the government and employers to take action to recover the fertility level. What policy options are available to this end?

Policy options

National policy responses in these contexts may be responding to the needs of a stagnant society, for example through reforms to reduce costs of social security systems, or they may seek to increase fertility, or some mix of these two approaches.

In order to stop falling fertility it is important to raise the specific or total fertility rate. And in order to raise the fertility level, governments have to reconcile work and family life for both individuals and society by facilitating those who wish to work to earn an income while participating in social life, and providing the best care and nurturing for children. These aspirations of work and family life need not be mutually exclusive.

A failure to balance work and care commitments has implications for labour and family decisions: parents – or would-be parents – may decide to delay having children, have fewer than they really want, or not have children at all. Or they may change their labour market behaviour. Some who are out of the labour market, for either short or long periods, may prefer to look after their children full-time, regardless of employment opportunities. But others, who would like to work, or work more, may be unable to do so because they cannot get the childcare services they need in order to continue their careers.

In order to balance work and family life, parents face many issues: their preference for providing parental care; formal and informal childcare; family income in and out of work; their access to family-friendly workplace arrangements and child-related leave programmes.

To raise the specific fertility rate is a key issue for nations to maintain population size. Change in the fertility rate are related to:

1   the youth labour market;
2   the costs of raising a child;
3   women's work participation;
4   the environment where the children are raised;
5   public policy to support and assist couples in raising children.

The French National Institute for Statistics and Economic Studies (INSEE) reported that 807,400 children were born in 2005, showing a continuing increase for the previous consecutive three years (Richet-Mastain 2005). Its specific fertility rate was 1.96 per cent, and was second only to Ireland (1.99) in the European Union. Of all newly born babies, 48.5 per cent are from non-wed couples. In France, besides operating a flexible family system, parental leave is allowed for three years at maximum, and other public assistance is provided to support childcare.

In contrast, the Danish policy model is aimed towards gender-equitable labour force participation on a full-time and universal basis (OECD 2002). To that aim comprehensive family support is provided, workers can access generous child-related programmes and childcare is accessible to almost all children from the age of six months. The tax/benefit system generates a high degree of horizontal equity. Paid parental leave is a family entitlement, and the Danish policy model generates the highest degree of equity in employment across the genders. Interestingly, the new Danish government stresses the need for parents to have a real choice about whether they work with good quality childcare or whether they stay at home with their children (Danish Government, Ministry of Social Affairs 1995). A new payment to families making the latter choice may be introduced at the discretion of local governments.

Another policy option is allowing foreigners to come into the job market to replace missing local labour. Citizen groups may well be concerned about the nature of these immigration policies. Policies may be selective, like requiring the migrants to have competent knowledge of local language and customs, or/and proof of the ability to support themselves; these are described in more detail in Chapter 58.

Conclusions

Very different policy responses are required to deal with the demands of rapidly growing populations, as against contexts where populations are ageing and where demographic stagnation dominates. But even within this broad distinction there are very wide variations in policy responses to demographic challenges. Demographic crises in sub-Saharan Africa demand different responses from those that are appropriate in India, where there has been a sustained tradition of intervention in population planning. And in demographically stagnant European nations, a similar diversity of policies has been enacted. Despite international recognition of the central importance of managing population trends, practice on the ground is still largely driven by local geography and politics, and the kind of demographic policy framework that emerges still reflects local and national concerns.

Notes

1 An Age-Specific Fertility Rate (ASFR) is calculated as the number of births in a year to mothers of a specific age per woman of the same age at midyear. The Total Fertility Rate (TFR) is a summary measure which represents the average number of children a group of women would have by the end of their reproductive years.

Further reading

Casey, B., Oxley, H., Whitehouse, E., Antolin, P., Duval, R., and Leibfritz, W. (2003) *Policies for an Ageing Society: Recent Measures and Areas for Further Reform* (OECD Economics Department Working Paper). Paris: OECD.

Danish Government, Ministry of Social Affairs (1995) *Social Policy in Denmark: Child and Family Policies.* Copenhagen: Ministry of Social Affairs.

DFACS/DEWR (2002) *Australia's Country Note for the OECD Project – Family Friendly Policies: the Reconciliation of Work and Family Life.* Canberra: Commonwealth Departments of Family and Community Services, Employment and Workplace Relations.

Japanese Ministry of the Cabinet Secretary (2005) *Korei Shakai Hakusho (White Paper for Ageing Society).* Tokyo: Ministry of the Cabinet Secretary.

——(2005) *Shoshika Shakai Hakusho (White Paper for Low-Fertility Society).* Tokyo: Ministry of the Cabinet Secretary.

Nyce, S.A. and Schieber, S.J. (2005) *The Economic Implications of Ageing Societies: The Costs of Living Happily Ever After*. New York: Cambridge University Press.

Nyce, S. A. and Schieber, S.J. (2005) *The Economic Implications of Ageing Societies: The Costs of Living Happily Ever After*. New York: Cambridge University Press.

OECD (2000) *Trends in International Migration*. Paris: OECD.

Riley, J.C. (2001) *Rising Life Expectancy: A Global History*. Cambridge: Cambridge University Press.

United Nations Population Division (2003) *World Population Policies 2003*. New York: United Nations.

——(2005) *World Population Prospects 1950–2050, 2004 Revision*. New York: United Nations.

World Bank (2005) *Improving Health Nutrition and Population Outcomes in Sub-Saharan Africa*. New York: World Bank.

References

Ainsworth, M. (1994) *Socio-economic Determinants of Fertility in Sub-Sahara Africa*, Washington DC: World Bank, Research Project, Policy Research Department.

Bhagat, R.B. (2002) Integration of demographic issues in sustainable development: reflections on India's population policies. *Population Geography* 24 (1 and 2), 21–30.

European Union (2004) *EUROSTAT*. Luxembourg: EU.

Indian National Commission on Population (2000) *National Population Policy 2000*. Available at http://populationcommission.nic.in/npp_intro.htm

Japanese Ministry of Welfare and Labour (2004) *Vital Population Statistics*. Tokyo: Ministry of Welfare and Labour.

Malthus, T.R. (1992) *An Essay on the Principle of Population, Selected and Introduced by D. Winch using the text of the 1803 edition*. Cambridge: Cambridge University Press.

Nippon Keizai Shimbun (2005) [Survey results] 22 August.

OECD (2002) *Babies and Bosses: Reconciling Work and Family Life, Vol. 1: Australia, Denmark, and the Netherlands*. Paris: OECD.

Register General of India (2000) *Population and Human and Social Development, Facts – I, II, and III*. Available at http://www.go.in/population/

Richet-Mastain, L. (2005) *Bilan démographique 2005: En France, la fécondité des femmes augmente toujours*. Paris: INSEE. Available at http://www.insee.fr/fr/ffc/docs_ffc/IP1059.pdf

Riley, J.C. (2001) *Rising Life Expectancy: A Global History*. Cambridge: Cambridge University Press.

United Nations Population Division (2003) *World Population Policies 2003*. New York: United Nations.

——(2005) *World Population Prospects 1950–2050, 2004 Revision*. New York: United Nations.

United States Department of Health and Human Services (2003) *National Vital Statistics Report*. Washington DC: US Department of Health and Human Services.

53

Exploiting

Power, colonialism and resource economies

Gavin Bridge

Hot gravel scatters as a truck blasts north on the Pan-American. I'm standing on the edge of the highway in the late morning sun, looking up and out across the long, dry slope that stretches inland from the Pacific towards the Andes. Buried beneath these gritty sands of Peru's central coast, running from the mountains to the sea, is a pipeline. And somewhere under my feet this pipeline cuts beneath the Pan-American in the final stage of a journey that originates 300 kilometres away and 4,000 metres up at a massive copper and zinc deposit. High up in the Andes in a wide open pit, a consortium of international mining firms have realized one of the world's largest mining investments: after spending two billion dollars to develop the project, these firms now extract and crush rock, concentrate the valuable ore, and feed it into the pipeline for a journey downhill to the Pacific. Here on the coast, the pipeline surfaces in a tidy block of industrial buildings that are fenced and guarded. There are no ships in today, but from the highway I can see the dock and long, grey-green loading boom that reaches out over the water: copper and zinc concentrates will flow from the boom into the holds of cargo vessels, bound for customers in Canada, Korea, Australia, Germany and Bulgaria. This is a thoroughly modern activity: nothing spectacular to see, even the pipeline is hidden; no toiling workers or roaring machinery; no sense of industrial process dominating the desert: all is order, containment, attention to detail, and multiple distant ties.

Difference: making here and there

From the side of the road, one begins to gain a sense of the network of geographical transfers that make up *distanciated resource geographies* – simultaneously local and global, here and there – of which the pipeline is only part: mineral concentrates transferred from the highlands to the coast, from east to west, then from global South to global North; a diaspora of finished copper and zinc from smelters and refineries in Germany, Korea and Bulgaria that transformed into pipes, wiring, galvanized sheets and all manner of other applications is scattered to the four corners via the medium of the market; millions of dollars in investment capital transferred from banks in London, New York, Japan and Toronto to the mining consortium in Lima, and then passed on (and back) in equipment orders, contracts for project management, and salaries; tax revenues and royalty payments from the mine to the regional government and the national treasury in Lima, and then on to service debts owed to international banks; the standardizing trail of certificates, approvals and audits associated with international best practice such as the global environmental management standard, ISO 14001; and skilled personnel who, nominally from Australia, Canada or Peru, circulate among the world's mining regions and whose collective experience creates its own unique geography.

A mental map begins to take shape: extensive regions extracting, cultivating and shipping resources elsewhere; industrialized areas importing these raw materials, metabolizing them, assembling new products, and shipping them on; a scattering of places producing new knowledge about the location, use and value of resources; and the vast spaces and chokepoints of transit. The map is now a richly textured geography, a world of difference woven together by physical flows of ships, copper, people and money. *But is this right?* What is the relationship between geographical unevenness and connections across these differences? Do geographies of resources – the spaces and flows associated with producing, trading and consuming products of the Earth – simply express uneven natural endowments? Or might the flows that connect places actively *make difference*, and generate the geographical unevenness that we ascribe to place?

These are more than philosophical questions about the 'production of uneven development' when it comes to resources. Of the twenty-five countries that are most dependent on the export of minerals for their income, twelve are classified by the World Bank as 'highly indebted, poor countries'. Will further development of their resources create the conditions for economic growth, the reduction of poverty and inequality, and improvement in measures of economic, social and human health? Peru, like many poor countries, hosts significant resources: gas, gold, timber, fish, copper, lead, zinc and biodiversity to name a few. Is the mobilization of these resources a way for Peru to move out of poverty? Or has Peru somehow been made poor – and, even more provocatively, is it being kept poor – because of the way its natural resources have been controlled?

The purpose of this chapter is to examine the patterns and processes of natural resource extraction at the global scale. Trading resources across space – i.e. the geographical separation of production and consumption – is a fundamental feature of resource geographies. Some resource movements – tropical spices, exotic animal furs and precious metals – have taken place over vast distances for a very long time. Others play a core role in the contemporary economy: oil, for example, is the single largest commodity traded and every country on Earth is involved in the international oil trade in some form. For some other resources – like water, stone and coal – traditionally short supply chains have become dramatically stretched over recent years. These 'econo-natural networks' sustain the conditions of everyday life for producers and consumers (Castree 1995): consider, for example, the ways in which your experience of daily life would change if transfers of water, fuels and food were to cease. These flows give rise to distinctive global geographies such as geographies of development and/or environment. In the mid-nineteenth century agricultural chemistry re-interpreted the trade of food from rural to urban areas as a geographical transfer of nutrients that had great social significance: harvesting crops exported nutrients from the fields (decreasing soil fertility) and accumulated these nutrients in the city (improving nutrition but also increasing water pollution). Thus important social and environmental differences between rural and urban areas were produced via the production and trade of crops. Like the flows of food, water and energy that produce the differentiation of 'country' and 'city', the movement of copper from Peru to manufacturing customers in Europe or East Asia is a process that does not simply play out over space, but is the stuff through which space and place are produced.

The central argument in this chapter is that the extraction, trade and consumption of resources can tell us a lot about the social relations of uneven development. The value of a geographical perspective on resources is not primarily the ability to know how much copper (or fish, or cotton) a country like Peru produces (around 1 million tonnes of copper, 10 million tonnes of fish and 65,000 tonnes of cotton at the beginning of the twenty-first century). Instead it is understanding the social relations expressed and reaffirmed by these flows. Resource flows bring a particular type of order to the world and these patterns of resource production, trade and consumption can tell us much about power and control. A characteristic of many resource flows, for example, is that resources tend to flow 'uphill' against any process of geographic equalization: the flow of copper from Peru, for example, is directed towards the already vast accumulations of refined copper in manufacturing centres (the amount of copper and zinc that is already pooled in urban areas gives rise to a density of metal occurrence exceeding the richest mines). We turn now to consider an enduring way of thinking about resources and place: the idea of 'exploitation'.

Development or exploitation: resources as relations

In the armoury of words describing social relations, 'exploitation' is surely one of the most potent. It is also a curiously flexible term, able at once to convey affirmation and opprobrium about the same process. Exploitation is kinetic: it is about the application of energies – intellectual, technical and manual – to achieve a change in state, and is only intelligible in a world in which humans are understood to possess free will and in which fate has assumed a minor role. In its progressive sense, then, the concept has its roots in the Enlightenment's application of reason, science and technology to improve the human condition. More particularly – as Williams (1976) points out – the word was still a novelty in English as late as the 1820s, and its popularization came about during the massive industrialization drive of the nineteenth century. It was at this point that the word became used to describe newly emerging social relations with the natural world, the relations of commerce and capitalism that were being formed during industrialization. Towards the end of the nineteenth century, 'exploitation' was being used in English to refer to the extraction and development of non-renewable resources by those in positions of wealth and power.

These progressive connotations focus on exploitation as a means for transforming landscapes and severing humankind from the drudgery of nature: for many, the exploitation of mineral resources, for example, was of not only historic but also existential significance since 'without mining, man would still be just another animal, seeking nothing more than a full belly and a refuge against other animals more savage than himself' (Heath 1975). The censorious connotations of the term, however, focused on the social relations through which this practice takes place. Exploitation-as-critique draws on the philosophical traditions of classical Marxism (exploitation via the expropriation and transfer of surplus value) and the Frankfurt School (exploitation via the application of instrumental reason and technologies of domination).

Over the last couple of decades, muscular exhortations to resource exploitation as 'the fine flower of industrial achievement' have largely given way to a different trope of utilization based on stewardship and sustainable forms of development (Rickard 1932). Yet in many contemporary resource conflicts one can find both meanings – progressive utilization and unjust forms of control – attached to resource exploitation. The provincial government in Quebec, for example, promoted exploitation of the hydro-power potential of the La Grande River (which flows into James Bay, at the southernmost tip of Canada's Hudson Bay) as a way to drive industrialization and development in the province. Yet the indigenous people of the region – the James Bay Cree – successfully opposed further hydro-power development on the neighbouring Great Whale River arguing that exploitation of its water power was tantamount to exploitation of the Cree. In a campaign aimed at major customers of the hydro-project's electricity in Boston and New York, the Cree made an explicit connection between technological control of the river for electricity generation and the subjugation an indigenous population's economy and culture (Howitt 2001).

The language of exploitation-as-critique is potent, then, because it recognizes how resources are not simply things shuttled around the world in response to supply and demand but that resources also produce and sustain significant social relations: the water sliding and foaming down the La Grande or Great Whale Rivers becomes a power resource only when it can be put into a particular relation with concrete, turbines and markets (see also White 1995). The electricity that would be generated by the dams may be available for all, but it is more particularly a means for industrial interests to advance their agenda in Quebec *vis-à-vis* rural interests. Thus a relation with the natural world – that we conventionally describe as resource utilization – is also a socio-spatial relation. Much of the work on resources by geographers starts from precisely this premise. Resources can be more productively analysed as a set of social relations between (often distant) groups rather than as discrete 'things'. Such a 'relational approach' turns the analytical lens back on to society: what is it about needs and wants, and the way a society is organized, that transforms a component of the non-human world into a resource in a particular time and place? Thus a relational approach denaturalizes resources by drawing our attention to how a resource is at least as much a function of social, political and economic conditions as it is of any intrinsic properties.

Building on this understanding of resources as a social category (into and out of which slip various components of the physical environment), a central argument of recent work is that resources are *inherently* political. Resources are an epistemologically specific outcome of competing claims over access to, control over and definitions of nature: to produce nature *as resources* is an exercise of power (Bakker and Bridge 2006). And taking this argument a step further, although resources are inherently political, only some of these relations become politicized in ways that present a challenge to extractive activities. It is at such moments of politicization that social concerns are mobilized in ways that impinge on established extractive practices. We are currently witnessing one such moment, a moment in which it is the *geographies* of resource extraction that are in the spotlight, and in which issues of exploitation – which have lain dormant for some considerable time – are once again being raised.

Modern-day alchemy: resource exploitation as wealth creation

From the Middle Ages until the late 1700s the Holy Grail of (what today we would call) chemistry was alchemy, the transmutation of base metals into gold. The alchemists' art lay in determining the secret by which great wealth could be generated from an abundance of common materials. Alchemy died with the birth of modern chemistry and metallurgy, yet the dream of transmuting resource abundance into wealth – of creating value from Earth – found a new expression in the 'extractive paradigm' (Slack 2001) of resource-based development See Plate 53.1.

Plate 53.1. The extractive paradigm: a copper mine in New Mexico. Photograph by Gavin Bridge.

Resource exploitation is a narrative of domestication and improvement that is closely bound to notions of development and state formation, and it continues to play a role in the organization of contemporary society. Territorial development strategies often position exploitation of natural resources as the foundation for economic growth. At the beginning of the twentieth century, for example, Winston Churchill stood at Owens Falls on the northern shore of Lake Victoria and noted how 'so much power running to waste ... such a lever to control the natural forces of Africa un-gripped, cannot but vex and stimulate the imagination', adding 'and what fun to make the immemorial Nile begin its journey by diving into a turbine' (cited in McNeill 2000: 149). There are multiple examples of how the objectives of regional (or national) development have been harnessed to resource exploitation, from the multi-dam Columbia River project in the US Pacific northwest for electric power and irrigation (White 1995), to Khrushchev's Virgin Lands campaign to plough up the northern steppes of Kazakhstan during the 1950s, or to the UK government's current efforts to exploit the country's wind power opportunities to help meet its obligations under the Kyoto Convention. Policy makers in developing countries often describe investment in their resource sectors as a key that will unlock the country's 'buried treasure' (Bomsel 1990) and set in motion a virtuous cycle of socio-economic change.

The common-sense view of resource exploitation as an 'engine of (national) growth' finds support from the export base model developed by Douglass North, co-winner of the 1993 Nobel Prize in Economics. North's model (1955) drew on his analysis of the US economy in the period before the Civil War and showed how regional exports from cotton plantations stimulated development in other sectors, leading to regional specialization and interregional trade. After the Second World War, mainstream development economics – which was dominated by modernization theories such as the Stages of Economic Growth model articulated by W.W. Rostow (1960) – argued that poor countries which were resource-rich could create economic growth by developing their resource endowments for export to the wider economy. The development and export of raw materials was also tied to so-called 'big push' theories of growth, in which a broad and sustained stimulation of demand (via revenues from resource exports, for example) could move poor countries out of a low-income equilibrium trap: resource development would create the conditions for economic 'take-off' by 'providing the catalyst for low income countries to overcome the fixed costs of industrialization' (Sachs and Warner 1999). Proponents of resource exploitation therefore spoke of 'sowing the oil' (or other non-renewable resources) and looked to the historical experience of countries where mineral extraction and processing had played a major role in driving industrialization. Despite vigorous critiques of modernization theory since the 1960s, resource-based industrialization remains a relative constant of development policy and draws its justification from a remarkably diverse array of intellectual traditions (Bridge 2004).

But sustainable economic growth based on resource production has proven elusive. Some countries with rich resources, and with large resource exports, are among the poorest in the world and have higher poverty rates and worse health conditions than more diverse economies. Nigeria, for example, is a major oil exporter, yet four out of ten children are malnourished. Table 53.1 demonstrates this correlation between resource exports and limited economic and social development by comparing the ranking of selected mineral-dependent states (defined as those states in which oil or non-fuel mineral exports account for a high percentage of GDP) in the UN's Human Development Index. Dynamic comparisons are equally striking: as a group, *resource-poor* countries grew two to three times *faster* than resource-rich countries in the period 1960–1990 (Ross 2001). An earlier generation of scholars referred to outcomes like these as the 'baffling paradox', noting how, after centuries

Table 53.1. Selected mineral and oil dependent states and their ranking in the Human Development Index

State	Mineral or oil dependence	HDI ranking 2003
Angola	68.5	160
Kuwait	49.1	44
Yemen	46.2	151
Nigeria	39.9	158
Botswana	35.1	131
Sierra Leone	28.9	176
Zambia	26.1	166
Mauritania	18.4	152
Papua New Guinea	14.1	137

Source: Adapted from Ross (2001).

of colonial mineral extraction in Latin America (and decades in Africa), these regions were still beset with grinding poverty (Lanning and Mueller 1973).

A uniquely difficult form of development

Like alchemy, resource-based development has an intuitive appeal: demonstrating the concept in practice, however, is rather more challenging. Unlike alchemy, however, successful resource-based development is not impossible: alongside the historical examples of Sweden, Canada, the United States and Australia, one could consider Chile and Alaska as cases in which resource exports have contributed substantially to improvements in economic and social conditions. There is, however, widespread recognition that extractive economies present a 'uniquely difficult form of development', and some analysts go further to argue that 'oil and mineral exports do not simply fail to alleviate poverty; they appear to make it worse' (Ross 2001: 5). From this perspective the exploitation of natural resources can create a development trap, ensnaring regions that attempt it in a state of dependency that undermines efforts to achieve broad-based, sustainable forms of economic growth. This line of argument draws from several strands of research, the most explicitly geographical of which is the so-called 'staples theory of growth' developed by Harold Innis in the first half of the twentieth century (Barnes 1996). Innis (1956) sought to explain the peculiarities of Canadian development – which he regarded as truncated and incomplete – by reference to the country's role in the British colonial economy. Canada's specialization in the production and export of basic goods – fishing in the maritime provinces, mining on the Canadian Shield, agriculture in the Prairies, oil and gas in Alberta, and forestry in British Columbia – drove her economy into a 'staples trap' where it was dependent on external influences and remained on the margins of the global economy (Barnes 1996). Analyses like this lay the foundation for a view of resource development as an exploitation of one region or group of people by another.

The extractive paradigm in the spotlight

Extractive activities have come under increased scrutiny since the early 1990s. There have long been critiques of specific oil, gas and mining projects and practices – extraction has never been a politically unproblematic affair because of the social re-shuffling of rights associated with 'making resources' – but over the last decade isolated critiques have coalesced into a broad scepticism regarding the ability of resource extraction projects to deliver 'development'. Thus single cases have come to stand for resource extraction *as a whole*. Each new case becomes a round in an unfolding drama, a modern-day morality play in which the protagonist (usually an extractive enterprise) encounters various abstractions – ideas of progress, development, wealth and ethics, for example – in the guise of actors, such as an endangered species, a band of indigenous peoples, shareholders seeking a return, or government regulators. The choices the protagonist makes – the drama of the play – serve an instructional purpose, a 'teachable moment' about the essential nature of resource extraction. This is clearly expressed in the following commentary from the *Oil and Gas Journal* (1999: 18) on Occidental Petroleum's experience in Colombia, where an indigenous tribe (the U'wa) threatened to commit suicide en masse if Occidental did not give up a proposal to drill on disputed land:

> What's at stake here goes beyond a potential billion-barrel oil field, beyond whether an exploration license is honored in Colombia, or beyond whether Bogota can stir up foreign investor interest in [its] petroleum sector ... the continuing standoff with the U'wa has escalated to a critical mass, to the point where the next step by either side could put the white-hot spotlight of the world on a single well.

So extractive activities have become rallying points for critiques of economic globalization and the role of multinational corporations in the developing world. At the core of contemporary debates over mining and the environment is a struggle to define mining's role in the context of sustainable development and increasing claims for local resource control. It is widely accepted that cleaner process technology and environmental management practices geared towards pollution prevention will be important as the mining industry seeks a social licence to operate. Yet the most contentious issues are far less susceptible to technological solutions, and involve issues of land rights, resource control and cultural perceptions of the value, meaning and significance of mining relative to other land uses.

The contemporary scepticism surrounding resource extraction as an agent of development has become institutionalized through the networked activities of a range of non-governmental movements, the incorporation into state policies of multiple development criteria and higher thresholds for acceptance, and through the emergence of supranational initiatives that increase oversight of extractive activities. In Europe, at the World Bank and at the United Nations, policy makers have begun to develop governance mechanisms for managing the effects of extractive enterprises (see, for example, the World Bank's Extractive Industries Review; the UK government's Extractive Industries Transparency Initiative; the Equator Principles for commercial bank lending to oil, gas and mining projects; and the UN-initiated Kimberley Process for diamond certification).

Coupling/uncoupling: resource extraction and development

'Why this is happening now' is an interesting question. Historically the wage relation has been politicized in extractive industries, making class conflict a primary axis for understanding relations of exploitation. Politicization of these relations led to the rise of working-class movements in the extractive sector. During the formal colonial period, resource extraction activities were relatively untroubled by concerns about 'development'. Resource exploitation was not understood as 'development' but as the establishment of commercial relations, the introduction of technology, or as efforts to instil labour discipline. With the flourishing of development as a concept in the post-war period, however, resource extraction had to justify itself by reference to these emergent social norms and, in particular, to a formal de-colonization which saw resource rights transfer to new sovereign powers (Esteva 1992). Extractive enterprises sought to contribute to national development goals largely by reference to economic metrics: tonnages, value of exports, contribution to GDP. Over the last couple of decades, development discourse has shifted in ways that make the challenge of development more acute. While the effects on extractive communities of contemporary resource exploitation are no worse than in the past – and by many measures they are significantly better – social expectations of the development benefits that extraction should deliver have undergone a significant transformation.

There are two phases to this ratcheting up of the development stakes for resource extraction. The first centres on calls for resource extraction to contribute to the goals of 'sustainable development' in the wake of the 1987 Brundtland Report. In the early 1990s, issues of air and water pollution dominated the discussion of extractive industries: as a prominent editorial in the mining industry press put it in 1990, 'let there be no doubt: the mining industry worldwide is at a turning point. In a relatively few years the environment has become the single most important issues facing executives in every sector of the extractive industry' (*Mining Journal* 1990: 1). Questions about the environmental performance of extractive enterprises evolved during the 1990s towards a broader concern with their effects on cultural and biological diversity: critics charged that extractive enterprises increasingly were operating in pristine areas and so were having a disproportionate effect on biodiversity and indigenous peoples (World Resources Institute 2004; Bowles *et al.* 1998).

The debate over extraction has shifted again, and extraction increasingly is judged by its capacity to achieve poverty reduction and contribute to forms of growth that are 'pro-poor'. Fairness, inequality and exploitation are now central concerns and the challenge to extractive industries is explicitly geographical: the phenomenon of grinding poverty amid resource wealth, for which oil extraction in the Niger delta is the iconic example. Capital-intensive forms of resource extraction are on a sticky wicket here. The technological and managerial strategies by which firms successfully addressed earlier concerns about pollution are much more difficult to replicate for poverty. Geographically uneven forms of development are a fundamental feature of resource economies, and the mining, oil, timber and fishing sectors have always sought spatial fixes to rising costs of production and squeezed margins.

Scaling up: making a global resource economy

Economies are 'giant materials processing systems' that draw in resources from the environment, transform these into a range of products, and deposit these products back into the environment (Geiser 2001). At the global scale, population and economic growth have driven increases in resource production and consumption during the twentieth century. Growth in the world economy's appetite for resources over the last hundred years is unprecedented: the environmental historian J.R. McNeill describes how the twentieth century was 'prodigal and peculiar' in terms of the use of resources and environmental impacts, and saw a '*screeching acceleration of so many processes that bring ecological change*' (McNeill 2000: 4, italics added). The material basis of the economy retains many of those characteristics that marked the twentieth century as historically distinctive (see Table 53.2).

Two other measures of change in resource production during the twentieth century are also worth noting. The first is the introduction of entirely new resources and a net increase in the range and complexity of global resource movements. Novel resources are associated

Table 53.2. The increasing scale of resource production in the twentieth century

Measure	Factor of increase
World economy	14
Industrial output	40
Coal production	7
Copper production	26
Nickel production	> 500
Chromium production	> 250
Forested area	0.8 (20% decrease)
Energy use	16
Water use	9
Carbon dioxide emissions	17
Fin whale population	0.03 (97% decrease)

Source: Adapted from McNeill (2000: 360).

with developments in organic chemistry (giving rise to persistent organic pollutants like PCBs, CFCs and DDT); the 'neotechnic' metals – chromium, nickel, manganese and even aluminium; and new fuel minerals like natural gas, uranium and oil shales. In many cases these novel resources have driven resource rushes around the world, such as the massive bauxite discoveries in Australia in the 1960s, or the 'dash for gas' in the last few years. The second measure is that the scale of several anthropogenically driven resource flows now rivals many geomophological activities: annual human-induced mobilizations of sulphur, for example – via the burning of fossil fuels and the smelting of sulphide ores – now exceed the rate of natural sulphur mobilization, while the volume of soil and rock moved by humans approaches the volume of material eroded, transported and deposited by water (McNeill 2000).

Geographical expansion and the spatial separation of production and consumption

Economic geographers, when in the company of economists, knowingly observe how production and consumption do not take place on the head of a pin. Increases in the volume and complexity of resource flows have played out geographically, so that during the twentieth century the global resource map was constantly re-drawn. For example, the Middle East dominates the contemporary map of oil reserves and oil production but was a minor player as little as sixty years ago. Tied to natural endowments, resource industries are generally quite 'sticky' in space, yet geographical shifts do sometimes take place over relatively short time scales: the map of global coffee production, for example, changed dramatically during the 1990s as Vietnam emerged from nowhere as the world's second largest coffee producer. The economic historian Karl Polanyi (2001: 42) observed that the significance of the industrial revolution lay not primarily in its technologies but in the habits of mind it introduced: 'the new creed,' he wrote, 'was utterly materialistic, and believed that all human problems could be resolved given an unlimited amount of material commodities'. Expanding the availability of commodities has required the expansion of resource supply, and the primary mechanism for doing this has been sourcing additional resources from increasingly distant areas. While other strategies are possible – for example, increasing efficiencies of use (e.g. recycling) or by substitution – and have been used from time to time (e.g. Napoleon Bonaparte's sponsorship of sugar beet as a substitute for tropical sugar, or the synthetic fuels programmes of Nazi Germany or South Africa), geographical strategies for securing supply are the dominant mode.

870

The result of these geographical strategies has been a stretching of economies, an increasing separation of production from consumption so that the distance over which resources are moved has become longer over time (Chisholm 1992). To take a simple example, at the beginning of the twentieth century the UK used to consume coal from British pits and most of its fish from the North Sea. The UK now consumes coal from as far away as Australia and a variety of fish species from the world's oceans. This process has deep historical roots, but a general pattern can be discerned. The geographical mobility of all resources increases over time so that formerly localized resource trading becomes regional or even global in scale. As mobility increases, so potential new sources of supply open up. This places regions in competition with each other, favouring larger, low-cost suppliers and leading to the closure of many traditional sources of supply.

Rural sociologist Jack Kloppenburg and colleagues (1996) have adapted the concept of the watershed to understand contemporary geographies of food, observing how the 'foodshed' of many commonplace agro-food products has become global. If the general proposition is that resource flows have scaled up geographically over time, we can also observe an historical sequence. The first 'resource-sheds' to be re-scaled through global trade were luxury items: long-distance trade in spices, silk or precious metals has been a feature of the world economy for over 500 years (and provides a basis for the claim by economic historians that globalization is not that new). The core lineaments of the contemporary global resource economy were laid, however, in the middle of the nineteenth century when bulk commodities – wheat, coal, iron, copper; later cement, oil, bauxite – began to be traded over long distances, following a dramatic fall in the cost of sea-freight in the mid-1850s. More recently, perishable commodities have seen a lengthening of the supply chain: resource-sheds in the vegetable and fruit sector, for example, now frequently extend from one hemisphere to the other. Even milk, the archetypal perishable commodity, is now traded in fresh form over long distances. Resources also can move from one category to another over time and space. For example, copper was traded over long distances as a finished metal long before the long-distance trade of intermediate products (ores, concentrates) began in the mid-nineteenth century. Some food commodities – sugar is an exemplary case – moved from luxury commodities to bulk commodities during the nineteenth century, while many tropical fruits have made this transition during the second half of the twentieth century. Indeed, a strategy of reducing weight and/or increasing exchange value can enable resources to overcome the friction of distance. From 'moonshine' in the hills to the production of hydroelectricity, finding a resource form that will travel across distance is a key component of resource-based strategies of development.

A second cut at capturing the significance of these re-scaled geographies of resource supply is the notion of an 'ecological footprint' (Wackernagel and Rees 1996). For a given geographical unit this concept describes the area required to produce the food its population consumes, to sustain its energy consumption, to provide space for infrastructure and the surface needed to absorb wastes associated with consumption. The ecological footprint provides a rough guide to the environmental load exerted by an area. The value of the concept is that it enables calculation of the 'ecological deficit' – the extent to which an area draws on resources beyond its bounds. The stretched and extended nature of resource geographies is neatly captured by the notion of the 'ghost acreage' developed by Borgstrom (1965) to refer to food imported from outside national borders. The term was subsequently extended as the 'fossil acreage' by Catton (1980) to describe the energy obtained from coal, petroleum and natural gas and the additional acreage of farmland needed to grow organic fuels with equivalent energy content. Footprints calculated at the global scale indicate that the average ecological footprint is around 2.3 ha per person. If all human beings lived like Europeans, the figure would be closer to 6 ha per person to provide for current levels of consumption and absorb wastes. Even the global average, however, exceeds the approximately 2 ha per person available from a crude division of global land area by population. This 'ecological deficit' is the result of drawing on resources in ways that exceed biological capacity and via borrowing from the future though deforestation and biodiversity decline, overfishing, ozone-layer depletion and climate change.

Manufacturing core and resource periphery?

History hangs heavy around global resource geographies. The plunder of the slave trade, the forced labour of gold and silver mining in New Spain, the whaling economies that roamed the Atlantic and Pacific, the plantation economies of the nineteenth century: by the middle of the nineteenth century these and other activities had produced a distinctive spatial division of labour, in which a vast range of resources drawn from increasingly distant regions converged on the industrializing and urbanizing economies of Europe and North America. At the centre of these flows were agricultural and mineral commodities and, in the case of European nations, much of the trade and investment to procure these flows was channelled through formal colonial ties. These patterns of global trade laid down the contours of a manufacturing core and a resource periphery, a division of labour in which colonial possessions specialized in the production of raw materials that were transformed into manufactured goods in the industrial core. In the light of significant global shifts in manufacturing that became apparent in the 1960s, this split between manufacturing core and resource periphery has come to be known as the Old International Division of Labour.

To what extent does this geographical division of labour still hold true? Much of the contemporary critique of extractive industries raises the issue of fairness and justice in an explicitly geographical way. It argues that the benefits of resource extraction accrue to those who consume them, while the costs – as measured by the transformation of livelihoods, pollution or social dislocation – fall on extractive communities. Muradian and Martinez-Alier (2001), for example, argue that geographical shifts in resource extraction following structural adjustment and the adoption of neo-liberal economic reforms in many countries during the 1990s mean that resource-rich developing countries are being integrated into the world economy in very particular ways. Reduction in the barriers to trade and investment has confirmed the predictions of neo-classical theory by driving increased economic specialization. Yet to specialize in natural resources is to specialize in economic activities that are environmentally intensive. Analyses like this argue that globalization is leading to a 'peripheralization' of the environmental effects of international consumption that exacerbates existing inequalities between North and South. At their most critical, these critiques proclaim the reassertion of a colonial resource economy (dominated by multinational corporations) and argue that developing countries are being vigorously exploited in a new round of plunder and control.

To assess the global geography of resource production for all resources is a challenging if not impossible task: any aggregate picture will be the product of multiple, overlapping geographies. So let us try with a single commodity – copper – which was central to the formation of the old international division of labour and remains one of the most economically significant and heavily traded metals. Figure 53.1 compares the global distribution of production and consumption of copper in 2004. It suggests that a manufacturing core and a resource periphery still exist. Three developing economies – Chile, Peru and Indonesia – account for 50 per cent of global copper production, with the bulk of this traded to manufacturing

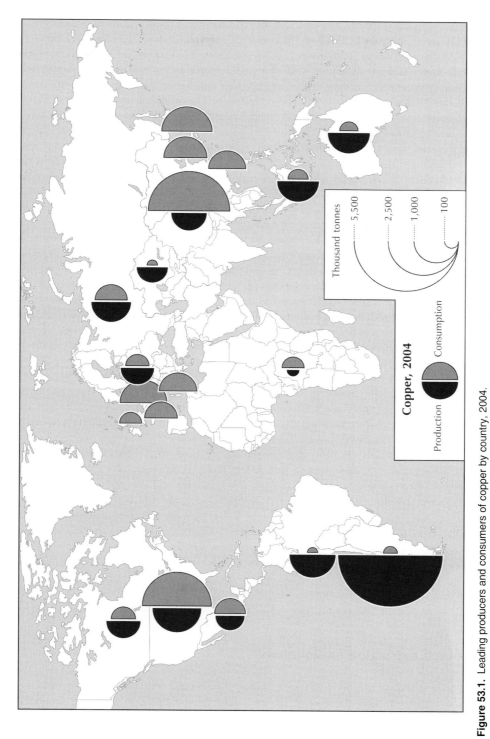

Figure 53.1. Leading producers and consumers of copper by country, 2004.

Source: Produced by author from data in World Bureau of Metal Statistics (2006).

economies, of which the traditional manufacturing centres of Europe, Japan and North America account for nearly half of demand. In common with most resources, the geography of production is more concentrated than that of consumption. The case of Chile, the dominant copper producer, is instructive: Chile produces over a third of the world's copper but exports over 95 per cent of this, with the largest shares going to China and Japan.

On closer inspection, however, these figures reveal significant departures from the model of an international division of labour based on a European manufacturing core and a colonial resource periphery. These departures make it difficult to sustain the argument that the current resource economy (for copper, at least) can be adequately understood as a reassertion of colonial patterns of resource trade. There are four points to make here. First – and most obvious in Figure 53.1 – the centre of gravity for copper consumption has shifted. The rise of manufacturing in east Asian economies – the New International Division of Labour, based on exports of manufactured goods rather than primary resources – has turned countries such as Taiwan, South Korea and China into major importers of copper. China, which as recently as the 1980s used to be a net exporter, now accounts for over a fifth of global copper consumption and is the world's leading consumer. Second, some of the world's largest economies are major resource exporters. While both Canada and Botswana export minerals – and in this sense both may be considered 'resource peripheries' – the latter is specialized around resource production (and is resource dependent) while the other is much less so.

Third, the category of developing countries is increasingly unhelpful, as it obscures a great deal of diversity in terms of the countries' relationship to resources. To take an instructive example, Indonesia – which is a member of the Organization of Petroleum Exporting Countries (OPEC) and which for many resources (timber, coal, copper) presents a classic case of a primary resource exporter – has made the transition to a net importer of oil as a result of economic growth and a slowing in its rate of oil production. From a resource standpoint, the concept of the BRIC economies – Brazil, Russia, India, China (Wilson and Purushothaman 2003) – is a more helpful distinction since it identifies economies which are developing in a way, and at a rate, which will change their relationship to resources: as effective demand grows and their range of exports increase, these economies may cease to look like resource peripheries. Fourth, while multinational corporations remain the primary vehicle for developing resources, there are a number of new entrants that reflect the growing economic muscle of former 'resource peripheries'. The aggressive pursuit of global oil and gas opportunities by the Chinese National Offshore Oil Company (CNOOC) and the Oil and Natural Gas Corporation (ONGC) of India are cases in point, as is the growing global presence of firms like the Russian bauxite miner and aluminium producer RUSAL and Venezuela's PDVSA. These firms stretch their geographies of production across space in the pursuit of strategic objectives and competitive advantage. Their mode of entry is primarily economic power: CNOOC, for example, has demonstrated its willingness to pay a premium for access to oil and gas deposits, and an ability to lever the financial muscle of the Chinese state to gain access to oil supply from Angola or provide military support to Nigeria in exchange for access to oil.

Is resource extraction exploitation?

In the previous section we reviewed geographies of resource trade and suggested that, with significant caveats, a basic division of labour could be identified in which a number of developing countries specialized in the production of primary resources. But do these geographic patterns amount to exploitation? They may be profoundly uneven and unequal, but are these geographies 'unfair' and, if so, on what grounds is that claim made? The case for contemporary resource geographies being exploitative can be difficult to make in the abstract. To take a simple example, an observation that over 90 per cent of the coffee consumed in the UK is harvested in countries that rank lower than the UK in measures of human development fails to distinguish between the different social relations constructed by fair trade initiatives and those associated with standard importation. Similarly, Germany may import nearly 40 per cent of its gas supplies from Russia, yet this relationship is rarely framed as an unfair exploitation of Russian resources. Indeed, it is often assumed that any exploitation is the other way around: Russia has power over Germany as its primary source of supply. Popular claims that resource extraction is exploitative typically focus on the resource-seeking investments of multinational corporations in the developing world. These claims are, however, often vague about precisely why the relationship constitutes exploitation. It is possible to identify at least five distinctive arguments about exploitation and natural resources, each of which draws attention to a different aspect of the social relations associated with resource control, extraction and trade.

Appropriation: land as property, resources as theft

There is a robust tradition of critical inquiry within geography which acknowledges that 'natural resources are not naturally resources' (Hudson 2001: 300). While the physical materials we term resources are not made by human hands – they are, by definition, the product of geological, biological and hydrological processes – the status of these materials *as resources* is an outcome of social processes. How, then, are resources made? Classical political economy provides us with the useful concepts of 'appropriation' and 'enclosure', which in their original form describe the process through which private landowners gained rights to lands, forests, waters and wildlife that hitherto had been in the public domain. In Britain, the classic example of this process is the Parliamentary Acts of Enclosure of the 1700s which enclosed a broad swath of England between Dorset and Yorkshire. For those who used or had access to these lands before, appropriation and enclosure imposed restrictions on their rights of use and access.

One way of thinking about whether resource extraction is exploitative, therefore, is to examine acts of enclosure and appropriation as the 'original moment' in the making of a resource. A number of authors have argued that enclosure and appropriation lie at the heart of the expansionary dynamic of contemporary capitalism. The concept of primitive accumulation (elaborated by Marx) provides a useful bridge between the institutional processes of enclosing and appropriating lands and resources, and the ways in which these processes enable accumulation. In its original form, primitive accumulation described the process of seizing control over land and resources, thereby separating traditional users from these means of production: the Spanish conquistadors' predations on New Spain in the sixteenth and seventeenth centuries provide a vivid example (Galeano 1973). But geographers have been at pains to argue that this process is persistent and ongoing: it is for this reason that Harvey (2003) has chosen to refer to the process as 'accumulation by dispossession'. One of the most salient moments in primitive accumulation concerns the privatization of resources, the process by which rights to resources formerly held in common are reassigned to individuals. In the last few years, geographers have started to analyse neoliberal privatization, commodification and enclosure of public assets by reference to the language of primitive accumulation. The critique of this process focuses on the uncompensated taking of resources and the social and geographical transfers of value that it involves.

875

Production: resource development as a transfer of surplus value

Structural political economy has had a long-standing engagement with resource exploitation, and with mining in particular. This may be seen in debates over European imperialism in the early twentieth century, in the extensive literature on Latin American and African under-development that formed around the 'dependency school' of development theory in the 1960s, and in contemporary work in political ecology, anthropology and environmental justice which pays particular attention to the political interests and struggles that form around mining projects. Whereas 'primitive accumulation' draws attention to the original or primary moment in accumulation, the focus of much structural political economy has been on the 'normal' process of accumulation: the extraction of surplus-value created by producers and its capture by a particular class. In the 1950s a number of thinkers began to consider how the expropriation of surplus – and its subsequent transfer abroad – might condition the possibilities for national development, particularly in economies where the extraction and export of natural resources were controlled by multinational enterprises (Baran 1957). At the centre of this process lies the distribution of revenues from the extraction of resources between investing firms (in the form of profits) and the state (in the form of rents or royalties). The use of transfer pricing and other techniques to minimize tax obligations in the host country, for example, highlights how the relationship between extractive firms and states is at best 'precarious, given the unresolved contradictions in their respective goals', and can be characterized by profound asymmetries in economic and political power (Vernon 1998: ix).

A classic statement of surplus value extraction as applied to natural resources is Frank's (1969) account of how the development of Chilean nitrates systematically benefited the core rather than the periphery. The extraction and shipping of Chilean nitrates netted British capital £16 million between 1880 and 1913 while Chile retained only £2 million, enabling Frank to conclude that the development of European agriculture came at the expense of Chile. Observations like these provided empirical evidence for the argument that under-development in Latin America, Africa and Asia was the necessary corollary of development in Europe, North America and Japan.

Unequal exchange: deteriorating terms of trade for resources

This line of argument centres on the international trade between developing and developed countries, and makes the case that the mutual exchange of manufactured goods and primary resources is unequal. The terms of trade – the ratio of import prices to export prices – fluctuate over time, but the long-run trend has been a deterioration for many primary producers. This means that to obtain the same value of (manufactured) imports, more (primary) exports have to be shipped. One reason for this is that the growth in demand for manufactured goods has exceeded the growth in demand for primary goods. Advanced initially by Prebisch (1950), unequal exchange is an explicit critique of Ricardo's theory of comparative advantage, which asserts that countries with relatively favourable natural resource endowments should specialize in resource extraction and export. Deteriorating terms of trade for resource exporters mean that inequalities within the global economy between the manufacturing 'core' and the resource-producing 'periphery' widen over time. For some, it is these structural inequalities resulting from trade that enable the exploitation of the periphery by the core. By the early 1970s many resource producers were calling for a New International Economic Order to address these power asymmetries. They sought to maximize their returns on resource exports through a combination of price supports, the indexing of commodity prices to the prices of manufactures, and the co-ordination of production to exert greater control over price: by 1979, for example, around 50 per cent of the world trade in bananas, rubber and copper was controlled by cartels (Crow and Thomas 1985).

Bad governance: exploitation through state failure

Over the last few years a number of non-governmental organizations have vividly illustrated serious environmental degradation and human rights abuses associated with mineral commodity chains. Global Witness's 'Blood Diamonds' campaign, for example, exposed the role of the diamond trade in financing wars in Angola, Sierra Leone and Congo and led to the UN-sponsored Kimberley Process for diamond certification. Along with similar initiatives around oil, gemstones and timber, these campaigns have highlighted how – in the absence of an effective state or other forms of institutional oversight – resource extraction and trade can promote factionalization and significantly undermine efforts at economic and social development. The primary dynamic of exploitation here is not between states and firms, but *within* states: it concerns the extent to which elites are able to seize and/or entrench power by monopolizing control of resource revenues via corruption, theft and other opportunities for looting that are associated with a lack of revenue transparency. Rather than exploitation stemming from the way global forces impinge on marginalized, developing countries, domestic elites exploit their local populations and actively utilize global connections to exercise power (Bayart 2000; Duffy 2005).

From this perspective exploitation is not a structural feature of the extractive paradigm, but is understood to be a consequence of state failure. Work on 'blood diamonds' suggests the ways in which states can fail catastrophically when it comes to managing the revenues and social costs of extraction. Increasingly, however, a whole host of issues associated with the extractive paradigm – environmental degradation, persistent poverty, corruption – are being explained by reference to the capacity of the state and the quality of governance. As an editorial in the *Mining Journal* (2006: 2) puts it, 'dependency on natural resources, poor economic performance and conflict are all the result of the same underlying factor: bad governance'. The governance of resources, therefore, is fast becoming a way of explaining national variation in development associated with the extractive paradigm. The concept of governance repositions the axis of exploitation so that it no longer highlights the tensions between firms and states, but the 'democratic deficit' between governing elites and the populations they claim to serve.

Instrumentalism: resources and the domination of nature

In this account, the core of exploitation is the epistemology of environmental knowledge that produces nature *as resources*. Resources are a very particular way of understanding the value and significance of the non-human world that is based on an instrumental appraisal: recognizing the particularity of the 'resource imaginary' reveals the operation of multiple value systems through which to interpret and interact with the world. The exploitative moment to resources lies in its denial or silencing of these alternative valuations or rationalities. The 'resource imaginary', then, is a colonial vision: resource definitions originate in the global North and they frequently 'discount the environmental practices of indigenous and local communities' (Robbins 2004: 10). To describe bauxite as a resource overlooks pre-existing land uses and land ownership that must be undone to establish mines and realize the exchange value of the ore (Howitt 2001). It is for this reason that a number of authors refer

877

to the 'violence' of the resource imaginary, thereby placing resources at the centre of human geography's encounter with post-colonialism (Peluso and Watts 2001; Braun 1997).

This perspective draws, in part, on the Frankfurt School's critique of instrumental reason which highlighted the ways in which exerting control over nature can become a means for exerting control over people. It also draws on recent work on governmentality and rationalities of rule, the diffuse interweavings of knowledge and power that produce assemblages of plants/animals as political units such as 'forests' or 'wetlands' (Bakker and Bridge 2006; Mitchell 2000). Similarly Peluso and Vandergeest (2001) document how the practices and rationalities of forest management in SE Asia – mapping, zoning and the enacting of land and forest laws – provided the colonial state with a way to control populations by criminalizing previously common practices. This perspective illuminates why debates over the role and effects of multinational resource firms in the developing world can be so intractable. Once issues of environmental performance have been addressed, the debate is ultimately about the value system one uses to judge whether the use of resources is justifiable or not.

Conclusion

Where does this leave Peru, its subterranean pipeline and the quiet infrastructure of resource export? With its low green buildings, orderly fencing and ISO 14001 'best practice' designation, the copper and zinc concentrate facility on the Pacific Coast hardly looks like the sharp end of exploitation. But the geographies of uneven development that create the conditions of possibility for large international mining operations like this – limited domestic markets, low market values attached to alternative, non-mining land uses, external indebtedness, booming external demand, external sources of surplus capital – are increasingly at the core of the 'new critique' of resource production. After a decade or more of primarily 'environmental' concerns, it is the social relations of extraction that are (again) assuming centre-stage with demands for resource extraction to alleviate inequality and contribute to pro-poor forms of growth.

The purpose of this chapter was to introduce a number of ways to think about the global geographies of resources. Geography's understanding of resources as a social relation, and its recognition of practices of resource production and consumption as distanciated geographies, is uncommonly in tune with popular critiques of resource extraction as a socially embedded process that tends to replicate – rather than transform – unequal social relations. The dominant strain of critique is that resource extraction does not deliver on the hopes and expectations of development for large numbers of people, and that the social relations around extraction need to be re-worked to ensure that resource activities contribute to economic and social goals. The diversity of challenges to resource extraction makes this a particularly interesting moment to witness the social redefinition of established economic practices.

Exploitation is a rhetorically potent and often politically effective weapon for naming and shaming some of the social relations around extraction. To date, however, it has shown itself to be a much blunter instrument for analysing these social relations, distinguishing among them, or for understanding the extent to which resource extraction is possible outside of exploitative relations. There are some intriguing parallels between the pattern of colonial resource economies and contemporary resource geographies, but there are also significant differences which limit the analytical value of claims regarding the reassertion of colonial *forms* of resource control. If claims that the extractive paradigm is exploitative are to be substantiated, there is a need to move beyond simple geographical correlations of production

878

in the periphery and consumption in the core to specify the mechanisms through which exploitation may occur.

Acknowledgement

Fieldwork associated with this chapter was supported with a grant from the US National Science Foundation SBR 9874837.

Further reading

Bakker, K., and Bridge, G. (2006) Resource regulation. In K. Cox, M. Low and J. Robinson (eds) *Handbook of Political Geography*. London and New York: Sage.

Howitt, R. (2001) *Rethinking Resource Management: Justice, Sustainability and Indigenous Peoples*. London: Routledge.

McNeill, J.R. (2000) *Something New Under the Sun: An Environmental History of the Twentieth Century World*. New York and London: Norton.

Mitchell, T. (2000) *Rule of Experts: Egypt, Techno-Politics, Modernity*. Berkeley and Los Angeles: University of California Press.

Rostow, W.W. (1960) *The Stages of Growth: A Non-Communist Manifesto*. Cambridge: Cambridge University Press.

White, R. (1995) *The Organic Machine: Remaking of the Columbia River*. New York: Hill and Wang

World Bureau of Metal Statistics (2006) *World Metal Statistics* 59 (1). Ware, Hertfordshire.

References

Bakker, K., and Bridge, G. (2006) Resource regulation. In K. Cox, M. Low and J. Robinson (eds) *Handbook of Political Geography*. London and New York: Sage.

Baran, P. (1957) *The Political Economy of Growth*. New York: Monthly Review Press.

Barnes, T. (1996) *Logics of Dislocation: Models, Metaphors, and Meanings of Economic Space*. New York: Guilford.

Bayart, J. (2000) Africa in the world: a history of extraversion. *African Affairs* 99, 217–67.

Bomsel, O. (1990) *Mining and Metallurgy Investment: The End of Large Projects?* Paris: OECD.

Borgstrom, G. (1965) *The Hungry Planet*. New York: Collier.

Bowles, I., Rosenfeld, A., Sugal, C. and Mittermeier, R. (1998) *Natural Resource Extraction in the Latin American Tropics: A Recent Wave of Investment Poses New Challenges for Biodiversity Conservation* (Conservation International Policy Briefs 1 (Spring)). Washington DC: Conservation International.

Braun, B. (1997) Buried epistemologies: the politics of nature in (post)colonial British Columbia. *Annals of the Association of American Geographers* 87 (1), 3–31.

Bridge, G. (2004) Contested terrain: mining and the environment. *Annual Review of Environment and Resources* 29, 205–59.

Castree, N. (1995) The nature of produced nature: materiality and knowledge construction in Marxism. *Antipode* 27 (1), 12–48.

Catton, W. (1980) *Overshoot: The Ecological Basis of Revolutionary Change*. Champaign: University of Illinois Press.

Chisholm, M. (1992) The increasing separation of production and consumption. In B. Turner, W.C.J.F. Clark, R.W. Kates, J.F. Richards, J.T. Mathews and W.B. Meyer (eds) *The Earth as Transformed by Human Action*, pp. 87–101. Cambridge: Cambridge University Press.

Crow, B. and Thomas, A. (1985). *Third World Atlas*. Milton Keynes and Philadelphia: Open University Press.

Duffy, R. (2005) Global environmental governance and the challenge of shadow states: the impact of illicit sapphire mining in Madagascar. *Development and Change* 36 (5), 1–19.

Esteva, G. (1992) Development. In W. Sachs (ed.) *The Development Dictionary: A Guide to Knowledge as Power*. London and New York: Zed Books.

Frank, A.G. (1969) *Capitalism and Underdevelopment in Latin America*. New York: Monthly Review Press.

Galeano, E. (1973) *Open Veins of Latin America: Five Centuries of the Pillage of a Continent*. New York: Monthly Review Press.

Geiser, K. (2001) *Materials Matter: Toward a Sustainable Materials Policy*. Cambridge, Mass.: MIT Press.

Harvey, D. (2003) *The New Imperialism*. Oxford: Oxford University Press.

Heath, K.C. (1975) Foreword. In M. Jones (ed.) *Minerals and the Environment: Proceedings of an International Symposium,* organized by the Institution of Mining and Metallurgy, with the cooperation of the Institute of Quarrying and the Institution of Mining Engineers, held in London from 4 to 7 June 1974, pp. x–xi.

Howitt, R. (2001) *Rethinking Resource Management: Justice, Sustainability and Indigenous Peoples*. London: Routledge.

Hudson, R. (2001) *Producing Places*. New York: Guilford.

Innis, H. (1956) *The Fur Trade in Canada: An Introduction to Canadian Economic History*. Toronto: University of Toronto Press.

Kloppenburg, J., Hendrickson, J. and Stevenson, G. (1996) Coming in to the foodshed. *Agriculture and Human Values* 13 (2), 33–42.

Lanning, G. and Mueller, M. (1973) *Africa Undermined: Mining Companies and the Underdevelopment of Africa*. Harmondsworth, England: Penguin Books.

McNeill, J.R. (2000) *Something New Under the Sun: An Environmental History of the Twentieth Century World*. New York and London: Norton.

Mining Journal (1990) Environment – the bottom line. *Mining Journal*, supplement to 23 February edition. London.

Mining Journal (2006) Helping the poor. *Mining Journal*, 10 February. London.

Mitchell, T. (2000) *Rule of Experts: Egypt, Techno-Politics, Modernity*. Berkeley and Los Angeles: University of California Press.

Muradian, R. and Martinez-Alier, J. (2001) *Globalization and Poverty: An Ecological Perspective*. World Summit Papers of Heinrich Boll Foundation. Available at http://www.worldsummit2002.org/publications/WSP7.pdf

North, D. (1955) Location theory and regional economic growth. *Journal of Political Economy* 63, 243–58.

Oil and Gas Journal (1999) Potential oil industry flashpoint centers on OXY's Colombian rainforest wildcat. *Oil and Gas Journal* 29 November, 18.

Peluso, N. and Vandergeest, P. (2001) Genealogies of the political forest and customary rights in Indonesia, Malaysia, and Thailand. *The Journal of Asian Studies* 60 (3), 761–812.

Peluso, N. and Watts, M. (eds) (2001) *Violent Environments*. Ithaca: Cornell University Press.

Polanyi, K. (2001) *The Great Transformation: The Political and Economic Origins of Our Time*, Foreword by J. Stiglitz and Introduction by F. Block. Boston, Mass.: Beacon Press.

Prebisch, R. (1950) *The Economic Development of Latin America and Its Practical Problems*. New York: United Nations.

Rickard, T.A. (1932) *A History of American Mining*. New York and London: McGraw-Hill.

Robbins, P. (2004) *Political Ecology: A Critical Introduction*. New York: Blackwell.

Ross, M. (2001) *The Extractive Sector and the Poor*. New York: Oxfam America.

Sachs, J. and Warner, A. (1999) The big push, natural resource booms and growth. *Journal of Development Economics* 59, 43–76.

Slack, K. (2001) Foreword. In M. Ross (ed.) *The Extractive Sector and the Poor*. New York: Oxfam America

Vernon, R. (1998) *In the Hurricane's Eye: The Troubled Prospects of Multinational Enterprises.* Boston: Harvard University Press.

Wackernagel, M. and Rees, W. (1996) *Our Ecological Footprint: Reducing Human Impact on the Earth.* Gabriola Island, British Columbia: New Society Publishers.

White, R. (1995) *The Organic Machine: Remaking of the Columbia River.* New York: Hill and Wang.

Williams, R. (1976) *Keywords: A Vocabulary of Culture and Society.* Oxford: Oxford University Press.

Wilson, D. and Purushothaman, R. (2003) *Dreaming with BRICs: The Path to 2050* (Global Economics Paper 99). New York: Goldman Sachs.

World Resources Institute (2004) *Mining and Critical Ecosystems: Mapping the Risks.* Washington, DC: World Resources Institute.

54

Counting

Finance, debt, banking and the global casino

Michael Pryke

Introduction and context: the world of money and finance

The world capitalist economy is a vast and complex entanglement of processes. For goods and services to be designed, produced and transported, for investment to take place in factories and offices – in effect, for the whole geo-economic system to work – payments have to be made. The sums involved are so large that they seem to take on a fictitious quality. For instance in 2004, the value of world merchandise trade stood at $8.89 trillion and world commercial services trade was around $2.10 trillion (World Trade Organization 2005). So the world economy needs financing; there is a need for 'world money'. During two significant periods in recent history, two currencies functioned as form of world money backed by gold – the gold-sterling standard of 1870 to 1914, and the gold-dollar exchange from 1945 to 1971. Both systems aimed to facilitate market-based economic exchange through the workings of financial markets. The explosive growth of the world economy is unimaginable without these forms of world money and the processes of economic 'globalization' described in Chapter 12 depend on global finance (Hirst and Thompson 1999; Temin 1999). Indeed, what really seems to epitomize present-day globalization are not the cross-border inter-connections made through trade in manufacturing and the production of goods, but the flows of *finance* and the workings of *financial markets*.

From around the globe, financial stories link globalization and various forms of finance. Shanghai shares on a rollercoaster ride; the Brazilian real plummets against the US dollar ... In the UK, it seems that each news bulletin ends with a money-related jingle – 'In the City the FTSE [Financial Times Stock Exchange] was up 40 at 4980' – as if to drive home the everydayness of a world made through private sector global financial flows.

The financial sums involved in these flows are truly vast. The Bank for International Settlements (BIS) estimates that in the fifteen years to 2000 the outstanding stock of cross-border bank lending rose from just over $2 trillion to over $10 trillion. In April 2004, average *daily* turnover in traditional foreign exchange markets was $1.9 trillion, while global *daily* turnover in foreign exchange and interest rate derivatives – another two key forms of global finance – was recorded at $2.4 trillion. The sums of nominal absolute value of all deals concluded and still open in derivatives transactions at the end of June 2004 was estimated to be $220 trillion (BIS 2005) (Figure 54.1).

It seems as if these sums have little to do with underlying manufacturing of goods or anything tangible. By 1992, for instance, the stock of international bank assets was over twice the volume of world trade (Akyüz 1995: 62). Indeed, a growing number of financial transactions take place between financial organizations and have little to do with the real

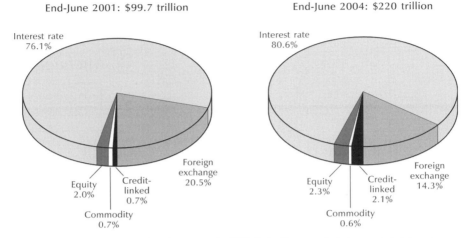

Figure 54.1. Reported global notional amounts in OTC derivatives markets by market-risk category.

Table 54.1. A typology of financial market internationalization

Inward liberalization	Outwards liberalization
Capital movement liberalization Liberalization of rules governing foreign direct investment, including sectoral restrictions, screening practices and performance requirements	Deregulation of outward direct and portfolio investment by nationals
Liberalization of foreign access to domestic equities and real estate	Liberalization of restrictions on repatriation of capital and disinvestment by foreign nationals and firms
Liberalization of rules governing foreign borrowing by domestic firms and the international operation of domestic banks	Liberalization of restrictions on payments for invisibles, including profits and dividends
Deregulation of sale and purchase of short-term domestic securities by foreigners	Deregulation of domestic foreign currency accounts for residents and non-residents Deregulation of sale and purchase of short-term foreign securities by domestic residents
Entry liberalization Liberalize entry of foreign banks, securities firms and other non-bank financial intermediaries	Permit or encourage domestic banks, securities firms and non-bank financial institutions to establish foreign branches and networks

Source: Adapted from Haggard and Maxfield (1996).

economy of production. Trading between banks and financial customers – the new significant players in the 'casino economy' (Strange 1986) such as hedge funds, asset managers and commodity trading advisers – now stands at around one-third of total financial market turnover (BIS 2005).

Some would argue that the dominance of current global financial markets is simply a sign that we are living in the midst of the latest surge of financial market activity (Arrighi 1994; Hirst and Thompson 1999; Neal 1990). The world of finance seems to have floated free of the world of production in a political economic environment shaped by the ideological triumph of neo-liberalism, a triumph that dates from the early 1980s. This project places private sector thinking and marketization of almost everything at centre-stage. The liberalization of financial markets, the key elements of which are highlighted in Table 54.1, was to have significant impact from the 1980s onwards.

A second undeniable aspect of the financial market surges lies in their marked *spatial expression* (Arrighi 1994; Harvey 1989; Swyngedouw 1996). The workings of financial markets make geographies. As the headlines noted earlier suggest, the everyday escapades of global finance seem to be inherently geographical. Spatialities emerge from the way that the

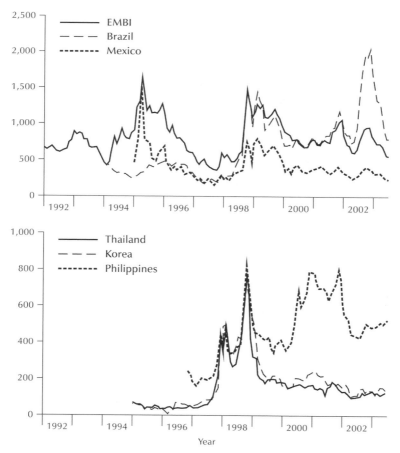

Figure 54.2. Bond spreads for selected emerging markets.
Source: Adapted from White (2004).

885

financial system mixes *flows* of national money (from national currencies such as sterling, to high street bank accounts and consumer credit) and international finance (such as foreign exchange dealings in 'global currencies' like the US dollars, to so-called financial derivatives, and corporate bonds, noted in Figure 54.1 previously) and *territories*. Territories may vary from specific locations such as New York's financial centre, Wall Street, to nation-states such as Brazil. The churning together of flows and territories in a system of globalized finance is seemingly tireless and gives expression to money's geographical character. Yet a key trait of this character is its selectivity (see Figures 54.2 and 54.3).

Financial flows are uneven. Moreover, financial interconnections may at times bring more disbenefits, in the form of financial crises, than net gains. The Latin American debt crisis of the 1980s is one example of the string of financial crises that hit many major 'developing' and 'transition' economies from 1994 to 2001, from Mexico, Thailand and the Russian Federation to Brazil, Turkey, Argentina and Malaysia (Mathieson *et al.* 1998; World Bank 2005; White 2004: 5–7). As the effects of financial volatility on these and other countries testify, while the sums may seem unreal financial flows hold potentially very real consequences such

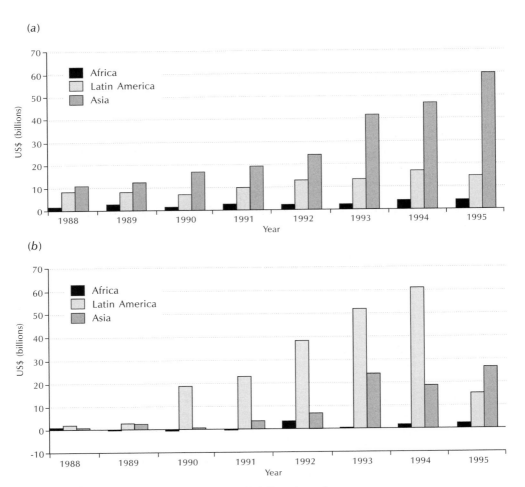

Figure 54.3. (a) FDI inflows by region; (b) portfolio inflows by region.

as unemployment, rocketing consumer prices and severe and sudden cutbacks in public sector expenditure.

Financial territories and flows are at the heart of this chapter. The later sections examine the significant spatial changes that have accompanied the latest surge in financial flows that followed re-regulation of international and global financial markets after the collapse of the gold–dollar standard in 1971. The present system of global financial markets has its roots in these times. From the 1970s there emerged not only a consolidation of private sector power in financial markets but, as the previous figures suggest, there was an accompanying 'explosion of new financial instruments and markets' and a growth of technical support for coordinating these markets on a global scale (Harvey 1989: 94). Within this system, financial markets were linked with the latest information and communication technology (ICT) and gave scope for finance to roam the globe. Against this background, I address three related sets of questions about financial flows and territories.

First there is something of a spatial paradox relating to the longevity of key *financial centres*, Wall Street in New York, Tokyo and the City of London, which are perhaps the most prominent symbols of global finance. Why do these places remain so important to global financial markets when numbers suggest that everything to do with finance is all about flows?

Second, there are the questions of how best to understand the emergence of the forms of global finance that began to appear in the 1970s, and how their geographical and temporal reach can be accounted for. There is a need to resist the invitation to view technology as *the* causal mechanism that has allowed global finance to achieve its current spatial reach. There is the important issue of the *financial architecture* that supports and regulates the global financial system. The present system of financial flows is certainly not set in stone. Its architecture, the routing of the flows and their relationship to nation–states, for example, is the outcome of ideas and political decisions. There are arguments for and against this latest architecture of so–called *liberalized flows*. In a brief final section, the chapter concludes by asking whether the present financial market system and its architecture is inevitable.

Spaces of financial organization: digitized finance and the need for coordination

We live in a market economy and market exchange is key to that system, as is money: quite simply, 'money makes the world go around'. Increasingly, finance and financial markets that are central to the operation of this system of exchange have become concentrated in a few places such as the City of London and New York's Wall Street (Sassen 1991, 2004). In these places financiers, bankers and a host of other financial market traders and dealers make markets in a growing range of sophisticated forms of global finance such as financial derivatives (LiPuma and Lee 2004).

Global financial markets deal with flows of financial assets and financial information that cross the territorial borders and are intricate combinations of technologies and human organizations located in specific places (Knorr-Cetina 2003).

Why are such places required, particularly in the days of instantaneous communication described in Chapter 60? Global financial markets are both complex and, in the way they operate today, arguably distinct from earlier financial markets, notably in the manner in which they rely upon information and communication technologies to assemble, not gold and silver coins, but flashing, multicoloured electronic signs that stream across computer screens. Stripped of any notion of the material and social worlds associated with other markets, financial markets centre on de-materialized flows. This de-materialized quality arguably stems from a process of *digitization* (Sassen 2004: 227) in which finance and the latest forms of ICT have been crossed and which has affected financial markets in at least three ways.

First is the use of sophisticated software to facilitate market operations. The use of software provides a constant real-time update of markets and prices; financial organizations can track global movements in key markets and listen to market rumour 'twenty-four seven'. Moreover when applied to financial market innovation and trade in financial products, such software can boost market growth and further innovative financial products. An example of the latter is the growth of financial derivatives that are made through decomposition and recomposition of different types of financial risk. These products have helped to transform capital flows within 'developed' *and* between developed and 'developing' economies (see Chapter 11; White 2004: 2).

Second, the application of digital technologies allows financial flows and territories to be interwoven and thickens interconnectedness and interdependencies between places and flows. Software enables previously separate markets to be woven together through instantaneous transmission of price movements. The intensity of this process has been heightened by the liberalization of financial markets. These markets now surge together, one potentially influencing the performance of the next. Moreover, such intensity is boosted further because of the ways in which sophisticated analytics – such as IBM's Informix IDS database software or the Numerical Algorithm group's 3D visualization software – enable real-time assessment of the performance of any one of these markets as they aid traders' assessment of advantages or disadvantages of holding or selling financial products. This real-time trading instantaneously brings distant territories on to screens in the heart of key financial centres (Sassen 2004; Knorr-Cetina 2003).

Third, the form of present-day financial transactions has changed, as Sassen reminds us:

> because finance is particularly about transactions rather than simply flows of money, the technical properties of digital networks assume added meaning. Interconnectivity, simultaneity, decentralised access, all contribute to multiply the number of transactions . . . and thereby the number of participants.
>
> (Sassen 2004: 228)

What results is a complex geography of financial transactions (Swyngedouw 1996).

Altogether, these factors make geographies that are arguably markedly different from those of the past: interconnections are the outcome of digitized finance flowing in real time. This in turn signals an altered relation between territories and flows and specifically between financial centres and other territories. Global finance plus the latest software is a truly 'geographical project' (Swyngedouw 1996: 135).

Yet something rather odd seems to be happening. While digitization has dispersed financial flows unequally across the globe, affecting the nature of interconnections and interdependencies between territories, the same process appears to have led to the concentration of the most significant global financial markets (Sassen 2004; BIS 2005). The chief reason for such concentration is that all of these flows need to be *coordinated*. The geography of one significant form of global finance – global equities – helps to illustrate this point.

Equities are financial instruments that form part of global stock markets. Together, the stock markets of New York (NYSE and the Nasdaq), Tokyo and London account for around 68 per cent of the world's capitalization of *stock market* trade (Sassen 2004: 234; see also BIS

2005). This is a clear sign of a concentration rather than a dispersal of power that accompanies financial flows. London, New York and Tokyo account for 33 per cent of global institutional equity holdings. The same three territories account for just under 60 per cent of the *foreign exchange* market (ibid.: 235). By 2004 just seven financial centres – London (the dominant centre), New York, Paris, Tokyo, Frankfurt, Singapore and Hong Kong – accounted for 75 per cent of overall over-the-counter (OTC) derivatives trading (BIS 2005: 21). This trend towards concentration in key global financial markets is captured in Figures 54.4 and 54.5

Why do only a handful of financial centres continue to matter? It seems that there has to be somewhere, to 'place your bets' (Pryke and Lee 1995). As Nigel Thrift notes, there has to be somewhere to meet and discuss market rumour, to assess confidence and generally to judge the state of play (Thrift 1994: 333–4; see also Pryke 1991: 1). London, Tokyo and Wall Street, and exchanges such as New York's Nasdaq and the Chicago Mercantile Exchange, are the key places where the intermingling of information, values, expertise and contacts around global finance is most strongly exhibited. In an attempt to make sense of what is going on, to figure out just what these flows of real-time information might imply for particular markets, experts and market players form themselves into social networks which work on the basis of trust and more information (Thrift 1994). All of this calls for more face-to-face meetings. People active in the market and the organizations they work for, together with the institutions regulating their activities, need a physical material presence to work through endless complex financial flows. The more dematerialized and digitized finance becomes and the more able it is to flow, the greater the need for places where the flows can be played. To be able to flow financial markets require making. It is not just software but people, organizations such as investment banks and brokers, and buildings that help to put the flow into global finance.

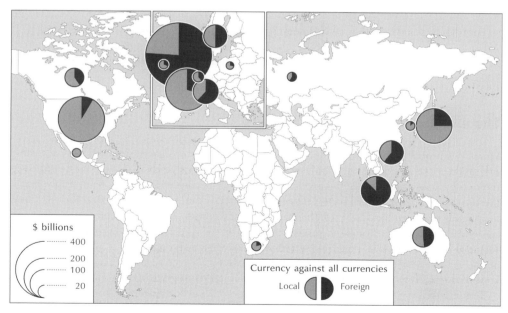

Figure 54.4. Forex trading by currency and country, daily average, April 2001.

Source: Adapted from Laulajainen (2003: 144).

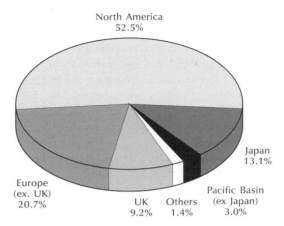

Figure 54.5. The leftover financial world: capitalization of world stock markets as a percentage of global total ($23,492.4 billion, February 2002).

Moreover, as work by Sassen (1991, 2004) shows, the vast offices crowding the financial centres of such cities as London and New York continue to symbolize a demonstrable political economic power. It is within such territories that financial elites employ technical connectivity to thicken their ability to direct flows globally. While centres such as São Paulo and Bombay may be regionally significant, they are in effect minor nodes when set against the City of London or New York (Sassen 2004). The authority to make sense and direct global flows stems from within these western financial enclaves.

Yet something more gives to Wall Street financiers, bankers, brokers and their like the scope and the authority to move vast sums of private finance around the globe. The freedom to coordinate the movement of financial flows cannot be simply ascribed to the latest ICT. 'Liberalization' signalled a significant change in the rules and regulations, the financial architecture, governing the flow of private finance and the role of markets (Tickell and Peck 2003), and it is to these regulatory frameworks that I now turn.

The architecture of financial markets

Finance is probably the best example of economic globalization with its swift moves around the globe in search of profit. Those managing private finance seek out the best returns as they mobilize global money. Finance needs to flow; it needs motion if it is to multiply. But if the movements are too swift, crises may follow. There cannot be a market free-for-all. Thus, historically, nation-states have sought to control movements of finance, and have sometimes succeeded. There are, though, different visions of freely flowing versus highly territorialized financial systems. Hence there is a need to consider what might be at stake in deciding between these visions – as free a scope as is possible for finance to move across territories, or a more territorially constrained system – and in implementing whichever vision is preferred.

Tensions between free trade and state regulation have dominated discussion of national economic policy for over a century. These tensions increase when considering finance. At the beginning of the twenty-first century, the advocates of free flows of finance seem to be winning the argument, but this orthodoxy has not always held sway. In the twentieth century the 'financial architecture' changed from free trade when sterling backed by gold was the world currency, to a high degree of state control during the period of gold–dollar standard, before swinging back towards free markets (Strange 1994; Leyshon and Thrift 1997; Leyshon and Tickell 1994; Panic 1995; Vines and Gilbert 2004).

The choice between a state- or market-led movement and the consequent relationship between territories and flows is not down to mere chance. The term 'financial architecture' is meant to convey this point. As with any architecture, imagination and decisions are involved: people sit in front of screens in London or Frankfurt; others attend meetings from New York through to Tokyo, or Washington, DC, and have to draw up, agree and implement designs. There has to be agreement about how markets should be regulated and whether the state or the private sector should do the regulation. Whatever the technology, groups of people have to make and agree the rules and regulations that shape the markets and the flows and how these will affect territories. One such group met in a small town in the USA in the early 1940s.

Geographies of finance from Bretton Woods to neo-liberalism

In July 1944, finance ministers from the major Western countries met in Bretton Woods, New Hampshire, USA, to establish the architecture for the post–world war international financial system. This was to be an architecture agreed by state power, not private bankers. The idea was that markets were to be subordinate to states in the new planned and managed international financial system. The two key proponents of the new system, John Maynard Keynes and Harry Dexter White, drew up what is now known as the 'Bretton Woods Agreement', the blueprint for the post-war financial system (Leyshon and Tickell 1994; Panic 1995).

Bretton Woods produced a global financial architecture to help the world recover economically and financially from the Second World War and prevent the recurrence of the depression of the 1930s that followed the Wall Street crash of 1929. In short, the 'world market economy could not be left to work by itself. Rules were needed' (Strange 1994: 53). In fact, Bretton Woods saw for the first time in history governments of the leading economies meeting explicitly to agree a set of rules for collective management (Strange 1994: 55). The governments agreed to provide stability to the international financial system, in which national economic agendas would be recognized and respected. Finance was to continue to move around the globe, but movements were to be regulated. The negotiated solution, technically known as a system of 'fixed but adjustable exchange rates', lasted until the early 1970s. Two international institutions, the International Monetary Fund (IMF) and the World Bank, lasted much longer. During this period currencies were fixed in terms of the US dollar, with any significant exchange rate disequilibrium between countries made good by the actions of the IMF.

The Bretton Woods system gave national territories room for manoeuvre to establish policies in relation to the international markets. Importantly, national controls over financial inflows and outflows were in place for the whole of the period that the agreement was in force. The Bretton Woods Agreement provided a largely state-led regulatory architecture to facilitate the stable passage of financial flows (Panic 1995; Strange 1994). What was distinct about this vision was that it established ideas for how financial flows might move between territories with the minimum of *volatility* and *risk* to the countries involved and their populations. Financial flows should be linked to trade and not directed towards the casino.

The appropriateness of the financial architecture agreed at Bretton Woods was contested at the time of its inception and throughout its relatively short life. The system did not last, and collapsed in the early 1970s. With cracks appearing in the regulatory architecture, finance increasingly escaped regulated territories – at first opportunistically, then by arguing for a new architecture (Leyshon and Tickell 1994). More and more, commercial banks found ways to circumvent state controls on financial flows. The development of 'Euromarkets', in which dollar deposits and loans were made outside the USA by banks from a variety of countries, is the prime example of such regulatory circumnavigation and the creation of 'stateless money' (Martin 1994).

The collapse of Bretton Woods signalled a systemic change in the world of international finance. The fantastic growth of private financial assets, quickly outstripping the volume of world trade, is remarkable and significant in itself. Yet perhaps most notable is the change in the *composition* of flows of stateless finance that came with the 'liberalization' from the 1970s onwards (Hirst and Thompson 1999), and the impact this had on the interdependencies between flows and territories at a global level (Akyüz 1995). The breakdown of Bretton Woods and the accompanying move from exchange rates fixed by the state to flexible exchange rates also signalled a shift in power from states to markets, and can be viewed as heralding the era of neo-liberalism (Leyshon and Tickell 1994).

Neo-liberalism is a significant international political project that seeks to transform a host of key agreements established at the end of the Second World War (Tickell and Peck 2003). The liberalization of finance is part of this project. Financial liberalization involves three interrelated measures: to expose a country to the free flow of international finance; to remove controls and restrictions on the functioning of domestic banks and other financial institutions in an effort to integrate countries into world financial markets; and to make a country's central bank, such as the Bank of England, independent – that is, to take it out of the political process (Patnaik 1999).

Yet what did this shift signal for the relationship between flows and territories? This question raises issues about the power wielded by the key financial centres over others in the context of liberalized financial flows. The key arguments in the debate between those who argue for and against financial liberalization are now summarized.

Arguments for financial liberalization

Advocates for the free movement of all types of private finance, from short-term portfolio to long-term direct investment, have a number of aims. One is to produce a world where there is a greater degree of financial integration that, they claim, benefits from access to more varied sources of private finance. This is achieved by a marked increase in cross-border flows of finance as investment funds flow to the places where they can be invested most efficiently (Wolf 2004: 278–306).

Those who are pro-liberalization view it as potentially beneficial to less developed countries. As the costs of important factors of production, such as labour, land and buildings, are lower in the less developed world, investors should, in theory, tend to invest more in poor countries. Such investments would be economically efficient (because the goods and services would be cheaper and hence in high demand) and tend to reduce the disparities in development which were maintained by controls over capital movement between countries.

Those within private finance organizations and working for international institutions such as the IMF argue that free flows of finance will tend to be from capital-rich industrial countries, where there is an abundance of private finance, to capital-poor developing countries, where finance is needed to develop (Kose and Prasad 2004). The claim is that there will be benefits all round: investors in developing countries will be rewarded by higher returns, and developing countries in receipt of financial inflows will quickly see the benefits that accrue from economic growth, such as growing employment and rising living standards. In short, there would seem to be no reason to be 'fearful of finance' (Wolf 2004: 278).

Moreover, whereas in the past many governments created problems, and even crises, by intervening unwisely in their economies, it is claimed that the rules of financial liberalization will ensure that countries will subscribe to the ideas and practices of sound economic management, since those rules are monitored and supervised by private financial organizations as well as international institutions like the IMF. Should national economic policy be seen to break the rules, then investors would withdraw their finance. Private finance would, in other words, head for more secure territories.

According to the advocates of liberalization, the relationship between territories and private financial flows could not be clearer. Countries, particularly in the 'developing world', have a lot to gain by making themselves attractive to private financial flows.

Arguments against financial liberalization

Critics of financial liberalization argue that the picture painted by its proponents is far too rosy, as it points to potential benefits to less developed countries but ignores the effects of changing composition of private finance – the mix of short-term 'portfolio flows' and long-term finance, for example (see Corbridge 1993; Griffith-Jones 1998) – and some of the actual disbenefits of financial liberalization, such as the strong tendency for capital to flow from less to more developed countries.

Patnaik (1999) helps to draw our attention to the new interdependencies between territories produced by financial liberalization, particularly in the face of the growing influence of private sector financial flows and the decline in 'official flows' of finance administered by the likes of the World Bank (see Corbridge 1993; Vines and Gilbert 2004; World Bank 2005). He uses the case of financial sector reforms in India to illustrate his argument about the consequences of a country becoming a liquid part of globalized finance. Patnaik stresses that one needs to distinguish between capital inflows in the form of FDI, which benefits the productive capacity of the economy, and short-term flows (see Figure 54.6).

The latter he views as 'essentially speculative in nature', and he argues that they damage rather than serve the needs of developing countries. Figure 54.6 captures this exposure 'to the vortex of speculative capital movements' – that is, to the flows of short-term finance in search of quick profits (Patnaik 1999; World Bank 2005). Patnaik also stresses developing countries must offer what he calls 'blandishments', such as lower tax rates than those to be found in developed countries, if they are to attract funds. And as private finance is moved around the globe searching for the best returns, the process creates a new set of interdependencies between nation-states as each tries to offer higher returns to private finance than its neighbour in an effort to make itself more attractive. This process brings with it potential social costs. The price of the new interdependencies is often borne by the poor. Reductions in tax mean that less money is available to spend on health and education.

In this new world of flows, governments no longer have the options that existed when capital could be controlled. To raise taxes would mean driving away corporations. These firms are relatively free to relocate. To increase government expenditure, say, would fall foul of the rules laid down by IMF and would not be looked on favourably by private sector banks and investment houses in London, Tokyo or New York. This type of action would frighten short-term investors, because they would be unsure whether their investments would be safe in a country where the government was pursuing 'unsound policies'

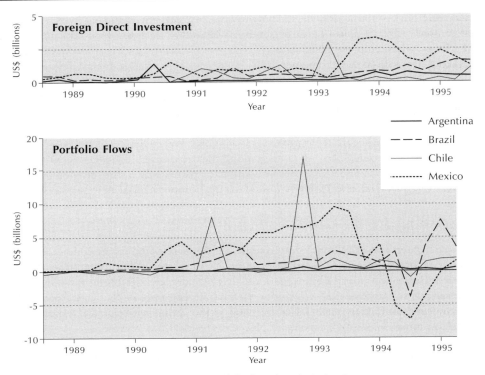

Figure 54.6. Foreign direct investment and portfolio flows in selected nations.

(Griffith-Jones 1998: 39–46). Nor does a single government have a realistic option of restoring controls on capital movements, particularly in a financial world ruled by private sector monitoring and rating agencies. Such agencies range from specialist firms such as the world leaders Standard and Poor's, Moody's, and Fitch, based in the USA, offshoots of the IMF such as the International Finance Corporation's emerging market indices, and private sector investment banks indices such as the influential Morgan Stanley 'All Country Far-East Ex-Japan Index and Emerging Market Free Index', to organizations such as the Institute of International Finance, Inc. (IIF), created in 1983 to provide 'high-quality, timely and impartial advice' for its membership of largely European-based financial institutions on emerging markets in developing countries. The influence of such organizations is considerable. It is easy to imagine the effect on government policy of such financial policing or of being placed in the category of 'most investor-friendly emerging market countries' by such an influential organization as the IIF.

The impact on developing countries of volatile private sector financial flows, and the workings of the system of private sector surveillance carried out through indices such as those noted above, has even encouraged some critics to challenge the claim that neo-liberalism is characterized by 'free markets'. Economic geographer Ron Martin articulates the central issue when he states that 'financial markets are as much political as economic in character, founded on and shaped by unequal relations of power between lenders and borrowers' (Martin 1994: 271). The theory that informs the neo-liberal position, Martin argues, is removed from what actually takes place in the world. In practice, he asserts, powerful private sector organizations, such as the big investment banks and securities houses, pension funds, mutual funds, multinational corporations, institutions like the IMF and the leading group of capitalist countries operating as G7, G8 or G10, are the financial system's dominant conductors. Goldman echoes these points:

> The production of actually existing neo-liberalism was (and remains) a transnational dialectical process, a product of tension, struggle, and negotiated compromise among World Bank, IMF, powerful bankers and political elites, and scores of actors working in corporations, governments, and professional societies around the world.
>
> (Goldman 2005: 93)

It is such economic actors, rather than the myriad of small, equally powerful, decision makers assumed in neo-liberal theory, that make the markets that move finance from territory to territory (Martin 1994: 272). Indeed, recent research suggests that private sector financial organizations such as mutual funds and hedge funds exercise more power and influence than do the likes of the IMF and World Bank (Harmes 1998: 101–8). Far from 'ending geography', as early commentators on a flow-based world economy expected, Martin concludes that financial globalization is 'reconfiguring geographies of money, power and dependency' (Martin 1994: 274). Yet it is important to remember that these western institutions did not develop their ideological and economic power against a clean backdrop. Michael Goldman, an ex-World Bank employee, writes that this power:

> was constituted in post colonial capitalist North–South relations from the start. It built upon the power relations embedded and embodied in the former colonial capitalist relations; wove its way through the World Bank's development regimes of poverty alleviation, debt management, and structural adjustment; and now thrives in the Bank's version of environmentally sustainable development.
>
> (Goldman 2005: 8–9)

The new system is highly contentious, with powerful supporters, mainly from more prosperous parts of developed economies, and many vociferous critics, mainly from less affluent groups and less developed countries. Maybe there is nothing inevitable about the present financial architecture and its markets, rules and regulations, and the resulting geographies.

Towards a conclusion: the inevitability of markets?

After the triumph of markets in the 1980s it may seem strange to find that private financial flows, so central to today's globalization and a key facilitator of the neo-liberal agenda, flow unevenly around the world. There are *'left over places'* (Lee 2003: 74). Global financial markets, are dominated by three currencies – the US dollar, the Yen and increasingly the Euro – and financial transactions describe a world in which vast areas of the world, such as sub-Saharan Africa, are effectively left off the map. The marginalization of large parts of Africa and the Middle East continues and is exacerbated by the trend for 'official lending' from the likes of the World Bank to decline markedly, and for capital market flows to developing and emerging markets to be replaced by potentially volatile and more selective flows of private credit and equity. What is more, even *within* 'highly developed' countries such as the USA and the UK, localities within nation-states may be bypassed by private financial markets (Leyshon and Thrift 1994; 1997: 225–59; Lee 1999). These different scales of 'financial exclusion' can be traced back to the growing influence of neo-liberalism and the accompanying tendency to rely on private sector financial organizations and flows, rather that public sector funding or 'official' flows of finance. Both processes in effect describe a political programme channelled through private finance, and neither spells the 'end of geography'. On the contrary, as Swyngedouw (1996: 162) writes, the present financial system is a 'new power geometry' that propels some to new commanding heights and disempowers others.

It would seem that liberalized financial markets and flows are not perfect. Nevertheless, are they inevitable? One leading proponent of the 'global market economy', Martin Wolf, is adamant that, despite its blemishes, 'Globalization works'. In his eyes and in the eyes of those who share his views, global financial markets collectively are a key means to achieve a market economy at a global level: 'the market economy is the only arrangement capable of generating sustained increases in prosperity, providing the underpinnings of stable liberal democracies and giving individual human beings the opportunity to seek what they desire in life'. What is more, 'it is in the *long-run* interest of countries to integrate into global financial markets. But they should do so carefully, in full understanding of the risks' (Wolf 2004: 319, emphasis added). Integration may well be a path to secure prosperity and may 'in the long run' mean that 'left-over geographies' are a thing of the past. However, as noted by the Bank for International Settlements, an international organization charged with monitoring the stability of the global financial system, global financial market integration over recent years has increased the vulnerability of the system to financial turbulence (BIS 2005).

The 'long run' may be quite a lengthy and costly time for some people as volatile, contagious flows of finance pour unequally across the globe, impacting even supposedly strong, financially sophisticated countries of the OECD. As Glynn notes: 'The real economies of the US and Japan have been scarred by financial excesses and the whole system can be threatened by the unrelenting search for "value" through ever more complex financial trades' (Glynn 2005: 35). Perhaps then, alternative architectures should be sought to provide a more even flow of finance and more socially responsible markets. Even international institutions such as the G7 industrial countries and the G22 are calling for reform of the system that supports global financial markets (Cartapanis and Herland 2002; Group of Seven 1999; IMF 2000, 2001).

While it would be foolish to argue that simple alternatives to the present organization of the 'market economy' exist (Helleiner 2003; Hirst and Thompson 2002) and that the market is 'all bad', there are nonetheless alternative ways to organize and run the 'global economy'. The point of talking about the discursive construction of key global economic and financial arrangements such the Bretton Woods' financial architecture and its key institutions, the World Bank and the IMF, is to underline that there is *nothing natural* about such arrangements. Financial architectures, their rules and regulations that enable the movement of financial flows and the design of markets, all stem from ideas, decisions and policies. The acceptance that free-flowing mobility is a 'good thing' stems from legislation shaped by international institutions and the accompanying 'legitimation work' of certain (Western) nation-states (see Best 2003). Moreover – and this is key to appreciating the geographies of finance and their unevenness – such ideas have very specific geo-histories. They build upon particular worldviews (such as the imperial West, in the case of Bretton Woods). They find routes along geographies of trade quite often established in colonial times. Calls for the expansion of markets, insisting that there is a need 'for more, not less globalization', fail to recognize that making markets is based on past geographies of inequalities and Western dominance, a fact not lost on some of the participants at the Bretton Woods conference who 'knew enough to articulate their needs in ways that emphasized imperial self-interest' (Goldman 2005: 53).

As political economic developments in several Latin American countries at the start of this century suggest, alternatives to a global market dominated by the Northern Hemisphere are imaginable. For instance, in 2003 twenty-five members of the Brazilian parliament, drawn mainly from the Workers' Party, called on colleagues to form a 'parliamentary front' on international financial institutions (IFIs). They declared that: 'The legislative power in Brazil cannot afford any longer not to question and debate technical aspects and political implications of the operations of the IFIs'. The group's proposals and objectives include coordination of national parliaments across Latin America and recommendations that improvements are made to the international financial architecture (Bretton Woods Project 2003). In 2004, 170 parliamentarians worldwide signed a petition demanding a more significant role in assessing the operations of IFIs within their nations in an attempt to reassert the 'sovereignty of legislatures in parliamentary democracies' (Bretton Woods Project 2004).

And beneath the dominant rhythm of global finance, similar reimaginings are happening in diverse ways. For example, alternatives to Western financial systems are being put forward within Islamic banking; cooperative banks are being established in India and Bangladesh; and local currencies are being established in the UK and the USA (Corbridge and Thrift 1994: 17) At an international level, an alternative financial architecture undoubtedly will be required. So why not consider reforming or replacing the IMF? Why not reorient the 'goals of lending' by bringing moral issues into the frame as well as technical economic terms that dominate and constrain debate (Best 2003)? Altogether, change in the rules that guide counting practices of Wall Street and the City of London may well produce alternative, more *socially responsible* (Massey 2004) geographies of interconnectedness made through financial flows.

Further reading

Arrighi, G. (1994) *The Long Twentieth Century*. London: Verso.

Corbridge, S. (1993) *Debt and Development*. Oxford: Blackwell.

Häusler, G. (2002) The globalization of finance. *Finance and Development* 39 (1), 10–12.

Hirst, P. and Thompson, G. (1999) *Globalization in question*, second edition. Cambridge: Polity Press.

Kose, M.A. and Prasad, E.S. (2004) Liberalising capital account restrictions. *Finance and Development* September, 50–1.

Laulajainen, R. (2003) *Financial Geography: A Banker's View*. London and New York: Routledge.

Leyshon, A. and Thrift, N. (1997) *Money/Space: Geographies of Monetary Transformation*. London and New York: Routledge.

——(2005) *Financial Derivatives and the Globalization of Risk*. Durham and London: Duke University Press.

——(ed.) (1999) *Money and the Space Economy*. Chichester: John Wiley and Sons.

Martin, R. (ed.) (1999) *Money and the Space Economy*. Chichester: John Wiley and Sons.

Neal, L. (1990) *The Rise of Financial Capitalism*. Cambridge: Cambridge University Press.

Strange, S. (1986) *Casino Capitalism*. Oxford: Blackwell.

Wolf, M. (2004) Fearful of finance. In M. Wolf, *Why Globalization Works*, Chapter 13, pp. 278–306. New Haven and London: Yale University Press.

References

Akyüz, Y. (1995) Taming international finance. In J. Michie and J. Grieve Smith (eds) *Managing the Global Economy*, pp. 55–92. Oxford: Oxford University Press.

Arrighi, G. (1994) *The Long Twentieth Century.* London: Verso.

Best, J. (2003) Moralizing finance: the new financial architecture as ethical discourse. *Review of International Political Economy* 10, 3579–603.

BIS (2005) *Triennial Central Bank Survey: Foreign Exchange and Derivatives Market Activity in 2004.* Basel: Bank for International Settlements.

Bretton Woods Project (2003) *Parliamentary Front on IFIs*, 26 May. Available at http://www.brettonwoodsproject.org/article.shtml?cmnd[126] = x-126-4430 (accessed 31 January 2006).

——(2004) *Parliaments Reign in IFIs: International Campaign Gains Momentum*, 21 September. Available at http://www.brettonwoodsproject.org/article.shtml?cmnd[126] = x-126-4430 (accessed 31 January 2006).

Cartapanis, A. and Herland, M. (2002) The reconstruction of the financial architecture: Keynes' revenge? *Review of International Political Economy* 9, 271–97.

Corbridge, S. (1993) *Debt and Development.* Oxford: Blackwell.

Corbridge, S. and Thrift, N. (1994) Money, power and space: introduction and overview. In S. Corbridge, R. Martin, and N. Thrift (eds) *Money, Power and Space*, pp. 1–25. Oxford: Blackwell.

Glynn, A. (2005) Imbalances in the global economy. *New Left Review* 34, 5–37.

Goldman, M. (2005) *Imperial Nature* Yale: Yale University Press.

Griffith-Jones, S. (1998) *Global Capital Flows: Should They Be Regulated?* New York: St Martin's Press.

Group of Seven (1999) *Strengthening the International Financial Architecture* (Report of 87 Finance Ministers of the Kohn Economic Summit, Cologne, 18–20 June). Cologne: Group of Seven.

Haggard, S. and Maxfield, S. (1996) The political economy of financial internationalization in the developing world. *International Organization* 50 (1), 35–68.

Harmes, A. (1998) Institutional investors and the reproduction of neoliberalism. *Review of International Political Economy* 5, 92–121.

Harvey, D. (1989) *The Condition of Postmodernity.* Oxford: Blackwell.

Helleiner, E. (2003) Economic liberalism and its critics: the past as prologue. *Review of International Political Economy* 10 (4), 685–96.

Hirst, P.Q. and Thompson, G.F. (1999) *Globilisation in Question*, second edition. Cambridge: Polity.

——(2002) The future of globalization. *Cooperation and Conflict* 37 (3), 247–65.

IMF (2000) *Progress in Strengthening the Architecture of the International Financial System.* Washington DC: IMF.

——(2001) *Reforming the International Financial Architecture.* Washington DC: IMF.

Knorr-Cetina, K. (2003) From pipes to scopes. *Distinktion* 7, 7–23.

Laulajainen, R. (2003) *Financial Geography: A Banker's View.* London and New York: Routledge.

Lee, R. (1999) Local money: geographies of autonomy and resistance? In R. Martin (ed.) *Money and the Space Economy*, pp. 207–24. Chichester: John Wiley and Sons.

——(2003) The marginalization of everywhere? Emerging geographies of emerging markets. In J. Peck and H.W. Yeung (eds) *Remaking the Global Economy: Economic-Geographical Perspectives*, pp. 61–82. London: Sage.

Leyshon, A.and Thrift, N. (1994) Access to financial services and financial infrstructure withdrawal: problems and policies. *Area* 26, 268–75.

——(1997) *Money/Space: Geographies of Monetary Transformation.* London and New York: Routledge.

Leyshon, A. and Tickell, A. (1994) Money order? The discursive construction of Bretton Woods. *Environment and Planning A* 26, 1861–90.

LiPuma, E. and Lee, B. (2004) *Financial Derivatives and the Globalization of Risks.* Durham, NC, and London: Duke University Press.

Martin, R. (1994) Stateless monies, global financial integration and national economic autonomy: the end of geography? In S. Corbridge, R. Martin and N. Thrift (eds) *Money, Power and Space*, pp. 253–78. Oxford, UK, and Cambridge, Mass.: Blackwell.

Massey, D. (2004) Geographies of responsibility. *Geografiska Annalar* 86 B, 5–18.

Mathieson, D.J., Richards, A. and Sharma, S. (1998) Financial crises in emerging markets. *Finance and Development* 35 (4, December), 28–31.

Neal, L. (1990) *The Rise of Financial Capitalism: International Capital Markets in the Age of Reason.* Cambridge: Cambridge University Press.

Panic, M. (1995) The Bretton Woods system. In J. Michie and J. Grieve Smith (eds) *Managing the Global Economy*, pp. 37–54. Oxford: Oxford University Press.

Patnaik, P. (1999) The real face of financial liberalisation. *The Hindu* 16, 4.

Pryke, M. (1991) An international city going global. *Society and Space* 9, 197–222.

Pryke, M. and Lee, R. (1995) Place your bets. *Urban Studies* 32, 329–44.

Sassen, S. (1991) *The Global City.* Princeton: Princeton University Press.

——(2004) The local and institutional embeddedness of electronic markets. In M. Berir and F. Trentmann (eds) *Markets in Historical Context*, pp. 224–46. Cambridge: Cambridge University Press.

——(1994) From Bretton Woods to the casino economy. In S. Corbridge, N. Thrift and R. Martin (eds) *Money, Power and Space*, pp. 49–62. Oxford: Blackwell.

Swyngedouw, E. (1996) Producing futures: global finance as a geographical project. In P.W. Daniels and W.F. Lever (eds) *The Global Economy in Transition*, pp. 135–63. Harlow: Longman.

Temin, P. (1999) Globalization. *Oxford Review of Economic Policy* 154, 76–89.

The Economist (1999) Global finance survey: time for a redesign? *The Economist*, 30 January, 1–22.

Thrift, N. (1994) On the social and cultural determinants of international financial centres. In S. Corbridge, N. Thrift and R. Martin (eds) *Money, Power and Space*, pp. 327–55. Oxford: Blackwell

Tickell, A. and Peck, J. (2003) Making global rules. In J. Peck and H. Wai-chung Yeung (eds) *Remaking the Global Economy*, pp. 163–81. London: Sage.

Vines, D. and Gilbert, C.L. (2004) The IMF and international financial architecture: solvency and liquidity. In D. Vines and C.L.Gilbert (eds) (2004) *The IMF and its Critics: Reform of Global Financial Architecture*, pp. 8–35. Cambridge: Cambridge University Press.

White, W.R. (2004) *Are Changes in Financial Structure Extending Safety Nets?* (BIS Working Papers No. 145, January). Basel: Bank for International Settlements.

Wolf, M. (2004) *Why Globalization Works.* New Haven and London: Yale University Press.

World Bank (2005) *Global Development Finance 2005: Mobilizing Finance and Managing Vulnerability,* Washington DC: World Bank.

World Trade Organization (WTO) (2005) *International Trade Statistics.* Geneva: WTO.

55

Producing

Changing patterns of work

Jane Holgate

The following reports from a British newspaper, on the transfer of jobs from the UK to various parts of the world, highlight the shifting geographies of capital as it seeks to minimize its labour costs. The level of savings to be made by relocating from the industrialized north to the less industrialized south are immense: workers in UK call centres, for example, earn on average ten times the rate in India.

> Unions today accused Dyson of betraying British workers as the pioneer of the bagless vacuum cleaner announced plans to shift manufacturing operations to Asia.
>
> (Cacanas and Collinson 2003)

> HSBC has announced plans to cut 7,500 jobs in Britain, with about 4,500 of those the result of a decision to move work to countries where labour costs are less, such as India and Malaysia.
>
> (Tran 2002)

> As if India were not enough of a threat, the 400,000 Britons employed in call centres are facing new and growing competition for their jobs from eastern and central Europe.
>
> (Tran 2004)

> With daily wage rates that wouldn't pay for a Big Mac meal in Britain, it's little surprise that UK companies are shifting call centre jobs to India at an alarmingly rapid rate. This week Norwich Union joined the list, revealing that it wants to outsource 2,350 jobs in admin posts to India in a move union leaders condemned as 'deplorable' but which prime minister Tony Blair called 'the way the world is today'.
>
> (Cacanas and Collinson 2003)

Prime Minister Blair's comment that this is 'the way the world is today' appears to suggest that the increasing flow of capital and the transfer and (re)creation of jobs across the globe is an *inevitable* consequence of economic markets and that politicians (and trade unions) have little power to moderate or challenge the power of global capital. Yet the landscapes of capital *and* labour are in a state of flux. While it is true that capital has gained the upper hand over labour since the last decades of the twentieth century, through the creation of new geographies of production, exchange and consumption, capital still has to contend with challenges from workers and their unions, albeit in much weakened forms (Herod 2001). At the same time, consumers of products and services are increasingly making their voices heard through initiatives such as ethical trade, corporate codes of practice that cover supply chain working conditions, minimum labour standards and ethical investments (ETI 2005).

Reports from newspapers and research papers suggest that the moving of call centres to India and other countries in Asia has not been without labour problems (Taylor and Bain 2004; 2005a). One of the benefits of call centres locating and relocating in less developed countries is the lack of trade unions in the sector. While there are no trade unions representing call centre workers in India at the moment, there are some small scale attempts to collectivize workers (Bain and Taylor 2004; Taylor and Bain 2005b; UNI Finance 2004) and it is unlikely the industry will remain union-free indefinitely. Further, companies outsourcing from the UK and the US to India have had to contend with a 'backlash' from some of their customers whose racism, xenophobia and sheer frustration at cultural misunderstandings make it difficult to communicate with call centre operators in India. Worker attrition rates have risen considerably in recent years as a consequence of working conditions and extremely rapid growth rates, which have enabled staff to move between companies to gain better pay and conditions (Taylor and Bain 2005a). The official industry body in India admits that average turnover is between 25 per cent and 40 per cent per annum (Nasscom 2005) and in reality these are conservative estimates. Central to all these examples are issues that are profoundly geographical – the battle for control of place and space.

The intention of this chapter is to discuss changing patterns of work and how the tensions between capital and labour are played out at different scales across the economic landscape. While popular rhetoric about the new forces of globalization suggests that capital is free to move butterfly-like around the globe seeking its 'spatial fix' wherever it should choose to (momentarily) rest, the reality is somewhat different (Dicken 2003b). Capital needs labour in order to produce profit, and while it is true that in comparison to capital labour has much less spatial mobility, grounded as it is in the social relations of home, work, family and leisure, capital does nevertheless also have a need to fix itself and the labour process (however temporarily) in place(s) in order to take advantage of workers in global and local labour markets.

The sheer scale of change in geographies of employment since the Industrial Revolution is immense. The early textile factories located in the north of England are long gone and most clothing and manufacturing goods for the British market are produced in countries of the Far East. At the same time, high-skilled and knowledge-intensive sectors remain stubbornly grounded in places like the City of London. The examples before show how companies today operate in a greatly advanced globalizing labour market. This chapter explores the scales at which the labour process operates today and how this is contested by capital *and* labour as each seeks to challenge the other's 'right' to control the labour process. It also explains how spatial divisions of labour are used to create fissures between workers who are concerned with defending jobs in their localities. The gendered and racialized division of labour becomes an increasingly important issue as greater numbers of women enter the paid labour market. The movement of migrant workers has also increased because of war and social disruption and become easier as a result of (relatively) cheaper travel and the need to move to where jobs are located if workers are to have access to paid work.

Global labour markets: the changing scale of labour processes

Few would disagree with the premise that the world economy today operates within a framework of global labour markets, although the extent to which world markets have *globalized* is nevertheless contested by those who argue that what we have are *globalizing* forces at work, where the processes of the world economy are ongoing, uneven and spatially differentiated, and that there is, instead, a coexistence of internationalization and globalization (Dicken 2003a). The rapid expansion of global trade over the last fifty years has occurred because firms have been able to take advantage of technological developments in transport and communications, which have led to what David Harvey refers to as a process of 'time–space compression' (Harvey 1990): a process readily exemplified by air travel and the Internet (see Chapter 60), which have both reduced the relative distance between places and compressed the relationship between time and space.

Firms have taken advantage of this compression of time and space to re-orientate the way that they organize and structure the labour process. When capital first brought workers into the factory to maximize production and to keep control over the work process as a means of increasing profits, the scale at which production took place was, in general, localized. While raw materials and finished goods were perhaps sourced and sold in distant markets, the process of production in the factory – the labour carried out by workers – tended to be drawn from local sources. These historical geographies of work have left their imprint on the industrial landscapes of the world, from the early textile factories of northern England to the US steel towns of Pittsburgh and Youngstown (Linkon and Russo 2002). These areas were spatially differentiated in a physical sense from other towns by their distinctive factories and steel plants, but also in a social sense by the way that workers developed particular skills required by the work they were expected to perform.

Other disciplines studying the world of work have often paid little attention to the significance of geography in the *production* of industrial space. Yet a basic contention of economic and labour geography is that labour markets and places of work are *actively constructed* by capital and labour who both seek to 'routinize' the social relations necessary for production and reproduction (see Chapter 22). This creation of place and the scale at which the labour process takes place is never static; it continues to shift and evolve in a characteristically uneven form as firms establish themselves, grow, merge and sometimes close according to the requirements of the market and potential for profit. Smith (1984: 99) developed a geographical approach to the theory of uneven development in order to theorize not simply 'the geography of capitalism but also [the] uneven rates of growth between different sectors of the capitalist economy'. As he notes, uneven geographical development has rapidly increased in the post-war period as new markets have been developed and expanded, particularly in the 'global south'.

This can be seen most starkly in developed countries, where the number of routine and 'low-skilled' manufacturing jobs has declined massively since the 1950s, leaving cities like London and New York and older industrial regions as post-industrial production sites (Sassen 1991). Conversely, countries such as Japan, Taiwan, Singapore, Korea, Hong Kong and more recently China have seen a dramatic expansion in labour-intensive, low-technology manufacturing, particularly in garment production and basic product assembly. This uneven development is also expressed in the (re)scaling of the labour process where the various functions of firms have been separated out and distributed locally, regionally, nationally and internationally in order to take advantage of geographically specific and dispersed labour markets. For example, the separation of research and development functions has been a particular feature of the computing and software sector, where 'high tech' computer development companies are clustered around places like Silicon Valley. In places like this employers are able to benefit from the close proximity of similar companies as well as the concentration of skilled labour. Other business functions are then located along 'commodity chains' that, in the case of personal computers, for example, are made up from component parts manufactured throughout the world. But as Walker (2000: 116) notes, 'economic geographers find the linkages binding such production systems to be more significant than the bits and pieces considered separately'. In other words, geographers are interested in the way that capital develops a 'spatial strategy' by using differentiation and difference amongst the labour force to material benefit. A detailed division of labour is therefore designed and constructed in complex hierarchical forms where functions are spread out over place creating an assembly of segmented sub-markets, each having its own geography (Castree *et al.* 2004).

It is these 'spatial divisions of labour' (Massey 1995), mapped according to skills, sector, occupation, power, region, gender, ethnicity, history, etc., which create their own distinct geographical patterns on the landscape – in relation to work and to the reproduction of labour in the home. Yet these are more than mere patterns. The labour process and spatial divisions of labour are, according to Massey, a product of 'stretched out, intersecting' and 'power filled social relations' where capital and labour actively creates space in the organization and living of life (1995: 1). By this she means that there are no pure spatial processes and conversely that there are no non-spatial social processes. It is, therefore, the task of geographers to understand the process through which places and spaces are produced and reproduced.

Producing place: the significance of class, gender, ethnicity and skills in shaping spatial divisions of labour

It was not until the early 1970s that economic geographers turned their thoughts to gender and the differing roles of men and women in the labour market and how these created distinct geographies of employment. Feminists argued that a preoccupation with class relations in employment had tended to ignore other social divisions such as gender and ethnicity and therefore failed to examine the diverse geographical contexts within which women and minority ethnic workers live their lives (Oberhauser 2000). A particular aspect of feminist work has been to highlight the gendered nature of work itself (see Chapters 24 and 62 for further development of these ideas). The traditional image of productive labour – the male manual worker going out to work in mines, docks and large scale factories – is often contrasted with that of reproductive labour, where women remained at home, shopping, cooking, cleaning and looking after children. While this scenario is essentially a myth, as women have always worked outside the home, it is nevertheless true that the twentieth century saw an increase in the number of women in the labour market, such that now in Britain, for example, women constitute half the labour force.

These changes have brought with them a greater interest in the processes shaping the gendered division of paid and unpaid labour (Hanson and Pratt 1995; McDowell 1991, 1997; Pratt 2004). We can see, for example, the gendered nature of the labour process at the scale of the workplace where certain tasks are constructed as 'women's work' and others are the preserve of men. Repetitive production line work has, for example, at times been socially constructed such that women are valued for their 'feminine qualities', their nimble fingers, their ability to do boring repetitive work and the fact that they could be paid less than men

(Pollert 1981). This latter quality has commonly been justified by employers on the basis that men earned the 'family wage' and women worked for 'pin money' or a little extra on top of the husband's wage.

Other writers have described the division of work*space* within factories and how this is imbued with gendered meanings. For example Cavendish's (1982) study of women workers at a factory producing components for the motor industry describes how nearly all the charge-hands were men and that they were divided from the women workers by skill and pay:

> I knew the sexual division would be like that, but it still shook me every day. You would see the differences so clearly on the shop floor: everyone who was working was a woman and the men in the white coats were standing around chatting ... It was obvious that the only qualification you needed for a better job was to be a man.
>
> (Cavendish 1982: 78)

This aspect of the gendered hierarchical scale of work is something examined by McDowell (1997) in a different context in her research into the career histories of merchant bank workers. While these workers are clearly distinguishable by their class status (high paid, middle class, many Oxbridge educated) and location (the City of London), she notes that the deregulation of the financial markets was bringing about changes to work practices, albeit slowly. In narrowing the scale of her study from the City to the firm, McDowell was able to examine the class and gender implications of these changes. As a place, the City of London is characterized in masculine terms: men in smart suits, a heavy drinking culture and the development of career progression through male social networks. Women of the 'right' social class, however, have been able to make inroads as merchant bankers, but to 'fit in' they attempt to do so by becoming 'honorary men', attempting to adopt masculine standards of style and behaviour. Nevertheless, these women are only partially successful. As McDowell (1999: 135) explains, the 'material differences still have an impact and masculine performance by a man is still more highly valorised than that by a woman'. Further, she argues: 'both the external and internal design and layout of the city symbolize male power and authority and men's legitimate occupation of these spaces ... In these spaces, feminine bodies are "out of place" ... the female body is "othered", (McDowell 1999: 145). Thus even in an increasingly feminized labour market, the gendered and spatial segmentation of labour is enduring – both in the workplace and at home.

In spite of the fact that women increasingly have full-time jobs and contribute equally to family finances, most women still find that they undertake the bulk of housework and childcare, which impacts upon the decisions they make when looking for work. In necessitating the construction of 'time–space regimes' – the balance between waged and non-waged work across space – the notion of 'geographical entrapment' is useful in describing women with dependent children who find themselves with a limited travel-to-work area, because of the need to remain in close proximity to home and schools (Castree *et al.* 2004). England (1993: 230), in her research into suburban clerical workers in the US, cautions about a simplistic approach to the spatial entrapment thesis when she argues against the claim that the segregation of some women into 'low-paid, low status waged work means that they are not sufficiently well-paid to "justify" lengthy commutes'. In fact, England found the opposite: women *with* dependent children had longer daily commutes than women *without* children. The 'complex web of socio-spatial relations' meant that working mothers found themselves bound to a particular neighbourhood so that even if their firm were to move some distance, they made a decision to remain and commute rather than move nearer to the job. In England's study, this contrasted with women without children living alone, who had a less complex web of social relations and therefore were more likely to move with the job.

The link between space and daily lives of women workers is therefore complex. It is though, further differentiated by ethnicity throughout the labour market. In successive periods of immigration, different ethnic groups in the UK, for example, have developed distinct spatial patterns of settlement as a result of historical ties, the availability of jobs and housing and cultural, social and ethnic networks (Fryer 1984). For historical reasons, the port areas of Britain are the places where the longest established migrant communities are to be found, but since post-war immigration new geographies of ethnicity have been created (Fieldhouse 1999). During the post-war period, successive ethnic groups established themselves in different regions of the UK, but the majority chose to settle in the south-east.

In the UK, London, as the largest metropolitan area and a point of entry, is the main destination for many overseas migrants. Two-thirds of all foreign workers live in the south-east, with half of these in London itself, demonstrating a distinctively uneven geographical distribution across the UK (Salt and Clarke 2001). Although a common feature of cities, 'ethnic enclaves' are not confined just to neighbourhoods: they are also to be found in labour markets and labour process segmentation, a process that has been ongoing since the time of slavery. In Sassen's (1991) work on the global cities of New York, London and Tokyo, she shows how people from black and minority ethnic groups (and migrants from the global south) are disproportionately concentrated in low-paid manufacturing and service sector jobs, where even second- and third-generation Caribbean and Asian groups remain economically marginalized.

The nature of uneven development can thus be characterized primarily in terms of unequal wealth and class/gender relations, but it is, at the same time, also acutely racialized. Uneven development is, notes Smith (1984: 155) 'social inequality blazoned into the geographical landscape, and is simultaneously the exploitation of that geographical unevenness for socially determined ends'. It is in the nature of capital to contribute to this uneven development, creating social and spatial differentiation between different groups of workers and residents. This unequal spatial distribution results in concentrations of low-paid (and often non-unionized) workers in districts where unemployment and poverty are also greatest. Allen et al. (1998: 105) have described the displacement of social groups by neo-liberal policy as 'spaces of exclusion', which have not only worked themselves out along class and gender lines, but where 'ethnicity and "race" had a central part to play, too'. Capital and neo-liberal policies have created spatial discontinuities between groups of workers, in the type of work undertaken and in areas where black and minority ethnic communities live. This is seen in the spatial distribution of black and minority ethnic *and* migrant communities which, as noted, are particularly marked in parts of London and other global cites.

The patterns of employment undertaken by migrant workers are particularly uneven and, despite popular misconceptions about migrant labour, overall their employment in the UK, for example, is weighted towards jobs at the top end of the labour market. This is unsurprising given the nature of immigration policy, which favours migrants with professional qualifications. Over the last decade, the UK government has adopted a more liberal attitude to (some) migration than previous governments as a result of specific skill shortages and the expansion of key sectors of the economy, but these jobs are of a particular kind. Ninety-six per cent of all work permits issued in 2000 were given to those in managerial positions or in professional and technical occupations, with only a small number going to people in low-paid work. The remaining migrants (including settled communities and those seeking asylum), however, are to be found at the bottom of the income distribution, either in low-paid jobs or unemployed and more likely to be from black and minority ethnic groups. It is this group of migrants who are geographically concentrated in areas of high unemployment and deprivation.

This then reflects socially constructed differences between ethnic groups in different sectors of the labour market. During the recent period of low unemployment in places like London, employers in some sectors, like distribution, hotels and catering, found it difficult to fill vacancies as these jobs often involved low pay and unsociable hours. Consequently, these jobs become unattractive to the 'indigenous' workforce and employers tend to fill them with workers (often recent migrants) who are unable to obtain other work. As Allen *et al.* (1998: 105) point out, an ethnic division of labour has therefore sprung up in places like London, particularly in cleaning work (but also in hotels, retail and catering) where workers are in these jobs 'primarily because of their ethnicity – regardless of their skill capabilities'.

These sectoral patterns of employment can also impact upon patterns of trade unionism. Historical traditions are reflected in the current geographies of trade unionism (Wills 1998) but, as would be expected, changing patterns of work are profoundly important in re-making geographies of labour.

Labour power and workers' organization

In many developed countries, trade union density still to a large extent reflects geographies of previous trade union heartlands, when union strength was concentrated in manufacturing, engineering, mining and dockyards. However, over the last quarter of a century, manufacturing and production in these countries have been in continuous decline, while the largely non-unionized service sector has grown. Public service jobs tend now to be the most highly unionized in these contexts. This has led trade unions to reconsider their approaches and to develop new strategies to recruit from outside traditional constituencies. Capital and labour are engaged in a continuous struggle to shape the landscapes of labour in their own particular interests. Yet these struggles take place not only between capital and labour, but also between workers and employers as they seek to gain advantage over weaker sections of the labour market:

> There can be bitter conflicts between groups of workers as well as between capital and labour as the working class is torn between the contradictory pressures of homo-genization (which sets it against capital), and differentiation (which sets different factions of it against one another).
>
> (Hudson 2001: 225)

At the heart of this contradictory pressure is the issue of power. When strong, workers and their trade unions can exert pressure to gain concessions from employers by the threat of withholding their labour or engaging in other forms of industrial action. When weak, there is a tendency for workers (and unions) to seek to defend their own workplaces or industries at the expense of other workers in other places. And, in the worst circumstances, workers can resort to sexism, racism and xenophobia as a means of defending jobs locally that they identify as their own. As noted in the examples at the beginning of this chapter, the movement of jobs to different places (particularly to the 'global south') is often a source of conflict between sections of the world's working class.

This conflict and the power battles between labour and capital have become of particular interest to geographers in recent decades (Herod 1997, 1998; Massey and Painter 1989). While early studies focused on how geographies of labour were constructed, latterly there has been a shift of focus to studying the *production* of 'labour geographies' – a subtle change of discourse, perhaps, but one which suggests the ascription of causal power to workers as *active* geographical agents, rather than as passive occupiers of space and place as (pre)-determined by capital. As Herod (1997: 2) has pointed out, workers have a 'vested interest in attempting to make space in certain ways' in an attempt not only to defend their working conditions, but to 'ensure their self reproduction and ultimately, survival'. Put another way:

> locations that, for capital, are a (temporary) space for profitable production, are for workers, their families and friends, places in which to live; places in which they have considerable individual and collective cultural investment; places to which they are often deeply attached.
>
> (Peck 1996: 13)

This attachment to place is sometimes seen as a barrier to workers' power in their struggle against capital, yet workers, as well as capital, are capable of developing their own 'spatial strategies' by up-scaling their activities to challenge exploitation. In cases where there is a geographical embeddedness to capital, such as mining or extraction, it is sometimes found that trade unionism is at its strongest. Coal miners in Britain were, until the closures of most of the pits in the 1980s and 1990s, seen as the most militant and organized group of union members in the country. Located in small mining villages, these groups of workers had a social and cultural cohesiveness from which a long historical tradition of high union density had developed. Because of this and the inherently place-based nature of industrial action, they were able to draw upon local support networks in the community in order to sustain strikes and disputes.

So, too, dockworkers are noted for their militancy, but added to this is the often international dimension to their industrial action. As a result of the nature of work undertaken in docks and ports, international connections are made across the world by seafarers, who not only travel overseas but also may remain in other countries in order to continue their trades. Consequently, place-based disputes in one locality can quickly develop an international dimension as other workers add their support to local actions. This 'up-scaling' of labour action or solidarity is evident in a number of high-profile disputes. For example, Castree (2000) recounts the story of the Liverpool dock dispute where 350 dockers were 'locked out' by their employer. He also charts the action the workers took in an attempt to regain their jobs. By sending union delegations from Liverpool to ports around the world, workers managed to co-ordinate international action around the world to boycott Liverpool-bound ships.

In another example, Herod (2001) describes how longshore workers in the US went about constructing new scales of labour relations to respond to technical innovations such as containerization. After a long struggle, the International Longshoremen's Association (ILA) agreed in 1971 to an industry-wide contract to conduct national bargaining. Yet during the 1980s this broke down as dockers in the Gulf and South Atlantic became convinced that local bargaining might serve their interests better, while North Atlantic dockers saw the national agreement as a way of preventing the transfer of their jobs to cheaper southern ports. In the end, the ILA negotiated a solution that took on board the concerns of all union members in the different localities. As Herod explains:

The union's pursuit of an explicitly geographical strategy to address the issues of job security and income maintenance for dockers not only highlights a particular sensitivity to the spatial restructuring of the industry and the geographical diversity of conditions found throughout East Coast ports, but it also suggests that rank-and-filers and union officials were acutely aware that space and scale can be shaped in particular ways to serve political end economic ends.

(Herod 2001: 124)

The important point evident in these two examples is that the scale at which action should be taken to defend working conditions is always relative and contingent. In most cases, worker or union activity will be place-based – often the place of work – but, as noted earlier, the increasing scale(s) of economic activity sometimes demands that new spatial structures are developed by labour to counter the power of capital's (often) superior command of space. One way this is achieved is through the development of international organizations. The International Confederation of Free Trade Unions (representing most national trade union centres), the Global Union Federations (international representatives of unions organizing in specific industry sectors or occupational groups) and the more anarchic groupings that came together in the protests against the World Trade Organization in Seattle and other places, all represent differently scaled organizations, formed to challenge capital and defend workers' rights (see Chapters 18–24 for more in-depth considerations of the scalar politics of action).

'From the local to the global' is a phrase often used to evoke the need to upscale worker action to respond to increasing globalization. Yet the process is more dialectical than the phrase suggests. It is not linear or simple and depends on the historical, geographical and economic situation in which workers find themselves. This may involve a complex mix of organizing approaches – some local, some global, but not necessarily in that order. As Waterman (2001: 118) explains: 'Indeed, the very significance of economic, political, geographical and other contingencies in any particular dispute means that there cannot ever be a single formulaic guide to workers' praxis.'

The nature of some global companies can often be brought to a standstill by intensely *local* actions. The example of a protest at the Flint General Motors plant in Michigan, USA, is a case in point that shows the power of the local in a global economy. The company used 'just in time' (JIT) production (a form of lean production which minimizes waste and the stockpiling of components while at the same time maximizing labour production by team working and the allocation of work to exploit the strengths of different workforces by using a system of continent-wide production). But workers subverted this process for their own benefit. When 3,400 workers went on strike to protest about the company's efforts to change local working rules, a further 2,800 workers had to be laid off by the company because of JIT production. Within two weeks 121 assembly and component plants had partially or totally closed through lack of work, resulting in over 100,000 workers being laid off (see Waterman 2001 for full discussion of this dispute).

The example of the dispute at the Ravenswood Aluminium Corporation, also in the US, is a further example of a local dispute taking on a global dimension. The United Steel Workers of America used connections between the plant, its owner and his connections with the international commodity trades to execute a well-organized global campaign to resolve a particularly local dispute. By linking up with the International Metal Workers' Federation, the International Confederation of Free Trade Unions (ICFTU) and unions throughout the world, they were able to get their concerns heard at a global scale by persuading supporters to take action in twenty-eight countries.

As such, globalization can bring with it a number of paradoxes and contradictions for workers: on the one hand there is the evident power of global capital which can undermine workers' own sense of power. But as these examples show, workers who are able to understand and tap into global networks and resources can also use them to their own benefit. The shrinking globe may lead to greater competition between places and workers as many spatial barriers are dismantled, but at the same time it may also facilitate greater contact between workers and allies in the anti-capitalist movements, particularly where trade unions have found it difficult to establish themselves in developing countries. Here, it has been non-governmental organizations (sometimes with trade unions) that have come together to form alliances to campaign for labour rights. The international anti-sweatshop movement – campaigning against conditions in the apparel industry – has grown significantly in recent years, helped by greater access to the Internet and email, which have facilitated the development of non-union struggles where students, campaigners *and* workers have taken the opportunity to build world-wide campaigns against global companies such as Nike and Gap. United Students Against Sweatshops, for example, have taken on US university administrators, demanding they be accountable to the conditions of workers who produce goods for the university, and this campaign has spread to over a hundred campuses. Such campaigns are replicated throughout the world in other sectors.

Developing a geographical imagination to understand the labour process and the response of workers to changing patterns of work

Although some writers have argued that unions need to 'enlarge the playing field' upon which trade unions organize (Wever 1998), understanding different scalar strategies has not been a major feature of other academic fields. For example, the importance of developing an appropriate scale at which to organize workers is something that has been given little consideration in recent debates around union revitalization. Despite trade unions being geographically constituted, mostly structured on a national, regional and local base, the reasoning behind these spatial arrangements is more often to do with historical legacy than any contemporary rationale. While there may still be many reasons for continuing with these particular forms of scalar organizations, examples given in this chapter and elsewhere suggest that unions and workers' organizations perhaps need to reconsider how their spatially constituted structural forms affect their overall approaches to organizing workers in changing and globalizing labour markets.

In contrast to traditional industrial relations and labour process approaches, geographers (as might be expected) have talked about the need to develop more 'spatially sophisticated' understandings of modern capital. These concerns have included the need to create new and more appropriate scales of collective bargaining that are able to match changes in global markets. Countering the growth of multinational corporations and contingent urban labour markets that are less based around the work*place* is another important research focus. Furthermore, as Herod *et al.* (2003: 176) have explained:

> Axiomatic for labour geographers is the claim that spatial factors – such as the inescapably uneven geographical development of capitalist economies, the geographical scale and scope of legislation, the role of distinctive regional 'cultures' of industrial relations practices, the structure and dynamics of local labour markets, the spatial hierarchies of trade union organization, the locally-differentiated processes of social reproduction,

gender and race relations, the shifting landscape of political activism and labour-orga-
nizational capacities – really *matter* in the practice of industrial relations and in the
trajectories of workplace politics.

The point being made here is that neither workers nor capital are passive in the geographies
of labour relations: both actively construct the world around us. The control of space and
place is thus crucial to the way that jobs are exported, created, lost and fought over. As
Hudson (2001) puts it, capital can be thought of as trying to *disorganize* labour by means of
segmenting the labour market (by place, gender, ethnicity, etc.) whereas labour seeks to
organize (through trade unions and other worker organizations) in order to improve conditions. It is impossible to fully understand the dynamics of such struggles without consideration of how capital seeks its 'spatial fix' and at the same time developing an understanding of
the geographical contexts within which workers live their lives.

Further reading

Castree, N., Coe, N., Ward, K. and Samers, M. (2004) *Spaces of Work*. London: Sage.
Dicken, P. (2003a) *Global Shift: Reshaping the Global Economic Map in the 21st Century*. London: Sage.
Herod, A. (2001) *Labour Geographies: Workers and the Landscapes of Capitalism*. New York: Guilford.
Hudson, R. (2001) *Producing Places*. London: Guilford.
McDowell, L. (1997) *Capital Culture. Gender at Work in the City*. Oxford: Blackwell.
Treanor, J. (2004) Union pickets HSBC over plan to move jobs abroad. *Guardian* 29 September.

References

Allen, J., Massey, D. and Cockrane, A. (1998) *Rethinking the Region: Spaces of Neo-liberalism*. London:
    Routledge.
Bain, P. and Taylor, P. (2004) No passage to India? UK unions, globalisation and the migration of call
    centre jobs. Presented at Work, Employment and Society Conference, 1–3 September 2004,
    Manchester University.
Cacanas, Z. and Collinson, P. (2003) The Indian takeaway based on Big Mac salaries. *Guardian* 6
    December.
Castree, N. (2000) Geographical scale and grassroots internationalism: the Liverpool dock dispute
    1995–98. *Economic Geography* 76 (3), 272–92.
Castree, N., Coe, N., Ward, K. and Samers, M. (2004) *Spaces of Work*. London: Sage.
Cavendish, R. (1982) *Women on the Line*. London: Routledge and Kegan Paul.
Dicken, P. (2003a) *Global Shift: Reshaping the Global Economic Map in the 21st Century*. London: Sage.
——(2003b) 'Placing' firms: grounding the debate on the 'global' corporation. In J. Peck and H. Wai-chung
    Yeung (eds) *Remaking the Global Economy*, pp. 27–44. London: Sage.
England, K. (1993) Suburban pink collar ghettos: the spatial entrapment of women? *Annals of the
    Association of American Geographers* 83 (2), 225–42.
ETI (2005) http://www.ethicaltrade.org/ (accessed 11 September 2005).
Fieldhouse, E.A. (1999) Ethnic minority unemployment and spatial mismatch: the case of London.
    Urban Studies 36 (9), 1569–1999.
Fryer, P. (1984) *Staying Power. The History of Black People in Britain*. London: Pluto Press.
Hanson, S. and Pratt, G. (1995) *Gender, Work and Space*. London: Routledge.
Harvey, D. (1990) *The Condition of Postmodernity: An Enquiry into the Origins of Cultural Change*. Oxford:
    Blackwell.

Herod, A. (1997) From a geography of labor to a labor of geography: labor's spatial fix and the geography of capitalism. *Antipode* 29 (1), 1–31.

——(1998) *Organizing the Landscape. Geographical Perspectives on Labor Unionism*. Minneapolis: University of Minnesota.

——(2001) *Labour Geographies: Workers and the Landscapes of Capitalism*. New York: Guilford.

Herod, A., Peck, J. and Wills, J. (2003) Geography and industrial relations. In P. Ackers and A. Wilkinson (eds) *Understanding Work and Employment: Industrial Relations in Transition*, pp. 176–94. Oxford: Oxford University Press.

Hudson, R. (2001) *Producing Places*. London: Guilford.

Linkon, S. and Russo, J. (2002) Reading the landscape: conflict and the production of place. In S. Linkon and J. Russo (eds) *Steel Town USA: Work and Memory in Youngstown*, pp. 9–66. Kansas: University of Kansas Press.

McDowell, L. (1991) Life without father or Ford: the new gender order of post-Fordism. *Transactions of the Institute of British Geographers* 26 (4), 448–64.

——(1997) *Capital Culture. Gender at Work in the City*. Oxford: Blackwell.

——(1999) *Gender, Identity and Place: Understanding Feminist Geographies*. Cambridge, UK: Polity Press.

Massey, D. (1995) *Spatial Divisions of Labour*. London: Macmillan.

Massey, D. and Painter, J. (1989) The changing geography of trade unions. In J. Mohan (ed.) *The Political Geography of Contemporary Britain*. London: Macmillan.

Nasscom (2005) *Strategic Review, 2005: The IT Industry in India*. New Delhi: Nasscom.

Oberhauser, A. (2000) Feminism and economic geography: gendering work and working gender. In E. Sheppard and T. Barnes (eds) *A Companion to Economic Geography*, pp. 5–76. Oxford: Blackwell.

Peck, J. (1996) *Work-place: The Social Regulation of Labor Markets*. London: Guilford.

Pollert, A. (1981) *Girls, Wives, Factory Lives*. London: Macmillan.

Pratt, G. (2004) *Working Feminisms*. Philadelphia: Temple University Press.

Salt, J. and Clarke, J. (2001) Foreign labour in the United Kingdom: patterns and trends. *Labour Market Trends* October, 473–83.

Sassen, S. (1991) *The Global City: New York, London, Tokyo*. Princeton: Princeton University Press.

Smith, N. (1984) *Uneven Development*. Oxford: Blackwell.

Taylor, P. and Bain, P. (2004) Call centre offshoring to India: the revenge of history? *Labour and Industry* 14 (3), 15–38.

——(2005a) India calling to the far away towns: the call centre labour process and globalisation. *Work, Employment and Society* 19 (2), 261–82.

——(2005b) Work organisation and employee relations in Indian call centres. In J. Burgess and J. Connell (eds) *Developments in the Call Centre Industry: Analysis, Policy and Challenges*. London: Routledge.

Tran, M. (2002) Dyson to shift manufacturing operations to Asia. *Guardian* 5 February.

——(2004) From Bangalore to Bucharest. *Guardian* 16 August.

UNI Finance (2004) http://www.union-network.org/unifinance.nsf (accessed 18 August 2005).

Walker, R. (2000) The geography of production. In E. Sheppard and T. Barnes (eds) *A Companion to Economic Geography*, pp. 113–31. Oxford: Blackwell.

Waterman, P. (2001) Trade union internationalism in the age of Seattle. In P. Waterman and J. Wills (eds) *Place, Space and the New Labour Internationalisms*, pp. 8–32. Oxford: Blackwell.

Wever, K. (1998) International labor revitilization: enlarging the playing field. *Industrial Relations* 37, 358–407.

Wills, J. (1998) Space, place and tradition in working-class organization. In A. Herod (ed.) *Organizing the Landscape. Geographical Perspectives on Labor Unionism*, pp. 129–58. Minneapolis: University of Minnesota.

56

Competing for power

Making local places in a global world

Simon Dalby

Geopolitics

Geopolitics is about the struggle to control spaces, dominate trade routes and ensure a form of order favourable to those who strive for global power. Geopolitical change may be read as an outcome of a competitive process in which different actors engage and from which flow social, economic and environmental processes. Geopolitical thinking and action is also about knowledge. It relates how political elites conceptualize and enact their interests and identities in a world of competing political and economic agencies. This concerns how political realities are defined and controlled to facilitate certain types of action (Ó Tuathail and Agnew 1992). The categories them and us, rich and poor, peaceful and violent enter into political debate and are used to justify foreign policy and military activities (Agnew 2003; Ó Tuathail 1996).

Just as elites attempt to control the terms of debate and the practical arrangements of politics and economics, so those subject to these arrangements may resist and invoke different identities and interests as alternatives. These may legitimize struggles against hegemonic power and empires. Local virtue is frequently depicted as the antithesis to perceived evils of foreign rule. Discourses of nationalism and regional cultural identity are frequently mobilized in struggles for self-determination. But, as recent scholarship in geopolitics has made abundantly clear, the specification of who is entitled to determine their own future is part of the construction of political discourse in the first place. Constructing identities as exclusive and insisting on their controlling territory can be a violent practice, as the wars in the Balkans in the 1990s showed (Campbell 1998).

In the aftermath of the cold war, in an era frequently specified in terms of globalization, these issues are now complicated by the global war on terror. New political specifications of dangers and new antagonists have been identified. The American state in particular has been quick to invoke the logic of the war on terror to encourage counter-insurgency operations in many places, most notably in parts of Russia, India and Indonesia. We need to understand how geographical identities are invoked in struggles against the encroachment of global corporations. We need to explore the contexts of opposition in rural areas where indigenous peoples and nomadic cultures still try to maintain traditional ways. Here too, however, what is classed as indigenous is not nearly so simple as assumptions of regional separation and autonomous cultures have all too frequently suggested.

One of the greatest difficulties in understanding contemporary geopolitics stems from the fact that hegemonic, dominant political scripts result from narratives written by the winners. But the history of the last few hundred years has also been about opposition to imperial power and the construction of national and local identities in the face of dominant colonial or multinational discourse. Indeed, many political struggles, not least in Europe after the end of the Cold War, and across the globe in response to globalization, are much more interesting when alternative possibilities are explored, instead of taking hegemonic representations and structures for granted.

In short, the terms of political discourse are contested in many ways and those that are dominant can change very quickly indeed in a crisis situation, as 11 September 2001 illustrated (Dalby 2003). Likewise, it is not always clear which key political texts will emerge to mobilize support in a crisis and then shape subsequent institutions.

The rest of this chapter suggests that moments of geopolitical transition are matters, in part, of this clash of geopolitical scripts. It explores differing approaches to this placing of power, contrasting global scales of analysis implicit in much of the literature with more local political action. It also suggests that geopolitics is about accommodation and resistance too, and that politics emerges at a variety of scales where identities are invoked in many different ways. The political process creates its own very distinct geographies.

Key to much of this geopolitical discourse is the invocation of threats to identity, and the insistence on institutions to secure an order that keeps these threats at bay. My argument starts with charting the progress of geopolitical change.

Geopolitical change

The recent history of the world exemplifies the contested nature of geopolitical categories and simultaneously shows how conflict shapes geographies in an increasingly interconnected world. The end of the Cold War in Europe opened up all sorts of possibilities for rethinking the space that could then once again be called Europe; indeed, activists in the 1980s explicitly demanded such a possibility in the face of the superpower division of the continent. But once the Cold War ended there was an intense debate about the future of Europe that was in large part about the geographical construction of security and political order. The emergence of the subsequent geopolitical order in the 1990s did not play out exactly as any of the scenarios discussed in the immediate aftermath of the collapse of the Berlin Wall suggested. Struggles over identity and notions of place were key to both analysis and policy prescription.

Through the 1990s increasing protests occurred against the international institutions implicated in the processes of globalization, and in particular against institutions that implemented and enforced neo-liberal agendas of business-led globalization (see Chapter 57). This led to protests and opposition that challenged the agenda of corporate leadership at international summit meetings, and led to numerous initiatives on the part of civil society. Most recently the geopolitical map has once again shifted in the aftermath of the events of 11 September 2001 (Dalby 2003). The remilitarization of international relations by the US in response to what it specified as the 'war' on terror, and its invasion of Iraq in the face of considerable international opposition, suggests the military dominance of the superpower, but also the political limitations of military action in conquering and pacifying places far from home.

While much of geopolitics has been concerned with global power and the invocation of geographical depictions of the world to justify military action and political manoeuvring, it is important to recognize that power may also be inscribed at smaller scales by more local communities and invoke richly variable national and ethnic specifications of identity. Most nationalist struggles aim to remove foreign troops and rule from local soil, a form of 'anti-geopolitics' that disputes imperial claims by invoking authentic locality. But nationalisms can also be about the imposition of rule on other people's territory, frequently justified by some claim to antecedent possession. It is also important to note that definitions of what is local are frequently a matter of specific connections to events far away, rather than a matter of things that happen within a small geographical radius. Identity is frequently constructed by the intersection of stories in particular locales, rather than just by the invocation of locality. Local struggles are often inspired by examples from elsewhere which provide a repertoire of slogans, arguments and tactics. In short, geopolitics is about geographical reasoning in political debate at many *different* scales.

To illustrate this argument, this chapter looks back to the end of the Cold War. It describes opposition to nuclear weapons systems and to the division of the continent, from activists on both sides of the geopolitical divide. Invoking a renewed notion of Europe, they argued against the presence of both superpowers in the continent, insisting instead that Europe should be freed from the weapons of cold war and allowed to decide its own fate, without the military presence of either the Soviet Union or the United States. But as the Cold War ended and the geopolitical divide was removed it wasn't at all clear what kind of a place this new Europe should, could or would become. Much of the debate was about how the new Europe should be conceptualized and whence threats to this identity might arise, a long theme in geopolitical thinking (Heffernan 1998).

Subsequently much of the discussion about geopolitics has been around globalization and resistance to change in specific places. Geopolitical reasoning has also been invoked in suggesting changes to the new international order of neo-liberalism, global media and consumption culture. It has also been tied into different state adaptations to these new circumstances, in terms of administrative changes to the new political economy and to the appropriation of universal political motifs to promote local and particular political agendas. Struggling to gain local control over the economic benefits of globalization has produced all sorts of local identities claiming all sorts of grievances and rights, nowhere more clearly than in the tragic case of the Nigerian state (Watts 2004).

In each of these cases what is key to understanding the political debates is the specification of the appropriate geographical terms for the discussion. Fixing appropriate geographies defines the terms of the agenda and impels us to discuss certain desirable outcomes, such as aspirations for autonomy, a desire for inclusion, or other local forms of conduct.

Geography matters in political discourse. But the crucial point is that this is a much more complicated process than is usually recognized and that the task of critical geopolitics has been to contest the taken-for-granted geographical assumptions. In so doing we can show how the unquestioned and taken-for-granted geopolitical categories of political discourse are important in arguments over identity. These processes are frequently clear in times of rapid geopolitical change and rarely more dramatic than the events at the end of the Cold War in Europe in the late 1980s and early 1990s.

Europe after the Cold War

The Cold War division of the continent was unacceptable to many Europeans, including dissidents on both sides of the divide who argued for a Europe 'beyond the blocs'. Dissenting discourses were important to any discussion about European identity, not least because they clearly showed the margins of conventional cold war discourses, but also because they pointed to the possibilities of alternative geopolitical arrangements with new identities and criteria for patrolling the geographical and ideological frontiers of a post-cold war world (Dalby 1991).

Most prominent among dissenting political voices were the intellectuals and dissidents connected, albeit sometimes rather loosely, with the European Nuclear Disarmament (END), the Dutch IKV organization and groups like Charta 77 in Czechoslovakia. END coalesced initially in Britain but their 'END Appeal' of 1980 was widely circulated (Thompson and Smith, 1980). The analysis in this appeal focused on dangers of nuclear arms build-ups and how the superpower competition functioned to maintain a divided Europe dominated by superpowers. The END appeal called for Europeans on both sides of the geopolitical divide to resist these arrangements and to act as though the division had been transcended. Its prefigurative strategy pointed to the possibilities of re-imagining Europe beyond the geopolitical divide, as a place in which a democratic civil society allowed for the discussion of political matters beyond the intrusion of state power.

In Eastern Europe these themes met with considerable scepticism amongst dissidents. They were suspicious of appeals to peace, and often saw the West with its military potential as an ally in their struggle for increased freedom. But the analysis did strike a chord with at least some of the subsequent leaders of the social movements active in the collapse of the communist regimes in 1989. Among others, George Konrad's (1984) *Antipolitics* and Vaclav Havel's (1990) writings on 'the politics of the powerless' were broadly congruent with de-alignment, with the democratization of security and with the dismantling of war machines and instruments of repression. At the end of the 1980s bloc divisions rapidly gave way in Europe and the Berlin Wall was pulled down.

But while the Cold War division had rapidly unravelled, at the time it was not at all clear what the future of an entity called Europe might look like. This emphasizes that the invocation of a geographical term as simple and supposedly obvious as Europe is a powerful political act. It is so precisely because one simply cannot take its meaning for granted. At least four loose scenarios were discussed as politicians and pundits, not to mention activists in the streets, tried to promote their vision of the future for the continent, defining the local at a continental scale (Buzan *et al.* 1990; Hyde-Price 1991).

Three Europes

The first scenario suggested that American influence would continue to decline and that European integration would stall. In these eventualities Europe might become a continent dominated by a small number of rival powers. Mearsheimer's (1990) pessimistic assessment of 'Back to the Future' suggested a reassertion of traditional European politics, with clashing military forces and partisan political ambitions searching for of national aggrandizement. The upsurge of nationalist rhetoric once the Soviet forces were withdrawn from former Eastern European nations suggested that nationalism remained a potent political force. The most obvious contenders for dominance were Germany, France and, in the long run, Russia (Buzan *et al.* 1990). German economic power, after the painful indigestion of the 1990 *Anschluss* had been overcome, was viewed as a possible hegemonic force. Fear of this result spurred many advocates of closer European integration to argue that further institutional links were needed to curtail German power by institutional entanglement. A French leadership role in the Western European Union, based in part on its nuclear arsenal and the absence of an American presence on the continent, might make the British and Russians decidedly nervous. Finally, a revived Russian presence was also a possibility, although in the short and medium term any military threat from that quarter seemed unlikely given its internal political and economic problems.

A second scenario suggested that Europe could remain part of an Atlanticist world order, becoming a second 'pillar' of the 'new world order', with Japan possibly forming a third. The attraction of membership in such an order was clear to policymakers in Eastern Europe as, to the dismay of some peace activists in END and the subsequent Helsinki Citizens' Assembly (Kaldor 1991), former dissidents turned politicians and then advocated the retention of the NATO alliance as a useful anchor for future East European security arrangements, possibly formulated around a redesigned Conference on Security Cooperation in Europe (CSCE) process (Dientsbier 1991). The geopolitical construction here is clearly between stability and economic progress on the one hand, and instability and economic chaos on the other hand; Europe supported by NATO is understood in antithesis to nationalist parochialism and militarist ambition.

In making the arguments for the reformulation of NATO rather than allowing its termination, Manfred Worner, then NATO's secretary general, constructed a role in which the institution expanded its mandate to one of global management of 'threats' to the Western dominated world order (Worner 1991), comprising instabilities and also global environmental threats emanating from the 'third world'. Once again geopolitical understandings of security contrast domestic political identity with perceived external threats that need to be deterred and controlled, if necessary, by military force.

In this scenario, however, non-Western states and instabilities are the threat to the political order of modernity. As it turned out, this was in some ways prescient, although no-one in the early 1990s would have predicted that a decade later the NATO treaty would be invoked after the 11 September 2001 attacks in Washington and New York and that as a consequence NATO troops would be dispatched to – of all places – Afghanistan.

A third scenario for geopolitical realignment after the Cold War was the rise of a European superpower after a successful Maastricht Treaty and subsequent integration of European defence and security planning, through either a revamped Western European Union (WEU) or some other organization. Such a European superpower could all too easily become engaged in economic rivalry with the USA and Japan. The prospect of a militarized version of the European community intervening in either the Middle East or Africa in search of oil supplies or political influence is a theme that worried critics of European militarism during the Cold War (Kaldor and Falk 1987). Coupled to xenophobic fears of Islamic influences within Europe, the spectre of a new version of European imperialism, buttressed with geopolitical rationales for interventionism premised on a revived 'Orientalism', gave cause for concern to critics of European integration that were subsequently in part borne out in the aftermath of 11 September.

In both of these latter cases, the boundary lines between Europe and 'not-Europe' had fairly clear geopolitical demarcations, albeit ones of economic criteria and tariff walls rather than military fortifications. The liminal group here, those on the boundary of inclusion and exclusion, might well be the states of Eastern Europe, doomed to peripheral status if they failed to remake their economies quickly. Russia and Turkey were clearly outside this project. Turkey was the only NATO member with a dominant Islamic tradition. It was a state with a decidedly 'undemocratic' record, and historical rivalries with Greece and Bulgaria. It had, however, often aspired to EEC membership. Important too are the questions of how 'Others' – migrants, ethnic minorities and refugees – within the boundaries of what was

917

then still the EEC, might be treated: as welcome guests and participating social groups, or as potentially subversive elements to be monitored, policed and controlled by authoritarian apparatuses (Bunyan 1991) (see Chapter 58).

Each of these three scenarios suggested a traditional 'realist' interpretation of future possibilities, in which territorial control of demarcated spaces within boundaries would be controlled by military power. What matters in this debate is where the boundaries might be, and at what scale this mode of organizing political space would occur. Each of these three scenarios assumed that the clashing spaces of geopolitical rivalry would continue to dominate European politics and possible futures. Tragically these modes of reasoning did play out, but only in Yugoslavia (Campbell 1998).

These three scenarios may, however, be contrasted with a fourth that directly challenges assumptions of territorial sovereignty and border controls with a rethought notion of security dependent less on borders and force and more on common actions. These actions might be designed to protect a more inclusive political order, through a process of demilitarization.

Demilitarizing Europe?

The fourth 'alternative security' scenario was short of advocates among the political decision-makers of most European states in the early 1990s. It was, however, considered possible, despite the power and influence of business elites in contemporary European politics (Ross 1992). This scenario envisaged a revitalization of cooperative and common security themes, and an enlargement of trans-boundary civil society which dissident intellectuals and activists established in the late 1980s (Federowicz 1991; Kaldor 1991; Spencer 1991). Drawing on the experience of the Conference on Security and Cooperation in Europe (CSCE), the recent Conventional Forces in Europe arms control agreements, strategic arms reductions and the Helsinki Accords, which established commonly agreed political standards of conduct and provided fora to negotiate political solutions to potentially troublesome conflicts, this liberal internationalist position pointed to the collective benefits of demilitarization and the possibilities of common security (Booth 1990). A possible more militarized variation on this theme pointed to limiting national states to 'non-offensive defence' forces, while a pan-European multinational 'police force' offered the possibility of military intervention in the event of internal turbulence or a clear common external threat (Moller 1992).

This fourth scenario, derived in part from the peace movement's programmes and ideas articulated by more progressive political forces, suggested that the opportunity presented by the end of the Cold War allowed politicians to rethink security drastically. Specifically it implied a resistance to exclusionist ideologies and imposed military solutions in the form of intervention or deterrence against external threats (Booth 1991; Campbell 1993). The CSCE process, the 'anti-geopolitical' arguments of END and, to a certain degree, Gorbachev's notions of a common European home, suggested down-playing military roles and shifting the geopolitical horizon to one informed by environmental and global considerations (Tairov 1991). There were few places for external threats. Geopolitical distinctions are replaced with analyses of militarization and the dangers of reliance on violence in the face of the new threats to human society. In particular, such thinking required taking seriously the political, economic and environmental difficulties in Eastern Europe, as a part of a common European security project (Schneider 1991; ZumBrunnen 1992). In these formulations aid and political and economic cooperation were more important than military preparation.

While some aspects of all these scenarios have played out, the point to be drawn from this analysis of discussions of post-Cold War possibilities in Europe is that there were a *variety* of options available. The future of the continent was not clear, and in the rhetorical battle specific visions of the kind of place Europe ought to be played an important part of the debate. Invoking a form of locality was central to articulation of alternatives; identity at a continental level was a rhetorical resource of considerable importance that challenged simplistic assumptions of an expanded NATO, or Western European or American expansion of control over the territory of the former Warsaw Pact states. Nonetheless, these states have gradually joined Western institutions, security alliances and the now enlarged European Union. They have, however, joined whilst being subjected to repeated discourses of othering, in which their non-Western Europeanness was portrayed as making them less than fully European (Kuus 2004a).

However, some of the peace movement's fondest hopes were partly realized by default. European states simply do not wish to spend large amounts of money on military matters, and hence cooperative security policies and substantial demilitarization have occurred, or at least in comparison to cold war levels of expenditure. Events in the Balkans in the 1990s and the American war against terror have challenged the tendency to de-militarization, but nonetheless Europe is less militarized now than it used to be. The possibility of war between its major states is now nearly unthinkable, given the integration of Europe's institutions and economy. Nonetheless, nationalist sentiments continue to be an important factor in European politics, especially when mobilized against the seemingly impenetrable bureaucracy in Brussels, by local politicians anxious to build careers on the European stage. More worryingly these sentiments have also increasingly been launched against immigrants from outside the continent (Dijkink 1996). These immigrants, most of whom end up in large urban centres, are very much part of the processes of globalization that fundamentally challenge the geographical categories of contemporary politics (Gupta 2005). A second set of contexts is needed to explore how geopolitics is played out at a more global scale.

Glurbanization

The contemporary human condition is increasingly urban. Resources to feed and fuel what can now be termed 'the global city' are the product of practices of what might best be termed 'glurbanization', and come from all over the world (see Chapter 58). Tourists and remittance payments flow back to the more rural parts of the globe, enmeshing agricultural zones into the global economy. We are now an urban species and have wired and paved the planet to move food, timber, oil, electricity, minerals and all sorts of commodities from the rural areas into these burgeoning cities (Dicken 2003). In a way analogous to earlier imperial arrangements, the flow of commodities inevitably disrupts traditional forms of economic life (see Chapter 53). Just as wheat flowed from Africa to Rome, so now does oil flow from the Middle East to other parts of the new imperium. Being networked in many parts of the world means being tied into patterns of commodity extraction (Hugill 1999). The Roman Empire built roads to facilitate communications and integrate the empire into an efficient network of supplies and military preparation, and modern states and global corporations also create infrastructure. Communications systems, media, the Internet and phone systems now link people all over the planet: a sense of 'globality' is part of the identity politics of the new millennium.

The global has also spawned a process in and of itself, simply called globalization. This term came to prominence in the aftermath of the Cold War. It rapidly displaced earlier specifications of contemporary social circumstances. It implied connections and cultural homogeneity, while occluding specific local patterns of change. It supposedly promised much but prevented most people from actually doing anything about how their circumstances changed as a result of its planet-spanning processes.

Inevitable change followed: cultural transformation, connections to a rapidly shrinking world where everything was speeding up, territorial boundaries repeatedly transgressed. All these features of the new age were expressed breathlessly by commentators and academics caught up in the new networks of instant exchange and communication. Novelty, acceleration and connection, a sense of the planet as a single place enhanced by communication technology, and humanity as sharing a common fate emerged in these discourses. Ways of life were determined increasingly by business rather than the nation-state, or so the narrative went. All these sorts of ideas encapsulate meanings imputed to 'the global' (Scholte 2000). All of these generalizations are open to numerous empirical critiques given their degree of generality (see Chapters 12 and 60 for further consideration of these issues).

Ideological disputation followed, from those who understand the global as a powerful discursive device in the hands of corporations and their state backers who conflate contemporary neo-liberal policies with a supposedly unstoppable and inevitable 'global' process of economic, political, cultural and social change. But the dimension of this being a single place is crucial to the geopolitical designation of the current period as one of globalization.

The invocation of cosmopolitan ideas as the universal human condition also suggests a global politics (Archibugi 2003) that draws on histories of liberal internationalism. But this cosmopolitanism is very much for the urban citizen, the person tied into the global circuits of capital and the long commodity chains that supply the metropolitan world with commodities and status symbols that make universal civilization possible. This invocation of global citizenship also links to the struggles of social movements in Eastern Europe in the 1980s and elsewhere, where movements called for political liberty and the extension of democratic rights. It does so in insisting on the universal as the appropriate category for political action in favour of human rights and economic liberty.

Glocalization

A sense of a unique place is also frequently described as local resistance to globalization in one form or another. Localities are invoked frequently in these discussions. The precise nature of locality is highly variable. Opposition to economic globalization gathered force in the 1990s and had a highly visible presence at a number of world trade organization meetings and summit meetings of political leaders. It has been rather more subdued since 11 September 2001, although the movement was reborn in the form of world-wide opposition to the American invasion of Iraq in 2003 and in the protests at the G8 meetings in July 2005. Nonetheless, the anti-globalization movement raises many important questions about how geopolitics is now conceptualized. The local and the global are two rather difficult political categories to specify, and there is a huge irony in the presence of such an entity as a global anti-globalization movement.

Universality and a supposed common human fate are key themes in the globalization debate, but these have run into opposition in many locales (Klein 2002). In part this is because social and economic changes inevitably have variable consequences in particular places. Some of these universal concerns focus on technical issues such as genetically modified foods and attempts by corporations to impose such technologies on farmers.

920

Elsewhere the urbanization of the rural, involving further appropriations of traditional hunting and commons access, or the wholesale appropriation of land and water for such things as golf courses and eco-tourism resorts, has run into a multiplicity of specific 'local' resistances tied at least loosely to matters of environment (see Peluso and Watts 2001 and Chapter 57). The mobility of production plants and the ability of corporations to switch production across national frontiers has long brought opposition from labour organizations concerned to protect their members' ability to earn a living wage (Mander and Goldsmith 1996 and Chapter 55).

What Esteva and Prakesh (1998) term opposition to the 'global project' has many manifestations. But insofar as these are understood as being parts of single opposition to a global process the irony of a global movement of localities points to the difficulties of an appropriate political language and strategy of resistance. A global movement of indigenous peoples makes the contradiction especially clear; common conditions are the premise for shared activities. But these conditions inevitably change the identities of the 'indigenous' participants in such activities (Mackenzie and Dalby 2003). The irony in such formulations simply reflects the unavoidable recognition of how impossible it is to be purely 'local' in a 'global' world.

The ironies of the Internet and cell phone technology, the symbols of the new global interconnectedness, are especially clear when they are considered in terms of political resistance to many things labelled 'globalization'. Through the late 1990s 'anti-globalization' activists were using websites and email to coordinate actions at international protests. In many protest actions activists were staying in touch and coordinating their activities using the flexibility of the cell phone. All of this suggests that protests in Seattle, Genoa, London, Quebec City, Washington and many other places were much more a critique of the depredations of neo-liberalism and unrestrained capitalism than specifically protests against 'globalization' *per se*. But the phrase 'anti-globalization' nonetheless shows how important 'global' interconnections had become by the late 1990s.

Juxtaposing indigenous resistance and global economics suggests that the impact of globalization has in some ways been global, but in doing so it denies the specifics of particular places. Different forms of local resistance to the global economy frequently have in common some form of opposition to the dispossession and appropriation of local resources by distant economic operators (Gedicks 2001). Again, this is not a new issue. The historical pattern of the expansion of empires, and European empires in the nineteenth century in particular, is a story of the appropriation of land and materials from conquered lands, and the destruction of indigenous peoples in the process (see Chapter 53 and Hochschild 1998). That these processes are now principally carried out by local elites in post-colonial states in collaboration with foreign 'investors' doesn't fundamentally change the pattern.

What it does do is challenge the conventional geographical assumptions of politics and the assumption that political space is about citizenship and hierarchical arrangements of political space (Magnusson and Shaw 2002). Nonetheless, some of the more intriguing patterns of contemporary politics are various attempts to re-impose territorial modes of rule that invoke notions of locality, community and sovereignty in the face of a dynamic global political economy. Two examples of these processes suggest the importance of a political vocabulary of identity tied to place, and the immense difficulty of imagining politics without commonsense understandings of proximity and community.

In the case of Nigeria, the link between the global economy and the politics of identity has played itself out in a complex territorial process of regional state construction. Group after group has mobilized on ethnic lines to lay claim to a territory and then to a share of the oil revenues dispersed by the central government (Watts 2004). In this case it isn't a matter of local resistance to external depredation that drives politics. Instead, groups organize to ensure that they can lay claim to the global wealth trickling back to the nation-state. In contrast, in Ogoniland activists mobilized to try to assert control over Shell Oil's operations in the Niger delta and prevent destruction of land and livelihood. This suggests, on the face of it, a more conventional story of locals wanting to protect their space from external threats. But the politics of this episode needs to be understood as part of a larger pattern of state-making. Oil in Nigeria is a national resource and is used by central government as a major source of revenue and hence political power. Communities in many parts of Nigeria want a share of the wealth and set about getting it by making claims for political rights to rule their local areas. Claims to indigenous rights become linked to matters of place and are frequently articulated on the basis of ethnic claims. 'Only in this way can one understand how, between 1966 and the present, the number of local governments has grown from 50 to almost 1000, and the number of states from 3 to 36' (Watts 2004: 210). Discussions of local resistance to central government simply don't explain this complex political geography of state and identity construction.

Another example in a very different place emphasizes the importance of understanding how complex the geographical invocation of political identity can be. In Scotland, following the election of a New Labour government there has been a reassertion of Scots identity and the devolution of powers to a new Scottish parliamentary assembly. This devolution is happening simultaneously with a confrontation with the legacy of feudal land tenure arrangements reflected in the rural crofting system. Questions of local identity are directly linked to property relationships and struggles to control who uses local resources to what end (Mackenzie 2004). The remaking of different Scots identities must therefore also be understood as being tied to the history of local communities and confronts questions of who controls the terms of modernization. Public art and symbolic representation in Scotland is a key part of this public discussion. All of this emphasizes how important it is to understand that the politics of place is a highly contingent process. Storytelling and narratives of location frequently turn out to be about the history of links to other events elsewhere, the local being a particular emplacement of those wider connections (Doubleday *et al.* 2004).

Writing the world

Europe, Nigeria, Scotland and the complex outcomes of change suggested in Chapters 25–33 suggest that it is important to think very carefully about the spatial categories used in political advocacy and academic analysis; graphing the geo is complex, fraught and unlikely to result in any *single* valid explanation of the political organization of our world (Sparke 2005). Thinking about how we invoke places and power impacts on political argument and policy action. Local and global appear to be commonsense expressions but turn out to be both very useful and very complicated. They are useful precisely because they are apparently commonsensical but actually mean many different things to different people. Ironically, also, it can be argued that some of the apparent victories of the 'West' and globalization might be better interpreted as discursive triumphs. Those who wish to gain the economic benefits of modernization have simply learnt how to use the geopolitical language of the dominant institutions for their own purposes (Kuus 2004b).

Presupposing autonomous localities turns out to be a geographical convenience with considerable political power, but not one that can in any way be taken for granted in an interconnected world. While locality is invoked in many struggles against globalization, these local people are frequently part of larger global struggles against the disruptions of neo-liberalism. Neither is there any good reason to assume that either local or global is necessarily more worthy. Global NGOs may help people in many places, while elsewhere dictators may invoke local culture and sovereignty to repress political opposition and stifle change. Contrastingly, indigenous groups may invoke the virtues of the local in their attempts to prevent the destruction of ecosystems by mining and forestry companies. Instead, it is time to realize that geographical concepts are key to political discussion. The ways in which they are invoked and used is both a political question and a scholarly matter, concerned with the use of language and geography.

Further reading

Agnew, J. (2003) *Geopolitics: Revisioning World Politics*. London: Routledge.
Bunyan, T. (1991) Towards an authoritarian European state. *Race and Class* 32 (3), 19–27.
Dalby, S. (2005) Political space: autonomy, liberalism and empire. *Alternatives: Global, Local, Political* 30 (4), 415–41.
Dijkink, G. (1996) *National Identity and Geopolitical Visions: Maps of Pride and Pain*. London: Routledge.
Hyde-Price, A. (1991) *European Security beyond the Cold War: Four Scenarios for the Year 2010*. London: Sage.
Johansen, R.C. (1991) Real security is democratic security. *Alternatives* 16, 209–42.
Klein, N. (2002) *Fences and Windows: Dispatches from the Front Lines of the Globalization Debate*. New York: Picador.
Ó Tuathail, G. (1996) *Critical Geopolitics: The Politics of Writing Global Space*. Minneapolis: University of Minnesota Press.
Peluso, N. and Watts, M. (eds) (2001) *Violent Environments*. Ithaca: Cornell University Press.
Smith, D. and Thompson, E.P. (eds) (1987) *Prospectus for a Habitable Planet*. Harmondsworth: Penguin.

References

Agnew, J. (2003) *Geopolitics: Revisioning World Politics*. London: Routledge.
Archibugi D. (ed.) (2003) *Debating Cosmopolitics*. London: Verso.
Booth, K. (1990) Steps towards stable peace in Europe: a theory and practice of coexistence. *International Affairs* 66 (1), 17–45.
——(ed.) (1991) *New Thinking about Strategy and International Security*. London: HarperCollins.
Buzan, B., Kelstrup, M., Lemaitre, P., Tromer, E. and Waever, O. (1990) *The European Security Order Recast: Scenarios for the Post Cold War Era*. London: Pinter.
Campbell, D. (1993) *Politics Without Principle: Narratives of the Persian Gulf War and the Ethicality of Operation Desert Storm*. Boulder: Lynne Rienner.
——(1998) *National Deconstruction: Violence, Identity, and Justice in Bosnia*. Minneapolis: University of Minnesota Press.
Dalby, S. (1991) Dealignment discourse: thinking beyond the blocs. *Current Research in Peace and Violence* 13 (3), 140–55.
——(2003) Calling 911: geopolitics, security and America's new war. *Geopolitics* 8 (3), 61–86.
Dicken, P. (2003) *Global Shift: Reshaping the Global Economic Map in the 21st Century*. London: Sage.
Dientsbier, J. (1991) Central Europe's security. *Foreign Policy* 83, 119–27.
Doubleday, N.C., MacKenzie, A.F.D. and Dalby, S. (2004) Reimagining sustainable cultures: constitutions, land and art. *The Canadian Geographer* 48 (4), 389–402.

Esteva, G. and Prakesh, M.S. (1998) *Grassroots Post-Modernism: Remaking the Soil of Cultures.* London: Zed Books.

Fedorowicz, H.M. (1991) Getting beyond the cold war 'from below': east–west dialogue towards democratic peace. *Peace Research Reviews* 11 (6), 1–80.

Gedicks, A. (2001) *Resource Rebels: Native Challenges to Mining and Oil Corporations.* Boston: South End.

Gupta, D. (2005) Migration, development and security. In F. Dodds and T. Pippard (eds) *Human and Environmental Security: An Agenda for Change,* pp. 115–27. London: Earthscan.

Havel, V. (1990) The power of the powerless. In W.M. Brinton and A. Rinzler (eds) *Without Force or Lies: Voices from the Revolution of Central Europe in 1989–90,* pp. 43–127. San Francisco: Mercury.

Heffernan, M. (1998) *The Meaning of Europe: Geography and Geopolitics.* London: Arnold.

Hochschild, A. (1998) *King Leopold's Ghost: A Story of Greed, Terror, and Heroism in Colonial Africa.* Boston: Houghton Mifflin.

Hugill, P.J. (1999) *Global Communication since 1844: Geopolitics and Technology.* Baltimore, MD: Johns Hopkins University Press.

Hyde-Price, A. (1991) *European Security beyond the Cold War: Four Scenarios for the Year 2010.* London: Sage.

Kaldor, M. (ed.) (1991) *Europe from Below: An East–West Dialogue.* London: Verso.

Kaldor, M. and Falk, R. (eds) (1987) *Dealignment: A New Foreign Policy Perspective.* Oxford: Blackwell.

Klein, N. (2002) *Fences and Windows: Dispatches from the Front Lines of the Globalization Debate.* New York: Picador.

Konrad, G. (1984) *Antipolitics.* New York: Harcourt, Brace Jovanovich.

Kuus, M. (2004a) Europe's eastern expansion and the reinscription of otherness in East-Central Europe. *Progress in Human Geography* 28, 472–89.

——(2004b) Those goody-goody Estonians: toward rethinking security in the European Union candidate states. *Environment and Planning D: Society and Space* 22, 191–207.

Mackenzie, A.F.D. (2004) Reclaiming place: the Millennium Forest, Borgie, North Sutherland, Scotland. *Environment and Planning D. Society and Space* 20, 535–60.

Mackenzie, A.F.D. and Dalby, S. (2003) Moving mountains: community, nature and resistance in the Isle of Harris, Scotland and Cape Breton, Canada. *Antipode* 35 (2), 309–34.

Magnusson, W. and Shaw, K. (eds) (2002) *A Political Space: Reading the Global in Clayoquot Sound.* Montreal and Kingston: McGill Queen's Press.

Mander, J. and Goldsmith, E. (eds) (1996) *The Case Against the Global Economy, and for a Turn to the Local.* San Francisco: Sierra Club Books.

Mearsheimer, J. (1990) Back to the future: instability in Europe after the cold war. *International Security* 15 (1), 5–56.

Moller, B. (1992) *Common Security and Nonoffensive Defense: A Neorealist Perspective.* Boulder: Lynne Rienner.

Ó Tuathail, G. (1996) *Critical Geopolitics: The Politics of Writing Global Space.* Minneapolis: University of Minnesota Press.

Ó Tuathail, G. and Agnew, J. (1992). Geopolitics and discourse: practical geopolitical reasoning in American foreign policy. *Political Geography* 11, 190–204.

Peluso, N. and Watts, M. (eds) (2001) *Violent Environments.* Ithaca: Cornell University Press.

Ross, G. (1992) Confronting the new Europe. *New Left Review* 191, 49–68.

Schneider, H. (1991) The threat from environmental destruction in eastern Europe. *Journal of International Affairs* 44, 359–91.

Scholte, J.A. (2000) *Globalization: A Critical Introduction.* Basingstoke: Macmillan.

Sparke, M. (2005) *In the Space of Theory: Post Foundational Geographies of the Nation State.* Minneapolis: University of Minnesota Press.

Spencer, M. (1991) Politics beyond turf: grassroots democracy in the Helsinki process. *Bulletin of Peace Proposals* 22, 427–35.

Tairov, T. (1991) From new thinking to a civic peace. In M. Kaldor (ed.) *Europe from Below: An East–West Dialogue,* pp. 43–8. London: Verso.

Thompson, E.P. and Smith, D. (eds) (1980) *Protest and Survive.* Harmondsworth: Penguin.

Watts, M. (2004) Antimonies of community: some thoughts on geography, resources and empire. *Transactions of the Institute of British Geographers* NS 29, 195–216.

Worner, M. (1991) Global security: the challenge to NATO. In E. Grove (ed.) *Global Security: North American, European and Japanese Interdependence in the 1990s,* pp. 100–5. London: Brassey's.

ZumBrunnen, C. (1992) The environmental challenges in Eastern Europe. In I.H. Rowlands and M. Greene (eds) *Global Environmental Change and International Relations,* pp. 88–121. London: Macmillan.

57

Protesting and empowering

Alternative responses to global forces

Paul Routledge

Resisting networks

On 1 January 1994, media vectors around the world carried the dramatic news that ski-masked guerrillas had captured the town of San Cristobal de las Casas (in the Mexican state of Chiapas) and declared war on the Mexican state. As the drama unfolded, it became apparent that the EZLN (Ejercito Zapatista Liberacion National) or Zapatistas, as they became known, differed from the recent guerrilla movements such as the FMLN (Farabundo Marti Liberacion National) movement in El Salvador, and the FSLN (Frente Sandanista Liberacion National) in Nicaragua. Unlike them, the EZLN did not see itself as the vanguard directing a struggle to seize state power. Rather, it demanded the democratic revitalization of Mexican civil and political society, and autonomy for, and recognition of, indigenous culture. The struggle ignited the imagination of many social movements, NGOs and other actors within civil society around the world. This was because the Zapatistas articulated both a critique of the globally dominant economic process of neoliberalism, and a vision of an alternative politics. This vision asserted the importance of cultural/indigenous integrity and autonomy, the reclamation of commonly owned resources such as water, land and forests, and the need for collective international resistance against the neoliberal project.

Whilst providing an important catalyst, the Zapatista revolt was only the most dramatic (and media-covered) of a series of resistances that had peppered the previous decade. A range of international initiatives had already begun to cohere against the threat posed by neoliberal globalization, including the riots against the IMF's structural adjustment programmes (which entailed the privatization of communal/collective commons) throughout the global South during the 1980s; the international anti-corporate boycott of Nestlé, organized by INFACT between 1977 and 1984; and the formation, in 1992, of Via Campesina – an international farmers' network, including farmers from Asia, Latin America and Europe (Starr 2005).

As a result of the impact of the Zapatista rebellion on the popular imagination of resistance movements around the world, when the Zapatistas organized an international encounter in Chiapas, in 1996, it was attended by activists, intellectuals and journalists from around the world. At the encounter Subcommandante Marcos – the articulate, humorous and poetic spokesperson of the Zapatistas – issued a call for a network of transnational resistance against neoliberalism:

> [W]e will make a collective network of all our particular struggles and resistances. An intercontinental network of resistance against neoliberalism, an intercontinental network of resistance for humanity. This intercontinental network of resistance, recognizing differences and acknowledging similarities, will search to find itself with other resistances around the world. This intercontinental network of resistance is not an organizing structure; it doesn't have a central head or decision maker; it has no central command or hierarchies. We are the network, all of us who resist.
>
> (Subcommandante Marcos quoted in Notes from Nowhere 2003: 37)

The reasons for this call to resist can be deduced from a brief discussion of the ideology and practice of neoliberal economics. This chapter will first outline the basic contours of neoliberalism, before reviewing the emergence of grassroots globalization as a response to it. It will then discuss some of the specific forms of resistance which pose alternatives to transnational forms of economic and political power.

Neoliberalism and its opponents

The ideology of neoliberalism articulates an overarching commitment to 'free market' principles of free trade, flexible labour and active individualism. It privileges lean government, privatization and deregulation, while undermining or foreclosing alternative development models based upon social redistribution, economic rights or public investment. Neoliberalism has seen a shift from 'roll-back neoliberalism' during the 1980s – which entailed a pattern of deregulation and dismantlement (e.g. of state-financed welfare, education and health services and environmental protection) to an emergent phase of 'roll-out neoliberalism'. This emergent phase is witnessing an aggressive intervention by governments around issues such as crime, policing, welfare reform and urban surveillance with the purpose of disciplining and containing those marginalized or dispossessed by the neoliberalization of the 1980s. Nevertheless, neoliberal gobalization is neither monolithic nor omnipresent, taking hybrid or composite forms around the world, i.e. different markets, different aspects of society integrating at different rates, etc. (Peck and Tickell 2002).

Neoliberalism entails the centralization of control of the world economy in the hands of transnational corporations and their allies in key government agencies (particularly those of the United States and other members of the G8), large international banks and international institutions such as the International Monetary Fund (IMF), the World Bank and the World Trade Organization (WTO) (see Chapter 18 for further consideration of the changing role of international agencies as global actors). These institutions enforce the doctrine of neoliberalism enabling unrestricted access of transnational corporations (TNCs) to a wide range of markets (including public services), while potentially more progressive institutions and agreements (such as the International Labour Organization and the Kyoto Protocols) are allowed to wither (Peck and Tickell 2002).

Although the effects of neoliberalism have been uneven in different countries, global trends are instructive. One billion people live on less than US $1 a day, and the disparities between rich and poor continue to grow: by 1997 the richest 20 per cent of the world's population received 90 per cent of global income (an increase from 70 per cent in 1960), while the poorest 20 per cent received 1 per cent (a decrease from 2.3 per cent in 1960). The combined annual revenues of the largest 200 TNCs are greater than those of 182 countries that contain 80 per cent of the world's population (Ellwood 2001). According to the World Bank, in 1998 the income of the richest 1 per cent of the world's population equalled that of the poorest 57 per cent (Callinicos 2003). Overall, neoliberal policies have tended to result in the pauperization and marginalization of indigenous peoples, women, peasant farmers and industrial workers, and a reduction in labour, social and environmental conditions on a global basis. These processes have been accompanied by what some have termed a 'democratic deficit' such as declining voter turnout, declining membership of political parties, reduced confidence in governments and politicians, and hostility to corporations and global institutions (Clark 2003).

In response to this, new forms of trans-local political solidarity and consciousness have begun to emerge, associated with the partial globalization of networks of resistance. These formations – consisting of diverse networks of social movements, trade unions, NGOs and other organizations – inhabit a political space outside of formal national politics (political parties, elections), and address a range of institutions across a variety of geographic scales (local, national, international). Mary Kaldor argues that such networks are involved in establishing a global civil society that is about 'democratizing globalization, about the process through which groups, movements and individuals can demand a global rule of law, global justice and global empowerment' (2003: 12). Social movements are increasing their spatial reach by constructing multi-scalar networks of support and solidarity for their particular struggles, and also by participating with other movements in broad networks to resist neo-liberal globalization, exemplified by the slogan 'our resistance will be as transnational as capital'. While such solidarities across borders are not new phenomena – e.g. in the nine-teenth and twentieth centuries international solidarity was forged in the anti-slavery, women's suffrage and communist movements – contemporary international alliances are characterized by the means, speed and intensity of communication between the various groups involved.

Grassroots globalization

The growth of anti-neoliberal globalization protests – and the networks that participate in them – has excited much academic and media attention in recent years. They have been conceived of as 'grassroots globalization' (Appadurai 2000) – attempts by marginalized groups and social movements at the local level to forge wider alliances in protest at their growing exclusion from global neoliberal economic decision-making. While establishing global networks of action and support, they attempt to retain local autonomy over strategies and tactics.

Grassroots globalization involves the creation of networks: of communication, solidarity, information sharing and mutual support. The core function of networks is the production, exchange and strategic use of information – for example, concerning oppositional narratives and analysis of particular events. Many information exchanges are informal such as by tele-phone, e-mail, and the circulation of newsletters and bulletins through a variety of means including by hand, post and the internet. Such information can enhance the resources available to geographically and or socially distant actors in their particular struggles and also lead to action (Keck and Sikkink 1998). The speed, density and complexity of international linkages have grown dramatically in the past twenty years. Cheaper air travel and new electronic communication technologies described in Chapter 60 have speeded up information flows and simplified personal contact among activists. Indeed, information-age activism is creating what Cleaver (1999: 3) terms a 'global electronic fabric of struggle' whereby local and national movements are consciously seeking ways to make their efforts complement those of other organized struggles around similar issues. Such networks, greatly facilitated by the internet, can at times enable relationships to develop that are more flexible than traditional hierarchies. Participation in networks has become an essential component of collective identities of the activists involved, networking forming part of their common repertoire of action and recruitment (Castells 1997).

The consolidation of a global system of financial regulation – as one of the means of neoliberal global control – has prompted the 'upscaling' of previously local struggles between citizens, governments and transnational institutions and corporations to the international level. Grassroots globalization is resulting in the forging of new alliances as different social movements representing different terrains of struggle experience the negative consequences of neoliberalism. By identifying structures of power within the global political field, social movements have established common targets of protest, exemplified by global days of action against targets which symbolize neoliberal power such as the G8, WTO, World Bank and IMF. Such protests have been celebrated for bringing together formerly disparate and often conflicting groups, such as trade unionists, environmentalists, indigenous peoples' movements and non-government organizations. Underpinning such developments is a conceptualization of protest and struggle that respects difference, rather than attempting to develop universalistic and centralizing solutions that deny the diversity of interests and identities that are confronted with neoliberal globalization processes.

The scale of grassroots globalization

In order to materialize collective struggle, grassroots globalization networks attempt to prosecute transnational collective political action, exemplified by the aforementioned global days of action. The first global day of action took place in 1998 when 10,000 people protested the WTO meeting in Geneva, and simultaneous protests were held in thirty other countries on five continents. There followed protests against the G8 summit in Koln in 1999 (in forty-three countries), against the WTO in Seattle in 1999 (70,000 protestors) and subsequent protests against the IMF World Bank in Prague in 2000, G8 in Genoa 2001, and subsequently whenever and wherever the architects of neoliberalism have held their meetings (see Starr 2005).

Such protests brought together political actors from different countries within a particular place (e.g. Seattle) while also witnessing solidarity actions in many other places around the world. For example, during the demonstrations against the World Bank and IMF in Prague in 2000, solidarity actions took place in over forty countries around the world. Many social movements, although engaged in grassroots globalization networks, nevertheless remain locally or nationally based, since this is where individual movement identities are formed and nurtured. However, when locally based struggles develop, or become part of, geographically flexible networks, they become embedded in different places at a variety of spatial scales. These different geographic scales (global, regional, national, local) form mutually constitutive parts, becoming links of various lengths in the network. Networks of agents act across various distances and through diverse intermediaries. However, some networks are relatively more localized while others are more global in scope, and the relationship of networks to territories is mutually constitutive: networks are embedded in territories and at the same time, territories are embedded in networks (Dicken et al. 2001).

However, certain scales of political action may provide more appropriate means than others for movements to measure their strength and take stock of their opponents. For example, many movements in the global South see defence of local spaces, and opposition to national governments (pursuing neoliberal policies) as their most appropriate scales of political action (Mertes 2002). Moreover, movements that are local or national in character derive their principal strength from acting at these scales rather than at the global level. For example, transnational corporations such as Nestlé, McDonald's and Nike have usually been disrupted primarily as a result of the efficacy of local campaigns (Klein 2000). Even where international campaigns are organized, local and national scales of action can be as important as international ones (Herod 2001). For example, the Liverpool dockers' international campaign was grassroots-instigated and coordinated (by Liverpool dockers) and operationalized by dockers beyond the UK working within established union frameworks (Castree 2000). See Chapter 55 for further examples of the scaling of labour disputes.

The diversity of grassroots globalization

Grassroots globalization involves a variety of political actors as well as strategic foci. In such networks, different groups articulate a variety of potentially conflicting goals (concerning the forms of social change), ideologies (e.g. concerning gender, class and ethnicity), and strategies (e.g. violent and non-violent forms of protest). As a result, a diversity of place-specific solutions to economic and ecological problems is articulated. For example, Kaldor (2003) posits that at least six different types of political actor can be identified – more traditional social movements (e.g. trade unions and anti-colonial and revolutionary movements); more contemporary social movements (e.g. women's and environmental movements); NGOs (e.g. Amnesty International); transnational civic networks (such as those resisting the construction of large dams, e.g. International Rivers Network); 'new' nationalist and fundamentalist movements (e.g. Al Qaeda); and the anti-capitalist movement (e.g. People's Global Action). Meanwhile Starr (2000) identifies at least three different strategic foci, namely:

1. *contestation and reform*, which involves social movements and organizations that seek to impose regulatory limitations on corporations and or governments, or force them to self-regulate, mobilizing existing formal democratic channels of protest (e.g. Human Rights Watch, and the fair trade network);
2. *globalization from below*, whereby various social movements and organizations form global alliances regarding environmental degradation, the abuse of human rights, labour standards, etc., to make corporations and governments accountable to people instead of elites (e.g. the Zapatistas, labour unions, the World Social Forum and People's Global Action);
3. *delinking, relocalization and sovereignty*, whereby varied initiatives articulate the pleasures, productivities and rights of localities and attempt to delink local economies from corporate-controlled national and international economies (e.g. permaculture initiatives, community currency (LETS), community credit organizations, sovereignty movements especially those of indigenous peoples, and various religious nationalisms; see also Hines 2000).

Despite such diversity, certain key areas of agreement have emerged, such as: (1) the cancellation of the foreign debt in the developing world (which amounted to US $3,000 billion in 1999); (2) the introduction of a tax on international currency transactions, and controls on capital flows; (3) the reduction in people's working hours and an end to child labour; (4) the defence of public services; (5) the progressive taxation to finance public services and redistribute wealth and income; (6) the international adoption of enforceable targets for greenhouse emissions and large-scale investment in renewable energy; (7) policies which ensure land, water and food sovereignty for peasant and indigenous people; and (8) the defence of civil liberties (Callinicos 2003; Fisher and Ponniah 2003). At the root of such demands is the perceived necessity to reclaim and protect common resources.

Reclaiming and protecting the commons

Reclaiming and protecting the commons concerns the defence of common resources such as land, water, forests, seeds and biodiversity against their exploitation and privatization by TNCs and national governments; and their communal management to ensure equitable access for direct uncommodified use by communities, and restraints on over-use. The defining struggles of grassroots globalization are the intense struggles of villagers to maintain control over their lives and protect ecologies against oil exploitation, dams, large landholders and their paramilitaries, agricultural, pharmaceutical and biotechnology companies, commercial fishing, aquaculture and forest preserves. Such struggles link community crises to the processes of neoliberal globalization.

One of the key responses to neoliberalism by many movements around the world has been that subsistence lifestyles are more secure, independent and self-determining than modern (neoliberal, market-driven) ones. As a result, social movements' demands include reorienting economies in the global South from the emphasis on production for export to production for the local market; defending those local markets; income and land redistribution; de-emphasizing growth and maximizing equity; not leaving strategic economic decisions to the market, but making them subject to democratic choice; and subjecting the private sector and the state to constant monitoring by civil society.

Movements have been involved in creating new institutions and practices which transform from the ground up the relations of production (e.g. fair trade, producer cooperatives); creating community cooperatives, small businesses and state enterprises and excluding TNCs; nurturing cultural and political autonomy within communities in the global South and global North; articulating the decentralization of productive activities; promoting mutual aid, community self-determination, direct democracy, worker self-management of factories and indigenous controlled education, healthcare, economics and politics (Starr 2005). The following examples will exemplify some of the practices that comprise grassroots globalization.

Water commons: anti-dam struggles

The Narmada Bachao Andolan (NBA, Save Narmada Movement) has, since 1985, been coordinating the resistance against the Narmada River valley project in India. (See Plate 57.1.) This river, which is regarded as sacred by the Hindu and tribal populations of India, spans the states of Madhya Pradesh, Maharashtra and Gujarat, and provides water resources for thousands of communities. The project envisages the construction of thirty major dams along the Narmada and its tributaries, as well as an additional 135 medium-sized and 3,000 minor dams. When completed, the project is expected to displace up to 15 million people from their homes and lands. While the dams were first envisaged as being financed by the Indian state, the processes of their construction have become increasingly entwined with

Plate 57.1. Narmada Bachao Andolan boat demonstration, Narmada River, India 1999. Photograph by Paul Routledge.

those of neoliberal globalization, as investment was sought from international corporate investors such as the World Bank, the US-based Ogden Energy Group and the German transnational corporation Siemens. For a variety of reasons, each of these investors has withdrawn.

The NBA is an exemplar of grassroots globalization because: (1) it is a long-term struggle for common (water, land) resources; (2) the movement is itself a network of multi-scalar connections and support; and (3) the movement is part of international grassroots networks against neoliberalism. The NBA is a social movement that comprises – in the Narmada valley – cash-cropping and tribal peasants and rich farmers, organized by a core group of activists, who originate mostly from outside of the valley. The movement is also a network as it has constantly attempted to forge an associational politics consisting of individuals, NGOs and other social movements that have prosecuted conflict on a variety of multi-scalar terrains, including both material places and virtual spaces. In so doing, the NBA has also participated in transnational networks such as the World Social Forum and People's Global Action (see later). The collective visions shared by all actors within this network are those of resistance to the construction of mega-dams, and their desire for development processes that are socially just and economically and environmentally sustainable.

The NBA has initiated a programme of 'our rule in our villages', which asserts autonomy from the state and its developmental apparatus, and seeks to engage with alternative development practices; has actively engaged in alternative energy projects (such as micro-hydel dams), conservation work, tree planting and agricultural initiatives in the valley; and has established ten *Jeevan shalas* (schools for life) for *adivasi* (tribal) children, whereby they are taught about their own society, heritage and knowledge systems in their own tribal languages.

The NBA has conducted its resistance simultaneously across multiple scales. It has grounded its struggle against the dams, in the villages along the Narmada valley, mobilizing *adivasi*

933

peasants, cash-cropping peasants and rich farmers to resist displacement. The NBA has been able to use their local knowledge of the valley to facilitate communication between disparate communities, and to mobilize, at times, tens of thousands of peasants to resist the dams. The NBA has also taken its struggle to non-local terrains, including the national and international levels. Nationally, the NBA has served writ petitions to the Supreme Court of India, and has established, and participated as a convener in, the National Alliance of People's Movements – a coalition of different social movements in India collectively organizing to resist the effects of liberalization upon the Indian economy. Internationally, the NBA has forged operational links with various groups outside of India, such as the International Rivers Network (IRN) and the International Narmada Campaign. International solidarity work has been conducted by groups such as IRN, Environmental Defence Fund, Friends of the Earth; human and indigenous rights groups such as Survival International; development organizations such as the Association for India's Development; and groups formed explicitly around the Narmada issue such as the Narmada Solidarity Coalition of New York. These in turn are also part of larger networks such as the Narmada Action Committee and Friends of River Narmada, which are mainly US-based collectives of South Asian, development and environmentalist activists which have developed links with other groups through flows of common experience, writings and materials such as documentaries (Routledge 2003a).

Struggles against the privatization of the commons

Struggles against privatization are now taking place in many countries in the global North and global South. Here I provide two brief examples. In April 2000, an insurrection and general strike in Cochabamba, Bolivia, by a movement of farmers, unions, students and small business people, demanded the cancellation of water privatization plans by which the Bolivian government would sell water to a US TNC, Bechtel, in cooperation with the World Bank. The movement claimed that: (1) water belonged to the Earth and all species and was sacred, hence it should be conserved, reclaimed and protected for all future generations; (2) that water was a fundamental human right and public trust and thus should not be privatized, commodified or traded for commercial purposes; and (3) water is best protected by local communities and citizens. During the protests government forces shot protestors, killing several. However, the protests forced the cancellation of the project and the Coordinadora del Agua y la Vida now administers the local water system. In another example, in 2000, the Soweto Electricity Crisis Committee (SECC) was formed in response to massive cut-offs of people unable to pay for electricity. This was a response to the privatization of the South African state-owned electricity commission. The SECC performed reconnections, disconnected politicians' home lines, removed pre-pay meters. Later the Anti-Privatization Forum was founded, embracing issues of water, electricity and evictions from people's homes (Notes from Nowhere 2003).

Struggles for land and cultural commons

Since 1985 the Movimento dos Trabalhadores Rurais Sem Terra (MST, Landless Workers' Movement), working independently of both the church and political parties, has undertaken large-scale occupations of unused land in order to de-commodify land and establish autonomous life for poor Brazilian communities. After maintaining the occupation (often against private armies) and establishing a settlement, the MST works in the courts demanding that the community be given legal status. In their first ten years the MST resettled 350,000 families in twenty-three of the twenty-seven Brazilian states. In 1999 alone, 25,099 families occupied land, building sixty food cooperatives, independent schools and healthcare facilities.

For the MST the act of occupying land – what they term 'cutting the wire' – is the cornerstone of their movement. As MST activist Darci Maschio argues: 'Land that we conquer through struggle is land that we win without the help from anyone. We don't have to go down on our knees to give thanks to anyone. This allows us to fight for other things' (quoted in Notes from Nowhere 2003: 123). The occupations confront the system of neoliberal modernization and urbanization, articulating the collective desire of underemployed people to have their own land, community and economic autonomy (Starr 2005). The MST produces beans and rice for the Brazilian government's anti-hunger programme, participates in the creation of a National Plan for Agrarian Reform, has expanded to Bolivia, and is working with movements in many parts of the world such as in the World Social Forum (see below).

In 1992 the indigenous U'wa people in Colombia decided that they would resist the drilling of petroleum in their homeland by Occidental Petroleum. Indigenous peoples blockaded roads into U'wa territory to prevent oil company vehicles entering, but were frequently tear-gassed by the Colombian military. In 1995, the U'wa threatened to commit mass suicide if oil extraction continued on their land. They argued that U'wa cultural integrity and autonomy – which was intimately tied to their land – would be destroyed by the massive exploitation and despoilation of their land for oil. Articulating grassroots globalization, many international environmental organizations supported the U'wa struggle, using shareholder activism, applying public pressure to the US Democratic Party for Al Gore's ties to Occidental Petroleum, and organizing massive public and student campaigns to pressurize the Colombian government. In 2002 Occidental Petroleum finally withdrew from U'wa territory (Starr 2005).

In Thailand, the Assembly of the Poor consists of a 2-million person-strong network of farmers, anti–dam activists, indigenous people, slum dwellers, fisherfolk and workers who have been resisting destructive development practices since 1995. In 1997, 20,000 dam-affected villagers, small farmers and fisherfolk constructed a 'village of the poor' outside the main government building in Bangkok to protest the displacements caused by the Pak Mun Dam. They camped in the city for ninety-nine days, growing vegetables illegally along the banks of the city's river. As a statement by the Assembly stated at the time:

> The most important thing for us now is dignity. Physical assets such as houses, farm-land and resources can be taken away from us. But we'll never let ourselves be looked down upon. Though deprived of wealth, we'll not let our human dignity be wrenched from us.
>
> (Assembly of the Poor 2003: 148)

In addition to demonstrations and rallies, movements within the Assembly continue to engage in land occupations in various parts of the country (Notes from Nowhere 2003). (See Plate 57.2.)

Struggles for political and social autonomy

As a result of the economic collapse of the Argentinean economy – precipitated by a massive external debt and structural adjustment policies (privatization) – a general insurrection took place in the country in 2001, including both working and middle classes. Through a growing

Plate 57.2. Meeting of members of the Northern Farmers' Alliance, a member of the Assembly of the Poor, Thailand, 2004. Photograph by Paul Routledge.

recognition of the limitations of representative/electoral politics, protestors demanded, '*Que se vayan todos*' (get rid of them all). Workers took over viable factories and the unemployed developed enterprises in abandoned ones. Networks of solidarity were forged between communities, between the working and middle classes and between peasants and indigenous peoples. Working-class *piqueteros* began to block roads to bring the country to a standstill, organizing by neighbourhood. Autonomous zones were created whereby educational, food and healthcare provisioning were organized by communities, using collective decision-making. The middle class *asembleas* movement initiated neighbourhood meetings and coordinated occupation of buildings, creating community meeting places whereby meals, information and skills are shared and pooled for communal use.

Elsewhere, in Europe (especially Italy) and Latin America, social centres have been established in many cities. People directly challenge private property and the commodification of everyday life by occupying unused buildings, factories, warehouses and other urban spaces. Such social centres provide accessible spaces for community- and group-organized and managed art production and exhibitions, musical events, community kitchens, movies and performance theatres, infoshops (community-run libraries), workshops, bars, legal advice, alternative media and childcare. In Italy alone there are approximately 262 social centres, which maintain networks with one another and with other sympathetic organizations both in Italy and elsewhere in Europe. Moreover, they are engaged in a variety of solidarity campaigns with struggles around the world and have mobilized thousands of people to participate in the global days of action against neoliberal international institutions (Mudu 2004).

Another attempt at autonomy are the independent media centres (IMCs) which were first established at the Seattle WTO protests in 1999, to provide a shared space for activist reporting of protests. They provided photos, text, audio and video/digital footage which were all placed on the activist website alongside a newswire with live reports updated by the minute. Enacted as a response to the misrepresentation of the anti-globalization movement by corporate mainstream media, the IMCs became an archive of video, photo and audio materials. By 2004 there were 130 IMCs operating in seven languages (fifty in the US). Indymedia emphasizes news over commentary, prioritizing coverage of activism and encouraging direct reporting and witnessing from activists. Indymedia recognizes alternative media as part of social movements creating virtual and material networks between movements.

Convergence of common interests

Whilst myriad struggles in defence of the commons continue to take place around the world, at least two important recent transnational initiatives have emerged, both inspired by the Zapatistas' encounters – People's Global Action and the World Social Forum. Both represent important – but by no means the only – convergences of common interests between diverse social movements, NGOs, trade unions and other actors within civil society.

People's Global Action

People's Global Action (PGA) represents a network for communication and coordination between diverse social movements, whose membership cuts across differences in gender, ethnicity, language, nationality, age, class and caste. It acts as a facilitating space for communication, information-sharing, solidarity, coordination and resource mobilization (Routledge 2003b). The network articulates certain symbolic unifying values – what I would term 'collective visions' – to provide common ground for movements from which to articulate common opponents (e.g. neoliberalism) and coordinate collective struggles. The broad objectives of the network are to offer an instrument for coordination and mutual support at the global level for those resisting corporate rule and the neoliberal capitalist development paradigm, to provide international projection to their struggles, and to inspire people to resist corporate domination through civil disobedience and people-oriented constructive actions. PGA has also established regional networks – e.g. PGA Latin America, PGA Europe, PGA North America and PGA Asia – to decentralize the everyday workings of the network. The principal means of materializing the network have been through the Internet (PGA has established its own website (http://www.agp.org) and email list in order to facilitate network communication); global and regional conferences; activist caravans (organized to enable activists from different struggles and countries to communicate with one another, exchange information and participate in various solidarity actions); and global days of action. (See Plate 57.3.)

The World Social Forum

The World Social Forum (WSF) emerged out of the various initiatives that protested the World Economic Forum (WEF). Activists in the Brazilian Justice and Peace Commission and the French Association for the Taxation of Financial Transactions for the Aid of Citizens (ATTAC) suggested the establishment of a gathering for NGOs, trade unions, social movements and other resistance networks involved in civil society worldwide. The purpose of the gathering was to protest the WEF and particularly neoliberal globalization, and to discuss and present concrete alternatives to it. The notion of the WSF was to engender a process of

Plate 57.3. Women of the Bangladesh Kisani Sabha (Women's Association) — a participant movement in the People's Global Action network, Bangladesh, 2002. Photograph by Paul Routledge.

dialogue and reflection and the transnational exchange of experiences, ideas, strategies and information between the participants regarding their multi-scalar struggles. In 2001, the first WSF was held in Porto Alegre, Brazil, and attracted almost 20,000 participants; the second, in 2002, attracted 55,000 participants, and the third, in 2003, 100,000 participants (Fisher and Ponniah 2003). The participants included diverse social movements, NGOs, trade unions, solidarity committees, and farmers' networks from the five non-polar continents (see Sen *et al.* 2004).

In addition, the WSF has decentralized into regional and thematic forums that are being held in various parts of the world. The principle among these have been the Thematic Forum on Neoliberalism in Argentina (2002), the European Social Forum in Florence, Italy (2002), the Asian Social Forum in Hyderabad, India (2003), and the Thematic Forum on Drugs, Human Rights and Democracy in Cartagena, Colombia (2003). In addition, myriad local events have been organized under the WSF banner around the world. The WSF also played an important role in building global opinion against the 2003 war in Iraq, not by taking a position itself but by being an arena where anti-war activists could meet and discuss transnational collective protests. As a result, in part, of this process there were global protests against the war on 15 February 2003 (amounting to as many as 30 million people worldwide).

Despite the success of such transnational convergences – not least in the rejoining of the concerns of the politics of identity and redistribution – significant differences remain in the type of specific alternatives to neoliberal capitalism articulated by global Northern and global Southern movements. Northern activists articulate alternatives that are conditioned by their embeddedness within – and alienation from – an already industrialized capitalist society. The fundamental concerns of Southern activists are with the defence of livelihoods and of communal access to resources threatened by commodification, state take-overs and private appropriation (e.g. by national or transnational corporations). Their alternatives are rooted, in part, in some of the local practices being undermined by neoliberal globalization (Glassman 2002).

By stressing the importance of connection, diversity and solidarity, such convergences, and the struggles which they comprise, are engaging in prefigurative action, i.e. embodying visions of transformation as if they are already achieved, thereby calling them into being and forging the notion of mutual solidarity – constructing the grievances and aspirations of geographically and culturally different people as interlinked. Mutual solidarity enables connections to be drawn that extend beyond the local and particular, by recognizing and respecting differences between people while at the same time recognizing similarities (for example, in people's aspirations) (Olesen 2005). It is about imagining global subjectivities through similarities of experience, recognizing the shared opportunities and techniques of struggle (Starr 2005). Through collective action and transnational networks of solidarity, the poor and dispossessed of the world are empowered to create and live out alternatives to neoliberal globalization, attempting to bring new worlds into being that are economically just and environmentally sustainable.

Further reading

Glassman, J. (2002) From Seattle (and Ubon) to Bangkok: the scales of resistance to corporate globalization. *Environment and Planning D: Society and Space* 19, 513–33.
Klein, N. (2002) *Fences and Windows*. London: Flamingo.
Notes from Nowhere (ed.) (2003) *We Are Everywhere*. London: Verso
Olesen, T. (2005) *International Zapatismo*. London: Zed Books.
Roy, A. (2004) *The Ordinary Person's Guide to Empire*. London: Flamingo.
Starr. A. (2005) *Global Revolt*. London: Zed Books.

References

Appadurai, A. (2000) Grassroots globalization and the research imagination. *Public Culture* 12 (1), 1–19.
Assembly of the Poor (2003) Peace message to the public. In Notes from Nowhere (ed.) *We are Everywhere: The Irresistible Rise of Global Anti-Capitalism*, pp. 148–9. London and New York: Verso.
Callinicos, A. (2003) *An Anti-Capitalist Manifesto*. Cambridge: Polity Press.
Castells, M. (1997) *The Power of Identity*. Oxford: Blackwell.
Castree, N. (2000) Geographic scale and grassroots internationalism: the Liverpool dock dispute 1995–98. *Economic Geography* 76 (3), 272–92.
Clark, J. (2003) *Worlds Apart: Civil Society and the Battle for Ethical Globalization*. London: Earthscan.
Cleaver, H. (1999) *Computer-linked Social Movements and the Global Threat to Capitalism*. Available at http://polnet.html atwww.ecoutexas.edu
Dicken, P., Kelly, P.F., Olds, K. and Yeung, H.W.C. (2001) Chains and networks, territories and scales: towards a relational framework for analysing the global economy. *Global Networks* 1 (2), 89–112.
Ellwood, W. (2001) *The Non-Nonsense Guide to Globalization*. London: Verso.
Fisher, W.F. and Ponniah, T. (eds) (2003) *Another World is Possible*. London: Zed Books.
Herod, A. (2001) *Labor Geographies*. New York: Guilford.
Hines, C. (2000) *Localization: A Global Manifesto*. London: Earthscan.
Kaldor, M. (2003) *Global Civil Society*. Cambridge: Polity Press.

Keck, M.E. and Sikkink, K. (1998) *Activists Beyond Borders*. Ithaca, NY: Cornell University Press.

Klein, N. (2000) *No Logo*. London: Flamingo.

Mertes, T. (2002) Grass-roots globalism. *New Left Review* 17, 101–10.

Mudu, P. (2004) Resisting and challenging neoliberalism: the development of Italian social centers. *Antipode* 36 (5), 917–41.

Notes from Nowhere (2003) Tomorrow begins today: invitation to an insurrection, by Sub-commandante Marcos. In Notes from Nowhere (ed.) *We Are Everywhere*, pp. 34–7. London: Verso.

Peck, J. and Tickell, A. (2002) Neoliberalizing space. *Antipode* 34 (3), 380–404.

Routledge, P. (2003a) Voices of the dammed: discursive resistance amidst erasure in the Narmada Valley, India. *Political Geography* 22 (3), 243–70.

——(2003b) Convergence space: process geographies of grassroots globalization networks. *Transactions of the Institute of British Geographers* 28 (3), 333–49.

Sen, J., Anand, A., Escobar, A. and Waterman, P. (eds) (2004) *World Social Forum: Challenging Empires*, pp. 183–90. New Delhi: The Viveka Foundation.

Starr, A. (2000) *Naming the Enemy: Anti-corporate Movements against Globalization*. London: Zed Books.

——(2005) *Global Revolt: A Guide to the Movements against Globalization*. London: Zed Books.

58

Moving

Migration, mobility

Ronald Skeldon

Every person moves unless physiologically unable to do so. The freedom of the individual to move was enshrined internationally in Article 13, paragraph 2 of the Universal Declaration of Human Rights adopted by the General Assembly of the United Nations in December 1948 which states that 'everyone has the right of freedom of movement and residence within the borders of each state' and that 'everyone has the right to leave any country, including his own, and to return to his country' (United Nations 1998: 11). A universal punishment for wrongdoing is to deny the right of people to move by imprisoning them. Although everyone and every human group moves, some move more frequently and farther than others. Those who study population migration and population mobility essentially attempt to explain how this comes about: why some people and some groups move more than others, and what the implications of these movements are. These implications range from the impact of migration on development or poverty, and the impact of development and poverty on migration, through to the relative participation of migrants in community or state institutions, to more abstract issues such as identity and sense of belonging. Migration in the current discourse has virtually come to signify movement across an international boundary (see Cohen 1995; Castles and Miller 2003; Weiner 1995, for example) with internal population movements known as 'population redistribution' and largely associated with urbanization. However, international migration is but a subset of total human population mobility and the discussion of moving, migration and mobility provides an opportunity to present all forms of population movement within a single framework.

Definitions, concepts and types of movers and migrants

Some of the movements are daily, commuting to work; others are weekly or monthly to centres of marketing or recreation, others annually to holiday resorts, while yet others are irregular and for long periods of time that are often associated with a change of residence. A change in the place of residence 'resets' the pattern of daily and weekly movement from a new base. Roseman (1971) perhaps still provides the classic statement on these forms of movement. The longer-term movements associated with a change of residence are generally considered to be a 'migration', whereas shorter-term movements around the residence are thought of as 'mobility' although, in practice, it is difficult to distinguish between the two. Regular seasonal shifts in residence associated with nomadism, for example, typify a society in a permanent state of migration, and at one time the migratory nomad was seen as a total contrast to the 'sedentary' peasant. The peasant was often associated with immobility but, as we now know, the idea of the sedentary peasant in pre-modern society was one of the myths of migration. Settled societies were usually highly mobile, often within fairly restricted areas based upon parish and market, but also over longer distances to centres of pilgrimage or on military expeditions. Migration and mobility did not begin with the industrial revolution and the advent of modern systems of transportation, even if they were profoundly affected by such innovations: they are as old as humankind. Perhaps one valid theoretical distinction that can be drawn between nomad and peasant mobility is that the former move within a uniform and self-contained system while the latter move in a complex society, where mobility creates links between different types of societies and economies. These types of mobility, unlike those associated with nomadism, can facilitate and engender change.

Migration, unlike the other two basic demographic variables, fertility and mortality, is not a discrete and unique event but is a continuous process across space and through time. One of the preoccupations of those who study migration and mobility has been definition. The volume of mobility that is measured by techniques such as population censuses and surveys depends entirely on the criteria employed. Clearly, mobility as defined by an absence from a household of twenty-four hours or more that involves leaving the settlement will include very many more people than if it is defined as an absence of at least three months and involves crossing the nearest provincial boundary. Hence, before any analysis of data on mobility can be made, one needs to know just how it is defined. The characteristics of those who are short-term and short-distance movers are usually different from those who move more definitively and over long distances. In some societies, the former flows may include greater proportions of women, for example, and larger numbers of unskilled movers compared with longer-term, longer-distance movers. Definitions that make so much of mobility and migration a statistical artefact make comparison across countries particularly difficult. Rarely can we say from census data that the citizens in country X are more or less mobile than those in country Y.

The idea of immobility, too, persists (see, for example, Hammar *et al.* 1997). However, this idea is predicated upon restricting a migration to a movement between large spatial units. For example, the total number of international migrants in the world around the year 2000 was estimated by the United Nations (2002) at around 150 million, a large number by any standard but representing less than 3 per cent of the world's population. Even given a large margin of error in the calculation of the figure, only a tiny minority of the world's population move across an international boundary. Most people move but do so within the borders of their country, with the majority moving locally. Linkages between local, regional and international population movements, and how these change over time, have formed a key area of enquiry for population geographers (Zelinsky 1971; Skeldon 1990) as migration and mobility form a critical human link between local and global societies and economies.

Not only do the spatial and temporal dimensions used to define mobility and migration vary markedly but so, too, do the reasons for moving. The image of 'the migrant' as someone who leaves his or her home to set up a new home elsewhere, either as a permanent resident in a town or as an immigrant to another country, represents today a minority of those who move. Perhaps they always did represent a minority, as people seldom move definitively with no thought of return. The process of migration consists of complex systems of back, forth and onward movements that defy easy categorization. Also, people move for many reasons other than just changing their home or becoming an immigrant to another country. Individuals move to continue their education or to work on specific jobs, or are sent by their companies. For this reason, specific mobility or migration systems are often identified, each with their own particular gender, educational or skill characteristics. Marriage migration and settler migration would perhaps come closest to the original ideal of what a migration actually is, but there are also patterns of student migration, contract labour migration and skilled migration. Within skilled migration itself, different sub-systems might be identified to distinguish those who were sent to a destination for a specific period of time by their company and those highly skilled who moved independently to find a job. The patterns of the mobility might also vary by profession: those in service provision, such as health professionals, may have different characteristics and patterns of movement from engineers, for example.

Separate from these movements that are essentially controlled by conditions in the labour market, people are also forced to move for reasons of persecution. Where that movement crosses an international boundary, those who are forced to move are classified as 'refugees'; if the movement is within a country they are classified as 'internally displaced persons'. The former are clearly the responsibility of the international community whereas the latter, while 'of concern' to international agencies, fall within the jurisdiction of a sovereign state in which outside powers are reluctant to interfere. However, the international refugee regime itself changed, too, over the last decades of the twentieth century, from a policy based upon the resettlement of those displaced towards one of creating conditions that will allow the displaced to return. In terms of human mobility, the policy shifted from one of migration to one of circulation and return. This shift was associated with a global refugee population that increasingly changed from being dominated by people of European extraction in the aftermath of the Second World War, towards a pattern dominated by forced migrants from developing countries in Asia and Africa. After the debacle in Rwanda in 1993, the international community began to involve itself in the internal affairs of specific states, perhaps most notably in the former Yugoslavia in Kosovo (see Chapter 18) and in Afghanistan, but also in Sierra Leone. One of the objectives was to limit the number of international migrants arriving in the developed world and to foster regional and local return movements. Now that the precedent of intervention in state sovereignty has been set, it seems likely that it will continue even if tempered by *realpolitik* that will see little intervention in the internal affairs of large and powerful countries.

The distinction between forced and more voluntary movements is, as in so many issues dealing with migration, not a clear-cut division. Among those movements influenced by labour markets, whether a transfer from one country to another is a voluntary or a forced move that is controlled by the particular needs of a company seems a moot point. Market forces, too, may be among the root causes of conflict, and factors bringing about forced and voluntary population movements may overlap. Development itself can directly impel movement through the expansion of urban and industrial areas on to agricultural land, the construction of roads or, most obviously, the flooding of river valleys consequent upon the building of a dam for the generation of power, for irrigation or flood control. The construction of the Three Gorges project in China, for example, is likely to displace more than 1 million people. In this case those displaced can never go home. Yet others are displaced by environmental catastrophes such as earthquakes, tsunamis or through volcanic activity (see Chapter 41), or more man-made activities that destroy local habitats. Most of these conditions result in local movements only. Some have coined the term 'environmental refugees' for this type of forced migration, although the term 'refugee' denotes a very specific type of forced migrant (Black 1998). Despite any continuum between forced and voluntary population movements, people fleeing from persecution mark a significant group, with a clear international definition and consequent legislative apparatus. The term 'refugee' should be left, without dilution, to apply to these cases alone.

Mobility systems, migration and development

The social spaces in which movers operate and live their lives, 'mobility spaces', extend and contract over time and reflect the nature of our society and economy. These spaces represent human linkages between areas, important conduits through which information, money and goods, as well as people, flow. Mobility spaces vary greatly in type and scale. The most ubiquitous are daily movements from places of residence to places of employment, commuting in the modern developed economy. Advances in transportation (described in Chapter 13) have allowed the separation of home from work to spread outwards from major urban centres, relieving densities in the urban core but spreading urban ways of living far into what were once rural areas. The difference between day-time and night-time populations of leading metropolitan areas can be substantial. For example, the daytime population of Tokyo in 2000 was, at 14.7 million, some 2.6 million greater than the night-time population (Japan 2004). Origins and destinations of commuting are tightly bound together as the diurnal waves of population movement spread a uniformity of lifestyle across a wide area, eroding senses of local village community and promoting global metropolitan mores. On a more practical level, differences in daytime and night-time populations have significant implications for energy consumption and the provision of appropriate services in origin and destination areas.

Limits to the amount of deconcentration that commuting can allow may exist. The ratio of day-time to night-time populations of Tokyo increased steadily from 116.4 in 1980 to 124.4 in 1995 but subsequently showed a slight decline to 122.0 in 2000. However, these data need not necessarily indicate the beginnings of a shift away from a commuter lifestyle. One of the very few generalizations that can be made about migration and mobility is that the majority of those who move are young adults. As populations age and the proportion of those in the cohorts most likely to move declines, we can expect the number of those who move, too, to decline. Thus, important linkages exist between shifting patterns of fertility and mobility that are yet poorly understood and clearly apply not just to patterns of commuting but to all forms of population mobility.

Longer-term circular mobility, often seasonal migration, can have a significant impact, and especially in the developing world where agriculture is still a significant source of employment. Bangkok is a city of anywhere between 5.7 and almost 9 million people, but one of the difficulties in estimating its population is that the difference between the wet- and dry-season populations is thought to be around 10 per cent (Chamratrithirong et al. 1995). Villages in the northeast of the country are closely tied to the capital through this regular human circulation and are transformed, not just by the money that the migrants bring back with them but by the ideas and new practices that they have learned while away from their villages. Of course, population mobility is not the only factor bringing about change in more isolated rural parts of the country. Government education policies, the role of the mass media, the extension of roads and electricity, and so on, are all part of the matrix of transformation that is known as 'development' (see Chapter 11). Mobility is, however, an essential component of this change as young people may have to move to an adjacent settlement if they want to pursue their education. Once this has been obtained, they may have to move to an urban area if they want to receive benefit from that education. Circular migration brings the money that allows the purchase of radio and television sets and of the bicycle and the pick-up truck. The army, one of the pillars of the construction of the state, takes young men out of the local community to regional and national training centres to instil in them communal national values. It is impossible to envisage development without changing patterns of population mobility but, rather than reflecting a failure of development, migration and forms of short-term mobility indicate and underlie development itself.

The great migrations out of Europe over the second half of the nineteenth century were a function of a period of globalization and rapid economic development in that continent. They were generally not a flight from poverty or a migration of the poorest. Poor people did migrate, as they do today, but the poorest do not move very far as they cannot afford to do so. Many of those who left Europe ostensibly as settlers to North America, like so many in the developing world today, did not leave definitively but with the idea of return. Some never did return, but estimates place rates of return for Europeans of up to 50 per cent (Baines 1991; Nugent 1992; Hatton and Price 2005). Today, increasing migrations from the developing to the developed world are not from the poorest countries but from those that are undergoing rapid development. Many of the migrants from those countries, too, return to their home countries. Hence, development is associated positively, perhaps not with an age of migration in a narrow sense but with the growing volume and increasingly complex forms of mobility.

With development and a transition to low fertility, a transition in mobility has also occurred in some countries with a consequent shift from out-migration towards in-migration and a change in the relative balance between net emigration towards net immigration. In Europe, even such traditional countries of emigration as Ireland and the southern European countries of Portugal, Spain, Italy and Greece have become net importers of population (Zimmermann 2005). A parallel process has been observed in the developed economies of East and Southeast Asia as South Korea, Taiwan, Malaysia and even Thailand have shifted from being economies that essentially sent labourers overseas on short-term contracts to economies that import labour on both a longer and a short-term basis (Abella 1994). Not all economies necessarily follow exactly the same pathways through a transition, but the result is a more interconnected and urban world. Globally, the proportion of the world's population that lived in urban areas was estimated at 29.1 per cent in 1950. By 2000, that proportion had increased to 47.1 per cent, and by 2025 some 58.3 per cent of the world's population will live in towns and cities. In the developing world, those proportions grew from 17.9 in 1950 to 40.5 in 2000. Expected to rise to an estimated 54.2 in 2025 (United Nations 2004: 23).

The transition from a predominantly rural to an urban society is truly one of the great transformations of our time and is built upon intersecting circuits of population mobility. Mobility between rural and urban areas is fundamental to this shift but, perhaps more importantly, circulation between among urban areas across international boundaries helps to drive the process. Skilled migrants, many as representatives of transnational corporations, extend the global economy outwards from core developed economies in Europe, North America and East Asia, spreading common labour practices, labour standards and legal agreements into areas that were once the realm of customary law. They establish the nuclei of offshore processing that provide the opportunities for local and national migrants. The representatives of international organizations and international banks consolidate this process, all serviced by an expanding network of health, educational and retailing facilities to cater to expatriate populations. Expatriates, however, are but one component of these transnational

945

elites (Sklair 2001) as return members of the diaspora community play a growing role in the economic and political life of their homelands. The geographical and social implications of these circuits of mobility is marked out in changing local contexts.

Landscapes of migration and mobility

It could be argued that all landscapes result from population and environment interrelations, and hence stem from mobility. However, some landscapes are more obviously associated with mobility than others. The deserted villages of late medieval England, the empty valleys of the Scottish Highlands following the Clearances, or the severely depopulated rural municipalities (*kaso*) of Japan, all bear mute testimony to a rural exodus the various causes of which lay far beyond their immediate areas. These causes mainly revolved around the demand for labour in new industrial economies or the landowners' power to create more viable commercial rural economies. In the case of the Highland Clearances, the image is perhaps stronger than the reality. Permanent migration from Scotland came predominantly from the prosperous southern and eastern parts of the country, with the lowest rates from the poorer northern and western regions most affected by the Clearances (Richards 2000). Yet the invisible links between rugged terrain in Scotland and present-day communities in Canada remain a powerful emotional image of forced migration and abandoned livelihoods with parallels across rural areas of many parts of the world, both developed and developing.

Other markers of landscapes of mobility are found in new construction in villages of origin: modern houses totally at variance with the traditional ancestral village dwellings. The 'sterling' houses built in the villages of the New Territories of Hong Kong from the 1960s with money from migrants in the United Kingdom (Watson 1975) find their counterparts in the houses of the 'Londoni' in Sylhet in Bangladesh or the houses in Kerala in southern India built with monies from contract labour in the Gulf States. Some of the migrants return to occupy their houses, others never do, but the idea of return is another powerful force linking the local with the global: 'global migrants, local lives' (Gardner 1995). Money and goods sent back by migrants in towns and overseas, and their impact on development, have become one of the major themes in current migration research. Estimated at some US $182 billion in 2004, of which US $125.8 billion flowed to developing countries, remittances represent the largest source of external financing in the developing world after foreign direct investment (Maimbo and Ratha 2005: 3–4). These estimates represent only those remittances sent through formal channels and in some countries it has been estimated that as much again comes through informal channels. Remittances are important as they are a direct flow of funds to migrants' families. The use of this money, whether for investment or for consumption, has been a matter of some concern. Remittances are the economic foundation of local households with global transnational linkages. Apparent expenditure on conspicuous consumption such as a house or even a local festival can have important multiplier effects for employment and production in the local area. Remittances are not a panacea for development: they tend to flow back only to a few parts of a country of origin and can exacerbate interregional and intra-community disparities in wealth, for example, but they are one of the most powerful effects of migration on development in specific areas.

Landscapes of mobility are also found in destination areas where markers indicate the origins of those who have settled and worked the land. Types of house and barn and forms of human settlement in parts of rural North America indicate the history of European occupation of the land. European cultures were not completely transferred: no single Scottish,

French or Spanish culture exists, and a rapid adaptation to new contexts is mapped out in styles, customs and new dialects adopted in complex response to specific conditions of the new environment (see Foster 1960). The settlement of eastern North America from the early seventeenth through to the late eighteenth century was characterized by four distinct migration flows that can be generalized as follows: from the eastern counties of England to Massachusetts; from the southern counties towards Virginia; from the northern Midlands towards Delaware; and from highland Britain to the backcountry of the American colonies (Fischer 1989). Those four flows gave rise to four separate culture regions, 'folkways', in terms of vernacular architecture, agricultural practices and social attitudes and behaviour that can still be discerned in the eastern United States today. Folk architecture, cultural transfer and adaptation to the land have all been prominent themes in studies in human and cultural geography in North America (see Zelinsky 1992; Meinig 1986).

It is in the global city, however, that the landscapes of mobility are writ most large. J.K. Rowling, the author of the best-selling Harry Potter novels, was allegedly told not to set her first novel in her home city of Edinburgh because 'Edinburgh is Edinburgh, but London is anywhere' (cited in Stenhouse 2005: 190). Although net migration is only one component in the growth of any city, along with natural increase and reclassification, it is the one that gives the city its most distinctive face. Migration brings together people from different parts of the country and, in the case of global cities, from different parts of the world. Ethnic neighbourhoods and diversity mark the global city, and such cities have become an ethnic mosaic and melting pot for peoples from all around the world. In London at the beginning of the twenty-first century, some 2.2 million people, or 30 per cent of the population, had been born outside England, a figure that excludes the children of immigrants born in England (Benedictus 2005). Of the social and linguistic groups that could be identified in London as non-indigenous, some fifty communities had populations of 10,000 or more. Over 300 languages were identified as spoken by the residents of the city. A macabre reminder of how multicultural London society has become was illustrated in the bombings on 7 July 2005: almost twenty different nationalities were represented among the fifty-two victims killed.

Centres of global capitalism such as New York, London, Los Angeles, Paris and, increasingly, Tokyo, have brought in workers, both skilled and unskilled, to service the world economy (Sassen 2001). Migration and mobility bring migrants to the cities and link them back to their communities of origin. The resultant circuits of mobility bring local communities in areas of origin into contact with a wider world through their communities in the global city. Not that these ethnic communities are exact reproductions of their home areas. They are not. Nor are destination enclaves hermetically sealed. The migrants interact and intermarry with other groups. The migrants act as a channel for global influences back to the local areas of origin through the transmission of ideas, as well as the material remittances. Skilled people move onwards from global cities to settlements further down the urban hierarchy, to oversee the expansion of economic endeavour into the developing world. Global cities are not just centres of attraction for migrants, they are centres of a circulation that reaches to the farthest parts of our world. They have also become icons of our time, with architectural monuments and a cultural and artistic life that makes them a magnet for tourist and terrorist alike.

Mobility, identity and belonging

The mobility of populations among economies at different levels of economic development and of very different cultural values raises fundamental issues with who the migrants think they are and raises questions of migrant identity and belonging. It is only when we encounter 'the other' that we can truly know ourselves, and the multicultural environments of some destinations generate new hybrid cultures and identities. Variations depend on the types of migrants, their cultural heritage, and particularly their education and skill background. The nature of the destination area is also critical to the outcome: whether, for example, policies of integration or multiculturalism are promoted or not. Linkages between origin and destination, and the circulation of migrants between them, have given rise to the idea of transnational communities that can challenge both the state of origin and the state of destination as a primary source of identity and belonging. Migrants from India to the United States, for example, are neither Americans nor Indians but some hybrid kind of person that combines a bit of both cultures and can, chameleon-like, shift from the one area to the other. It is only upon return to the place of origin that migrants realize the extent to which they have changed. The origin, too, may have changed in their absence, and they feel 'at home' neither in their origin nor in their destination. A literature on 'exile' has emerged to give expression to feelings of loss for a – usually idealized or even mythical – origin, and alienation towards the destination (Robertson *et al.* 1994; Simpson 1995)

Abstract perceptions of belonging and a lost sense of place have generated more practical and policy concerns that evolve round the issue of security. Origin states may see migrants as coming from disaffected or minority groups that establish cells abroad that might seek to raise funds for separatist movements. Sikh or Sri Lankan Tamil migrants in North America and Europe, for example, have been seen at various times to have acted not in the best interests of their states of origin. Destination states may also seek to use migrant groups to achieve geopolitical aims in regions of origin. Conversely, origin states or self-declared transnational religious groups may use migrants to try to achieve objectives within states of destination. Thus, transnational circuits of mobility have emerged as a major political challenge to states and the established global order and are at the root of the current drive for the more effective management of migration. Irregular migration and trafficking have emerged as major issues on the international agenda, not simply to eliminate practices that lead to the exploitation of migrants in vulnerable situations but also to attempt to control exactly who can enter a state. In an era of globalization, the nature of state is changing (see Chapter 19).

The idea of the transnational community finds expression in a concept that has become increasingly common in studies of international migration: the diaspora. Originally applied to the expulsion of the Jewish peoples from Israel or to other cases where the majority of a population was forcibly expelled into exile, in modern discourse the term has come to be used for virtually any group of migrants living beyond their homeland. Diaspora also incorporates second, third and further generations of migrants in specific ethnic communities. Implicit in the use of the term 'diaspora', however, is the idea of the migrant as victim and of populations living in exile waiting to come home. Not all migrants are victims, as the earlier discussions should have made clear. Many are skilled and highly entrepreneurial, and the majority are better educated and wealthier than those who remain, even if these differences in education and wealth are relative. Poor people do move, even if the very poorest move only locally and over the short term: the wealthier, the restless and the innovative move further and more often, usually seeking an improvement in their livelihood. Not all migrants wish to return, at least on a permanent basis. Assimilation or some form of integration with destination communities does take place. Migration does engender subtle shifts in identity and ways of thinking. Women migrants may appreciate being away from patriarchal societies, and all may appreciate political and cultural freedoms of wider, more flexible societies away from the local networks of the peasant community. Migrants move into the relative political freedoms of the global, in contrast to the constraints of the local. Not that all migrants are free. Work in regimented factories is hardly 'freedom', but for many the experience of migration and the participation in a greater world than the purely local engender a sense of hope that cannot be attained in the area of origin.

Today, the diaspora is seen as a powerful 'tool' for development (Newland and Patrick 2004). Remittances from the members of the diaspora and the drawing on diaspora communities for skills needed at home are seen to combat the loss of highly skilled people from developing countries (the so-called 'brain drain'). While the impact of the brain drain is neither so general nor so deleterious as might first be assumed, migrant communities overseas and the circulation between destinations and origins do form an important source of capital and expertise for the developing world. The diaspora, however, is not as homogeneous as many assume: it is highly heterogeneous and diffuse and rarely will have populations that exactly mirror those of the state of origin (Skeldon 2001). Migrants are not randomly selected from areas of origin but tend to be self-selected by wealth and ability. More importantly, they often tend to come from very specific parts of the state of origin, with one region, one ethnic group, even one class more heavily represented than others from the same state. Diaspora members, although living and working in a more global context overseas, may have more local concerns when they look towards their homeland. The security concerns outlined above and the specific origins and destinations of international mobility systems fracture any attempt to create easy divisions between global and local concerns with respect to a sense of identity or belonging.

Conclusion

The mobility of people in the early twenty-first century is one of the more obvious signs of globalization. While migration and the movement of people are certainly not new, improvements in the technology of transportation and communication have allowed more people to move in a greater variety of ways than ever before. The international movement of people is the result of regional differences in wealth, relative rates of growth of labour forces and the demands for labour. Internal movements, too, are often the result of global forces of international investment and of political change. Unlike the movement of capital, goods and information, the movement of people is subject to a much greater degree of control. The number of open borders in the world is few, within the countries of the Schengen Agreement, or between Ireland and the United Kingdom in Europe, between the United States and Canada and between India and Nepal, for example. Borders are important and states are seeking to increase their powers to manage migration more successfully according to some kind of immigration policy. Despite calls to 'think the unthinkable' (Harris 2002) and do away with border controls altogether, it seems unlikely that national controls in favour of a more global economy will disappear in the near future. Even more limited proposals to work towards introducing greater flexibility in globalizing labour markets through such institutions as the World Trade Organization, by facilitating the movement of 'natural persons' in specified occupations through GATS mode 4, seem unlikely to be reached. Existing commitments to liberalize movement under GATS mode 4 refer primarily to highly skilled workers moving within the network of transnational corporations and foreign direct investment (Winters et al. 2002). Developing countries have the comparative advantage to supply workers at lower cost but the developed world is unlikely to agree to any proposal on trade that will facilitate the increased movement of labour, as this is a backdoor to immigration. This tension between labour and immigrants is one of the inherent contradictions in globalization and, in liberal democratic political systems in which governments must be responsive to their electorates, it seems that local state interests will override more global interests. One way of resolving the tension between labour and immigration is to look to outsourcing, mode 2 of GATS. In this scenario, clients move to services, and what were once local services such as routine health care and some levels of education move overseas and thus become global (Kapur and McHale 2005; Skeldon 2005).

Although the mobility of people is the 'stickiest' of the major global flows of capital, goods, information and labour, it may also be the most persistent. Should we witness a collapse of globalization and a return to a more nationalist world (Saul 2005), migration might slow, but the communities created through prior migration seem destined to remain. It would take an extreme reversal in the values of liberal democracies, based as they are upon human rights, to seek to expel ethnic communities. And expel them to where? For those born in destination societies or who came as young children, the destination society is home. The idea of non-indigenous peoples living in diaspora is deceptive indeed. Idealized and mythical homelands are very different from destinations with the actual right of residence. Irrespective of the direction of global forces, the lack of integration of migrant and ethnic groups into destination economies and societies is a failure of local (national) policy, and any retreat from the global towards the local may have positive benefits for migrants, paradoxical though this might at first appear. Nevertheless, it is difficult to see migration and mobility disappearing from the global agenda. The demographic inertia created by declining fertility and an ageing population will maintain a demand for certain types of labour in areas where ageing is most acute. Ultimately, a global ageing of population is likely to see a reduction in the absolute numbers of movers simply as a result of the decline in the numbers of those most likely to move. However, the process of ageing does not occur uniformly across space or through time and, over the medium term, will maintain mobility to more-developed from less-developed parts of the world even in the face of increasing attempts to control or manage the flows of migrants. This global force of demographic change (described in Chapter 9), while not completely independent from economic and political change, is less volatile and will continue to affect the direction and volume of population mobility irrespective of the direction of the latter. However, the local response to these global forces in terms of types and frequencies of movers and types of national responses towards management of migration and integration will continue to be highly complex and varied, no matter whether the tide of globalization is flowing or ebbing.

Further reading

Boyle, P., Halfacree, K. and Robinson, V. (1998) *Exploring Contemporary Migration*. London: Longman.

Castles, S. and Miller, M. (2003) *The Age of Migration: International Population Movements in the Modern World*, third edition. London: Macmillan Palgrave.

Cornelius, W.A., Tsoda, T., Hollifield, J.F., and Martin, P.L. (eds) (2003) *Controlling Immigration: A Global Perspective*, second edition. Stanford: Stanford University Press.

IOM (2005) *World Migration 2005*. Geneva: International Organization for Migration.

Massey, D.S., Arango, J., Hugo, G., Kouaouci, A., Pellegrino, A. and Taylor, J.E. (1998) *Worlds in Motion: Understanding International Migration at the End of the Millennium*. Oxford: Clarendon Press.

McKeown, A. (2004) Global migration, 1846–1940. *Journal of World History* 15, 155–89.

Migration Policy Institute (2005) http://www.migrationinformation.org

Siddique, M.A.B. (2001) *International Migration into the 21st Century: Essays in Honour of Reginald Appleyard*. Cheltenham: Edward Elgar.

——(1997) *Migration and Development: A Global Perspective*. London: Longman.

Skeldon, R. (2001) The dangers of diaspora: orientalism, the nation state and the search for a new geopolitical order. In M.A.B. Siddique (ed.) *International Migration into the 21st Century: Essays in Honour of Reginald Appleyard*, pp. 109–25. Cheltenham: Edward Elgar.

UNHCR (2000) *The State of the World's Refugees: Fifty Years of Humanitarian Action*. Oxford: Oxford University Press.

Zlotnik, H. (1999) Trends of international migration since 1965: what existing data reveal. *International Migration* 37, 21–61.

Zolberg, A.R., Suhrke, A., and Aguayo, A. (1989) *Escape from Violence: Conflict and the Refugee Crisis in the Developing World*. New York: Oxford University Press.

References

Abella, M.I. (ed.) (1994) Turning points in labour migration. *Asian and Pacific Migration Journal* 3 (special issue).

Baines, D. (1991) *Emigration from Europe 1815–1930*. London: Macmillan.

Benedictus, L. (2005) London: the world in one city. *Guardian* 21 January (special supplement).

Black, R. (1998) *Refugees, Environment and Development*. Harlow: Longman.

Boyle, P., Halfacree, K. and Robinson, V. (1998) *Exploring Contemporary Migration*. London: Longman.

Castles, S. and Miller, M. (2003) *The Age of Migration: International Population Movements in the Modern World*, third edition. London: Macmillan Palgrave.

Chamratrithirong, A., Archavanitkul, K., Richter, K., Guest, P., Thongthai, V., Boonchalaksi, W., Piriyathamwong, N. and Vong-ek, P. (1995) *The National Migration Survey of Thailand*. Bangkok: Mahidol University, Institute for Population and Social Research.

Cohen, R. (ed.) (1995) *The Cambridge Survey of World Migration*. Cambridge: Cambridge University Press.

Cornelius, W.A., Tsoda, T., Hollifield, J.F. and Martin, P.L. (eds) (2003) *Controlling Immigration: A Global Perspective*, second edition. Stanford: Stanford University Press.

Fischer, D.H. (1989) *Albion's Seed: Four British Folkways in America*. New York: Oxford University Press.

Foster, G.M. (1960) *Culture and Conquest: America's Spanish Heritage*. Chicago: Quadrangle Books.

Gardner, K. (1995) *Global Migrants, Local Lives: Travel and Transformation in Rural Bangladesh*. Oxford: Clarendon Press.

Hammar, T., Brochmann, G., Tamas, K. and Faist, T. (eds) (1997) *International Migration, Immobility and Development*. Oxford: Berg.

Harris, N. (2002) *Thinking the Unthinkable: The Immigration Myth Exposed*. London: I.B. Tauris.

Hatton, T.J. and Price, S.W. (2005) Migration, migrants, and policy in the United Kingdom. In K.F. Zimmermann (ed.) *European Migration. What Do We Know?* pp. 113–72. Oxford: Oxford University Press.

IOM (2005) *World Migration 2005*. Geneva: International Organization for Migration.

Japan (2004) *Japan Statistical Yearbook 2004*. Tokyo: Statistics Bureau, Ministry of Internal Affairs and Communications.

Kapur, D. and McHale, J. (2005). *Give Us Your Best and Brightest: The Global Hunt for Talent and its Impact on the Developing World*, Washington DC: Center for Global Development.

Maimbo, S.M. and Ratha, D. (2005) Remittances: an overview. In S.M. Maimbo and D. Ratha (eds) *Remittances: Development Impact and Future Prospects*, pp. 1–16. Washington DC: World Bank.

Massey, D.S., Arango, J., Hugo, G., Kouaouci, A., Pellegrino, A. and Taylor, J.E. (1998) *Worlds in Motion: Understanding International Migration at the End of the Millennium*. Oxford: Clarendon Press.

Meinig, D.W. (1986) *The Shaping of America: A Geographical Perspective on 500 Years of History. Volume 1, Atlantic America, 1492–1800.* Yale: Yale University Press.

Newland, K. and Patrick, E. (2004) *Beyond Remittances: The Role of Diaspora in Poverty Reduction in their Countries of Origin.* Washington DC: Migration Policy Institute.

Nugent, W. (1992) *Crossings: The Great Transatlantic Migrations, 1870–1914.* Bloomington: Indiana University Press.

Richards, E. (2000) *The Highland Clearances: People, Landlords and Rural Turmoil.* Edinburgh: Birlinn.

Robertson, G., Bird, J., Curtis, B., Mash, M. and Tickner, L. (eds) (1994) *Travellers' Tales: Narratives of Home and Displacement,* London: Routledge.

Roseman, C.C. (1971) Migration as a spatial and temporal process. *Annals of the Association of American Geographers* 61, 589–98.

Sassen, S. (2001) *The Global City: New York, London, Tokyo,* second edition. Princeton: Princeton University Press.

Saul, J.R. (2005) *The Collapse of Globalism.* London: Atlantic Books.

Simpson, J. (ed.) (1995) *The Oxford Book of Exile.* Oxford: Oxford University Press.

Skeldon, R. (1990) *Population Mobility in Developing Countries: A Reinterpretation.* London: Belhaven.

——(2001) The dangers of diaspora: orientalism, the nation state and the search for a new geopolitical order. In M.A.B. Siddique (ed.) *International Migration into the 21st Century: Essays in Honour of Reginald Appleyard,* pp. 109–25. Cheltenham: Edward Elgar.

——(2005) *Globalization, Skilled Migration and Poverty Alleviation: Brain Drains in Context* (Working Paper T15). Brighton: University of Sussex, Development Research Centre on Migration, Globalization and Poverty.

Sklair, L. (2001) *The Transnational Capitalist Class.* Oxford: Blackwell.

Stenhouse, D. (2005) *How the Scots Took Over London.* Edinburgh: Mainstream Publishing.

United Nations (1998) *International Migration Policies.* New York: United Nations Population Division, Department of Economic and Social Affairs.

——(2002) *International Migration 2002.* New York: United Nations Population Division, Department of Economic and Social Affairs.

——(2004) *World Urbanization Prospects: The 2003 Revision.* New York: United Nations Population Division, Department of Economic and Social Affairs.

Watson, J.L. (1975) *Emigration and the Chinese Lineage: The Mans in Hong Kong and London.* Berkeley: University of California Press.

Weiner, M. (1995) *The Global Migration Crisis: Challenge to States and to Human Rights.* New York: HarperCollins.

Winters, L.A., Walmsley, T.L., Wang, Z.K. and Grynberg, R. (2002). *Negotiating the Liberalization of the Temporary Movement of Natural Persons* (Discussion Papers in Economics No. 87). Brighton: University of Sussex.

Zelinsky, W. (1971) The hypothesis of the mobility transition. *Geographical Review* 61, 219–49.

——(1992) *The Cultural Geography of the United States,* revised edition. Englewood Cliffs: Prentice Hall.

Zimmermann, K.F. (2005) *European Migration. What Do We Know?* Oxford, Oxford University Press.

59

Dwelling

Pau Obrador-Pons

One of the main concerns of human geography is the relation between human culture and the natural environment. How we live on and with the natural world, the impact of our activities on the environment and the social meaning of nature have been for a long time at the centre of the discipline. The interest of human geographers is not limited to nature. It extends to all facets of human life, which are all bound up with questions of space and place. Human geography is uniquely concerned with the spatiality of social life: that is, with the way human beings encounter, know, co-construct and experience the world in which we live. This is not an abstract facet of human life. Encounters with the spatiality of the world permeate our everyday lives.

In recent years, notions of dwelling have been proposed as an alternative style of thinking about many aspects of spatiality. Many commentators have made use of this concept to think of nature and landscape (Ingold 1995, 2000; Macnaghten and Urry 1998; Franklin 2002; Cloke and Jones 2001; Wylie 2003; see also Chapter 2), place and space (Thrift 1999; Urry 2000; Casey 1998), the role of objects (Lury 1997), tourism (Obrador-Pons 2003) and surfing (Shields 2004). Notions of dwelling, however, are not new to geography, but have been used before mainly in humanist approaches. Dwelling features strongly in the work of David Seamon (e.g. Buttimer and Seamon 1980; Seamon and Mugerauer 1985; Seamon 1993) and Yi Fu Tuan (e.g. 1976, 1977) but rather fell out of fashion in the disciplinary retreat from humanistic approaches during the cultural turn of the late 1980s and 1990s. The resurgence of dwelling as a motif responds to a growing unease with conventional epistemologies and, in particular, with the common separation of people and space. Notions of dwelling are by no means alone in responding to this sense of unease as other theoretical developments have demonstrated, most notably Actor Network Theory (Latour 1999; Law and Hassard 1999), Non-Representational Theory (Thrift 1999, 2004) and notions of performativity (Rose 1999; Dewsbury 2000) and hybridity (Haraway 1991; Whatmore 2002). All of these approaches defy the idealism that dominates Western thought.

The sense of unease to which these theories respond stems from the inadequacy of conventional approaches to 'making sense' of the spatiality of human life. Dominant ways of thinking in geography are often premised upon the severance of subjects and objects. The same division is replicated between culture and nature. These binary divisions are not simply physical demarcations; they are first and foremost ontological separations. Conventional approaches assume a distal and idealistic form of knowledge wherein a detached subject contemplates the world from an outside point of view. In this scheme of thought the emphasis is placed on a penetrating gaze seeking the a priori order of things, their intrinsic foundations and underlying meanings and structures. Such spectatorial epistemologies have left us with a de-materialized and disembodied view of the world and are described in more detail in Chapter 36. Giving priority to detached forms of knowledge, human relations with the environment are reduced to an intellectual and visual exercise, leaving little space for skilful, embodied coping or engagement with the environment. In this context the material world seems only to exist either as an unavoidable precondition – a mere container of human activities – or as the product of social construction.

This chapter considers the so-called dwelling perspective in geography. The aim is two-fold: first, to comment upon recent developments that make use of dwelling; and second, to assess the value of dwelling. The underlying question is whether notions of dwelling provide a useful framework for understanding the complex relations between human culture and nature. This chapter is structured in four parts. The first presents the theoretical development and traces its philosophical roots. The fundamental experience of involvement is identified as the primary focus of this approach. The second part looks at how dwelling has been deployed in re-materializing and re-embodying landscape, an entity previously reduced to symbols and representation. While bridging the Cartesian gap between the material and the ideal, dwelling does, however, risk erecting new binaries between vision and embodied practice. A third section returns to the original question and considers what makes dwelling attractive as an alternative framework for understanding relations between people and nature. Geographers and other social scientists have turned to dwelling in search of an interconnected and embodied view of these relations that can still retain a notion of place. The final part considers the limitations of the dwelling perspective. If dwelling is to be a useful concept in geography, its interpretative scope has to be extended beyond its original usage. It should register the fleeting as well as the enduring, the mobile as well as fixed, the modern as well as the traditional.

The dwelling perspective

In geography, the concept of dwelling owes its reputation to the work of Tim Ingold (1995, 2000), an anthropologist with an interest in hunter-gatherer societies, human–animal relationships and human ecology. He turned to the phenomenological writings of Heidegger and Merleau-Ponty searching for more adequate ways of understanding the relations between people and the environment. Ingold felt uneasy with the conventional belief that humans inhabit intentional worlds, in which life is designed prior to its material realization. This belief prompts the unreasonable conclusion that human beings develop a dual existence as organisms and as persons, that is half nature and half culture, half body and half mind (Ingold 2000: 172). In suggesting a split-level existence, conventional ways of thinking effectively reintroduce a Cartesian dichotomist epistemology.

Notions of dwelling provide a valuable route for those seeking to move beyond dichotomist ways of thinking such as those troubling Ingold. Dwelling leaves no place for theories that perpetuate a Cartesian division between the material and the ideal, the brain and the body. Instead, a sense of proximity and togetherness, of staying with things, is presupposed. The embeddedness of human beings in the world is the primary focus of this approach (Dreyfus 1991; Casey 1998; Ingold 2000; Cloke and Jones 2001; Wylie 2003; Thrift 1999).

Being is always being-in-the-world: that is, a situated and contingent process of engagement with the environment. For Heidegger, to be-in does not primarily refer to the spatial location of human activities – that is, to sheer containment – but refers to the involvement of humans with things (Dreyfus 1991: 42). Dwelling connotes taking care, being familiar with, cherishing or looking after, which according to Heidegger are the primordial meanings of the term. It is worth noting that some of the usages of the preposition 'in' still have an existential sense which expresses involvement, as in being in love or being in business (Dreyfus 1991: 46). By giving emphasis to involvement, notions of dwelling argue against the severance of human beings from the material environment. 'Dwelling is about the rich intimate ongoing togetherness of beings and things which make up landscapes and places, and which bind together nature and culture,' Cloke and Jones point out (2001: 651). Human beings reside somewhere alongside things in an intense relationship with the environment.

Recognition of dwelling implies a shift from the so-called 'building' perspective, where ideal mental constructs are imposed on the world. Notions of dwelling reverse the normal order of priority of form over process. 'Life ... is not the revelation of pre-existent form, but the very process wherein form is generated and held in place,' Ingold points out (2000: 173). Conventional 'building' approaches sees humans as unique beings occupying intentional worlds. Contrary to animals, whose relations with the environment consist of practical absorption into the landscape, human engagement in the world is thought to be designed in the imagination, in webs of meaning, prior to the material realization. Humans appear to cover the world with a 'tapestry of meaning' (Ingold 2000: 177). The trouble with building perspectives is that a pre-given order before life is presupposed. As Ingold points out: 'Something ... must be wrong somewhere, if the only way to understand our own creative involvement in the world is by taking ourselves out of it' (Ingold 1995: 58). A dwelling perspective does not deny the importance of processes of social construction, but sees them as possible only because we are engaged in the world. 'Any act of building, living, or even thinking, is formed in the context of already being-in-the-world' (Cloke and Jones 2001: 651). What a dwelling perspective denies is the possibility of representing the world, of extracting an image of some naturally present, externally given reality. Human imagination does not pre-exist human practices. 'People do not import their ideas, plans or mutual representations into the world, since that very world ... is the homeland of thoughts they do' (Ingold 1995: 76). Consciousness does not precede the act of dwelling, but emerges from it.

In their current usage, notions of dwelling take for granted the primacy of pragmatic involvement. Central to the work of Ingold is the idea that our commitment with the world is mainly practical and not cognitive. Being-in-the world consists of an everyday skilful, embodied coping or engagement with the environment. A dwelling perspective suggests that the world is disclosed without resorting to deliberate consciousness. According to Dreyfus, 'Subject–object epistemology is secondary to what may be termed "the directly given and fundamentally experience of involvement"' (1991: 42). However this interpretation of dwelling may be read as an alteration of the original meaning. Dwelling as formulated by Heidegger in his essay 'Building, dwelling, thinking' (1993) does not imply simply the primacy of the practical activity. Heidegger does not overcome Cartesianism by eliminating the spiritual components of our lives. Instead he integrates it. In his later writings, Heidegger makes space for dwelling in depth: that is, for the invisible and spiritual components of our lives (Casey 1998: 273). It is by means of dwelling that humans become humans. And not only because they are practically involved in the world in a constant manipulative frequently unreflexive relation (participation) with things and people, but also through bringing the fourfold elements, earth, sky, divinities and mortals together in one entity (Harrison 2007: 17) since we-are-in-the-world life is preserved from dispersion and dis-integration.

Despite the lack of concern for movement, a dwelling perspective can be aligned with relational and performative approaches to place, for example those of Massey (2005) and Thrift (1999). Within a dwelling perspective, place is considered as a situated and relational phenomenon wherein humans and non-humans are bounded together co-constituting and performing the world. These are not abstract relations, but material interactions between people and their environment, 'relations which are necessarily embedded material practices that have to be carried out', Massey explains (2005: 9). Place emerges as a lived entity that is always in the process of being made. It is always under construction, never finished or closed. A relational and performative notion of place (see Chapter 5) does not necessarily exclude in-material elements. Places are the result of multiple relations, including invisible and spiritual ones. 'The ecology of place is a rich and varied spectral gathering, an articulation of presence ... and seething absences' (Thrift 1999: 316–17). Places haunt us at the same time that we haunt them. That is, places frequently visit us in the form of ghosts, since they are constituted through human and non-human dwelling. By leaving space for the invisible in the visible, an understanding of place as a lived and autonomous entity is made possible.

Dwelling and landscape

In geography notions of dwelling have been extensively deployed in re-materializing and re-embodying cultural geographies of landscape (Ingold 2000; Cloke and Jones 2001; Wylie 2003). Many commentators have turned to dwelling as a means to renovate the conceptual basis of a field which was felt to be 'sliding out of sight' with the performative turn and nascent critiques to representation. Its main appeal comes from the fact that it provides a passageway between the 'cultural turn' and theorizations of praxis and performance (Wylie 2003: 141–2). In re-conceptualizing landscape as a 'milieu of involvement', a 'kinaesthetic medium of practices' (Wylie 2003: 155), dwelling is able to transcend the theoretical impasse of culturalist approaches to landscape and re-materialize an entity that has often been reduced to texts, representation and ways of seeing.

Tim Ingold was the first to use notions of dwelling to think of landscape. For Ingold the 'Landscape is constituted as an enduring record of – and testimony to – the lives and works of past generations, who have dwelt within it, and in so doing have left there something of themselves' (2000: 189). Landscape is presented as something different from land and space. It is neither quantitative nor homogeneous but qualitative and heterogeneous, it is the world as known to those who inhabit it. This means that landscape is neither just a 'way of seeing' nor simply an object of contemplation, but the sedimentation of mundane everyday practices of humans and non-humans. As Ingold explains:

> A place owes its character to the experiences it affords to those who spend time there – to the sights, sounds and indeed smells that constitute its specific ambience ... It is from this relational context of people's engagement with the world, in the business of dwelling, that each place draws its unique significance.
>
> (2000: 192)

We are not spectators of landscape but participants in it, not just with the eyes, but with the whole of our body. Landscapes are felt through the senses

Ingold provides illustration of his dwelling approach to landscape through an analysis of a European rural scene called *The Harvesters*, painted by Pierre Brueghel in 1565 (Ingold 2000: 201–7). In this analysis, landscape is presented as the historical record of human dwelling. Rather than focusing on the symbolism of the scene, Ingold brings to the fore how landscape is felt as it is incorporated into our bodily experience. Particularly illuminating is his analysis of the paths that traverse the landscape. For Ingold, paths reveal the accumulated imprint of countless journeys. They are the sedimentation of the mundane activity of an entire community over many generations.

> Taken together, these paths and tracks 'impose a habitual pattern on the movement of people' (Jackson 1989: 146). And yet they also arise out of that movement, for every path or track shows up as the accumulated imprint of countless journeys that people have made . . . as they have gone about their everyday business.
>
> (Ingold 2000: 204)

At the centre of the painting there is a pear-tree, around which the landscape is ordered. Echoing Heidegger's analysis of the bridge (1993), Ingold suggests that the very place arises out the solid presence of that tree. In part the tree constitutes the scene.

> But this is not just a tree. For one thing, it draws the entire landscape around it into a unique focus: in other words, by its presence it constitutes a particular place. The place was not there before the tree, but came into being with it.
>
> (Ingold 2000: 204)

A commentary of a church, the hills, the valley, the cornfields and the people complete the analysis of the painting. Two elements are central in this rural landscape: the solid materiality of non-human elements such as the tree and the everyday imprint of the people who live and work in it.

The notion of landscape developed by Ingold is considered in combination with temporality. For Ingold, landscape 'unfolds the lives and times of predecessors who, over the generations have moved around in it and played their part in its formation' (2000: 189). Landscape is not only saturated with the lives and practices of those who have lived there in the past, it also gathers many projections into the future. In his account the present is not detached from the past and the future; instead, all three are gathered together in the landscape 'like refractions in a crystal ball'. Landscape is a place of memory that tells multiple stories, evoking different temporalities and spatialities. Central to Ingold's approach to landscape and temporality is the notion of taskscape, which refers to the array of 'practical operations carried out by a skilled agent in an environment as part of his or her normal business of life' (2000: 195). The so-called taskscape is what confers the social character to landscape, what saturates the place with memories. For Ingold the temporality of the taskscape is neither chronological nor historical, but social. Time is not an external abstract frame that covers up the world but is something that emerges from the engagement of people in the manifold tasks and practical activities of dwelling. As he points out, 'the notion that we can stand aside and observe the passage of time is founded upon an illusion of disembodiment. This passage is, indeed, none other than our own journey through the taskscape in the business of dwelling' (2000: 196). For Ingold, temporality and landscape are quintessentially performed, enacted.

Drawing on notions of dwelling, Ingold manages to transcend the theoretical impasse of conventional approaches to landscape and re-materialize an entity that has often been reduced to texts, symbols and representations. While bridging the Cartesian division between the material and the ideal, his dwelling perspective risks erecting new binaries between vision and embodied practice, in which vision is defined negatively. As Wylie points out: 'The sense remains that the "dwelling perspective", and notions of embodied practice and performance more widely, in some sense involve a rejection of the visual gaze' (2003: 145). In the work of Ingold there is what Hinchliffe terms an 'earthy romanticism' that gives priority to embodied practices and the know-how that makes living possible, and marginalizes the textual and the visual (Hinchliffe 2002: 220). A disdain for the visual, together with its rustic romantic connotations, has been singled out as the main weaknesses of the dwelling perspective.

If it is to be a useful concept, a dwelling perspective must not eliminate the visual. In his critique, Wylie speaks to the need to re-sensitize seeing by recasting it as bodily sensuous experience. Although vision is often identified as external and detached, it still is part of the sensuous apparatus of the body and as such is one of the ways through which we experience and co-construct landscape. For Wylie, the dwelling perspective must not reject the visual but reconfigure it as a practice of dwelling.

> Rather than focusing upon a critique of particular cultural forms of visuality, and their association with, for example, discourses of objectivity, control and authority, the task of a dwelling perspective upon landscape should involve a reconfiguration of vision such that . . . the activity of gazing is itself understood as a practice of dwelling.
>
> (Wylie 2003: 146)

Neither should a dwelling perspective reject texts. As Hinchliffe points out, texts such as landscape paintings are not simply representations but experiments that make places habitable. They are actions that produce connections. Rather than arguing for fewer texts, textualities can actually be pursued, for the production of an inhabitable and affective world. 'Rather than looking for things that exist outside texts, the aim becomes one of gaining understanding of how texts (perhaps among other means) can enable what Latour calls a "learning to be affected"' (2002: 216)

Notions of dwelling are valuable ideas for cultural geographies of landscape. However, they cannot be taken uncritically. To do so would risk erecting new binaries, and would exclude some legitimate modes of engagement with the world, in particular vision and textuality.

Human–nature relations

Notions of dwelling provide a valuable route for those seeking to re-theorize human–nature relations. Its main value comes from its ability to transcend the theoretical and methodological impasse of conventional approaches, which envision nature either as an unavoidable precondition – a mere container of human activities – or as the product of social construction (Franklin 2002; Macnaghten and Urry 1998). Emphasizing performativity, involvement and togetherness, notions of dwelling have the potential to break up this sterile dichotomy, paving a way between naturalist and culturalist approaches (Ingold 2000: 189). A dwelling perspective offers an interconnected and embodied view of human–nature relations, which acknowledges the complex, diverse and overlapping ways humans experience the environment.

Nature came to be seen as a collection of always localized and relational phenomena embedded in particular times and spaces. This interconnected view of the world is not detrimental to a notion of place as is the case of Actor Network Theory (Cloke and Jones 2001). Humans and non-humans are interwoven together, co-constructing and performing the world without stripping either of its own agencies.

Moreover, notions of dwelling offer the opportunity to move beyond an occulocentric view of nature. Much writing on nature takes for granted a visual and cognitive relation with the environment. Human experience of nature is often reduced to a practice of visual consumption, wherein a detached subject has the privilege to observe nature from a vantage point. Nature transpires as a collection of views, which are extraordinary and separated from everyday life. This means concealing the complex and contradictory ways people inhabit the world around them. The reduction of nature to visual representations and its conversion into spectacle participate in the occulocentrism that since modernity has dominated not only the experience of nature but also the whole Western culture (Jay 1994). When notions of dwelling are employed, the visual is no longer treated as a disembodied relation with the world and nature is no longer reduced to visual representations. In a dwelling perspective, being is always being-in-the-world, a situated, embodied and contingent process of engagement with the environment. To be in nature is not only a question of being 'located' in nature or 'representing' nature but of practising and performing nature. A dwelling perspective assumes that nature is always experienced in sensual and embodied terms. Encountering nature is a complex and diverse process in which vision smell, touch, sound and kinaesthetics overlap.

By taking into account what exceeds the rational and the visual, notions of dwelling have the potential to unveil new dimensions of the human engagement with nature. Such is the case with the beach. An account of the tourist experience of the beach is uncompleted if it focuses only on the visual consumption of the beach even when considering this already as an embodied practice. Working within a visual framework neither exhausts the experience of the beach nor overcomes the limitations and contradictions of vision. On the beach there are other articulations of senses, movements and taskscapes that penetrate the surfaces and superficialities of modern visual natures. Most of the time the beach is experienced in sensual and embodied terms, through a combination of visual and non-visual senses, distal and proximal modes of engagement. What makes the beach a distinctive and pleasant experience is the direct exposure of the skin to the sun as well as the possibility of manipulating the sand and moving the body into the water. Swimming, sunbathing and building sandcastles – the most characteristic beach activities – suggest a haptic order of the sensible, as well as a visual one. The beach shares with other leisure activities such as hunting and angling (Franklin 2001, 2002), walking (Edensor 2000) and adventure sports (Cloke and Perkins 1998) a performative character.

Nature is something material, not ideal, that is socially constituted through both discursive and non-discursive everyday practices. 'Each such nature,' Macnaghten and Urry argue, 'is constituted through a variety of socio-cultural processes from which such natures cannot be plausibly separated' (1998: 1). Nature is not an external and pre-given reality, it is always a localized and relational phenomenon embedded in particular times and spaces. This means that there is no singular nature but a diversity of different natures. In using the notion of dwelling, Ingold (2000) and Macnaghten and Urry (1998) are able to eschew the unproductive tension between naturalistic and culturalist approaches. Nature is not conceived as a neutral, external backdrop to human activities that has the power to produce unambiguous, observable and rectifiable outcomes – the point of view of environmental realism; nor is it seen as a particular cognitive or symbolic ordering of space – the point of view of environmental idealism (Ingold 2000: 189; Macnaghten and Urry 1998: 1). As Franklin points out, 'nature is always and everywhere socially constructed but it is also a performed as well as a lived and dwelt experience' (2002: 7).

Notions of dwelling offer an interconnected view in which humans and non-humans are bounded together, co-constituting and performing the world. In a dwelling perspective, human culture and the natural environment are not independent from each other, but blended together and often confused. The focus is not the borders of nature and culture but the interface and hybridization of both realities. There are at least two common grounds between dwelling perspectives and hybrid geographies (described in Chapter 41): a radical opposition to Western dualisms and constituted totalities like the binary opposition between nature and culture; and an argument 'for pleasure in the confusion of boundaries and for responsibility in their construction' (Haraway 1991: 154). Dealing with the interface of people and nature means considering 'transgressed boundaries, potent fusions and dangerous possibilities' (Haraway 1991: 154). Human societies cannot be thought of as apart from things, whether natural environments like the beach or manmade things like a house or a car. In a dwelling perspective this interconnected and hybrid view of the world is not detrimental to a sense of place and agency, as is often the case in Actor Network Theory (ANT). Cloke and Jones locate here some of the main differences between these two perspectives. Notions of dwelling:

> could provide a fruitful framework for giving notice to the physical active presence of actants other than humans; doing so in a way similar to ANT, but yet acknowledging the creative agency of particular entities, and taking into account the common ground that is place.
>
> (2001: 654)

Humans and non-humans are bounded together without losing their agency.

Authenticity and dwelling

There are major downsides in the dwelling metaphor that considerably narrow the interpretative scope of the concept. The main trouble derives from its common association with authenticity. Traditional modes of dwelling are often presented as the authentic mode of being-in-the world. In so doing, dwelling carries romantic and rustic connotations, which do not correspond with the way we live in the contemporary world. This links with other concerns such as the 'partial eschewing of the visual' (Wylie 2003: 145), the ignorance of bodily movement (Urry 2000: 133) and the 'framing of the landscape (Cloke and Jones 2001: 663). Dwelling can only be useful if is adapted beyond its original nostalgic usage to explain not only pre-industrial rural communities but also contemporary fleeting societies.

Dwelling was not originally conceived to embrace contemporary urban life. In its original usage, dwelling is almost impossible under the conditions of modernity. In much of the literature (including Macnaghten and Urry 1998) a rural pattern of life rooted in a particular earth and world is taken as the model form. Modernism is presented as alienating and destructive, whereas stable rural communities are commonly identified as genuine and authentic. The prominence of the traditional over the modern itself stems from Heidegger. Cloke and Jones point out that 'A sinister (nationalistic) rustic romanticism ... pervades Heidegger's ideas' (2001: 661). His argument takes for granted a close relationship between authenticity and dwelling. The discrimination between authentic and non-authentic modes of dwelling suggests nostalgia for fictitious pre-industrial societies as well as a desire to live in a harmonious and stable place. In the work of Heidegger there is a persistent anxiety for the stranger, the uncanny and the unfamiliar (Casey 1998). The 'original' sense of dwelling puts forward important questions about the relation between human culture and the natural environment in contemporary conditions. Taken to their extreme, such arguments lead, paraphrasing Cloke and Jones, to 'a view of true nature, or authentic landscape, or communities, as consisting of diminishing pockets of harmonious authentic dwelling in an ever-encroaching sea of alienation' (2001: 657). Without adaptation notions of dwelling are unable to explain the contemporary world.

In its original usage, only territorial forms of engagement create dwelling and produce spaces and temporalities. There is a coincidence between place, community and landscape, which leads to a locality-based and 'presentist' sense of place (Hinchliffe 2002: 220). Assuming the oneness of people and the environment, dwelling commonly implies physical proximity and spatial fixity, neither of which corresponds with the fleeting reality of today's globalized world. There is the risk of obscuring the multiple and complex connections and virtualities that transcend local boundaries, thus mistaking place and landscape as solely a local achievement. An emphasis on the proximal and the static pervades much of the literature on dwelling. The kind of dwelling that Heidegger has in mind is a 'dwelling in nearness' (Casey 1998: 281): enduring, self-contained and time-deepened. This vision of a local bounded harmonious community corresponds with his vision of the idyllic peasant life in the Black Forest. There is no dwelling in the urban, mobile, fragmentary life of the city. Ingold's pursuit of dwelling also contains a certain degree of romanticism (Urry 2000; Cloke and Jones 2001; Wylie 2003). The societies upon which Ingold rests his notion of dwelling are hunter-gatherers, apparently unaffected by the shrinking of the planet, the acceleration of Western life and increasingly global flows and mobilities. Ultimately Ingold's work emphasizes spatial fixity and physical proximity and the prominence of bounded local space. As Urry points out:

> In the painting described by Ingold, propinquity, localness and communion thus coincide. But in the contemporary world they almost never coincide. The emergence of new, often more or less instantaneous mobilities mean that the patterns of dwelling described by Ingold require extensive reconceptualization.
>
> (Urry 2000: 136)

The oneness of people and the environment is equated to a reciprocal face-to-face interaction.

A useful employment of dwelling in geography must extend its interpretative scope beyond the analysis of traditional pre-industrial societies. In the Western world only a tiny bit of human experience corresponds with such a romantic and rustic view of dwelling. It is a matter of fact that our societies are no longer arranged as bounded, face-to-face communities. Place, community and landscape often do not correspond. Central to modernity is a variety of bodily movements and interconnections that extend all over the world. Travel and tourism, migration and diasporas, instant communications and other technologies are now everyday experiences, at least in the West. Even quotidian objects we live with in proximal close relationships incorporate many mobilities. As Chapter 61 implies, only a tiny proportion of what we consume is local. As Massey points out, these complex networks and mobilities, far from destroying the local sense of place, are often what make these places unique and different (Massey 2005). Without the ethnic mix of people, exotic cuisines and communication technologies, our cities would not be the interesting and exciting places they are today. We must neither comprehend the contemporary world as an inauthentic way of dwelling, nor treat modern societies as if they were hunters and gatherers, avoiding their mobile and fluid reality. As Urry points out:

> There are ... a variety of ways of dwelling, but once we move beyond that of land, almost all involve complex relationships between belongingness *and* travelling, within and beyond the boundaries of national societies. People can indeed be said to dwell in various mobilities.
>
> (2000: 157, italics in original)

A relationship between belonging and travelling is not exclusive of modernity. Traditional societies also involve complex relationships between them. The gypsy and Jewish communities are good examples of dwelling-in-mobilities.

If dwelling is to be a useful concept in geography it should register the fleeting as well as the enduring, the mobile as well as fixed, the global as well as the local. Promising insights can be gained by articulating transitory experiences such as tourism in terms of involvement rather than location or detachment (Obrador-Pons 2003). Doing tourism is not only a matter of being in space or representing the space. It is, above all, a matter of practising space and practising through space. That is, tourists are not only in place but also involved with the place, although not in the same manner that non-tourists are. Tourism is a form of dwelling that often corresponds with what Urry and Macnaghten term 'leisure landscapes'. This kind of 'dwellingness' is distinctive in the exceptional power of the visual sense, the pre-eminence of an aesthetic sensibility and the temporal and geographical estrangement from everyday life. 'In such leisure landscapes,' Macnaghten and Urry argue, 'work, leisure and domestic routines are geographically and temporally estranged from each other and the physicalities of the situated body are leisured and have nothing to do with those of land per se' (1998: 7–8). Most holidaymakers do not engage with the places they visit as insiders, like the peasant does, working the land as a way of economic survival. Their 'dwellingness' is not that of the land, but that of the 'landscape'. They approach the environment as consumers and pleasure-seekers through practices that not only pursue the visual consumption of the place but also allow them 'to get away from it all' and re-live a simpler and more natural life. In considering transitory and banal experiences such as tourism, the challenge is to grasp this reality as dwelling without concealing the flows, networks and connections that make it possible. The non-bounded character of tourism cannot be an excuse to reintroduce a de-specialized, ungrounded subject.

Conclusion

This chapter has examined the possibilities and limitations of the so-called dwelling perspective. It has been conceived as both an introduction to recent developments that have made use of dwelling, and as a critical review of the concept. Dwelling provides a valuable route for those seeking to move beyond dichotomist ways of thinking that sever the material and the ideal as well as culture and nature. Its main value is the provision of an alternative style of thinking about the spatiality of human life, including human–nature relations. A dwelling perspective takes for granted an interconnected and embodied view of the world that still retains a notion of place (Cloke and Jones 2001). Place, nature and landscape emerge as situated, localized and material phenomena wherein humans and non-humans are bound together, co-constituting and performing the world. By emphasizing involvement over detached contemplation, scholars such as Ingold (2000) manage to re-materialize and re-embody cultural geographies of landscape, thus renovating the conceptual basis of a field that was felt to be 'sliding out' of sight with the performative turn and the nascent critiques to representation (Wylie 2003).

Despite its enormous potential, the use of notions of dwelling in geography is not without pitfalls. There are major downsides in the dwelling perspective that considerably narrow the scope of the concept, the main one being its rustic and romantic overtones. Dwelling was not originally conceived to embrace contemporary urban life. In its original usage, dwelling is almost impossible under the conditions of modernity. Other concerns refer to the 'partial eschewing of the visual' (Wylie 2003: 145), the ignorance of bodily movement (Urry 2000: 133) and the 'framing of the landscape' (Cloke and Jones 2001: 663). While bridging the Cartesian division between the material and the ideal, the dwelling perspective risks erecting new binaries between vision and embodied practice, fleeting and enduring life. All these weaknesses ultimately derive from its common association with authenticity. While some particular forms of being-in-the-world seem to create dwelling, others appear to destroy dwelling. If dwelling is to be a useful concept in geography it should register the fleeting as well as the enduring, the mobile as well as fixed, the global as well as the local.

Further reading

Cloke, P. and Jones, O. (2001) Dwelling, place and landscape: an orchard in Somerset. *Environment and Planning A* 33, 649–66.
Heidegger, M. (1993) Building, dwelling, thinking. In M. Heidegger, *Basic Writings*, revised and expanded edition, pp. 344–63. London: Routledge.
Ingold, T. (2000) *The Perception of the Environment: Essays in Livelihood, Dwelling and Skill*. London: Routledge.
Obrador-Pons, P. (2003) Being-on-holiday: tourist dwelling, bodies and place. *Tourist Studies* 3 (1), 47–66.
Wylie, J. (2003) Landscape, performance and dwelling: a Glastonbury case-study. In P. Cloke (ed.) *Country Visions*, pp. 136–57. London: Longman.

References

Buttimer, A. and Seamon, D. (eds) (1980) *The Human Experience of Place and Time*. New York: St Martin's Press.
Casey, E.S. (1998) *The Fate of Place: A Philosophical History*. Bloomington, IN: Indiana University Press.
Cloke, P. and Jones, O. (2001) Dwelling, place and landscape: an orchard in Somerset. *Environment and Planning A* 33, 649–66.
Cloke, P. and Perkins, H. (1998) Cracking the canyon with the awesome foursome: representations of adventure tourism in New Zealand. *Environment and Planning D: Society and Space* 16 (2), 185–218.
Dewsbury, J. (2000) Performativity and the event: enacting a philosophy of difference. *Environment and Planning D: Society and Space* 18, 473–97.
Dreyfus, H.L. (1991) *Being-in-the-World: A Commentary on Heidegger's Being and Time, Division 1*. Cambridge, Mass.: MIT Press.
Edensor, T. (2000) Walking in the British countryside: reflexivity, embodiment and ways to escape. *Body and Society* 6, 81–106.

Franklin, A. (2001) Neo-Darwinian leisures, the body and nature: hunting and angling in modernity. *Body and Society* 7 (4), 57–76.

——(2002) *Nature and Social Theory.* London: Sage.

Haraway, D. (1991) *Simians, Cyborgs, and Women: The Reinvention of Nature.* London: Free Association Books.

Harrison, P. (2007). The Space between Us: Opening Remarks on the Concept of Dwelling. *Environment and Planning D.*

Heidegger, M. (1993) Building, dwelling, thinking. In M. Heidegger, *Basic Writings*, revised and expanded edition, pp. 344–63. London: Routledge.

Hinchliffe, S. (2002) Inhabiting – landscapes and natures. In K. Anderson, M. Domosh, S. Pile and N. Thrift (eds) *Handbook of Cultural Geography*, pp. 207–25. London: Sage.

Ingold, T. (1995) Building, dwelling, living: how animals and people make themselves at home in the world. In M. Strathern (ed.) *Shifting Contexts: Transformations in Anthropological Knowledge*, pp. 57–80. London: Routledge.

——(2000) *The Perception of the Environment: Essays in Livelihood, Dwelling and Skill.* London: Routledge.

Jackson, M. (1989) *Paths Towards a Clearing: Empiricism and Ethnographic Enquiry.* Bloomington, Indiana: Indiana University Press.

Jay, M. (1994) *Downcast Eyes: The Denigration of Vision in the 20th Century French Thought.* Berkeley: University of California Press.

Latour, B. (1999) *Pandora's Hope: Essays on the Reality of Science Studies.* London: Harvard University Press.

Law, J. and Hassard, J. (eds) (1999) *Actor Network Theory and After.* Oxford: Blackwell.

Lury, C. (1997) The objects of travel. In C. Rojek and J. Urry (eds) *Touring Cultures: Transformations of Travel and Theory*, pp. 15–95. London: Routledge.

Macnaghten, P. and Urry, J. (1998) *Contested Natures.* London: Sage.

Massey, D. (2005) *For Space.* London: Sage.

Obrador-Pons, P. (2003) Being-on-holiday: tourist dwelling, bodies and place. *Tourist Studies* 3 (1), 47–66.

Rose, G. (1999) Performing space. In D Massey, J. Allen and P. Sarre (eds) *Human Geography Today*, pp. 247–59. Cambridge: Polity Press.

Seamon, D. (ed) (1993) *Dwelling Seeing and Designing: Towards a Phenomenological Enquiry.* Albany, NY: New York University Press

Seamon, D. and Mugerauer, R. (eds) (1985) *Dwelling Place and Environment: Towards a Phenomenology of Person and World.* New York: Columbia University Press.

Shields, R. (2004) Surfing: global space or dwelling in the waves? In M. Sheller and J. Urry (eds) *Tourism Mobilities: Places to Play, Places in Play*, pp. 44–52. London: Routledge.

Thrift, N. (1999) Steps to an ecology of place. In D. Massey, J. Allen and P. Sarre, (eds) *Human Geography Today*, pp. 295–322. Cambridge: Polity Press.

——(2004) Summoning life. In P. Cloke, P. Crang and M. Goodwin (eds) *Envisioning Geography*, pp. 81–103. London: Arnold.

Tuan, Y.F. (1976) Humanistic geography. *Annals of the Association of American Geographers* 66, 266–76.

——(1977) *Space and Place.* Minneapolis: University of Minnesota Press.

Urry, J. (2000) *Sociology Beyond Societies: Mobilities for the Twenty-First Century.* London: Routledge.

Whatmore, S. (2002) *Hybrid Geographies: Natures Cultures Spaces.* London: Sage.

Wylie, J. (2003) Landscape, performance and dwelling: a Glastonbury case-study. In P. Cloke (ed.) *Country Visions*, pp. 136–57. London: Longman.

60

Communicating

Barney Warf

Geography – the study of how human beings are stretched across and utilize the surface of the Earth – inevitably involves some account of how people communicate with one another. All social processes necessitate communications in one form or another, including flows of ideas, data and information through space and time. This process is central to the manner in which social formations are structured and change spatially, and in changing experience of time and space. Despite this obvious importance, communications have, however, long been relatively 'invisible' in the discipline of geography (Hillis 1998).

Starting in the 1960s, geographers began to supplement models of transportation with models of communications that began to underscore a more plastic and mutable view of space. Janelle (1969) offered a seminal analysis of how declining transportation times brought places closer together via time–space convergence. Ronald Abler (Abler and Falk 1981, 1985; Falk and Abler 1980, 1985) played a key role in shifting attention from transportation to communications, particularly the role of public services in facilitating interaction over space. Brunn and Leinbach (1991) edited an influential volume, *Collapsing Space and Time*, which took this theme further, opening up the geographical analysis of new technologies (e.g. satellites) and markets (e.g. finance). Geographers have also been vitally interested in the ways in which communications are used to represent spaces in media such as film and place marketing for tourism. By virtue of its one-way flow of information, the analysis of media is necessarily somewhat removed from communications.

A highly influential contemporary interpretation of the impacts of communications has been Castells' (1996) notion of a 'space of flows', a digital context of interaction replacing the older 'space of places' where people live and work. As Castells emphasizes, the network society of contemporary capitalism has led to new political formations, forms of identity and spatial associations; he notes (1989: 349), for example, that whilst 'people live in places, power rules through flows'. Castells' ideas reflect the growing concern for the political nature of communications, the fact that all images (ranging from photos to literary descriptions) are inherently tied to a purpose. This also reflects a growing interest in humanistic geography and the symbolic nature of space and the increasing political sophistication of social science. Value-free approaches were becoming more problematic and social discourse was increasingly seen as being tied to political interests. Thus, the political economy of communications, and its geographic dimensions, has close theoretical ties to attempts to reveal all spatial discourses, such as maps, as inherently value-laden, with social origins and consequences (Harley 1989; Wood 1992; see also Chapter 36).

This chapter situates communication into this social context. It charts the impacts of technological change on telecommunication, focusing in particular upon the micro-electronics revolution as a major facilitator of global communication. I then move on to consider urban and economic consequences of these profound changes, with particular focus on office location, before describing the huge potentials for communication occasioned by the spread of the Internet and the rise of e-commerce. The central concern is the extent to which these changes are leading to the ostensible 'end of geography'.

Geography and telecommunications

Telecommunications are not a new phenomenon. As Hugill (1999) demonstrated, communication systems have been deeply interwoven with global and local geopolitics for more than a century and a half. In 1844, telecommunications began with Samuel Morse's invention of the telegraph, which allowed communications to become uncoupled from transportation. The telegraph made possible the worldwide transmission of information concerning commodity needs, supplies, prices and shipments – information that was essential to national and international commerce. Starting with the first trans-continental telegraph wire in 1861, the telegraph was important in the American colonization of the West, where it helped to form a national market by allowing long-distance circulation of news, prices, stocks and other information (Pred 1973). In 1868, the first successful trans-Atlantic telegraph line was laid, part of the round of international time–space compression that accompanied the Industrial Revolution (Standage 1998).

For decades after Alexander Bell's invention of the telephone in 1876, telecommunications were synonymous with telephone services (de Sola Pool 1977). Just as the telegraph was instrumental to the colonization of the American West, in the late nineteenth century the telephone became critical to the growth of industrial city-systems, allowing firms to centralize headquarter functions while they spun-off branch plants to smaller towns. Corporations with operations across different sites used the telephone to coordinate production and shipments. In the 1920s, the telephone, like the automobile and the single-family home, became a staple of the growing middle class (Fischer 1992). In the 1950s, direct dialling eliminated the need for shared party lines. Swept by neoliberal waves of deregulation in the 1980s, the telephone industry underwent profound changes with the break-up of AT&T in 1984, the introduction of new firms (e.g. MCI, Sprint) and massive technological change.

Even today, despite the proliferation of new technologies, the telephone remains by far the most commonly used form of telecommunications for businesses and households. Internationally, access to telephones is a common measure of a nation's communications infrastructure. Telephone penetration rates – the availability per 1,000 people – mirror and reinforce geographies of wealth and poverty around the globe. The United States and Canada have almost 50 per cent of the world's telephones, yet together, comprise only 4 per cent of the world's population. Africa has less than 1 per cent of the world's telephones and comprises 15 per cent of the world's population. Half of the world's population has never made a telephone call.

The introduction of the cellular phone ushered in a new wave of change in this regard. Given how widespread this technology is, surprisingly little is known about its social and spatial dynamics and impacts, such as the blurring of the distinction between the private and public domains. By allowing communication person-to-person rather than person-to-place, the cell phone offers unprecedented flexibility and access to communications. Today, more than half of the world's telephones are cell phones, with the fastest growth in the developing world, where it allows users to bypass expensive or out-of-date landlines.

Telecommunications and the microelectronics revolution

The microelectronics revolution of the late twentieth century was particularly important for the telecommunications industry, which is arguably the most rapidly expanding and dynamic industrial sector today. As data were converted from analogue to digital form, computer services merged with telecommunications. The digital format suffers less degradation over time and space, is much more compatible with the binary constraints of computers, and allows greater privacy. In response to the growing demand for international digital data flows beginning in the 1970s, the United Nations International Telecommunications Union introduced Integrated Service Digital Network (ISDN) to harmonize technological constraints to data flow. ISDN has since become the standard technical model of telecommunications worldwide.

Exponential increases in the ability of computerized systems to analyse and transmit data were crucial to post-Fordist 'digital capitalism' (Schiller 1999). No large corporation can operate in multiple national markets simultaneously, coordinating the activities of thousands of employees within highly specialized corporate divisions of labour, without access to sophisticated channels of communications. Thus, telecommunications are important to understanding broader issues pertaining to globalization and the world economy, including the complex relations between firms and nation-states (see Chapters 19 and 22).

Today, two technologies – satellites and fibre-optics – underpin the global telecommunications industry. Transmission capacity grew rapidly in the late twentieth century as the microelectronics revolution unfolded. Multinational corporations, banks and media conglomerates typically employ both technologies, often simultaneously, either in the form of privately owned facilities or as leased circuits from shared corporate networks. The skein of fibre lines linking the world constitutes the nervous system of the global financial and service economy, linking cities, markets, suppliers and information vendors around the world (Graham 1999).

Because international finance has become so inextricably intertwined with electronic transfer of funds worldwide, it presents the global system of nation-states with unprecedented difficulties while simultaneously attempting to avoid its risks. Friedman (1999: 90) writes of the 'Electronic Herd', which consists of:

> all the faceless stock, bond and currency traders sitting behind computer screens all over the globe, moving their money around with the click of a mouse from mutual funds to pension funds to emerging market funds, or trading from their basements on the Internet.

Global finance today is dominated by this vast assembly of large and small investors. In the context of electronic money, Kobrin (1997: 75) notes that:

> e-cash is one manifestation of a global economy that is constructed in cyberspace rather than geographic space. The fundamental problems that e-cash poses for governance result from this disconnect between electronic markets and political geography. The

967

very idea of controlling the money supply, for example, assumes that geography provides a relevant means of defining the scope of the market. It assumes that economic borders are effective, that the flow of money across them can be monitored and controlled, and that the volume of money within a fixed geographic area is important. All of those assumptions are increasingly questionable in a digital world economy.

Travelling at the speed of light as nothing but digital assemblages of zeros and ones, global money dances through the world's neural networks in astonishing volumes (well over $1 trillion per day in 2005 in the foreign exchange markets). National borders mean little in this context: it is far easier to move $1 billion from New York to Tokyo than a truckload of grapes from California to Arizona.

Urban impacts of telecommunications

There exists considerable confusion about the real and potential impacts of telecommunications on urban structure, in part caused by the long history of exaggerated claims. Often such views hinge upon a simplistic, utopian technological determinism that ignores the complex, often contradictory, relations between telecommunications and local economic, social and political circumstances. For example, repeated predictions by post-industrialists that telecommunications would allow everyone to work at home via telecommuting, dispersing all functions and spelling the obsolescence of cities, have fallen flat in the face of the persistence of growth in dense urbanized places. In fact, telecommunications are generally a poor substitute for face-to-face meetings, particularly when the information involved is irregular, proprietary and unstandardized in nature. Most managers spend the bulk of their working time engaged in face-to-face contact, and no electronic technology can yet allow for the subtlety and nuances critical to such encounters. For this reason, a century of technological change, from the telephone to fibre-optics, has left most high-wage, white collar, administrative command and control functions clustered in downtown areas.

In contrast, telecommunications are ideally suited for the transmission of routine, standardized forms of data, facilitating the dispersal of functions involved with their processing to low-wage regions. In short, there is no *a priori* reason to believe that telecommunications inevitably leads to the dispersal or deconcentration of functions; by allowing the decentralization of routine ones, information technology actually may enhance the comparative advantage of inner cities for non-routine functions (albeit with jobs generally filled by suburban commuters). Thus, telecommunications facilitate the simultaneous concentration *and* deconcentration of economic activities.

Contrary to popular claims that telecommunications would render all places equally accessible, the transformation to global, financially propelled post-Fordism accentuated the status of 'world cities', including London, New York and Tokyo, as well as, to a lesser extent, Paris, Toronto, Los Angeles, Osaka, Hong Kong and Singapore (Sassen 1991). These centres, which offer powerful agglomerative economies, play a disproportionate role in the production and transformation of international economic relations. London, for example, remains the largest centre of currency exchange in the world and the largest European financial centre. Similarly, New York has become the premier centre of the Americas. Tokyo likewise is the apex of Asian capital accumulation despite the prolonged recession of the Japanese economy. Such metropoles reveal the geographies of centrality and peripherality that accompany the birth of a neoliberal, digitized world system.

The new hypermobile capital markets also include new centres of offshore banking, a reflection of the shift from traditional banking services (loans and deposits) to lucrative non-traditional functions, including debt repackaging, foreign exchange transactions and cash management (Roberts 1994). The growth of offshore banking, usually in response to favourable tax laws, has stimulated banking in such previously unlikely places as Panama, Bahrain and the Netherlands Antilles. Offshore centres are the 'black holes' in the global topography of financial regulation, a status that emanates directly from the enhanced ability of large financial institutions to shift funds electronically to take advantage of lax regulations, freedom from taxes and currency controls, and other restrictions to be found on the periphery of the global financial system. Such centres reveal that as the technical barriers to moving money around have declined, the significance of political ones rises.

Within cities, telecommunications have contributed to an on-going reconstruction of urban space (Graham and Marvin 1996). For example, teleworking or telecommuting, in which workers substitute some or all of their working day at a remote location (almost always home) for time usually spent at the office, is often touted as the answer to traffic congestion (especially at peak hours), demands on energy, the need for office space, and environmental impacts such as pollution. The self-employed do not count as teleworkers because they do not commute. Telework is most appropriate for jobs involving mobile activities or routine information handling such as data entry or directory assistance. At present, only 2 per cent of the US labour force is engaged in telecommuting, although that share is likely to grow rapidly.

However, as Graham and Marvin (1996) point out, there are reasons why telecommunications may *increase* the demand for transportation rather than decrease it. First, while telecommuters spend fewer days at their workplace, it is not at all clear that they have shorter *weekly* commutes overall; indeed, by allowing them to live farther from their home, the total distances travelled may actually rise. Second, time freed from commuting may be spent travelling for other purposes, such as shopping or recreation. Telecommuting may alter the reasons for travel, but not necessarily the frequency or volume. Third, by reducing congestion, telecommuting may lead to significant induced effects, whereby others formerly inhibited from driving may be induced to do so. In short, whether or not a trade-off between telecommunications and commuting takes place may not be clear-cut.

Transportation informatics represents another significant and growing set of impacts. It encompasses a variety of improvements in surface transportation such as smart metering, electronic road pricing, synchronized traffic lights, automated toll payments and turnpikes, automated road maps, information for trip planning and navigation, travel advisory systems, electronic tourist guides, remote traffic monitoring and displays, and computerized traffic management and control systems, all of which are designed to minimize congestion and optimize traffic flow, enhancing the efficiency, reliability and attractiveness of travel. Wireless technologies such as cellular phones also allow more productive use of time otherwise lost to congestion.

Telecommunications and back office relocations

Another economic activity heavily affected by telecommunications is back office functions. Back offices perform routine data entry of office records, telephone books, library catalogues, payroll and billing, bank checks, insurance claims and magazine subscriptions. These tasks involve unskilled or semi-skilled labour, primarily women, and frequently operate on a 24-hour-per-day basis. Back offices have few of the inter-firm linkages associated with headquarters

969

activities and require extensive computer facilities, reliable sources of electricity and sophisticated telecommunications networks.

Historically, back offices have located near to headquarters in downtown areas to ensure close management supervision and rapid turnaround of information. However, as central city rents rose in the 1990s and companies faced shortages of qualified computer-literate labour in the cores of metropolitan areas, many firms began to uncouple their headquarter and back office functions, moving the latter to cheaper locations on the urban periphery. Given the flexibility afforded by satellites and fibre-optics lines, back offices also relocated on a broader, continental scale, making them increasingly footloose. In the USA, for example, many financial and insurance firms and airlines moved their back offices from large, coastal metropolitan areas to low-wage, small cities in the Midwest and South.

Internationally, this trend has taken the form of the offshore office. Offshore back offices are established not to serve foreign markets, but to generate cost savings for US or European firms by tapping low-cost Third World labour pools. Many firms with offshore back offices are in industries facing powerful competitive pressures to enhance productivity, including insurance, publishing and airlines. Several New York-based life insurance companies, for example, have relocated back office facilities to Ireland. Likewise, the Caribbean, particularly Anglophone countries such as Jamaica and Barbados, has become a particularly important locus for American back offices. American Airlines paved the way in the Caribbean when it moved its data processing centre from Tulsa to Barbados in 1981; through its subsidiary Caribbean Data Services, it expanded operations to Montego Bay, Jamaica, and Santo Domingo, Dominican Republic, in 1987. The rapid growth of call centres in Bangalore, India, is a similar reflection of this trend. Indeed, theatres in Manhattan can now use ticket sellers in Ghana, and offices there may employ security guards in Liberia (Worth 2002). Such trends indicate that telecommunications may accelerate the offshoring of many low-wage, low-value-added jobs with dire consequences for unskilled workers (see Chapter 55).

Geographies of the Internet

In the late twentieth century, as the cost of computing capacity dropped and processing power increased rapidly, telecommunications steadily merged with computers to form integrated networks. Like the railroad system of the nineteenth century and the interstate highway system of the twentieth century, the information highway of fibre-optic cables, satellites and wireless grids facilitates communication between people and places. It now includes billions of computers, telephones, faxes and other electronic products all over the world.

Among the various networks that comprise the world's telecommunications infrastructure, the largest and most famous is the Internet, which is, more accurately, a vast web of electronic networks. The Internet originated in the 1960s under the US Defense Department, which designed ARPANET to withstand a nuclear attack. The ability to make such a network function even if random nodes and links were removed or out of service was made possible by the technique of packet switching, which broke up messages into different groups and sent them separately, and by the Transmission Control Protocol/Internet Protocol (TCP/IP), in which individual messages may be decomposed, the constituent parts transmitted by various channels, and then reassembled, virtually instantaneously, at the destination. Through the National Science Foundation (NSF), a high speed data transmission 'backbone' for the US was created by the early 1990s. Similarly, a European Internet backbone emerged in the 1990s. Local Area Networks (LANs) operating in workplaces grew throughout in the 1990s, which saw the diffusion of the personal computer and Internet service providers such as America Online.

The growth of the Internet has been phenomenal; indeed, it is the most rapidly diffusing technology in world history. In 2005 an estimated 1.08 billion people, in more than 200 countries, were connected (Click Z Statistics 2005). However, there are large variations in the Internet penetration rate (percentage of people with access) among the world's major regions, ranging from as little as 0.9 per cent in Africa to as high as 62.2 per cent in North America. Inequalities in access to the Internet internationally reflect the long-standing bifurcation between the First and Third Worlds. While virtually no country is utterly without Internet access (although portions of Africa come close), the variations among and within nations in relative accessibility are huge. Given its large size, the US – with more than 185 million users, or 63 per cent of the population – dominates when measured in terms of absolute number of Internet hosts. The highest penetration rate is in Sweden (75.8 per cent), and connectivity rates are high in wealthy nations such as the Netherlands (63.7 per cent), Britain (58.2 per cent), and Germany (53.9 per cent); Eastern Europe lags considerably behind, and in Russia a mere 4.2 per cent of the population uses the Internet. In Asia, access is greatest in Taiwan (49.1 per cent) and Japan (46.4 per cent); about 5 per cent of China is hooked up. In Latin America, the largest numbers of users are found in Brazil (8 per cent) and Mexico (4.6 per cent). The Internet in Africa is essentially confined to South Africa. In all cases, per capita incomes are the key. Variations in the number of users are also reflected in the geography of Internet flows (although flow data are much harder to come by than are place-specific attribute data): 80 per cent of all international traffic on the Internet is either to or from the US.

Internationally, access to the Internet is deeply conditioned by the density, reliability and affordability of national telephone systems. Most Internet communication occurs along lines leased from telephone companies, many of which are state-regulated (in contrast to the largely unregulated state of the Internet itself). Prices for access vary by length of the phone call, distance and the degree of monopoly: in nations with telecommunications monopolies, prices are much higher than in those with deregulated systems. The global move towards deregulation in telecommunications will likely lead to more use-based pricing (the so-called 'pay-per' revolution), in which users must bear the full costs of their calls, and fewer cross-subsidies among different groups of users (e.g. between commercial and residential ones), a trend that will likely make access to cyberspace even less affordable to low-income users.

Within the US, significant discrepancies exist in terms of access to the Internet, largely along the lines of class, wealth and race (Chakraborty and Bosman 2005). While 50 per cent of US households have personal computers, only 20 per cent have modems at home. Access to computers linked to the Internet, either at home or at work, is highly correlated with income; wealthier households are far more likely to have a personal computer at home with a modem or high bandwidth connection than are the poor. White households used networked computers three times more frequently than did black or Latino ones. The elderly likewise often find access to the Internet to be intimidating and unaffordable, although they comprise the fastest-growing demographic group of users. American Internet users thus tend to be white and middle class, well educated, younger than average, and employed in professional occupations demanding college degrees.

Social and spatial differentials in access to the skills and equipment necessary to get on to the electronic highway threaten to create a minority underclass deprived of the benefits of cyberspace (Warf 2001). This phenomenon reflects the broader growth in inequality throughout industrialized nations generated by labour market polarization (i.e. deindustrialization and growth of low-income, contingent service jobs). Modern economies are increasingly divided between those who are comfortable and proficient with digital technology and those who neither understand nor trust it, disenfranchising the latter group from the possibility of citizenship in cyberspace. Despite falling prices for hardware and software (basic entry-level machines for Internet access can be purchased for less than $1,000), this remains an excessive amount for low-income households. Internet access at work is also difficult for many: for employees in poorly paid service jobs (the most rapidly growing category of employment) that do not offer access to the Internet at their place of employment, the obstacles to access are formidable. Even within the most digitized of cities there remain large pockets of 'off-line' poverty. Those who need the Internet the least, already living in information-rich environments with access through many non-Internet channels (e.g. newspapers and cable TV), may have the most access to it, while those who may benefit the most (e.g. through electronic job banks) may have the smallest chance to log on.

Social implications of the Internet

In an age in which social life is increasingly mediated through computer networks, the reconstruction of interpersonal relations around the digitized spaces of cyberspace is of the utmost significance (Kitchin 1998; Crang *et al.* 1999). However, the fact that cyber-contacts differ from face-to-face one serves as a useful reminder that telecommunications change not only *what* we know about the world, but also *how* we know and experience it.

Most of the Internet's uses revolve around simple entertainment, personal communication and other ostensibly apolitical purposes. However, the Internet can also be used to challenge established systems of domination and to publicize the political claims of the relatively powerless and marginalized. The Internet has given voice to countless groups with a multiplicity of political interests and agendas, including: civil and human rights advocates, sustainable development activists, anti-racist and anti-sexist organizations, gay and lesbian rights groups, religious movements, those espousing ethnic identities and causes, youth movements, peace and disarmament parties, nonviolent action and pacifists, animal rights groups, and gays living in homophobic local environments (Warf and Grimes 1997). By facilitating the expression of political positions that otherwise may be difficult, or impossible, the Internet allows for a dramatic expansion in the range of voices. In this sense, it permits the local to become global. Within the Internet itself one finds all the diversity and contradictions of human experience: cyberpolitics mirrors its nonelectronic counterparts, although the boundaries between the two realms are increasingly fuzzy. Indeed, in a socio-psychological sense, cyberspace may allow for the reconstruction of 'communities without propinquity', groups of users who share common interests but not physical proximity.

There is also what may be called the 'dark side' of the Internet, in which it is deployed for illegal or immoral purposes. Hackers, for example, have often wreaked havoc with computer security systems. Such individuals are typically young men playing pranks, although others may unleash dangerous computer viruses and worms. Most hacks – by some estimates as many as 95 per cent – go unreported, but their presence has driven up the cost of computer firewalls. The dark side also includes unsavoury activities such as identity theft of counterfeit drivers' licences, passports, social security cards, military IDs, securities swindles and adoption scams. Credit card fraud is a mounting problem: 0.25 per cent of Internet credit card transactions are fraudulent, compared to 0.08 per cent for non-Internet transactions. Some Internet sites even offer credit card 'marketplaces', such as in Russia and the Philippines, where people who hack into merchant accounts may steal large numbers of cards and sell them wholesale.

One of the most hotly debated dimensions of cyberspace concerns the widespread prevalence of pornography. Pornography in cyberspace is an extension (and for some, a substitute for) the physical sexuality of the body, revealing that the mind is the most erotic organ of all. Computer pornography combines aspects of the public and private spheres: in the privacy of the home, consumers can participate in Usenet discussion groups, WWW sites, private chat rooms and bulletin-board services (BBS). No aspect of cyberspace has generated as much political friction as cybersex, particularly the ease with which children may have access to explicit pictures and stories about sexual acts.

Digital capitalism also involves a reconfiguration of the body (Warf 2000), including its ability, through telecommunications, to be in more than one place at a time (Adams 1995). While bodies typically appear as 'natural', they are in fact social constructions deeply inscribed with multiple meanings, 'embodiments' of class, gender, ethnic and other relations (see Chapter 24). Digital technology allowed for a far-reaching rescripting of the 'natural' body (Kitchin 1998; Crang *et al.* 1999), in which simple dichotomies such as 'off-line' and 'online' fail to do justice to the depth to which they are shot through with one another. Nguyen and Alexander (1996: 116) argue: 'As cyberspace erases the boundaries of time and space, it also erases the materiality of our bodily boundaries. Online, we seem to break free from the limitations of bodily existence.' Like identity, the social construction of the body is thus part of the contemporary wave of time–space compression, reflecting capitalism's reach from the most abstract of spaces, the global economy, to the most personal.

E-commerce

The impacts of telecommunications upon businesses include a variety of activities often lumped together under the term 'e-commerce', which comprises business-to-business transactions and those linking firms to their customers. Information technology lowers transactions costs among corporations, which helps to spur productivity. Such systems were instrumental in the restructuring of many corporations in response to mounting global competition, as they 'downsized' in favour of flatter corporate hierarchies. Many firms sought improved productivity by accelerating information flows within the firm and lower costs by reducing intermediaries and distribution costs.

One important version of e-commerce concerns Electronic Data Interchange (EDI) systems, which are generally used in business-to-business (B2B) contacts. Common uses of EDI include advertising, on-line product catalogues, the sharing of sales and inventory data, submissions of purchase orders, contracts, invoices, payments, delivery schedules, product updates and labour recruitment. E-commerce reduces delays, marketing and delivery costs, and has led to a greater emphasis on connectivity, ideas, creativity, speed and customer service.

In the same vein, 'E-tailing' or electronic retailing reveals the growing commercialization of the Internet: in 1993, 2 per cent of all websites were commercial, i.e. 'dot com' sites; by 2002, 50 per cent were so categorized. Shopping by the Internet requires only access (e.g. a modem), a credit card and a parcel delivery service, and allows effortless comparison shopping. The most successful example perhaps is Amazon.com, started by entrepreneur Jeff Bezos, which now is responsible for 60 per cent of all books sold on-line. Other examples include on-line auctions (e.g. eBay), Internet-based telephones (voice over Internet telephony, or VOIP) and Internet music (e.g. downloading of MP3 music files as in Napster), which has provoked a firestorm of opposition from music companies complaining about infringement of their intellectual property rights. Internet sales have provoked worries about tax evasion and sales of illegal goods, e.g. pharmaceuticals from abroad. Despite predictions that 'click and order' shopping would eliminate 'brick and mortar' stores, e-tailing has been slow to catch on, however, comprising in 2004 only 3 per cent of total US retail sales, perhaps because it lacks the emotional content of shopping. Shoppers using this mode tend to be above average in income and relatively well educated. Web-based banking has also experienced slow growth, even though it is considerably cheaper for banks than automatic teller machines, as have Internet-based bill payments, mortgages and insurance. Internet-based sales of stocks (e.g. E. Schwab, E★Trade) now comprise 15 per cent of all trades. One particularly successful application has been in the travel reservation and ticketing business, where growth in web-based purchases of hotel rooms and airline seats (e.g. through services such as Travelocity, Priceline.com and Expedia.com) has led to a steady decline in the number of travel agents. Electronic publishing, including more than 700 newspapers worldwide, has been extended to ebooks, which unlike printed text can be complemented with sound and graphics. Other services offer Internet searches of databases and classified adverts. Webcasting, or broadcasts over the Internet (typically of sports or entertainment events), demands high bandwidth capacity but comprises an increasingly significant share of Internet traffic today.

Internet advertising has proven to be difficult, in part because the Internet reaches numerous specialized markets rather than mass audiences. Cyberspace does, however, allow specialized companies to reach global niche markets. E-advertising comprises only 1 per cent of total advertising revenues in the US, and is heavily focused on computer and software firms. Indeed, many users are now wary of 'spam' email (unwanted commercial messages, often pornographic), which constitute an ever-larger, and increasingly annoying, share of email traffic.

Another version of e-commerce concerns universities, many of which have invested heavily in web-based 'distance learning' courses. Although such programmes are often designed to attract non–local and non–traditional students, they also reflect the mounting financial constraints and declining public subsidies that many institutions face, which may see distance learning as a means of attracting additional students, and tuition, at relatively low marginal costs. The most spectacular example of web-based teaching is Phoenix University, based in Arizona but with students located around the world; with more than 100,000 students, Phoenix is now the largest university in the world. Distance learning has provoked fears that it opens the door to the corporatization of academia, while others have questioned whether the chat rooms that form an important part of its delivery system are an effective substitute for the face-to-face teaching and learning that classrooms offer. It remains unclear whether web-based learning is an effective complement or substitute for traditional forms of instruction.

Concluding thoughts: the end of geography?

Clearly, the growth of dense telecommunications networks has dramatically changed the nature of space and the significance of geography, a theme commonly exaggerated as 'the death of distance' (Cairncross 1997) or 'the end of geography' (O'Brien 1992). However, popular notions that 'telecommunications will render geography meaningless' are simply naïve. While the costs of communications have decreased, other factors have risen in importance, including local regulation, the cost and skills of the local labour force, and infrastructural investments. Moreover, far from eliminating space, the impacts of tele-communications are increasingly understood to be geographically specific. This unevenness reflects differential access to different communications technologies (e.g. the telephone, Internet) as well as the varying uses to which the same technology can be put (cell phones in Japan and Africa have very different impacts).

The literature on time–space compression or convergence (Harvey 1989, 1990) reveals a much more complex set of relations. Although space and time appear as 'natural' and outside of society, they are in fact social constructions; every society develops different ways of dealing with and perceiving them. Capitalism has generated successive rounds of improvements in transportation and communications that markedly reduced transaction times and costs. Telecommunications represent the latest, and perhaps most profound, in the long series of episodes of time–space compression, effectively reducing to zero the communications time among places. Relative space, in which distances are measured through changing metrics of time and cost, becomes a more useful way of understanding such a world, in contrast to notions of absolute space, the traditional Cartesian form that characterized most Enlightenment forms of geography. Spatially, this process endlessly generates new geographies of centrality and peripherality, bringing some places closer together and others relatively less so. Generally, elites tend to enjoy the earliest and often the greatest advantages from reduced costs and transmission times of transportation and communications.

Moreover, because the economy cannot be detached from other realms of social life, time–space compression is more than a simply economic phenomenon. By changing how people use their time and space on a daily basis, the constraints they face, the meanings they attach to them, time–space compression is simultaneously cultural, social, political and psychological in nature. Cyberspace, for example, has changed the everyday lives of hundreds of millions, if not billions, of people, altering not simply what we know but how we know it, creating a prosthetic extension that fuses person and machine (see Chapter 33). Globally, in a shrinking world distant strangers become less and less distant or strange.

Geographic space, in short, will not evaporate because of the telecommunications revolution. It is true that networks such as the Internet allow some professionals to move into rural areas, where they can conduct most of their business on-line, gradually permitting them to escape from their long-time reliance upon large cities where they needed face-to-face contact. Yet the full extent to which these systems facilitate decentralization is often countered by other forces that promote the centralization of activity. This is particularly appropriate given the importance attached to tacit knowledge and face-to-face contact in high value-added functions in metropolitan regions. Thus, exactly how telecommunications are deployed is contingent and depends upon local circumstances, public policy, culture and ideology within the national and world economy.

Further reading

Dodge, M. and Kitchin, R. (2001) *Mapping Cyberspace*. London: Routledge.

Graham, S. and Marvin, S. (1996) *Telecommunications and the City: Electronic Spaces, Urban Places*. London: Routledge.

Hugill, P. (1999) *Global Communications since 1844: Geopolitics and Technology*. Baltimore: Johns Hopkins University Press.

Kitchin, R. (1998) *Cyberspace: The World in the Wires*. New York: John Wiley and Sons.

Schiller, D. (1999) *Digital Capitalism: Networking the Global Market System*. Cambridge, MA: MIT Press.

Standage, T. (1998) *The Victorian Internet*. New York: Walker.

Warf, B. and Grimes, J. (1997) Counterhegemonic discourses and the Internet. *Geographical Review* 87, 259–74.

References

Abler, R. and Falk, T. (1981) Public information services and the changing role of distance in human affairs. *Economic Geography* 62, 59–67.

——(1985) Intercommunications technologies: regional variations in postal service use in Sweden, 1870–1975. *Geografiska Annaler B* 67, 99–106.

Adams, P. (1995) A reconsideration of personal boundaries in space–time. *Annals of the Association of American Geographers* 85, 267–85.

Brunn, S. and Leinbach, T. (eds) (1991) *Collapsing Space and Time: Geographic Aspects of Communication and Information*. London: HarperCollins Academic.

Cairncross, F. (1997) *The Death of Distance*. Boston: Harvard Business School Press.

Castells, M. (1989) *The Informational City*. Oxford: Blackwell.

——(1996) *The Information Age, volume I: The Rise of the Network Society*. Oxford: Blackwell.

Chakraborty, J. and Bosman, M.M. (2005) Measuring the digital divide in the United States: race income and personal computer ownership. *Professional Geographer* 57, 395–410.

Click Z Statistics (2005) *Population Explosion*. Available at http://www.clickz.com/stats/sectors/geographics/article.php/5911_151151

Crang, M., Crang, P. and May, J. (eds) (1999) *Virtual Geographies: Bodies, Space and Relations*. New York and London: Routledge.

de Sola Pool, I. (ed.) (1977) *The Social Impact of the Telephone*. Cambridge, MA: MIT Press.

Falk, T. and Abler, R. (1980) Intercommunications, distance, and geographical theory. *Geografiska Annaler B* 62, 59–67.

——(1985) Intercommunications technologies: the development of postal services in Sweden. *Geografiska Annaler B* 67, 21–8.

Fischer, C. (1992) The telephone in America. In C. Fischer, *America Calling*, pp. 33–59. Berkeley: University of California Press.

Friedman, T. (1999) *The Lexus and the Olive Tree*. New York: Farrar Straus Giroux.

Graham, S. (1999) Global grids of glass: on global cities, telecommunications, and planetary urban networks. *Urban Studies* 36, 929–49.

Graham, S. and Marvin, S. (1996) *Telecommunications and the City: Electronic Spaces, Urban Places*. London: Routledge.

Harley, J. (1989) Deconstructing the map. *Cartographica* 26, 1–20.

Harvey, D. (1989) *The Condition of Postmodernity*. Oxford: Blackwell.

——(1990) Between space and time: reflections on the geographical imagination. *Annals of the Association of American Geographers* 80, 418–34.

Hillis, K. (1998) On the margins: the invisibility of communications in geography. *Progress in Human Geography* 22, 543–66.

Hugill, P. (1999) *Global Communications since 1844: Geopolitics and Technology*. Baltimore: Johns Hopkins University Press.

Janelle, D. (1969) Spatial reorganization: a model and concept. *Annals of the Association of American Geographers* 59, 348–65.

Kitchin, R. (1998) *Cyberspace: The World in the Wires*. New York: John Wiley and Sons.

Kobrin, S. (1997) Electronic cash and the end of national markets. *Foreign Policy* summer, 65–77.

Nguyen, D. and Alexander, J. (1996) The coming of cyberspacetime and the end of the polity. In R. Shields (ed.) *Cultures of the Internet: Virtual Spaces, Real Histories, Living Bodies*. London: Sage.

O'Brien, R. (1992) *Global Financial Integration: The End of Geography*. Washington: Council on Foreign Relations.

Pred, A. (1973) *Urban Growth and the Circulation of Information: The United States System of Cities, 1790–1840*. Cambridge, MA: Harvard University Press.

Roberts, S. (1994) Fictitious capital, fictitious spaces: the geography of offshore financial flows. In S. Corbridge, R. Martin and N. Thrift (eds) *Money, Power and Space*. Oxford: Blackwell.

Sassen, S. (1991) *The Global City: New York, London, Tokyo*. Princeton, NJ: Princeton University Press.

Schiller, D. (1999) *Digital Capitalism: Networking the Global Market System*. Cambridge, MA: MIT Press.

Standage, T. (1998) *The Victorian Internet*. New York: Walker.

Warf, B. (1995) Telecommunications and the changing geographies of knowledge transmission in the late 20th century. *Urban Studies* 32, 361–78.

——(2000) Compromising positions: the body in cyberspace. In J. Wheeler, Y. Aoyama and B. Warf (eds) *Cities in the Telecommunications Age: The Fracturing of Geographies*, pp. 54–68. London: Routledge.

——(2001) Segueways into cyberspace: multiple geographies of the digital divide. *Environment and Planning B: Planning and Design* 28, 3–19.

Wood, D. (1992) *The Power of Maps*. New York: Guilford.

Worth, R. (2002) In New York tickets, Ghana sees orderly city. *New York Times* 22 July, A1.

61

Shopping

The terminal form of public life?

Jon Goss

Introduction

Shopping is a complex social activity that involves looking at goods on public display, judging quality, estimating value and, in some contexts, negotiating their price, before decisions are made on their purchase. As lived experience it has long satisfied material needs and offered primordial pleasures of interpersonal interaction, public display of the self, and fantasies of transcendence. Historically, however, shopping has been confined to particular places and times, first in occasional fairs and periodic markets, in 'shops' themselves since the thirteenth century (Paquet 2003), and subsequently in department stores, urban shopping centres and suburban shopping malls during regular hours of retail operation. Now, however, shopping seems to be everywhere at all times: it has infiltrated almost every institution of everyday life, and is no longer out of place in train stations, airports, hospitals, schools, museums, sports facilities and even churches. Shopping has arguably become the dominant form of public life, although the catalogue retailers have offered rural populations access to urban and seasonal shopping since Montgomery Ward distributed its first 'dream book' in 1872, thanks to the Internet we can now also shop '24/7' from the privacy of our own homes. As Sze Tsung Leong (2001: 129) puts it, 'not only is shopping melting into everything, but everything is melting into shopping'.

We spend more time watching television, but shopping is our next most time-consuming leisure activity, and in any case much of television's programming and advertising depicts commodities and lifestyles that are calculated to incite shopping. Certainly it is hard to think of any other leisure activities that can be properly pursued without shopping for the appropriate accompanying products or services. Shopping is not just a leisure activity, of course, for it is also an everyday domestic duty and an expression of affection for others and the self: it is sometimes simply provisioning and sometimes an act of love (Miller 1998: 18). Some would even deem shopping part of a national duty in support of the economy and 'our way of life', such as President George W. Bush, who is claimed to have said in response to the events of '9/11' (11 September 2001): 'We can't let the terrorists stop us from shopping' (quoted in Norris 2004).

How is it that shopping has become such an important part of our everyday lives that it is a moral duty, and not only political but a war by other means? In the following, I provide a partial history of shopping and the retail built environment, focusing on the emergence of consumer society and its contemporary elaboration. Subsequently, I consider some of the anxieties that shopping produces, and the polemical arguments it inevitably engenders. I suggest that shopping involves an exchange between antagonistic partners, and that much of its history has been the struggle to obscure the antagonism that is the source of these anxieties.

The world of shopping

The rise of commodity aesthetics

The consumer shops not only for things to satisfy material needs, but also to make social meanings and metaphysical connections. The use of 'fashion' to mark social status, for example, is said to have been established during the 'first consumer revolution' in the court of Elizabeth I during the sixteenth century when nobles competed for royal attention with flamboyant clothes (McCracken 1988: 11–15), but it becomes more generally institutionalized in urban capitalist society where there is regular interaction among strangers and status is determined by wealth. In this context, consumer goods are immediately visible and interpretable signs of social status, and shoppers' choices rarely involve personal taste alone but necessarily constitute a form of 'position-taking' within a hierarchy of competencies distributed largely according to class (Bourdieu 1984: 136).

Following the 'democratization of luxury' that occurred in England during the seventeenth century, luxury goods were no longer associated with decadence and pretension, because they were seen to stimulate shopping and in turn generate commerce and employment. Once freed of this stigma, the emulation of elite tastes created demand to meet the expansion of international trade and industrial production that in turn reduced commodity prices (Berry 1994). Several developments also contributed to the elaboration of a display aesthetic in that the development of long-distance trade in commodities, combined with the move from open markets to shops, effected the separation of production and consumption, while permanent stores also favoured visual over verbal display (Welch 2005). Both of these developments are essential to the so-called 'fetishism of commodities' whereby objects are displayed innocent of their material origins – the geography and social relations of production and distribution – and so 'emptied out' can be invested with aura through semiotic associations within the context of display (see Sack 1992). At this time what may be taken as the first 'shopping centres' were developed. In the late sixteenth century, contemporary accounts tell in awe of jewellery, textiles and intimate articles like girdles on display in the luxury shops of Cheapside, close to but separate from the nearby workshops where they were produced, and in 1609 King James opened the New Exchange on the Strand, a project financed by Robert Cecil, Earl of Salisbury, consisting of two ornate galleries of stores complete with milliners, mercers, haberdasheries, china houses and booksellers (Knowles 1997: 14). In such contexts, shopping became not only the means to acquire goods, but also the means to display them and their owners as objects of desire. Thus shoppers began to show off their luxuries such as jewellery on their person and to display food, furnishings and pottery in their homes (McKendrick *et al.* 1983). Domestic interiors were progressively penetrated by the 'commodity aesthetic' and made into a public showcase for personal possessions (Agnew 1989: 135).

Subsequently, department store displays, retail catalogues and advertisements, together with ancillary popular culture productions such as movies and television, have instructed shoppers on how they should dress, decorate their homes and spend their time and money, establishing the idea of stylistically and functionally related 'constellation of commodities' (McCracken 1988). Market and advert exploited the idea of fashion to create anxieties over obsolescence (Robbins 1999: 15–16) so intensifying the need to shop and 'keep up appearances'. At the same time, such 'cultural intermediaries' worked to restructure expectations and habits of consumers, mobilizing notions of hygiene, comfort, cleanliness, convenience and style, for example, to escalate consumption. The global acceptance of business suit and toothpaste are examples of the standardization of such qualities, to which we might add more recent innovations such as bottled water, cell phones and credit cards. Cars and televisions are 'leading objects' in modern society (Lefebvre 1971: 102), but many other commodities trigger complementary demands to accessorize, and the so-called 'Diderot effect', whereby the purchase of a new commodity provokes the stylistic obsolescence of related possessions and so sparks a round of further acquisition to match its newness (McCracken 1988).

Identity is more than keeping up with the Joneses, however, and shopping is also a means to individual self-actualization. Colin Campbell (1987) suggests that a 'second consumer revolution' occurred in the eighteenth century when consumer goods came to represent the material means to pursue happiness and realize fantasies of the self. Religion and art were displaced, and commodities became focal points of desire for transcendence and the 'dream world of mass consumption' was born (Williams 1982: 64). Shopping combined with the 'Romantic ethic' to create 'a new propensity to consume' based on a controlled form of hedonism. A contemporary example of this phenomenon is the consumption of commodities such as cosmetics, fitness programmes and pharmaceuticals, in which pleasure is based on individual desire constrained by a moral discourse of personal well-being, autonomy and self-possession (Sassatelli 2001). Again, consumers had to be educated in the project of the self. Pick up any consumer catalogue, magazine or 'magalogue' and you will be exhorted to shop for this somewhat paradoxical combination of self-improvement and hedonism, denial and pleasure, discipline and indulgence.

Department stores and commodities

Even with the help of cultural intermediaries, nations of shoppers did not emerge simply from the operation of social envy and desire for self-actualization, and historical studies reveal how states long promoted regimes of consumption (Collins 2000; Glickman 1997; Calder 2001). Trade, wage and credit policies, for example, helped fashion the first 'consumer republics' in which shopping was central to political life (Cohen 2003) and later underpinned the development of today's consumer society. A whole series of institutional changes accompanied the commercialization of society, but perhaps most visible was the retail built environment, first in the form of arcades, then the department store, and ultimately the shopping mall. It was in these contexts that shopping became a socially sanctioned form of leisure, and the shopper became the object of increasingly sophisticated observation and management, as well as solicitous hospitality services that cultivated what we now know as 'consumer sovereignty' (Robbins 1999: 15–16). Here shoppers were enticed into a fantasy space, moved physically through object displays according to spatial principles of retailing, and exposed to 'merchandizing pictures' that entertained their exotic/erotic fantasies and enhanced the value of commodities, in order to move them to make impulse purchases. Marketers came to know the desires and behavioural propensities of shoppers in more and more intimate detail through the disciplines of retail psychology and anthropology (Zaltman 2003; Underhill 1999), and may yet know more through 'neuromarketing', or the use of

Magnetic Resonance Imaging (MRI) to monitor the emotional response of consumers to products and displays (CBC Marketplace 2002). Eventually, it seems, people went out to shop when there was nothing they wanted to buy, happy to allow the shops to take them in and make decisions for them, trusting they would be presented with something they did not realize they desired (Pooler 2003: 5).

The department stores – which began with Bon Marché in Paris in 1852, Macy's in New York in 1857, and Whiteley's in London in 1863 – became vast grandly appointed empor-iums hosting spectacular cultural events and providing diverse public services to shoppers. These 'palaces of consumption' evoked exotic and utopian worlds, and were already sight-seeing stops offering their own tours, a combination of retail and tourism that has perhaps reached its architectural apotheosis in the huge destination malls, like Mall of America (Goss 1999). If the retail built environment works to obscure the geographical origins and pro-duction relations of most mundane commodities, it also highlights the exotic nature of others, especially 'travelling objects' whose value lies precisely in their displacement from authentic 'elsewheres' and other times (Lury 1997).

Once restricted to promotion of patent medicines, advertising grew rapidly in the late nineteenth century as industrial manufacturing demanded a means to differentiate and market standardized commodities such as canned foods and soap. Brands were then first deployed as symbols of commercial trust and loyalty to customers: H.J. Heinz, for example, popularized manufactured foods by appealing to health, hygiene and convenience for working women, and by exploiting gendered and racialized images of 'purity' (Domosh 2003). Department stores not only used advertising to sell brands, but they advertised themselves as brands, marked by the social status and lifestyles of their customers: Marshall Field, the Chicago retailer, built his brand on images of solicitous service to all classes of female customers (Koehn 2001). Today, we live in a full-blown 'brand culture,' where we go 'brand shopping' and identify ourselves through loyalty to labels that represent complex articulations of abstract values (Klein 2000). Shoppers acquire a considerable amount of practical knowledge about the meaning of brands and labels, and shop selectively among styles and fashions for things that fit and suit perfectly, so as to seem made just for them. Many would probably be able to claim, like James Twitchell (1997: 45), 'tell me what you buy, and I will tell what you are and who you want to be'. It is upon this basis that our shopping identities have themselves become commodified objects sold by geo-demographic corporations and mass marketers.

The department store also pioneered new technologies of light and glass to display goods as aesthetic objects with the power to transform the consumer into a more desirable person. Glass, in particular, is a 'technology of desire' that works by the interplay of proximity and distance (Taylor 2000), and the task for the shop window was, in the words of Frank Baum, author of *The Art of Decorating Windows and Dry Goods Interiors*, to 'arouse in the observer a cupidity and longing to possess the goods' (cited in Leach 1989: 110). Baum's *Wizard of Oz* stories feature objects that, once removed from the magic of the window, rapidly lose their lustre, and he well knew that the dialectic of desire and disappointment is an essential and inevitable part of the experience of shopping.

The department stores offered a fixed-price system and provided credit, effectively elim-inating bargaining and local vendor loyalty, but new shopping skills were required and these were taught explicitly to women as part of their duties of domestic science. Successful shopping involves judgment of quality, price and value. The satisfactions of comparison shopping and bargain hunting may complement more libidinal pleasures, but they may also become disciplines to be mastered and tantamount to a form of work. Recently, it seems, 'tyranny of choice' has intensified sufficiently that the effort required is disproportionate to the satisfactions, even to the point of clinical depression and suicide among shoppers (Schwartz 2004).

Ideologies of shopping

If shopping as we experience it today was born in the profane spaces of the department stores of the nineteenth century, it was rapidly articulated to popular religion, most obviously in the carnivalesque celebration of Christmas. In fact, to a large extent religious holidays were regularized and devotional practices standardized by merchants and advertisers, most obviously in gift giving, greetings cards and ritual consumption of foods. By now, in the United States, for example, Christmas shopping, which begins on 'Black Friday', the day after Thanksgiving, is central to the ritual experience and is a vital economic stimulus to the national economy. Many observers lament the commercialization of Christmas, of course, but even as the promotion of 'devout consumption' in family-oriented seasonal window-displays, by the likes of John Wannaker, exploited religion for material ends, it also brought Christianity 'into the marketplace for praise and homage, and in turn, the Philadelphia store took on a peculiarly hallowed aura' (Schmidt 1997: 167). And it is not just during religious holidays that the retail built environment functions as sacred space, with roles similar to those described in Chapter 15, as shoppers ostensibly make regular pilgrimages to department stores, shopping malls, theme parks and other 'Cathedrals of Consumption' to practise collective rituals of identity and to commune with a higher meaning (Ritzer 1999).

In fact, the connection between shopping and religion is ancient, for the market is a magical place, a context for transformation and exchange between the material and spiritual realms. Shopping requires a faith, or at least the suspension of disbelief, in the power of objects and the possibilities of transcendence. Various observers have remarked on the similarity of the commodity aesthetic to religion (Miller 2003), and the functional equivalence of advertising to primitive magic systems (Twitchell 1997); the similarity of consumer practices to religious rituals (deChant 2002); the role of the brand as a totem, object of devotion and badge of belonging (Atkin 2004); and, most especially, the equation of the commodity with the religious fetish, as it appears to be animated, possessed of aura and powers of transformation, and even invested with 'soul' (Dichter 1960).

If shopping is not only about the purchase of objects, it does not necessarily require a purchase at all, and typologies of shoppers include categories like fantasy shopping and vicarious shopping, as well as window-shopping. Shopping implies precisely the freedom to select among potential purchases and not to make a selection after all. Shopping also implies the readiness of the shopper to invest time and money in purchasing decisions, and a principled openness towards objects and their meanings, to the spatial, semiotic and rhetorical persuasions of the retail environment. Shopping thus describes a disposition: a willingness to take a look, to taste something different, and to try something on.

Nor is shopping necessarily based on an actual or potential commodity transaction, since we 'shop' whenever we relatively freely and deliberately make any kind of choice. We do not merely shop for commodities, but adopt a 'consumer attitude' to life (Bauman 1990: 204), so that whether as patients in healthcare facilities, students in educational institutions, voters in electoral politics, and even in our selection of romantic partners, our experience increasingly resembles the exercise of choice between 'brands'. We have thus been consumed by the 'ideology of shopping', whose governing principle is 'consumer sovereignty' and the right to freely choose among convenience, price, quality and value. Shopping subsumes all other ideologies, as we shop in a dream of social equality in discount stores, of social mobility and self-improvement in name-brand and designer stores, and of unmediated relations with the Other, Nature and History in stores that sell 'ethnic products', 'Endangered Species' or objects of idealized pasts (Zukin 2004; Goss 1999).

Needless to say, the ideology of shopping is unevenly developed, but the collapse of communism in the Soviet Union and Europe, and the market reforms in China of the late twentieth century, extended and intensified the ongoing 'global transformation of desire' (Stearns 2001) such that shopping is becoming a more or less universal way of life. The spread of shopping malls and the multinationalization of brands are evidence of the globalization of shopping as a leisure activity (Farrell 2004: 254). Myers and Kent (2004: 3–4), claim that there are at least 1.1 billion people with their foot on the 'affluence ladder', who, no longer 'preoccupied from dawn to dusk and from birth to death … seek … after ever increasing, indeed limitless consumption … [and] the holy grail to which all the new consumers aspire, a western lifestyle'. Perhaps we should be concerned about the social environmental consequences of them all going shopping!

The authors of the *Harvard Design School Guide to Shopping* (Chung *et al.* 2001) conceive of shopping as a living organism, one that is able to progressively colonize our lifeworlds by constantly adapting, and by evolving ever more complex forms in response to innovations in construction and marketing technologies, advances in the arts of display and representation, and most especially to the changing desires and needs of shoppers. Even if we desire less, there seems to be no escape: we can only resist the excesses of conspicuous consumption by shopping more self-consciously, thus only reproducing the consumer attitude. Dissent is progressively commodified, becoming a style among the others that we shop for, such as when someone like William Burroughs (a counterculture homosexual drug addict who killed his wife) becomes a spokesperson for Nike Corporation (Frank 1997). We can shop ironically by creatively appropriating commodity meanings, but there is no escape 'outside' of shopping (Klein 2000: 33). Indeed, Jean Baudrillard (1988: 29n) argues that shopping represents the terminal condition of life itself:

> We have reached the point where 'consumption' has grasped the whole of life … work, nature and culture all previously dispersed, separate, and more or less irreducible entities that produced anxiety and complexity in our real life, and on our 'anarchic and archaic' cities, have finally become mixed, massaged, climate-controlled, and domesticated into the single activity of perpetual shopping.

In part, whether this condition is frightening or comforting depends upon your conception of the relationship between buyer and seller, subject and object, material and spiritual, but it seems inevitable that shopping creates a certain amount of anxiety because of the dynamic tension between the categories through which exchange occurs.

Anxieties of shopping

The dominant discourse on shopping is generally disdainful of its unproductive pleasures, its role in the displacement of public life by commerce, the replacement of community by consumer identities, and especially the corruption of basic needs by 'false needs' (Marcuse 1964). This view is at least as old as ancient texts of the Christian tradition where there are excoriations of Mammon and materialism, and a futile gesture to drive the money-lenders and merchants from the temple, and it is also consistent with the 'depth ontology' of Western metaphysics whereby object, artifice and display are presumed to obscure and corrupt the naturalness of the person (Miller 1995: 25). In this tradition, there is a deep-seated suspicion of commerce, as if all transactions were exploitative, and shoppers therefore victims of manipulation. There is a long history of effort by medieval municipal and mercantilist national governments to rationalize commerce and protect shoppers from misrepresentation and unfair trading practices.

It is harder, however, to protect shoppers from themselves and their desires for objects as means of social distinction and personal satisfaction. The social-conservative critique of consumption includes, for example, Thorstein Veblen (1902) on the phenomenon of 'conspicuous consumption'; Daniel Boorstin (1974) on the loss of American collectivity to 'consumption communities'; and Christopher Lasch (1991) on the development of 'culture of narcissism', the decline of public life and politics into consumerism, demographics and opinion polls. Modern expressions of the 'anxieties of affluence' (Horowitz 2004) were equally likely to come from the 'New Left', however, particularly in the 1950s and 1960s under influence of the Frankfurt School's critique of mass consumption, the power of the 'consciousness industries' and the problematical relationship between materialism and democracy (Marcuse 1964). Daniel Horowitz (2004: 252) suggests that the 'purchase' of Marxist social analysis was reduced in the intervening decades, when American politics shifted to the right, and following changes in the publishing industry and the rise of self-help psychology – shopping for personal solutions to social problems – but he identifies a 'reassertion of the new moralism' among contemporary public intellectuals and the return of 'impassioned, morally charged critiques of consumer culture'.

According to Boris Groys (quoted in Hollein 2002: 13) 'nothing in modern consumer society is consumed with such relish as the criticism of consumption', and there is a whole raft of recent best-selling jeremiads against shopping and consumer culture: on the social and personal psychological consequences of overspending and compulsive shopping (Schor 1999 and 2000; Manning 2000); on the seduction and manipulation of consumers by the spatial and semiotic strategies of the shopping mall (Farrell 2004); on the pernicious effects of advertising, brands and fashion (Klein 2000; Lee 2003); on the 'commercialization of childhood' (Schor 2004); on the operation of commodity chains, the iniquities of the food provision system and the 'shocking power' of supermarkets (Young 2004; Blythman 2004); on the deleterious health effects of 'fast food' (Schlosser 2001; Critser 2004); and on the negative environmental consequences of shopping decisions (Myers and Kent 2004).

The most extreme accounts consider shopping to be nothing less than a generalized pathological condition. For example, de Graaf *et al.* (2002: 2) identify 'an epidemic of overconsumption' in the United States, and diagnose the condition of 'affluenza', which is 'a painful, contagious, socially-transmitted condition of overload, debt, anxiety and waste resulting from the dogged pursuit of more'. Similarly, Fredric Jameson (2003: 77) equates shopping to a mysterious virus 'spreading like a toxic moss across the known universe' to infect us with an empty existential condition where we can only seek meaning within the very meaningless of commodified existence. For George Ritzer (2004) shopping has a deadening effect, replacing what is unique and real with the 'non-places' like shopping malls, 'non-things' like credit cards, and 'non-people' like sales associates, tantamount to the 'globalization of nothing'. Finally, Lacanian philosopher Zlavoj Žižek (quoted in Grunenberg and Hollein 2002: 91) likens shopping to masturbating in public, by which I presume he means to condemn its narcissistic self-absorption.

There are, of course, real dangers in excessive and compulsive shopping (Benson 2000), but I think this 'morality of negation' perhaps says more about the anxieties of the (mostly) masculine critics than the motivations and pleasures of shoppers themselves. The reluctant shopper thus betrays both a Puritanical suspicion of the sensual pleasures of shopping and a rationalist resistance to its seductions for fear of being taken in or suckered in a sale.

The majority of shoppers are women, of course, and the libidinal economy of consumption affects how we think about the links between femininity, sexuality and the commodity, so it is not surprising that mass culture is persistently gendered as female, and that shopping evokes fears of unbridled, 'hysterical' desire (Nava 1996). In the Victorian era, for example, shopping threatened the established sexual order as women gained unprecedented access to fantasy life and public life through shopping. Shopping established norms of female appearance, making the body into an object of disciplinary care and visual desire, but also provided escapes from domestic servitude and the promise of romantic love, so transforming modern gender relations. Naomi Wolf (2003) argues that shopping remains a feminist issue since it provides one of the few remaining opportunities for women to socialize and fashion the self – it is nothing less than 'women's last safe inner space, their cultural vulva'. Critiques of consumerism are, in fact, misogynistic, because 'to hate shopping and all of its representations is to hate women'.

The class biases of the cultural condemnation of shopping have also been exposed by cultural studies of consumption which reveal the complexity of motivations among shoppers and their active appropriation of commodities and meanings. While the retail industry and its vast armies of cultural workers would like to predict and control shopping behaviour, consumer motivations are so various and complex that they are more or less 'unmanageable' (Gabriel and Lang 1996). As James Twitchell (1999: 273) argues, 'there are no "false needs"', only 'false critiques of consumption'. 'Cultural populists' even celebrate shopping as a form of resistance to dominant culture, involving acts of inversion and appropriation of meanings by otherwise marginal groups. Also, criticizing shopping, or certain kinds of shopping, marks social distinction through appeal to the same abstractions – like taste, quality and authenticity – that structure the experience of shopping itself, so again reproducing the consumer attitude.

If there has been a redemption of shopping in post-critical studies, it is only partial, however, as the dominant negative connotations have long been internalized by shoppers themselves. Bumper stickers may proudly proclaim 'Born to Shop' or 'Shop 'Til You Drop', but they rely on irony for effect because we all to varying degrees acknowledge the authority of the rationalist critique of shopping which they invert. Opinion polls show that the American public has 'serious reservations' about consumerism, the vast majority agreeing that 'most of us buy and consume far more than we need' (Farrell 2004: 269). Whether we are worried more immediately about our compulsive behaviours or consumer debt, or more generally about the morality of materialism, environmental sustainability or social justice, shopping is always something of a guilty pleasure. There are means to assuage this guilt through more rational forms of consumption. We might, for example, seek to curb impulses by learning to distinguish want from need; or by adopting alternative consumer lifestyles such as 'Voluntary Simplicity' and 'Slow Food'; or by shopping for sustainability and social justice, buying products certified by the Fair Trade Federation and Global Exchange.

There are cases where politically and socially conscious shopping does make a difference and there are well-organized contemporary campaigns against international brands that source from sweatshops, engage in animal testing, create toxic waste or deplete groundwater (Klein 2000). Geographers, in particular, have been exhorted to 'get behind the veil, the fetishism of the market and the commodity, in order to tell the full story of social reproduction', and so to expose the real geographical and social origins of goods (Harvey 1990: 422; see also Sack 1992: 118). Otherwise, it is felt that consumers cannot understand the consequences of their choices because systems of production and distribution are 'virtually obliterated' in the abstract and perfected 'context of the commodity' (Sack 1992: 200).

Although consumers express unease about consumerism and producers are vulnerable to negative publicity, there are limits to the effectiveness of critical research around commodity chains which focuses on exposing the 'backstage' of the commodity. First, there is a widely observed 'attitude–behaviour gap': shoppers are unwilling to pay premium prices for cause-related products, lack the information to make effective choices, respond to short-term negative publicity more than long-term positive campaigns, and suffer from 'care fatigue'. Second, consumer guilt is easily exploited by marketers: ethical retailing is often more about public relations (for example, 'greenwashing') than transforming relations of production. Third, consumer activism only targets particular products and brands or particular styles of consumption, not the extension and intensification of commodification itself.

The fact that there is limited purchase for resistance to consumerism leads some observers to advocate a more playful engagement with shopping, like so-called 'ironic consumers' who acknowledge the pleasures and guilt of consumption, and understand that there is no alternative to this contradictory condition. If consumption and guilt are two sides of the same cultural coin, Daniel Akst (2004: 43) wonders whether 'perhaps even God is in two minds about materialism'. Some theologians and marketers have even sought to redeem shopping as an authentic form of spirituality, in which 'people pay for meaning more than they pray for it' (Atkin 2004). Shoppers are thus 'soulfully hungry persons' and brands are objects of devotion, sources of collective identity under the sign of a greater power (Beaudoin 2003). Nevertheless, the prescription for an authentic life involves conscious recognition of the spiritual content of collective material desires, beyond the abstract and fragmented form in which they appear in the marketplace, and the free celebration of the joys of desire itself (Miller 2003: 13). Such a theology reminds me of Walter Benjamin's call for the 'dreaming collective' to wake up from its unconscious and distracted state, and to recognize in commodity consumption its wish images, the desire of the collective for an alternative order of production, and the means of their repression (Buck-Morss 1989: 318).

Conclusion

Shopping is in many ways a contradictory activity, but at its heart is the necessarily antagonist relation between buyer and seller. The history of shopping is in part the 'working out' of this antagonism, its progressive displacement from the site of purchase. Contemporary branding, advertising and credit cards, among other techniques and technologies of consumption, work to distract us from what is involved in the market transaction: an exchange of material and symbolic value. Retail laws and the ideology of shopping, with its myth of consumer sovereignty, distract us from the potential inequalities of this exchange, while the design of the retail built environment – shop windows, floor displays, climate and lighting control, retail concepts and spectacular themes – obscure the centrality of its purpose (see Goss 1993, 1999). It seems that one is never just shopping, and never just buying some 'thing' from someone, for there is always something else going on.

In the spectacular contexts of consumption it is easy to forget the ethical issues involved in market transactions. It is easy to forget that shopping is not only a means to personal transformation through the acquisition of objects, but is also potentially a means to realize a better society. It is hard to see through the aesthetics of commodity display and the ideology of consumer sovereignty to reveal how shopping might work to 'contain' collective visions of that better society. In the fantasy world of contemporary shopping, it is easy to be distracted from the real conditions of exchange, and it is hard to maintain an ethical position and to act constantly. We may work hard to be well informed and sincerely pursue personal ideals and social values, but we must inevitably make compromises between quality and price, rationality and pleasure, materiality and symbolic meaning, because there is no unequivocal conception of 'value'. We always risk making the wrong choice. As Sharon Zukin (2004: 276) cautions, 'a shopper's life isn't easy'.

Further reading

Berry, C.J. (1994) *The Idea of Luxury: A Conceptual and Historical Investigation.* Cambridge: Cambridge University Press.

Gabriel, Y. and Lang, T. (1996) *The Unmanageable Consumer: Contemporary Consumption and its Fragmentations.* Thousand Oaks: Sage

Paquet, L.B. (2003) *The Urge to Splurge: A Social History of Shopping.* Toronto: ECW Press.

Pooler, J. (2003) *Why We Shop: Emotional Rewards and Retail Strategies.* Westport, CT: Praeger.

Ritzer, G. (1999) *Enchanting a Disenchanted World: Revolutionizing the Means of Consumption.* Thousand Oaks, CA: Pine Forge Press.

Sack, R. (1992) *Place, Modernity and the Consumer's World: A Relational Framework for Geographical Analysis.* Baltimore: John Hopkins University Press.

Underhill, P. (1999) *Why We Buy: The Science of Shopping.* New York: Simon and Schuster.

Zukin, S. (2004) *Point of Purchase: How Shopping Changed American Culture.* New York: Routledge.

References

Agnew, J.-C. (1989) A house of fiction: domestic interiors and the commodity aesthetic. In S.J. Bronner (ed.) *Consuming Visions: Accumulation and Display of Goods in America 1880–1920,* pp. 133–55. New York: W.W. Norton.

Akst, D. (2004) Buyer's remorse. *Wilson Quarterly* 28 (1), 42–7.

Atkin, D. (2004) *The Culting of Brands: When Customers Become True Believers.* New York: Portfolio Press.

Baudrillard, J. (1988) Consumer society. In M. Poster (ed.) *Jean Baudrillard: Selected Writings,* pp. 239–57. Stanford, CA: Stanford University Press.

Bauman, Z. (1990) *Thinking Sociologically.* Cambridge, MA: Blackwell.

Beaudoin, T. (2003) *Consuming Faith: Integrating Who We Are with What We Buy.* Lanham, MD, and Oxford: Sheed and Ward.

Benson, A.L. (2000) *I Shop, Therefore I Am: Compulsive Buying and the Search for Self.* Lanham, MD: Jason Aronson.

Blythman, J. (2004) *Shopped: The Shocking Power of British Supermarkets.* London: Fourth Estate.

Boorstin, D. (1974) *The Americans: The Democratic Experience.* New York: Vintage

Bourdieu, P. (1984) *Distinction,* trans. R. Nice. Cambridge, MA: Harvard University Press.

Buck-Morss, S. (1989) *The Dialectics of Seeing: Walter Benjamin and the Arcades Project.* Cambridge, MA: MIT Press.

Calder, L. (2001) *Financing the American Dream: A Cultural History of Consumer Credit.* Princeton: Princeton University Press.

Campbell, C. (1987) *The Romantic Ethic and the Spirit of Modern Consumerism.* Oxford: Blackwell.

CBC Marketplace (2002) *The Science of Shopping*. Available at http://www.cbc.ca/consumers/market/files/money/science_shopping/

Chung, C.J, Inaba, J., Koolhaas, R. and Leong, S.T. (2001) *Project on the City 2: Harvard Design School Guide to Shopping*. Cologne: Taschen.

Cohen, L.(2003) *A Consumer's Republic: The Politics of Mass Consumption in Postwar America*. New York: Knopf.

Collins, R. (2000) *More: The Politics of Economic Growth in Postwar America*. Oxford: Oxford University Press.

Critser, G. (2004) *Fat Land: How Americans Became the Fattest People in the World*. Boston, MA: Mariner Books.

de Graaf, J., Wann, D. and Naylor, T.H. (2002) *Affluenza: The All-Consuming Epidemic*. San Francisco, CA: Berrett-Koehler.

deChant, D. (2002) *The Sacred Santa: Religious Dimensions of Consumer Culture*. Cleveland, OH: Pilgrim Press.

Dichter, E. (1960) *The Strategy of Desire*. New York: Boardman.

Domosh, M. (2003) Pickles and purity: discourses of food, empire and work in turn-of-the-century USA. *Social and Cultural Geography* 4 (1), 7–26.

Farrell, J.J. (2004) *One Nation Under Goods: Malls and the Seductions of American Shopping*, Washington DC and London: Smithsonian Books.

Frank, T. (1997) Why Johnny can't dissent. In T. Frank and M. Weiland (eds) *Commodify your Dissent: Salvos from The Baffler*, pp. 31–45. New York: W.W. Norton.

Glickman, L.B. (1997) *A Living Wage: American Workers and the Making of Consumer Society*. Ithaca: Cornell University Press.

Goss, J. (1993) The magic of the mall: form and function in the retail built environment. *Annals of the Association of American Geographers* 83, 18–47.

——(1999) Once-upon-a-time in the commodity world: an unofficial guide to Mall of America. *Annals of the Association of American Geographers* 89, 45–75.

Grunenberg, C. and Hollein, M. (eds) (2002) *A Century of Art and Consumer Culture*, pp. 13–37. Ostfildern: Hatje Cantz.

Harvey, D. (1990) Between space and time: reflections on the geographical imagination. *Annals of the Association of American Geographers* 80 (3), 418–34.

Hollein, M. (2002) Shopping. In C. Grunenberg and M. Hollein (eds) *A Century of Art and Consumer Culture*, pp. 13–37. Ostfildern: Hatje Cantz.

Horowitz, D. (2004) *The Anxieties of Affluence: Critiques of Consumer Culture, 1939–1979*. Amherst and Boston: University of Massachusetts Press.

Jameson, F. (2003) Future city. *New Left Review* 21. Available at http://www.newleftreview.net/NLR25503.shtml

Klein, N. (2000) *No Logo: Taking Aim at the Brand Bullies*. New York: Picador.

Knowles, J. (1997) Cecil's shopping centre: the rediscovery of Ben Jonson's masque in praise of trade. *Times Literary Supplement* 7 February, 14–15.

Koehn, N.F. (2001) *Brand New: How Entrepreneurs Earned Consumers' Trust from Wedgwood to Dell*. Harvard: Harvard Business School Press.

Lasch, C. (1991) *Culture of Narcissism: American Life in an Age of Diminishing Expectations*. New York: W.W. Norton.

Leach, W. (1989) Strategists of display and the production of desire. In S.J. Bronner (ed.) *Consuming Visions: Accumulation and Display of Goods in America 1880–1920*, pp. 99–132. New York: W.W. Norton.

Lee, M. (2003) *Fashion Victim: Our Love–Hate Relationship with Dressing, Shopping, and the Cost of Style*. New York: Broadway Books.

Lefebvre, H. (1971) *Everyday Life in the Modern World*, trans. S. Rabinovitch. New York: Harper and Row.

Leong, S.T. (2001) . . . and then there was shopping. In C.J. Chung, J. Inaba, R. Koolhaas and S.T. Leong (eds) *Project on the City 2: Harvard Design School Guide to Shopping*, pp. 129–35. Cologne: Taschen.

989

Lury, C. (1997) The objects of travel. In C. Rojek and J. Urry (eds) *Touring Cultures: Transformations of Travel and Theory*, pp. 75–95. New York: Routledge.

McCracken, G. (1988) *Culture and Consumption: New Approaches to the Symbolic Character of Consumer Goods and Activities*. Bloomington: Indiana University Press.

McKendrick, N., Brewer, J. and Plumb, J.H. (1983) *The Birth of a Consumer Society*. London: Hutchinson.

Manning, R.D. (2000) *Credit Card Nation: The Consequences of America's Addiction to Credit*. New York: Basic Books.

Marcuse, H. (1964) *One-Dimensional Man*. Boston: Beacon Press.

Miller, D. (1995) Consumption as the vanguard of history: a polemic by way of introduction. In D. Miller (ed.) *Acknowledging Consumption: A Review of New Studies*, pp. 1–57. New York: Routledge.

——(1998) *A Theory of Shopping*. Oxford: Polity Press.

Miller, V.J. (2003) *Consuming Religion: Christian Faith and Practice in a Consumer Culture*. London and New York: Continuum.

Myers, N. and Kent, J. (2004) *The New Consumers: The Influence of Affluence on the Environment*. Washington DC: Island Press.

Nava, M. (1996) Modernity's disavowal: women and the department store. In M. Nava and A. O'Shea (eds) *Modern Times: Reflections on a Century of English Modernity*, pp. 38–76. London: Routledge.

Norris, T. (2004) *Hannah Arendt and Jean Baudrillard: pedagogy in the Consumer Society*. Infed Archives. Available at http://www.infed.org/biblio/pedagogy_consumer_society.htm

Paquet, L.B. (2003) *The Urge to Splurge: A Social History of Shopping*. Toronto: ECW Press.

Pooler, J. (2003) *Why We Shop: Emotional Rewards and Retail Strategies*. Westport, CT: Praeger.

Ritzer, G. (1999) *Enchanting a Disenchanted World: Revolutionizing the Means of Consumption*. Thousand Oaks, CA: Pine Forge Press.

——(2004) *The Globalization of Nothing*. Thousand Oaks, CA, and London: Pine Forge Press.

Robbins, R. (1999) *Global Problems and the Culture of Capitalism*. Harlow: Allyn and Bacon.

Sack, R. (1992) *Place, Modernity and the Consumer's World: A Relational Framework for Geographical Analysis*. Baltimore: Johns Hopkins University Press.

Sassatelli, R. (2001) Tamed hedonism: choice, desires and deviant pleasures. In J. Gronow and A. Warde (eds) *Ordinary Consumption*, pp. 93–106. New York: Routledge.

Schlosser, E. (2001) *Fast Food Nation: The Dark Side of the All-American Meal*. Boston: Houghton Mifflin.

Schmidt, L.E. (1997) *Consumer Rites: The Buying and Selling of American Holidays*. Princeton: Princeton University Press.

Schor, J.B. (1999) *The Overspent American: Why We Want What We Don't Need*. New York: Harper.

——(2000) *Do Americans Shop Too Much?* Boston, MA: Beacon Press.

——(2004) *Born to Buy! The Commercialized Child and the New Consumer Culture*. New York: Scribner.

Schwartz, B. (2004) *The Paradox of Choice: Why More is Less*. New York: HarperCollins.

Stearns, P. (2001) *Consumerism in World History; The Global Transformation of Desire*. New York: Routledge.

Taylor, M.C. (2000) Duty-free shopping. In C. Grunenberg and M. Hollein (eds) *A Century of Art and Consumer Culture*, pp. 39–53. Ostfildern: Hatje Cantz.

Twitchell, J.B. (1997) *Adcult USA: The Triumph of Advertising in American Culture*. New York: Columbia University Press.

——(1999) *Lead Us into Temptation: The Triumph of American Materialism*. New York: Columbia University Press.

Underhill, P. (1999) *Why We Buy: The Science of Shopping*. New York: Simon and Schuster.

Veblen, T. (1902) *The Theory of the Leisure Class: An Economic Study of Institutions*. New York: Macmillan.

Welch, E. (2005) *Shopping in the Renaissance: Consumer Cultures in Italy 1400–1600*. New Haven: Yale University Press.

Williams, R.H. (1982) *Dream Worlds: Mass Consumption in Late Nineteenth-Century*. Berkeley: University of California Press.

Wolf, N. (2003) Anti-consumerism equals anti-womanism. *eXile* 174. Available at http://exile.ru/174/174080000.html

Young, W. (2004) *Sold Out! The True Cost of Supermarket Shopping*. London: Fusion Press.

Zaltman, G. (2003) *How Customers Think: Essential Insights into the Mind of the Market*. Boston, MA: Harvard Business School Press.

Žižek, Z. (1997) *Plague of Fantasies*. London and New York: Verso.

Zukin, S. (2004) *Point of Purchase: How Shopping Changed American Culture*. New York: Routledge.

62

Engendering change

Janice Monk

Over the last three decades, awareness that gender shapes the ways in which people think about, experience and shape space and place has become widely acknowledged. Prompted especially by women scholars, whose consciousness was raised by the revitalized women's movements of the 1970s, geographers began to ask new questions about theories, methods and purposes of the discipline (Monk and Hanson 1982) and to conduct research on the implications of gender, especially for women's lives. Initially, studies emphasized differences between women and men without making further distinctions within those groups, though there was an early awareness that place was an important aspect of difference. As the field expanded, sensitivity developed to the importance of considering how other social distinctions, such as class, ethnicity, 'race', nationality, religion or point in the life course intersected with gender (see also Chapter 24). Concurrently, women's lives have been changing. In many areas of the world their participation in the paid labour force has increased, partly in response to global changes in the spaces of production and the expansion of service economies. Their burdens for reproductive work have grown with the retreat of social welfare supports in both Western and Third Worlds. International migration has brought many women into new places. Political conflicts have disrupted and harmed the lives of others. As a result, both women's and men's lives have become more complex. So too the circulation of research across disciplines and various parts of the world, especially from the global 'South', made evident that not only did experiences differ, but also ways of understanding them.

This chapter cannot offer a comprehensive synopsis of gender research or of the ways in which gender identities, roles and relations have changed. By presenting examples, I aim to address key issues and to provide enough detail to clarify subjectivities, actions and differences. They will illustrate how other social distinctions intersect with gender, highlight the importance of place, space and time, and demonstrate how multiple geographic scales are implicated in understanding gender roles and relations in the social, economic and political arenas of the contemporary world. I focus on women, still neglected by too much research, though the implications for gender relations will be apparent. Women continue to be subjected to oppression and are disadvantaged in many settings, but my choice is to emphasize their agency – their strategies for coping and how they work for change – and to demonstrate some complexities of that change. I begin with the scale of the body, then progress to household, community and national scales, and finally, to the transnational. Though organizing the chapter on these scalar dimensions, it will be evident that interpretation generally involves crossing scales, that the global and national have implications for the local and vice versa (Nagar *et al.* 2002). I conclude with some remarks on gender and empowerment.

Body politics

The concept of gender was introduced into research to demonstrate how women's and men's lives are socially and culturally constructed, rather than immutably fixed by a dichotomous sexual (biological) division. Subsequently, research has made it apparent that bodies also need to be understood through social, cultural, economic and political lenses, that sexualities and mind/body are not simple binaries. Two examples from Asia illustrate how individual women express agency over their bodies even as that agency is not always in conditions of their own choosing. Lily Phua and Brenda Yeoh (2002) explore ways in which pregnant Chinese women in Singapore resist and negotiate political, medical and cultural discourses that attempt to regulate their choices and behaviour. Though women may give lip service (as in survey responses) to the state's pro-natalist policies, at the private level they often express that they are 'stopping at two' (children), prioritizing personal economic concerns or values about children's education. By drawing on advice from their social networks or reading they will contest and negotiate medical practices and discourses proffered in clinic spaces where the right to regulate the pregnant body is assumed. By evading familial contacts they may resist cultural traditions that see the pregnant woman's body as 'property' of the lineage and container of the foetus, a body whose diet and spatial activities should be constrained in particular ways. As Phua and Yeoh point out, the individual expressions are not directed to making structural changes in the social order, yet they may have potential for revising discourses which have wider impacts. Certainly, the shifts that have taken place in Singapore over thirty-five years from policies to limit population growth, then to eugenics and later to pro-natalism, reflect not only the state's visions of its needs but also the realities of women's attitudinal and behavioural responses.

That bodily autonomy may be more constrained than it is for these Singaporean women is evident in Marten's (2005) research with commercial sex workers near the Thai border in Cambodia. Their situation demonstrates differences in power among women while still revealing the exercise of agency in self-interest to mitigate the risks of contracting and spreading HIV. The women in her study, mostly internal migrants in Cambodia, are poor, have little education and low self-esteem; they are removed from familial supports and are highly vulnerable to potential abuse from clients and employers. Government policies mandate use of condoms by sex workers in brothels. Marten examined women's engagement with an educational programme offered by the nongovernmental agency (NGO) Médicins sans Frontiers Holland, designed to teach about disease protection and condom use. Her research revealed that participating sex workers have been substantially successful in persuading their clients to use condoms by persistent and resourceful 'soft' and 'sweet' talk, emphasizing the benefits of disease protection to the male client and his family. Yet their exercise of control is limited. Women who are indebted to brothel owners may not be able to insist on condom use if the owner places more value on the client's payment than on the women's health. Those who have regular ('boyfriends') or affluent clients such as 'healthy-looking' government officials are less able or willing to require usage. Most vulnerable are self-employed sex workers who lack economic or physical protections of a brothel owner and are not subject to the law for compulsory use. Marten also found that Vietnamese immigrant women working in brothels were the most in control. She attributed this to their capacities to sustain familial ties and to their expectations of turning to other lives in the future. Context and differences among women thus have demonstrable effects on agency. Notably these women's agency was individual, not collective, limited by their low status and economic dependence. It also reflected support from an international NGO. As Marten points out, more might be accomplished if the women could receive assistance to organize, gain independent access to financial support, or have opportunities for other sources of income. In the next section, I turn to examples that begin to illustrate efforts to cope with economic and political stress which may generate collective action at the community scale.

Changing the spaces of action: work, household and community

A key insight of geographers studying gender is that spaces of action, once seen as separated into 'private' and 'public', the former associated with women, the latter with men, are integrated, fluid and contested. In this section, I will examine a range of contexts and spheres of action in which challenges to separation of spaces are offered. Focusing on the intersections of work, household and community, I highlight implications for gender identities and actions. In so doing, I link these changes to larger-scale spaces. My illustrations draw on a range of settings with a view to demonstrating the pervasiveness of change, its uneven gains, and the significance of context.

Restructuring has brought profound change to many regions that were long dependent on agricultural, extractive and industrial economies in western Europe and the United States. As old ways of making a living have declined, new ways have emerged in such regions; women have taken up new forms of productive work and of contributing to their households. Though they have always laboured in these settings, much of what women did went unrecorded and unpaid as they took care of families or worked on family farms. The development of agro-tourism in Spain in the 1990s represents an endeavour that is heavily dependent on women's work and that links public and private spaces (Cánoves et al. 2004). Promoted by regional governments and with European Union support, the intent is to enhance rural incomes, to preserve and promote local cultural heritages and environments. Not surprisingly, the appeal and accessibility of places varies so engagement is uneven. Additionally, how much women assume formal leadership in agro-tourism apparently reflects the extent to which men have other economic options. In some regions, the majority of recorded business owners are women, in others men own as many as 50 per cent of the establishments. Agro-tourism requires that women's traditional domestic responsibilities continue and indeed expand as they welcome and serve guests in their homes. But it also brings a public dimension into what were previously private spaces, as women not only meet clients but negotiate, for example, for public financial support. Many women rate highly that they are generating an income without leaving the house, having their work become visible to the rest of the family, widening their world and experiencing enhanced self-esteem. Yet the benefits remain constrained: work load increases, income is modest and fluctuates. If younger women have other options because of their mobility, it appears they do not find the industry attractive. Thus the outcomes of taking up agro-tourism are mixed in terms of supporting social change.

In the old coal-mining regions of rural Appalachia in the United States the distinctions between public and private spaces are also becoming increasingly blurred. There has been a widespread engagement by women in isolated rural areas in a variety of home-based work to

995

generate new income for themselves and their families (Oberhauser 1995, 2002). Offering services such as telephone marketing, grooming and training pets, child and elder care and hairstyling, or producing commodities such as animals for sale, crafts or baked goods, women often draw on traditional female skills. The benefits they report overlap with those indicated by the Spanish women: generating income, being able to maintain family responsibilities, increasing self-worth. But stresses vary among women if paid work infringes on home space, problems arise in meeting work schedules while continuing family care, or women experience associated feelings of guilt or inadequacy. Additionally the husband's sense of identity as breadwinner may be threatened, though some men demonstrate flexibility and increase their share of caring work. The Appalachian case further demonstrates how home-based work can connect women beyond the household. By participating in work-related networks, such as Appalachian By Design, the women's non-profit cooperative that offers contracting, educational and marketing services for home knitters, members move not only further into the public realm but through collective action they enlarge the scale of change.

The remaining examples in this section, from Ghana, Australia, India and Peru, illustrate how economic issues may serve as a stimulus not only to women's engagement in that sphere but prompt activism in other arenas of life and cut across scales. In examining women's organizations in two communities in Ghana, Mensah and Antoh (2005) identify those that have economic agendas and others that are more generally involved with community development, political, religious and educational programmes. Women have long engaged in collective activity in Ghana, but the bases for organization and scope of activities have been significantly altered as they attempt to cope with the effects of Structural Adjustment Programmes (SAPs) imposed by the World Bank and International Monetary Fund. These programmes prompted retrenchment of public services and removal of food subsidies while rendering employment more precarious, thus increasing stresses on households. They are widely recognized as having disproportionately created burdens for women. In this circumstance, women have increasingly initiated collective action. In the two districts studied, more than half of sixty-six women's groups focused on economic concerns. Market women, for example, provided mutual support through such means as purchasing in bulk, manipulating prices, giving crisis assistance to members, or offering intergenerational training. Other economically oriented organizations brought together women traders or artisans or set up rotating credit groups. In addition to demonstrating how local women respond to the negative impacts of global scale economic policies, Mensah and Antoh identify a range of organizations that address humanitarian concerns beyond the private or directly economic spheres: community development organizations that are pressing for adult education, literacy programmes for women or family planning, and that involve young girls in their work; religious organizations that are challenging male domination in churches. By working together, the women's groups are shaping change, though the authors are careful to point out how activism varies between the two districts they studied reflecting community size, history and religious orientation.

Panelli (2002) offers yet another perspective on blurring the boundaries of public and private that has recursive effects. In her research with the Australian 'Women in Agriculture' movement, she shows how women sought to address the lack of recognition of their work on the farm and their marginalization by local farming organizations, rural media, and business and governmental bureaucracies. By forming supportive networks, coming together in conferences and workshops and promoting their stories in press releases, they heightened recognition for the fundamental importance of their roles in sustaining rural industries. They moved beyond the local scale, mobilizing not only to challenge state and industry organizations and to host the First Women in Agriculture International Conference. Simultaneously, engagement in these public activities prompted personal consciousness-raising and re-shaping of identities, so that individual women began to function differently not only in public and in relation to the state, but to become more vocally involved, confident in decision making and taking on new tasks on their own family farms. The binary of 'public–private' at once became more complex, multi-dimensional and multi-scalar.

An Indian example highlights how specific spatial strategies that emerged as an instrumentally oriented project designed to empower poor rural women economically were enlarged into a widespread campaign against domestic violence towards women in villages in Uttar Pradesh, India (Nagar 2000). A programme of Mahila Samakhya was designed to train women as hand-pump mechanics in a region of water scarcity. Developing new skills not only empowered women technologically but fostered their desire for formal literacy, initially so as to be able to keep their own work records as they became increasingly conscious of gender inequalities. As literacy advanced, women created and disseminated stories, poems and songs for which they received national as well as local recognition. In the process, a new but related organization, Vanangana, was formed to address the disjunction between women's enhanced standing in the work sphere and their continuing subjection to violence, rape and burnings that disempowered them in homes and communities. With support from the NGO Oxfam and assistance from Delhi-based NGOs, Vanangana created street theatre performances to protest violence against women. Clear spatial strategies were identified in selecting sites, with distinctions between those designed for villages where performances were addressed to violence in marital/conjugal homes and those in victims' natal homes. Nagar relates the evolution of women's consciousness, identities and discourses in dramatic performances that demanded taking of responsibility for gendered injustices by local authorities, families and neighbours. She highlights the significance of specific caste, class and familial relationships. Again, we see the indivisibility of the public and private spaces in expressions of women's activism and the importance of attending to the specificities of contexts and social categories.

In Peru, the armed conflict between government and Sendero Luminoso (Shining Path), beginning in the impoverished rural Department of Ayacucho in 1982, could not successfully be contained or resolved by the repressive traditions of government or the confrontational politics of Sendero Luminoso. Though men were the primary targets of both sides, with greater mobility than vulnerable women who had familial responsibilities, men could more readily leave dangerous communities. In this context, women initiated a movement for survival and resistance that brought them to 'transcend confinement to traditional roles and consolidate themselves as social and political actors' (Hays-Mitchell 2005: 597). Through their networks, they initiated spatial strategies to facilitate relocation of their husbands and adolescent children in refuge communities as far away as possible, and of their middle children to homes of relative and friends in more secure locations, while keeping elders at home to retain a stake in the local. In the face of economic collapse, they created new income-generating activities such as communal gardens and food services. Most telling was the collective resistance to violence, initially fomented furtively at the local level, but blossoming into a Federation of Mothers' Clubs coordinated at sub-regional, regional and national scales. These groups organized relief programmes, coordinated searches for the missing, disappeared and deceased, and were themselves subjected to violence. At first dismissed as inconsequential by Sendero Luminoso, then attacked by them, the Federation persisted to become central in turning around the conflict. As Hays-Mitchell points out, it is misleading to represent women primarily as victims in conflict situations and also to overlook women engaged in supporting conflict. She highlights the transformation of poor *campesinas* into critical social actors, demonstrates ways in which the familial identity of 'mother' can be brought into public life and warns that reversion to masculinized models of power in the post-conflict period would be unjust and ineffective. To sustain peace-making, reconciliation and development, specific gender interests and contributions must be recognized.

Crossing national borders

The previous sections have illustrated some of the dynamics of change in women's gender identities and their agency in engaging with their bodies, their homes, workspaces and communities. Many more examples could be offered, especially from North America and Britain, of ways in which gender is implicated in managing the spatial challenges of responsibilities for juggling care-giving and paid work (see e.g. England and Lawson 2005). Likewise, a substantial literature exists on the structural constraints within which women operate within urban areas (see e.g. Preston and Ustundag 2005) and as they are subjects of unequal impacts of development programmes (see e.g. Momsen 2004). In this section, however, I want to turn from the more local to aspects of women's agency as they cross national borders, seeking not only to change personal lives (and those of their families and communities) but to organize for wider political change. I will emphasize transnational activism, especially within the context of the United Nations, but also engage with local ramifications of the transnational. In so doing, I take up the question of universalisms and particularisms as they emerge in debates about women's rights.

The 1970s resurgence of feminism saw not only local expressions but the initiation of the UN Decade for Women in 1975 and a related series of international conferences. As Ruth Pearson has commented, '[o]ver the last years of the twentieth century, women's organisations and lobby groups emerged as the transnational political actor *par excellence*' (2000: 15). Not only was their engagement in deliberations at the UN women's conferences enlarged and transformed, but so too were their concerns integrated into UN environmental, population and human rights agendas as women demonstrated the interconnections between economic, social, and political change. Friedman (2003) offers a detailed analysis of the strategies women devised to influence outcomes and the resistances they encountered. I will draw on her research to highlight processes that reflect evolving transnational engagements. Several points are key. First is the expansion of participation by women representatives of NGOs who created spaces outside the official sessions to share their views and formulate ways to influence the discourse. At the Mexico City conference in 1975, 'only two representatives per accredited NGO were permitted to participate on a limited basis in the governmental conference' (Friedman 2003: 317). By decade's end, some 30,000 women from across the world gathered in the NGO Forum ancillary to the Beijing Fourth World Conference on Women, not only working with each other, but shuttling back and forth between the NGO and governmental sites, communicating deliberations and lobbying for the inclusion of their perspectives in the Platform for Action. The transformation reflected local organizational development in diverse national settings, international networking that grew among women and their associated strategy of intensive engagement in preparatory conferences to formulate their positions. Also important were geopolitical shifts. Women of the North and South who had been divided at the first two conferences (1975 Mexico City, 1980 Copenhagen) by nationalist politics and different understandings of the nature and causes of women's oppression found paths to commonality. Friedman (2003) attributes the reconciliation to the efforts of feminists from North and South engaged in development studies who came to recognize the importance of contextual differences. Additionally, she sees the process enhanced as allegiances and priorities shifted in the post-Cold War period.

Perhaps the most notable outcomes from this transnational women's activism have been their successes in shifting the discourse, integrating gender perspectives into the documents that emerged from the UN conferences on the environment, population, and human rights. Thus at the 1992 Rio Conference on Environment and Development, by emphasizing 'women's roles as stewards of the environment and expertise in sustainable development' (Friedman 2003: 320) women activists were able to insist on the inclusion of gender content into the final Agenda 21 document. Nevertheless, there remained considerable differences in the perspectives presented in Agenda 21 and those articulated at the preceding women's conference, notably, according to Brú Bistuer and Agüera Cabo (2004) that the women's agenda saw gender as cross-cutting social, economic and ecological issues with linkages from the global to the personal, whereas the Rio document compartmentalizes women, continuing to construct them as 'other' rather than as subjects in their own right. Brú Bistuer and Agüera Cabo also argue that Agenda 21 places more faith in technological solutions to environmental sustainability in comparison to the women's more critical views of such approaches.

At the 1993 Vienna Conference on Human Rights, where women's groups promoted the position that 'Women's Rights are Human Rights', they brought about a fundamental conceptual change in the mainstream discourse through their intensive lobbying. More contentious politics permeated the 1994 Cairo Conference on Population and Development. Though women's health advocates from North and South shifted the limited focus on fertility to a broader interpretation of women's reproductive health, they faced strong opposition from religiously based coalitions, including the Vatican, with its anti-abortion stance, and Islamic groups mobilizing against challenges to traditional family roles. Still, as Pearson notes, the interventions in these conferences generated more than mere lip service to politically correct opinion.

> [T]he recognition that women have the right to freedom from violence and bodily integrity as a basic human right has been translated into the addition of rape as an international war crime, and several war trials following the conflicts in the Balkans and in Rwanda have concretely reflected this change in public policy.
>
> (Pearson 2000: 15)

These international challenges by women open up the need to examine thinking about universalisms and particularisms in addressing the engendering of social change. Struggles in Morocco over attempts to establish a Moroccan Plan for Action to Integrate Women into Development and to ratify the Convention on the Elimination of all Forms of Discrimination against Women illustrate the tensions in perspectives (Freeman 2004). While some groups of Moroccan women organized in support of the universalist underpinnings of these two documents, others, still aiming for progressive changes that would enhance women's rights, took positions identified as Islamist on the grounds that the Moroccan Plan for Action imposed imported values. In support of their arguments the divergent groups adopted the spatial tactics of sponsoring two simultaneously scheduled and well-publicized marches, one in Rabat, the other in Casablanca. As Freeman narrates the positions and local politics, she reveals some of the complexities of thinking about what is universal and what is particularistic. To what extent, she asks, were the Islamist perspectives expounded in Morocco themselves transnational? How did women supporting universalist positions strategize by co-opting local religious and cultural discourses in order to frame their positions?

Such complexities are explored in some depth by Geraldine Pratt (2004) in her work with immigrant communities in Vancouver, especially with Filipinas who have entered under the Live-In Caregiver programme. In their struggles to gain recognition for the credentials they brought to Canada as registered nurses, they had to consider whether to take up the Canadian discourse of multiculturalism and form alliances with other immigrant groups. The Philippine Women's Centre, however, maintained that they should organize separately in order to acknowledge their specific historical and material circumstances. In another example, Pratt explores women's fluidity in defining, redefining and expressing identity in transnational communities as they move from one space to another in Vancouver. Why might a young locally born Chinese-Canadian woman on the one hand feel disempowered in a downtown shopping mall by being identified with recent affluent Chinese immigrants, yet also derive a sense of empowerment from belonging to the enlarged Chinese community that recent migration has created?

In these examples of transnational organizing and experiences, I have aimed to indicate both the achievements of expanding collective action by women and the continuing challenges that reflect differences among women on such bases as their cultural and political perspectives, religion or national origin. I have also attempted to illustrate that gains are partial, contested and involve personal and group ambivalences.

Gender and empowerment

In this chapter, I have periodically referred to women's empowerment. This concept has increasingly been invoked not only by feminist activists and scholars but by such international bodies as the World Bank and many NGOs. In considering the engendering of change, it is important to reflect on how empowerment has been interpreted, in what ways it might have been achieved and what major challenges remain. Townsend *et al.* (2004: 886) draw attention to an *Oxford English Dictionary* definition from the seventeenth century which included the meaning 'to gain or assume power' but note that the more common long-standing meaning is 'to confer power upon'. They and others writing about engendering change commonly include the former of these two interpretations. Staeheli and Kofman add another dimension in defining empowerment as the 'struggle to reposition marginalized groups in webs of power that organize life' (2004: 7), thus recognizing the importance of networks and webs of relationships. Feminist aims in empowerment include undoing internal oppression and fostering a more equitable sharing of resources, in the ways they are organized, distributed and claimed at multiple scales (Nagar and Raju 2003). What is less clear is how the process works, though it is recognized that the aspects are not, or need not be, mutually exclusive. Again, we see the acknowledgement of feminist thinking that it is valuable to think beyond dichotomies.

That empowerment may involve ambiguities and contradictions and is not necessarily a linear process may be inferred from the cases I have presented in preceding sections. Engaging women in paid work in or beyond the home, for example, may enhance their incomes, options and self-esteem while also increasing work loads and responsibilities. It may heighten their consciousness of the needs for public and collective action to challenge economic, political or cultural disadvantage, oppression and bodily integrity, but women may continue to be marginalized in setting agendas. Yet as Mensah and Antoh concluded in their examination of the women's organizations in Ghana empowerment can occur:

despite the debilitating impacts of patriarchy, poverty and illiteracy, women in both districts have managed to use their grassroots organizations to improve the socioeconomic circumstances of their members in particular and their communities in general.

(Mensah and Antoh 2005: 82)

A complex issue is assessment of the roles of NGOs in fostering empowerment. As governments have adopted neoliberal policies and retreated from providing public services, local, national and international NGOs have taken on these responsibilities or been prompted by governments to do so. New questions emerge. Who is setting the NGOs' agendas? To what extent are they becoming primarily involved in delivering services rather than challenging the structures that disempower women? Where do these organizations find funds and how can they be maintained? How do requirements for accountability and reporting to funders promote a professional culture whereby power within NGOs is held by people with the greatest resources in terms of education and skills to manage financial and linguistic demands of national or international relations? Evaluations of the effectiveness of NGOs in fostering change suggest that their roles and capabilities have diminished as they have come to take on increasing burdens for delivering services and responding to bureaucracies, though some remain committed to working for structural change (Nagar and Raju 2003; Townsend *et al.* 2004).

An examination of the representation of women in arenas of formal politics presents another perspective on empowerment. Bashevkin (2005), drawing on work by Voet, proposes that such representation can be examined from three perspectives. First is looking at the representation of women in elected offices, reflecting the liberal feminist position that having women in office is a precondition to equality. Second is an analysis of the representation of women and women's issues in bureaucracies, including special women's units, under the assumption that women hold different values and have different needs than men. Third is the analysis of discourse in political representations. Applying these perspectives in a comparative study of urban government in London and Toronto in the wake of decentralizing the system in the former and centralizing in the latter, Bashevkin finds more presence and support for women in the decentralized and leftist-led London than in the centralized and conservative-led Toronto. The percentage of seats held by women rose after decentralization in London, but fell after centralization in Toronto. In London, it was recognized that gender-blind language was inappropriate and that women's particular needs should be identified. Appointment of a women's policy advisor prompted gender-aware approaches in housing, employment and transportation programmes. In Toronto, earlier bodies such as the Safe City Committee that had been women-oriented were replaced by a task force on community safety whose members largely came from groups other than women's organizations. Language related to women disappeared from Toronto planning documents.

Women's political representation varies widely internationally (Seager 2003). The granting of voting rights, for example, has spanned over a century, with rights often being granted to men before women and to white women before people of colour. As of 2002, in no country were women equally represented in national legislatures, and in only twenty-two did they hold 25 per cent or more of seats. Those with the highest shares were countries that enforce explicit policies promoting equality (Seager 2003: 94). Similar analyses in the United States reveal wide state-level differences in women's representation in elected office and in their records of participation as voters (Institute for Women's Policy Research 2004).

Contextualized research would be required to explore the underlying conditions of space, place, histories, cultures and variations in demography that give rise to the patterns observed.

In summary, in my examination of engendering change, and especially of the empowerment of women, five themes recur. First, to understand and work for change it is critical to consider specificities of context: of place, time, culture and distinctions among women such as those of religion, economic status, ethnicity or citizenship. Second, change takes place at multiple and interconnected scales, from the body to the transnational. Third, individual changes in consciousness are integral to fostering wider social change, but so too can wider social change shape the ways in which an individual comes to the consciousness that engenders change. Finally, although much that could be considered progressive for women has been witnessed over the last three decades, disadvantages persist. Many challenges remain.

Further reading

Nagar, R., Lawson, V., McDowell, L. and Hanson, S. (2002) Locating globalization: feminist (re)readings of the subjects and spaces of globalization. *Economic Geography* 78, 257–84.

Nelson, L. and Seager, J. (2005) (eds) *A Companion to Feminist Geography.* Malden, MA, and Oxford: Blackwell.

Seager, J. (2003) *The Atlas of Women: An Economic, Social and Political Survey,* revised third edition. London: The Women's Press.

Staeheli, L.A., Kofman, E. and Peake, L. (eds) (2004) *Mapping Women, Making Politics: Feminist Perspectives on Political Geography.* New York and London: Routledge.

References

Bashevkin, S. (2005) Training a spotlight on urban citizenship: the case of women in London and Toronto. *International Journal of Urban and Regional Research* 29, 9–25.

Brú Bistuer, J. and Agüera Cabo, M. (2004) A gendered politics of the environment. In L.A. Staeheli, E. Kofman, and L. Peake (eds) *Mapping Women, Making Politics: Feminist Perspectives on Political Geography,* pp. 209–25. New York and London: Routledge.

Cánoves, G., Villarino, M., Priestley, G. and Blanco, A. (2004) Rural tourism in Spain: an analysis of recent evolution. *Geoforum* 35, 755–69.

England, K. and Lawson, V. (2005) Feminist analyses of work: rethinking the boundaries, gendering, and the spatiality of work. In L. Nelson and J. Seager (eds) *A Companion to Feminist Geography,* pp. 77–92. Malden, MA, and Oxford: Blackwell.

Freeman, A. (2004) Re-locating Moroccan women's identities in a transnational world: the 'woman question' in question. *Gender, Place and Culture* 11, 17–41.

Friedman, E.J. (2003) Gendering the agenda: the impact of the transnational women's rights movement at the UN conferences of the 1990s. *Women's Studies International Forum* 26, 313–31.

Hays-Mitchell, M. (2005) Women's struggles for sustainable peace in post-conflict Peru: a feminist analysis of violence and change. In L. Nelson and J. Seager (eds) *A Companion to Feminist Geography,* pp. 590–603. Malden, MA, and Oxford: Blackwell.

Institute for Women's Policy Research (2004) *The Status of Women in the States.* Washington DC: Institute for Women's Policy Research.

Marten, L. (2005) Commercial sex workers: victims, vectors, or fighters of the HIV epidemic in Cambodia? *Asia Pacific Viewpoint* 46, 21–34.

Mensah, J. and Antoh, E.F. (2005) Reflections on indigenous women's organizations in sub-Saharan Africa: a comparative study in Brong Ahafo region, Ghana. *Singapore Journal of Tropical Geography* 26, 82–101.

Momsen, J.H. (2004) *Gender and Development*. London: Routledge.

Monk, J. and Hanson, S. (1982) On not excluding half of the human in human geography. *The Professional Geographer* 34, 11–23.

Nagar, R. (2000). *Mujhe Jawab Do!* (Answer Me!): women's grass-roots activism and social spaces in Chitrakoot (India). *Gender, Place and Culture* 7, 341–62.

Nagar, R. and Raju, S. (2003) Women, NGOs and the contradictions of empowerment and disempowerment: a conversation. *Antipode* 35, 1–13.

Nagar, R., Lawson, V., McDowell, L. and Hanson, S. (2002) Locating globalization: feminist (re)readings of the subjects and spaces of globalization. *Economic Geography* 78, 257–84.

Oberhauser, A.M. (1995) Gender and household economic strategies in rural Appalachia. *Gender, Place and Culture* 2, 51–70.

——(2002) Relocating gender and rural economic strategies. *Environment and Planning A* 34, 1221–37.

Panelli, R. (2002) Contradictory identities and political choices. In B.S.A Yeoh, P. Teo and S. Huang (eds) *Gender Politics in the Asia-Pacific Region*, pp. 17–40. London and New York: Routledge.

Pearson, R. (2000) Moving the goalposts: gender and globalization in the twenty-first century. *Gender and Development* 8, 10–19.

Phua, L. and Yeoh, B.S.A. (2002) Nine months: women's agency and the pregnant body in Singapore. In B.S.A Yeoh, P. Teo and S. Huang (eds) *Gender Politics in the Asia-Pacific Region*, pp. 17–40. London and New York: Routledge.

Pratt, G. (2004) *Working Feminism*. Philadelphia: Temple University Press.

Preston, V. and Ustundag, E. (2005). Feminist geographies of the 'city': multiple voices, multiple meanings. In L. Nelson and J. Seager (eds) *A Companion to Feminist Geography*, pp. 211–27. Malden, MA, and Oxford: Blackwell.

Seager, J. (2003) *The Atlas of Women: An Economic, Social and Political Survey*, revised third edition. London: The Women's Press.

Staeheli, L. and Kofman, E. (2004) Mapping gender, making politics: towards feminist political geographies. In L. Staeheli, E. Kofman and L. Peake (eds) *Mapping Women, Making Politics: Feminist Perspectives on Political Geography*, pp. 1–13. New York and London: Routledge.

Townsend, J.G., Porter, G., Mawdsley, E. (2004) Creating spaces of resistance: development NGOs and their clients in Ghana, India and Mexico. *Antipode* 36, 871–90.

63

Performativity

Identity and its geographical significance

Jan Penrose and Susan J. Smith

Introduction

The history of social and political geography revolves around the way people are categorized by others, and how they identify themselves. There has been a tendency to regard these social groupings (in practice if not in theory) as more given than made, so that major divisions and inequalities – around class, race, nation, gender, religion, disability, age and so on – are often taken for granted either as axes of oppression or as rallying points for resistance. While anti-racist, feminist, disability rights and other anti-essentialist scholarship sometimes imagines and often strives for a world without these lines of difference, the path from here to there has proved contentious, complicated and occasionally tortuous.

Something of a roadmap may, however, be contained in a new set of ideas about the way the social world works. Simply stated, these new ideas are bound up with the theory of performativity which argues that individual and social identities are in a constant process of becoming; that they are not fixed or as easily categorized as people have come to assume. The notion that categories of identity are not stable is encouraging testimony to the possibilities for change (offering the real hope that the future may be both different from, and better than, the past). However, this notion is also dangerous and destabilizing because it undermines attempts to use these categories as rallying points against entrenched and essentialized patterns of marginalization and disadvantage. So although some scholars are exploring how feminist politics might be pursued without presuming the category of women (e.g. Rose 1993 and Lloyd 2005), and how the just cause of anti-racism can be advanced without the category of race (e.g. Gilroy 1998, 2005; Smith 2005a), these ideas have yet to permeate popular perspectives and movements. To some extent, problems of imagining a world without categories like gender and race are a reflection of just how deeply seated a category-based perspective on the world has become. At the same time, if people choose to identify themselves as, for example, 'black', and seek to use this to engage politically or to secure social rights, this should not be dismissed lightly. For this reason, the new ideas discussed below may, in the end, be judged as much on whether they advance or delay the implementation of some important normative goals around equality and diversity, as on whether or not they are 'essentially' true.

To explore the liberating and transformative potential of the performative understanding of identity – and discuss the limitations of this approach – this chapter is divided into three main sections. First, we briefly outline what is normally understood by the term 'identity', consider its relevance to geography, and show how explanations of its constitution and significance have changed over the past fifty years or so. This is followed by a discussion of ideas about performativity and performance which highlights the innovative conceptions of identity that they support, and explains their geographical significance. The third main section considers what is distinctive about a performative approach to the geography of identity by inserting it into debates around structure and agency; drawing out its non-representational, embodied and affective (or emotional) qualities; and showing how it helps understanding of the ways in which social groups make and are shaped by the environments, technologies and material circumstances in which they live.

Identity

Until very recently, the concept of identity has been remarkably unproblematic – identity is who people are. This conceptual simplicity belies an enormously complex range of ideas about what actually constitutes individual identities and about how their definitive qualities are formed. Nevertheless, it is possible to advance some general comments about identity. The first is to suggest that identity connotes the way in which people more or less self-consciously locate themselves in their social world (cf. Penrose and Mole, forthcoming). The second key point is that people's capacity to know who they *are* also implies knowledge of who they *are not* and this makes it clear that all identities are relational (Massey 2004: 5). Third, it is immediately apparent that processes of social location and the designation of who people are/ are not rely heavily on social categories (Smith 2005b). These categories currently serve as means of making sense of the world – including human positions within it – and of communicating this understanding to others. In the process, however, they also *represent* the world as coherently structured and this reinforces the power of certain categories and of those who benefit most from them. Given that one of our goals in this chapter is to disrupt the power of fixed categories of identity, it makes sense to look at why categories are so dominant in the contemporary world.

Part of the power of categories comes from the ways in which scientists and academics have portrayed them. According to some social psychologists, for example, human beings have an instinctive need to categorize humanity into distinct social groups and to ascribe each with a unique identity (see, for example, what might be termed Social Identity Theory and Self-Categorization Theory described by Tajfel 1981; Tajfel and Turner 1986; and Turner 1987). They argue that processes of categorization are necessary because the social world has very few explicit lines of division. Social entities and the boundaries between them are fuzzy and fluid; they appear chaotic and unstructured because, for the most part, they are. Constructing categories, so this argument goes, is something that helps people to cope with the infinite stimuli of their worlds by imposing order on them. By making life less inchoate, categories also make it more predictable and this – according to this line of reasoning – makes it easier for human beings to locate themselves in the world. At the same time, the processes of categorization and representation render 'experience[s] of the world subjectively meaningful' and help us to behave in ways which are appropriate to the norms of the groups to which we or others belong (Hogg *et al.* 1995: 261).

The prevalence of this perspective, and its contribution to the reification of social categories as inevitable, makes it worthy of note. However, others are less sanguine and, like us, would argue that the creation of social categories is about inclusion and exclusion, empowerment and disempowerment see for example Chapter 62. In our view, claiming that some people are alike (because they share phenotypic traits, presumed histories, similar geographies) and that some are different (because they do not share these attributes) is a convenient way of deciding who gets what, where, and of legitimating any resulting inequalities.

Either way, categorization implicitly involves a process of accentuation: to create boundaries between social categories, so that 'like' needs to be grouped with 'like'. People therefore perceive entities within specific categories to be more similar to each other, and more different from entities in other categories, than they actually are. The processes of categorization and accentuation promote a perception of uniformity and, at the same time, create sharp divides between in-groups and out-groups, that do not exist in any objective sense. Nevertheless, 'the cognitive divisions we impose on the world do not seem arbitrary to us but instead a reflection of seemingly objective breaks and discontinuities' (Theiler 2003: 260). This apparent objectivity has historically been reinforced by geography, in the sense that where someone lives, or originates, is often used as an index of who they are: certainly this is how racial, national and ethnic identities have come to seem to be real.

This fixation with breaks and discontinuities, whether spatially or socially defined, is a product of the process of 'hegemony' which allows those in positions of power to convince subordinate others to accept the dominant group's moral, political and cultural values as the 'natural' order (Jackson 1989: 52–3, after Gramsci). The categories that structure much of human existence – particularly categories of identity – are a manifestation of these unequal power relations. Thus, even though the *process* of category formation may be instinctive, the resultant categories – and the values that are ascribed to them – are not 'given' or natural in any way (Penrose 1995). Instead, the categories that constitute contemporary worlds – including the division of humanity into various groupings – are a reflection of the perceptions, priorities and aspirations of those people who have the power to construct categories and promote them as 'natural' or superior. The same is true of representations of those people who are associated with specific categories; these representations are not 'givens' but constructions that reflect the power relations that exist within any specific social, geographical and historical context.

The glimmer of hope here lies in the fact that dominant positions are always contested; attempts at persuasion are always met with some resistance. Nevertheless, the categories that become entrenched through hegemony often set the parameters of contestation such that the content or significance of categories can be discussed but the category itself – as a legitimate division of the world – cannot (Penrose 1995). Thus, even though the meaning of identities is not fixed, the dominant categories of identity – things like 'race', gender, class, religion and nation – have proven very difficult to challenge, let alone dislodge.

In part, the relative fixity of *categories* of identity is reinforced when individuals who are assigned to a particular category accept this group membership as a key element of their personal identity. This happens when people look to categories of race, class, gender and so on as mechanisms for generating a sense of belonging, maximizing self-esteem, and/or claiming a fair share of resources. This process entails identification with an in-group (as defined by any given category or combination of categories) and with this in-group's dominant group norms, as well as its differentiation from the out-group. All identities – both individual and collective – are thus defined with reference to both Self and Other. Given the importance of group membership for self-definition, human beings tend to internalize their own group categorization; as the individual becomes part of the group, the group becomes part of the individual. It is this internalization of identity that helps to make categories of identity so important, and consequently so powerful. Those categories that inspire the greatest internalization, that become personal and perceived as key to the survival of the self, are those that assume the greatest significance in structuring divisions of people and space as well as the power relations and the structures of power that mediate them.

The recognition that categories are social constructions which are intimately bound up with power relations, marked a major transition in the understanding of identity. If categories are not natural, then they can be resisted, changed and/or replaced in ways that, potentially at least, generate greater equality and justice. This prospect has been cause for hope but, as long as identity is conceptualized exclusively in terms of categories, much of the messiness of identity remains unacknowledged and hidden from view. This concealment also means that alternative and potentially liberating ways of thinking about identity, and about transforming its geographical significance, remain overlooked as well.

It is partially out of concern about the limitations of category-based, or representational, notions of social construction and identity formation that ideas about performativity and performance find their origins. The realization that societal infrastructures and power distributions not only set up the boundaries and characteristics of specific identities, but also provide the contexts which shape (and are shaped by) their roles and practices, constitutes a huge change in perception. From this perspective, identity is no longer simply about who people *are* and where they fit into some broader system of social classification: it is also very much about what people *do*; about how their everyday lives, their practices and experiences actively constitute society.

Performing identities

Performativity is about the way ideas, events and things in general – and identities in particular – are made. To say that economics is performative, for example, is to recognize that economic ideas have a bearing on, and are incorporated into everyday life; it is to argue that economic theories and models have an effect on how economies work; and it is to suggest that economic processes are themselves influenced, perhaps radically changed, when economic ideas are put into practice (Mackenzie 2006). Likewise, to claim that identities are performative is to recognize that entrenched social categories have a bearing on how lives are lived; it is to argue that when people act as if categories are real, these acts have real, material effects; and critically, it is to recognize that once the essentialism of social categories is challenged then putting this challenge into practice can change the social geography of the world.

Consider for example the question of disability. At one time the term 'disabled' figured as a politically correct alternative to the derogatory label 'crippled'. However, to regard people as disabled itself implies that certain kinds of bodily impairments are necessarily limiting. But the practices – the performance – of disabled people, excelling in sport, in scholarship, in art, as well as managing creatively in the routine of daily life – made this presumption false. Some people *are* disabled, but this is because they live in social and physical environments which are actively disabling. For example, people who rely on wheelchairs for their mobility are stripped of their independence when they cannot easily enter buildings where the only access is by using stairs. The source of this disability is clearly not located in bodily impairments, because the technology of the wheelchair enhances mobility. Instead, the limitation comes from the lack of social and economic will, on the part of those in positions of power, in the institutions of an 'ableist' society, to *en*able and include a wider range of people by improving access through the addition of ramps. It is, then, ableist societies, and not just those who are 'disabled' that perform disability. Political recognition of this has, in some jurisdictions, meant that a growing range of environments and institutions are required by law to be enabling and this is encouraging – and expressing – some quite radical transformations in the social geography of disability. In other cases, the performance of disability by people with bodily impairments is changing the parameters of what disability means. A good example here is the rapid expansion of Paralympic sports where people who were once told to fear ice and snow now ski and curl and play a game called sledge hockey which, by virtue of its equipment, is impossible for the supposedly 'able' to play. All of these changes and challenges mean that the tenacity of disability as a social category and as a means of identification is being challenged (Butler and Parr 1999). In the process, the ways in which places and power relations support the formulation of identities is also changing.

It is worth noting, in light of this, that the notion of *performativity* refers to something that can be distinguished usefully from performances, as they are commonly understood (i.e. from performance as a special, practised, often professionalized, event). Performativity is not necessarily theatrical and performances are not necessarily performative (Sedgewick and Parker 1995). There is a great deal of confusion in the literature around performance and performativity, especially when approached for the first time. So although it is not strictly necessary to distinguish the two *terms*, it is worth recognizing the two different meanings that are (not always consistently) associated with them. Performance, in commonsense terms, refers to a situation where one or more people act out particular roles and/or demonstrate particular skills through a public exhibition or demonstration, usually with the intent of engaging an audience. In geography, this understanding of performance has enjoyed a recent upsurge in attention because of the potential for the study of performances to advance geographical knowledge in a number of ways (Thrift 2000: 577).

Most importantly, the significance of performances lies not just in what they represent but in their capacity to permit access to knowledge that can only be shared in and through practice (Smith 2001: 35). This, for example, is why Edward Said (1992) attaches such importance to the concert hall in his account of the relevance of music and musicians to the elaboration – to the maintenance and change – of social life. In this sense, the act of performing 'is as much about what is done as about what is said: it is a way of recognising that ways of being include the unknowable and the unsayable' (Smith 2001: 35). So, performances as 'special events' offer innovative opportunities for conveying, accessing and interpreting information. Given that performances *are* communicative events, it is not surprising that they also have an intrinsic and very powerful political dimension. This can be deployed in a wide variety of ways, ranging from the deceptively benign reproduction of the status quo to the overt challenge of it. Where the former reinforces the dominance of particular conceptions of the arts or of high culture, and the power of those who promote and benefit from this view, the latter seeks to alter these power relations by introducing new artistic forms or subverting old ones. Crucially both kinds of performances are interrelational because they are dependent on one another for their existence. Finally, performances achieve many of their impacts through the manipulation of time and space (Thrift 2000), not least because they take people out of their usual routines. Here, performances can transform spaces, for example the physical location and facilities in which they occur, and they can bring new places into being by producing imagined worlds that are created in the process of doing the performance. The spaces of performance may, then, be regarded as a microcosm of life itself, and as such they have much wider significance than might be imagined. In all of these ways, it is easy to see why performances have relevance to geography.

On a more theoretical level, the notion of *performativity* recognizes these important qualities of performance as a special event, and extends the notion of what constitutes a performance into the realms and regimes of everyday life. Thus, theories of performativity define a performance as 'any event, action, item or behaviour' (Smith 2001: 35). Lives are lived performatively; but within limits. So human subjects (performers, if you like) and the world in which they live are continuously constituted through the regulation and repetition of certain practices (stylized) and norms. In other words, people continuously perform the conventions of any given time and place and, in the process they actually produce these conventions and make them appear necessary and natural. For example, students attend lectures and seminars, prepare assignments and write essays (and sometimes party with abandon) and in the process of doing these things they define what it means to be a student. According to Judith Butler (1990, 1993), these performances are largely unconscious, and this means that any changes to identity and 'reality' can only come about through an accidental slippage in the performance or inaccurate reproduction of texts (Gregson and Rose 2000: 437; Lloyd 2005).

This is quite different from the commonsense understanding of performance which views performers as subjects that exist outside of their performance and grants them powers of agency and intentionality (cf. Gregson and Rose 2000). In these performances, actors can change their lines and alter their character. But where society as a whole is regarded as being constituted performatively, this is not possible in the same ways for two reasons. The first is because performers only exist through the act of *doing* the performance (so they cannot be outside it); students are only students when they do what students do. Second, actors are not (always) conscious of their citational practices or repetitive actions. So, to extend the same example, students seldom stop to question the practices that make them students and they have to keep doing these things to remain students. Nevertheless, the act of doing contains the possibility of change. It is precisely because the constitution of identity is iterative that there is always the possibility that the repetition will not be successful and that change or subversion may occur (Butler 1990:25). This is most obvious where performers are reflexive but it is also present in the very processes of repetition through which identities are constituted. So some students through the act of 'studenting' may, as time goes on, turn themselves into, for example, physicists – an outcome which is only possible by virtue of their location within the performative practices that constitute an educational institution.

Importantly, these two applications of the notion of performance – the theatrical and the everyday – do not need to contradict one another. The very different explanations of the subject and of how change occurs can, however, produce real tensions and must be recognized. Some scholars argue, like Gregson and Rose (2000: 433), that 'performance is subsumed within and must always be connected with performativity – that is, to the citational practices which produce and subvert discourse and knowledge, and which at the same time enable and discipline subjects and their performances'. They think this for the very sound reason that the subjects of performances and their performative practices cannot exist without the already established knowledges that they cite. This is because being black or female, for example, is dependent upon the repetition of practices that have come to define race and gender. By the same count, changing what it means to be black or female requires the existence of these norms in order to have something to change.

Where authors like Butler (1990, 1993) and Gregson and Rose (2000) stress the disciplining aspects of performativity, others like Smith (2001) are more interested in how a performative perspective reveals new insights into how identities are formed, maintained and changed and why people act in the ways that they do. For Smith (2001: 35) 'the idea that identity is repeatedly negotiable is as old as social science itself'. She argues that what is really exciting about performance is that it introduces the idea that identity is 'something that can only be accessed – that only exists in – performance, precisely because it is an expression, an enactment, of what is not "knowable"' (in other ways) (Smith 2001: 35). Moreover, performativity makes it clear that people can and do act (to make things change *or* to keep them the same) on the basis of how they feel as well as because of what they think (see below). This chapter is not the place to attempt a reconciliation of the wide range of ideas about performance and performativity; but it is the place to illustrate why performative identities are significant and how they offer new hope as a means of transforming entrenched power relations. This is what we turn to next.

The distinctiveness of a performative approach to identity

The literature on identities is buzzing with ideas about the way performativity theory and performance practice enlarge understandings of human life. Three themes in particular stand out. First, performative approaches to social identity emphasize process over structure, assigning agency to individuals and groups, recognizing the capability and capacity that human subjects have to enact or resist change. So they speak to the enduring, unresolved and probably irresolvable 'structure–agency' debate. Second, performance is a non-representational style of being and knowing, and this allows for the extent to which knowledge is visceral and sensory: life is as much about what is felt as about what can be said or written. So the study of performance enhances understanding of how social relations and social life are underpinned, or animated, by an emotional dynamic. Finally the performativity of identities is a product not just of the way humans experience and interact with themselves. It is also part and parcel of their entanglement with the nonhuman world; with objects, equations, technologies and a range of other materials of life. So it is in a sense about the forging of 'hybrid geographies' – alliances of humanity and technology which may, in the end, change the character of social identity and, indeed, of human life itself. We consider these three themes in turn.

Between structure and agency

It is often thought that what is distinctive about a performative approach to identity is the recognition that social divisions and distinctions are continually and routinely worked at: that social reproduction requires constant and consistent activity. But as Smith (2001) has noted, while this may be a useful and refreshing shift from recent preoccupations with how enduring entrenched inequalities are, it is not that new. Anthropologists have for years noticed how rewarding it can be to concentrate on the fuzzy edges of social groupings rather than on their homogenized interiors (Barth 1969), on the negotiable and contested aspects of identity rather than on their taken-for-granted core. From this perspective, some discussions of performativity might indeed be criticized for presuming that principles of inclusion and exclusion are routinely, repetitively and barely consciously reproduced. What is novel, on the other hand, about a performative take on identity is that it contains the seeds of change; what happens in practice may be more of the same, but there is always the possibility that things could be different – that gender could be reworked, classes restructured, race redefined. Importantly, it is precisely because identities are embedded in and produced by established performative practices that their subjects have the potential – though not necessarily the inclination, motivation or opportunity – to effect change.

Yet performativity theory has surprisingly little to say about what might change, when, where, why or how. Most attention has been afforded to the routinization of the status quo, the reproduction of the old. More excitement is expended on the qualities of the 'now' than on the present as a point of articulation between a past that is fixed and a future which is uncertain and has at least some degree of openness. So the constraints on performing the new, the actancy of inertia, are much better appreciated than the mechanisms by which things change. But just as inertia is a force worth reckoning with, so small acts can be forceful in other ways too: by accident, by design, or by some mix of the two. For example, Hille Koskela (1997), drawing on the narratives of Finnish women, shows how the performance of 'bold walk' undermines the gendered division (and masculinization) of public space that is routinely enforced through fear of crime. Likewise, Smith (1999) shows how all kinds of local politics are addressed in the rhythm and routine of daily living; change is not just effected at the ballot box or through common alternatives such as social movements or pressure group activities. The performance of everyday life has its own very powerful political agenda, and this is part of the way identities change.

More generally, though, the means by which things change rather than stay the same are only weakly understood. Among the ideas that might be drawn on to remedy this situation are Max Weber's notions of the qualities of charisma in effecting institutional change; work from management on leadership; from business studies on innovation niches; and no doubt many others. This is not the place to weigh up the arguments. Rather, our point here is that, across the whole of life – from the actions of charismatic individuals to the normative ideas developed as people routinely live out their hopes and fears – a performative perspective on identity opens up radical possibilities. It is in allowing for agency, in referring to future possibilities, in practising the new, that theories of performativity are given their most critical, creative and political edge.

Affective embodied geographies

Performing identities is a non-representational activity, and this is a second claim to originality for this approach. For many years now the dominant explanations of most social and cultural phenomena have concentrated on how ideas, identities and events are represented: these approaches have interrogated where identities have come from and described what they have become. To this end, they have worked with written and visual accounts of all kinds. In contrast a non-representational approach to identity is concerned with practice, with performance.

This is most obvious in the study of formal performances because, at first glance at least, they seem to be very distinctive forms of communication, ones that rely on relationships between artists and audiences that are quite different from those between the normal actors of academic inquiry, namely author and reader, or interviewer and interviewee. On closer scrutiny, however, the distinctive attribute of performance is the need to focus on doing – a performance only exists in process (and possibly in memory). Crucially, this attribute is equally present in all other academic research: the processes of reading, writing, and interviews all produce meaning – much of which is sensory – through doing, and this is true of virtually all activities that constitute life.

This concern with *doing* draws attention to the physicality of people's lives. To state the obvious, people live through and with their bodies; they experience their life, and engage with other people, with and through a wide range of sensations and emotions. And when social encounter is conceived of and practised in this way, it becomes much more diverse and textured than many of the earlier written accounts of identity imply. Bodily appearances, capacities and capabilities – the materiality of bodies – evince more variety than similarity. And relationships in practice are inflected with all kinds of passions and affects: love, hate, shame, hope, fear, and so on. It is perhaps not surprising that the growing number of studies which attend to the practicalities of human encounter are producing some quite radical new ideas about the patterning of social life and the process of identity formation. For example, the feminist writer Elizabeth Grosz (1993) and the social geographer Arun Saldanha (2004), working respectively with ideas about sex and gender on the one hand and race on the other, have argued that there is no basis in practice for the old binaries man/woman or black/white. Rather, they urge us to recognize the realities of a 'thousand tiny' sexes and races. While this does not amount to dissolving social categories altogether, it has enormously radical political implications. Recognizing a thousand tiny races, for example, undermines the hegemonic status of being 'white', since being 'white' – even if it survives this splintering of affinities – is just one of thousands of possible affiliations and identifications and there are thousands of ways of being it.

Hybrid identities

Finally, performing identities provides a glimpse into a social world formed not just from the interaction of human subjects, but from the engagement and entanglement of the human and non-human worlds. There are several ways to think about this.

First, people's experience of who they are is being radically affected by advances in medical science, in the areas of, for example, human molecular genetics, proteomics, neuroscience, brain imaging and body scanning. Catherine Nash (2005) thus writes about the reframing of geographies of relatedness, the rekindling of kinship affinities, prompted by widening access to certain kinds of genetic testing (to trace ancestry). Finding new ways to think about lineage and kinship opens up new ways to experience family and the suite of identities around it. Perhaps it heralds a new kind of 'togetherness' across time and space that displaces old national and racial boundaries, that gives people a stake in a new kind of belonging. In contrast, the proliferation of predictive and diagnostic testing for a wide range of health conditions has the potential to set up new geographies of distancing, avoidance and exclusion. Far from seeking to identify with family members who carry, for example, a genetic marker for breast cancer, people looking to access certain kinds of employment or particular financial services (life, health, unemployment insurance, for example) may stress the difference between themselves and other family members, precisely to avoid the potential costs, possible stigma and likely prognosis that goes with being 'the same' as their relatives. Either way, the basis of human relationships, the performance of identity, all seem set to change.

Second, what people themselves consist of is open to change as they team up with medicine and technology in ways that alter bodily appearances, functions and capabilities: changing, for example, the experience and enactment of health and illness. Tagging criminals, 'chipping' employees, bar-coding identity cards, transferring biometrics into passports may equally create – perhaps 'actualize' is a better word – new classes or categories of identity which it is much harder to perform otherwise (see Dodge and Kitchin 2005). It is possible, if rather ironic, that new markers of identification, embedded in science, indexed by technology, whether chosen or conferred, may be more entrenched and less open to challenge even than gender and race.

1013

Finally, how people operate is increasingly encased in, driven and mediated by technology and technological change, with profound implications for the social character of identity. People are social beings, but they also form relationships with and cement their identities in relation to things. Michel Callon (2006), for example, inspired in part by the philosophers Gilles Deleuze and Felix Guattari, writes about the way markets are performed by, and experienced as, 'agencements': a seamless mix of bodies, objects, tools, technologies and algorithms which have the capability or capacity to act in different ways – to perform the world differently – depending on their location and configuration. This captures the way credit ratings, software sorting and all kinds of other technologized markers of inclusion and exclusion are beginning to change the shape of the social landscape to an extent that has yet to be fully explored; how identities are created and shaped, what options and alternatives are performed, remains to be seen. What is clear, though, is that old conceptions of identity are no longer sufficient to capture what is happening, whereas a performative perspective may increasingly be coming into its own.

Conclusion

Identities have never been stable, but in the past they have been conceptualized, and to an extent experienced, in ways which emphasized the enduring natures of certain social divides, especially those around the essentialisms of class, gender, race, disability and so on. This has been an important tradition because it has not only secured recognition for the extent of a wide range of exclusions and inequalities, but it has also provided a basis from which to make claims in the interests of social justice. However, as the world moves on and as the pace of change of all kinds accelerates, an approach to identity that pays attention to how differ-ence is made, practised and reconfigured seems more promising. Although performativity comes without a clear theory of just what the mechanisms are that reshape old divides into new social forms, it does provide for the possibility that such shifts can happen. There is no guarantee that the new will be better than the old; but here, in this moment between the past and the future, there is at least a space of potential.

Further reading

Callon, M.(2006) What does it mean to say that economics is performative? In D. MacKenzie, F. Muniesa and L. Siu (eds) *Performing Economics: How Markets Are Constructed*. Princeton: Princeton University Press.

Dewsbury, J.-D., Harrison, P., Rose, M. and Wylie, J. (2002) Enacting geographies. *Geoforum* 33 (4) (special issue).

Gregson, N. and Rose, G. (2000) Taking Butler elsewhere: performativities, spatialities and sub-jectivities. *Environment and Planning D: Society and Space* 18 (4), 433–52.

Latham, A. and Conradson, D. (2003)The possibilities of performance. *Environment and Planning A* 35, 1901–6.

Rose, G. and Thrift, N. (eds) (2000a) Spaces of performance, part 1. *Environment and Planning D: Society and Space* 18 (4) (special issue).

——(2000b) Spaces of performance, part 2. *Environment and Planning D: Society and Space* 18 (5) (special issue).

Sedgwick, E.K. and Parker, A. (eds) (1995) *Performativity and Performance*. New York: Routledge.

Smith, S.J. (2001) Doing qualitative research: from interpretation to action. In M. Limb and C. Dwyer (eds) *Qualitative Methods for Geographers*, pp. 23–40. London: Edward Arnold.

Thrift, N. (2000) Performance. In R.J. Johnston, D. Gregory, G. Pratt and M. Watts (eds) *The Dictionary of Human Geography*, p. 577. Oxford: Blackwell.

References

Barth, F. (1969) *Ethnic Groups and Boundaries*. London: Allen and Unwin.

Butler, J. (1990) *Gender Trouble*. London: Routledge.

——(1993) *Bodies that Matter. On the Discursive Limits of Sex*. London: Routledge.

Butler, R. and Parr, H. (eds) (1999) *Mind and Body Spaces: New Geographies of Illness, Impairment and Disability*. London: Routledge.

Callon, M.(2006) What does it mean to say that economics is performative? In D. MacKenzie, F. Muniesa and L. Siu (eds) *Performing Economics: How Markets Are Constructed*. Princeton: Princeton University Press.

Dewsbury, J.-D., Harrison, P., Rose, M. and Wylie, J. (2002) Enacting geographies. *Geoforum* 33 (4) (special issue).

Dodge, M. and Kitchin, R (2005) Codes of life: identification codes and the machine-readable world. *Environment and Planning D: Society and Space*, 23 (6), 851–81.

Gilroy, P (1998) Race ends here. *Ethnic and Racial Studies* 21 (5), 838–47 (special issue on 'Rethinking Ethnic and Racial Studies', edited by M. Bulmer and J. Solomos).

——(2005) *Postcolonial Melancholia*. New York: Columbia University Press.

Gregson, N. and Rose, G. (2000) Taking Butler elsewhere: performativities, spatialities and subjectivities. *Environment and Planning D: Society and Space* 18 (4), 433–52.

Grosz, E. (1993) A thousand tiny sexes. Feminism and rhizomatics. *Topoi. An International Review of Philosophy* 12 (2), 167–79.

Hogg, M., Terry, D. and White, K. (1995) A tale of two theories: a critical comparison of identity theory with social identity theory. *Social Psychology Quarterly* 58 (4), 255–69.

Jackson, P. (1989) *Maps of Meaning*. London: Unwin Hyman.

Koskela, H. (1997) Bold walk and breakings. Women's spatial confidence versus fear of violence. *Gender, Place and Culture* 4 (3), 301–19.

Latham, A. and Conradson, D. (2003)The possibilities of performance. *Environment and Planning A* 35, 1901–6.

Lloyd, M. (2005) *Beyond Identity Politics. Feminism, Power and Politics*. London: Sage.

Mackenzie, D. (forthcoming 2006) *An Engine, Not a Camera: How Financial Models Shape Markets*. Cambridge, Mass.: MIT Press.

Massey, D. (2004) Geographies of responsibility. *Geografiska Annaler* 86 (B), 5–18.

Nash, C. (2005) Geographies of relatedness. *Transactions of the Institute of British Geographers* 30 (4), 449–62.

Penrose, J. (1995) Essential constructions? The 'cultural bases' of nationalist movements. *Nations and Nationalism* 1 (3), 391–417.

Penrose, J. and Mole, R. (forthcoming) Nation-states and national identity. In K. Cox, M. Low and J. Robinson (eds) *Handbook of Political Geography*. London: Sage.

Rose, G. (1993) *Feminism and Geography: The Limits of Geographical Knowledge*. Minneapolis: University of Minnesota Press.

Rose, G. and Thrift, N. (eds) (2000a) Spaces of performance, part 1. *Environment and Planning D: Society and Space* 18 (4) (special issue).

——(2000b) Spaces of performance, part 2. *Environment and Planning D: Society and Space* 18 (5) (special issue).

Said, E. (1992) *Musical Elaborations*. London: Vintage Books.

Saldanha, A. (2004) Psychedelic whiteness: rave tourism and the materiality of race in Goa. Unpublished PhD thesis, Milton Keynes, Open University.

Sedgwick, E.K. and Parker, A.(eds) (1995) *Performativity and Performance*. New York: Routledge.

Smith, S.J. (1999) The cultural politics of difference. In D. Massey, J. Allen and P. Sarre (eds) *Human Geography Today*, pp. 129–50. Cambridge: Polity Press.

——(2001) Doing qualitative research: from interpretation to action. In M. Limb and C. Dwyer (eds) *Qualitative Methods for Geographers*, pp. 23–40. London: Edward Arnold.

——(2005a) Black:white. In P. Cloke and R. Johnson (eds) *Spaces of Geographical Thought: Deconstructing Human Geography's Binaries* (Society and Space Series) pp. 97–118. London: Sage.

——(2005b) Society–space. In P. Cloke, P. Crang and M. Goodwin (eds) *Introducing Human Geography*, second edition. pp. 12–23. London: Hodder Arnold.

Tajfel, H. (1981) *Human Groups and Social Categories*. Cambridge: Cambridge University Press.

Tajfel, H. and Turner, J.C. (1986) The social identity theory of intergroup behaviour. In S. Worchel and W.G. Austin (eds) *Psychology of Intergroup Relations*. Chicago: Nelson Hall.

Theiler, T. (2003) Societal security and social psychology. *Review of International Studies* 29, 249–68.

Thrift, N. (2000) Performance. In R.J. Johnston, D. Gregory, G. Pratt and M. Watts (eds) *The Dictionary of Human Geography*, p. 577. Oxford: Blackwell.

Turner, J.C. (1987). *Rediscovering the Social Group: A Self-Categorisation Theory*. Oxford: Blackwell.

64

Thinking and acting

Academic, policy and civil society response – a gallery of maps

Danny Dorling

How we think of the world determines how we act in and on the world. Academia helps shape that thinking. Geography especially can encourage a particular imagination that sees the world as one. The apparatus of academic writing can, however, sometimes hide the need for action – bibliographies, citations and academic rigour can make it harder to see *why* the research matters.

The painting of pictures fuels the geographical imagination and visual images provide better fuel than do metaphorical ones. Cartographers know this; most geographers are still learning. This chapter is a cartographic plea for action, without the distractions. The chapters in this book present us with evidence and with moral imperatives. But research and books like this should not exist in a policy vacuum. *You* can think and act. Change can be powered by rhetoric and the mapped form of the world can evoke a persuasive call.

Be moved by these striking global images!

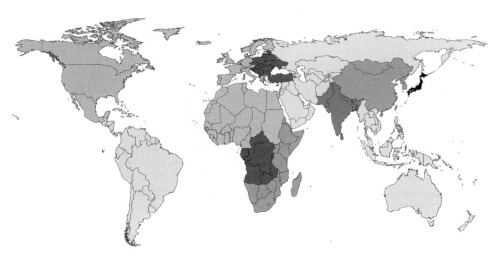

Figure 64.1. Territory drawn in proportion to land area.

Rolled out on a map the entire surface of the globe is clear – a view even the few human beings who have walked on the moon could not see. The image is often centred on Europe and stretches out the high latitudes but that is not how it most distorts your mind. The map can make you think that it is *land* that matters – rather than *people*. Draw a map of people and you begin to think a little more imaginatively. Draw a map of people you hope will be alive in three centuries' time and you begin to think even more carefully.

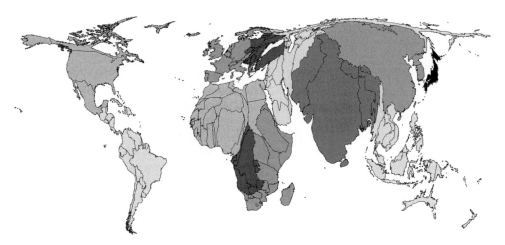

Figure 64.2. Territory drawn in proportion to population estimated by the UN for the year 2300.

Draw a map, not of people but of what people have, and you perhaps begin to think a little more openly. Where are all the cars on the planet? To where is the petroleum flowing and from where are the exhaust fumes rising? How many cars are needed if all are to have what the rich have now in three centuries' time?

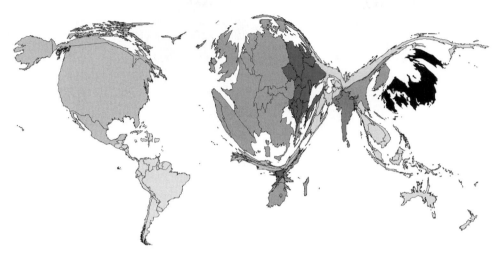

Figure 64.3. Territory drawn in proportion to numbers of passenger cars.

What means of transport do most people use in the world? Where are two wheels not used because most folk can afford more or none? Again, where does the fuel come from? Where does the pollution go? How many lives are lost when the scooters come off the roads and the motorbikes don't mix with cars? From and to where are all these people moving?

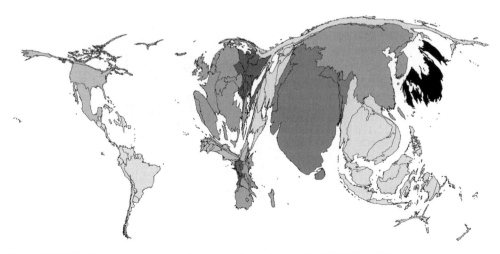

Figure 64.4. Territory drawn in proportion to numbers of mopeds and motorcycles.

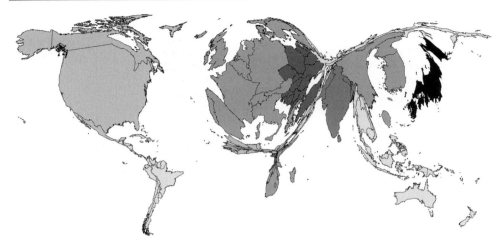

Figure 64.5. Territory drawn in proportion to value of crude petroleum imports in US dollars.

Like minds, some vehicles require more fuel than others. Some homes are better heated than others. In some places without petroleum there would be no plastic and without plastic there would be a great deal missing. So with what do those who need the petrol (and so much more) pay? What pays for the petrol to flow to where the cars run? For the steel to be taken to where the cars are made? For all that comes to those who have the most?

What do the rich have to offer the poor for their resources?

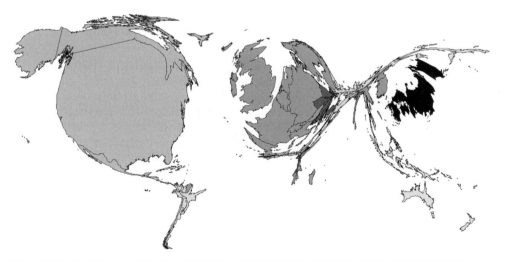

Figure 64.6. Territory drawn in proportion to the value royalties and licence fees export earningss.

Everything that matters most, when counted in dollars, comes from the richest areas of the world. That is why they are rich. Increasingly, they own the most expensive products of all – ideas – which they license for sale. Ideas that make songs, ideas that make cars, ideas that make medicines. And what do they want for their ideas? What could the poorer territories of the world have that could possibly be of value to the wealthy?

And for what do they sell their financial advice, their insurance and their ideas that make songs, cars and medicines? What could there be outside their territories that they need? From where do the songs, the cars and the medicines come, or even the wood to pulp for paper on which to write their ideas?

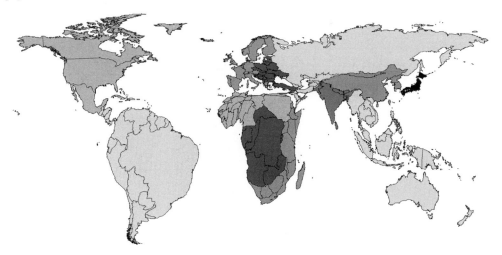

Figure 64.7. Territory drawn in proportion to the area of forests 1990.

And from where have they taken what the rich think they need? Equally from everywhere? Or do they keep their forests, the copyrights to their songs, their iron for their steel for their cars and their ideas for their medicines to themselves?

Surely the map of what is taken from the world does not paint a picture of the richest territories squeezing out what they value from the lands of the poor?

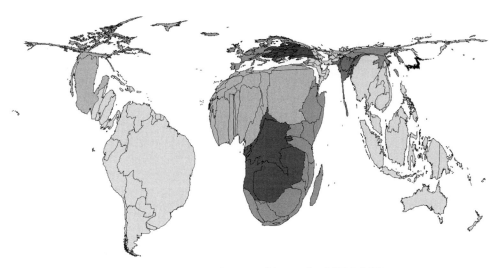

Figure 64.8. Territory drawn in proportion to the area of forests 'lost' 1990–2000.

1021

Surely not?

But at least the rich can use their knowledge, their ideas, their wealth, to help those whose resources they plunder. Without wealth 'creation' we would never attain the progress needed to improve all our lives – to bring music round the planet, to cover the lands with cars, and to make medicines that everyone can use?

People would never be that selfish.

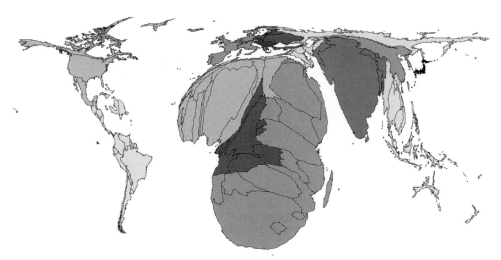

Figure 64.9. Territory drawn in proportion to the numbers of people dying from HIV-associated disease.

Would we?

Acknowledgements

Maps derived from Http://www.worldmapper.org. For further information and images on these topics access this site.

Index

'ableist' society 1008–9
Abler, R. 32, 965
Aboriginal art, different aesthetic to Western map of same area 564
Aboriginal people, Midnight Oil's pro-land anthem 'The Dead Heart' 400
Abu-Lughod, J.L. 393, 395
accessibility of multimedia 629–30
Accessional accessibility planning tool – Accession 2006 210
accidental relationshps, sedimentary records and 8
acid rain 87
Ackroyd, P. 707–8
Actor Network Theory (ANT) 60, 953, 959–60
Adams, P.C. 521, 973
adapting to climate variability and change 663; climate-related changes in other physical environmental variables 664; (nature and types of climatic variability 663–64); current and projected future responses to global warming current and future change and response in tropical rain-forest areas 674–79; examples of societal impacts and responses in the past (example 1: societal impacts and response in Classical times and subsistence societies 668–69; example 2: the Little Ice Age in Europe 669; example 3: human impacts of the Sahel drought phase since 1965 in semi-arid Sudan 669–72); general context 672–73; hurricane frequency changes and dilemmas for planning responses in North Atlantic/Caribbean region 679–80; (predicted changes and likely impacts and responses in the UK and Europe 673–74); human responses to climatic variability and change: overview 665–68
adiabatic temperature changes 113

advertising, grew in late nineteenth century 982; Western consumerist values and 594
aerial photographic images 588
aesthetics, definition 574
Afghanistan 136, 293, 549, 943; NATO troops dispatched to after 11 September (2001) 917; The Taliban enacted restrictive civil policies 232
Africa 81–82, 132, 169, 179, 186, 208, 304, 435, 487, 841; cell phones 975; city of Great Zimbabwe 218; decolonization 301; financial marginalization 895; high fertility 136–37, 850; images of 541; increase in water withdrawals 754; internet users 192; inward investments in cities 334; legacies of late colonialism 305; less than 75 per cent of population have access to safe water 747; malaria and economic growth 651; mineral extraction and poverty 867; people seek refuge in 487; population expected to rise 847; reading of African 'classics' influenced by publishers such as Heinemann 548; southern and water stress 759; tropical and ENSO year 740; youth 145
African-American hip hop aesthetic 617
African Writers Series 548
aftermath of 9/11 and 7 July bombings in London, anti-Muslim feelings 238; change in national security 310
Agarwal, B. 355, 359
agency, women and 995, 998
Agenda 21 828, 999
'agglomeration economies' 472
Agnew, J. 43, 282–83, 289, 300, 306
agricultural landscape, makeover by human influences 8
agriculture 8, 263; achievement was to free some people from getting their own food 7; affects hydrological system 745; buffer zones 693;

religious places 236–37; integration of with environmental concerns 1
People's Global Action *see* PGA
performances, special events opportunities for interpreting information 1009
performativity 1005–6; conclusion 1014; the distinctiveness of a performative approach to identity 1011; affective embodied geographies 1012–13; between structure and agency 1011–12; hybrid identities 1013–14; identity 1006–8; performing identities 1008–11
Perkins, C. 1, 21–22, 27, 73, 556, 561, 565; golf mapping 566
Perkins, C and Gardiner, A., how visually impaired people read tactile maps 566
Personal Digital Asistants (PDAs) 629, 636
personal photography, 'snapshots' 590, 597
Peru 121, 484, 872, 878, 996; Federation of Mothers' Clubs 997–98; hosts significant resources 862–63
pesticide use, issues arising from 686
Peterson, R.A. 616–17, 619
Pethick, J.S. 788–89
Petts, G.E. 79, 723, 725
PGA 931, 937
phenomenon of urban reconcentration, reconcentration of poverty 484
Philippines 140, 151–52, 189, **266**, 972
Philippine Women's Centre, separate organization 1000
Phillips, R. 540–41, 547–48, 558; Smokey Mountain waste dump and others 713
Philo, C. 37, 328
Phoenicia 770
Phoenix, in-migrants 381
Phoenix University (Arizona) 974
photographic evidence, employed as 'source material' in historical geographies 588
photographic genres **590**
photographic images, manipulated in packages such as PhotoShop 599
photographs, as art **591**; carry multiple meanings 591; composition may be important influence on what the image comes to mean 590; part of military armour 592; use of in adverts 594–95
photography 587–88; compositional qualities: art and the aesthetic 590–91; conclusions 599; consuming passions: persuasion 594–97; cultural power of: race, class and gender 591–94; photographic truth 588–90; practices 597–99
photojournalism rely on implied correspondence between image and reality 589
physical geographer, scientists' tool kit and 27
physical landscapes, always dynamic 397
'physical phenomena', nature 3
Pickard, G.L. 771, 776
Pickles, J. 556, 558, 562

PIE 10–11
Pilkey, O.H. 787, 795
Pimm, S.L. 822–23
Pinder, D. 564, 567
Pitcairn Islands **807**
Pittsburgh (USA) 333
place, cultural facets 19; experiential 31; major source of profit and loss 47; moral concept 35; representation of 44; Schiphol Airport (Amsterdam) 39
'place-ballet' 33–34
place building, role of transport 208
place as landscape, place and space 19–20
placelessness, postmodern capitalism and specifically globalization 221
place as network 57–60, 62–65; coda 67; conclusion 66–67; place in network 60–62; place as relational effect 65–66
places, actively constructed through actant networks 64; always in process 53; conceptualized as intersections or nodes interacting with networks 62; networks, not simply open or perforated intersections 67; outcome of relationships 2; part of our biographies 40; people form bonds with 20; provide a locus for identity 43; segments of landscape with physical form 1
places as networks, Bodies-without-Organs 63; never given they are always becoming and performed 64, 67
planning policy, aim to increase development of 'brownfield' rather than 'greenfield' sites 474
planning for population growth 847; ageing nations and their policy options, the ageing trend 855–57; conclusions 859; nations of continuing growth and their policy options 851; India: over-urbanization and the two-children policy 851–53; policies for sub-Sahara Africa 853–55; projection of population growth 847; the demographic transition model 848–49; the specific fertility rate 850–51; the three components of population projection 849–50; world and regional population trends 847–48 stagnating nations and their policy options 858–59; problems of population decline 857–58
plants and animals, labelled as 'weeds' and 'pests' 8; transferred from continent to continent 13
plastics, 1950s offshoots of refining of oil 11
plastics manufacturers, polychlorinated bipheny (PCBs) as flame retardants 87
plate tectonics, changes in palaeogeography 119
Poland 714
Polanyi, Karl 343, 870
polar cell 'index cycle' 112
political dimension, 'unchanging places' 386

processes 903–4; labour power and workers' organization 907–10; producing place: the significance of class, gender, ethnicity and shills in shaping spatial divisions of labour 904–7
production, small units as result of IT 255
'production of uneven development' when it comes to resources 862
product life cycle 423
'property', cultural concept 217
protected areas 410–11
protesting and empowering,; convergence of common interests 937; people's global action 937; the World Social Forum 937–39; grassroots globalization 929–30; diversity of 931–32; scale of 930–31; neoliberalism and its opponents 928–29; reclaiming and protecting the commons 932; struggles against privatization of the commons 934; struggles for land and cultural commons 934–35; struggles for political and social autonomy 935–37; water commons: anti-dam struggles 932–34; resisting networks 927–28
protests, key areas of agreement 931–32
public-private partnership, urban policy 331 public space, segregated according to gender and age 52
public transport, still important in cities 208
Pullman, G., worker control 451, 454, 464
Puranen, J., photographs of Sami people 579–80

Quantitative Revolution (late 1960s and early 1970s), spatial concepts and 19, 555
Quaternary climatic change 119
Quebec (Canada) 305; anti-globalization protest 921; exploitation of hydro-power potential of La Grande River 864
Quinn, M, sculpture of Alison Lapper 46
Quito 110
Quorn, single-cell protein 274–75

racism 43
Radburn (America), as garden city 460
radiative-convective models (RCMs) 113
Raju, S. 1000–1001
Ramamurthy, A. 594, 597
Raper, J. 626–27
rap music 617, 621–22
Ravenswood Aluminium Corporation (USA) 909
Reagan, Ronald (USA), market-led policies 174
reconcentration 483; by city centre living in western cities 490; conclusions 492–93; from rural economic change 483–84; Argentina: the rural crisis and increasing poverty 484–85; outcomes of in Rosario

(Argentina) 486–87; gentrification in Stockholm – case study 492; movement back to city centres after dispersal 483; refugees from war, civil conflict and environmental disasters in towns and cities 487–90; in UK's regional centres 490
Redford, K.H. 821, 825
Red Sea, Butler's model of life cycle of tourism 791
Reed, D.J. 789, 795
Rees, W. 837, 871
refugees, 'hands-off' ideology in economically advanced world 427; living in Ugandan capital Kampala without UNHCR assistance 488; people forced to leave 943
regenerating places 467; the change makers 471–75; sort of urban renaissance 467–71; so what? 478–79; who lives in the city centres? 475–76
regenerating places moving beyond the centre 476–78
Regional Development Agencies 318
regional initiatives and responses 313; conclusions 323–24; devolution, constitutional change and economic governance 315–18; economic governance post-devolution 319–21; economic governance pre-devolution 318–19; implementation: new regional responses 321–23; new regional agendas: geography and states 313–15
Regional Planning Association of America (RPAA) 460
religions, definitions difficult 228; importance of pilgrimage 235; natural features may be venerated by 233–34; painted as stabilizing forces in society 230; popular 983; rituals of death on landscape 234; social and political views linked to 237; world **229–30**
religious barriers, family planning programmes and 148
religious belief, landscape 26; reflected in nature of places 232
religious differences, genocides in Armenia, Rwanda and Bosnia 231
religious identity, complexities of place 237
Relph, E. 19, 31–32, 35, 63, 65, 521; *Place and Placelessness* 39, 221
remittances, economic foundation of local households with global transnational linkages 946; effective at grassroots level 141
renewal water resources 78
renting property 475
representations, have material weight 44
reservoir impoundments, significant effects on downstream flow regimes 745
reservoirs 81–82
'resilience', socio-economic practices 658–59